DEATH FROM THE SKIES

DEATH
FROM THE
SKIES

HOW THE BRITISH AND
GERMANS SURVIVED BOMBING
IN WORLD WAR II

DIETMAR SÜSS

Translated by Lesley Sharpe and Jeremy Noakes

OXFORD
UNIVERSITY PRESS

OXFORD
UNIVERSITY PRESS

Great Clarendon Street, Oxford, OX2 6DP,
United Kingdom

Oxford University Press is a department of the University of Oxford.
It furthers the University's objective of excellence in research, scholarship,
and education by publishing worldwide. Oxford is a registered trade mark of
Oxford University Press in the UK and in certain other countries

First published in German as *Tod aus der Luft. Kriegsgesellschaft
und Luftkrieg in Deutschland und England*
By Dietmar Süß
© 2011 by Siedler Verlag, a division of Verlagsgruppe
Random House GmbH, München, Germany.

The translation of this work was funded by Geisteswissenschaften
International–Translation Funding for Humanities and Social Sciences
from Germany, a joint initiative of the Fritz Thyssen Foundation, the
German Federal Foreign Office, the collecting society VG WORT,
and the Börsenverein des Deutschen Buchhandels
(German Publishers & Booksellers Association).

© in this English translation Oxford University Press 2014

The moral rights of the author have been asserted

First Edition published in 2014

Impression: 1

Published in the United States of America by Oxford University Press
198 Madison Avenue, New York, NY 10016, United States of America

British Library Cataloguing in Publication Data
Data available

Library of Congress Control Number: 2013940850

ISBN 978-0-19-966851-9

Printed in Italy by
L.E.G.O. S. p. A.–Lavis TN

Links to third party websites are provided by Oxford in good faith and
for information only. Oxford disclaims any responsibility for the materials
contained in any third party website referenced in this work.

Acknowledgements

It is a pleasure to thank those who have supported me generously in the writing of this book. Many people—more people than I can thank individually—have given me their time, pointed me in the right direction, and discussed this project with me. It is one of the great myths about academic research that it inevitably leads to isolation.

The origins of this book lie in the 'air-war group', of which Barbara Grimm, Nicole Kramer, and Hans Woller were also members, at the Institute for Contemporary History in Munich. I discussed with them the initial drafts and much more besides.

In Jena Norbert Frei offered me the opportunity to continue working on the air war. He supported the project energetically and constantly spurred me on to ponder the subject afresh. What more could one wish for?

This study was accepted in the summer semester of 2010 as a second doctorate (*Habilitation*) by the Philosophical Faculty of the Friedrich Schiller University in Jena. The *Habilitation* scholarship awarded me by the Bavarian State Ministry for Education and the Dilthey Fellowship I was given by the Volkswagen Foundation enabled me to complete the work free from material concerns.

The Department of History at the University of Exeter very kindly acted as my host during my stay in the UK. As a Fellow of the Alexander von Humboldt Foundation I spent an unforgettable year working with Jeremy Noakes in Exeter. I am very grateful to the Foundation and to my wonderful host. He taught me many things that cannot be found in the archival documents and yet are so important to anyone writing about another country.

Richard Overy provided me with the opportunity to present and discuss my research at the University's Centre for the Study of War, State, and Society from which it greatly benefited. I am also grateful to all the British and German archives I used for their assistance. Jörg Arnold, Neil Gregor, Christiane Kuller, Armin Nolzen, Kim Christian Priemel, Sybille Steinbacher, and Malte Thiessen sacrificed a great deal of time to give me critical comments. I made particularly heavy demands in this respect on Daniel Maul and on my brother Winfried.

Katja Klee and Mathias Irrlinger were very a great help with the final edit. Siedler, the German publisher, and its managing editor Tobias Winstel, supported the project from an early stage, for which I am also very grateful.

I completed the German text in October 2010 and have only been able to incorporate a few references to more recent literature in the English edition. The translation was made possible with the generous aid of 'Geisteswissenschaft International' and I would like to thank the two translators, Lesley Sharpe and Jeremy Noakes, for their excellent translation.

Rosmarie Scheidhamer-Süss is familiar with all the highs and lows in the history of this piece of work. It is dedicated to her.

Augsburg, 2013

Preface to the English Edition

For me the air war conjures up memories of football. Although I am no longer certain, it must have been during the World Cup semi-final between England and Germany in 1990 that I first heard the song 'There were ten German bombers in the air', though as a 16-year-old schoolboy on a language course I did not grasp its meaning fully. I only knew that the atmosphere in the pub suddenly changed and we realized we would do well to keep our delight about the missed penalties strictly to ourselves.

I was reminded of this many years later when, some ten years ago, controversy over the air war raged for months in the press on both sides of the Atlantic. My first tentative thoughts about this project date back to that time, but the weightiness of the topic did not come home to me until I first read extracts from Jörg Friedrich's *The Fire* in the German newspaper *Bild*, the equivalent of *The Sun*, and the heated responses to it in the British press.

The arguments surrounding the legitimacy of the air war and Churchill himself as an alleged 'war criminal' produced a fair amount of intemperate comment and since then the German extreme Right in particular has repeatedly referred in emotive terms to the 'Allied bombing holocaust' and attempted to mobilize its supporters on the anniversaries of the bombing raids. This still goes on and thus the history presented in this book is one with an open ending.

The controversy regarding the 'taboo' subject of the air war and the legitimacy of Allied tactics did not, however, come from nowhere but was rather connected to a boom in literature about the air war, which from the mid-1990s onwards gave increasing prominence to the perspective of the victims and to the 'history of German suffering' in the Second World War. This book is therefore not only about the war as a set of past events but also about the 'new' Germany that arose after reunification and about British–German relations almost seventy years after the end of the war. While almost every British crime series is shown on German television, one of the most

popular and (in the author's view) most wonderful British series about the
Second World War has never appeared on German TV, namely *Dad's Army*.
This fact may well be of more than just anecdotal interest.

The controversy over *The Fire* has since died down and it has become
even more evident how far memories of the air war have been adjusted to
fit the present, thus becoming freshly relevant and acquiring new meanings
in relation to current controversies. This was shown when NATO forces
intervened in Libya. Are air raids effective in preparing for the deployment
of ground forces? How can 'collateral damage' be avoided? And is this possible, in any case? And, whether intentionally or unintentionally, are these
weapons systems not always directed against the civilian population?

As in Britain, where for many years the overarching 'myth of 1940',
which was created for propaganda purposes, obscured the deep divisions in
wartime society, in Germany the air war fed into the construction of a new
national identity that was meant to reflect the Germans' past not only as
the perpetrators of the war but also as its victims. In spite of the vast quantity of books on the history of the Second World War, in spite of the many
studies of the Blitz, there have up to now been few attempts to give an
account of the air war as part of the history of violence in Europe in the
modern era and thus to investigate the shared and distinctive experiences
of war on the part of the civilian populations. For many decades this perspective was at odds with the established traditions of national historiography; it was at odds also with the public and private narratives of the past.

In addition, there are reasons why this kind of comparative project is
problematic. The asymmetries of the war are, of course, one problem: the
differing levels of destruction caused by the air war and the differing phases
of the war in which the raids took place. On first consideration, given the
images of Dresden and Hamburg that have become fixed in the collective
memory, a comparative study of urban life seemed an unproductive approach.
From autumn 1944 the Allied air forces' command of the skies gave them
greater and greater power to inflict damage, for the Americans and British
could now attack German towns and cities at will by day and night. The US
air force concentrated on targeting German industry, while the RAF continued with its strategy of night-time area bombing. The Ruhr in particular
experienced a new intensity of bombing from September 1944 onwards, in
the course of which industrial plant, fuel depots, and large parts of the road
and rail network were seriously damaged. Fairly small and medium-sized
towns were now the targets of Allied raids, which, apart from destroying the

infrastructure and industry, were supposed to create widespread fear and panic in the population in order to destabilize the regime and at the same time support the advance of ground troops in the west after the Normandy landings. At the latest from 1943/4 onwards the raids completely disregarded the already hazy boundaries between military and civilian targets. From the start of the war to the spring of 1945 British Bomber Command was able to quadruple its total of bombers and increase tenfold the quantity of explosives they carried. At the same time the Allies could mobilize greater and greater economic and technical resources, with the result that they could significantly increase their number of operations and have long-range fighters accompany their bombers. So while the German daytime and night-time anti-aircraft defences, hitherto so dangerous, were slowly being paralysed, the Allies, boosted also by their advance in Italy, were able constantly to extend the range and precision of their raids.

Anyone wanting to find out more about Allied strategies or about the Luftwaffe may well find this book a disappointment, for its focus lies elsewhere, namely on day-to-day life during the war, on the experiences of those who went through it and the attempts of both nations to deal with this new threat from the air and its dire consequences. This is therefore a book about wartime morale, about ideas of the 'right' and 'wrong' ways to respond to war situations, about populations' powers of endurance and the daily struggle to cope with crisis. Hence it is also a history of the fear of 'death from the skies'. In spite of the gulf between democracy and dictatorship, the story of this sense of threat determined the reactions of both nations and their responses to it showed both similarities and fundamental differences. This book is not therefore concerned with the long-running conflict between Germans and the British over 'guilt' and 'expiation', nor does it aim to pass judgement on the issue of the legitimacy of the air war, as other studies, including most recently some by British writers, have done. British involvement in Iraq has left its mark on this debate and at the same time contributed to a change in perspective on the past. This book is concerned with something else: by probing what lies beneath the terms 'national community' and the 'People's War' we may reach an understanding of those ambivalent forms of social organization that characterized both societies at the time of the air raids. Such a comparison reveals even more clearly than hitherto what distinguished the German 'national community'—a divided and unequal, increasingly extreme society based on violence—so fundamentally from other forms of social organization of the inter-war and war periods.

Contents

List of Illustrations

Glossary

Gau Term used by the Nazi Party to designate districts in its organization. These varied in size, e.g. East Prussia and Essen as two extremes, and were headed by a **Gauleiter**.

national community (*Volksgemeinschaft*) The term used by the Nazis to designate the society of the 'Third Reich' embodying their version of *völkisch* (see below) values and operating in accordance with *völkisch* norms.

national comrade (*Volksgenosse*) A member of the 'national community' and so subject to its norms and values. Those who failed to conform were excluded as 'community aliens' (*Gemeinschaftsfremde*) and were subjected to its penalties.

Oberbürgermeister Mayor of a city possessing substantial executive powers.

prefect (*Regierungspräsident*) Civil service official in charge of a district roughly the size of an average English county.

state secretary (*Staatssekretär*) The senior civil servant in a ministry.

sub-prefect (*Landrat*) Civil service official in charge of a district roughly the size of an English rural district council.

völkisch Term dating from *c.*1900 denoting nationalist ideology and movement that stressed the importance of ethnicity in determining national identity and considered that human mentalities, behaviour, and national cultures were largely determined by 'race'/ethnicity ('blood') and that there was a qualitative hierarchy of ethnicities (Völker). These beliefs were usually accompanied by anti-Semitism. In the Nazi context it was used to designate what was seen as a set of quintessentially German values, which were considered superior to and threatened by 'Jewish' western liberal/capitalist and 'Jewish' eastern 'Bolshevik' ideas. However, unlike the pre-1918 *völkisch* movement, of which Hitler was critical, the dominant Nazi version of *völkisch* did not look back to a Teutonic past and did not fear and dislike the modern world, but instead envisaged a special German path to modernity, including the enthusiastic adoption of modern technologies and the pseudo-science of eugenics or, in its German version, 'Racial Hygiene', to purify the 'national body'.

Introduction

Ludwig Mankowski can still remember the boots. As he fled from the flames one of them got stuck in the asphalt. He managed to hang on to the other. And even in 2006, more than sixty years after the bombing raids on Hamburg, he kept the old boot by him: 'I've still got it. I use it now to keep my savings in.'[1]

The air war has left its traces up to this day: ruined buildings, advertisements for British beer, or items of family history. They may be shoes, candlesticks, table cloths, or even a pair of champagne glasses—all are bound up with memories of the war and are regularly brought out again on festive occasions so that the children and grandchildren can be told stories about 'the old days'. Memories of the bombing raids have thus remained part of the present day, for they contribute to an individual family's search for its identity and form part of the background against which war and violence in today's political conflicts, for example in Afghanistan and Iraq, are viewed.

A few years ago ZDF (the second state-sponsored German television channel) showed 'Dresden', a love story about a German nurse and British pilot who had been shot down in the inferno of the air war—sentimental but at the same time an attempt, in a form suitable for popular family viewing, to tackle the question of the effects of violence and of the nature of British–German 'reconciliation' sixty years after the end of the war. A British–German history of the air war carries the baggage of cultural memory in both countries, and in a certain sense it also forms part of an ongoing historical enquiry, beginning with the question of which parts of history are to be recounted and what terms will be used to do so.

War from the Skies

One thing at least is certain: from the beginning of the twentieth century the deployment of aircraft fundamentally changed how war was waged.

Conflicts between states were henceforth conducted in the air as well as on land and at sea. Aircraft opened up new opportunities for destruction and new forms of killing. At the beginning of the First World War the limited technology meant that bombing was very largely a hit-and-miss affair. By the Second World War that had changed: cities and their inhabitants were the targets of carpet bombings and the deaths of hundreds of thousands of civilians were factored in. This book deals with the consequences of these attacks, the morale demonstrated in the communities being bombed in Britain and Germany, and their attitudes to these events since 1945.

At the outbreak of war in 1939 no decision had yet been taken to wage war in the air against the civilian population.[2] Although political leaders from Berlin to Washington had spoken out against such attacks, strategists were anticipating aerial warfare. Their main concern was not to be branded as war criminals in the eyes of the world. In Britain even more than in Germany it was assumed that all that was needed was a pretext and raids would then be targeted even at densely populated areas. It was less a question of scruples and more one of tactics that caused Hitler and the Luftwaffe to shrink from a strategy that made the civilian population the target of 'terror attacks', as they were called then. After the German victory in the west over France and the chaotic retreat of the British Expeditionary Force at Dunkirk in 1940 the 'Führer' was still hoping to induce Britain to make peace.

Contrary to Hitler's calculations, Winston Churchill, who became Prime Minister on 10 May 1940,[3] was not interested in rapprochement. From the outset he made it clear that he would fight implacably against the tyranny of National Socialism. The German raid on Rotterdam on 14 May 1940, in which 800 people lost their lives, was for London only the final proof to add to the accumulated evidence of the depravity of German warfare.[4] British propaganda had a field day with this raid and the very next day Churchill gave Bomber Command the order to attack the German 'home front'.

On the other side of the Channel preparations were being made from mid-June 1940 for an invasion. The 'Battle of Britain' began in July 1940 with attacks on convoys in the Channel and in the Thames Estuary; on 13 August major raids against Royal Air Force bases on the south-west coast were initiated, followed by raids on the north of England and the Midlands. From 7 September 1940 the Luftwaffe even conducted daytime raids on London—as a 'reprisal' for an RAF raid on Berlin. Although these raids, which involved heavy losses, ceased in October, the provisional end of the

Battle of Britain, the night raids went on up until May 1941, the end of the period commonly known as the Blitz.

Having lost the aerial battle, the Luftwaffe set about attacking the cities of the north and Midlands in order to strike at the heart of the British armaments industry; one of the heaviest raids was on the city of Coventry on 14 November 1940. Even though the tally of destruction was lower than was to be the case in Germany, it was nevertheless considerable: in total some 20,000 lives were lost in London alone, and apart from the capital and Coventry numerous other British cities suffered significant damage.[5]

German planning for the invasion and the conquest of the skies over Britain was improvised and ill organized; the raids were neither carefully prepared nor part of a comprehensive strategy. The Luftwaffe underestimated its opponent, while massively overestimating its own effectiveness.[6] Initially the German raids were not strategically planned as pure 'terror attacks' on the civilian population but as operations aimed at military and economic targets.[7] The victims of the bombings were not, however, interested in the strategic motives of their attackers when their homes were burning and communities being destroyed—and in the autumn and winter of 1940 many communities were targeted. In retaliation for attacks on military and industrial targets Bomber Command struck above all at the west of the German Reich and, as an irritant, at Berlin. It could now pursue the policy it had been intending to pursue since the start of the war.

Yet the results at first were far from satisfactory; on the contrary, the Butt Report, a government report that came out in the summer of 1941, provided evidence that hardly a single aircraft had succeeded in finding its target with any precision. The number of hits was alarmingly small.[8] For Churchill, however, there was no alternative to aerial warfare and so he disregarded the critical voices in his own ranks complaining about its high costs. These costs resulted from the poor technical standard of the bombers as well as from the robust German air defences, which in 1941 caused the British attackers significant losses.[9]

The decision to target German morale is frequently associated with the name Arthur Harris, who in February 1942 was made head of Bomber Command. But the tactic of carpet bombing had already been adopted by then and offered at least a glimmer of hope in the fight against the Nazi regime, which in the meantime had redirected its resources to concentrate fully on the war of annihilation in the east.

Harris was not the bloodthirsty butcher that German propaganda liked to present him as. He was fully aware that German 'morale' was not a clearly defined target and could not be easily broken. But it was in his view necessary to do so if the Germans' 'material capacity for war'[10] were to be destroyed. Industrial centres, workers' housing, factories—all had to be bombed before an Allied invasion could be attempted.

The massive fatalities among the civilian population did not thereby become the aim in itself but they were at the same time a not unwelcome by-product, not collateral damage but rather an important component of the strategy. From 1942 onwards Harris and Bomber Command were helped by the fact that several technical innovations could finally go into production.[11] In addition, Harris improved the training of the bomber crews and the organization of the bomber squadrons. In the meantime the latter had 'Pathfinder' at their disposal, which guided bombers to their target.

With the United States' entry into the war in December 1941 the relative strengths in the air war changed. The RAF raids the following spring on Lübeck and Rostock and on Cologne at the end of May 1942 were in line with the new strategy of area bombing, yet Bomber Command's losses were still enormous. German retaliation, the attacks on Exeter, Bath, Norwich, and York in April/May 1942 known in Britain as the 'Baedeker Raids', was little more than a series of desperate reprisals, although they caused considerable distress in Britain.

In January 1943, therefore, when Churchill and Roosevelt along with their Chiefs of Staff met in Casablanca, the development of a common air-war strategy was on the agenda along with the issue of when a second front should be opened. The directive arising from the meeting on 21 January 1943 summarized the objectives clearly: aerial warfare had the aim of destroying the military, economic, and industrial infrastructure of the German Reich and of undermining morale among the population until resistance collapsed.

The Combined Bomber Offensive envisaged British night bombing and American daytime raids. The latter were to be aimed through 'precision bombing' at strategic targets.[12] Although in theory and in the perception of the population British and American policies towards aerial warfare differed, the basic strategic assumptions were closer than was often claimed after the war. Churchill, Roosevelt, and their supreme commanders shared the view that the raids must target enemy 'sources of strength', that is industry and the civilian population, in order to inflict the maximum damage and achieve the desired objective, namely the complete collapse of the dictatorship.

At the start of the combined Allied air offensive against Germany code-named Pointblank in 1943 the situation for the RAF and the US Army Air Force was very unfavourable, for up to that stage German air defences had inflicted heavy losses on the enemy. From the spring of 1942 onwards the British had concentrated on the Rhine–Ruhr area, and starting in the spring of 1943 the British and Americans carried out raids on targets in the west of the Reich. They were equipped with the latest radar and target-finding technology and the range and bomb-carrying capacity of their four-engined long distance bombers was immeasurably greater than at the outbreak of the war.

Between March and July 1943 Bomber Command stepped up its raids. The Battle of the Ruhr was at first directed at Essen and the Krupp works, but numerous other cities suffered significant damage. While Bomber Command was able to report the lowest losses of the year and hail the massive raids as great successes, for the Germans they were a catastrophe: at least 34,000 people perished as a result of Operation Gomorrah (the raids on Hamburg at the end of July 1943).[13]

From September 1943 the attention of Bomber Command turned increasingly towards the Reich capital, but compared with Hamburg the distance was greater and the approach more dangerous. Those factors, added to the reorganization of the German air defences, resulted in heavy losses, as had occurred at the beginning of the year. Nor did the US air fleet at first notch up consistent successes. On the contrary, the attacks on aircraft factories and industrial sites in the course of 1943 led to serious losses. From the spring of 1944, however, the Luftwaffe had less and less to throw at the US forces in the early stages of what had become a battle of matériel and thus in the skies over Germany the Allies met with little resistance. The bombing offensive had achieved its greatest effectiveness and so could destroy cities, factories, and infrastructure in the 'Third Reich' almost at will.

In addition to the Ruhr, now even towns and cities in the south, south-west, and east of Germany experienced their worst raids so far.[14] The damage inflicted on German centres of production was huge and attempts to deal with the problem by relocating plant or by the brutal use of forced labour became less and less successful. In particular the serious damage done to oil refineries and hydrogenation plants, the backbone of the German war machine, weakened the economy and so delayed the war of annihilation in the east.[15]

The Allied bombing raids had direct and indirect consequences: they forced German industry to curtail the production of bombers in favour of fighter planes, which were required to defend Reich territory. As a result the Wehrmacht in the west had to go on the defensive and in the east it lost a weapon which had inflicted heavy losses on Soviet troops and had worn down their defences. Even so, the Reich collapsed markedly more slowly than the high commands in Washington and London had expected; in Britain in particular it was feared that Hitler still had an ace up his sleeve and could strike back with poison gas or a secret weapon. That was one of the reasons why the Allied forces persisted with their strategy of carpet bombing and alternatives were dismissed.

Thus it was that in January 1945 Nuremberg and Magdeburg suffered their heaviest night bombing raids with the highest number of fatalities. From February onwards the range of towns and cities was extended: not only was Berlin, already seriously damaged, bombed several times more, but also cities and regions which up to that point had been largely untouched by air raids, chief among them being Dresden, which was bombed in the night of 13/14 February. Between 18,000 and 25,000 lives were lost in the Dresden raids.[16]

This did not mark the end of the bombing campaign, however, though even in Britain an increasing number of voices were heard expressing doubts about its strategic and military necessity. On the other hand, the German Wehrmacht and the Nazi leadership were still fighting what was now a hopeless war, thus escalating its cost. It was above all this last phase of the war, from the autumn of 1944 to April 1945, that turned the German Reich into rubble. Eighty-five per cent of Würzburg was destroyed, while Cologne, Dortmund, Hamburg, and Leipzig lost as much as 70 per cent of their housing stock.

According to official estimates approximately 410,000 civilians, 32,000 'foreigners' and prisoners of war, and 23,000 members of the police and Wehrmacht—a total of 465,000 people—died in air raids in the German Reich as defined by its 1937 borders.[17] By adding refugees to the total number of bombing victims the German Office of National Statistics estimated that 635,000 died in the Reich in its 1942 borders. In October 1945 the Allied staffs arrived at a different total on the basis of their own calculations and their evaluation of statistical material from the Reich government: they referred to at least 420,000 German victims of bombing, while assuming that there was an unknown number of victims whose bodies were never recovered and that half a million dead was a realistic figure.[18] New calculations put the total at about 380,000 dead.[19] The figures for Britain can be established more reliably: the consensus is that 60,000 civilians were killed by bombing and by V-1 and V-2 raids.[20]

The Battle over Morale: Methods and Perspectives

The controversy over whether the Allied bombing campaign was a 'war crime' goes back to the war years. The Nazis made the term an important topos of their propaganda at home and abroad in order to distract attention from their own tyrannical policies. By invoking international law they aimed to make the Germans 'recognized' victims of the war and thus present the German policies of expansion and annihilation as 'self-defence'—an important precondition for the myths of German victimhood after 1945. The term 'war crime' itself was hardly unambiguous, for it concealed a wide variety of interests and meanings. International law itself added to this by admitting different interpretations of aerial warfare.[21]

Although at the outbreak of war there were no rules ratified by all the combatants it was the custom in war to exclude the bombing of civilians, with the result that everyone was aware of infringements. Thus in October 1939, for example, the international law experts in the Wehrmacht High Command were already considering how German or enemy violations of international law should be dealt with in propaganda.[22] Bombing was one part of their considerations. At this point the precepts of international law were not completely jettisoned, but the experts explained in their comments that, in spite of the ban, air raids or gas attacks could be justified as soon as the enemy used them. It is evident that at this early stage the Wehrmacht High Command was already making infringements of international law part of their calculations and envisaging new levels of violence that would make violations of the rules a matter of 'wartime necessity'.

On both sides of the Channel the expectation was that the enemy would cross the legal boundaries. In Britain no one doubted that the Germans were ready to do so. For what could vague international laws of war signify to the Nazi war leaders? For the British General Staff the military threat was more important than worrying about opaque international rules, though the fact that a strategy of deliberate bombing of cities and civilians posed a significant ethical problem remained a dilemma.

In many respects the question of whether the war in the air constituted a war crime leads into a blind alley, for it merely reproduces the arguments of the one-time enemies and their mutual accusations. This book takes a different approach. Aerial warfare represents a specific form of violence in advanced societies in the twentieth century. The history of aerial warfare should therefore focus more sharply than before on 'war as a social condition'[23] and thus on the history of how Britain and Germany came to terms with the bombing in respect of leadership, culture, and experience. At the heart of this history are two constitutionally different political systems: British democracy and National Socialist dictatorship.

When speaking of societies in war in this context we are looking at the dynamic through which societies are transformed from peacetime to war and at the consequences of this transition for social relationships, forms of control, social inclusion, and experiences of violence.[24] Societies were not inevitably changed into 'societies in the grip of fate' or 'emergency societies', terms that Joseph Goebbels was fond of using to describe the defence of the 'national community'.[25]

Even before 1939 horror scenarios put out by the military and the media gave an inkling of what war would bring even to remote areas. And in fact the aerial war did mobilize all the resources of society in a way hitherto unimagined. It combined economic and technical modernity with state-imposed discipline and thus became one of the pinnacles of industrialized warfare in an 'age of extremes' (Eric Hobsbawm). Bombing was to test the population's moral resilience, its 'steadfastness'. Morale was the glue that both nations, Britain and Germany, believed they needed to win the war. A decline in morale, or so it seemed, could be the Achilles heel of industrial societies and that fact had to be turned to advantage in the war. A disintegrating home front was the nightmare of all politicians and military leaders in the inter-war period.

What made the Second World War a 'total war' was not primarily the mobilization of the whole of society but rather the increasing disregard for the inviolability of non-combatants[26] and thus the removal of limits on violence, something that determined not only how the war was waged abroad but also the politics of how it was dealt with at home and the question of morale. In the controversies surrounding the war in the air and the consequences of Allied bombing the term 'morale' acquired key significance: the view taken post-1945 held that the home front had remained stable amid the bombing and that the population in Germany and Britain had united properly only as a result of the air raids.

On the other hand, this view ignored the pitfalls associated with the term *Kriegsmoral* or 'wartime morale'. One is the assumption that it is possible to dictate what the behaviour of the civilian population in wartime must be. Such an approach carries a large amount of contemporary ballast, for underlying it is an assumption, which had been developing since the First World War, that the merging of front and homeland had turned the population into 'civilians in the front line'.[27]

In Germany the controversy over bombing has frequently got no further than stating that the raids were unsuccessful because the Allies failed in their objective of weakening morale in the population. Yet this is where the real questions begin: what was meant when people spoke of morale being 'high' or 'low' or by 'community' and 'endurance'? Was there a yardstick valid across national boundaries and political systems for measuring feelings and behaviour in aerial warfare according to the degree of loyalty of the population to the state?[28] And how close were Germany and Britain, dictatorship and democracy, in this regard? In reality reactions were ambivalent and the consequences of the bombing so contradictory that they elude simple formulae such as the notion of social 'cohesiveness'. In both societies conflicts arose during the war from the quest to maintain 'stability' and 'correct bearing'. Thus morale always stood for many things at once: it was the object of contemporary academic investigation, a term used in the propaganda war, a military objective, and finally, after 1945, a historiographical point of reference and the blueprint for future wars.[29]

Whenever morale, 'mood', and 'bearing' were spoken of or analysed in Germany or Britain specific presuppositions came into play that had largely arisen from debates surrounding the consequences of the First World War. The history of its 'invention', the politics of morale, points to differences in social experience, to crisis situations and prognoses regarding democracy and dictatorship in a period of extreme threat; it directs attention to the social construction of reality and to social practice in wartime, and it helps us map out the competing interests of the individual's experience of war and the population's collective understanding of itself.

The years 1939 to 1945 are at the heart of this study. In order, however, to reach an accurate understanding of the continuities, discontinuities, and contradictions at work in the way the consequences of bombing were coped with and appropriated in cultural, social, and political terms in both countries, there will be some examination of earlier and later history and also of the various phases in the development of the culture of memory since 1945 and up to the present day.

A comparison of this kind can adopt various perspectives. This book will not focus on military theories of aerial warfare, on operational decision-making, the technological history of armaments or of the air forces and their staffs, for all these things have been well researched elsewhere.[30] The purpose of comparing and contrasting democracy and dictatorship is rather to uncover the different strategies for coping with crisis[31] and the different types of community formed in and as a result of the war.[32]

Germany and Britain were two advanced industrial nations that in the First World War had already made use of new military possibilities and dropped bombs on enemy cities. For a long period comparative studies across different political systems were unusual within the tradition of comparative history, particularly in the field of contemporary history and were overshadowed by the theoretical battles during the Cold War over the validity of the concept of totalitarianism.[33] If comparisons were attempted at all, it was fascism[34] and communism[35] that were used as foils to each other in the analysis of totalitarian power, not democracies such as Britain, Sweden, or the United States.

Only since the late 1970s have attempts been made to compare National Socialism with liberal democracies as part of the history of the crisis of modernity[36]—not in order to relativize Nazism but rather to expose convergences, differences, and the contradictory capabilities of modern societies; in other words, the aim is to show what was specific about Nazi society—a society based on violence—at war, but also to show the susceptibilities, inner conflicts, and forms of inner stability of democratic societies as they struggled with an opponent who was (correctly) believed to be capable of anything.[37] The precise advantage of a comparison consists in gaining insight into the internal structures holding dictatorships and democracies together in a continuing state of emergency.[38] Thus the focus here, unlike in other comparative studies, is not an analysis of what causes democratic social structures to break down. It is how different political systems cope with war itself, with the historical study of morale as the *tertium comparationis*, the comparative test case.

This history of bombing can be defined as part of a comparative social and cultural history of war[39] that investigates the resilience and resourcefulness of industrial societies. Aerial warfare crosses boundaries and had consequences that were bound up with the history of British–German relations as well as with each nation's individual and particular experiences over a specific historical time span. In addition to a comparative study of these

experiences, selective instances in the history of how both societies influenced and perceived one another during the war and the post-war period
will be examined in order to highlight what interactions took place, what
distinctions were drawn, how the societies were viewed from abroad, and
how they saw themselves. This approach creates the opportunity to extend
the analysis of aerial warfare as a European phenomenon, an aspect of the
era of total war, beyond the boundaries of a specific era, without being stuck
in the groove of British–German controversies both then and now over the
moral and political question of bombing and 'guilt'.[40]

Beyond this a comparative approach promises answers to the question of
what constituted the core of the German *Volksgemeinschaft* (national community) in wartime, for the specific mixture of National Socialist integration and violence, mobilization and terror, comes into focus when Britain
is also borne in mind. Last but not least, it raises the possibility of finding
answers, both specific to and independent of any particular political system,
to questions connected with the threat from the air: were the organization
of air-raid defences and air-raid shelters, the methods of coping with crisis
among local communities, and the rituals of death something specifically
'National Socialist'? Did the strategies and interpretative models, the rituals
and myths of collective life in other industrial societies have similar characteristics, and were they therefore parallel answers to the threat from the air?
Was there an idea independent of political systems of how the civilian population was to be protected in wartime and how enemy morale was to be
destroyed? This study is in a sense a plea to see the history of British society
at war and of National Socialism in international and in comparative
terms.[41]

At the heart of this book are the differing ways in which Britain and
Germany coped with crisis, gave the war meaning, and instituted forms of
cultural commemoration after 1945.[42] In other words, it deals with the social
practice of power, with mechanisms of political and social inclusion and
exclusion, with death, the process of dying, and with the contest surrounding the memory of bombing that began even during the war in both societies and went on after it.

Particular attention will be paid to the relationship between the public
sphere and the formation of opinion in war. If in this context different forms
of the public sphere in democracy and dictatorship are investigated, this contradiction is only an apparent one. The term 'public sphere' was long held to
denote the normatively defined core of a civil society based on Enlightenment

values.[43] But even dictatorships such as National Socialism recognized spaces and (semi-) public spheres that amounted to more than the sum of press briefings from party offices or staged mass demonstrations.[44] The air raids in particular created such new 'informal public spheres'[45] in which a struggle for dominance and public image took place and which were crucially important to the stability of the regime. The offices of the war damages agencies, where applicants made their claims for damages and where, by contrast with the Nazi press, there was no doubt about the extent of the total damage inflicted by the air raids, were one example; the networks of underground air-raid shelters, which offered space for social interaction as well as for the exchange of information and of rumours, which the regime attempted to regulate but could not suppress, were another.

Changes to these spaces will be one subject of this study, as will an investigation of the connection between morale and violence.[46] In this context violence is not an abstract term but means the physical injuries, pain, and fear experienced by various sections of the population in the face of sustained bombing or the threat of it, which made bombing a vivid sensory experience of violence.[47] Even during the war numerous medical and psychological experts in both Britain and Germany attempted to delve into the significance and effects of these events, whose consequences stretch far beyond 1945.[48]

Alongside many advantages such an approach also involves a number of methodological problems. The degree of destruction was significantly different in the two countries and even the phases of the raids were not synchronized. The bombing of Britain reached its peak in 1940/1, there were raids in the early summer of 1942, and finally the last phase was in 1944/5 with the V-1s and V-2s. Germany's losses were of a different order altogether; the bombing of Hamburg alone was more extensive than all the raids on most British towns and cities put together. That in itself might make a comparison inappropriate. To focus on quantity alone is, however, deceptive. For among British leaders the fear of air attacks and of German V-weapons endured up to the last months of the war and remained a major political factor. Even though Britain did not suffer a wave of attacks comparable to what Germany suffered from the summer of 1944 onwards in raids far more intense than the British experiences of destruction, the worry that Hitler might have a final trump card never abated. This fear shows how up to the last the bombing war played an important role not only as an actual danger but also as an imagined one.

Moreover, although not as many cities had been destroyed as in Germany there was serious loss of life and of residential property, not only in London but in numerous coastal and industrial cities, and thus problems arising from the state of emergency in urban areas in Britain and Germany are very comparable. It is precisely these instances where bombing was concentrated or was particularly intense for a specific period of time that are especially suitable for comparison for they give indications both of similarities and differences in people's realms of experience and in strategies for coping that arose from the escalation of the bombing.

Not all questions can receive a comparable amount of attention in relation to every region in Britain and Germany. While this method is a product of the documentation and the type of sources that are available, there is another important reason for it. In the final analysis my aim cannot be to trace in detail every variation in organizational structures and every issue arising from differences in the specific urban and religious environments. The comparative method requires systematization. In the case of Germany the regions selected for study follow the course of the bombing. Cities in the west and north of the Reich that were bombed early and over a long period are investigated, as well as cities in the south that were not attacked until the second half of the war and thus able to take advantage of the fund of knowledge and experience gained in other regions. Thus Stuttgart, Nuremberg, and Munich are analysed as well as Rostock, Berlin, Hamburg, Kiel, Cologne, and Düsseldorf. In the case of Britain this study is based on the overwhelming majority of the major cities that were bombed. Apart from London these are, for example, Southampton and Plymouth, Bristol and Exeter, Coventry, Manchester, and Hull.

However much scope such a comparison offers, its limitations must also be borne in mind. This is true first of all of the choice of regions to be examined: this study focuses primarily on urban societies and thus (in the case of Germany) above all on bombed regions in the *Altreich* (Germany within the frontiers of 1937). At various points this restriction will be set aside, when it is a case of showing how bombing changed the public sphere in both societies and the bombs even contributed to a blurring of the boundaries between city and countryside.

Secondly, there is a danger that comparisons of dictatorships with democracies tend imperceptibly towards obliterating the constitutional differences between the two societies through functionally orientated comparisons. It is even more important therefore to include in the analysis long-term influences and features of the social structure extending beyond the war period and to pursue the forms of community found in wartime beyond the end of the war.

Thirdly, caution is needed: specific social practices, (relative) success in coping with crisis, and state provision of various kinds cannot allow direct conclusions to be drawn about an individual's trust in and the loyalty of various groups in the population towards the regime.

Aerial War, the National Community, and the People's War: Research Problems

The effects of the bombing raids on the German 'national community' attracted the interest of American and British sociologists even during the war. Members of the United States Strategic Bombing Survey visited German towns in the spring of 1945, questioning those with decision-making powers and Nazi Party members and collecting anything that came their way as possible evidence. The outcome of their investigations was, however, in many ways sobering: the attempt to crush morale had failed. Although they pointed to the sum total of the economic destruction caused by the raids, they concluded that neither side had achieved its strategic goal, namely the demoralization of the enemy's civilian population.[49]

In the 1950s and 1960s in Germany those formerly engaged in anti-aircraft duties for the Nazi state as well as local historians, archivists, and international law experts began to write the history of the bombing war, making use to a considerable extent of interpretative models and terms from the Nazi period, according to which the German Reich became the defenceless object of Allied 'air gangsters'. It took until the late 1970s for German military historians, with the Research Centre for Military History (MGFA) at the forefront, to turn their attention to the aerial war against Germany. Their focus was principally on the preconditions for and the strategic planning and implementation of the bombing raids and thus on the comparative history of the Luftwaffe internationally. They perforce repeatedly engaged with the highly contentious question (contentious just then in Britain as well) of which country had been the first to use carpet bombing and thus was responsible for the escalation of the air raids. The proportionality of means used and also the issue of Allied 'war crimes' were disputed, but the effects of the raids on German society were virtually ignored.[50]

It was the historians of specific cities and localities who, often to mark the anniversary of the bombing raids, produced studies from a different perspective. Until the late 1980s, however, these accounts showed little sign of a conscious methodology.[51] That has changed in recent years: taking Nuremberg as their example, Neil Gregor and Ralf Blank have shown to what extent the bombing of the city led to the dissolution of social cohesion and to the growing significance of local and family networks independent of Party and state.[52] Other local studies provided evidence of how crucial local communities were to the stability of the Nazi system of control, to people's ability to cope with the crises caused by the bombing, and to the Third Reich's politics of exclusion.[53]

Although war was one of the constitutive elements of the National Socialist dictatorship,[54] up to now there have been no studies of its significance as a component of the increasingly radicalized National Socialist social policies.[55] It has taken those general historians of Nazi Germany oriented towards social history in particular a long time to grasp the significance of the bombing for the Nazi system of control.[56] This is why the war and its effects on the home front remained an interpretative gap that was slow to be filled.[57] The essays collected in volume nine of the series 'Das Deutsche Reich und der Zweite Weltkrieg' represent an attempt to provide a synthesis.[58]

In the meantime large and ambitious histories of the air war as a whole have been written by Richard Overy, Horst Boog, Rolf-Dieter Müller, and Olaf Groehler.[59] They all have excellent qualities but Groehler's remains the only one that, though details may be criticized, accords the social history of bombing significant space. Thus what Jeremy Noakes regretted many years ago is still the case, namely that there is still no comprehensive social and cultural history of the bombing war.[60]

In addition, the history of bombing must be linked to more recent discussions in the historiography of National Socialism, and in particular the potency of and the transformations that took place within the 'national community' must be explored.[61] Only then can the 'core problem'[62] be identified, namely the internal structure ordering German society during the war, the regime's methods of ensuring cohesion, and the forms of inclusion and exclusion. To dismiss the term 'national community' as nothing more than a Nazi propaganda slogan leads nowhere, for after all the 'national community' tapped into a great variety of societal models, the focus of which was the harmonization of social conflicts. This made participation in the Nazi state possible for diverse groups.[63] Even those who saw themselves as opponents of National Socialism could still be actively engaged in the 'national community'.

Above all it is confusing that various terminologies converge in this discussion: Nazi plans for a new social order, forms of social practice that were supposed to create the 'national community' and were at the same time locations for social self-mobilization and disciplining, as well as the social structure of the 'Third Reich'.[64] The attempt to use the notion of the 'national community' as a tool with which to investigate the cohesiveness of the regime, what drew people in and (crucially) what marginalized them, must not be confused with a 'concept' of any particular kind. My aim is to use a comparative perspective in order to investigate the mechanisms of coercion and consent in societies in wartime—at bottom a very old problem in research into National Socialism that has none the less lost none of its relevance. Yet, as far as the central phase of the war is concerned, we are still a long way from having a convincing account.

The experiment suggested here of comparing the 'national community' with a variety of different societies in other European countries (in this case Britain) offers a way out of the terminological confusion.[65] Even liberal democracies such as Sweden and Britain were familiar with projects for collective organization and creation of communities as a response to the crises of the inter-war years.[66] The term 'The People's War' in Britain was in this respect both answer and alternative to the Nazi 'national community'. The term 'People's War' first emerged in the early nineteenth century to denote a new form of civilian quasi-democratic organization of militias during the Napoleonic War.[67] It evoked a defensive struggle on the part of the whole nation that overcame class barriers and created a very special 'community spirit'.[68]

Before the twentieth century Britain had been primarily involved in colonial wars, and, by contrast with France and Germany, up until the First World War there had been little debate about international wars. That changed around 1890 with the fear of a German invasion and then finally in 1914. Military ideas of the nation gained influence and so too did the 'People's War' as a vision of an armed civil society fighting together in the munitions factories and communal shelters. The notion of a 'People's War' that prevailed from 1939 onwards seemed to have been born in the tunnels of the London underground; a national project for creating a community that not only offered moral armour for the fight against National Socialism

but also contained the promise that this war would be followed by the construction of a new society based on a welfare state.[69]

British contemporary history, like its German counterpart, has concentrated attention on its national narrative,[70] and for this reason hardly any
empirically well-founded comparative studies exist.[71] The first official histories of the Second World War based on documentary evidence appeared
sooner in Britain than in Germany. As early as 1961 Noble Frankland and
Charles Webster published their history of the strategic air offensive,[72] which
to this day is an important point of reference for numerous studies of the
military history of bombing, one of the most productive historians in this
field being Richard Overy.[73] Their focus, however, was overwhelmingly on
training and production, strategy and effectiveness, and much less on the
social consequences of aerial warfare.

Broadly speaking, two distinct though of course interconnected strands
of debate are apparent in the British historiography of the home front:[74]
first of all the relationship of war and social change. Did the war increase the
state's sensitivity to the dire problems of the working class? In the end, was
it the experience of war that led to the creation of the British welfare
state?[75] In addition to social policy there was a second group of related questions that focused on the 'People's War', and asked whether the war, and in
particular the Blitz,[76] had created a new British 'sense of community'.
Numerous studies written from the immediate aftermath of the war into
the 1960s took this as their basic idea.[77]

The definitive study of the social history of the war period and the one
that remains to this day the most influential is Angus Calder's monumental
The People's War.[78] His pioneering work was the first to use the records of
Mass Observation and made the everyday experience of the 'little people'
during the Blitz his focus. He was no longer concerned exclusively with
military successes but with the problems of everyday life in wartime, with
administrative failures and the concerns of individuals, about which up to
that point almost nothing was known.

It was also remarkable how much the myth of the 'People's War' gathered
momentum through the book's reception and took on a life of its own, with
the result that from the 1980s a veritable flood of studies appeared that
turned the social and political history of the war into a hotly contested battlefield. The battle lines were drawn, to put it in abbreviated form, between
those who saw the war as a vital engine of social change and the welfare
state as essentially the product of the post-war consensus, and others who,

not least from the perspective of gender,[79] emphasized the rigid social hier-archies, the differing political aims of the coalition partners, the continued discrepancies in wages between men's and women's work, the dominance of patriarchal role models, and the longevity of the class structure.[80]

Whereas there is a long tradition of social and political history for the years 1939 to 1945 and research began to open up—faster than in Germany—to the increasing influence of cultural history, it is astonishing how little resonance these debates had in British histories of cities and regions during the war. There is no comparable tradition in Britain of the political and social history of localities such as was highly influential in the history of National Socialism from the 1980s onwards.[81] In many cases Lon-don is the exclusive focus and so studies often end in 1941—as a result of which the consequences of the war and the connection between the war and the post-war world are lost from view.[82]

Thus the differing national and regional cultures of commemoration in Britain and Germany after 1945 will form the final section of this book.[83] It will focus on the adaptation and alteration of contemporary narratives about bombing, their distortion and political instrumentalization, ending with the debate surrounding *Brand* (The Fire). Jörg Friedrich's history of the bombing war, published in 2002, triggered a major controversy about 'taboos' and the 'traumatizing' of the Germans and put aerial warfare on the front pages of the popular press. This was a debate that, even though con-ducted in a variety of contexts, produced lively discussion on both sides of the Channel about the morality of war and war crimes, about the legitimi-zation of and necessity for the use of extreme violence in the fight against the world's dictators, and gave rise to the 'new' history of the Second World War with Germany as victim. This history has no end point, only many intertwined paths connecting the past, present, and future of war.

I

The War of the Future
1900–1939

The Shock of London

When the aerial war was over New York City lay in ruins. The global battle had turned human beings into barbarians and civilizations into violent feudal societies. This bloody, apocalyptic picture of war was painted by the young British science fiction author H. G. Wells in his 1908 novel *The War in the Air*.[1] At the end of it the cities of Europe and the American metropolis on the Hudson lay in rubble. Along with the rising Asian powers Germany was the dangerous warmonger aiming for world domination, whose aeroplanes brought death and destruction. The terror from the skies caused fear and panic among the population and heralded the end of the world.

At the beginning of the twentieth century aerial warfare was a subject for novelists and futurologists. And the dream of flying spurred on the pioneers of this new technology—a technology that from its beginnings aroused great interest among Europe's general staffs, for airships and planes offered the chance of revolutionizing the way wars were fought, of striking behind enemy lines and of gaining information about enemy troop movements. Civilian enthusiasm for technology and strategic military war games projecting the future of war went hand in hand and even before the First World War were to extend what was militarily conceivable and practicable in Europe and the USA. Yet in spite of initial experiments by Spain and then Italy—in 1911/12 during the war against Turkey bombs were thrown by hand from an aircraft—neither in London, nor Paris, nor Berlin did anyone have clear ideas about the implications of such a war in the 'third dimension' (in addition to land and sea).

At first the German Kaiserreich had concentrated on airships and neglected other options, whereas at the start of the First World War France created its first bomber group, which was capable of attacking its enemy across the border on the latter's own soil. With the naval aircraft of its Royal Navy Air Service Britain too had at its disposal a weapon first deployed in the autumn and winter of 1914 against Cologne and Düsseldorf and also against the airship bases in Friedrichshafen and Cuxhaven.[2] When the German advance was halted by the trench warfare of the western front and the British blockade first began to bite, Berlin started to search for alternatives and to attempt to regain the ground lost in aircraft production. Through massive injections of materials and money the Reich increased production. Apart from Zeppelins it focused on new types of aircraft such as the Gotha-IV bombers, which, although they carried fewer bombs, had better defences and were more powerful.

In spite of this they were unable to catch up with the Allies. At the end of the First World War Germany's enemies had the first bombers that carried enough munitions and fuel to attack industrial plant and ports. As yet the struggle for air supremacy was far from being decisive for the war's outcome, but nevertheless the strategic significance accorded to aircraft had increased from month to month. From 1918 the British Air Ministry possessed the first detailed lists of potential targets in the north and west of the Reich, above all for Berlin and the Ruhr area. Munitions factories were regarded as the most important target and hopes were high that with the use of the new types of bombers industrial plant and submarine production could be paralysed.[3] As yet, however, the required technology did not exist and there was a lack of instruments for precision navigation and of qualified personnel capable of achieving more than a very few chance hits. The actual damage to infrastructure and also the number of victims resulting from the first military air operations were therefore limited.[4] Up to the end of the war Germany suffered 729 fatalities while the armaments industry was virtually untouched; plans to bomb Berlin came to nothing.[5] In Britain 1,414 people were killed and 3,416 were injured.

Even so, what at first glance appears a small number of fatalities is deceptive. For in the case of Britain in particular the significance of the German attacks was not limited to the comparatively slight loss of life. For the first time in centuries the United Kingdom had been attacked on its home soil. London, the heart of the Empire, had been hit and it had proved impossible to protect the population. German zeppelins had attacked the British capital at the end of May 1915; in 1916 a further 123 raids followed, until finally in 1917 the first bombers attacked London. In the heaviest of these attacks, on 13 June 1917, 162 people were killed. There were numerous reports about discontent, fear, even panic in some of the areas of London that were bombed. There were no effective early warning systems, and, as German observers reported, a simple rumour often sufficed to make crowds of Londoners flee into the underground tunnels. Night raids, they said, seemed to affect people most powerfully: women especially shrieked hysterically and there was general 'shouting and scurrying'—a state of 'total madness', as a German businessman wrote at the beginning of December 1917 to the German Admiralty.[6]

The Chief of the Imperial General Staff remarked after the raids that many people seemed to think that 'the end of world had come'.[7] London policemen reported that people fought to get a secure place in the underground and could be made to see reason only with difficulty; it was above all the unaccustomed sense of helplessness and defencelessness that made many people 'nervous'.[8]

In many cases this sounded like a self-fulfilling prophecy. H. G. Wells had already imagined people fleeing in panic outside Madison Square Garden and on Brooklyn Bridge, crushing their neighbours in the process. The idea that masses in a state of terror ceased to behave humanely and became transformed into a violent mob verging on the bestial was a widespread assumption among social psychologists and military theorists, whose ranks had been expanding since the turn of the century. It was an assumption founded on observations of human behaviour during major natural catastrophes or based wholly on anthropological theory.[9]

What seemed clear was that in extreme situations civilians, precisely those who inhabited great cities, were particularly vulnerable to all forms of fear, neurasthenia, and panic and that in wartime in particular collective reason was fragile.[10] It was the modern city-dweller, the anonymous proletarian in the crowd, who was believed by many representatives of what was still the young science of sociology to be particularly liable to react inappropriately in the crisis of war. Whereas in country areas old ties kept the social fabric intact, cities were regarded as jungles in which bombs could wreak real havoc.[11] In 1914 the *Journal of the Royal United Services Institute* was already warning about the disastrous consequences of an enemy attack on the British Isles: it was quite possible that a massive enemy strike might lead not only to panic but even to protests by the masses, who might force the government to make peace on the enemy's terms.[12] Medics and psychologists considered it at best a matter of time before the feeble backbone of the home front crumbled and people succumbed to nervous illnesses,[13] not least because modern warfare had created a completely new potential for destruction.

Visions of Aerial Warfare

What was to be the outcome of all this? The plans made in 1915 by the Chief of the British bomber fleet, Brigadier General Hugh Trenchard, for the bombing of Germany were above all for attacks on infrastructure linking the western front with the Reich. Apart from the Ruhr additional targets included the industrial sites of Alsace-Lorraine. The shock of the zeppelin and Gotha bomber attacks on London led to intensive debate about future bombing strategy and the choice of potential targets.[14] Should the Germans be paid back in kind? And what were the moral boundaries? After the attacks of summer 1917 public calls in Britain for retaliation were growing ever louder. 'Political bombing' (the supposed German strategy) without regard for civilian victims was now seen as typical Teutonic behaviour and sufficient legitimization for any form of retaliation,[15] although in fact the German air force was too inaccurate to be particularly terrifying. However, when during an attack in June 1917 more than a hundred schoolchildren were killed, shock at this type of warfare turned into public outrage and a clamour for retaliation.[16]

Whereas Great Britain was still conducting the war in a chivalrous manner, concentrating its bombing on military targets,[17] it was claimed that German air raids aimed at the innocent were 'cruel' and 'inhuman'. *The Times* described the search for the remains of the bodies of dead children in exhaustive detail, drawing attention to the lack of warning systems, which, had they been set up, might have saved the children's lives.[18] In October 1917 the Minister of War, Lord Derby, declared that at least the raids had failed to weaken British morale. Though a considerable number of those affected had in fact sought shelter from the raids in the underground stations, he said, most of what was said there had been incomprehensible. In other words, only fearful foreigners had done a bunk, but not the British.[19]

Along with the demonization of the enemy, cautious criticism of the preventive measures, and the appeal to British wartime morale a new kind of discussion got under way in the defensive propaganda battle with Germany, one that distinguished between 'justified' and 'unjustified', 'military' and 'civilian' bombing, though without drawing clear boundaries between them. For in spite of all protestations to the contrary they were in fact indistinguishable. In June 1918 Hugh Trenchard informed the War Cabinet about his bomber units' future targets: Germany was to be crushed by an assault on the core of its physical and psychological strength, and that meant systematically bombing its densely populated industrial areas.[20] Underlying this was the assumption that as a result of the lengthy sea blockade German morale overall was already low and air raids would finish the enemy off.

This line of argument was extremely dangerous because, following the attacks on London at the latest, the view had taken hold among the British public and large sections of the military that Germany lacked any sense of chivalry and that German aggression would be aimed primarily at the home front, at vulnerable women and the working class. In Britain's eyes it seemed not only strategically necessary but legitimate from the point of view of morality and the laws of war to repay the Germans in the same coin. That meant that even attacks on civilian targets, which were considered to be the enemy's real weak spot, were justified. Nevertheless, Trenchard rejected 'terror bombing', the use of bombers purely to destroy the civilian population, and this was an important qualification that was to have an impact on the controversies surrounding the British bombing strategy reaching into the Second World War.[21] On the other hand he was a vehement advocate of the bombing of factories and the workers in them as a means of stoking social unrest and forcing the enemy to make peace.[22] Factories were seen as legitimate targets and in the end, he assumed, the workers would abandon the works for fear of further attacks and thus restrict the manufacture of armaments.[23]

Fascination with the possibilities of a new technology, the assumption that the Germans had no moral scruples, combined with the supposedly instructive experience of the summer of 1917 and the wavering support of the civilian population produced a distinct surge of enthusiasm for the comprehensive deployment of the air force. These impulses were at first merely interrupted by the end of the war and Germany's capitulation, in which, it must be said, aerial bombing played only a tiny part. But the hope was that in future conflicts this would be very different. This at least was the view noisily put about after the war by leading theorists of aerial warfare, though one that was not undisputed by other branches of the military, who at most were prepared to concede that the air force could support land and sea operations. Whereas the German air force's brief boom was for the time being brought to an end by the Treaty of Versailles and it remained uncertain how, given the new restrictions, Germany could still keep up in the field of aviation, American and British strategists in particular considered it a foregone conclusion that bombs were the new miracle weapon of war and pilots their modern-day crusaders. As the future agents of 'total war' they were the ones who could fly over mountains and seas to strike at the enemy's heart.

Yet this type of warfare did not exactly fit the self-image of German and British pilots: 'Knights of the air' such as Manfred von Richthofen regarded war more as a sporting duel, a fight man to man as in a tournament in which the best and bravest man wins. While in the trench warfare of the First World War the powerful machine guns battered each other, aerial warfare and the pilots' battles seemed like the last remaining manifestation of chivalry in an industrial war and the airmen thus as a special class, heroic as well as sporting, more individualists than soldiers, who fought a 'clean' war.[24]

The war in the air gave an impression rather of being, as the pilot Cecil Lewis put it in his autobiography, a noble confrontation, a contrast to the bloody battlefields the airmen could observe beneath them. This cult of the honourable knight of the skies was so strong on both sides of the Channel that the Allies sent a delegation to Germany in November 1925 to pay their last respects in the presence of the German President Paul von Hindenburg to Manfred von Richthofen, the dead First World War ace, when his remains were brought from France to Germany and interred at a state funeral.[25] At the same time the autobiographies of German airmen were reaching a mass audience not only in Germany but also in Britain and romanticizing the airman as mythic figure. The men sitting in the planes were thus not murderers but men whose masculine and heroic role contrasted with industrialized war and its anonymous mass fatalities.[26] The negative counterpart to the 'knight of the skies' had already emerged in British propaganda during the war; he sat at the controls of zeppelins and German bombers, killing women and children in a ruthless and cowardly fashion and ignoring the rules of sportsmanship.[27]

This new type of airman dreamt about, for example by Ernst Jünger, was in fact a long way from the ideals of 'sportsmanship'. What was lauded by

Jünger and others was a man firm and unflinching with nerves of steel who had been tempered by the noise and machinery of aircraft and who, together with the other pilots of his squadron, did not shrink from attacking the enemy, while keeping any strong emotions under control.[28] War and the industrial age demanded a new man and warrior who carried out his mission coolly and with total control. In such a war your comrades died and death was routine and a calculated risk. An airman, however, was too disciplined and iron-willed to be deterred by this, for these were the characteristics of celebrated pilots such as Oswald Boelcke and von Richthofen, and were more necessary to 'modern warfare' and popular patriotism, so Jünger thought, than exaggerated (British) sportsmanship.[29]

War in the third dimension therefore changed the 'warrior' himself. But what was the significance of the new technologies for the way in which future wars would be planned and successfully waged? And what sort of category was it that had found its way into military orthodoxy, namely the 'population'? The most radical of these visions of aerial warfare was put forward by the Italian General Giulio Douhet, whose experiences while serving in North Africa were recorded in his book about 'air supremacy'.[30] More than any other theorist of aerial warfare of the inter-war years Douhet conjured up an image of the omnipotence of bomber fleets, whose deployment he gauged to be more efficient and cost-effective than, for example, constructing air defences or attempting over many years to expand ground forces. The coming of bombers had revolutionized warfare and that also meant that it was now possible to attack the enemy with maximum force at his weakest point and so to take advantage of speed and total mobilization. He argued that there was no answer to these new weapons and to the unrestrained use of gas in aerial warfare and only those who opted for them unreservedly could exploit their effects fully in a 'total war'.

Air supremacy was therefore crucial in future wars, for the new power relations in the sky made possible something many military strategists had dreamt of: defeating the enemy not at the front but at home. And to do so it was not only permitted but positively necessary to attack the enemy's morale—with bombs or poison gas—in order to minimize one's own risk while maximizing the damage inflicted.

Virtually no other aerial war strategist went as far as Douhet. In Britain, moreover, little attention was paid to foreign countries and the main focus was on internal discussions about the role of the RAF within the military as a whole. Thus Douhet's influence remained slight in the 1920s. In Germany hardly anyone took notice of him and his book was not finally translated until 1935.[31] In Britain it was much the same story: hardly anyone had read the book in the years following its publication and if anyone did then it aroused marginal interest at best.[32] This was not to change until the mid-1930s, when important theoretical debates had already taken place in Germany and Britain and Douhet was valued, as it were, retrospectively, as a seminal predictor of the future of warfare.[33]

Across Europe, in France and Britain as well as in Germany, there was palpable scepticism concerning these radical plans. Apart from considerable doubts about the use of poison gas and the possible escalation resulting from that, this scepticism sprang above all from the reduced significance of the army and navy, for which Douhet envisaged no role and which would have had to be subordinated completely to the air force. None the less, military staffs were in no doubt that the air force would fundamentally change the next war. For wars in the future would no longer be decided solely by victory over the enemy's armed forces. The victor would be the nation with the greatest military, economic, and civilian resources, and that could only be the nation that was capable of eliminating the enemy's resources in the enemy's own territory.

That was what the nations were preparing for. Britain was the only country where the experience of using an air force in the First World War had led to the establishment of a service in its own right. This in turn ensured that discussion about the purpose of aerial warfare from the 1920s onwards gained increasing weight, notwithstanding the continued reservations on the part of Britain's army and navy. After the heavy losses suffered in the battles of the First World War with its millions of casualties 'total war' from the air seemed to offer Britain the potential to engage in military conflict without at the same time having to pay a commensurate price in terms of bloodshed. This was an alternative acceptable not least to the Treasury, as the RAF promised to wage a war that was not only efficient but also inexpensive.

Hugh Trenchard's prediction that the effects of an air attack on morale had the ratio of 20:1 was supported by many Conservative politicians and military leaders for the simple reason that they wished to believe that he would be proved right.[34] There was no evidence for it; at best there were the horrors depicted by some science fiction authors and the predictions of leading military theorists discussing the future of warfare in military journals. These predictions applied of course primarily to 'civilized' countries.

Colonial practice is hard to overestimate.[35] For all European colonial powers air supremacy had, at the latest since the beginning of the 1920s, been the primary instrument for the control and subjection of non-European nations. Policies of occupation and pacification changed as a result of the new technology, allowing the colonial masters to refine their use of force in such a way that they could restrict themselves to selective destruction. The costs to the European powers varied, however, according to their opponents. Italians and Spaniards, who at an early stage had adopted 'police bombing' and, as in Morocco, had tried out poison gas, were facing considerable military resistance that quickly sent the material and civilian costs soaring.

This was not the case with Britain, which thus could get worked up about the cruel use of air power by other European countries: in the Middle East, Africa, Iraq, and Afghanistan British pilots had chalked up initial and, as far as the experts were concerned, promising successes in the struggle against the indigenous populations. In Egypt, Nigeria, South-West Africa, and many other parts of the Empire the RAF had used bombs and machine guns in aircraft against insurgents, protesters, and rebellious tribes. These weapons were not to be deployed against white people but they were used against indigenous 'uncivilized' populations, to whom the same standards of international law would not apply.

The use of aircraft developed quickly from the 1920s into an important element in imperial policy, one that from the standpoint of leading politicians in the colonies was inexpensive and efficient, efficient above all because the results—usually the suppression of uprisings against colonial power—spoke for themselves. The consensus was that the effect of bombs on 'morale' had been impressive and the losses huge.[36] From the point of view of the RAF such attacks showed how effective this new military instrument could be and thus how important it was to establish bombing of the indigenous population as a component in the stabilization of imperial rule, and not least to ensure lasting security in the most distant corners of what was now a financially burdened Empire. A handful of pilots and their planes could replace expensive armies and maximum success could be achieved with only a few bombs.

This strategy was admittedly controversial.[37] Yet in spite of critical voices, in particular from the growing pacifist movement, neither Trenchard nor the Foreign Secretary Austen Chamberlain was prepared to make concessions. Speaking in Parliament in July 1933, Chamberlain argued, not least with an eye to aerial warfare in the colonies, that as a weapon the aeroplane

was 'the most humane instrument that you can employ'.[38] The great attraction exerted by the prospect of ending a war swiftly could be seen even in
the case of a liberal, and thoughtful, individual such as the influential military theoretician Basil Liddell Hart.[39] He too saw in aircraft the chance to
hit a modern state where it particularly hurt, namely deep in its interior.
Yet what he envisaged was far from being a final war of annihilation. He
rather believed that this type of warfare could save lives and prevent a move
to total war, as experienced in the First World War. In the end, he claimed,
it was in the interest of the power pursuing the war to combine two aims:
forcing the enemy into submission and at the same time inflicting on him
as little lasting damage in terms of loss of life and destruction of the industrial infrastructure as possible. After all, he said in conclusion, the enemies
of today were the customers of tomorrow and also potential allies.[40]

Regardless of such distinctions, what made a lasting impression was the
notion of a future war that involved the total mobilization of all societies
and in which civilians would also become a new target. Even before the
development of concrete military plans this vision had established itself
among large sections of the military and the public, and damaging the
enemy's morale was now seen as an objective. In addition to destroying
factories and transport networks, targeting actual places of work and destroying the means of production and the workforce itself were now seen as
offering the chance of making a major impact.

The implications of that vision for Britain's own society turned out to be
ambivalent. On the one hand it was firmly believed after the battles of the
First World War that British courage was superior; on the other, there was
considerable doubt about whether large sections of the working classes
would actually stand firm under pressure. Concern about the reliability of
women and of the proletariat was certainly an unmistakable element in
virtually all discussions and memoranda[41]—and not only in Great Britain.

On the German side General Erich Ludendorff's vision of 'total war' had
already established the connection between warfare and the population.[42]
The people, he explained, were the key element in total war.[43] Wars were no
longer simply conflicts between two sovereign states that sent their forces to
fight each other; wars were existential struggles of entire nations in the
service of a higher moral justice. This 'total conflict' between nations created
the foundations for comprehensive mobilization and total commitment
when it came to both ends and means. Aerial warfare, Ludendorff believed,
was a crucial weapon in this respect and at the same time an important

factor in ensuring domestic integration and in propaganda, both of which were necessary for survival in 'total war'. The essential issue was how industrial nations were to stand the test in the new age of war—and where they were most vulnerable. In this context the term 'nation' could have a wide variety of meanings. For Douhet a nation being subjected to attack from the air was nothing more than a helpless mass that could do nothing but flee and try to overthrow the government. If bombing was ferocious enough, no air defences could be too extensive to guard against rebellion.

Thus aerial warfare became part of the struggle of modern industrial nations, attempting to strike where they thought each other weakest, namely on the margins of society. Bombing, industrialization, and social integration thus became even more closely associated: first, because the raids were intended to destroy sources of economic strength and so prevent a first strike of an unknown kind; secondly, because the working class, which was not sufficiently integrated into society, was regarded as the real weak spot of modern societies. Thus conflicts between modern industrial societies were marked from the very outset by the fact that the border between economic and military targets on the one hand and political and civilian ones on the other was becoming more and more fluid. Even for those involved it was increasingly unclear where the borderline should be, in so far as they had come to see this new kind of total war as indispensable. And what, in the final analysis, was the difference between munitions workers, who kept the machinery of war in motion, and the soldiers at the front? Both were part of the same war.

Air Defence and the Nation

When morale and the civilian population were being discussed there was frequent talk of 'nerve centres', main arteries that had to be severed, attacks on the enemy's 'heart' and 'brain'. Since the inter-war years the vocabulary of destruction had featured terms such as insects, gnats, or mosquitoes, which depersonalized the civilian realm and turned the enemy into a biological object which could be eliminated without any scruples. At most it was an anonymous body or an organ necessary to the whole that was being destroyed, not human beings. There was no mention of pain and even the calculation of the number of victims appeared at best as a statistic, a piece of mathematics designed to demonstrate military strength.[44]

If morality was ever discussed, then it was not in order to legitimize this kind of warfare. For to large sections of the British public and military such a legitimization seemed to have low priority simply because the Germans as the future enemy had after all already shown their true nature. This perception made it possible to claim moral superiority over the enemy, while at the same time thinking him capable of anything and preparing one's own response as a preventive measure.

Naturally even in Britain, especially in the Labour Party and in pacifist circles, which had been growing rapidly since the end of the war,[45] voices were raised in opposition, predicting an escalation of violence and therefore promoting the creation of a new international order rather than the RAF as a first-strike weapon. Yet these groups were not in the majority, as became evident not least when a civil air defence and secure shelters were established. In fact Douhet's notion of the 'defenceless masses' was by no means universally accepted. For however great the reservations with regard to a radical and undisciplined working class may have been, the civilian decision-makers did not want to succumb to a feeling of inevitability, regarding all defence as pointless and so giving up all their responsibility for non-military options.

Since the beginning of the 1920s British government officials had been considering civilian preparations for war. What sort of war was on the way? Could people defend themselves against the new weapons? Did air defences, underground bunkers, and evacuations make sense? What sort of security was even possible? The scenarios discussed by the military and in the Air Raid Precautions Committee (ARPC) formed especially for this purpose in 1924 were as frightening as they were extraordinary. The image lodged in people's minds was of total devastation: buildings in ruins, refugees in their millions, bodies lying everywhere, the capital in flames, starving, marauding hordes fighting for survival—that was what an attack on London would bring.[46] The quantity of explosives likely to be dropped was calculated and the numbers of wounded extrapolated; in addition, it seemed not inconceivable that whole cities might be razed to the ground. An apocalypse most certainly seemed a real possibility.[47]

What could be done to defend people? Nothing, was the view of Hugh Trenchard, chief of the air force General Staff. Thus he rejected all objections raised by John Anderson, the civilian chair of the ARPC and Permanent Under-Secretary of State at the Home Office, to the plan of dispensing with air defence precautions solely because they might in any case not be capable of withstanding an attack.[48] The conflict continued to smoulder for years, military leaders and ministries renewing debates about new predictions of destruction: What use were bunkers if within a few days enemy bomber squadrons could destroy the water supply? Who was to assume responsibility for civil defence in an emergency? Meanwhile, a controversy was continuing in the background, not about finances or responsibilities, but about British morale and about what might happen if the enemy were to strike with full force. In the view of the Conservative elites the first warnings of the unruly behaviour of the masses had come during the General Strike of 1926. The escalation of that conflict had, in their estimation, made clear the unpredictability of the working classes. Not least the question of what methods of military coercion would be acceptable to the population in an emergency was a moot point after the General Strike.

It was not only the elites who were fearful of aerial warfare. Magazines and mass circulation newspapers were full of reports about the future of war. The next war, it seemed certain, would be an aerial war—with catastrophic results.[49] For that reason plans for the development of air defences proved controversial. Numerous academics and architects criticized the plans, for even though in committee rooms catastrophic scenarios were repeatedly evoked, the concrete strategies that had been worked on since the mid-1930s led, according to critics, at best to minimal protection for the population under threat. If there was a genuine desire to protect people that would mean above all investing more money in defence installations. Instead, the Conservative government's plans seemed confined to extending the numbers of air-raid wardens and air defence observers and in the event of war to undermining parliamentary democracy and establishing a semi-authoritarian form of government.

The question of the population's morale touched on a further sensitive spot, however. In the event of a raid what rights should pass to the military? At what point did the situation become an emergency and when should the civil authorities relinquish power? These issues caused much conflict.[50] Anderson, the chair of the ARPC, for example, took the view that martial law could be declared only in the most extreme emergency, and that meant in the event that none of the civil institutions was still operational. Admittedly, even Anderson could not resist the argument that in the case of a massive panic quasi-military agencies would be required in order to restore order in the country—though he insisted such agencies should be under civil control. Even the military resisted taking over civil functions, not least on the grounds of cost.

In the end—and this was crucial—every effort was to be made to avoid declaring martial law because this would not only seem like a defeat but would create huge conflicts among the organizations designed to ensure consensus and continuity. Even though fear of aerial warfare was an important political battlefield, the government had the confidence to promote air defence actively only from about 1933. Up to that point the deliberations had been largely kept out of the public domain because there was concern that otherwise fear would increase and become uncontrollable. Now for the first time resources were made available in the budget, concrete plans began to be developed, and even local authorities put the topic of air defences on the agenda.

Germany

In Germany the preconditions for an extension of air defences were different, not least as a result of defeat in the First World War and the stipulations of the Treaty of Versailles, which had banned the possession of military aircraft and multi-engined planes. Yet in spite of numerous attempts to avoid reparations, the creation of Lufthansa in 1926, and the development of civil aviation, Germany after 1933 was lagging behind with regard to long-haul aircraft. Even if the attacks on cities such as Freiburg[51] or Düsseldorf had not led to violent national agitation, such as had occurred in Britain, the future of aerial warfare and the protection of the population was an important aspect of domestic politics and the scene of conflicts concerning the future order and the relationship between the military and civil society. It was assumed that bombing and gas attacks during the coming war would mean that the German people would face an even more severe test of their endurance than in the First World War from 1914 to 1918. Leading representatives of the Defence Ministry regarded air defences as being as important as securing the eastern border and hence as a matter of national survival. The extension of air defences therefore seemed from the middle of the 1920s to be particularly pressing because the population had been deprived of the will to defend itself as a result of the demobilization and demilitarization imposed by the Allies. While other nations were preparing for war Germany was suffering from a lack of knowledge and wilful ignorance.[52]

Air defence organizations began to drum up support for activities to be extended and the population to be informed, continually conjuring up the horror scenario of a future 'total war' and the need for the nation's 'self-preservation'. The German Air-Defence Association (DLS) appealed to the Reich government not to leave the 'defenceless' population in ignorance about the dangers threatening them but to be active in keeping them informed. Air defence was a humanitarian project and a national duty, part of a struggle for survival and a 'democratic' self-mobilization. This latter idea of 'democratic self-mobilization' was seen as something that should develop as complementary to the activities of state and bureaucratic organizations.[53] At the end of the 1920s pressure increased on the Reich government to play a more active role in air defence matters and to invest more money in them. Air defence was regarded as the symbol of the commitment to national survival and the cross-party attempt to overcome the chaos of conditions in the Weimar Republic. This was, at any rate, the view of the members of the German Air Defence League, founded in 1931. Mayors of numerous German cities who wished to inform their inhabitants about the calamitous nature of gas and air attacks belonged to it, seeing themselves as the nucleus of a movement that would transcend party boundaries.[54]

From the end of the 1920s state and local government organizations and various other associations tried with renewed energy to draw attention to air defence and to secure responsibilities in this field, the significance of which steadily increased both within politics and in the public sphere, with the Right staking a particular claim. The states governed by the German Social Democratic Party kept a very watchful eye on attempts by fringe groups of air defence activists to form paramilitary organizations and Social Democrats and pacifists alike warned of a creeping militarization of the Republic. On the political Right it was difficult to distinguish between genuine concern, hysteria, and deliberate attempts to cause panic. The debate about air defences increasingly revolved around ideas of a national 'awakening' and around combating the delusory longing for peace current in German politics. In a world in which no one was willing to abandon aerial warfare and peace could not be guaranteed the response could only be self-defence and readiness for conflict.

At the beginning of the 1930s less and less was being said about peace, while voices were increasingly raised in favour of a more extensive mobilization of all sections of the population in conjunction with the Reich army. The responsibility for air defence still lay in the hands of the executive. The

Reich Ministry of the Interior fended off all attempts to hand over tasks that came under its jurisdiction and had begun from 1931 to create preliminary organizational structures for air defence, starting at Reich level and spreading down to the states and local authorities. The Reich Finance Ministry also succeeded in blocking any increase in financial support for the air defence organizations. Pressure was nevertheless growing, particularly as the cause was taken up in the Reichstag by the Nazi Party and the DNVP (German Nationalists).

The extent to which the climate was beginning to change from the early 1930s was indicated not least by the growing number of apocalyptic studies and fictional stories of aerial warfare that were being published. As in Britain, though appearing a little later, they painted vivid and horrifying pictures of future aerial warfare and repeatedly referred to the risk of panic breaking out and people fleeing en masse.[55] *Gas over Austria*, for example, was the title of a study by the Viennese senior medical officer Arthur Zimmer, in which he relates the injuries caused by gas in the First World War and makes the gloomy prediction that 'aerial warfare will affect the whole country and threaten the lives of all the inhabitants indiscriminately'.[56] In *Europe Gone Mad 1934* Hanns Gobsch tells the story of the future bombing war between Fascist Italy and France.[57] It is remarkable not only for the brutality with which the war is waged but also for the end result, which Gobsch evokes as a horrific scenario. By the end both countries destroy each other. St Peter's, the Arc de Triomphe, and the Eiffel Tower, symbols of European culture, collapse and in the end the real winner is the communist Soviet Union.[58]

It was not, however, only their poor literary quality that distinguished works such as these or Axel Alexander's *The Battle over Berlin*[59] or Johann von Leer's *Bombs Fall On Hamburg*[60] from the scenarios described in H. G. Wells's science fiction. For a start the Reich is now the victim of 'Bolshevist' terror from the air, and secondly the bombs hit a nation that has been underestimated and is now slowly reawakening, and which in the moment of crisis and led by a resolute government unleashes the whole of its might and shows discipline in coping with the cowardly bombing war. These were tales of oppression and national rebirth, of communist threats, self-discipline, and German morale in wartime, which posited that an essential element in Germans' ability to survive and in their superiority lay precisely in their fighting character. Air defence propaganda could be smoothly fitted into the anti-republican revanchism of the *völkisch* Right, which claimed that

Germany was an encircled Reich under external threat, whose industrial centres moreover lay in border regions and thus represented an easy target for enemy aircraft. It was a nation for which 'self-defence' was an elixir, restoring the people to health and preserving the 'nation's body' (*Volkskörper*). Moreover, in von Leer's story it is the combination of the fighting spirit of the city community and the peasants showing solidarity with them that succeeds in thwarting the cowardly bomb and gas attack on the Hanseatic city and overcomes the class divisions in society.

By the end it seems as if the bombing and the external threat that have been survived through a collective response have formed a new kind of community, stronger and tougher than democratic society. Although such sentiments did not necessarily originate from the mainstream of the air defence movement, their resonance had increased significantly by the beginning of the 1930s. The air defence movement was now characterized by its growing radicalization and militarization, combining these with the demand that the nation's oppression through the Treaty of Versailles should end and the Germans' 'preparedness to fight' in a world full of enemies be restored. 'The fighting community' and 'morale' went hand in hand and should be the driving forces of this rebirth.

In spring 1933, a few days before the National Socialist takeover of power in Bavaria, a travelling exhibition dealing with self-defence during air raids was opened in Munich. There were maps and tables, posters and leaflets aimed at educating citizens about the threat from the air and preparing them for a military emergency. In its report on the opening ceremony the *Bayerische Staatszeitung* left no doubt that in its view air defence was a patriotic duty and a vital necessity in the face of external enemies: 'There are 10,000 planes based on the German borders; ¶ 198 of the Treaty of Versailles condemns Germany to defencelessness: So Germans, look up at the skies.'[61]

In the first few weeks of the new regime the conditions under which air defence was operating changed.[62] It did not take long for Göring to gain formal authority over this area of activity, first as Reich commissar and then as Reich Air Minister. As far as those involved in air defence were concerned the impact of this was ambivalent. On the one hand, it signified a further upgrading and extension of their activities, which they had long dreamt about and for which there was, in spite of a tiny budget, now a basis; on the other hand, the consequence of the amalgamation of all the organizations into the newly created Reich Air Defence Association

(Reichsluftschutzbund = RLB) was a simultaneous loss of independence and freedom of action, for the RLB was subordinated to the Reich Air Ministry. In addition, many organizational problems were still unresolved, in particular how police functions in relation to air defence were to be handled and how the areas of responsibility were to be demarcated between the police and the Reich Air Ministry. Moreover, the Nazi Party and its various sections regarded the RLB and its bureaucratic structure with considerable scepticism, since the latter was to its mind too sclerotic and a refuge for conservative military men.[63]

In addition to the constant stepping up of air defence propaganda and an increasingly open policy of rearmament, what changed was above all the involvement of the civilian population. As a result of the Air Defence Law of 1935 'self-defence' had become a duty.[64] Any man or woman could be called to serve in the air defence service, if their health permitted and they were not committed to serve in another capacity. The 'self-defence' to which the law committed people, imposing sanctions on non-compliance, recognized various roles: air-raid wardens and dispatch runners, auxiliary helpers and house firemen. People served in the building in which they lived. This was, so to speak, the nucleus of the national community, the place where it stood its ground, and the heart of the 'air defence community'; it was at the centre of propaganda activities and of practical air-raid training. The latter had been immensely extended by the RLB from the mid-1930s and its development had been the result of close cooperation between the RLB and other sections of the Nazi Party. At the premises of the RLB the members (about 15 million at the start of the war) learned everything necessary to survive a future war from the air: putting out fires and blackouts, rescue and coordination. Gigantic demonstrations put on from Berlin to Vienna[65] were, in addition, designed to demonstrate to the last sceptic the significance of air defence for the new state.

As early as spring 1933, for example, the Nazis in Munich prepared the population for future aerial warfare by putting on a bizarre show. While members of the Hitler Youth and SA activists lined the streets of the 'movement's capital city', eagerly rattled collection tins for donations for the recently founded RLB, and handed out leaflets about the correct way to behave in an air raid, specially chartered planes circled over the centre of the city. At about 10.45 the first plane dropped paper bombs filled with sand on the inner city. Written on them was 'Air defence is self-defence'. At the same time sirens went off, traffic came to a halt, and SA men equipped with gas masks, along with firemen, set about making the 'bombs' safe. Up on the balcony of the town hall, as the newspapers noted, the new Nazi masters of the city, along with their departmental heads, contentedly watched this propaganda spectacle.[66]

This show was not simply exaggerated activism or clumsy propaganda but rather it reflected the conviction shared by large numbers of those involved in air defence and within the NSDAP that, in contrast to what Douhet had asserted, the mass of the population could, through education and discipline, mature into an air defence community and that a 'national community' thus steeled and strengthened would, compared with feeble democracies, be better prepared for the fight to sustain the population's 'morale'.[67]

For the Nazis the term 'morale' thus contained several highly disparate levels of meaning: first, there was the danger that, as in 1918, a weakened home front could cost the country victory; at the same time, however, morale was regarded as an important asset of the national community that, once restored and consistently maintained, would constitute a key strategic advantage in the struggle. Some 6.5 million people—at least that is the number recorded by the RLB on the fifth anniversary of its founding—had attended air-raid courses by 1938, and about 650,000 officials had been given additional, focused training on several occasions.[68] Though these figures may have been somewhat massaged, it was nevertheless clear that in the view of the Nazi Party possession of the technical skill to deal with threats from the air represented an important contribution to the 'will to defend oneself' and thus was part of the canon of Nazi indoctrination.[69]

Thus, as in Britain, during the immediate pre-war years air defence became a classroom activity: in art and handicraft classes pupils were already painting the future of warfare in the form of bombs, bunkers, and blazing barracks.[70] Psychologists analysed the strengths and weaknesses of young people's constitutions in a state of emergency,[71] and in special classes teachers drilled pupils on how to make an orderly evacuation when the siren sounded and how to use gas masks and fire beaters. In Munich, as in many other cities and large towns in the Reich, the education authorities organized their own air-raid practices and mass events simulating emergencies: at the end of July 1938 some 90,000 pupils were drilled by these methods in the 'correct' responses.[72]

If for most people war was no more than a vague idea, the courses left no one in any doubt about how seriously the will to defend oneself and morale in the 'national community' were taken by the 'Third Reich'. They meant mobilization, not least of the female population, who in special courses run by the Nazi women's organizations, the *NS-Frauenschaft* and the *Deutsches Frauenwerk*, acquired the necessary know-how and were to be trained as 'defence fighters' on the home front. These women, the dream come true of National Socialist air defence propaganda, were female heroes of a new type:[73] in *The Siren*, the journal of the RLB, contented young women were to be seen performing their duty on the 'fire beating front', working with good humour but also seriously and preserving their femininity even in uniform.

Ernst Ohliger described what women could achieve in a future war in his novel *Bombs Fall on Kohlenstadt*.[74] He recounts the story of an air raid on the Ruhr from the perspective of Mrs Hellmann, a woman as courageous as she is level-headed, who is at first afraid, then pulls herself together, and finally rescues her children and those living in the same building. In the course of the story this air-raid warden's wife is transformed into a true heroine, calm and confident, yet also full of empathy and as strong as her husband would have been at such a moment—principally because, as the narrator tells us, from the beginning she regularly attended the air-raid courses and stuck to what the men in those courses had taught her.[75] If men showed them the way, according to the rather obvious message, then even women could be heroines of air defence. This propaganda, which was given little literary embellishment, and the training sessions in barracks could produce a wide variety of effects. Sometimes women themselves voiced their reservations about being exploited in propaganda about 'self-defence fighters', which obliged them to serve dutifully with gas masks, fire beaters, and protective clothing.

At the same time, the promotion of the training courses aroused considerable interest, and even women who were otherwise not enthusiastic Nazis felt that communal fire-fighting was a case of 'self-evident solidarity', 'the national community in action', and an 'enjoyable experience' that strengthened their sense of patriotic duty and made them regard their air-raid service as a means of fulfilling it.[76] Here and in other instances the power of the supposed external threat to integrate people was considerable and brought about a mobilization of the population that was not based on compulsion alone.

That was, admittedly, only one side of the story; another and quite different one could be found in the order of 1937 implementing the Air Defence

Law[77] and in the decree issued a year later by the Reich Air Ministry. At first it was envisaged that Jews and *Mischlinge* (those who were partly Jewish) would be entrusted with a task in air defence only if it were connected with their own property or the protection of their own person; then Göring's ministry ruled that Jews and *Mischlinge* could not hold any leading positions in air defence. Moreover, they were not allocated any space in the 'air defence community', even when their lives were in danger.

The war that Hitler was pushing for so single-mindedly and for which German society was being so radically mobilized was not, however, planned as a strategic aerial war. In spite of its great attractions very few military personnel in London and Berlin believed this type of warfare had impressive prospects. In addition, both sides were fearful of its dire consequences. All planning exercises worked on the assumption that the civilian population was the enemy's real vulnerable spot but it was the weakness in one's own defences at the same time. Military theorists of a *völkisch* turn of mind considered that the danger would be reduced the faster a 'national community' that confronted the threat from the air in a disciplined and steadfast manner could be formed from a deeply divided democratic society.

The 'national community' thus seemed to have a competitive advantage in modern warfare, as it had sufficient resources at its disposal and also the necessary 'irrepressible will' to repel even the most extreme threat. Humane ideas did not at any rate play a significant role in military and strategic thinking; and the law of armed conflict offered adequate scope for 'terror bombing' to be rejected but for the bombing of 'defended' cities to be judged rational and legitimate. Both sides saw the other as capable of crossing the Rubicon, only nobody wanted to be the first to embrace indiscriminate bombing under the world's gaze.

The Lessons of Guernica

The Spanish Civil War, which offered the Luftwaffe the opportunity of trying out in practice what had hitherto only been possible in theory, represented an initial and crucial testing ground for a future emergency.[78] In 1935 Germany's fascist ally Italy had already gained some early practical experience with bombers in Ethiopia and had deployed them to gas soldiers and the civilian population.[79] Although air support for ground troops had not brought the hoped for breakthrough, the government in Rome considered the use of mustard gas to have been effective, given the fact that the Ethiopian army was militarily inferior and so incapable of countering it.

The Germans lacked this kind of experience in the use of gas as a weapon, and although people wished to avoid it, it was playing an ever greater role in simulations.[80] To begin with they had assisted the rebel insurgents around General Franco with organizing supplies and troop transports. The deployment of the Condor legion now offered the opportunity for Germany to gain experience and to try out new technologies and new types of aircraft. The results were very mixed. Whereas medium-sized, twin-engine H III bombers lacked precision and these were therefore used primarily to provide support for the army, the single-engine Ju 87 dive bombers with their loud sirens, deployed in Spain from spring 1937 onwards, were considered a particularly effective weapon against the republican forces. In reality, however, civilian and military targets could hardly be distinguished in aerial warfare. In fact, towns and villages reckoned to be under the control of the enemy 'Reds' were considered legitimate targets for the bomber and fighter pilots of the Condor legion. In this respect Guernica in no way marked a break with previous practice, nor was it an especially brutal bombing. Rather, it conformed exactly to what had become the norm, as indeed the bombing raids on Madrid, for example, had demonstrated.

Admittedly, even the heads of the Luftwaffe regarded the 'random' terrorization of the civilian population as illegitimate and, as before, the primary aim remained defeating the enemy's troops. At the same time, this led directly to attacks on 'defended' cities and thus to bombing raids targeting the morale of the civilian population. For in the final analysis the place where victory was going to be won was behind the enemy's lines. In theory distinctions might remain, but in practice all those concerned realized that air raids on cities were never aimed solely at military sites. Thus the death of civilians was not some kind of collateral damage but always an integral part of the inner logic of strategic bombing.

In the run-up to the Spanish Civil War this precept had been formulated in the Luftwaffe's General Regulations: aircraft were to be deployed to target the enemy's combat strength and should aim to strike the enemy's population and territory at 'their most vulnerable' points. Unintentional collateral damage was unavoidable,[81] an assessment by no means unique to Germany and one that could have been accepted by the majority of air force commanders. The contentious issue was rather whether a strategic bombing war dominated by bombers could be successful or whether—and this was the primary lesson drawn from the Spanish Civil War—the secret of success lay in the Luftwaffe's assuming a supporting role in close cooperation with the army and navy.

In the end this disagreement had far-reaching consequences: the Luftwaffe, not least under pressure from the Four-Year Plan, rapid war preparations, and tight financial resources, decided against building four-engine planes for strategic bombing and concentrated instead on mid-range aircraft. Huge increases in production since the mid-1930s fed the illusion of being suitably prepared for a future bombing war. The decision in favour of the He 117 twin-engine dive bomber, which it was hoped would combine precision with calculable financial risks, rapidly turned out at the beginning of the war to be a disaster, for it was totally unsuitable for creating a credible threat of strategic aerial warfare against Britain or the United States.[82]

Britain

In Britain the Spanish Civil War and the young republic's fight for survival had electrified the British Left. The reports from the Iberian peninsula seemed to give a foretaste of how wars would be in future. Everything pointed to Spain being, as it were, the prelude to this new, modern type of warfare—with its dire consequences, its brutish violence, and its cruel destructiveness. What Germans and Italians had been doing in Spain from the summer of 1936 onwards left no doubt about what aerial warfare would henceforth mean. Under attack from fascist bombers the republican capital, Madrid, seen as representative of all democracies, underwent what Alfred Kantorowicz called 'the West's descent into hell'.[83] In the British and American press horrifying reports came thick and fast about the 'sadistic' and 'barbaric' bombardment, the collapse of civilization taking place on the Iberian peninsula, and the unrestrained violence to which the centre of Spanish life, hitherto so peaceful and friendly, was exposed. London and Paris would be the next victims of the fascist alliance, there seemed no doubt of that.[84] After the bombing of the small Basque town of Guernica on 26 April 1937 the floodgates seemed effectively to have been opened. At first there was talk of more than 1,600 deaths, for which the Condor legion was responsible.

From the late autumn of 1936 onwards the Luftwaffe had tested the effects of strategic bombing away from the main front lines. From the beginning the issue of the morale of the 'Reds' was a critical element in the Germans' and

Italians' assessment of their success. How would the population react? Would people flee, leaving their weapons behind? Since the beginning of the war the bomber squadron under Wolfram von Richthofen had been straining at the leash to get started on its test raids, even if consideration for the civilian population meant that at the start the plan was for no 'destruction by fire bombing', as Richthofen confided to his diary.[85] Then 'undermining the morale of enemy forces' was one of the operational orders issued to the legion when it set out in mid-December 1936 to bomb Andalusian villages, causing considerable devastation. In their detailed reports the legion's fighter pilots wrote of houses destroyed and people fleeing, creeping in terror through the streets days after the attacks. Even if at this early stage a few people felt scruples for a short time, there was still a general consensus that strategic bombing would be central to future warfare.

It was not, however, until the destruction of Guernica and ultimately the iconic representation of the bombing by Pablo Picasso, first shown at the Paris World Fair of 1937, that aerial warfare and the immense, if very abstractly depicted, suffering of the civilian population became the focus of public attention.[86] Now it was no longer just a matter of strategy; now the apocalypse of aerial warfare and the power of bombing to destroy civilization seemed to be displayed in all its brutality and, especially to those in Britain, to confirm what, ever since the raids on London, the Germans had been deemed capable of. Immediately after the attack *The Times*' correspondent George Steer had travelled from nearby Bilbao to Guernica to gain an impression of the force of the bombing. His article 'Tragedy of Guernica',[87] which caused outrage when it also appeared shortly after in the *New York Times*, gave a penetrating account of the people's suffering and left no doubt about the Germans' brutal will to destroy. The Hitler regime's only concern, he wrote, had been to demoralize the civilian population and to destroy the Basque nation. To begin with Spanish Nationalist propaganda met the wave of international indignation that followed in the days after the attack with an attempt to deny everything; then, when that failed, it put out the lie that the 'Reds' had set fire to the town themselves in order to sabotage the 'national liberation' by Franco's troops.

It was not only concern about European democracy, however, that worried the political Left in Britain. In the perception of the British military and government officials the civil war had underlined the need to build up air defences in the face of the fascist threat. After the Munich crisis of 1938 and the failure of the British policy of appeasement to halt Hitler by means of political and territorial concessions and so avert war, Chamberlain's government stepped up its efforts, amongst them the distribution of some 38 million gas masks. No household could continue to be in doubt as to how seriously the authorities viewed the threat and that London itself was patently expecting a gas attack. There was a deep-seated fear of aerial warfare and thus in September 1939 Chamberlain's government took great pains, even after the declaration of war, to avoid anything that at this stage might cause the war to escalate. Pamphlets were to be dropped over Germany but no bombs as yet. It was a case of waiting for the right moment and there was a desire to avoid creating the impression in the eyes of the world of striking the first blow—that would be left to the Germans. Nevertheless, it was clear to the General Staff that if an escalation should occur the RAF must proceed with maximum effectiveness to be successful.[88]

Chamberlain's government had in the past already attracted considerable criticism for its air defence policy. As far as Labour was concerned it was precisely air defence and the building of shelters that proved the complete failure of the Conservatives and also their ignorance about the working classes.[89] Criticism flared up over underestimates of the shelters needed and over the attempt to transfer some of the costs to the local authorities. And even a 1939 initiative, the mass production and distribution of around 2.5 million steel structures (quickly named Anderson shelters) that could protect people against shrapnel and be put up in the garden, by no means met with wholehearted support. Although they offered rudimentary protection and were distributed quickly and efficiently to households in the regions affected, this operation at the same time signified the abandonment of plans to extend the provision of urgently needed and distinctly safer shelters. And what were workers in the East End of London or the tenements of Manchester and Birmingham to do with these mini-shelters, when there was no room anywhere to put them up? Safety from bombing had thus become a matter of class, and it was above all left-wing academics and architects who from the mid-1930s onwards bemoaned the social disparity in the provision of protective equipment.[90]

In 1938 the Left Book Club published a comprehensive assessment of British air defences. Its author was J. B. Haldane, a former member of the Cabinet committee for air defence and an ARP expert. He had travelled to Madrid, Barcelona, and other parts of Spain to study the effects of the air raids there.[91] What he had seen appeared to him to be the precise opposite of British policy and prompted him to write a damning report. Whereas the republic with its tight budget had focused on driving safe underground bunkers into the base of rocks and thus made the safety of individuals its priority, Britain had negligently put all its eggs in the basket of rearmament. That was as dangerous as it was irresponsible and blinkered, because it primarily benefited industry to the detriment of the population. He suggested building a bunker system in London six metres deep that would deter an attacker from wearing Britain down by bombing.

This utopian programme did not, however, find majority support and it had no influence on government plans. Official pressure to extend Civil Defence with its volunteers and to boost the local authorities' responsibility had nevertheless increased on the eve of war. For one thing was believed to be certain right across party boundaries: the war that was looming would surpass anything that people had previously experienced, particularly if the enemy, as in the First World War, was Germany. Nazi propaganda had in the end succeeded in giving an impression of Germany's resources that was not borne out by the reality of its production and technical equipment. On the outbreak of war the Luftwaffe was ill equipped for a strategic air war, for priority had been given to rapid troop movement on the ground.

People in Britain were nevertheless very afraid, in the first place, because since the First World War the Germans had been considered capable of any kind of excess, but also because the enemy's forces were being massively overestimated. In addition, Britain's own current capability of conducting air warfare was—still—far from adequate. The RAF's range was too limited and the technical equipment and the quality of the pilots were not up to inflicting serious damage on the German Reich. However, when the war began, contrary to the fears of military theorists and science fiction writers, there was neither a massive first strike nor an out and out 'terror bombing' campaign, nor were there millions of victims. The only thing that happened in London on 3 September 1939, the day war was declared, was the wailing of the air-raid sirens, driving people into the shelters—a false alarm, as was quickly established, set off by two British pilots. London remained quiet during these days and so did Berlin. For the time being.

2

Bombing, the Public Sphere, and Morale

The Struggle to Win Trust and Maintain Morale

During the first weeks of September 1939, although bombs were not yet falling on Britain, people were already very worried about the threat of gas attacks and bombing. Panic had to be avoided at all costs. At this point Britain found itself facing numerous problems. The attempt to tame German aggression had failed and so the hope of avoiding another conflict after the costly battles of the First World War had proved illusory. Political unrest was growing on the boundaries of the Empire and consuming substantial financial and military resources. Britain had been badly affected by the economic crisis of 1929 and heavy industry in particular was suffering from a loss of markets. During the 1930s, as a 'saturated nation', the British Empire had had to observe how the rising powers of Japan, Italy, and Germany threatened the balance of power and sought to revise the post-war international order.

For a long time London had underestimated the ambitions of the fascist powers. It was only when, in March 1939, Hitler dropped his mask and occupied Czechoslovakia, contrary to the provisions of the Munich treaty, that the sceptics such as Winston Churchill, who had been warning about Germany and had rejected the policy of appeasement, could feel vindicated. On 10 May 1940, the King called on Churchill, hitherto First Lord of the Admiralty, to form a new War Cabinet as Prime Minister in place of Neville Chamberlain. The German occupation of Denmark and Norway, which began on 9 April, had been a disaster for the latter's already weakened government and led to growing calls for a change of leadership. Although Churchill had been partly responsible for the abortive Norway operation, his reputation as a strong opponent of Nazism was impeccable and this provided an essential precondition for bringing the Labour Party, which had been vigorously opposed to Chamberlain, into a grand wartime coalition. Thus, apart from several well-known Conservative politicians such as Lord Halifax, who remained Foreign Secretary, the new cabinet also contained leading Labour figures such as Clement Atlee, Ernest Bevin, Arthur Greenwood, and Herbert Morrison.

At this point, however, Churchill's position was not unchallenged. For even his Conservative colleagues considered him too unpredictable and some remembered his time as an unsuccessful Chancellor of the Exchequer in the mid-1920s, when he was a member of Stanley Baldwin's Conservative government. At any rate, at this existential moment when Churchill became Prime Minister it was not yet clear how the country would respond to the major defeats of the first year of the war. Might it not put out cautious feelers for peace in order not to lose everything?

In fact the new government could hardly have begun under worse auspices. German troops had overrun Denmark and Norway and on 10 May the Wehrmacht crossed the Belgian border and advanced into France at an astonishing pace. The western campaign had begun, the Allied troops had to withdraw and, by 25 May, the only harbour to remain open and offer the British expeditionary force the chance of escape was Dunkirk. Around 340,000 British and French soldiers were bottled up there. While Hitler and the army leadership held back from delivering the decisive blow in order to concentrate their forces for the further advance into France, a large-scale evacuation of British troops got under way under the codename 'Operation Dynamo'. This operation was soon being described as 'the miracle of Dunkirk' in order to gloss over the reality of Britain's helplessness at this point and how close it had been to total defeat.

In his first brief speech, emotionally charged and exuding confidence in ultimate victory, to the House of Commons on 13 May, Churchill embarked on the attempt to unite Parliament and the public behind the war with Hitler's Germany.[1] However, although his 'blood, toil, tears and sweat' speech left no doubt about Britain's new uncompromising stance towards the German tyrant, it was in fact not he but Chamberlain who received the loudest applause in Parliament that day.[2] At this time, there were still those among the Conservatives who were looking for alternatives to a war with Germany and were putting out feelers to Italy.[3]

At this critical moment at the end of May 1940, while British troops were fleeing from the continent and the Belgian army was about to surrender, it was Churchill who, in a series of dramatic meetings, persuaded the War Cabinet not to compromise. In the final analysis it was his rhetorical skill and courage that in this desperate situation were the key factors in the British decision to continue the struggle and to reject any attempt to reach an agreement with Germany and so give Hitler a free hand for further conquests. Now, although weakened and on its own, Britain was still in the war. Moreover, as Hitler knew only too well, behind the British Empire stood the United States and all its military resources. Churchill was convinced that he could win over the United States for the war against Germany. Until then he concentrated on increasing armaments production, strengthening the Royal Air Force, and exploiting the resources of the British Empire. Moreover, he assumed that the Nazi–Soviet pact was a marriage of convenience and would not last long.[4] He believed that time was not on Hitler's side and that in the summer of 1940 the latter was now confronted with the choice of either defeating Britain militarily through a successful invasion and bombing campaign or, by attacking the Soviet Union, attempting to determine once and for all who was to dominate the European continent. By defeating the USSR he could remove Britain's 'continental sword', force her to make peace, and prevent the United States from intervening.

In any event it seemed as if Churchill's uncompromising stance had frustrated Hitler's plans. It appeared that once again the democratic world had found a strong voice.[5] This is clearly demonstrated by the response to his speeches, and not least to the fact that he was able to sum up the current state of the war and the future prospects. In his 'we shall never surrender' speech of 4 June 1940 in the House of Commons Churchill made no bones about how critical the situation was: Dunkirk was a military disaster and there was an acute threat of invasion. Wars could not be won by evacuations even if, as the news reports had already indicated, Dunkirk had been carried out by a flotilla of small ships which had heroically thwarted the German plans. Thus, according to Churchill, Britain's only response would be an uncompromising determination to achieve victory: 'We shall fight on the beaches, we shall fight on the landing grounds, we shall fight in the fields and in the streets, we shall fight in the hills, we shall never surrender.'[6]

Mass Observation and morale

This struggle was also one for the hearts and minds of the British people, without whose willingness to make sacrifices the war could not be won. And, in view of the extent of the threat, it appeared all the more necessary to control knowledge and information about the course of the war. For, in the light of the experience of the First World War, leading air defence experts assumed that there was a threat of mass bombing of British cities leading to hundreds of thousands of casualties. The working class was seen as particularly vulnerable to defeatism. Thus, in the view of the Ministry of Information, it was vital to create trust and thereby to win the struggle for hearts and minds. The Ministry of Information had been established on 4 September 1939, the day after the declaration of war, and made responsible for all matters involving the media, for censorship and publicity, and for internal and external propaganda.

The main focus was on morale[7] and, as the head of the Home Intelligence Division in the Ministry asserted, this involved not only ensuring that people's material needs were met in the shape of food, work, free time, sleep, and security, but there was also a psychological aspect to be considered: the need to create the impression that, despite all the rationing, things were being done fairly, that the sacrifices were being shared equally, and that the political leadership was working efficiently and with integrity.[8]

Without high morale it would be impossible to achieve a comprehensive mobilization of the nation's resources, to maintain trust in the War Cabinet, and to persuade people to bear the burdens involved in the war effort. More than any other term it was 'morale' that shaped the public perception of the air war, determined the semantics of propaganda, and the questions posed and the explanations given. However, those involved, above all social scientists and psychologists, were by no means agreed on what exactly lay behind the term, what 'high' and 'low' morale actually meant, and how they could be created and observed.

After the outbreak of war the British Home Intelligence Division initially considered the number of rumours and expressions of discontent as indicators of low morale. The social observers involved in Mass Observation worked along the same lines when, following an air raid on Glasgow in the spring of 1941, they asserted that morale did not mean merely 'keeping going' but rather 'seeing it through' with total commitment and being convinced of the need to make sacrifices, whether large or small and, in the worst case, to lay down one's life. 'High morale', therefore, meant hard and unrelenting work; it implied optimism, maximum unity and trust, and refraining from making any complaints.[9]

Mass Observation, which had been established in 1937, was initiated by three philanthropists who wanted to find out more about the British working class.[10] It was a documentary project to assess the milieu, but also a middle-class adventure and experiment inspired by a romantic view of the working class, aiming to examine the day-to-day life of the 'little people'. Its initiators, Tom Harrisson, Humphrey Jennings, and Charles Madge, were not part of the academic establishment, although they had had a good education.[11] Madge was a writer and film maker, a Surrealist and Freudian, who was interested in the role of the subconscious in daily life. Jennings was a documentary film maker and painter, while the third member, Tom Harrisson, was an anthropologist who had recently returned from field work among the cannibal tribes in the New Hebrides.

Participatory observation, exploration of the unconscious, was not an entirely new method. At an early stage Harrisson and his colleagues had sought contact with leading British social anthropologists such as Bronislav Manilovski. What Harrisson was looking for was this external perspective from which to find a key to understanding what had remained unseen and unheard in the class society of the inter-war years. This was a novel approach to the extent that British sociologists—unlike their German colleagues—did not have a tradition of this kind of social research, which assigned such importance to individual experience and to live conversation.[12]

Some of the ideas of the founders of Mass Observation were half-baked and lacked methodological rigour.[13] But that was not the crucial point.[14] What was important was not only the fact that the everyday life of the oppressed classes was going to be investigated but above all how and by whom. For in fact the number of volunteers involved steadily increased between 1937 and 1945: around 2,800 men and women took part in at least one of the questionnaire and interview panels of Mass Observation, rather less than half, some 1,100, several times. During the first years of the war around 200 of them kept diaries of varying length and intensity and sent them to the London headquarters, where reports on the political and general state of the nation were composed on the basis of these diary entries, and using scraps of conversation and extensive observations by participants.

The main point of the project was to provide an alternative to the dominant narrative of the political elites and thereby to assign historical importance to the problems of ordinary people who had hitherto not been considered significant. However, Mass Observation was not a working-class movement. The majority of diary entries and reports, which covered such topics as, for example, the drinking habits of the workers in Bolton or the coronation of King George VI, came from the middle class and revealed as much about their experiences and perceptions as about the 'real' history of the working class. Very few of the participants had been able to afford to go to university; only a few were workers; the majority were small shopkeepers and white collar workers, housewives and teachers. Many had become unemployed during the inter-war economic crisis, had had difficulty in finding work again, and stated that they were politically 'left of centre'.[15]

However, Mass Observation collected more information than it could process. During the first year around 600 men and women had participated in the diary programme and produced over two million words. These daily entries covered everything imaginable, from noisy neighbours to children who had brought sand into the bathroom. It may have been banal and everyday stuff, but that was precisely what was interesting and was intended to provide an insight into the inner state of Britain. Mary Adams, a friend and BBC colleague of Harrisson's and now director of the Ministry of Information (MoI) Home Intelligence department, now came up with the idea of using Mass Observation to provide regular reports on morale.

In consequence the project moved from the margins to the centre of British social affairs and those involved advanced from being laymen to becoming experts in social research. At this early stage in the war there was little knowledge of how the population might behave in an emergency, only horrific assumptions based on the experience of the First World War and on the first reports of the effects of air raids during the Spanish Civil War[16] and the Sino-Japanese War.[17] However, the Air Ministry did not consider this information an adequate basis for forming an opinion on how the population would behave in the event of a bombing campaign.[18]

The term morale, therefore, involved three assumptions: first, preconceptions about the military 'character' of the British nation, in particular compared with that of other nations. It also reflected the traumatic experience of the First World War, which with its mass casualties had extended the realm of what was conceivable to such an extent that any future war could only be imagined as an Armageddon. Thus, based on the reports they had received about the bombing that had already occurred in continental Europe, war veterans in the military and political agencies produced very pessimistic prognoses about future morale and about the devastation that would be caused and, in view of the numerous cases of shell shock during the First World War, advocated the establishment of special Neurosis Centres for the victims of bombing.[19]

Secondly, the term morale contained elite assumptions about the unreliability of the working class, assumptions that went back to the nineteenth century and which indicated the need to pay particular attention to this class. It was precisely because they regarded themselves as on the side of the working class that the Mass Observation movement had emerged in part as a consequence of these debates about the 'morale' of and the 'threat' posed by the lower classes. Their (empathetic) studies were intended at last to provide material about this 'alien' class.

Thirdly and finally, the term was based on an interpretation of military conflict as 'total war'.[20] One of its essential characteristics was the increasing blurring of the lines between the military front and the home front and the assumption that the reaction of civilians would mirror the behaviour of soldiers during the First World War. This interpretation also assumed that a wartime society differed completely from a peacetime society and did so in a variety of ways: in its subjection to total mobilization, in its powers of resistance, and, above all, in its ability as a nation at war to create social solidarity, bridging all classes and overcoming all social and political differences.

This militarization of the civil sphere also involved an assumption by the government and the military that the population could be influenced and controlled like soldiers on the battlefield. At the same time, they were aware that in a democracy wars required proper legitimization. They needed to win the population's support and trust. For various reasons the threat of air raids played a central role in this. In their view the ultimate test for the population was whether or not it could cope with the raids. This would determine whether morale was high or low. It was not a question of feelings, fear of what was to come, or grief at the loss of relatives, but rather what the individual would do immediately after a raid and how he or she would behave.[21] What counted as 'high morale' at the start of the air raids was not to panic or despair, to go on working hard, to make small or large sacrifices, and at the same time to be prepared to face the dangers that might come, and this was what shaped the reports on the air raids.[22]

But at the outbreak of war there were no clear guidelines for all this. To begin with, the Ministry of Information, which was responsible, found the going hard.[23] It was uncertain what information should be released and what should be censored, nor was there an effective organization, let alone a staff with journalistic experience and familiar with the ways of Fleet Street. Newspaper journalists and those in the BBC regarded the activities of the Ministry of Information with scepticism, particularly since it evidently had difficulty in retaining its senior personnel. The question was: what should be, what could be, reported in order not to undermine morale?

A week after the outbreak of war, one of the staff advocated in a paper for the Home Office that as far as possible people should be told the truth. Fear and panic occurred when the population sensed that they were not being told the worst. Speculation produced rumours and undermined trust.[24] However, the policy on censorship that followed in autumn 1939 pursued a different path. It was based on Defence Regulation 3,[25] which banned all citizens, and that included all members of the media, from spreading information that could be of assistance to the enemy.[26] Government departments then specified in Defence Notices those topics which could not be discussed or referred to in publications.

As far as much of the military were concerned, and this was particularly true of the Royal Navy, almost no information of any kind should be revealed to the public and therefore it would be best to follow a policy of silence. In practice, the system of censorship was based not only on the direction of news by the ministries, but also on the unavoidably close and often conflict-ridden cooperation between the press and government departments. The departments could reject or cut reports; they did not, however, alter or rewrite the text. Editors could also pick a fight with the censors if they were convinced that, contrary to the view of the MoI, a report or photograph did not contain militarily significant material.

As far as the public authorities were concerned, the beginning of the war had not turned out as expected: there had been no immediate air raid on London, no poison gas attack, no invasion. The 'phoney war', the first unexpectedly peaceful months of the war, to some extent disappointed the expectations of how the war would develop: it was taking place all over the continent but not where it had been anticipated, namely on the home front. The few sensitive pieces of information to emerge were subject to all the more strict controls, which came not from the official censorship, but rather from the voluntary action of the British press.

As far as the BBC was concerned, the start of the war had represented a caesura. It had switched its broadcasting onto a single channel and saw itself faced with the task not only of providing information but also, and increasingly, of having to entertain and to struggle for its listeners' favour.[27] This also had something to do with the fact that the English-speaking Nazi propaganda broadcasts from Radio Hamburg and using 'Lord Haw-Haw', alias William Joyce, provided new competition. At the end of 1939, after the Nine O'Clock News around 30 per cent of British radio listeners were switching to the enemy broadcasting station, with the news bulletin given by Joyce, whose entertainment programme was more attractive and whose news seemed more reliable.[28]

Paradoxically, the unexpected peacefulness and lack of air raids, together with the control of the news, contributed to growing discontent and to scepticism towards the information contained in the newspapers and radio. At the beginning of 1940, the MoI reporters were registering an increasing number of wild rumours: at one point it was claimed that Princess Elizabeth had fled from the impending air raids to Canada, another rumour had it that leading members of the royal family belonged to secret Nazi organizations. Other rumours claimed that invasion was imminent, that secret German commando units were operating, that senior French officers had committed suicide, or that there had been heavy British casualties.[29] The MoI responded by establishing an Anti-Lie office to collect rumours that were in circulation, to inform the ministries, and to develop strategies to counter the rumours.[30]

The weakness of the government was a constant theme. Its retreat from the victorious Germans appeared eminently plausible, and if the secret disappearance of the princess was considered feasible then morale was clearly not in good shape. A report by Home Intelligence of 24 May 1940 noted that these wild speculations were damaging and 'unhealthy' for people's response to the war and had to be stopped as a matter of urgency.[31] But how? The assessments continued to vary. Was the rigid control of information the price that a democratic society had to pay for the struggle against a dictatorship? Or were the rumours, as Tom Harrisson believed, a mechanism with which people provided themselves with a form of security against what the future might bring, a tranquillizer against the control of information?[32]

After February 1940 the problem increased: while military developments accelerated, with Germany celebrating one victory after another and Britain's allies crushed, the public was receiving only very limited information about the situation. At the same time, with the first bombs and the first casualties the war had arrived on British soil. Censorship imposed very strict limits on what the newspapers could report on these air raids. During the days following the raids the regional press did not report on the local damage inflicted or on the exact targets. The reports downplayed the casualties and during the summer of 1940 remained limited to vague statements.[33] Sometimes, although a raid had taken place, the morning news reported that it had been a quiet night, thereby encouraging the sense of insecurity and adding to the scepticism surrounding the official news.

At the beginning of July 1940, Churchill instructed the MoI to do something to stop the rumours,[34] thereby initiating an elaborate and counterproductive propaganda campaign that was designed to calm fears on the home front. Large posters reminded people of their duty not to talk. 'Keep it under your hat' was the cautiously humorous title of a series of posters, which reminded both men and women that careless talk could cost lives.[35]

Other aspects of the initiative were much more heavy-handed with an obvious moral gloss. One poster showed different 'types' of people who spread rumours: Mr Knowall, for example, a man who knew everything, who knew all about the strategy of the Luftwaffe, just as he knew about that of the RAF; 'Mr Glumpot', the professional pessimist; 'Mr Hush', who was always telling people he had 'the latest news' and that it was hush hush; and 'Miss Leaky Mouth', the gossipy neighbour, who felt she had to talk about everything. Neighbours, friends, and colleagues should tell all these people to 'Stop talking'. The campaign accused 'people who spread rumours', including in other words all those who wanted to form their own assessment of the war situation, of being potential security risks.

It soon became clear, however, that this rigid form of controlling opinion was a major mistake.[36] The posters had the reverse effect of that intended; sowing mistrust instead of trust, encouraging scepticism instead of improving morale, and providing more ammunition for the critics of the MoI in Fleet Street even before the air raids had got going.

The 'air defence community'

The Nazi propagandists did not have to fear criticism from the press and yet for the 'Third Reich' air raids also represented a major problem. After all, it was by no means clear how the regime's propaganda should deal with the threat from the air. For, as in the case of Britain, the regime was faced with the issue of trust: What could, what should the population be expected to put up with? And what sorts of information stabilized morale and what sorts threatened it? Moreover, the air raids were public events about which one could not simply keep quiet as if they were distant battles. During this initial phase of the air war, around the years 1940/1, when the Royal Air Force made only occasional raids with limited damage largely confined to the north and west of the Reich, little was done. Unlike in Britain, to begin with no clear propaganda instructions were issued for reporting on air raids.[37] Attention was focused on the rapid military successes in the west.

The way in which the reports were composed, the amount of information contained in them, and the choice of pictures used varied from region to region and, as far as the military and propaganda agencies in Berlin were concerned, they contained too much information.[38] For there was still uncertainty about how much public attention should be given to air raids and what language should be used in discussing them. For example, were the first victims of the raids to be regarded as soldiers killed in action (*Gefallene*)? And what instructions should be given to the press: should it report frankly about the threat from air raids and give detailed accounts of the destruction? Or should it dramatize the alleged breaches of international law by the British 'plutocratic clique'[39] and attempt to neutralize enemy propaganda?[40]

Following the first raids on Berlin, the Reich Propaganda Minister, Dr Joseph Goebbels, advocated that they should be open about the slight damage that had occurred since this would create 'a better impression' than if they 'tried to conceal it'.[41] Reporting on air raids should in future be 'unemotional' and 'not tendentious', although not as extensive as hitherto. Here Goebbels was responding to a trend in the regional press, above all in the areas in the west of the Reich most affected, for extensive reporting of the air raids. For example, in June 1940 the *Essener Nationalzeitung* reported the exact number of bombs dropped and gave an account of hits and misses.[42]

Photographs showed the destructive power of the raids: collapsed apartment buildings, blocked streets, deep bomb craters, but no dead or injured, merely funerals with Nazi functionaries beside the coffins. The main aim behind the choice of pictures was to show that these were attacks on civilian targets and as such illegal under international law, and so not only was the timing of the raid reported but also the location and function of the buildings hit. They included kindergartens, workers' housing estates, and hospitals. The British raids were to be depicted as Churchill's war 'against women and children',[43] as ruthless barbarism inflicted on a peaceful German people, who were only defending themselves. Their own raids on British targets were, by contrast, simply a morally appropriate response to British 'terror', legitimate under international law.

As part of the struggle against the internal enemy the focus was entirely on the role of the 'national community' in the air defence programme and on the morale of the population. According to Goebbels, the main task of politics and propaganda was to protect it and sustain it with all available means. Just as the soldiers at the front did not allow themselves to be frightened by any weapons, however terrifying they might be, so civilians must do their duty and become soldiers of the home front. Every air raid required a demonstration of the same moral qualities as a battle at the front: courage, cool-headedness, and a brave heart. The air war was 'a real test of nerves'. In this battle morale was no longer an individual matter but a task for the whole 'national community'.[44]

Inclusion and exclusion were important features of this programme and in the most serious cases the death penalty would have to be imposed on anyone who damaged morale, acted contrary to it, or threatened to harm it.[45] According to the Propaganda Minister, this would not require any clear regulations because, after all, everyone ought to know how to behave in wartime.[46] To have high morale was thus a Nazi form of behaviour that one could 'feel' was the right thing to do. Becoming an active participant in the air defence programme meant that one belonged to the 'national community'. In practice this meant participating in the exercises of the Air Defence League and learning how 'to take responsibility for protecting one's own home' (*Selbstschutz*) and how to deal with incendiaries.

With the increase in air raids this topic moved from the specialist journals of the Reich Air Defence League (RLB) onto the front pages of the local press. How should fire be tackled? How best to cope with the heat? How to use a hose?[47] At the beginning of 1940, air raids had become part of the daily life of the urban population and the deliberately calm instructions that were now issued made it clear that the days when the Nazi Party had carried out exercises by dropping paper bombs on town halls[48] were over. The 'national community' was becoming an 'air defence community', in which the focus was now on combating incendiaries and taking responsibility for protecting one's own home, discipline and obedience, self-sacrifice, and doing one's duty—norms that also formed the basis of British notions of morale.

Among the most urgent issues was the question of air-raid warnings.[49] The lack of clear guidelines had resulted in great uncertainty because it was never entirely clear at what point the alarm would be sounded.[50] This was particularly true in the western cities that were suffering most of the raids. Thus, during the first months of the war there were often chaotic scenes because responsibilities, priorities, and the development of the situation in the air were all unclear. The commanders of the air districts [*Luftgaukommandeure*] acted on their own initiative and, as a result, there was an increase in the risk of false alarms being given. For in 1940/1 the RAF attacked in combinations of single bombers in small groups, which prompted the alarm to be given on the way to their targets when there was actually no danger.[51]

From the start of the war control over what was being said was an important instrument for maintaining trust and discipline and all attempts to evade it were dealt with by the local Nazi Party agencies, which denounced those who claimed to have spotted a threat to the town from something they had heard in a conversation or had seen themselves and had then passed on at their workplace, in the pub, or to neighbours.[52] According to the Essen Nazi Party such observations were 'completely irrelevant'.[53] It was not up to individuals to assess the coming dangers, but rather it was the Party, military, and state agencies who were responsible, since they had a monopoly of the sources of information and were in charge of interpreting potential risks. This included the authority to determine the appropriate behaviour to be adopted during future air raids. From the summer of 1940 onwards, the local authorities throughout the Reich put up posters containing instructions in the event of air raids. This was a new source of information, which on occasion provided a much more realistic picture of future developments in the war than was provided by many of the Wehrmacht reports that were published or the newsreels in the cinema,[54] in which pictures of the 'Battle of Britain' were shown but little was to be seen of the bombing of German cities.

This 'Knigge'* for air raids was also available in a convenient edition that everyone could keep in their air-raid suitcase, which they had to carry during raids. The information it contained prepared people for life in an air-raid shelter, a period of nervous tension, of danger, and of blackout.[55] It was no longer a secret that their own town would soon be in the front line. For, after all, the police authorities were giving out information about where to take the injured and how to extinguish fires in the home. In their pronouncements the authorities also referred to the threat of homelessness and told people what they had to do if their property had been damaged or destroyed.

---

* Translators' note: Adolph Freiherr von Knigge (1752–96) was the author of *Über den Umgang mit Menschen* (On Human Relations), in which he provided a guide to behaviour and etiquette, and so his name has come to refer to books on etiquette.

Apart from focusing the propaganda campaign on an attack on 'British plutocrats', the government authorities and the Party created new forms of public space where official notices and 'Basic Instructions for the Victims of Bombing' became seismographs of the development of the war. To begin with, the announcements were limited to basic rules on how to behave in the event of air raids.

By May 1940, in response to the bombing, the Hamburg chief of police had already formulated a whole series of instructions, which were given out in the form of newspaper notices, posters, and leaflets and which in future had to be carried by everyone and frequently perused.[56] These included 'Make sure to blackout properly' or 'Clear the streets'. The air-raid shelter was the best place to take cover as soon as bombs could be heard falling or planes approaching. People should clear their attics and remove easily inflammable objects, offer help to neighbours, and not hamper the work of the rescue services during a raid through simple curiosity. Otherwise, the police would deal 'ruthlessly' with such troublemakers. At the same time, the police chief, as the person responsible for local air defence arrangements, announced that special aid centres would be established for the population in those parts of the city that were likely to suffer particularly from air raids.

It was clear that these announcements contained a series of assumptions, which then reappeared in people's day-to-day discussions about air raids. They included the assumption that the high point of the air raids had not yet been reached and that there would be heavy casualties. At the same time, the authorities responsible for air defence admitted that the methods used hitherto had not been adequate to deal with the threat of air raids and were seeking new ways of coping with the problem. These included, for example, the publication of regulations for 'the support of families in the event of injuries to persons or damage to property', instructions for the organization of assembly points and emergency accommodation, or rules for the allocation of emergency housing,[57] all of which were designed to document the regime's concern for the care and protection of its people.

Thus, one of the major aims of Nazi policy was to win the nation's trust. For, in the final analysis, the bombing campaign was challenging the regime's legitimacy. Looked at from this perspective trust had a double meaning. On the one hand, it involved subordination to the guardianship of the political leadership in whose care the population had to place itself and to whose absolute authority it must submit.[58] From this point of view the relationship of trust was one-sided and paternalistic. 'Trust in the responsible authorities'[59]

Figure 1. 'The Enemy can see your lights! Lights out!'

was what the regime demanded in the air war and in this it differed markedly both in tone and in its comprehensive claim to obedience from the
British approach which, despite its compulsory aspects, was based on a recognition of individual rights and not on totalitarian force rooted in the
notion of a 'national community'. Questions were not welcome and nor
were neighbourly exchanges about what had been seen or heard. Anyone
who did not trust in the strength of the air defences, anyone who did not
follow the instructions of the air-raid warden or was incapable of demonstrating in public his belief in the leadership, was part of that 'sceptical society' (Jan. C. Behrends) that the Nazi state was targeting.

At the same time, and this was the second aspect of the policy of seeking to ensure the population's trust in the authorities, the regime responded to the air raids by constructing a comprehensive network of surveillance and control agencies. It kept popular morale under constant review in order to gauge how to set priorities for its propaganda. This was necessary from the regime's point of view because, although the first air raids in 1940 had caused little damage, in the view of the Security Service (SD) they had caused a not insignificant loss of trust in the regime. There were reports of a 'mood of panic',[60] of a 'psychosis of fear' in the population, and of its being ground down both psychologically and physically in the areas in the north and west of the Reich that were affected. All in all, the SD claimed to observe a decline 'in work morale' and a loss of production. The workers were over-tired and blamed absenteeism on the effects of the war and the air raids.[61]

Above all, shortly before the beginning of the war Göring had declared that not a single enemy bomb would fall on the Ruhr.[62] Its inhabitants undoubtedly still had his boast ringing in their ears when the first air-raid warnings sounded and the first bombs started to fall.[63] There was thus a clear gap opening up between people's expectations and their actual experiences, although this varied from place to place. The SD was shocked to note that false alarms, delayed warnings, and inadequate protection could soon cause a loss of trust.[64]

The Policy on Rumours and the Representation of the State

The increase in the number of rumours noted by the SD represented a threat to the regime. So far, the rumours had been circulating in narrowly restricted areas, in places where initial raids had taken place, but where the regional press had not reported them or had done so in an obviously misleading way. From the early summer of 1940, when enemy planes were flying over almost daily and the first daylight raids had begun, there was an increasing number of reports of damage in the Rhineland and Westphalia and of the threat of more to come.

Thus, at the end of May 1940, the SD reported from Dortmund and Münster that the population was having agitated discussions about future British bombing raids. It was being rumoured that 5,000 pilots were standing by ready to bomb the Ruhr and they might even use gas. 'These rumours', reported the SD, were 'very widespread and were passed on in trams, trains, shops and in the streets'.[65]

This type of rumour had five characteristics.[66] First, it prophesied a raid; secondly, it gave a possible date for it; thirdly, it gave as its source a British leaflet or 'enemy radio station'; fourthly it used particular terms such as 'large-scale raid' or cited the number of enemy bombers to describe the scale of the future raid; and, fifthly, it referred directly or indirectly to the inadequacies of the air defences. This was a problem that also arose in connection with the children's evacuation programme. For with its plan to evacuate all children between the ages of 3 and 14 from Berlin and other cities threatened by air raids the regime had produced a shock,[67] which resulted in wild rumours being spread about impending gas attacks and massive air raids and led to 'the Berlin population being more concerned about this than anything else since the beginning of the war'.[68]

Rumours of this kind struggled to find the right words for what was to come, which evidently differed so markedly from what had been known about in the pre-war period. At the same time, they served to create a sense of safety through foreknowledge, integrating future air raids into people's imaginative horizons. This process also involved the description of further targets, which, like Augsburg and Munich in 1941, were not yet regularly attacked by British bomber pilots.[69] While these rumours referred to the future, others attempted to describe what had happened in the past. This referred, in particular, to raids that had already occurred, the size of the bomber fleets, or the amount of damage and the numbers of dead and wounded.[70]

In this way, the attempt retrospectively to structure past events and use them to create expectations could perform at least two functions: quantifying the damage established a yardstick for the violence to which people had been subjected and at the same time opened up the prospect of what was to come. Secondly, the attempt to establish the effects of air raids was a response to the regime's failure to communicate with the population and to provide it with information following the attacks. Goebbels had correctly gauged the dangers of this policy of silence when, following an air raid on Berlin in September 1941, he noted: 'I am concerned that from now onwards on the day after every air raid we should provide the population with a clear overview of the amount of damage caused and above all of the number of dead. That's necessary because otherwise we open the door to the spread of rumours which, as is well known, invariably paint things worse than they really are.'[71]

In fact it was indeed the case that the extent and range of the rumour-mongering had significantly increased following the start of area bombing in 1942, namely the raids on Lübeck, Rostock, and Cologne, the daylight raid on Augsburg, and the first heavy raids on Hamburg, Saarbrücken, and Nuremberg. After the raid on Lübeck at the end of March 1942, which above all had destroyed a considerable amount of housing, the SD informants reported not only 'the great shock' suffered by the population. They also noted rumours going round which spoke of 'huge losses', 'unprece-dented'[72] in extent, causing 'great concern' in large parts of the Reich. The SD noted a similar development following the 1,000-bomber raid on Cologne at the end of May 1942. According to the SD, assessments of the numbers of dead and of the damage caused were circulating which bore no relation to reality.[73] The number of available British pilots was deduced from the number of planes that had been shot down and this provided the basis for a prognosis of future raids, which had begun to affect the rural population as well.[74]

The expansion of the number of raids evidently increased the need to develop strategies for improving the regime's communication with its pop-ulation, though this threatened always to lag behind events and thereby acquired its own dynamic. At the end of September 1942, Goebbels noted with concern how 'rumour-mongering in the Reich' had 'reached an unbe-lievable extent'[75] and that people were increasingly talking of public figures who were allegedly ill, had crashed, or had died.[76] Even Hitler himself was caught up in this.[77] For, in the meantime, he had ceased to project the image of a 'Führer' who was close to his people. The regime's propaganda, there-fore, did everything possible to present Hitler as the great, albeit somewhat remote, pilot of the nation. Having to focus on the conduct of the war, he was above everyday problems and therefore could not be held responsible for the deficiencies of the home front and certainly not for the destruction in the cities. Nevertheless, it was not least the air raids, together with the disastrous course of the war in Russia and Africa and the deteriorating food supply situation, that were responsible for producing considerable cracks in the charismatic Führer image.[78]

Hitler's withdrawal from the public sphere, which occurred from 1942/3 onwards,[79] provoked annoyance and discontent. Goebbels, who was fully aware of the problem, tried to compensate for the Führer's absence by appearing in areas affected by air raids. At the same time, he was aware of how necessary it was, if the people's emotional links to the 'Führer state' (Norbert Frei) were to be maintained, for Hitler to show himself in the areas hit by bombing. Goebbels noted that in their letters numerous people raised the question: 'why does Hitler never visit the areas affected by air raids; why does Göring never show himself; above all, however, why does Hitler never speak to the German people in order to give them an idea of what is happening? I consider it very necessary for the Führer to do this despite the burdens he is carrying in the military sphere. One can't neglect the people for too long. For when all is said and done they are the core of our war effort.'[80]

Goebbels also pressed for the terms prescribed for discussing the air war to be revised for he believed that the population was no longer prepared to be fobbed off with press statements and announcements in which developments in the air war were even being described as signs of enemy weakness.[81] Following the raids on Lübeck he had already urged the Wehrmacht High Command (OKW) to stop downplaying the damage caused because otherwise 'the nation's trust in the Wehrmacht reports' would be 'undermined'.[82] Instead, they should document and 'emphasise in the strongest possible way' the 'desecration' of the nation's cultural possessions by the Allied 'air pirates', which is what then happened after almost every raid.[83]

The problems the regime was having in adjusting its propaganda strategy to the new realities of the air war became clear immediately after the raid on Cologne at the end of May 1942. Up until then newspaper reports on air raids had been largely confined to the back pages. But now the damage could no longer be hushed up. The destruction of the city was covered in numerous reports on the radio and in national, regional, and local newspapers. The leitmotif of these reports was, as had already been the case with previous raids on the Ruhr,[84] that these were terrible acts by 'murderous British arsonists', who would now have defenceless women and children and old people on their consciences. Pictures of destroyed hospitals, blocks of flats, and damaged churches were designed to underline the criminal nature of these raids. Above all, by emphasizing the destruction of churches the reports were designed to denigrate the actions of these British 'cultural vandals', who had no inhibitions about destroying cultural treasures that were hundreds of years old. This was a narrative which, in highlighting the damage to the 'old' and peaceful city, was to become an important interpretative model for the treatment of air raids[85] because it was able to associate people's local and religious sense of identity with Nazi anti-British, and later increasingly anti-Semitic, diatribes.

At the same time, the articles contained two more topoi of air-war propaganda: first, the continual emphasis on the successes of German air defences, which were quantifiable, and so on the high price the British were paying for their 'terror'; and, secondly, a narrative in which the 'German soul' displayed its mettle and solidarity, calmly surviving all the attacks with discipline and good sense. A number of individuals were chosen as 'heroes of the home front' to exemplify these qualities. Their, usually 'female', roles in air defence as air-raid wardens or nurses were portrayed in the most vivid colours as caring, motherly, and intrepid fighters for hearth and home and at the same time as kind and patient helpers.[86]

Apart from the quiet individual hero there was another heroic narrative, that of the intrepid city. 'Cologne together—a Team' was the message contained in a pamphlet that appeared shortly after the attacks and which, in addition to singing the praises of the city's self-sacrifice and steadfastness, also contained an encomium to the Nazi Party for its contribution.[87] The press was full of praise for the Party—for its indefatigable efforts to rescue property, its organizational skills, and its rapid and unbureaucratic aid after the raids. This praise was a response to the considerable discontent of, and criticism expressed by, the Cologne population, something that the Cologne Nazi Party organization was obliged to take on board. It was now necessary to create an authoritative counterweight to the rumours and discontent that were emerging.[88]

It was clear that with the intensification of the strategic air war against German cities after the spring of 1943 people's assessment of the number of victims was increasing and so they tried to adjust their notions of what was happening and what was likely to happen to correspond to the escalation of the air raids. Thus, according to the SD, after the attack on the Möhne dam on 16/17 May 1943, the population believed that between 10,000 and 30,000 people had been killed.[89]

In the west of the Reich a considerable number of people claimed that the Allied 'air campaign over the Ruhr' aimed to 'obliterate' [ausradieren] the cities, to destroy them completely and reduce them to rubble—a nightmare vision, which, on the one hand, was reminiscent of the inter-war scenarios of destruction, but on the other hand, in view of the pictures from Essen, Düsseldorf, or Cologne, appeared by no means completely exaggerated. Evidently rumours led people to adjust their day-to-day observations and perceptions to what might be experienced or anticipated. The same was true of the rumours of the deployment of gas: at the start of the war people's expectations were dominated by the language about and pictures of the use of gas in the First World War. Gas seemed to represent the essence of the impending threat of air warfare, of people's new sense of insecurity.[90]

However, during the course of the war the way in which the catastrophic experience of air raids was recounted came to correspond to the actual events. From 1942/3 onwards rumours of the Allied deployment of phosphorus bombs increasingly replaced reports about the threat of gas warfare. Above all, the heavy raid on Wuppertal, at the end of June 1943,[91] during which more than 4,000 people were killed, encouraged the spread of rumours about the deployment of chemical weapons.[92] Some people believed that phosphorus was even more effective than gas.[93] This was a scenario of impending doom that tried to integrate terror into the diagnosis of present and future. At the same time, however, it was also a response to the search for the 'truth' about bombing, which diverged so markedly from the propaganda slogans and their rhetoric of retaliation.

There is no doubt that the topic of air raids dominated domestic politics.[94] Rumours had developed a dangerous and destabilizing dynamic and, as Goebbels himself believed, it appeared vital to respond aggressively to them. To begin with, this meant changing the criteria for observing and assessing what, in the language of the Nazi state, was termed 'the population's mood and behaviour'.[95] In his instructions to the press, issued March 1943, with reference to the air war Goebbels had ordered 'that in future one should speak only of good behaviour'.[96] It was quite possible that the population might give way to resignation; after all no one knew when 'the gruelling air raids' were going to come to an end. Since houses were being burnt and cities devastated it was unlikely 'that people would start crying hurrah'.

A shift away from hushing things up

In contrast to German propaganda the British approach relied on a policy of hushing things up. Little was heard of German air raids and, if at all, then only after a considerable delay. The reports in the national and provincial newspapers only noted vaguely that there had been 'light' or 'heavy' raids on cities in north-west England which meant, for example, the bombing of Liverpool. In the first days of the air war most of the media restricted themselves to publishing government communiqués without covering the local situation in any detail.

This restrictive information policy caused considerable discontent among broad sections of the population, as it was quite clear which city had been the target of such a raid. The news reports sometimes mentioned some damage but no one ever appeared to have been killed or wounded. It was reported that people's behaviour had been admirable, calm, and prudent and the emergency services had invariably arrived 'promptly'.[97]

Editors and civil servants were aware of the growing problems concerning the censorship of news concerning air raids. Above all, the authorities outside London complained about the inadequate and misleading reporting. There were also, as was the case in Bristol and Liverpool, a growing number of reports of criticism of the authorities and increasing demands that, despite the danger of thereby providing the enemy with potentially valuable information, people should have their local pride restored by at least having their suffering adequately reported.[98]

After Brendan Bracken, Churchill's private secretary, took over the Ministry of Information in June 1941 from the luckless Duff Cooper,[99] there was a change of course. Unlike his predecessor, Bracken, who was an experienced newspaper man, was not convinced that restrictions and exaggeration were appropriate methods in the struggle to win the population's trust. Bracken believed that a 'people's war' required a different approach to people from that adopted in wars hitherto. For, in the final analysis, the war against Hitler could be won only with the support and the 'spirit' of the people. 'High morale', he declared in a memorandum for Churchill's War Cabinet in April 1940, could be achieved only by an open information policy, which explained to people the risks of war, including the threat of air raids. Otherwise, there would be a grave loss of trust.[100]

For example, Mary Adams, the head of an MoI department, complained strongly about the reporting of a raid on Swansea at the beginning of 1941: it was hardly conceivable that people who had just lost friends or relatives would be walking through the streets of the city wreathed in smiles.[101] In her view all the previous studies had indicated that, after air raids, people were initially downcast; a few were confused, others felt isolated or discouraged. Above all, those who had lost property or relatives often appeared in despair. In future, information policy must take account of this.[102] Thus people's experiences and reactions could be very different. What might depress some people could boost the self-esteem of others. But, as Adams pointed out, this increased the danger that the significance of the reports would not be played down but rather exaggerated.

It was dangerous to claim that morale was so high when there were large numbers of people who were frightened. Instead of exaggerated and, as a result, implausible generalizations, Adams argued that eyewitnesses should be given the chance to have their say and this would lend credibility to claims about the air defences. In her view credibility and trust were also reduced if, as was usually the case, reports on war damage bore little relation to reality. It was, therefore, important for the reports on the efficiency of the local emergency services to be more even-handed: praise for local heroes should be counterbalanced by criticism of administrative errors. At any rate, inadequacies should not be hushed up because otherwise this would only increase people's feeling that they could not trust the news if only positive experiences were being reported.

Adams's view of how to control information was based on the assumption that, although the war had turned people into 'civilians at the front', this did not mean that they had lost their right to hold and express opinions. It was precisely because support for the war could not be enforced that it was essential to pursue an active information policy and to keep emphasizing that in this critical situation every individual was being taken seriously and was not being deceived by false or exaggerated statements. In her view it was possible to talk of 'high morale' only when people could cope with unpleasant news, and trust in the government would actually increase if it reported the unvarnished truth about the war situation.

Despite the need to impose censorship during the war, Mary Adams, who was on the Left, insisted that the relationship between the individual and the state should not be subjected to a fundamental revision, with individual rights being suspended on the grounds that the war constituted a new 'social situation'. Thus censorship was double-edged: alleged military priorities versus public opinion and control. Support for the war had to be fought for and, if it had to happen at all, then the partial regulation of public debate could be only a temporary expedient.

However, the reports on which Adams relied for her analysis and which were also decisively to shape the views of the War Cabinet were of course themselves subject to their own linguistic conventions, which influenced what the informants chose to report and the questions they posed. For example, in February 1941 various forms of behaviour and expression that were taken to indicate 'low morale' were giving cause for concern: the Weekly Reports, but also psychological studies, interpreted all pacifist comments and all conversations expressing fear and concern about the future as clear indications of 'declining morale'.[103]

All reservations expressed about the war were interpreted as 'defeatism' and this was the term applied to behaviour that was out of line. It was accepted that there were such 'defeatists' and yet it was claimed that such socially objectionable behaviour was not widespread. The same was true of criticism of the authorities, which was registered in the reports under the rubric 'grumblers'. There were frequent references to such discontent in the Weekly Reports of the MoI, particularly in the years 1940/1, although these were considered minority views. That also applied to the growing number of anti-Semitic comments, which, from the end of 1940/beginning of 1941, were increasingly to be heard coming not only from London, but also from Liverpool and other cities. Jews were accused of a lack of 'discipline' and of behaving selfishly during and after air raids. This marked a further boundary between 'them' and 'us', between 'British' and 'un-British' behaviour.[104]

Thus the various interpretations of and assumptions about the term 'morale' shaped the response of the propaganda authorities and the media to the air raids and their assessment of the population's behaviour in a number of different ways. This also involved the question of how far a democracy should curb a free press in order to achieve a worthy goal. The difficulty of striking a balance was reflected both in Bracken's attempt to introduce a change of course, which was not uniformly welcomed either by the War Cabinet or in other ministries or by the military, and in the experience of the first two years of the war, when his ministry kept using questionnaires to test how far its activities were regarded as credible by the population. Although the government's information policy was generally accepted, at the same time a majority considered it inadequate and in part damaging.[105]

This was particularly true of the press reports on bombing, which, contrary to the wishes of the Ministry of Information, varied greatly from region to region and, as in Germany, despite attempts to control them from the centre, were able to retain a measure of independence. It was several days before the two Liverpool newspapers, the *Daily Post* and the *Express*, published their first reports and photographs of the air raids on the city. Up until then they had published only specific information required for the removal of debris in the immediate aftermath of a raid. Thus, both papers reassured their readers that everything was in place to look after those affected by the raids. The homeless were being cared for, an emergency plan was in place, and the distribution of supplies from the war damage fund was going smoothly.[106]

It was possible to glean bits of information from newspapers despite the censorship. Without referring to air raids directly both papers reported on soup kitchens,[107] on new air defence measures, and on people's unbroken morale. Light air raids on cities in the north-west were first mentioned at the end of October 1940, but there was nothing about damage or casualties. However, both papers provided space for city councillors to criticize the failure of the emergency committee to prevent the unauthorized use of public air-raid shelters.[108]

Criticism of the policy regarding air-raid shelters was evidently so widespread that the censors felt that they could not allow this sensitive topic to go unreported. However, the newspapers' readers were not permitted to know what exactly the problem was or who was responsible. After experiencing its first heavy raids, Manchester faced equally serious problems, but the *Manchester Guardian* responded by taking a much tougher line than the Liverpool press.

The city suffered its worst air raids just before Christmas Eve 1940. Around 30,000 dwellings were destroyed and around 380 persons were killed. A few days later the *Manchester Guardian* published a highly critical article.[109] The German bombs had inflicted serious damage on the city, numerous buildings had been destroyed and, as a result, important examples of Britain's cultural heritage had been wiped out. However, much of what had fallen victim to the flames could have been rescued if only the fire brigade and emergency services had been better organized. Often air defence personnel had spotted fires but had not been able to summon assistance. In many cases it was the people who had sought refuge in the air-raid shelters who had put out the fires. And if only those responsible for dealing with the fires had secured a vantage point high above the city from which to assess the situation much of the damage could have been avoided. This was damning criticism.

The issue of whether such criticism could contribute towards undermining morale or whether, on the contrary, a frank information policy was a necessary precondition for persuading the population to support the war was controversial right from the start of the bombing campaign. This question had also preoccupied the Research and Experiment Department of the Ministry of Home Security, which was responsible for researching the effects of bombing and which sought answers by assessing reports in the majority of provincial newspapers. However, the Ministry failed to reach a clear conclusion.[110]

Of course it was not only important what the newspapers wrote but also what they showed. Here too, despite the censorship, they had a certain amount of scope. While even months after the heavy air raids the Liverpool newspapers did not illustrate any of their reports with photographs of destroyed buildings, but rather concentrated on people and large portraits, a week after the Christmas raids readers of the *Manchester Guardian* were already seeing pictures of damage to the city centre. They showed a burnt-out house that was still smoking and of which only the outside walls were still standing. In among the ruins the true heroes of the situation were confronting the devastation with pickaxes and their bare hands. They did not appear to be radiating confidence in victory but rather an unbroken will to survive and a 'manly' determination to do their bit.[111] The first pictures of the air raids illustrated above all the self-sacrifice shown by the firemen, men who were attacking the flames, sweating, and fighting to defend their homeland at the risk of their lives.

At the end of November 1940, the Southampton *Southern Daily Echo* published on its front page a large picture of a burning building with the headline 'Towns Nazis tried to destroy still live'.[112] Firemen were trying to extinguish the large fires so that they did not spread and reach catastrophic proportions. The newspaper did not reveal the location of the fire so that the picture appeared to illustrate the way in which all the cities that were being hit at this time—Southampton, Birmingham, and Bristol—were being defended.

The selection of photographs of Southampton differed markedly from those used in other newspapers, for, in the first place, the large-scale pictures of damage were frequently printed on the front page and, secondly, the editor used not only photos of churches and buildings of cultural importance— symbols of Nazi barbarism—but also pictures of lifeless streets that resembled craters, buses that had been destroyed, and the shells of houses.[113] Although the articles printed on the same page might praise people's morale, the picture conveyed a different message. It was a gloomy and depressing scene of a city that that had been destroyed. Thus, presumably unintentionally, those people were proved right who, like the informants of Mass Observation, had noted that the mood after the heavy raids on Southampton had reached rock bottom and who had seen it as a city in agony.[114]

The visits of the King and Queen to the bombed cities were, by contrast, an attempt to portray the destruction in the public sphere in a new light and to project complete confidence in victory. From September 1940 onwards, the royal family criss-crossed Britain in order to underline its sense of solidarity with the British people. The image of the King and Queen not seeking refuge in one of their country residences but staying in London with their people at the heart of the Empire and giving them courage was projected in almost every newspaper. The Queen was the caring, noble mother, a people's queen in a royal family at the apex of a nation under threat.[115]

At the beginning of November, the King and Queen were once again by the side of those who had suffered. They visited one of the soup kitchens in Liverpool and were shown the damage that had been done to the cathedral and they commiserated with a woman who had lost her husband in one of the air raids. None of the pictures showed the location of the destruction, no sorrowful faces were to be seen, only cheering crowds. The visit was designed to show the King and Queen meeting ordinary people, the royal version of the 'People's War'. During the First World War, visits to hospitals and military establishments had already been standard practice for the royal family. Now the air raids were once again bringing monarch and people together in a demonstration of an Empire that bridged social class, was at peace with itself, and had only one aim—to withstand the attacks of a barbaric enemy. Despite air-raid warnings, the visit was not cancelled. The royals stuck to their programme, visited areas that had suffered damage, and inspected air-raid shelters. Given the strong criticisms that had been made beforehand, this was a particularly important gesture for, if even the King and Queen had praised the careful safety measures, who could dare to grumble about them?

According to the newspapers they were met everywhere with spontaneous applause. People presented flowers, schoolchildren lined the streets, women interrupted their housework when they heard that the royal couple was in the neighbourhood.[116] It was, in particular, the 'motherly', the female side of the home front that received particular emphasis in this royal visit. Apart from (local) male worthies, the pictures of the visit showed almost exclusively working-class women cheering. Sometimes the Queen spoke to a widow, sometimes to a woman who had lost her home. The royal visit was an act of ritual national integration; of a 'family' of which the royals were the head and to whom all those who had suffered could turn with their concerns and troubles, above all women who, it appeared, were having to bear the main burden of the air war.[117]

Evacuations and Rumours

Like Propaganda Minister Goebbels's visits to the areas threatened by air raids, the royal visits to the districts hit by bombing were important acts of public integration designed to overcome old inequalities between classes and regions and new inequalities between those who had been bombed out and those who had not been affected. However, that was not the only set of conflicts given new impetus by the air raids. Already, immediately after the beginning of the war, the extensive evacuation of schoolchildren from areas in danger of air raids had sparked a debate about the state of the nation. To start with, at the beginning of September 1939, there was much talk about the need to keep calm.[118] Nothing should be allowed to create the impression that war was unavoidable and that it was only a matter of time before air raids started. The government tried to get across the need for security and to take precautions. Herbert Morrison, the Chairman of London County Council, told children and their parents that they should cope with any problems that might arise with a 'cheerful British smile'.[119]

The newspapers informed their readers where the school classes should assemble, when the trains would leave, and above all that the evacuations of the, for example, around 750,000 London children were proceeding in a 'calm and orderly manner'. There was no mention of angry parents or of a lack of transport capacity. It was a triumphant example of British organizational skills and discipline.[120] Everywhere people had been ready to help to ensure that the transport of the children went like clockwork. To begin with, the newspaper pictures showed only happy children, who were experiencing the evacuation as a great adventure holiday and whose happiest dream had been of a stay in the country, where unlike in the city there was no war but instead only the warmth and peace of the countryside.

The BBC adopted a similar tone in its reports. In the news broadcast of 29 October 1940, for example, a young boy reported on the first cow he had encountered in his life and shared his magical rural experiences with the listeners.[121] The relationship between town and country touched on one of the core issues of what it meant to be 'British'. Criticism of the consequences of urbanization for the health of the British nation and glorification of the countryside were continually recurring topoi of the search for national identity. Anyone who wanted to discover the heart of the nation was expected to leave the city and head for somewhere like Sussex or Devon. Urban growth seemed to be encouraging national illnesses, to be the catalyst for criminality, poverty, hunger, and soullessness. By contrast, it was worth fighting for 'rural England'.

The search for the peace and quiet of country life had followed the horrors of the First World War.[122] H. V. Morton's *In Search of England* published in 1927 had sold a million copies and was one of the most successful books of the inter-war years. However, the association of Englishness with the countryside did not necessarily have anti-urban and anti-modern connotations and its interpretation could vary depending on class and regional factors. Morton, for example, could celebrate the peaceful qualities of the countryside and its inhabitants and consider it was the heart of England, while at the same time opposing the demonizing of urban life.

The reporting of the first phase of evacuation follows on from these older discourses in two ambivalent respects: in the first place, in terms of the rediscovery of rural idylls in the context of the war and of the justification for why it was worth fighting against Hitler. The evacuation was viewed as enabling the urban evacuees to become acquainted with the beauty of Great Britain and then to return to the cities with news of its romantic and peaceful qualities. At the same time, the evacuees from proletarian districts represented an invasion of the countryside by modern urban life.[123] People made fun of their accents and eating habits, joked about these strange figures from the big city, and noted with disgust how alien this 'other half' of the country was. These working-class mothers seemed incapable even of providing their children with a decent meal made with simple ingredients.

Secondly, the evacuation became part of a debate about the 'social question', which also went far back into the pre-war period. The fact that poor working-class children received not only adequate meals and clothing from the upper-class and middle-class families with whom they were staying, but also human warmth, formed an important topic within the discourse about the evacuation. For example, in the middle of September British Movietone News carried a report that the evacuees staying with the family of the Tory MP Oliver Lyttelton, who was to become Minister of War Production in 1942, felt at home being looked after by a member of the upper class. A girl wrote to her parents that she was being given things that she would never have been able to have at home. She was eating hare, roast venison, and pheasant.[124]

This kind of notion of social harmony was an essential element in the discourse of morale. The emergency situation created by the war was seen as providing the precondition for solidarity and for overcoming class divisions. At the same time, this analysis of the evacuation was challenged by other interpretations, which described the encounter of the classes as a kind of social shock and drew from it very different conclusions. To some extent, the descriptions of the children involved, with their torn clothing and shoes with holes in them, were reminiscent of Victorian interpretations of poverty as being the fault of the poor themselves. The evacuees, above all the women, were adding to the burdens of the middle-class families who were taking them in. Only very few women were considered 'acceptable', as a letter to *The Spectator* put it, and most of the mothers were 'on the bottom rung of slum dwellers'.[125]

Such assessments were by no means exceptional. In the late autumn of 1939 the letter columns of the *Glasgow Herald* were full of comments that the evacuees were responsible for 'polluting the cities' and complaints about the children's lack of discipline.[126] A helper working for the Liverpool city council also used the term 'pollution' when describing the invasion of 'orderly' city life by 'irresponsible' evacuees. Within a very short time they had wrecked the reception centres and in their treatment of the dwellings to which they had been assigned they had ignored basic standards of behaviour.[127] Observers blamed all this above all on the working-class mothers' lack of maternal care of their children. In this view it was not poverty or poor housing that was to blame for this regrettable situation but 'family problems', a lack of time and a lack of diligence on the part of the mothers in the way they treated their children.[128] Poverty from this perspective was above all the result of specifically female misbehaviour, which it was vital to correct, for if it continued it would damage morale.[129]

The power to define who belonged to the nation was an essential principle of the construction of a community at war and morale governed the way in which class and gender issues were viewed. More than any other domestic political topic the debate about the housing of the evacuees during this early phase of the war was a substitute for a debate about the essence of the British nation and 'correct' behaviour during the war. While military decisions were to a large extent subject to censorship, this was not true of expressions of opinion. Comment was largely unaffected by censorship.

This form of social and gender exclusion did not go unchallenged. There was a growing number of voices who saw in the fate of the proletariat and the conflicts concerning their accommodation a wake-up call for rapid social intervention.[130] A member of Liverpool social services complained that it was deplorable that in a Christian country egoistic house owners should turn away families seeking help and send them back to areas threat-ened by air raids.[131]

Those in local government held a variety of views. The Provost of Glasgow, Lord Darling, spoke out strongly against the abuse of evacuees who lived in poverty as 'polluters'. It was true that these children did not have aristocratic standards of hygiene, he noted caustically in his contribution to the *Glasgow Herald*. Nevertheless, they deserved more sympathy than they had received hitherto. After all, they were victims of an environment which in the past had paid more attention to profit and dividends than to family and the quality of housing.[132] All this opened up a wide-ranging debate about social reform that was to continue until the end of the war.

Evacuation in the Third Reich

The increase in the number of Allied air raids meant that more resources had to be devoted to the evacuation programme. From April 1943 onwards the central authorities attempted to exert a tighter control over the evacua-tions, which until then had often been uncontrolled and 'chaotic', in order to relieve pressure on the areas threatened by air raids. Although many of the ideas put forward during the planning process proved unrealistic,[133] the Reich Interior Ministry and, above all, the Propaganda Minister made it very clear that they wanted to follow a new path and that could only mean the substantial centralization of evacuation measures.

However, apart from the logistical problems involved, centralization had another consequence: it turned evacuation into a major public issue. The evacuation of children had begun as a kind of secret operation and, as a result, had provoked popular indignation. Goebbels now went on the offen-sive. The public was to be informed through the press, the Party, and other sources of information about the Gaus from which the children were to be taken and those to which they were to be sent and it was to be persuaded of the benefits of evacuation. That represented a 180-degree turn.

Information sheets issued to the hosts of the evacuees marked the bound-aries of what could be said in public about the air raids and revealed far more than the official statements in the press.[134] Anyone reading them could get an idea of how big the losses had been. They mentioned people who had had hardly any sleep, who had lost everything, not only personal pos-sessions but relatives and friends. The hosts should show understanding for their grief and their tense nerves and, above all, the children should be treated with great consideration. The information sheets also informed regions such as Tyrol or Lower Austria, which had not yet been affected by the air aids, of what was to come.[135]

Despite all the propaganda about the national community, the public statements issued in the host districts revealed the major rows that were going on between the local people and the evacuees.[136] The authorities appealed to the rural population to show consideration for the different habits of people coming from big cities and be tolerant if it took a little time for the outsiders to adjust to the new living conditions.[137] Given the tense situation, they advised caution in passing on information and reports about air raids to the evacuees in order not to add to their anxiety. In this they were effectively admitting that even what appeared to be exaggerated rumours could be very close to reality.

At the same time the regime attempted to redefine the concept of crisis management. According to the Party Chancellery, the words 'evacuation' and 'evacuees' should no longer be used because they smacked of compulsion.[138] Instead, more neutral terms should be employed such as 're-accommodation' and 'people who had been re-accommodated'. The Party Chancellery also wanted to dispense with the use of the phrase 'front line of the British terror bombing'. However, the Propaganda Ministry seriously doubted the efficacy of these proposals, given the fact that they reflected a policy of trying to win trust that in the eyes of those affected often appeared to have long been discredited by their own experience.

At any rate, Goebbels's colleagues advocated keeping both sets of terms; after all, in the first place, the terms had become established and, secondly, it could not in fact be done without a certain amount of moral pressure. They also advocated keeping the term 'front' because it provided 'a certain satisfaction' for those affected and it was commonly used in propaganda.[139] The re-visualizing of the ruined urban landscape as urban battle zones was very much in keeping with Goebbels's vision of 'total war' that he had already announced in his speech in the Sports Palace in Berlin on 18 February 1943 and which since then had become part of his new propaganda strategy for the air war.[140]

Thus, it was clear what sort of directives he would be issuing to the Gau propaganda offices: the air raids had to be 'always on our minds';[141] after all, at the moment they were the 'decisive problem of the war'. The propaganda agencies should ensure that the air raids were reported every day in the press and on the radio, not least in order to provide moral support to the population in the west of the Reich, who were suffering so much, and in order to document the 'national community's' sense of solidarity. Everybody must understand: 'There must be no grumbling; people must simply put up with the sacrifices demanded of them by the Government.' What was needed was a 'counterweight to stiffen morale' in the face of the threat of a disintegration of the home front and in view of the 'crucial test' to which the population was being subjected on a daily basis. According to the Propaganda Minister, many people in the less affected areas lacked 'generosity of spirit' towards the evacuees or sympathetic understanding of the consequences of what he described as the 'greatest migration of all time'. The biggest problem was not Stalingrad but the air raids.

The thing that prompted Goebbels to adopt this proactive strategy was probably his visit to the industrial cities of the Rhineland and Westphalia in June 1943. Apart from Düsseldorf, he also visited Wuppertal, which had been seriously damaged and where he attended the memorial service for those who had been killed.[142] The population there had 'lost its nerve', everything was lacking, and 'worst of all', people no longer knew where 'all these air raids were going to lead'. In the meantime, the population had even forgotten to cry out for revenge, 'because they know that at the moment it can't be achieved'.[143] From the middle of 1943 onwards, reports of anxiety, apprehension, and a considerable degree of nervousness came in from many parts of the Reich.[144] This was caused above all by the British raids on Hamburg between the end of July and the beginning of August 1943. After Operation Gomorrah the SD reported that there were estimates of hundreds of thousands of deaths; there were also reports of disturbances and demonstrations by people who had been made homeless. The city had been 'flattened'[145] and the police, SA, and Wehrmacht had had to crush the riots. A 'November mood'* was becoming widespread in the districts affected by air raids and it was hardly likely that the population would put up with this for long without rebelling.[146]

Similar reports were coming in from numerous towns and the further away these towns were and the less experience they had of this kind of catastrophe the more speculative were the attempts to assess the extent of the damage. Whereas in north Germany the estimates of the deaths in Operation Gomorrah ranged between 18,000 and 80,000 deaths, in the west the estimate was 50,000, in south Germany there were rumours of between 80,000 and 150,000, while in Silesia, which had hitherto been

---

* Translators' note: This refers to the German revolutions of November 1918.

completely unaffected by air raids, people were prepared to believe that up to 350,000 had been killed.[147]

More than any other previous event this mass bombing raid had made air raids the vital issue for the home front. In the eyes of the regime Hamburg exceeded anything that had happened hitherto. Goebbels observed a sort of 'panic'[148] invading public life, which, contrary to what had been hoped, was paralysing instead of 'strengthening' the will to resist, as the President of the Higher Regional Court in Munich put it in a report.[149] Reports of the fire storms, which spread throughout the Reich like a shock wave, contributed to this mood. The rumours picked up by the SD and the judicial authorities contained horror stories that make clear the extent to which ideas about the destructive power of air raids had grown. There was talk of people becoming burning torches and there was a report from Bayreuth that Hamburg women had taken the heads of their dead children with them when they were evacuated.[150]

By spreading awareness of the impact of air raids to regions which had not yet been penetrated by Allied aircraft, above all the rural areas in the south and east of the Reich, the evacuees helped to draw the whole of the Reich into the air war and to make of it a major event that was not simply mediated through propaganda but was transparent and out in the open.[151] In this process they were both subjects and objects. Thus combating rumours was a number one priority for the Nazi Party as a response to what was felt to be the inadequacy of the regime's ability to influence the public mood. As far as the Party Chancellery was concerned, it was no use simply remaining silent in the face of a combination of enemy propaganda, defeatism, and weakness.[152] Moreover, the tales about the effects of the air raids, the destruction of swastikas in the sky by divine intervention, and the reports about a breakdown of discipline, the misuse of public office, and the threat of defeat were all damaging the morale of the home front, undermining the Party's self-confidence, and weakening the relationship of trust between leadership and people.

In any case, it was part of the Party's leadership role (*Menschenführung*) to observe the development of rumours and to direct and control them more than had been the case hitherto. Nazi functionaries were informed that education and Nazi indoctrination ought to help to check the flood of rumours. This was to be carried out by the local branches through a combination of encouragement, political advice, and repression. At the same time, they should be cautious about using exaggerated propaganda.

It was sensible to be matter of fact because the population was above all receptive to rumours when, as had been the case with Stalingrad, they had proved to be quite close to the truth. Thus the Party Chancellery instructed its functionaries that it was better not to get involved in the discussion of concrete facts but instead one should refer to the 'great goals' of the war. If this failed then, as far as the Nazi Party was concerned, the only thing to do was to 'lock 'em up, lock 'em up without mercy'. After all, people who spread rumours were like 'bacilli in the nation's body' and so had to be isolated.[153]

During the autumn and winter of 1943 the regime was particularly concerned about rumours contained in leaflets that cited dates on which bombing was going to occur or the names of cities that were going to be spared.[154] For these not only represented an attempt to predict the strategic decisions of the Allies but also exposed the Nazi state to the accusation that it was taking inadequate precautions.[155] Thus the fight against rumours was also a fight against 'national vermin' and therefore an important propaganda task for the Party, to which, towards the end of the war, it was to devote more and more of its efforts.

The Image and Memory of the War

The Nazi regime's desire to establish total control over the way in which air raids were reported was not restricted to its attempt to reduce the number of rumours. As far as the Propaganda Minister was concerned, it was at least as important to establish the basis for an archive of memoirs of individuals who had been through the raids. In addition to demonizing the Allies through propaganda, the history of Germany's experience of sacrifice and survival was to become a collective, Nazi memory of the history of the air war, an archive, which, after the war, would serve as evidence for its national (völkisch) heroism and unbroken will to win.

Initial plans had been prepared in Hamburg and finally, in August 1944, Goebbels called on cities and local communities systematically to gather information and memoirs of people's experiences of air raids. After all, almost every day 'heroic acts had occurred', of which future generations should be reminded.[156] Recollection of the strength of the 'national community' and of the 'cultural barbarism' of the Allies were the two themes, which, for example, formed the basis of several plans for exhibitions, which were designed, even during the course of the war, to provide visual evidence of 'crimes' and underline the nation's unbroken determination to win.

Immediately after the heavy air raid on Lübeck on 28/9 March 1942, the artist Eduard Hopf was commissioned by the Nazi Party to produce drawings of churches and houses that had been destroyed, which a year later were being exhibited in the city and in other places in north Germany. Around one hundred pictures provided a variety of gloomy sketches of a Hanseatic city that had been 'destroyed by fire', of houses that had been demolished and burnt-out churches, all of which had become the victims of senseless violence and cultural destruction; the 'old' city and its history appeared to be a victim of the flames and, as a result, the history of the nation itself seemed to have become the target of Allied 'terror bombers'.[157]

In Hamburg, Hansa, the city's photographic service, documented the ruins in order to provide posterity with an impression of the blow to culture represented by the loss of traditional Hansa buildings,[158] and in other cities too photographers were active in recording the damage in the service of the Reich Propaganda Ministry, heritage or city authorities, or of the Wehrmacht.[159] Without express authorization photographs of military installations, armaments plants, and railways were subject to strict censorship. There was no express ban on photographing other public buildings, damaged houses, or streets; however, in practice what was permitted varied from city to city, particularly at the start of the air raids. In a criminal trial in Cologne involving a man who had taken photos of damage for his own use the court concluded that 'the photographing of private houses that had been damaged in an air raid' was not subject to any ban. Finally, with the increase in air raids that began in April 1942 a police regulation came into effect banning photographs of railway installations, autobahns, canals, and harbours.[160]

The invasion of Poland and the bombing of Warsaw had already been extensively covered by the Wehrmacht Propaganda units. The German press quickly published pictures of enemy streets and houses that had been destroyed. The use of pictures in the *Völkischer Beobachter*'s reporting of Britain from the middle of 1940 was dominated by two themes.[161] The photographs either illustrated the reach of the German Luftwaffe, its effectiveness and huge potency; or the themes were chosen in such a way as to demonstrate the crumbling morale of the British people. The photos showed crowds in front of tube stations: large, frightened groups, who seemed as if they had given up and were submitting to their fate. It appeared as if it would not be long before British resistance would be finally broken.

From 1940 onwards, the Reich Propaganda Ministry had insisted that, in order to document the damage, press reports on the bombing of Germany should include not simply text but also pictures and that the photos should be tagged with the slogan 'terror attack'. The Ministry considered such photographs so important that, at the beginning of the war, they were sometimes allowed to circumvent military censorship. It was arranged for the photos to be sent immediately to the Reich Photograph Archive in Berlin where they could be utilized for the propaganda battle at home and abroad. Air-raid photos represented a central element in the propaganda struggle for moral authority and for the establishment of Germany's political innocence. After the British raids on Berlin and Hamburg the reports were expected to 'hype up every detail' for the whole world to see and thereby underpin the justification for German revenge attacks in the future. 'Since, as expected, the British are using more and more atrocity propaganda, we for our own part in our press and radio broadcasts must point out emphatically that it was Britain who wanted the war and that everything that is now happening was provoked by Britain, despite all our repeated warnings. Moreover, we must keep emphasizing that, in contrast to the British, we are attacking only military targets, but that they simply have themselves to blame if, now that they have got the war they wanted, civilians come under attack.'[162]

Various pictorial themes played an important role in domestic and foreign propaganda. These included photographs of cultural monuments, schools, and churches that had been destroyed and served to depict the British once again as 'barbarians' and 'ruthless air bandits'. These were often photos which, using familiar picture postcard motifs, adopted traditional forms of representation and tried to underline the amount of destruction that had been caused through pictures of 'before' and 'after'. Another dominant pictorial theme was of aid workers and fire fighters working indefatigably and successfully to combat the 'terror'. Iconographically, these pictures differed hardly at all from photographs in British newspapers in showing the 'moral superiority' of one's own side and the depravity of the others.

As a rule, newspaper readers did not get to see either the ruins of individual houses or close-ups of grieving people; instead, everywhere there were helping hands eager to save people's belongings. From an early stage, first the Wehrmacht and then Goebbels had insisted that everything should be done to avoid people's enthusiasm for the war being undermined by pictures of violence.[163] The 'toughness', the 'greatness', and the 'self-sacrifice of war' should certainly be shown, as Goebbels emphasized in his guidelines for the press of 10 June 1940. But, at the same time, 'exaggeratedly realistic descriptions' should be avoided, since this, after all, 'merely encouraged a horror of war'.[164] To begin with, this meant 'correcting' the number of victims upwards so that the British could be once again branded as war criminals.

The pictures of the early memorial ceremonies did not contain any faces that could be seen, as was also the case in Britain. The perspective looked over the backs of the heads of the crowd towards the Party speakers, with the photographers following detailed instructions that remained the same for the rest of the war. However, the openness with which the air raids were being depicted came to an end with the disastrous 1,000-bomber raid on Cologne. The chaos produced by its devastating power and the extent of the destruction involved led Goebbels to demand that in future lengthy reports on air raids with pictures should no longer be published.[165]

Pictures of air raids could not only be seen in the newspapers; they were also shown in cinemas. For example, bombing, air-raid warnings, and the threat to the 'home front' formed the background for the plot of *Die grosse Liebe* (The Great Love).[166] With Zarah Leander in the starring role, it was the most commercially successful Nazi film of the war. Around 27 million people went to see the love story of the young fighter pilot, Paul Wendlandt, who while home on leave falls in love with the singer Hanna Holberg. They meet unexpectedly during an air-raid warning and this meeting in an air-raid shelter begins a dramatic love story with a happy ending. Finally united, at the end of the film they gaze into the sky where German bombers are circling overhead.

Die grosse Liebe tells a story of wartime duty, of the need to subordinate individual happiness to the fate of the nation, to what was required for Germany's victory; its message is of waiting for what one wants, that sacrifices are worthwhile, and that even desirable women like Hanna Holberg are prepared to make them. What was remarkable was not so much the propaganda message as the, by comparison with other 'home front films', unusual attempt to present an unvarnished account of everyday life in wartime. Air-raid warnings were part of the everyday life of the 'national community', just as was having to spend time in fear and apprehension in an air-raid shelter. It was there that everyone met and laughed together. Thus air-raid shelters appeared to represent a test for the 'national community', which the majority passed with flying colours; but they were also dangerous places in encouraging strong emotions, as in the case of Paul and Hanna. At the same time, the proud shelter community jeered at all the 'grumblers' and defeatists, who were never happy with what they had and only saw the worst in everything. Here it was the 'national comrades' themselves who decided who belonged to the 'national community' and who did not. And 'troublemakers' excluded themselves.

The fact that the everyday life of air raids played a part in this romantic film was exceptional and with the increase in bombing even such 'realistic' scenes, which were in fact clearly designed for their propaganda effect, disappeared from cinema screens. The German public was not shown the devastation of their homeland, which was in fact all around for them to see. Instead, the main subject of numerous films was the story of the heroic success of the German Luftwaffe and of its deployment over the Atlantic.[167] The pilots were the young heroes of the Nazi state, brave, manly, and calm. Emotions were for other people.

One of the best-known films of this genre was *Stukas* from 1941.[168] *Stukas* tells the story of a German officer who is shot down over France and afterwards suffers from depression. He is cured only after a visit to the Wagner festival at Bayreuth and can then return to his squadron and join in the Battle of Britain. Contemporary critics noted that it was a very thin plot and the script had serious dramatic flaws. But it was a historic battle on which everything depended and so it was felt that the story had to be told as authentically as possible. To achieve this, the director, Karl Ritter, cut scenes from the weekly newsreels and documentary pictures of planes landing and bombs falling and integrated them. The film did not have a conventional opening: 'Stukas' dive from the sky, every bomb is a hit, and the explosions come nearer and nearer—the Luftwaffe appears to be getting ever closer to a final victory over Britain. The scenes added from the newsreels gave spectators the impression of authenticity and allowed them to participate vicariously in the 'Air Battle against Britain'.

The film was made by men for men, a story of the great ethnic community of soldierly heroes who, with all their differences of character and variety of regional backgrounds, had placed themselves entirely at the service of the Fatherland. Relationships, girlfriends, women, all of that was of little significance for these men of steel and nothing seemed to be allowed to get in the way of their technical battle with the enemy. Although the plot was simple, the film's remarkable success may be down to its fast cutting and striking shots. By January 1942 it had earned an impressive 3.18 million Reich marks during its seven-month run.

Britain was the favourite subject for films about the air war and the more remote victory in the air was the greater the cinematic impact of bombers and fighters appeared to be. *Fernbomber über dem Atlantik* (1942) (Long-Range Bombers over the Atlantic) is the story of an attack on a British convoy, and *Einsatz* (1942/3) (Action) focuses on the fate of a squadron based near the English Channel which finally, after careful reconnaissance and photo analysis, launches an air raid on Southampton.[169]

There were no deaths in these films and, if a plane happened to be shot down, it was made clear that rescue was near at hand. The air war appeared to be primarily a matter of technology, of which the Luftwaffe was a master, confident in its technical modernity when taking on the enemy. However, after about 1942 the focus gradually began to shift. Now it was no longer primarily about the enemy being overcome by superior technology, but rather the national community's heroic determination to win and to survive and about its manly protagonists. Given Allied air superiority towards the end of the war, the Bavaria film company's plans for a film with the title *Invasion im Rücken der Front* (Invasion in the Enemy's Rear), involving an attempt to make up for the failure to secure a German landing in Britain, were completely anachronistic.[170]

Visualizing the Blitz

Invasion, bombing, heroic pilots—these were themes that, even during the war itself, were the focus of numerous commemorations and film productions on the other side of the Channel. Since 15 September 1942 Battle of Britain Day had become a fixed date in the calendar, commemorating the heroic defence of Britain by the RAF—those proud days when the German aggressors were put to flight. Whereas Battle of Britain Day was to a large extent based in London, from 1941/2 onwards other cities that had suffered air raids began to develop their own culture of commemoration with a focus on their suffering and survival.

A year after the first air raids many newspapers published large-scale pictures taken from above, with two different but related narratives of the Blitz: either, as was the case with Liverpool or Exeter, they showed the city in the present, largely cleared of rubble, brought back to life. Traffic was flowing and people's lives were back to normal; or the picture focused on the wounds inflicted on the city: wherever one looked the Germans had destroyed buildings and torn great gaps in the existing urban landscape. But the pictures showed not only the destruction but also, viewed as a whole, the silhouette of the city that the Germans had been unable to destroy.

Thus the city's indestructible sense of local identity was a foundation on which the work of reconstruction could build and, as the pictures showed, this reconstruction was already in full swing.[171] The photographs of the effects of the Blitz on Bristol, taken during the course of the raid, showed the fire, demonstrating what a huge and dangerous inferno it had been. But, while this picture from the previous year made readers shudder at the apocalyptic mood it conveyed, it also reminded them that even an inferno like this could be overcome. Had the picture, which the *Manchester Guardian* photographer took from the roof of its editorial offices,[172] been published the previous year it would probably not have helped boost morale. Now, however, people could look back at past events with a degree of distance, could reflect on the stories of heroism during the air raids and see the future a bit more optimistically. In Bristol local journalists and local government officials, city councillors and mayors of the two big parties, all cooperated as early as 1942 to publish the first account of the nights of horror.[173]

The cover picture could hardly have been more dramatic: the city was framed in dark red; a church and old houses were in the path of the flames; it was an apocalyptic vision printed in two colours. The book wanted to bear witness to how an 'old', in other words culturally rich, city with a past full of tradition was able to stand up to philistine barbarians. In other words, as in Germany, the 'old' city was an alternative vision to the current destruction, a space whose identity could not be destroyed overnight, and which possessed enough strength to stand up to the challenges of the present. While the city was burning, its inhabitants had proudly fought the fires; men and women, citizens of all classes, police, fire brigade, and soldiers had fought with all their strength against the flames and bombs. The book told the story of the almost superhuman struggle, documented the damage, reported how hospitals, doctors, and nurses had saved their patients and how the whole city had become a great community.

At the same time, there had been victims. Some had been disfigured, others had lost relatives, and, above all, the rescue services had risked their lives performing a task, the immensity of which, the book said, could never be fully related.[174] It was, therefore, all the more important to record the city's achievements and the stories of its citizens' heroism and to document them for eternity. However, the book was not only an attempt to link the 'old' with the 'new' and now scarred city, and to measure its historic greatness in comparison with the performance of other cities in defending themselves, it also aimed to honour the contribution to the British war effort made by its own victims. The Blitz was part of the city's own history, but it was also part of the history of the 'Free World' and it was necessary to spell this out as clearly as possible to their still rather shaky American ally.

Right from the start, the visual representation of the Battle of Britain and the Blitz played a vital role in the efforts to secure American support. The air war was being fought not only on the home front but also abroad. America should be made to see how resolute the British were in facing up to their sufferings but also how great was the threat from the barbaric Nazis. Could the United States afford to remain neutral when faced with this threat? In mid-August 1940 Winston Churchill remarked to General de Gaulle that the bombing of Oxford, Coventry, and Canterbury would cause so much outrage on the other side of the Atlantic that the USA would inevitably join in the war.[175] However, his confidence proved premature. Why on earth was the United States hesitating?

Whereas at home there was a dispute going on with the supporters of neutrality, the majority of the American journalists reporting on the war from London sensed that their country ought to become actively involved in trying to defeat Hitler. The advent of the air raids altered the style and tone of their reporting: the war against civilians brought violence into people's homes, not only those of the British but also those of American radio listeners and cinema goers. After the 'phoney war' came the war with the 'human touch'. In fact a number of patterns of interpretation had already become established before the first bombs had even fallen. Following the 'miracle' into which the flight from Dunkirk had been transformed and the Battle of Britain, the reports of leading correspondents were emphasizing the 'rebirth' that Britain was experiencing during this period under threat.

In a commentary from mid-August 1940 Ed Murrow, the chief European correspondent of CBS and one of the most influential American journalists, explained to his listeners what the United States could expect from Britain: a defensive fight which would still be talked about in generations to come and for which the British would long be admired.[176] It was also Murrow who ensured that, despite the continuing censorship, he and his American colleagues could gain access to information and air-raid sites in London and other bombed cities. While there was often friction between the American journalists and the MoI, Murrow and his newspaper colleagues did not find the self-censorship to which they submitted themselves[177] too arduous because they were convinced that in the final analysis they were on the same side as their British colleagues.

Selling the war to America had a high priority for the MoI so that when, in August 1940, for example, NBC and CBS expressed a wish to film a dog-fight between the Luftwaffe and the RAF live, it did not hesitate to give permission. At the end of August 1940, CBS organized a broadcast, together with the BBC, in which a number of correspondents reported live from various parts of London while the air-raid sirens were sounding and people were fleeing to the shelters.

Murrow had cleverly evaded censorship by recording sounds of a city under attack and inserting them into his commentary. *London after Dark* was a sensational success in the United States because it made the broadcast into an event that one could actually hear happening and in which everyone in the country could participate. Broadcasts in which journalists were reporting live during the bombing of London had a considerable impact on the shape of war reporting because they allowed the battles in the sky to be reported like a boxing match, with the result that the war acquired a sporting as well as a dramatic aspect. 'I'm standing on a rooftop looking out over London', announced Murrow in his broadcast on the night of 21 September. 'At the moment everything is quiet. For reasons of national as well as personal security I'm unable to tell you the exact location from which I'm speaking [...] Listen to them: You'll hear two explosions! There they are.'[178]

Rather than the printed word it was their radio broadcasts which turned some journalists like Murrow into mini-war heroes.[179] His broadcasts created a sensation in the United States because they turned the distant war being fought by the British 'cousins' into a confrontation that was now no longer taking place three thousand or more miles away somewhere in Europe but as if it were in one's own living room. Now one could listen to and feel Hitler's barbarism. That was particularly true, for example, of pictures of destruction and of casualties. While the censorship authorities forbade the British media to publish pictures of burnt corpses in Coventry, because they would undermine 'morale', the American press agency, UP, was permitted to use them and send them to America for publication.[180]

The photographic section of the MoI had early on taken steps to provide not only their own but also the American media with pictures and had engaged the best British photo-journalists to produce them. One of them was Cecil Beaton, who was highly regarded in the United States. Hitherto,

Beaton had worked mainly for *Vanity Fair* and *Vogue* and was one of the best-known society photographers in Hollywood. From the summer of 1940 onwards, working for the MoI, Beaton provided American magazines with a stream of new material from London. It was his vision more than any other that shaped the American view of the Blitz. Apart from pictures that could also be seen in the British media, apart from cheerful pilots and the smoking chimneys of armaments factories, it was above all the picture of 3-year-old Eileen Dunne that caused a sensation in the United States. With her dark eyes and clutching her teddy bear, she is looking straight at the camera. Overnight this innocent little girl had become a victim of an air raid. She had been hit by a shrapnel splinter and now she was sitting in a hospital bed with a bandage round her head. *Life* magazine published the picture on 23 September 1940 in the middle of weeks of heavy raids on London,[181] and soon it was appearing on all the posters appealing for the entry of the United States into the war.

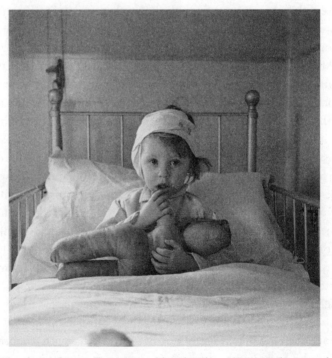

Figure 2. The face of war: the 3-year-old girl, Eileen Dunne, photographed by Cecil Beaton for *Life Magazine* on 23 September 1940.

The film department, which early on had also begun to develop a film language with which to sell the Blitz to the American market, played an equally important role in the pictorial history of the war. At the end of 1940 the MoI achieved a lasting success in both Britain and the United Success with *London Can Take It*. This short film lasting five minutes was part of a new series which had been running since July 1940 in British and American cinemas under the title *Britain Can Take It* and could also be seen at showings organized by the MoI. A number of well-known documentary film makers, such as Humphrey Jennings, worked on it.[182] Jennings, co-founder of Mass Observation, together with Tom Harrisson, provided documentary film of London under the Blitz and persuaded Quentin Reynolds, the London correspondent of *Collier's Weekly*, to provide a commentary.[183]

Jennings's film told the story of a city during the Blitz. It began with a picture of St Paul's Cathedral undamaged—a motif that Jennings used again and again and integrated into a picture of everyday life under the threat of bombing: men and women going to work and going home again, sirens wailing, young and old proceeding in an orderly manner to the air-raid shelters, firemen fighting the flames. The film had the authenticity of a documentary aiming to show what people were really thinking and experiencing. Bright searchlights flashed and anti-aircraft guns boomed, framed by the darkness of the night sky, and the following day the rubble of the night was removed in a mood of stoic calm. Reynolds accompanied the pictures with a commentary delivered directly to his American audience in his smoker's voice as if he was reporting live; the listeners were not aware that, while the film purported to be a documentary, in fact the scenes had been carefully selected and edited.[184]

'I am speaking to you from London', Reynolds informs his audience. In the middle of the fire fight Reynolds claims to be a neutral observer reporting everything exactly as he is experiencing it. He explains to his fellow Americans how unusual these events are that are taking place before his eyes, as if he could not believe how people could keep their nerve in the face of such violence. London shows no sign of fear, no panic, anywhere. Bravery, determination, and courage characterize the people on 'Churchill's island'. One feels bitter to see how much centuries-old culture can be destroyed in five minutes by bombs. But although bombs can destroy, although they can kill people, they can never break the irrepressible determination of Londoners. 'London Can Take It'—during Reynolds's final words off camera, in the background the film shows Westminster Hall with its windows blown out by bombs and in the foreground the bronze statue of Richard the Lionheart; and so the film ends with the theme of the unity of monarchy and people, as a hymn of praise to the British nation, her people, her past, and her future.

The film exudes the spirit of resistance and of the will to survive. Future in this context did not yet mean a new classless society. In the first instance it was about driving the enemy back and fighting together in the People's War, regardless of class and status. Even during the air war London had become a site of commemoration of a sense of national solidarity and it was the 'little people' who formed its backbone and its point of reference.

In contrast to many simplistic propaganda films, *Britain Can Take It* evidently struck a chord with audiences. After a showing in front of Scottish miners, who in general did not have much sympathy with the metropolis, an official of the Ministry of Information reported that it 'was by far the most successful film. The reasons, I think, were because of the neutral reporter, the emphasis on the common people and the fact that it showed what the war was like.'[185] An otherwise very critical Mass Observer reached a similar conclusion, saying it was 'the most frequently commented upon film, and received nothing but praise'.[186] In the United States it was estimated that, during the late autumn of 1940, the film had been seen by 60 million people. Around 12,000 cinemas showed the film with a generally positive response.

There was a second short propaganda film, made in a similar way especially for the American market, called *Christmas under Fire*. Once again, Reynolds, in his American accent and using documentary film excerpts, tells the history of the British nation and this time laced with even more emotion. The film was specially designed to suit the 'super sentimentalists' in the United States, a 'tear-jerker', as Watt, the co-producer put it.[187]

Jennings's films tied in with those made by the documentary film movement of the 1930s, creating a completely new genre of propaganda film. This linked the documentary iconography of the People's War with fictional narratives using a partly surrealist and highly sophisticated pictorial language, which intentionally differentiated itself from Nazi propaganda. This was true both of Jennings's short films and the feature films he made for the Crown Film Unit. *Fires were Started* was the most successful of Jennings's feature films dealing with the nation, the war, and morale. He had already begun researching it during 1941 in London and Liverpool. Jennings wanted to tell the story of the 'real' heroes, the firemen, and of how they saved the city and its population. As in his other films, once again the major roles in this story of a fire brigade unit were played by amateurs. He wrote the script in 1942 when heavy air raids were already in decline, although the Baedeker Raids were still a cause for anxiety in many other parts of the country. When the film finally arrived in cinemas in 1943 two years had passed since the Battle of Britain and the Blitz and British newspapers were now report-ing on the massive area raids by the RAF on German cities.

The audience discovers that the fictional story about London firemen is set back in the grey winter months of 1940. Barrett, a young recruit, is beginning his job at the fire station. Everything is new to him, but all the men with their different accents and quirks soon form a band of broth-ers. Individuality and a degree of eccentricity were essential elements in the People's War rather than something to be stamped out. This group give each other moral support, allow each other to get on with their jobs in their own way, respect personal boundaries, and stick together when things become serious, as happens in the second half of the film. London is in flames, fires are burning everywhere, and Barrett's brigade has been called out to deal with a life-threatening incident.

The action now begins to gather pace. Up until then the men have had time to chat and crack jokes, but now with the fire raging they need to pull together and to show courage. Jennings had recreated the fire in the London docks instead of, as it seemed to the audience, using documentary material. His shots turned the incident into a catharsis. The flames appear as timeless and fateful violence ending in pain and death. The fire they are fighting seems more like a natural catastrophe than part of a modern war. The film does not mention the Germans; there is nothing about the background to the bomb attacks and nothing about German terror. The people in the film do not express hatred or talk about revenge. It is all about heroic courage and comradeship in action. Above all, what made Jennings's film so extraor-dinary were the camera angles he used and his editing.

Some of his shots of the catastrophe are reminiscent of his surrealist work during the 1930s, for example when he makes a frightened horse gallop through the smoke; there are also close-ups of dramatic moments, when single firemen bravely stand on the roofs of burning houses or, tragically, when they can no longer hold on to the hand of a comrade and so are too weak to save him. The third part of the film, which to begin with shows the firemen in their fire station, focuses on death and on how they cope with the horror of these events. Each one tries to find an individual means of expressing his feelings at the loss of a friend. While the audience already knew that the fire had caused casualties, Jennings shows the wife of a dead fireman listening to the news of the heavy air raid on the radio, while not yet knowing that she has lost her husband. Finally, the film ends with his sad but dignified funeral.

However, superimposed on the grief of relatives and friends there is a final shot in which simultaneously with the funeral a munitions ship is shown sailing up the river—a last sign that their deaths have not been in vain and that they have secured the lives of the others. This was a message that left no room for nuances and no time for a lengthy period of grieving. Unlike in Germany, already during the war itself the air raids were providing a screen on which to project a national coming together, as they were already being historicized and seen as an important moment of national integration. Although the pictorial narratives of a heroic fire brigade and the solidarity of an air-raid shelter community were similar, in Germany the pictures of burning houses were part of a catastrophic present, while in Britain they appeared more as evidence of a past that had been painful but had now been victoriously overcome, and now offered scope for something new for which it had been worthwhile fighting.

Both in Britain and in Germany the aim was for the air raids to become an experience that would encourage a sense of social solidarity, of community. Whereas the British film produced this message in the present and could show it with a positive conclusion, Nazi feature films concentrated on a variety of historical topics and analogies in order to find their positive conclusion in the past. However, quite apart from its aesthetic, Jennings's film was more multi-layered than was suggested by its emotional conclusion. Jennings's version of the People's War involved, as was already the case with other films, ordinary people and their heroic courage. Solidarity and comradeship were firm components of the British sense of identity, and the war revealed these 'characteristics', possibly the nation's best, like no other event. At the same time, there was room for individualists, eccentrics, and pig-headed types, who nevertheless were prepared to pull their weight in an emergency.

Thus collectivist egalitarian ideas that reduced individuals to the status of numbers and mere functionaries doing their duty were completely alien to this vision. It was a narrative of solidarity among equals, a democratic and free social order that was in complete contrast to the totalitarian utopia of the 'national community' and one that was told in a poetic pictorial

language that integrated its subject within the great heritage of British culture. Jennings dealt openly with death and with the pain that people suffered. Whereas propaganda had kept quiet about it in 1940/1, two years later
Jennings took up the narrative of pain and retroactively gave it meaning. By
projecting it back to the first year of the war, it was also possible to reinterpret the original defensive battle as an offensive form of defence, at the end
of which the community would express its solidarity by being there for
those who were grieving. It was hoped that the end would not only be
marked by defiant resistance—that was the leitmotif of the Battle of Britain—but also by the dawn of a better society in the post-war world, one
based on team spirit, self-sacrifice, and responsibility.

The response to the film was euphoric. The newspapers praised this
'very moving', 'dramatic' work that was so sensitive in the way it handled
people and their fate.[188] The author of the *Documentary News Letters*
claimed that never before had the behaviour of ordinary people during
the war been described so precisely and so well. Only the *Daily Telegraph*
declined to join in the praise.[189] However, one Mass Observation observer
did not agree: 'The best war documentary ever', he wrote. And another
observer, summing up his impressions and that of his acquaintances, noted:
'Having lived through the London blitz we naturally enjoyed the film. We
were impressed with the way things were done and with the lack of
heroics.'[190]

The British public and the bombing of Germany

The Allied bombing offensive against Germany was intended to make a
decisive contribution towards ensuring that the war would end well. From
the very beginning the RAF's strategy against Nazi Germany was widely
discussed in the national press. However, hardly any of the editorial staff were
in a position to provide a remotely accurate assessment of the information
coming out of the Ministry of Information. Moreover, even if someone
wanted to try, he or she was still dependent on the reports on successes and
the figures for losses released by its press officers. The idea of providing access
to all news was thought not only a strategic mistake that would strengthen
the enemy, but also to constitute a threat to domestic morale.

It was considered to be crucial for morale that the conduct of the war
should reflect the difference in character between 'Huns' and British
'gentlemen'. For it was felt to be an essential characteristic of British

strategy in the air war that it should not be based on area bombing targeting innocent civilians, such as was being carried out by the Germans, but
instead concentrate on the precision bombing of military targets. Thus,
readers of *The Times* and the *Manchester Guardian* were informed that the
RAF was going to force the Germans to their knees and defend the country
by using precision raids.

From about the late autumn of 1940 onwards the debate slowly began to
shift. Up until then most newspapers had tried to avoid giving any indication that Britain had been making retaliatory raids on Berlin or on other
cities. 'Retaliation' was not a notion that fitted in with the type of warfare
that adhered to the rules of chivalry. Instead, the press preferred to refer to
RAF counteroffensives and, in an article published at the end of August
1940, *The Times* made it clear that launching raids in retaliation would be the
equivalent of a defeat, as they would mean that Britain was no longer pursuing its own strategic goals, but instead was simply copying enemy tactics and
so, in the final analysis, losing the initiative.[191] 'Retaliation' and 'revenge'
were words that were, above all, used to refer to the German raids, thereby
demonstrating their morally reprehensible character.

However, the *Daily Mirror*, with its predominantly working-class readership, soon began to raise questions about precision bombing. At the latest
following the heavy raids on London in September 1940 the press began to
report a growing mood among the population demanding a tougher
response, wanting a war that was not simply being fought against Hitler and
the Nazis but against the German 'master race' as a whole. However, while
the majority of the press was restrained, on 12 September the *Daily Mirror*
argued that modern bombers had abolished the old chivalrous forms of
warfare and, as a consequence, civilians were now on the front line. Britain
was not prepared passively to accept martyrdom and so it had to fight back.
And this could only mean casting off the bonds of traditional warfare and
accepting that it was hardly possible to make a clear distinction between
infrastructure targets and the enemy's 'nerve centres'. This 'merciless war'
was causing casualties, tens of thousands of deaths, most of whom were
workers in the war industries. All of them were now involved in the war,
whether in factories or at the front, and, as a result, potential casualties.[192]

In fact the High Command had been gradually coming to the conclusion
that the German war industry could not be destroyed by precision bombing. In August 1941 the Butt report had already made it abundantly clear to
the War Cabinet that British bombs had been depressingly ineffective.[193]

The RAF came under increasing pressure: what was the point of expending all these resources if the results were so meagre? Its response was the change in strategy inaugurated by Directive 22 of 14 February 1942, which now focused overwhelmingly on the area bombing of German cities and the attempt to weaken morale, and acquired a new face in the shape of Arthur Harris as the new Chief of Bomber Command.

However, the media's treatment of the intentional killing of German civilians presented a major dilemma. How was the destruction of others to be spoken of, what words should be used? After all, hitherto area bombing raids had been considered absolutely 'un-British' and in fact specifically German. For Harris the matter was clear cut: the bomber crews had the task of making normal life in Germany impossible and so bringing the war to an end. The destruction of German cities was thus directly linked to the killing of German workers, who kept the armaments industry going. Harris became involved in a major conflict with Sir Archibald Sinclair, the Secretary of State for Air, not so much over the objective as over how it should be communicated to the public. For, despite all the evidence of damage, the Air Ministry continued to differentiate between the destruction of industrial and military targets and the killing of civilians, although it was clear to all involved, as Harris pointed out, that this bore no relation to the reality of the air raids.[194] However, Sinclair stuck to his guns. For unlike Harris he was convinced that telling the truth about the bombing would not be good for people's morale, particularly for church people, despite the fact that from 1942 onwards the newspapers had been full of stories of the RAF bombing German cities.

Although, right up until the end of the war, official statements kept repeating that Allied area bombing targeted at German industries had nothing to do with 'terror attacks' and that, in the case of Berlin, the aim was not simply to frighten the civilian population but rather to eliminate the German capital as the centre of the German war machine, alert newspaper readers could none the less gain an impression of the results of these air raids. Moreover, with the British raids, which began in spring 1942, first on Lübeck and Rostock, and then, at the end of May, on Cologne and shortly afterwards on Essen, the majority of newspapers began to refer openly to what the new strategy in the air war implied: the destruction of German cities and the annihilation of their inhabitants. Although prominence was continually given to targets involved in the armaments industry, the majority of newspapers made no secret of their increasing sympathy for the RAF's new bombing strategy, which had now at last found its 'true' role. It was not only the popular press which talked about how each new bomb was 'paying the Germans back'. Cities were being 'obliterated' and houses 'shaved'. Now, as the *Daily Express* put it after the 1,000-bomber raid on Cologne, the day of 'vengeance' had come.[195]

Of course the pictures of the raid that passed the censor could be interpreted in a variety of ways. The *Daily Express* printed a photograph of the destruction of Cologne's city centre and a drawing of the area round the cathedral with the caption 'No part of Cologne escaped in the 1000-Bomber Raid'. *The Times*, on the other hand, saw the photographs as proof that Goebbels was wrong in maintaining that the bombing had been a 'terror raid' against the civilian population. The RAF had not been attacking people's morale but rather the Nazi city's shopping and business quarter.[196]

On a subsequent occasion the *Times* journalists used rather different language: the paper, which was close to the government, headlined a report on a raid on Hamburg at the end of July 1943: 'One of the best raids of the war'. According to the report, the RAF had dropped 175,000 bombs on one of the best-defended German cities and inflicted serious damage on the centre of the U-boat industry. There was mention of clouds of dense, dark smoke and the fact that Hamburg was in flames. Although the report stressed the military significance of the raid, after their experience with London everyone could imagine what it meant if huge fires had broken out in a city.[197] The reference to people's own experience of air raids and to the number of bombs that had fallen on British cities provided a marker emphasizing the RAF's new potential. Comparing their own experience with the fate of the German population provided people with a scale of the damage and injury that had been inflicted and in this respect Britain was now undoubtedly ahead.

The popular press did not let any opportunity pass to report new record raids and to celebrate sensational successes with big headlines. While the reporting in *The Times* and the *Manchester Guardian* generally endeavoured to stress the military character of the air raids, the *Daily Mirror* and the *Daily Express*, in particular, were dominated by stories of massive devastation with unvarnished reports of burning cities, the destruction of houses, and people in flight. After Operation Gomorrah readers of the *Manchester Guardian* were informed in cool and technical prose that Hamburg was now the most bombed city in the world.[198] Like '*coventrieren*' (to coventry), this raid came to be part of the language of war: a few months later, during the 'Battle of

Berlin', the *Daily Express* and the *Daily Mirror* reported that Berlin had been 'hamburged' by the RAF.[199]

From 1942 onwards, the issue of German civilian morale and thus the impact of air raids was a recurring topic in intelligence reports on the enemy. How many bombs would be necessary to break the back of the German war economy? And for how long could the Germans go on defying the raids, which were increasingly becoming a substitute for a naval blockade?

Evidence of declining morale was seen above all in the reports of floods of refugees and homeless people, with which the regime in Germany appeared increasingly unable to cope, and also in the population's 'apathy'. Readers of every newspaper were informed that a state of emergency had been declared in Berlin and Hamburg, the infrastructure had collapsed, water and electricity were in short supply, and people's everyday needs were no longer being met. In May 1944 the *Daily Express* published a photograph by a Swiss photographer, one of few coming directly from Germany itself, showing a 'dead' Berlin with its 'troglodytes': a city without a centre, gutted, destroyed, in which people were stumbling through the ruins of Kurfürstenstrasse.[200]

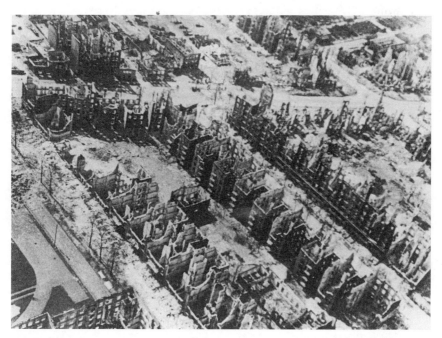

Figure 3. Aerial View of Hamburg after the British air raids (Operation Gomorrah).

From mid-1943 onwards there had been an increasing number of cautiously optimistic reports that German morale was declining. The information on which these reports was based came either in censored form
from the Air Ministry or from neutral, generally Swedish, journalists, who
were still able to report from Germany, albeit to a very limited extent. But
however much the reports alluded to the effectiveness of air raids, the
breakthrough failed to materialize. The escalating violence was legitimized
by the change in the character of the enemy. For the war being fought by
the British Empire was no longer directed solely against Hitler and his
clique but rather against the German nation and its pathological aggres-
siveness. And that meant there was no longer any need for kid gloves.
At the same time, the concept of 'civilians in the front line', which had
become accepted since the beginning of the war and which initially had
been part of a heroic self-image, made it easier to brand 'the other' as a
legitimate target. For if civilians, as a result of their work, were in the end
no different from soldiers, why was it necessary to offer them special protection? Only a few people, like Harris, were prepared to express this view
openly, but media reporting provided wide scope to channel this silent
consensus.

From the beginning of 1944 onwards, and at the latest with the Normandy invasion, there were far fewer euphoric reports of air raids as
people lost interest in the stories of bomber crews. It was not that public
criticism of the RAF's strategy had increased but rather that people had
come to regard other strategic issues as more important. The press did
not consider even the bombing of Dresden on 13 and 14 February 1945 as
of particular note. And so it was not surprising that, while the raid was
regarded as a very heavy one, it was not considered an unusually ferocious attack on the Nazi dictatorship. After all, as was stated in all the
reports during the days following the raid, the city was an important transport hub and link in the German defences against the Red Army. The *Daily
Telegraph* reported non-stop raids and 650,000 incendiaries dropped by the
RAF, while at the same time rejecting German propaganda's claim that the
Anglo-American raid had been a 'terror attack'.[201] *The Times* paid little
attention to Dresden, only referring to the raid in the context of its reports
on air raids on Chemnitz and Cottbus.[202]

The bombing of German cities during the last phase of the war no longer
produced much excitement because, despite some uneasiness, there was a
consensus that in the final analysis the bombing of cities and populations was

a necessary evil and, although on its own not necessarily decisive, was nevertheless imperative in order to bring the war to an end as quickly as possible.

Retaliation, Word of Mouth Propaganda, and the Struggle to Win Over a Sceptical Population

By contrast, the achievement of Allied air superiority and the increasing numbers of casualties posed a growing problem for Nazi propagandists. The regime now concentrated not only on taking a tougher line with 'rumour mongers' but also on developing a propaganda line promising retaliation through miracle weapons and intended to restore people's faith in victory over the Allies. Anti-Semitic clichés were an important element in this propaganda, which turned pilots into 'gangster bosses' and 'crooked negro boxers'. Basically, the Jews were behind the air raids as part of their cruel war of annihilation against the German people, whose morale, despite all the prophecies of doom, remained unbroken.[203]

From 1943 onwards, this theme increased in importance. Goebbels kept emphasizing the significance of the alleged Jewish-Bolshevik conspiracy and its influence on the Anglo-American conduct of the war and that of the 'Plutocrats', and that they were responsible for the German soldiers' suffering and for the army of dead German civilians. 'The Jews are Guilty'— this narrative of the war as a story of the Germans as victims of a Jewish conspiracy acquired increasing importance for propaganda, possibly also because the regime was noting with growing concern the increase in the number of those who were coming to associate the Allied bombing with its Jewish policy, and interpreting the raids as a response to the 'destruction of their temple'.[204]

After the raids on Hamburg in the summer of 1943 clergy were remarking on 'a sense of guilt' that was being felt by sections of the population. Air raids were taken to be the Allies' response to the anti-Semitic robberies and deportations. A Hamburg businessman made this assessment in a letter to an acquaintance: 'Despite all the anger being directed against the British and Americans because of the inhuman way in which they are waging war, objectively speaking it has to be admitted that ordinary people, members of the middle class and other groups, are repeatedly saying to each other in private and even in quite large gatherings that the raids are in retaliation for our treatment of the Jews.'[205] It is difficult to say how representative such statements were, but it seems not implausible that Nazi propaganda had the desired effect on, or was willingly accepted by, some sections of the population. For example, the SD reported from Schweinfurt that 'national comrades' who had been bombed out were claiming 'that if we hadn't treated the Jews so badly we wouldn't have had to suffer so much from the terror attacks'.[206]

The destructive air raids provided a welcome motive for the regime to divert attention from its own helplessness and from the Holocaust by radicalizing the language used in its propaganda. They also prompted people to write to the Propaganda Ministry to suggest, for example, ways in which the Jews could be made to pay for the raids or that they should even be used as human shields.[207] But not only that: the extermination of the Jews now appeared also as a response to the 'Anglo-American air terror', as the price which their 'race in Europe and perhaps far beyond' were having to pay for their 'absolutely outrageous behaviour'.[208] Within this context the concept of retaliation acquired a much more radical significance than in 1940. Retaliation now included the annihilation of the Jews and their Bolshevist partner.

At the heart of the rhetoric of retaliation was the threat of a strike back and also its blatant anti-Semitism. As early as the Stalingrad defeat Speer and Goebbels had recognized how important it was to divert attention from the threat of defeat, internal tensions, and the material superiority of the Allies and to make people believe that the future course of the war was still open by claiming that Germany possessed a new kind of miracle weapon.[209] On several occasions during his briefings Hitler demanded that 'terror must be broken by terror'[210] and the best way of doing so was by deploying a new type of weapon, which, unlike the, in Hitler's view, disastrous and 'slapdash' conduct of the air war against Britain, must result in effective and devastating attacks.[211] Hitler's tough and, given the situation, illusory demand was for permanent attacks against Britain carried out by radical and fearless pilots. And talk of 'retaliation' served both as an early warning and domestically as a diversionary tactic.

During 1943 and coinciding with the heavy Allied air raids during the summer, the Propaganda Ministry launched a campaign with the theme of imminent and decisive retaliation so that it came to form part of the Party's official reporting, was spread as a rumour, and became an important motif in memorial and cultic ceremonies. Thus, on the occasion of a funeral of air-raid victims in summer 1943, the Gauleiter of Westphalia-North, Dr Alfred Meyer, announced that the Reich must fight 'a war of extermination'. For 'we know that the war of retaliation is coming. And when the Führer decides to strike, Britain will have a fearful awakening.'[212]

The reference to the correct moment for retaliation and the Führer's right to decide it formed an important aspect of the Propaganda Ministry's attempt to control the course of the retaliation propaganda campaign as it suggested that, despite all the blows that were being suffered, the decisive strike by the Nazi state against Britain was still to come. The SD did in fact notice a growth in retaliation euphoria, but this was already storing up trouble for the future. For the more the regime announced that retaliation was coming, the more the population was reassured in newspaper articles, at Party meetings, and other rallies that it was on its way, the more urgent became the question of when and where, and whether all the talk of retaliation said more about the current weakness of the regime than about its future strength.[213] For although the air raids on London in spring 1943 were trumpeted as a great success, it was clear that they could only be a prelude to what the regime had promised. At any rate, the results, the amount of destruction caused, did not appear to have been sufficient to force the Allies to stop their air raids, let alone to have been seriously damaging. In large parts of the Reich the stepping up of retaliation and hate propaganda only increased people's desire to see words turned into action. And the longer this was delayed the more often the regime's intelligence agencies noted growing doubts about Germany's military potential.[214]

In winter 1943 even hard-bitten local Party cadres were afraid that, after the propaganda campaign had been running at full blast for over a year, the price to be paid for all these announcements could be high, indeed catastrophic, if retaliation did not happen in the foreseeable future. This prompted Goebbels to make the language being used about the war correspond more to reality and so to ensure that the failure to fulfil the promises, which he himself had been partly responsible for making, did not become quite so obvious. Thus, in December 1943, he decided to limit the use of the word 'retaliation', permitting it to be employed by the press only 'when it is used by official sources'.[215] It was not to be used about the Luftwaffe's air raids on London under any circumstances because it was obvious that these could not yet be the real retaliation.[216] At the beginning of June 1944, Goebbels himself, albeit somewhat guardedly, referred in a speech in Nuremberg to an act of counter-terror being imminent. His announcement was guarded not least because he knew that, since the tests of the flying bomb had been relatively unsatisfactory, success was by no means guaranteed and that another unfulfilled promise would turn public opinion even more against the regime and encourage the spread of the dreaded 'November spirit'.[217]

The radicalization of the hate propaganda against the 'barbaric war of cultural annihilation' being waged by the Allies was one of the ways by which the regime pursued its policy of negative integration through fear.[218] However, even those who no longer believed in the situation reports and the reports of air-raid damage could receive some benefit from reading the newspapers and listening to the radio. For apart from appeals for solidarity and self-sacrifice in the interests of the national community, there was an increasing number of articles giving practical tips for life during the air war and providing safety information. They included above all an attempt to guarantee people's legal security during the war. There were series in provincial newspapers providing information about the laws concerning compensation for war damage, the methods of removing air-war debris, about war claims, payments, and recent decisions of the Reich Administrative Court, which were applicable to an increasing number of people.[219]

This was true of those who had already lost property, but also of those who were threatened by the development of the air war and who were preparing for air raids, and in 1943/4 that applied to the overwhelming majority of the population. Compared with the columns devoted to banging the propaganda drum, the reports on the radicalization of the air war and the way in which the administration was coping with the crisis provided a much more sober impression of the effects of the air raids. For example, the main Nazi Party paper, the *Völkischer Beobachter*, referred to 'many national comrades' who had lost their possessions through air raids by spring 1943.[220] And it advised that not only those living in cities but in all parts of the Reich should 'take advantage of having their property valued by a bailiff' because that was the only way they would be able to make a claim effective in the event of an air raid. By admitting that they were incapable of defending the Reich the regime could hardly have been more frank about the dangers of the air war. At the same time, it appeared that, crossing every regional and social boundary, all 'national comrades' shared the same worries and were tortured by the same fears—in a sense then the air war saw the formation of a kind of *völkisch* community through loss and destruction.

The instructions for 'Self-Help During Air Raids' published in all provincial and national newspapers were on similar lines, providing information on how to deal with incendiaries and rules for behaviour in air-raid shelters.[221] They offered an interpretation of the past as well as a prognosis for the future development of the war. They indicated that the horrors of war had acquired a dimension that, as the *Völkischer Beobachter* put it in August 1943, immediately after Operation Gomorrah, was 'beyond comprehension'. The German language could no longer find words to describe this 'total war'.

The propaganda machine tried hard to provide new concepts with which to establish a framework for articulating the experiences of the air war and not to leave it to private reports. Thus, the policy of self-help was not intended simply to provide practical aid in dealing with phosphorus bombs and incendiaries, but was part of a continuing attempt to routinize catastrophe, to make dealing with it part of a new social praxis, and to create an air-raid semantics, which would get across to people the dangers of fire, the threat of air-raid shelters collapsing, and the need for appropriate clothing and the right equipment when dealing with flames and heat.[222]

From autumn 1944 onwards, the Nazi Party, together with the Wehrmacht propaganda units, placed more emphasis on propaganda by word of mouth in order to ensure the impact of this type of language. The aim was to 'increase confidence among the population and strengthen the conviction that this war must be won at any price and can end only in our victory'.[223] The regime was determined to regain trust and stabilize morale and was clear that it had much to do. However, by trust, what was meant above all was belief in final victory, in self-sacrifice for the 'national community', and in the power of 'holy fate', which, as Hitler put it apocalyptically in his Political Testament, might lead to ruin, but in any event the Germans would not go like sheep tamely to 'the slaughterhouse'.[224]

The Party concluded that soldiers who had been at the front were the best people to overcome the mistrust that was now so widespread. Their symbolic capital consisted above all in their experience of battle, in the authenticity they conveyed through having served at the front,[225] whereas the regular propaganda, public speeches, and last ditch calls to arms were felt to be feeble, indeed useless, because, in the end, they invariably met with 'more and more mistrust or complete rejection'.[226]

The regime required detailed reports on the conversations and mood of every section of the population and at the same time it needed to intervene in order to counteract rumours and spread morale-boosting messages. The initiative was taken by the Nazi Party: it aimed to provide a kind of substitute for the SD reports, which had been vilified by Goebbels and Bormann for their alleged defeatism. Initially, a number of big cities such as Vienna,

Berlin, and Nuremberg were selected, but after a dry run it was decided to extend the scheme to other Reich cities. The Party's propaganda headquarters prescribed the line that was to be taken and then passed it on to the Wehrmacht propaganda officers who organized the initiative in the strictest secrecy.

The soldiers were expected to produce unvarnished reports that gave a clear picture of the situation. The action was focused on locations which the regime assumed were centres of informal communication: public places such as trams, pubs, or cafés, notice boards displaying the Wehrmacht reports, cinemas, canteens, and, above all, the aid centres for air-raid victims and air-raid shelters because it was assumed that the population was 'particularly relaxed and talkative' there.[227] However, the regime evidently recognized that alternative structures of communication outside the official media had been building up with ever-increasing rapidity. Through them people tried to make sense of the situation, attempting to fill the gap that had opened up between what they had been promised and what was actually happening about retaliation.[228] The pressure arising from this vacuum was immense and engagement in word of mouth propaganda represented one of the last chances of the regime's dealing with a functional deficit for which it had only itself to blame.

What usually happened in this propaganda action was that two soldiers, one in civilian clothes and the other in uniform, appeared in various places, engaged people in conversation, listened to what they had to say, and noted down any rumours that were going round. They then passed on the official line urging people to stay the course and promising retaliation, relying on their credibility as front line soldiers to get the message across. When an air-raid siren sounded several squads would go off to perform their so-called 'terror raid duties' in parts of the city that had been particularly badly hit and where preparations had already been made.[229] However, rumours about the desperate war situation, about sickness, corruption, the effects of air raids, and the inadequacy of food supplies were spreading so fast that those involved in word of mouth propaganda were not even remotely capable of successfully challenging them. Many cities, such as Duisburg and Münster, where there were plans to campaign, had already been reduced to rubble. There was no longer any point in engaging in word of mouth propaganda there because, given the desperate war situation, any attempt to establish trust in the regime, let alone raise hopes of success in a 'final struggle' against the 'Bolshevist barbarians', was doomed to failure.

In addition to the numerous worries shared by what was now a society in a state of collapse, the expectations, raised by the regime but then disappointed, about the effects of the 'miracle weapons' led to people's increasing mistrust of its ability to cope. The failure of the Luftwaffe, of which people repeatedly and openly complained, contributed to this sense of disillusionment, as did the relative ineffectiveness of the V weapons, which people now wanted to be deployed in the war against the Soviet Union. During the last phase of the war, the Party's propaganda headquarters and the Wehrmacht were being given a picture of the situation by their propaganda agents that appeared increasingly ominous. Moreover, the soldiers involved were noting that, when talking to each other informally, people were showing a growing lack of respect for the regime's authority.[230] Although, even in February 1945, it was reported that the population in Berlin was still remarkably calm, it was nevertheless evident that the struggle for public opinion had been lost.

Allied air raids made a decisive contribution to this development. From the beginning of 1945 onwards, the raids increased in intensity and, apart from numerous small and medium-sized towns and cities, for the first time also hit those in the south and east of the Reich, which had hitherto counted as largely safe. Goebbels was fully aware of the erosion of trust in the regime and, from the end of 1944 onwards, had tried to respond by concentrating the efforts of his propaganda machine on emphasizing the atrocities being committed by the advancing Red Army. In addition, in January 1945 the Propaganda Ministry called on German embassies to try to raise international concerns about the 'Allied strategy of air raids'. The idea was to portray Germany as the victim of long-term Allied plans for its destruction and its own actions as a defensive response to an emergency. This was accompanied by an interpretation of the air war as symbolizing a form of cultural barbarism essentially aimed at destroying European and western values.[231]

While the German embassies were in the process of informing European governments about the raids, during the night of 13/14 February the Allies bombed the city of Dresden in a massive air raid. The following day, on 15 February—news of the attack, which caused around 18,000–25,000 deaths, had already reached the Reich authorities in Berlin—the German news agency, acting under orders from the Propaganda Ministry, issued an account of the raid that was to establish the propaganda guidelines to be followed for the rest of the war.[232] The terror raid on the world famous artistic centre and baroque city of Dresden was the final proof that, ultimately, the Allies were bent on destroying and annihilating the Germans rather than pursuing military goals. The report did not refer to casualties but rather contained a detailed account of the destruction of the Frauenkirche and the Zwinger, the Japanese Palace and the Hofkirche. The propaganda machine made a final effort to galvanize the 'national community' and persuade the population to carry on fighting on the grounds that if the war was lost it would mean Germany's complete downfall.

The reports that followed the attack on Dresden saw a change in the language with which the regime tried to dictate the interpretative framework within which the raid would be viewed both at home and abroad. This did not apply to the attacks on 'Allied air gangsters' so much as the reporting of the actual bombing itself. While, to begin with, the British media did not devote much attention to Dresden, the Allies were made aware of the consequences of the raid via the international reporting, which within a very short time had turned the raid into a symbol of the destructive power of Allied air raids; it was seen as a raid aiming to bring the enemy to its knees using overwhelming force and technical precision.

The raid had not, in fact, been planned as a model of a destructive blow[233] and yet, within a few days, the comments and reports on it, both in Europe and overseas, served to underline the prominent role that Dresden had acquired in judgements on the Allies' conduct of the war. It was the Swedish press, above all, which, guided by the German censors, provided information on the extent of the destruction. It referred to 'an unheard-of loss of human life', to a tragic city, to the misery of the refugees, who had been staying in the city at the time of the raid, and to the sheer endless number of deaths. On 17 February, the newspaper *Svenska Morgenbladet*, referring to confidential sources, reported 100,000 deaths and that around 2.5 million people had been in the city. Other newspapers, including American ones, adopted this figure and increasingly referred to the unimaginable extent of the destruction, and to the uniqueness of the Allied raid, which had turned a European city into dust and ashes. Now Dresden no longer appeared as just one military attack among many but as the quintessence of the catastrophe of war. While the military and strategic motives for the raid were increasingly lost sight of, interest focused more and more on the extent of the destruction.

Finally, on 27 February, *Svenska Morgenbladet* reported that the number of dead was nearer 200,000 than 100,000,[234] a figure which, from then onwards, not least based on tendentious German propaganda reports, established itself as an accepted fact, and was then used as evidence for the terroristic character of Allied air raids. The Allies then played into Goebbels's hands: a report by the AP news agency on a press conference held at the headquarters of the Allied Expeditionary Force (SHAEF), which was not stopped by the censors, referred to a change of strategy by the air force high command following the raid on Dresden: 'Allied air bosses have made awaited decision to adopt deliberate terror bombing of great German population centres as ruthless expedient to hasten Hitlers's doom.'[235] Although the Allies tried to stop and deny the report, once it had come out it appeared to confirm what Goebbels had been saying all along.

At this point, there was no mention of the number of casualties or the large flood of refugees on German radio or in the press. Instead, there were vague hints about the extent of the destruction, which, as had happened after the Hamburg raid, soon became known through informal communication networks and via refugees and evacuees. Well into spring 1945 public discourse on the air war was dominated by official statements calling on Germans to seek revenge and appealing for self-sacrifice and solidarity on the part of the 'national community'. The head of the German Labour Front, Robert Ley, took the same line in a furious article in Goebbels's Berlin newspaper *Der Angriff*.[236] The air war, which had been started by 'Jewish lackeys', had reduced half the nation to penury and destroyed one of Germany's 'most valuable jewels, the peaceful, artistically precious city of Dresden'. Like Hitler, Ley tried to reinterpret the consequences of the bombing as ultimately beneficial to the Nazi revolution. After all, the destruction had forced them to get rid of all bourgeois conventions, all boundaries and inhibitions, and to commit themselves totally to the struggle against the Jewish-Bolshevist warmongers; now there was nothing more to lose. Ley had given his article the title 'Without Baggage', and that meant that the losses caused by the bombing had really toughened up the national comrades and removed all their bourgeois pretensions and expectations.

Given the catastrophic situation, Goebbels considered these sorts of public expressions of cynicism disastrous.[237] In its response the Propaganda Ministry tried to introduce new emphases, moving away from the previous representation of the air raids and exploiting the benefits that had accrued from the international reporting of the destruction of a defenceless Dresden, an allegedly unimportant city full of millions of refugees. On 4 March, Goebbels's journal, *Das Reich*, which had some intellectual pretensions, published a contribution from Rudolf Sparing under the headline 'The Death of Dresden',[238] which provided a remarkably frank analysis of the

Allied raid, departing in several respects from previous reporting of the incident. The article engaged with a point current for some time in the foreign
press, namely that the destruction of Dresden was something unique, something different from previous air raids in terms of its impact and thus of
exceptional importance. Thus in his account of the event Sparing made no
bones about the 'catastrophe of Dresden'; on the contrary, he endeavoured
to provide a largely 'realistic' or at least authentic and plausible report. It
used a form of language that differed from Ley's abuse not least in that it
criticized the Allies without foaming at the mouth. His descriptions of the
raid were so detailed that even those who had only heard of it through one
of the numerous rumours could form an impression without panicking, but
at the same time have a sense of the impact of the bombing and of the
extent to which the civilian population had suffered.

A variety of strategies was used in reporting Dresden to try to counteract
Nazi propaganda's serious lack of credibility and people's unwillingness to
trust it. These included estimating the numbers of inhabitants and refugees,
and a figure of a million by no means seemed an exaggeration. They also
included discussing the subject of death in air raids, the anonymous mass
graves, and the people who could not be identified. However, in contrast to
propaganda directed abroad, domestic propaganda refrained from giving
exact numbers of casualties; it was vaguely suggested that the figure was
large but it was never made precise. Sparing did not place the main emphasis
on heroic death, which had been the refrain of Nazi propaganda for so long,
but rather on people's individual deaths, the willingness of neighbours to
help, the help of the sighted for the blind, the 'civilian population's self-
reliance', which despite or even because of the 'catastrophe of Dresden' was
stronger than ever. The home front was intact.

Looking at the overall situation, Sparing observed what had become a
familiar daily experience for his readers: 'the trip to the cellar has become
part of daily life for millions of people, being bombed out is just a fact of
war, or is a coolly calculated risk.' And yet, he wrote, the raid on Dresden
was quite different from anything that had occurred before. For it showed
what happened when 'western culture was abandoned in a spasm of self-
destruction'. Dresden, that symbol of western culture, that 'trustee of the
common values of the West', had been destroyed; it had fallen victim to
Anglo-American cynicism and to the air war's spiral of violence. Within a
few weeks Dresden had become for Nazi propaganda the symbol of the
senselessness of the war, of the removal of any limits to the use of violence,

of a unique catastrophe, a huge and sudden explosion in what was possible, a senseless destruction of western civilization, for which there was no military justification;[239] it was a moral bargaining chip that the regime no doubt intended to use not just for the final agonizing months, but also for the post-war period that was in sight and for the discussion about war guilt that was about to begin.[240]

3

Social Organization under
a State of Emergency

Institutions for Dealing with Emergencies

At the beginning of the war there was a great fear that Britain might soon be lying in ruins. It was therefore crucial to maintain morale through propaganda. Beyond that was the very practical problem of whether the prevailing administrative structures were adequate to cope with the air raids. This chapter therefore focuses on the organizational and legal responses both societies produced to the challenge of the air war, what traditions and guiding principles they followed, and what tensions determined the strategies for coping with crisis adopted in various phases of the war. In addition to administrative matters, the policy of keeping up morale involved the building of shelters and air-raid protection, legal issues and those involving social control, criminal justice, and bomb damage compensation.

In contrast to Germany, Britain at the start of the war had structures that had been established in the course of a lengthy process of negotiation, uniting the various participants in a consensus, and this framework hardly changed up to the end of the war. The Civil Defence Committee was one of several inter-ministerial committees charged by the War Cabinet with organizing home defence and was chaired by the Minister of Home Security. Even before 1939 civilian air-raid precautions had been his responsibility and now he enjoyed significantly greater influence.

As many as sixteen ministries and government bodies were represented on the Civil Defence Committee, which made decisions by consensus, although in addition to the Home Secretary the Ministers of Transport, Health, Education, Labour, and Food had the biggest say. From September 1940, as German air raids grew more extensive, the committee as an

Executive Sub-Committee was given additional importance in the informal network of ministries, in particular because, although John Anderson, Minister of Home Security since the outbreak of war, was not formally a member of the War Cabinet, he nevertheless in practice attended most of the meetings and thus gave greater weight to civil defence.[1] This development was reinforced when Anderson became part of Churchill's War Cabinet in October 1940 as Lord President of the Council.

The Civil Defence Committee chairman coordinated the work and had important powers. The committee was not, however, designed round a particular person with extraordinary freedom of action, nor had other ministries lost influence as a result or lost out in a polycratic power struggle, as occurred under the Third Reich.[2] For the Civil Defence Committee had no state apparatus of its own and its decisions were always integrated into the organizational structure of the individual ministries responsible for implementation. The committee thus fitted seamlessly into the existing structures, and even though it was a product of the war and a new institution in the otherwise very inflexible British civil service organization it was not regarded as a foreign body by those involved with it. On the contrary, it was positively in the interest of ministries that did not have a seat in the War Cabinet to discuss key problems of policy at the highest level and search for amicable solutions.

Thus its strength did not lie in providing rapid solutions to the crises caused by air raids; those remained the responsibility of the various regional administrations and ministries. These included the local authorities, in whose hands air-raid protection largely lay after the Civil Defence Act of 1939, as well as the Regional Commissioners, who worked as ministerial appointees and as an extension of the Ministry of Home Security in the regional defence zones. Only in a state of emergency, however—if there should be an invasion or the state should be in danger of collapse—were the Regional Commissioners to assume dictatorial powers in order to take executive decisions as stand-in ministers.

Until such a state of emergency was declared their function consisted in coordinating and passing on information both upwards to the ministry and Civil Defence Committee and downwards to the individual local authorities. Civil servants from a variety of ministries worked in the offices of the Regional Commissioners and if, for example, they were representatives of the Ministry of Health they took care of issues such as evacuation or hygiene in the air-raid shelters and were meant to be the interface for logistical matters between central government, the ministry, and the local authority.

While the practical coordination of aid agencies before and after air raids was a local and regional responsibility, the Civil Defence Committee served primarily to direct and coordinate knowledge about the dangers of the war. From the point of view of the leading air defence experts, the prerequisite for risk assessment was above all communications. For as was stated in a memorandum of April 1940, a war of such an unfamiliar kind as the one being fought with Germany required above all a new information system.[3]

Step by step the subjects in its purview had expanded since 1940 and so covered not only the organization of air-raid precautions, as up to 1939, but also everything to do with the air war: the building of shelters and evacuation, provision of food, and compensation legislation. Contentious topics that had caused public concern were put on the agenda: what form of entertainment should be permitted in air-raid shelters?[4] And was it not urgently necessary to open the underground tunnels to protect the population? How far must public pressure be bowed to and higher priorities such as the smooth running of local transport be put on hold?[5] Such decisions could not be made without the agreement of the Civil Defence Committee and this was true, for example, of the organization of air-raid shelters too.

There had, since the beginning of the bombing raids, been repeated complaints about the state of shelters, and in the Prime Minister's view these had to be dealt with urgently. There were complaints in particular about the fact that administrative responsibility was fragmented, split between the Ministry of Health and the Ministry of Home Security. The latter was responsible for policy regarding shelters, for the choice of location, and for construction.[6] Responsibility for hygiene, medical supervision, and the deployment of doctors and nurses was part of the Ministry of Health's remit. How could a compromise be found that did not bypass the accepted methods of reaching consensus? At first the two ministries concerned had been unable to agree on a division of powers. After intensive negotiations a compromise was finally found that allowed everyone to save face and yet at the same time, by as it were squaring the circle, advanced the centralization of decision-making.

A memorandum sent out by the Civil Defence Committee shortly before Christmas 1940 began by pointing the finger of blame. It claimed that it was not administrative friction between the two ministries that had produced the complaints but rather inefficient local authorities and the lack of available labour had held back the extension and proper running of the shelters. The document weighed up the pros and cons of placing all powers in one administrative body, finally arriving at the wise suggestion of keeping all responsibilities where they were, but transferring decision-making power to the London Regional Commissioner with his appropriate team of Health Ministry civil servants—a ruling that was to last until the end of the war and adhered to the wartime administrative practice of attempting only very gradual changes of direction that were based on the widest possible consensus.

Equally important as this attempt to balance competing interests was the practice of first-hand assessment and observation. Thus after heavy raids numerous ministers travelled the country in person, passing on, as did the Minister for Home Security, a first-hand impression of the state of the nation. After the raids on the Midlands, the industrial heartland, Herbert Morrison, the influential Labour Minister in the War Cabinet and successor to John Anderson as Home Secretary, travelled to the region in November 1940 in order to see for himself the situation in Coventry.

His verdict was thoroughly sobering.[7] Although the regional organization of air defences was, he believed, still intact and the city administration had also acquitted itself well, the sum total of the destruction was nevertheless 'immense'. In conversations with him local air-raid experts complained that because of scarce resources the city had been underprepared for war: the lack of anti-aircraft guns had left the skies clear for the Luftwaffe and thus had made the disaster possible in the first place. Morrison rejected these accusations, emphasizing instead the fact that supplying the city with food—the task of the Ministry of Food—had been difficult and yet vitally important in such a catastrophe. Considering the huge destruction, this operation had been rapid and successful.

As a rule it was not the ministers themselves who wrote the reports; instead, news from the bombed cities was based on information collated by the Home Office and the Ministry of Information, which undertook an initial analysis. The process of first-hand assessment was an important element in a policy of risk management that was struggling to gain credibility, and thus hardly a meeting passed without a discussion about what could be learned from the raids. As the Civil Defence Committee concluded at the beginning of December 1940, the raids on Southampton had shown that the use of volunteers had been totally inadequate to cope with the aftermath of the raids. Therefore, it was decided, it was high time for the Ministry of Food to create mobile canteens that could be sent quickly to the cities affected in order to plug the gaps in provision left by the overstretched local authorities.[8]

The ministries' reports on the management of the crisis offered one of the few if also informal opportunities to discuss problems. At the same time they were an important basis for the exchange of information, on the strength of which inadequacies in civil defence could be dealt with. In December 1940, two months after the start of the London Blitz, the ministries involved in the Civil Defence Committee under the leadership of Herbert Morrison presented reports on what they had learnt during the air war.[9] Contentious issues were identified such as the less than satisfactory provision for the homeless, the lack of emergency plans, and inadequate preparation for the reconstruction of bombed houses.

Similar points were made by the Ministry of Home Security, which was responsible for air defences; in its estimation the first months had shown that although solid work was being done numerous improvements were nevertheless feasible in all areas—the work of air-raid officials as well as that of the emergency rescue services, equipment, and regional cooperation. The ministers agreed that the results should be passed on as quickly as possible to the Regional Commissioners so that they could discuss these deficiencies with the local authorities. In addition, the Civil Defence Committee agreed that an interdepartmental committee should check the implementation of the suggestions and report on progress.[10]

Improved coordination also seemed necessary because from the autumn of 1940 public pressure to give better protection to the population had grown markedly. Up to that point much that had been debated in the ministries was purely a paper exercise. Although the planned building of shelters had been discussed extensively in memoranda, in practice the implementation was slow. These delays angered significant sections of the population, including the MPs whose seats were in the parts of London affected; in a two-day sitting of Parliament in October 1940 they gave full vent to their resentment. Their anger was directed chiefly at the Health Minister, Malcolm MacDonald, who was responsible for housing and feeding the homeless and for access to the shelters and who in the end was forced to apologize to Parliament for the failings of his ministry.[11]

A further area of conflict came under the responsibility of the Ministry of Health: the coordination of evacuations. Since before the war there had been plans for how to respond to the threat of German air raids. At first the projections and calculations had to remain vague, as no one could judge exactly what form of warfare this war would produce and what the consequences for the civilian population would be. It seemed certain only that extensive evacuations would be necessary to avoid panic and uncoordinated stampedes. From the beginning of 1939 these plans became more concrete and led to detailed agreements between the central government and the local authorities, which were obliged to check their housing stocks.

Deliberations were based on the assumption that in a bombing war it was impossible to guarantee everyone's safety.[12] A decision had therefore to be made on who took priority. The criteria were the degree of threat predicted for the region and the ability of people to protect themselves. That meant that first of all schoolchildren, mothers with small children, and pregnant women from the industrial centres in the north and south were to be evacuated to rural areas considered to be safe. It was anticipated that school classes would be accommodated with their teachers so as to lose as little schooling as possible. In consultation with the Ministry of Transport timetables were produced early and provision for the children seemed secure.

The early stages were not kept at all secret; numerous ministers and aid organizations were involved and early on teachers rehearsed with their pupils what they would do in the real situation; that meant having their gas masks to hand, a warm coat, and a change of underwear, not forgetting slippers![13] The Ministry of Health, which was responsible, was particularly keen to include head teachers and had drafted sample speeches that could be made if evacuations were imminent. Confidence in the government was a prominent theme; confidence in the protective function of the state's basic security provision and in the logistical capacity of the bureaucracy to remove children from the endangered areas and give them somewhere suitable (and free) to live.[14] For as yet the plans did not involve compulsion; parents could keep their children at home even in the danger zones and even if there was strong pressure to fall in with the instructions from the schools and the ministry.

In evacuation matters too the Civil Defence Committee remained a kind of clearing house[15] making decisions about logistics, finance, and future planning. And that was necessary, for the evacuation of children involved the areas of responsibility of numerous ministries, and, although the evacuation of more than 760,000 British schoolchildren had been largely successful, there was general recognition that the real problems began when they arrived at their destinations. The provision of health care was one example of this.

Numerous reports from the public health service, the Medical Officers of Health, and the School Medical Officers from the pre-war period turned out in fact to have been overoptimistic. From the autumn of 1939 onwards younger doctors in particular were blunt in their criticisms of the health of the children they examined on arrival for infectious and skin diseases. While during the inter-war years many of the relevant authorities had been able to turn a blind eye to the problems of working-class children, viewing their poverty as an individual problem of character, now the sheer scale of malnourishment gave rise to complaints and in many cases created a new sensitivity with regard to social issues.

Medical inspections up to this point had manifestly failed in their purpose and it seemed high time to extend state check-ups, though only, as for example a Birmingham doctor thought, if at the same time the social circumstances of the poorest children were improved.[16] Even in the Ministry of Health, which by no means adopted a particularly receptive attitude to the massive criticism, some civil servants at least changed their tone after the end of 1939. In circulars to the city authorities the Ministry now alluded for the first time to the fact that in some regions there were significant problems with skin diseases and lice. On the Board of Education also an increasing number of voices were heard saying that it was urgently necessary to get to the bottom of the reasons for the evacuated children's illnesses, which were often to be found in the family's social environment and for which the state therefore had to bear some responsibility.[17]

Precisely what the state's role and duties were vis-à-vis its citizens was one of the fundamental conflicts fought out in numerous areas of policy during the war years. What the argument over the efficiency of school medical provision clearly demonstrated, however, was the increase in public vigilance and the political pressure exerted in particular by circles close to Labour. They were stating unequivocally that people's willingness to fight the war was linked to an expectation that more would be done than hitherto to reduce social inequalities.

The conflicts surrounding the evacuations had not aggravated the problems, still less had they created them, but they had come to some people's notice, and not only that of members of the Left. This was true, for example, of the provision of clothing and shoes, which, contrary to the impression created by the fulsome declarations of the Ministry of Health, had failed to meet the needs of many children from poorer families. According to the arrangements made by the Ministry of Health it should have been the Local Education Authorities (LEAs), together with charities, that gave help in particularly pressing cases.

But in the first weeks of the winter of 1939/40 it became apparent that the resources of the LEAs were inadequate. State aid was needed, but in the first weeks of the evacuation the Ministry of Health persisted in working to the regulations as already set: it was the parents who were responsible for the children and for adequate provision for them; where their means were insufficient, organizations such as the WVS should arrange the aid. There was a fear in Whitehall of making sizeable financial commitments and after protests became ever more widespread in October and November it was agreed that at best minor concessions could be made.[18]

In a decree of November 1939 the Ministry of Health announced that in urgent cases school heads in the various evacuation areas could approach the Director of Education for emergency funds for those in particular need. The simmering conflict over the formation of a future welfare state that emerged as the direct result of the evacuation and the growing politicization of the issue of poverty was not thereby resolved; in fact it had just begun, for it was after all still an open question how far the state actually should, or indeed was obliged to, guarantee the welfare of the individual.[19]

Thus in November 1940, for example, the WVS was able to distribute clothing to the needy in London that came not from its own stocks but rather—and this was new—from the state and from stocks given by the American Red Cross.[20] In February 1941, when voices were still being raised about the pitiful state of some of the evacuees, the Board of Education for the first time accepted an application from the London County Council and approved a sum of £20,000 for clothing and shoes to be distributed by the WVS.

Initially, civil servants and the Board of Education maintained a sceptical attitude towards individual claims to state welfare as a result of bombing; there was, however, a growing public debate about the social fabric of the nation, about poverty, welfare, and state responsibility. The conflict over the diet and fitness of evacuated schoolchildren did not create willingness overnight to provide state welfare, still less was the view abandoned that poor relief was primarily the responsibility of charities. What did begin to change, however, was the debate, intensifying as a result of the threat of the air war, about the causes of poverty, the state of health of the weakest in society, and the role of the state.

Führer rulings and special agencies

There was no room under National Socialism for such a broad public debate. In the *völkisch* welfare state poverty was regarded as abolished or as the result of asocial behaviour. Evacuations served to demonstrate how great was the solidarity of the 'national community'. All the same, air defences were, as in Britain, a sensitive area; their organization had been subjected to considerable pressure with the expansion of the air raids and was character-ized by growing fragmentation. Whereas in Britain various bodies com-peted for responsibilities and decision-making authority but nevertheless were obliged in the end to come up with a consensual solution, German air defences were significantly shaped by 'Führer directives' and special agencies.[21]

Originally civil air defence had since the 'seizure of power' in 1933 been the sole responsibility of Hermann Göring and the Reich Air Ministry. In the towns and cities the local police chiefs as air-raid supremos were the most important coordinators in crisis situations. Yet the police and Luftwaffe as the two controlling authorities were from the outset confronted with two competing organizations: the Reich Air Defence League and—as the most powerful agency, whose influence was constantly growing—the Nazi Party and its local branches. Many of the problems encountered later by civil air defence were evident at an early stage, in particular the distribution of scarce resources.

Before the outbreak of war the Reich Air Ministry had limited its expenditure on civil air defence and pressed for local communities or indi-vidual citizens themselves to take precautions in order to preserve resources for armaments production. Owners of buildings were, for example, obliged through a decree for the implementation of the Reich Air Defence Law in May 1937 to build bomb-proof shelters in new and altered buildings and thus to bear a large part of the costs of privatizing the financial burdens of the war.[22]

At the same time, air defences were considered to be a Reich responsi-bility and local communities did not wish to be the principal ones to pay for them. As a result many of them did not invest in air defences. For as long as this question had not been definitively decided, and it was unclear where, for example, the iron for shelters was to come from, in many places nothing happened at all. A first step towards the organization of air defences came after Germany lost the Battle of Britain in autumn 1940. Hitler made Baldur von Schirach responsible for the expanded 'Kinderlandverschick-ung', the preventive evacuation of schoolchildren and their mothers to rural areas, thus responding to the growing threat even to the Reich capital from the air.[23]

A second consequence was the decision to introduce a 'Führer's Emergency Air Defence Programme', a response to the inadequate preparations and altered forecast of the danger of air raids. Berlin and the Ruhr were to be the centres of stepped-up building work intended among other things to extend existing shelters and boost the construction of public shelters. It was above all Fritz Todt, Reich Minister for Armaments and Munitions, and Erhard Milch, Inspector General of the Luftwaffe, who coordinated the work and in conjunction with the regional authorities categorized the possible threats and determined the scale of construction.

The gulf between ambition and reality soon became apparent, however. Substantial resources flowed not into the development of civilian shelters but into the armaments industry and the armed forces. There was a shortage of raw materials and building supplies as well as labour, and even the growing number of forced labourers could not compensate for the scarcity of resources. The ambitious schedule was soon obsolete and thus in many places building could not begin until the autumn of 1941, which meant that work on the additional shelters needed in cities at risk from air raids was further delayed.

From the summer of 1941 the regime attempted in stages to reduce the expectations it had itself created and to adjust the building programme to the conditions of wartime—the result of which was always to downgrade civil defence in favour of war mobilization and, for example, to finish only shelters that were already in progress but not to start new projects.

Another possibility was to lay more emphasis on the quantity of shelters than on their quality and to concentrate, as Milch had suggested in a discussion with Hitler at the end of January 1942, on extending cellars.[24] Although this policy of reduced protection in the end reinterpreted the 'Führer's will' in a very particular way and almost turned it into its opposite, this nevertheless seemed the only way of providing at least partial protection in a short time.[25] It was a strategy that in the face of intensified air raids and other grandiose large-scale projects would soon be halted.

The failure of the plans that had been proclaimed so noisily was obvious and local authorities complained repeatedly and vociferously about inadequate commitment on the part of the Reich and about being financially overstretched.[26] Instead of costly new shelters, in the second half of the war it was principally underground tunnels that, being cheaper to construct, were rapidly built and were, to quote Himmler, 'one of the most important protective measures against the danger of terror from the air'.[27]

The escalation of the air war from the spring of 1942 revealed that in the cities the organization shared up to that point by police, Luftwaffe, and local authorities was increasingly overstretched. With old city centres in flames and the passivity of the Reich Air Ministry repeatedly criticized, the call for new guidance and direction grew louder. The external trigger for the start of a heated controversy was supplied by the British attack on Lübeck on 29 March 1942. The attempt by the city and the Reich authorities to cope with the crisis was undermined by a dispute over responsibilities. Hitler was personally enraged about the chaos and quickly demanded that the situation be remedied. He took responsibility for direct aid in the regions damaged by bombing from the Reich Ministry of the Interior and transferred it to his Minister for Propaganda, who, he asserted, enjoyed 'unlimited powers' to deal with crises.[28]

Together with his state secretary, Leopold Gutterer, Goebbels called a meeting of state secretaries the night after the raid in order to organize the transport of what was required to Lübeck. He simultaneously interpreted the 'Führer command' as granting him the right in this acute emergency to give orders to the Gauleiters and, as in Mecklenburg, to deal with accommodation for evacuees. With Hitler's instructions in his pocket, Goebbels considered that the moment had come for him to claim a key role in steering internal policy, regardless of the regulations in force at the time concerning the handling of crises.

Organizing disaster aid offered him an excellent opportunity to make a name for himself as an energetic and unconventional expert on emergencies, particular where evacuation policy and the evacuation of children to rural areas were concerned,[29] and from the end of 1941 he had been attempting to gain control of them by trying to obtain powers 'directly from the Führer'.[30] Since the beginning of the air war Goebbels had been receiving information about damage, numbers of fatalities, and the mood of the population via the reports produced by the Party's regional propaganda offices. As the raids grew more intense he involved himself more and more frequently with local efforts to cope with problems. To begin with he was content to ask for reports. Later, from the winter of 1941, he sent his officials to the bombed cities to gather information[31] or took it upon himself to raise morale and provide additional deliveries of food.

Thus it was no accident that after the Lübeck disaster Hitler gave his Minister of Propaganda new personal authority. It was bold of Goebbels, however, to interpret Hitler's instructions as a far-reaching commission to take on the civil defence of the Reich and to infer that in particularly extreme disasters he could relieve local officials of their mandated functions and take over the general coordination of the mopping up operations himself.[32]

Goebbels was for the most part alone in his interpretation of his new powers and he was still a long way from having established himself as a new centre of authority as 'Minister for the Air War'.[33] The distribution of responsibility as far as protective measures and aid after bombing raids were concerned remained a contentious issue; thus the Propaganda Minister attempted to capitalize on his fact-finding and inspection tours[34] to bomb-damaged cities by being the driving force behind and organizer of the home front and so to improve his starting position in the ongoing negotiations among the various Reich ministries, which had been growing in intensity since the early summer of 1942. In the face of mounting destruction strong pressure for a new coordinating mechanism came not from Berlin but from the bombed regions of the west.[35]

In October 1942 the Deputy Gauleiter for Düsseldorf, Carl Overhues, gave free rein to his anger about the crisis in air defence at the time in a letter to the Party Chancellery.[36] Up to that point, he said, each Gau had made its own decisions about priorities. Above all the Reich Ministry of the Interior had pursued a policy of 'appeasement and improvisation' in its direction of the evacuations. Often regional initiatives failed because the Gaus and defence districts defended their own powers. Furthermore Overhues harboured no illusions about the progress of the war. There was no question of an early end to the air war; on the contrary, there were many indications that it had not yet reached its peak. For that reason he called for a radical change in structures. The time was ripe, he said, for a new strategy that no longer centred on the individual Gau and moved towards organization of support from the centre.

His suggestion was that one central office for the Reich should be the contact point for all authorities and party agencies, though it should not be visible to the public. As the person within the Gau headquarters responsible for mobilization Overhues criticized sharply the deficiencies in Robert Ley's housing policy and saw the need for action in a number of different areas: both in the preparatory phase as well as in the aftermath of raids a person equipped with 'adequate powers and authority' was needed to draw together the diverse interests, to control information, and then to organize help in a coherent way. The point was not only to improve coordination but to share the burdens more equitably. The regions that had up till then been free from raids should, after all, also open their storehouses and send out teams of tradespeople. Overhues's suggestion of a coordinating authority was soon circulating and was supported by his own Gauleiter, Friedrich Karl Florian.[37]

While Goebbels took this suggestion to relate directly to himself and the new responsibilities the Führer had given him, Martin Bormann weighed in in favour of Ley as the new home front supremo.[38] There was at any rate no doubt that any such new institution would be of decisive importance— providing too many ministerial interests were not undermined.[39] Goebbels was supported above all by Albert Speer and Hans-Heinrich Lammers, head of the Reich Chancellery, who in particular referred to the fact that this new position was the practical application of the 'Führer command' of March 1942 and its authority therefore had to be accepted.[40]

The new air-war committee that was created, the Interministerial Air War Damage Committee (Interministerieller Luftkriegsschädenausschuss— ILA), was supposed to be the interface for all participants and have the aim of arranging accommodation where it was lacking and obtaining building materials and food. To realize this, as Lammers indicated, a supraregional authority was needed outside the existing ones, though without any legislative role, which should remain with the ministries. At first therefore it was not a case of placing an area of policy under the control of a commissar directly appointed by the 'Führer', as for example in the field of health.[41] Instead this new committee, in form not unlike its British counterpart, was more a collegial body designed to boost efficiency.

This was certainly not exactly what Goebbels had been trying to achieve, but he headed up this new committee all the same. Now he had a forum in which he could make a mark and extend his powers—and in an area that was gaining in significance day by day as a result of the Allied air raids. Even without legislative powers he now through the new committee benefited from a marked extension in his scope for action outside the Ministry of Propaganda and his Berlin Gau.[42]

In contrast to Britain it had taken Germany three years for ministries, various organizations, and the Party to reach the point of creating a new body to take charge of the acute crisis. Crucial pressure for it had come from the bombed regions, while in Goebbels there was an ambitious player who was new to the field of air-raid policy and knew how to exploit his access to Hitler to fulfil those ambitions. As the air war intensified into a steadily mounting threat the Reich was still searching for an administrative response to a challenge that up to that point it had underestimated or subordinated to other priorities linked to armaments production. Virtually no one thought Britain had anything to teach them in this matter; there was no interest in the enemy's organizational structures. How effective the new controlling body would actually be remained to be seen.

The State and the National Emergency

Even though Britain enjoyed an administrative early warning system at an earlier stage this does not mean that it operated more efficiently or that conflicts did not arise.[43] It was at any rate evident that the state of emergency also demanded other institutional responses, which were accompanied by considerable administrative friction: Herbert Morrison had pushed forward a scheme, the forerunner of which went back to the 1930s and which through the experience of the huge blazes in London in 1940/1 had acquired new significance: the nationalization of the fire service.[44]

Responsibility for fire services lay with the local authorities and for a long time they had neglected to prepare for an emergency. There were extensive shortages of personnel and equipment. As early as 1937 the Air-Raid Precaution Act had called on town councils to set up an Auxiliary Fire Service, where volunteers were involved in fire-fighting. This initiative, it must be said, met with little enthusiasm on the part of professional fire brigades.

The sheer scale of the new fire brigades changed the nature and structure of traditional fire-fighting; at the end of the 1930s there were around 23,000 volunteer firemen, who threatened to burst the confines of the existing organization. The first German raids on British cities had shown that cooperation among the various agencies was difficult to achieve and that central control and coordination between regular and volunteer fire brigades were urgently needed. Even the Home Office had failed to take the risks seriously enough. At first the greatest disasters seemed likely not to be rapidly spreading blazes but German gas attacks. That was to turn out to be a mistake with fatal consequences.

The importance of central control had been demonstrated by the raids on London and other British cities that began at the end of 1940. Emergency plans were ineffective, equipment was missing, and many fires could not even be put out,[45] one reason being that although the local authorities had made plans on paper for coping with fires they had failed to engage professional staff and to train volunteers. When in April 1941 numerous British ports were bombed the extent of the damage was due in no small part to the fact that the fire services there had been made up of inadequately trained police units.[46]

As early as May 1941 the War Cabinet discussed a proposal from Morrison for a temporary nationalization of the fire service. During the war, the plan suggested, the local authorities should transfer their powers to the central government. The huge force of the raids and the organizational chaos of the previous months had led to a broad consensus about limited centralization of decision-making powers and contributed to the fact that in the autumn of 1941, after a little more than three months, the necessary administrative measures had been completed. Even if in practice the services were still regionally based and the local authorities were not completely stripped of their powers by the purely temporary transfer of responsibilities agreed on, the decision nevertheless signified a fundamental push towards centralization that added markedly to Morrison's influence.[47]

The National Fire Service did not, however, have to deal with a real emergency. After Germany invaded the Soviet Union in the summer of 1941 its priorities were focused completely on the east. The numbers of raids on Britain dropped and were to rise only once more for a short time during the Baedeker Raids between April and June 1942. Yet the fear of further German bombing did not diminish at all. After the experiences of the first two war years Whitehall was careful not to encourage a false sense of security. The possibility could not be excluded of the Germans developing high-flying bombers that could attack by day or in future having planes that could fly very low at night and thus increase their effectiveness. But were the precautions now adequate to defend the country against future threats? Had air defence in fact achieved its ambitious targets?

In the middle of 1941 the answer was mixed. According to the National Council of Social Service, in whose hands the coordination of the numerous volunteer organizations concerned with victims of bombing and with immediate relief lay, there were considerable gaps. The secretary of the NCSS stated in 1941 that many rescue and aid plans existed only on paper. Above all, the provision of food and shelter after raids was, he said, still inadequate, and if cities such as Liverpool were to be bombed for one or two days longer than hitherto panic and disturbances in the city would be the consequence.[48]

Almost simultaneously the NCSS took stock for the first time in an extensive memorandum.[49] In practice its diverse members, in particular the WVS but also various local initiatives, churches and clubs, participated in managing the crisis in numerous ways. Many looked after the rest centres (the first stop for those affected by bombing, where they were provided with clothing and hot meals) on behalf of the municipalities, and as a rule the staff at the Citizens' Advice Bureaux, where those bombed out could go for information and help, were volunteers from various social organizations.

In the NCSS's view preparations for a possible emergency were crucial. For only if procedures had been agreed between private and municipal help-givers could that help be given efficiently. And that, according to the NCSS, was precisely what was lacking. Experience of the bombing had shown that, contrary to planning, the rest centres in cities would not only have to guarantee provision for people's immediate needs but also be capable of accommodating them for several weeks. In most emergency plans, however, this had not been foreseen and so the rest centres lacked the necessary infrastructure and there was a shortage of clothing and food. At the same time, the experience of recent months had shown that most of those affected in urban areas did not make for the countryside but rather remained in the city, whereas in smaller towns the population was more apt to move to the country and thus create considerable problems for the adjacent districts—problems that were in many cases also unforeseen.

It was these and other complaints that caused voices to be raised in the summer of 1941, after the first, difficult year of the air war, demanding an overhaul of the organization of air defences,[50] and the creation of a ministry specifically for Civil Defence that would control the entire air defence operation: the fire service and fire prevention, provision of food for those affected by bombing, evacuation policy, shelters, and the reconstruction of destroyed towns and cities. According to the plan, the minister was to be given extensive powers to enable him to override regional autonomy and to make decisions by decree via his officials posted in the regions, if necessary even against the will of the municipalities. He would be a sort of 'home front commissar' of a kind Goebbels would have welcomed.

This centralization and concentration of power was considered the only suitable response to the policy of crisis management by local government, which seemed constantly overstretched. Two further hopes were attached to the new authority: that it would bring an end to the squandering of resources that resulted from powers being spread over different ministries and a strengthening of local morale; after all, the bond between city and nation would be consolidated by the centralization of power.

Yet neither Churchill nor Morrison, who up to this point had been responsible for large parts of civil defence, could warm to this proposal.[51] It would after all lead to a massive loss of power at local government level and the latter would, it was claimed, resist it. Whether centralization actually would bring about an increase in efficiency was also disputed for in the end two parallel structures would exist: one subordinated to the new ministry and one that was part of local government. Instead of a new ministry, it was regarded as more sensible, as a memorandum to the Prime Minister pointed out, to delegate additional powers to the Regional Commissioners. In this way existing shortcomings would be made the responsibility of a suprare-gional authority and at the same time the administrative network would not be ruptured by an abrupt change to the administrative structure. The pro-posal to create a new Civil Defence Ministry gained no sustained support in Parliament in June 1941, even if a whole string of MPs was dissatisfied with the existing organization and reported many inadequacies.[52]

To prevent the pressure from growing and to exploit the short period of respite in the summer of 1941 all leading ministries, responding to an initia-tive of the Ministry of Home Security, compiled eyewitness reports and suggestions for how air-raid precautions might be improved.[53] Most at risk in the view of the highest-ranking air-raid personnel were the ports. Their being bombed was the modern equivalent of the blockades of the past and would do considerable damage to the British war machine. The raids in spring 1941, as the internal analysis stated, had been directed first and fore-most at the working and living conditions of dock workers and had been extremely effective.

The example of Coventry had, in addition, shown that by deploying massive numbers of bombers the Luftwaffe was capable of inflicting signifi-cant damage on British industrial production. Keeping production going at all costs in port operations had to be an urgent priority. That applied not only to the protection of the plants but also to the dock workers and their homes, otherwise massive numbers of people would leave and thus restrict war production. In future every effort must be made to offer protection to industrial workers close to their plant, so that they could return to work as quickly as possible. To that end, the proposal stated, precautions in the regions affected in the north, on Clydeside, Merseyside, in the Bristol area, Hull, and all other ports should be checked once more and adapted to the German offensive strategy. The basic precondition for this was that the cities would increase the efficiency of their arrangements to repair damaged houses quickly and of all their other emergency plans.

In the Home Secretary's view the system of Regional Commissioners had proved its worth. Moreover, the responsibilities of the ministries should be delegated more fully to them, in order to speed up progress, for example, in building shelters. After checking the existing shelters the ministry decided to alter its priorities. Britain was to be split into three security zones, with the funding sent to those regions facing the greatest threat. In order to make an impact as quickly as possible Morrison focused not on building new shelters but on extending the existing ones. At the same time, there were plans to boost production of the more cost-effective indoor shelters and to enlarge the scope of those members of society entitled to them.

There was now more money available to privatize the risks of war. The creation of special zones was not only a response to a forecast of the hazards of the air war but also the consequence of a shortage of labour, the availability of which in the months to follow for building shelters for the local population was very limited because of war production. In the case of London this meant that 50 per cent of the planned new shelters and 30 per cent of the extensions were never built.[54]

This injection of funds was combined with a propaganda campaign aimed at making the purchase of private shelters more attractive.[55] But soon after the start of the war Morrison had to concede that a considerable proportion of the components ordered for the private shelters (Anderson shelters) could not be delivered because of production problems. This policy represented an unsecured cheque for the future and it could only be hoped that the Luftwaffe would not soon make it bounce. But not only scarce resources, a lack of personnel added to the Home Secretary's concerns. In spite of the tense war situation there were enough air-raid workers available to stave off smaller raids; things looked more complicated if, as feared, large-scale raids were to happen, because the pressure of recruitment to the armed forces was making itself increasingly felt. In future it would be difficult to avoid a situation where volunteer air-raid staff no longer served in one city but instead local authorities increased cooperation to cover shortages.

The Ministry of Health was also concerned by a lack of resources. In its analysis it highlighted the work of the rest centres for those affected by bombing and the search for alternative accommodation. When it became evident that what had been available hitherto could no longer meet the need the Ministry planned to create accommodation in hotels on the outskirts of the bombed cities, where up to 4,000 people could be housed at short notice, as in Hull, Plymouth, or Portsmouth. The aim was to make space for up to 200,000 people by the end of the year. This involved not only a considerable financial struggle but also a clear agreement between the central and local authorities to resolve all logistical friction as quickly as possible when accommodating the victims of bombing.

The Ministry emphasized its intention to use its right to remove from the accommodation provided anyone not entitled to be there. Apart from the immediate residents priority was to be given exclusively to workers from the neighbouring industrial cities and ports, who were to be accommodated without fail close to their places of work.[56]

Civil defence was therefore now not only being reformed administratively and made to adjust organizationally but was the locus of conflict in a struggle for scarce resources. The protection of the population had to be adjusted to fit the necessities of war and thus many high-flown schemes had to be put on ice as soon as they were announced. As early as autumn 1941 the decision was made to build new shelters only in the areas most at risk. The Ministry of Labour withdrew labour bit by bit from the construction of shelters. For the most part the workers had been employed to renovate existing shelters, to install lighting and heating and to make sure that in the winter the damp would not be unbearable. Even that, it must be said, was in many cases impossible, as the Ministry of Health was forced to state, because there was neither money nor labour. Thus in many places work was limited until the end of 1941 and beginning of 1942 to keeping the shelters passably clean.

Even before activities in this core area of civil defence were largely halted in the spring of 1942 and the resources channelled completely into war-related industries, the two responsible departments of the Ministry had in June 1941 been amalgamated into one, with significant reductions in staffing.[57] The Ministry of Home Security therefore looked with increasing displeasure on local initiatives that, in spite of the changed level of risk and the reduction in German bombing, continued with sizeable building projects and aimed to extend underground shelters or railway tunnels, thus depriving armaments production of labour.

When in November 1942 the Civil Defence Executive Sub-Committee met to discuss future priorities the building of shelters no longer played a prominent role.[58] Instead their use by various groups of the population as regular accommodation outside the alarm periods and during the day was now regarded as one of the home front's major security problems. This misuse had to be tackled vigorously so that the shelters were ready for emergencies and not occupied by unauthorized people. The review of tasks and organizational standards was based on two experiences: the German bombing raids from summer 1940 onwards and speculation about how the Germans would react to the altered British air-war strategy since the spring and to area bombing.

The Germans, it was assumed in the late autumn of 1942 in Whitehall, would focus in the coming months on attacking by day using low-flying planes and begin by concentrating the attack on coastal regions; heavy raids of a similar nature and using similar tactics to the Baedeker Raids on sizeable towns were expected, the purpose of the latter having been intended as retaliation for British destruction and as a means of pacifying the German home front. It seemed altogether plausible that the Luftwaffe would copy the British strategy and retaliate at night using incendiary bombs.[59] In the view of the Civil Defence Committee the most important task in the face of this threat was to secure the communications network during and after such bombardments. New people responsible for this should be appointed in all the regions, to control the safeguarding of the information flow at every level and consistently check the existing networks. These included the link between government offices and the police, the news coming in from the fire brigades, and cooperation with air-raid officials. At the end of 1942 the response to possible German retaliatory raids was not more money or increased air-raid precautions but an attempt to coordinate the existing organization more efficiently with declining resources. This was at any rate how those in charge of air defence policy interpreted the new priorities.

Although in propaganda terms air-raid precautions continued to enjoy a high profile they had none the less suffered organizationally and financially. There was no administrative loser in this process because, confronted with pressing problems such as the rebuilding of homes, the provision of food, and the management of labour, the ministries involved were not forced to negotiate with each other over responsibilities but rather were able to reorganize within the existing structures. Laborious negotiations could thus be at least partly avoided.

At the same time, the threat from the air had not disappeared entirely. The fear of gas attacks and the dreaded German miracle weapon was still too great for that. As early as 1939 there were reports, more numerous from 1942 onwards, that the Germans were working on a devastating weapon.[60] No details were known in Whitehall, however, and much of the information, which reached London by circuitous routes, was nebulous and vague, though according to the news agencies from April 1943 onwards the evidence was growing that such a weapon would pose a significant threat. There was therefore no reason to give the all-clear. Home Office calculations were based on the assumption that every rocket fired at London would make more than 8,000 people homeless and kill or injure about 400. Within a week a million people could lose their homes.[61]

In spite of these threatening scenarios Churchill stuck to his policy of not investing one individual, as in the case of Germany the Special Commissar, with extensive powers and thus changing the established processes of regulation. Instead he convened two committees of experts with representatives from all the important ministries with responsibilities for technical and military matters and for civil defence and they made decisions by consensus. Although there was a chairman, Sir Findlater Stewart, who coordinated the work, he was primarily the person who presented the information to the public in concise form rather than taking his own initiatives. In addition, this kind of committee work always had a time limit and nobody was brought into it who was not already familiar with the workings of government.

His first report in late June 1943 investigated once again all areas of civil defence, the feeding and housing of those bombed out, the preparation for evacuations, the warning system, the shelters, and the control of information. In spite of all the scepticism about the actual threat from miracle weapons,[62] plans were made for a new wave of evacuations of 100,000 Londoners from areas particularly at risk;[63] and for those who were not evacuated the Home Office kept at the ready near London a large quantity of compact air-raid shelters that could be put up in people's own four walls and could be delivered if needed.

It soon transpired, however, that the delivery of some 100,000 private shelters would take considerably longer than planned as a result of a lack of transportation, as these plans were in competition with the mobilization for the D-Day invasion, now in high gear, to which all other objectives were subordinated. In spite of the information that was in the meantime trickling through that the secret weapons were unmanned missiles, the War Cabinet decided to give no additional resources to defence, for the risk did not in the end seem great enough to justify reducing resources so important to the invasion.

The 'Baby Blitz' that hit the British capital in the first months of 1944 at first confirmed the correctness of this decision. The destructive capacity and range of the German Luftwaffe were not great enough to present the personnel involved, even though reduced, with a really sizeable challenge. The bombs and even the dreaded 'miracle weapon' had not been capable of holding off the 6 June invasion. When, a week after D–Day, the first V-1s finally reached Britain, they did not bring about the devastation feared. In contrast to 1940/1 the V-1s did not cause huge fires but rather explosions and impacts that destroyed homes over a wide area but did not kill nearly as many people as had at first been feared. By August 1944 there had been 5,000 victims.

Even so, in spite of their limited effect the V-1 attacks increased the feeling that Hitler's Germany possibly did in fact have a trump card up its sleeve. The information finally being received in July 1944 therefore aroused very deep concern in Whitehall.[64] The Home Secretary considered the threat to be serious and suggested concentrating strength and resources once again, in order to decide on concrete civil defence measures at the same time as matters of military defence.

The War Cabinet accepted this proposal and, yet again, formed an inter-ministerial committee, the Rocket Committee, later the Rocket Consequences Committee, which had the task of finding rapid solutions, above all of preparing for mass evacuations and the speedy reconstruction of housing. For in the face of raids without warning numerous air-raid precautions proved useless, as there was little time to locate shelters or give information to the population.

Paradoxically, there was at the same time some respite in this for air-raid defences. The V-1 and V-2 hits remained as a rule limited in scope and often only a few landed together in a single place at the same time, thus leaving the personnel on the ground enough time to rescue and care for those affected. The danger from 'miracle weapons' was by no means over when the Ministry of Home Security decided that civil defence conscription in numerous less threatened regions would be suspended. In the middle of September 1944 the ministry decided to discharge a large part of the permanent air-raid personnel.[65] Only three months later at the end of December 1944 the number of civil defence employees had been reduced by about a half and restricted to a small nucleus.[66] Of the 217,000 full-time air-raid auxiliaries only 146,000 were still in post at the end of January 1945. At the same time the strict blackout regulations were being gradually lifted and the Home Guard's regular air-raid training stopped.[67] Even before the last German rocket hit British soil on 27 March 1945 organized air-raid protection had begun to disappear.

Marginalization of institutions by agents of the Führer

At this point German air-raid protection was also dissolving—though for other reasons. For all the extensive attempts at organizational restructuring, National Socialist special agencies, and inspectorates had been able to do nothing or very little to combat superior Allied strength. In spite of all boastful assurances, aspiration and reality in this matter diverged dramatically.[68] The inter-ministerial committee for bombing damage (ILA) was supposed first of all to bring together all relevant agencies. Its membership included representatives of the highest Reich authorities, Party authorities, and also the Reich Labour Service, the Todt Organization, the Plenipotentiary for Construction, and the army high command (OKH).[69]

The committee's staff was drawn from the participating authorities and Party apparatus. Goebbels's representative was Alfred-Ingmar Berndt,[70] a deputy secretary (Ministerialdirigent) in the Propaganda Ministry. In the summer of 1943 Goebbels appointed the former mayor of Duisburg, Theodor Ellgering,[71] a National Socialist career civil servant experienced in administration and familiar with the ministerial bureaucracy in Berlin, as secretary and thus as the person who actually ran the committee. It was to take until the middle of 1943 for it to be sufficiently effective to establish its own agenda within the delicate area of air defence policy. The staff attached to it had first and foremost to respond to calls for help from local government after air raids and then to decide as a task force what sort of support was needed.

Thus the ILA did not possess its own powers as an institution. At the same time, however, it could exercise power above all over the control of information. The 'Air War Notices', express letters to all the highest government offices and first issued in the summer of 1943, were a means by which Goebbels could inform them of the committee's decisions, put the emphasis he wanted on the information being passed on and on how the crisis was being handled, and also forward instructions agreed by the committee. In contrast with Britain it was precisely this tendency to personalize decisions and to transfer responsibilities to new, power-hungry protagonists that characterized air defence policy from 1942/3 onwards.

In this process it was important not only how individual decisions were arrived at, but that decisions were made in the first place and that decisions led to further decisions, thus conferring authority on Goebbels. For the Air War Notices were more than just channels of communication. Goebbels exploited the medium of the 'express letter' to develop his claim to authority. He set himself up as Hitler's mouthpiece, translator, and foremost interpreter, reporting on his discussions with the 'Führer' and the decisions reached, for example, with regard to evacuees.[72]

It was precisely during the difficult initial phase of setting up the committee, when there was disagreement about the scope and limits of the 'Führer's command',[73] that the Air War Notices gave Goebbels the opportunity to present himself as the decisive and universally well-informed head of crisis management—and thus also to legitimize his organization and create its own official charisma.[74] Part of this process, in contrast to the practice of several Reich authorities, was not immediately to block regional initiatives and proposals, but rather to adopt suggestions for improvement in firefighting and disseminate them—which was also a means of controlling the flow of information and distinguishing between the important and the unimportant.[75]

The Air War Notices generated information and thus were not only an important tool in translating the 'Führer's will' but also helped to feed decisions from a multiplicity of Reich authorities along a single pathway from the centre to the periphery and so to make up for the polycratic fragmentation of air-raid protection services, which led to the build-up of information blind spots and administrative friction. By this means the information deficit caused by the National Socialist control of communications was counterbalanced by another institution, even though it was not yet firmly established, and through this the regime's prioritization of aid allocations was made easier.

A further factor came into play. The meetings of mayors, sub-prefects (*Landräte*), or municipal heads of section that were prompted or supported by the ILA during the war also quickly developed into important committees, consciously exploited by the municipalities, to further the interest-driven politics of local government in the air war and thus went some way to filling one of the gaps left by air defence policy up to that point.[76] For unlike in Britain, there was no one to act as a kind of Regional Commissioner, reconciling the rival interests of the various players at their interface, namely at regional level. And unlike in Britain, the local authorities as a rule did not enter negotiations over their problems directly with the Reich authorities but rather had had a wearisome battle to secure, via the German Local Government Association (*Deutscher Gemeindetag*), an institutional arena in which to exchange experience and information, though it had no legislative function. The regional nature of problems brought about by the air war and the centralization of decision-making powers created a vacuum of which Goebbels was aware and for which the ILA promised at least a partial remedy.

When on 21 December 1943 Hitler set up a 'Reich Inspectorate of Civilian Air Defence Measures'[77] by 'Führer decree' under the aegis of Goebbels, this development was part of the logic of the Reich Propaganda Minister's power politics and formalized the political practice visible in his early manoeuvres. The Reich Inspectorate was to produce an overall evaluation of civilian air defence in Germany and Austria: all types of damage limitation and of aid to the population and all preventive measures were to be examined and 'community help and self-help' were to be set in motion in the cities and rural areas—an ambitious programme to which Hitler had expressly appointed his Minister of Propaganda.

In Britain the responsible ministers and to some extent the Regional Commissioners had assumed similar functions, and yet the British practice of inspection and evaluation differed from the German above all in the fact that responsibilities for any given matter ended with that matter and there was no Reich Inspector who claimed responsibility for all questions concerning air defence and who therefore intervened—or considered doing so, at least—in the sovereign territory not only of other ministries but also of the Gau administrations and local authorities.

As chair of the ILA Goebbels had already made several visits to the regions affected by the air war in the course of 1943 and had done so asserting a claim to comprehensive information and regulation.[78] ILA staff such as Ellgering or Berndt and also the Gauleiter of Westphalia-South, Albert Hoffmann,[79] someone experienced in aerial warfare and especially esteemed by Goebbels, had been travelling the Reich on Goebbels's orders since the second half of the year in order in particular to examine the preparedness of the regions that had not yet been affected. In Goebbels's view their findings were in part, as in the case of Vienna, alarming.[80]

His attempt to create a super authority, his real aim, had failed—Bormann's opposition had been too weighty for that[81]—but even his new post considerably extended Goebbels's scope.[82] The inspection reports went via the Party Chancellery straight to Hitler, who thus had direct knowledge of Goebbels's initiatives. The Propaganda Minister firmly believed himself to be the recipient of a kind of mandate from Hitler that in his view legitimized his activities—even if they were unwelcome to this or that Gauleiter. For the Gauleiters the inspections remained an annoyance, as they regarded their obligation to provide information to the ILA staff as a curb on their autonomy and felt unjustly pilloried.

What distinguished the Reich Inspectorate from Hitler's other commissars was first and foremost the instrument it had been given through the 'Führer's decision': as an instrument of power and control the right to conduct inspections was exceptional for special authorities, ministries, and local government, because it did not reconfigure responsibilities and powers but rather left it to the experts to manage crises, while making every adjustment dependent on Hitler personally. At the same time the Inspectorate was instrumental in bringing transparency to a dysfunctional, overstretched section of the home front.

The attempt to learn from the experiences of other cities already hit by bombing and to align the expectations of what was to come with the reality of the comprehensive destructive capacity of Allied area bombing raids[83] was an important motive behind the Reich Inspectorate, whose staff all came from regions in which they had gained extensive expertise in emergency aid.[84] The right to conduct inspections not only embraced the opportunity of inspecting the damage but conferred on staff the right to require information about air-raid protection in practice from all authorities, Party offices, and, very unusually, from the Wehrmacht.

Neither the ILA nor the Reich Inspectorate, whose personnel was so closely linked to it, destroyed an institution of longer standing and yet their effect was to relocate at least some of the processes of negotiation about rational criteria and prioritization in the air war and so bring new players into the game, who gradually prised responsibility for air-raid protection away from the Luftwaffe and Göring. The right to inspect conferred on Goebbels by Hitler signified at best an indirect opportunity to intervene in the Gaus' strategy for the defence of the Reich. It was far from being central control and continued to require decentralized processes of negotiation below 'Führer level' to implement decisions. Hitler had not done anything to change that.

After a little more than four weeks, at the end of January 1944, Goebbels presented the Reich Inspectorate's first interim report.[85] His staff had visited six Gaus and the upshot in Goebbels's view was very mixed: whereas Saxony and its Gauleiter Martin Mutschmann had 'done extraordinarily competent work',[86] he was extremely dissatisfied with the state of preparations in Halle-Merseburg.[87] Goebbels's powers did not at this stage allow him to intervene on his own authority in the sphere of influence of the Gauleiters solely on the grounds of their inadequate preparations, and yet he appeared confident that Hitler would support his policy.[88] The Gaus had for their part evidently largely accepted the right to inspect as a legitimate new instrument of power. As in the case of Thuringia, criticism expressed itself principally in relation to political issues with symbolic significance.[89]

It must be said that only a few inspection reports contained anything approaching a sober appraisal.[90] For Goebbels, however, this was to a certain extent of secondary importance, as the Reich Inspectorate meant for him a real increase in the scope of his political power, on the basis of which he was able for example to curtail the Gauleiters' evacuation operations.[91] As far as evacuation policy was concerned, he pursued the aim of imposing the Reich's demand to exercise control even against the wishes of the most endangered Gaus. He aimed for a solution that strengthened restrictions on internal mobility in the Reich and increasingly limited the scope for evacuations from cities at risk from bombing. Simultaneously, as was reflected in Hitler's instructions, the central government, by now overstretched, began to make the air war a local government issue by increasing its demand for local self-help. The nationwide 'shake-up process',[92] as Goebbels called the evacuations from cities threatened with bombing to less endangered regions, had finally ground to a halt.

Several factors were decisive in this. First of all it was the result of the extension of the 'internal zone of combat' in the Reich, where, as Goebbels rightly thought at the beginning of 1944, there were hardly any more areas that could not be considered at risk of aerial attack.[93] Small and medium-sized towns not at risk from fire storms were in future to be more or less exempted from evacuations and the same was true of large cities deemed to have adequate precautions in place and whose layout made fire storms seem unlikely. This policy thus became a miracle formula, as simple as it was deceptive, and its persuasiveness allowed the Reich authorities to pass on responsibility for management of the crisis to local officials. Proximity to Allied bombers' potential targets was at any rate no longer a reason for evacuation, in particular because even at this stage the evacuations that had taken place had caused the authorities increasing problems and the social impact of rehousing people in practice quickly revealed the limits of the national community's solidarity.

Secondly, the change in the direction of evacuation policy pushed by Goebbels was the expression of the regime's priorities: in view of the hopeless war situation the transportation of the army and armaments took precedence over civilians and the risk of death through bombing was regarded as of lesser importance than the mobilization of the final military resources.[94] The Reich Inspectorate was one of the interfaces that supported and mediated this policy. Its most immediate effect probably consisted less in the concrete help it gave to the regions than in its creation of internal terror against those who tried to escape their 'air defence duty', broke blackout regulations, or caused disturbances at feeding stations.

Although some suggestions made by the authors of the reports on civil air defence were translated into a 'Führer decision' and thus became concrete policy,[95] for the most part the problems were marginal ones,[96] to the extent that they did not lead to serious differences with local institutions. Whereas the ILA concerned itself primarily with decisions affecting the distribution of resources, the Reich Inspectorate attempted to exert control mainly by means of information and the obligation to produce reports, though ultimately the course of the war made this fairly ineffective. After the first two waves of inspections between December 1943 and April 1944 the Inspectorate's enthusiasm visibly declined. The Reich Inspectorate and the ILA tried perforce to concentrate their resources again on immediate aid. Acute crisis management was their focus, day-to-day planning, the deployment of forced labour and concentration camp inmates, more and more new emergency programmes, but no coordinated thinking, let alone long-term planning. A consequence of this was that after pressure from the Gaus senior staff attempted to match what help the Reich had to offer more closely to the regions' needs and visited cities directly after bombing raids in order to agree on the spot what support was required.[97]

When the reports were written the work of the Reich Inspectorate seemed finished. Senior staff such as Berndt, the ILA secretary, had been looking around for a new task since July 1944, once it was clear that their present one was coming to an end.[98] In August Goebbels gave Hitler a final report on the Gaus that had been inspected and had up to that point been less affected by bombing. With pride he drew attention to the fact that the Führer's orders—in the final analysis his own work—had either been acted upon or were about to be.[99] He was, he said, thus in a position to return to Hitler the powers invested in him as Reich inspector.

What persuaded Goebbels to take such an unusual step? Several factors were involved. First of all, the Reich Inspectorate's instruments had turned out in the main to be blunt, which was most likely less the result of stubborn resistance by the Gaus than of the catastrophic military situation from the spring and summer of 1944 onwards. Secondly, some time before this Goebbels had lost interest in the role of Reich Inspector, for although it brought with it access to the Führer, in the final analysis no direct powers were attached to it. From the start of 1943 at the latest Goebbels's (like Speer's) response to the bombing had been total war. Now in the summer of 1944, after the heavy bombing of roads and railways and hydrogenation plants and the collapse of munitions production, the time had come to drop all internal political constraints and mobilize the population 'without exception' for the battle on the home front.

To this end, as he had already put it in a memorandum of 18 July 1944,[100] the existing bureaucratic systems in the Reich should be dissolved and a new controlling authority created for each sector of government: a person commissioned by Hitler who, responsible only to the Führer and freed from all existing spheres of competence, would possess absolute powers in a specific area; unencumbered by bureaucratic constraints and imbued with the spirit of the NSDAP's early years, he would be given the task as a special commissar of making all necessary decisions[101]—a form of improvised rule that Goebbels saw realized in exemplary fashion in the Reich Inspectorate. The dismantling of institutions and decision-making through the appointment of individuals and agencies directly responsible to the Führer: these were the components of a vision of the Nazi state mobilized for war, one that could not have been more different from the politics of consensus bound by formalized rules as practised in Britain.

For it was precisely the attempt to hold on to the existing structure of institutions and to cope with the state of emergency as far as possible by means of the existing administrative powers that was one of the key characteristics of British air defence policy. The government nevertheless made attempts, precisely as a response to the social emergency, to adjust the relationship between the state and local government, to centralize responsibilities, and—through the Regional Commissioners—to personalize them; this was a development that had operational similarities to the Nazi regime and was deliberate.

Strict limits were, however, imposed on this process and it was clear even to the advocates of placing a stronger emphasis on Whitehall and on individual appointees with special powers that there was no majority in favour of extra-legal structures outside of the existing procedural arrangements. Although they might at first sound tempting in a particularly critical moment in the air war, it was nevertheless obvious that such decisions would have to be publicly justified, thus costing more in terms of lost confidence than they would achieve in terms of efficiency. Nazi policy in the air war may have faced different challenges, but its distinguishing feature was to have redrawn the administrative map and to have created a system of institutions in which, as it were, might was right and decisions were made on the basis of authority derived directly from the Führer. The war had offered extraordinary opportunities for this feature to develop.

Justice and Repression

Even before the aerial war had reached Reich territory, regulations had come into force by which the Nazi state intended to maintain public order after bombing raids. The 'Decree against Public Vermin' (*Volksschädlinge*) of 5 September 1939[102] was the key element in the repression of the enemy within. The state secretary in the Reich Ministry of Justice and later President of the People's Court, Roland Freisler, had declared the aim of the new wartime criminal law to be 'to put a stop to unscrupulous vermin who seek out opportunities to carry out criminal and selfish attacks while our nation is defending itself, not to mention acts that damage our nation's powers of resistance, and to exclude them ruthlessly from our communities, which they have themselves betrayed, and if necessary eradicate them'.[103]

The Decree against Public Vermin covered several offences: it regulated 'looting in an exposed area', 'crimes during aerial threat', 'crimes against public safety', and 'exploiting the state of war as an aggravating factor'. The section on 'crimes during aerial threat' was explicitly formulated with bombing in mind. It provided for a prison sentence of up to fifteen years with hard labour, and in particularly serious cases for a life sentence or even execution, for anyone who 'exploited air-raid precautions to commit a crime or offence against the person, life or property'. The looter, according to Freisler, 'is the repulsive modern equivalent of the battlefield scavenger' and must therefore be punished mercilessly.

With the war the Nazis created a new set of laws making the criminal act dependent on the conditions of war, which could be redefined at any given moment and were liable to arbitrary interpretation. Society in wartime required increased control. In future there was no longer to be any distinction between an attempted act and an act committed. For sentencing this was crucial. Thus as early as 1939 two defendants being tried before a special court in Frankfurt for an attempted break-in during the blackout were not granted the possible mitigation.[104]

The sentence for 'exploitation of air-raid precautions' could now far exceed what had hitherto been the norm. As a rule the crimes in question were offences committed during the blackout (break-ins, thefts from air-raid shelters, the removal of air-raid equipment) or crimes that exploited the blackout during an air raid. And a further element was required for a guilty verdict: the perpetrator had to be characterized as 'vermin'.

Not all criminal acts were to be put into this expandable category—it excluded youthful misdemeanours and acts of pure desperation—but primarily those which, as Freisler considered, were an 'attack on the nation at war, a stab wound inflicted on the soldier at the front'.[105] The designation of 'vermin' was used to evaluate the deed and the doer in terms of the need to protect the 'national community'. Thus, just as the external war was being fought against 'Jewish Bolshevism' and the Anglo-American 'air gangsters', so the internal battle was being directed against agents of 'fungal decay' and, as a commentary on the new edict called them, 'air-war parasites',[106] and sentences were set accordingly.

The scope for prosecution had been significantly extended by the 'Decree against Public Vermin'. Virtually all crimes committed during the blackout were in future to be punishable by death. Even petty thefts were liable according to the norms of wartime justice to come under the scope of the Decree against Public Vermin and be sucked into the maelstrom of the special courts, whose jurisdiction enlarged as the air war continued. That was true in particular of cases involving alleged 'looters' who had, for example, removed from areas that had been voluntarily vacated property belonging to evacuees or to those who had been bombed out.

The sentence depended not only on the perpetrator being categorized as 'public vermin' but also on 'sound national sentiment' (*gesundes Volksempfinden*), which was to serve as the basis for judgment. Thefts of batches of army post or of materials belonging to the Reich railway were examples of where this applied. The edict was also directed against 'application offences' such as giving false information in connection with war damage claims, infringements of the coupon regulations or the war rationing system, and making an 'indecent proposal to the wife of a front-line soldier'.[107]

From the outset no limits were set to the latitude with which the edict was interpreted; after all, it was supposed to put an 'extremely sharp and, by virtue of its broad scope, readily usable weapon'[108] in the hands of the judiciary. Only a few weeks before the outbreak of war Franz Gürtner, the Reich Minister of Justice, had set clear parameters for criminal law in the special courts: 'In wartime we require that soldiers commit their persons and their lives heedlessly and without hesitation for the defence of their nation. At home too the fate of the individual in wartime must be ruthlessly subordinated to the idea of defending the nation. This radical intensification, this vivification of the notion of community results, to my mind inevitably, in a certain revision of peacetime values in the criminal law.'[109]

The 'Decree concerning radios', which also came into force at the outbreak of war and made it an offence 'intentionally to listen to foreign radio stations', was similarly conceived.[110] The spreading of news from foreign stations was to be prosecuted with particular harshness, for this was held to contribute not only to a 'maiming of the mind' as in the case of listening to foreign stations, but also to a 'poisoning of the mind' of the German nation—in the view of leading Nazi lawyers a particularly serious offence.[111] For passing on such information seemed liable to 'jeopardize the German nation's powers of resistance',[112] as was stated in the preamble to the edict issued by the Ministerial Council for the Defence of the Reich on 1 September.

The radio decree was similar in nature to the other offences covered by the special wartime legislation. It combined an at times positively panic-stricken anxiety about the effects of enemy propaganda and the population's vulnerability to it with an attempt to create solidarity in the national community by means of repression. In this the law was to be the tool by which distrust of the regime was to be penalized and loyalty extorted. In this respect the air war was one of the most important touchstones of and preconditions for the introduction of a new wartime criminal justice system. The threat of punishment and its execution formed part of an attempt to enforce the hegemony of Nazi interpretations of war and the home front. This involved suppressing by force any form of publicly voiced reservations about the credibility of Wehrmacht reports on the progress of the armed forces and preventing information and rumours about the air war, about cities that had been destroyed and the threat of raids, being passed on.

A direct connection was made between criminal justice and maintaining a public order legitimized by racial and *völkisch* ideology. From the point of view of the judiciary, however, the existing infrastructure of special courts was inadequate to achieve quick convictions; for them the bombing war and in particular the aftermath of the raids on Cologne at the end of May 1942 had made the situation critical and caused the number of 'looters' to rise so steeply that after the death of Gürtner, the state secretary in the Reich Ministry of Justice Franz Schlegelberger ordered the rapid establishment of special courts.[113]

A heavy raid on Düsseldorf shortly after had the same result. In the area covered by the higher regional court, to which Wuppertal and Duisburg also belonged, looters were to be prosecuted in future with the full force of the law. In the view of the Reich Ministry of Justice this was necessary if only because those who were experiencing at first hand 'the misery of the population and the vulnerability of their property' were best placed to pass judgment in cases of looting with the 'required severity'.[114] To lose no time, shortly after this the president of the Düsseldorf higher regional court called upon the individual regional courts to produce a staff roster that would guarantee that in the event of a raid the special courts were ready to sit the very same night.

After the heavy air raids of summer 1942 the special courts in the western cities of Düsseldorf, Wuppertal, Essen, and Duisburg, cities particularly under threat of bombing, were on the alert almost round the clock so that they could respond immediately to the criminal police's request for them to be capable, as 'drum-head courts martial on the internal frontline', of passing sentence on offenders the day they were arrested. This request had more to do with Nazi fantasies of criminal justice and as a rule could not be fulfilled even by the judicial terror system of the special courts.

With the appointment of Otto Georg Thierack as the new Reich Minister of Justice in late summer 1942 attempts to control the justice system escalated, as did interventions by the Party in the criminal justice system in cases involving bombing. In a speech in the Reichstag in April Hitler himself had expressed anger at what he held to be over-lenient judgments by the judiciary and had threatened serious repercussions.[115] The central importance accorded the Decree against Public Vermin and its implementation in the Nazi attempts to cope with the bombing crisis is illuminated by the *Judges' Letters* published immediately after Thierack's appointment. These were designed to guide the Nazi interpretation of justice and in the very first edition they stated what judicial practice was to be: the task of the law in wartime was 'to eliminate traitors and saboteurs on the home front'.[116]

Thierack demanded that 'noxious' elements be eradicated, the 'national community' protected, and sentences for looters be set as a deterrent. After all, he wrote, prevention is better than cure and over-lenient sentences carried the danger of 'spreading like a plague' and 'gradually causing the home front to disintegrate'.[117] Although in Thierack's view the majority of judges had shown they acknowledged their new responsibility, nevertheless—and this was the purpose of these attempts to guide from the centre—in 1941/2 there had been sentences passed on looters that he considered too lenient and for this reason had been heavily criticized in the Justice Ministry's instructions. Judges were praised for passing the death sentence, as in the case of a 29-year-old man who used the blackout to steal a handbag. In the end, he wrote, it was a matter of giving special protection to the population on the streets, bearing in mind the blackout regulations, and to give it a 'sense of security'.

Singlemindedness, preparedness for battle, severity—these were the values that guided a *völkisch* judge during the air war and had the purpose of keeping the home front united in the face of 'cowardly' bombing raids. A key element in this from the viewpoint of the Reich Ministry of Justice was the prosecution of 'looters'. But what did looting actually mean? The sentences passed could turn out to be very varied precisely in the phase when the special courts were expanding their work after air raids, and this was the result of the unclear definition of what constituted looting.

This fact had not escaped the attention of the judicial authorities. In their view the Decree against Public Vermin had from the start allowed a certain amount of flexibility[118] that depended on the discretion of the judges and on 'sound national sentiment'. So that judges would continue to pass judgment in the spirit of a *völkisch* justice system and sentencing not vary too greatly, in 1942 the Reich Ministry of Justice issued criteria: 'The national understanding of looting in general is the unprincipled appropriation of what belongs to others by right, in the course of which the perpetrator exploits a public disturbance or the helplessness, distress, confusion or terror of the population to carry out this act.'[119] According to the Reich Ministry of Justice the value of the stolen objects was immaterial; however small that might be, the 'wrongfulness of the act', the 'betrayal of the national community', was decisive.

The Reich Justice Minister identified grey areas when dealing with young or old people. A special court had condemned an 82-year-old pensioner to death because after an air raid he had found a horse's bridle and taken it to make a belt and braces. Even the Reich Justice Ministry considered this inappropriate, as the accused was suffering from dementia and was, it said, unaware of the significance of what he was doing. Modifications such as these may also have been a response to reports from the higher regional courts that members of the public considered the death penalty excessive in the case of petty crimes and in spite of prevalent thefts after air raids would not press charges because of the threat of a death sentence.[120]

Conversely, the 'mood' of the population could be used to justify the death penalty. In the case of Wilhelm Janowsky, the director of the Schleswig-Holstein office of the Nazi Party Welfare Organization (NSV), who after an air raid on Lübeck in 1942 misappropriated food and clothing on a grand scale and sold them on the black market to his friends in the Party,[121] the anger of the people was an argument that played an important role in his being condemned to death in December 1942. By contrast with its usual practice the regime published the sentence and execution in the press, aiming to lower the temperature of the public mood by this demonstrative act of 'justice'. Looting and wartime morale remained explosive subjects during the whole of the war. Just two years after his first set of instructions to the judges Thierack returned to them.[122]

He blamed looting more vigorously even than in 1942 on Allied bombing raids. If at the outset he had spoken only of damage and the loss of property, now he could not avoid acknowledging the reality of the destruction and the immense suffering of the population. At the same time, however, he made it clear that in this defence of the nation the German criminal justice system and its judges were acquiring a positively military mission. As in 1942 he emphasized the role of the justice system in preserving 'public order' as part of the home front and as a weapon in the battle against enemy attacks. The extension of the air war and the increasing destruction it brought raised afresh a number of questions regarding criminal justice, not least of which was what constituted looting.

The judicial authorities themselves, he said, were astonished to find that there seemed to be no clear profile of this category of perpetrator: there were those who had lived blameless lives up to that point and had succumbed to a 'sudden temptation'; thefts committed by those trying to survive seemed as numerous as those motivated purely by greed; some offences

were committed immediately following air raids while others were committed some time afterwards. What was not in doubt, in Thierack's view,
was that by now all German judges were convinced that 'looters' needed to
be punished severely. The number of death sentences passed during the war
reached a peak in 1944 and this was true as much in Berlin as in Hamburg,
Brunswick, Düsseldorf, Kiel, Mannheim, or Duisburg. But the judgments of
the special courts still did not go far enough for him, for he took the view
that there were cases in which judges had still not taken sufficiently to heart
the lapidary but also brutal principle: 'Anyone who in any shape or form
misappropriates the property of other national comrades after air-raids is in
danger of forfeiting his life.'[123] Contrary to his instructions, there were still
sentences determined by the value of what had been looted and not by the
act itself.

Given that the legislative authority had set criteria that were anything
but clear, the presidents of the regional courts and chairmen of the special
courts in the particularly heavily bombed areas of Essen, Dortmund, and
Bielefeld in the western Reich were moved to work out for themselves
transparent rules to apply in practice in passing sentence.[124] In January 1944
at one of their meetings they agreed that even those who had stolen goods
of little value were to be condemned for looting, for in the final analysis the
intention behind the act was the important thing. Clear guidelines were
required above all for the badly bombed regions, where cases of looting had
been on the increase since the start of the war. They did not at any rate think
there was any compelling reason to limit the punishment of looting in the
sense used by the Decree against Public Vermin to cases where the act was
committed immediately after a raid. Some areas in towns in the west of the
Reich lay in ruins in 1944 and in the rubble and in abandoned homes and
cellars were many objects. In the estimation of the Westphalian judges, anyone who removed items in 'evacuated areas'—and by that time this included
bomb-damaged buildings—could expect only one punishment: death.

There were, however, voices raised in opposition to the inflationary use
of the looting clause. In his report of August 1944 the president of the Kiel
higher regional court suggested re-examining whether a distinction should
not be made in sentencing between perpetrators with a 'decent' attitude,
'who in the agitation caused by a bombing raid succumbed to an unaccustomed temptation and stole items of little value, and other criminals who as
typical looters (hyenas of the battlefield, so to speak) exploit the situation
created by an air raid to enrich themselves, by allowing the possibility of a

prison sentence instead of the death penalty in cases of the first kind'.[125] In Hamburg too the president of the higher regional court drew attention to the fact that the clause on looting had arisen under different circumstances, before the air war had become so extreme.[126]

Even if verdicts given could vary from one region to another, such carefully formulated reservations had little impact on the devastating practice of the special courts. In the final analysis the attempts to direct the justice system had the effect of taking penalties to the limit and of escalating the measures taken to eradicate deviant behaviour. The subjectivization of the law that went with this, the latitude given to judges to interpret what constituted the imprecisely defined special category of looting, extended the range of tools of oppression available to the regime.[127]

Even at the end of January 1945, for example, an agreement was reached by the chief prosecutor for Munich, the chief of police, and representatives of the criminal and state police on a new scenario for prosecuting cases of looting.[128] Immediately after arrest the accused was to be transferred to a police station or the court building. The state prosecutor was to be called in as soon as possible and if possible was to speak only to the policemen who had conducted the interview. The main hearing was to take place no later than the second day after the arrest. By that time the charges would be drawn up, a defence lawyer engaged, and the accused transferred to a concentration camp or remand prison. As a result the trial could be held there without delay before the special court. As the chief prosecutor remarked, that procedure also had the advantage that executions by hanging could be carried out directly in the concentration camp, thus making it unnecessary for those condemned to be brought back to Munich.

By this stage the possibility that anyone might be acquitted seemed inconceivable. The penalty and above all whether it should be 'carried out immediately' were to be referred by the state prosecutor responsible in a brief written report to the Reich Minister of Justice. 'A strict interpretation of the law' should apply. After the Reich Justice Minister had made a decision the punishment was to be carried out at once and a further check made to decide whether the case should be posted up publicly. Thus at the end of the war the last vestiges of a criminal justice system operating in a state bound by the rule of law had disappeared.

Criminal justice in practice revealed its essentially racist character ever more clearly as the war progressed. In Hanover, for example, as in other special courts from 1942 onwards, a constantly rising proportion of those accused under the Decree against Public Vermin were foreign workers.[129] In 1941 it was 10 per cent, in 1942 15 per cent, in 1943 34 per cent, and in 1944 slightly more than 46 per cent.[130] As far as Poles were concerned, Thierack had instructed his judges that 'leniency as such is misplaced'.[131] The procedural practices adopted by the special courts, where in cases against foreigners the taking of evidence was often handled both ruthlessly and in an unserious and superficial way, did in fact demonstrate that many of the judges did not need instructions from him to sign death sentences willingly—for crimes such as taking half a dozen eggs or some worn-out shoes abandoned in a cellar.[132]

Even in branches of criminal law that were not covered by special wartime criminal law the Reich Ministry of Justice pressed for greater severity. Again and again the priority was to maintain 'public order' under air attack, for example in the way paragraph 330 C of the Reich Criminal Justice Code was interpreted. In this paragraph the Code stipulated that 'a failure to provide help' had occurred if help were refused in cases of danger or emergency 'even though sound national sentiment'[133] would regard this as a duty. The penalty was set at up to two years' imprisonment or a fine. The Nazi regime took the view that the air war had created numerous situations of this kind, where the 'national community' ought to demonstrate its willingness to help. Those who had lost their homes or had had to leave the place where they grew up and now had nothing ought in particular to feel the benefits of national solidarity. An essential part of the new Nazi morality was the duty towards the national community and this was to be inculcated with the help of the criminal law, with the result that those who for example refused to help victims of bombing were to be given prison sentences. The judge's task was to test whether the acts in question were simply inadequate efforts or were offences against 'sound national sentiment' and 'obvious duties to the community'.[134]

The first convictions on the grounds of 'refusing emergency aid' came after the heavy bombing of Rostock at the end of April 1942.[135] The extensive, centrally controlled evacuations of 1943 and the huge and constantly worsening problem of homelessness ensured that, as the Reich Minister of Justice commented, crimes falling into the category of 'omitting to give help' grew in significance. At the points where the 'national community' revealed its social boundaries—and in the relations between evacuees, local residents, and the homeless this was not exactly a rare occurrence—criminal justice was intended to help coerce people into doing what politics could not prescribe. There were frequent cases of those in need not being given accommodation or being given inadequate accommodation in spite of having official certification from the housing department. Landlords were accused of chicanery of a greater or lesser kind such as refusing to provide water or lighting, or pub landlords were accused of refusing to open their pub during closing hours to those seeking cover from bombing and anti-aircraft fire.[136]

There were, however, cases that came to court where air-raid wardens abused their power. In October 1942, for example, a woman with two children whose husband was at the front tried belatedly to get into a shelter. She was first given a severe dressing down by the air-raid warden and refused entry. A district court found the man guilty of omitting to give help and offending against air-raid regulations and sentenced him to four months' imprisonment—which in the view of the Reich Justice Ministry was almost too lenient. Air-raid regulations came under the system of administrative law rather than criminal law, but since being passed in 1935[137] and owing to the expansion of the air war they had undergone constant radicalization and the range of penalties had grown.[138]

Offences against the blackout regulations, against the regulations concerning the disposal of junk, and other 'duties to behave in a way conducive to air-raid protection' were punished with custodial sentences or fines of up to 150 Reich marks. Repeat offenders or anyone who prevented others from carrying out their air-raid duties were to be sent to prison, in particularly bad cases sentenced to hard labour. The police authorities were responsible for bringing prosecutions, and pursuing those who infringed the blackout regulations was an important tool they used to exercise discipline over the population.

As early as April 1941 the Munich police chief had decreed that in future a tougher line should be taken against infringements of the blackout regulations and that those who had ignored the guidelines repeatedly or 'malevolently' and had been caught red-handed were to be turned over to the Gestapo.[139] By getting actively involved in combating 'defaulters and the neglectful' the local branches of the Nazi Party acquired the main responsibility for supervision and reporting.[140] In addition to propaganda activities, this social control and constant supervision, which involved cooperating with the police in bringing prosecutions in the area of air defence law, became one of their main tasks.

In the summer of 1940 Hitler had already decreed that local Party members should be involved in supervising the blackout after numerous reports of inadequate observance of the regulations.[141] The Party Chancellery had passed on the Führer's wish to the Gau headquarters and made it clear they should become actively engaged, which might mean that individual repeat offenders or even whole communities could have their power cut off.

As far as one can tell, things did not get to that point, but the local Nazi Party membership took advantage of this instruction to extend their control significantly: this consisted in regular patrols and also in attempts to stigmatize negligent residents by posting their names in public. If that did not work, those accused could be summoned to the local Party office for a reprimand and required to pay a fine for 'blackout infringements'.[142] In other words, a police interview was no longer necessary to establish an offence, which could then be referred to the justice system, but rather local Party organizations used their growing powers to take over functions that were previously the prerogative of the state. This applied above all to spheres that, as in the case of the special wartime criminal code, epitomized the way the 'national community' coped with crisis, namely through terror and repression.

Looting and criminal justice in Britain

In Britain there was no special wartime criminal code, still less were there special courts—at least not to the extent that they existed in Germany and certainly not as part of a comprehensive policy of repression. Nevertheless, the Defence Regulation of 1939 equipped Britain with a wartime constitution that was time-limited and supported by the major political parties, and although it did not abandon everything that had existed pre-war it did provide for considerable changes in turning a civil society into a nation at war. The Defence Regulation invested the Prime Minister with extensive powers, limiting the prerogatives of Parliament and permitting the suspension of individual statutes of civil law.[143] Measures such as press censorship, the internment of enemy aliens, the introduction of new crimes such as looting after air raids, and also regulations concerning the blackout were introduced on this legal basis with the approval of Parliament. The various stages of criminal proceedings, however, and the rights of defendants and defence counsels remained unchanged. Even in wartime Britain remained a state governed by the rule of law (*Rechtsstaat*) with a functioning separation of powers. Even a growing sense of commitment on the part of those working in the justice system to protecting morale on the home front could do nothing to change this.

The blackout was one of the key areas resulting in new practices in the justice system. A set of uniform blackout regulations had been in force since the beginning of September 1939 and they restricted life in the public sphere significantly.[144] No flicker of light was to be seen coming from houses and blocks of flats in the evening, street lighting was turned off, cars and lorries were not allowed to use headlights. It was hardly surprising that within a few months there was a rapid increase in the numbers of deaths and injuries as a result of road accidents occurring during the blackout. Mass Observation reports recorded that in the late autumn of 1939 nothing annoyed people more than the blackout regulations[145] because they put restrictions on considerable areas of public life. This was at a point when many people had hardly been affected by the war and air raids had not yet begun.[146]

How could a balance be struck between the requirements of the military and the protection of the civilian population on the one hand, and, on the other, the desire to maintain 'normality' in spite of this state of emergency? As a response to growing discontent it was finally agreed at the end of 1940 to relax the regulations slightly and, for example, to allow shops and businesses to stay open for longer, torches to be used, and vehicles to be driven with dimmed headlights. It was nevertheless difficult to reach a compromise between air defence experts, businesses anxious about their productivity, and the expectations of the public. As in the case of other contentious issues, the way forward was to bring together the various interests in a special inter-ministerial committee in an attempt to minimize conflict.

Thus from the middle of 1943 onwards, on the initiative of the War Cabinet and under the auspices of the Ministry of Home Security, a number of ministries met to discuss the reform of the blackout regulations as they applied to industry.[147] The blackout was a key element in civil defence, a ritual that involved every individual in the battle to defend the country and at the same time made an example of anyone who through negligence, let alone criminal behaviour, tried to ignore or circumvent the state's requirements. As in Germany, in Britain the blackout was one of the key areas that offered the potential to impose discipline and ensure compliance through pressure and control.

Local air-raid workers were responsible for checking that the stringent requirements were met and for reporting habitual stragglers, such as householders who refused to cover their windows with black cardboard or owners of businesses who were not prepared to switch off illuminated advertising.

Infringements were very common and the police were under orders to act. In 1940 alone some 300,000 cases of infringements of the blackout regulations were heard in court[148] and in relation to the severity of the offence penalties were stringent: a man of 83 from North London was fined £2, which amounted to four times the average weekly pension, after his neighbours protested about light showing through his front door and called the police. In the case of shopkeepers who failed to comply with the rules the fines often exceeded £50, a little less than half the sum required to buy a small car.[149] By comparison with Germany, where practices in criminal law were constantly becoming more repressive and radical, this was still very lenient, and yet it was hardly a negligible penalty and was keenly felt by those affected.

The fact that in both Germany and Britain the blackout had such a great symbolic significance was due to two related problems in particular. On the one hand, there was a concern that morale would drop. The government was uncertain how far the population in town and country were prepared to accept restrictions to public life. On the other hand, restrictions were an indication that the dreaded air and gas war was now no longer a literary fiction but could soon be a reality. The sense of uncertainty, of waiting for a threatening danger no one could yet imagine, the fear of walking home in the evening in darkness—these were undoubtedly concerns the Metropolitan Police considered capable of lowering morale.[150]

At the same time, the Met wished to avoid overestimating the risks, for as long as basic leisure activities could carry on in daylight without lengthy interruptions, the cinemas could remain open, and the working classes could still talk about football after the week-end, the experts believed that morale would hold up. The reports from early October 1939 from various London superintendents on the effects of the blackout in their districts did not at any rate give rise to excessive concern. Most citizens understood that obeying the regulations was their patriotic duty and put up with a frequent cause for complaint, namely that women spent less time on household matters than their husbands wished.[151]

Concern about the consequences of a drop in morale went beyond changes to supper times and the number of shirts ironed, however. It focused on a problem that since the end of 1939 and beginning of 1940 had been causing increasingly intense public concern, namely the rise in criminal behaviour, the fear of robbery, burglary, and sexual violence under cover of the blackout.[152] Did turning off the street lighting result in criminal elements taking advantage of the national emergency to attack decent citizens and their businesses under cover of darkness? Since the outbreak of war the Met had in fact recorded a growing number of offences, in particular looting after air raids or burglaries during the blackout. These greatly agitated the public.

However necessary it was to protect people against the threat of German raids, the outbreak of war seemed to have opened the floodgates of criminal activity and citizens would have to take precautions against it. The Senior Officer at a London Youth Court, for example, blamed the blackout in large measure for the increase in criminality among the young, women as well as men, who had lost all sense of discipline.[153] The blackout was thus a hotbed of immorality. The controversy surrounding the removal of restrictions continued throughout the war, always acquiring new dimensions and creating new conflicts: civil defence and the defence of the home country, curbs on productivity and 'moral decay', state-provided protection and individual discipline. Offenders who exploited the blackout or misappropriated other citizens' property after air raids could not at any rate count on leniency. Their actions were not only criminal but also morally reprehensible, for after all these were shady elements who were committing crimes against the nation under cover of darkness.

At the same time as the German air raids the British press was publishing detailed reports on the seemingly dangerous increase in crimes[154] being prosecuted in courts from Liverpool to London. A London court, for example, sentenced a burglar to five years' penal servitude and this was completely in line with the Defence Regulation. There was no doubt, the judgment stated, that the accused had exploited the blackout to commit the crime and must therefore expect to feel the full force of the law. The sentence was therefore consciously used as a deterrent, for all criminals in the country should after all be aware that crimes committed during a national emergency must be punished especially severely.[155] The same principle applied in cases where men pestered women in an 'immoral' fashion and attempted to exploit the darkness to assault them or steal their handbag.[156]

Cases of looting also aroused public concern. These were also prosecuted under the Defence Regulation, but unlike in Nazi Germany they were not heard before specially created courts. The crime of looting had been created by legislation expressly to maintain morale at home. Every case of theft of property from bombed houses was to be treated differently from a normal burglary.

The public and politicians were very troubled by the rising number of crimes that the police and the government had been reporting since the outbreak of war. Looting was only one factor, and by no means the weightiest, in the increase in crime, but it called into question the image of a united and solid home front. At the end of August 1940 and even before the actual Battle of Britain a London judge had stated in his judgment that thefts after air raids must not be accepted under any circumstances, let alone treated as though they were trivial.[157] In Birmingham, Liverpool, Belfast, and London rumours began circulating early on that bomb-damaged houses and business premises were being looted by organized, professional gangs. After the raids of December 1940 on Sheffield it had taken two days for sentences to be handed down in all the cases of looting.[158]

In the overwhelming majority of cases reported in the press the perpetrators were juveniles, though, as the police noted, they proceeded like professionals. This circumstance fuelled the debate, which though by no means new was becoming more intense as a result of the war, about the moral decline of the young,[159] and it was particularly intense if children of 10 and 11 were caught breaking and entering and were subjected to corporal punishment.[160] There was another respect, however, in which looting seemed to be a social problem, for most of the burglars apprehended were working class. In many instances the items stolen were not very valuable and yet for the courts they had great symbolic significance. In autumn 1940 the Lord Mayor of London therefore felt compelled to use billboards to denounce such reprehensible behaviour and warn against exploiting this time when the nation was being put to the test to steal other people's property. 'Looters', it was stated, would be imprisoned or even executed; their crime was comparable to murder.[161]

British criminal law became in fact considerably politicized in response to growing public pressure to make an example of people who by looting had shown themselves to be 'un-British'. To do this it was not, however, necessary, as in Germany, to create a centrally controlled judicial policy sanctioned by law that challenged the autonomy of judges and annulled existing laws, and such a policy would not have been feasible. In October 1940 alone, immediately after the beginning of the London Blitz, the police chalked up 1,662 incidents of looting. For the period September 1940 to May 1941 New Scotland Yard estimated a good 890 reported cases each month;[162] in London alone there were thus around 4,600 incidents.

Admittedly all concerned knew full well that the underlying figure was much higher and that many of the victims did not turn to the police or that in spite of having a special unit 300-strong the police were incapable for lack of manpower of pursuing those responsible. They estimated that only one crime in four reported ended in an arrest. Anyone who was actually caught ran the risk of imprisonment or hard labour, even for minor thefts. In 30 per cent of cases recorded by the police in 1940 the value of the goods stolen was £2 or less; in 56 per cent of cases it was not more then £5.[163]

If members of the rescue services, volunteer firemen, or police were involved in looting there was particular outrage. Lengthy prison sentences were often handed down in such cases, for those concerned had after all, as stated in the charges against them, committed a particularly grievous offence by robbing those they were supposed to be helping. At the same time, in spite of the seriousness of the offence the criminal proceedings did not differ in any fundamental way from those in other trials. Although looting was a new category of crime, there was no change to the judicial process, to the hearing of witnesses, to police investigations, and to the independence of the judiciary—a complete contrast to Nazi Germany.

In the War Cabinet and civil defence cabinet the ministries involved were more concerned about the spreading of exaggerated rumours about the extent of looting, and no one seriously considered using the death penalty against such minor offences.[164] Even if one or two people spoke up for an even tougher line to be taken against criminal activities, the ministers involved, in part for tactical reasons, silenced them. After the first wave of public concern in 1940/1, looting became an issue in Parliament and among the public at the time of the V-1 raids, when civil defence officials were once more taken to court. In response the Civil Defence Committee turned to New Scotland Yard in July 1944 for information about the accuracy of the rumours, discovering quickly that the number of cases was well below the levels of 1940/1. There were no grounds for panic, at any rate. On the contrary, the ministries were strongly in favour of using press releases to warn the public against misleading rumours and dramatizing the situation, while in the same breath reminding people that looting was not just any old crime, but a particularly base crime that would continue to be vigorously prosecuted. Admittedly, not even the police authorities and ministers were certain whether in any given case charges were being brought for looting when a straightforward robbery had taken place—in this respect the Defence Regulation was vague, which had considerable consequences in practice for prosecutions.

There were at any rate no ministerial officials who intentionally played up cases of looting or worked at eroding established judicial practices in the interests of promoting an extra-legal policy. These factors were indicative of an essential difference between Britain and the Nazi dictatorship, in spite, for example, of a comparable ritual significance accorded to looting in both countries. The war might be a state of emergency but that was no reason to abandon core constituents of the rule of law.

The fact that the problem of looting had largely disappeared from the political agenda by the middle of 1944 was revealed by what was happening in another area of policy in competition with it. As a result of parliamentary questions and several newspaper reports the Civil Defence Committee decided in August 1944 to have the Board of Trade examine whether victims of lootings were entitled to state compensation. The answer was no.[165] 'Looting', it was decided, was, after all, not directly war damage. As a matter of principle the state provided no compensation for the consequences of 'criminality'. All told, this demonstrated a rather dispassionate attitude to British wartime morale.

War Damages and Wartime Morale

Compared with the conflicts surrounding compensation for private war damage the controversy over looting really was of marginal significance. The issue of damages had been a battleground since the end of the 1930s. What consequences of war was the state responsible for? How was war damage defined, in any case: the loss of income from rents as a result of evacuations? Loss of earning from being called to serve in the Home Guard or in air-raid protection? Municipal tax deficits or strictly direct damage such as the bombing of private houses? And what form might compensation take? Assistance from the public purse, loans, or direct pay-outs? What if the value of people's homes had dropped as a result of the damage? And what about home contents, which were likely to have been damaged as well?

Initial discussions at the Board of Trade in 1937 assumed that, as war was considered imminent, the state could not possibly insure against the risks of war and that the best protection lay in arming the military—in effect, a complete privatization of the consequences of war.[166] This approach had provoked powerful opposition at an early stage, and so at the end of January

1939 the Chancellor of the Exchequer, Sir John Simon, responding to an independent government report about possible war damage, announced that the government had reached the conclusion that the cost of war damage could not be borne by individuals but must be carried by society as a whole and therefore covered by public funds. This, however, did not settle the points at issue, because declarations of intent remained vague. Press responses and the reactions in Parliament were extremely negative. Criticism was aimed above all at the government's inadequate preparation and thus also at its lack of sensitivity to public worries.[167]

In the end it was Churchill himself who recognized the political explosiveness of the issue of war compensation and gave the Chancellor the task of framing a law that would strike a difficult balance between the limited resources of a nation at war and the requirement in a parliamentary democracy to legitimize war in material terms also. The War Damage Act of 1941[168] attempted to maintain this balance. Owners of houses and flats, landowners, and owners of businesses had to pay through the tax system a particular sum related to the size and value of their property. Charities and churches were exempted. In return for these insurance payments it was envisaged that war damage would be assessed by a state commission and compensation paid out in accordance with the degree of damage. The Act defined war damage first of all as damage caused directly by the enemy such as the impact of bombing, then secondly as damage resulting from the effects of war, such as when municipal authorities were forced to demolish houses that were no longer safe, and thirdly indirect damage from the accidental detonation of mines set along coastal areas to protect against invasion.

The state commissions were organized into regions and in the course of 1941 they opened offices across the country where claims for compensation could be submitted. The commissions checked the claims, assessed the damage, compared old and new values, and set the level of compensation, dealing in the first instance with a limited period fixed by law as the period between the outbreak of war and the end of August 1941. Setting the amount of compensation was a complex and contentious process, for situations where homeowners used public money to fund improvements, by, for example, having old houses expensively rebuilt, had to be avoided. The commissions therefore checked how far houses increased in value during renovation.

The procedure for compensation was therefore based on the principle of maintaining the owner's status and less on simply covering needs. The Act envisaged three categories of compensation payment. If the damage was reparable the claimant would receive a sum of money that could be used to restore the property to its former state. If on the other hand houses were completely destroyed and could not be repaired the state would assume the full costs, though not until after the war. Finally, there was also state support in cases where money for renovation was needed at short notice.[169] As air raids grew more frequent and it was feared that morale might suffer Churchill's government and the Chancellor withdrew the decisions made earlier to peg compensation for household contents and clothing in principle to income thresholds.[170] Depending on the severity of the loss, homeowners could receive up to £200 in compensation; married couples were entitled to an additional £100, with a further £25 for each child under 16.[171] From May 1941 an additional state insurance was introduced giving homeowners the option of insuring their property up to a value of £10,000, though in most cases money would not be paid out until after the war. The Act also limited the period for which claims would be valid, which at first went up to the end of August 1941, after which Parliament extended it at various points in the course of the war.

Compared with Nazi Germany the War Damage Act signified a fundamentally different form of insurance against the consequences of war in a mixed economy. Basic state cover for the most severe types of damage was linked to a system of contributions, paid also by businesses, and together with additional funding by the state these formed the basis for future compensation payments. The Board of Trade outsourced the drawing up of the insurance policies to the big insurer Lloyd's. The state did not, it is true, accept liability for private damage or for the loss of valuables beyond a minimum level and encouraged individuals in such cases to pay for additional cover. This hybrid form taken by the War Damage Act was based on a prediction of the costs of the air war that assumed that war damage would not exhaust the funds of the citizens or of the state and so would certainly not delegitimize the war itself.[172]

The legislators had left themselves several loopholes to limit costs. The compensation promised was linked to the Empire's wartime economic strength and a considerable portion was deferred to the post-war years. At the same time the legislators had designated the regions most at risk, these being, in addition to London, above all the towns on the south coast and the industrial centres of the Midlands, Liverpool, Sheffield, and Manchester, while other regions were excluded and so the number of possible claimants limited.[173]

Reactions to procedures for insurance and compensation, which were judged even by experts and proponents as extremely complicated, were far from unanimous. The view of the Chancellor of the Exchequer, Sir Kingsley Wood, was that considering the threat from bombing the Act contributed significantly to guaranteeing financial compensation and simultaneously to creating a financial basis for the war years to follow.[174] One thing was certain: it was impossible to fight this war without imposing additional financial burdens and insuring citizens at least to some extent against the demands that might be made on them in future. By contrast with Germany, public consent had to be sought even in the wartime state of emergency, and as a result those responsible for the Act had to face hostile questioning from MPs in session after session. The King's speech to Parliament just nine months after the Act became law in November 1941 praised what the War Damage Act had achieved. It had, the speech stated, brought great relief to many British subjects and the compensation payments had also strengthened the war economy.[175]

The King's speech was addressing one of the key elements in the conflict surrounding the War Damage Act: what financial contribution were property owners prepared to make to the war? And should it be given voluntarily or should war damage be dealt with by means of an unpopular compulsory levy disguised as a 'tax' and raised from businesses and homeowners? And if so, for how long? At any rate, the many anomalies in the Act, including its vague time limit, continued to provoke criticism up to the end of the war. Were the premiums not set too high, higher than a normal insurance policy on the open market? Did the Act have to apply to everyone or only to those in the regions affected?[176]

When the extension of the War Damage Act was debated in November 1941 there were opponents from various parties who nevertheless saw it as their patriotic duty in view of the war situation not to sound off too vigorously.[177] The War Damage Commission ran into difficulties in practice when working with local authorities to examine the damage and decide whether houses did in fact have to be demolished or could still be repaired. By the end of the war around two and a half million houses had been destroyed or damaged and all of these were the War Damage Commission's responsibility. No wonder, then, that by the end of 1943 the approximately 2,200 employees (after the war the number rose to over 3,300) had not managed to deal with all the cases of war damage from the years up to 1942, as had been hoped.[178]

For those affected the policy of deferment and the shortage of staff in the Commission were a serious problem, because scarce building materials could be obtained or an architect engaged to give a proper estimate of the costs only with the Commission's consent. It was also the Commission's decision what type of compensation would be given and when and how much money would be paid out.[179] In addition, the delays and uncertainties surrounding construction and compensation payments exacerbated the acute housing shortage from which Britain's urban areas had been suffering even before the war. Social security was on the agenda.

Attempts were made to adapt the hastily compiled set of guidelines to the changing war situation by means of amendments to the Act, but the amendments were confined to marginal issues.[180] The Chief Secretary to the Treasury countered fierce criticism from a few MPs during a debate on one amendment in August 1943 by saying that in the end it was not the war damage legislation that created unreasonable demands but the war itself.[181] Though he conceded that the Act was not ideal in every respect, nevertheless the government had taken great trouble to simplify the regulation of damage claims in stages and done all it could, given the pressures on the war economy, to keep the burdens imposed on homeowners to a minimum. Thus although individual MPs continued to complain, even in the last year of the war as a result of the V-1 and V-2 raids, there was no fundamental conflict.

One reason for this was that after the air war had peaked in 1940/1 the cases of damage dropped rapidly; the resources available were adequate to deal with emergencies and all other problems postponed to the end of the war. It is altogether possible, however, that if the bombing of British cities had continued, causing more destruction and raising the level of contributions, the resources of the War Damage Act would have been considerably drained and the system brought to the point of collapse. But in the final analysis this system of sharing the costs of war and their partial privatization was only one problem among many and did not present any serious challenge to the legitimacy of the war, even if as it continued the number of parliamentary questions consistently rose. Parliament—in contrast to the situation in the 'Third Reich'—at least provided a sort of public wailing wall where ministers still had to give an account of themselves. Debates did not maintain the standard of pre-war ones and the war situation was often used to suppress discussion of sensitive issues. However, the controversy surrounding how individuals would cope with war damage was seen as a test of confidence in government policy and of the limits of what the public would bear, given that its endurance had clearly not been exhausted by the destruction caused by the air war.

War damage compensation in Germany

Whenever the British War Damage Act was mentioned in Germany, legal experts in the Nazi administration saw it above all as an example of Anglo-Saxon faint-heartedness.[182] The lawyers in the Reich Ministry of the Interior confidently pointed to the latest achievement of National Socialism, so much more comprehensive, more equitable, and more robust than the outdated British model, which pushed a considerable part of the burden onto ordinary people. The War Damage Legislation (KSR: *Kriegsschädenrecht*), drawn up in 1940, was indeed an essential component of the Nazi state at war and an insurance against the 'Stab in the Back' of November 1918.

The KSR was designed to respond to the growing challenge of the air war and to be a key means of legitimizing the Nazi dictatorship in its struggle to retain the population's confidence. In the second year of the war, at the height of military expansion, after the Polish campaign, the occupation of Norway, and the defeat of France, on 30 November 1940 the Ministerial Council for the Defence of the Reich passed a law exuding the euphoria of certain victory.[183] Convinced of the invulnerability of the Reich's borders the War Damage Decree (KSV) regulated future compensation for all damage caused to civilians as a result of the war.

Admittedly, the Reich Interior Ministry, which was responsible for the legislation, did not envisage serious destruction from area bombing. Though the raids on the Rhineland had been unpleasant, the cost of the damage, in the regime's view, was far from being a serious blow to the Reich. There was no experience from the First World War that the administration and the Nazi leadership could draw on. In 1939 there had been some hesitancy, for the Decree on the Assessment of Damage to Property issued in the first week of the war envisaged that those affected would be given an advance payment only and anything further would be held back pending an overall settlement.[184] This ruling implicitly adopted a principle that had determined the compensation payments after the Franco-Prussian War of 1870/1, though these were hardly comparable: in the expectation of victory losses were to be fully compensated at a level required to replace or repair what had been damaged.

Priority was given to payments to prevent damage from closing businesses or reducing people's circumstances drastically, still more if the damage was about to cause bankruptcy. The legislators did, all the same, leave a get-out clause, by making payments dependent on whether they were economically justified. What this signified in individual cases the decree did not specify. Possible limits to the amount of compensation were also left open at this early stage and reserved for later rulings. There was merely a concise outline of the procedure.

Claims were to be lodged with the relevant mayor's office or sent directly to the Assessors' Office at the local authority responsible for making the assessment. What was new about the KSV of 30 November 1940 was first and foremost that it set down that a victim of war damage had a valid claim against the German Reich. There was an established administrative procedure, there were responsible authorities and staff and the beginnings of a body of case law—all designed so that individuals should receive 'speedy and generous' help,[185] as Wilhelm Stuckart, state secretary in the Reich Ministry of the Interior, emphasized. Compensation, as everyone agreed, was an essential means of strengthening the 'home front'.[186] If the Nazi state failed to provide extensive support, then in its own estimation it risked undermining people's assent to the war. Their power of endurance seemed to those in charge of the Nazi state to depend crucially on assistance that was as unbureaucratic and immediate as possible, for example, on those who had suffered damage after air raids being given something to eat, adequate clothing for the first weeks, and quick pay-outs to cover essentials.

State, Wehrmacht, and Party were to cooperate in clearing war damage and supporting those affected. Material compensation was a fundamental form of restitution for the burdens war imposed, chief of which were the consequences of bombing. The power of propaganda or rapid victories were not sufficient on their own to sustain people while the enemy was attacking them at home from the air. The promise of being safeguarded financially from the risks of war was an essential part of winning people's trust and securing their loyalty and readiness for battle. As Bernhard Danckelmann, one of the leading legal experts on war damage, explained, war was a matter that concerned the whole 'national community'. Thus its costs must be carried by all on an equal basis, for this was, after all, the essence of the 'national community', namely that the individual committed himself to it and made extraordinary sacrifices, but in return received support from it, should the burdens and losses the individual suffered go beyond what could be reasonably required.[187]

Yet what at first glance looked like comprehensive cover without any costs being met by the individual was revealed on closer inspection to be deceptive. First of all, whatever claims people were entitled to make, all pay-outs were to be dependent on economic developments and that meant on victory in the war and the constraints of the budget. In other words, the departments of the Reich Ministry of the Interior and the Reich Finance Ministry involved tried to put a stop to inflated claims from the word go. Securing the home environment and the loyalty of the national community versus politically and financially determined 'wartime constraints', the KSV was caught between the two and the tension between them made itself felt at the point when the intensity of the air war over Germany looked set to overturn the predictions about damage the authorities had been making since 1942. There was hardly another area of law at this time that was in such a state of flux, was struggling so hard to retain at least temporary coherence, and was overtaken so often by the omnipresence of bombing as the KSV.

The precondition for claims to one of the local authority assessment offices was damage resulting from a 'war-related event',[188] such as a combat operation involving enemy weapons: in other words, air-war damage such as homes destroyed or household goods lost. The decree made a distinction between damage to property and loss of use. Damage to property was to be compensated in full, according to whether what was damaged was replaced or repaired. If something could not be used because of war damage (for example, when income from letting property was lost) a claim for compensation specifically for loss of use could be submitted. For businesses, where the costs of lost production through bombing were considerably higher, the KSV provided for the possibility of individual grants, should works have to halt part or the whole of their production or if additional expenses were incurred that the business could not cover from its own funds.[189]

Although the KSV ruled that in cases where as yet damage could not be repaired or the item replaced, for example as a result of shortages of construction materials, payments could be withheld or deferred to a point in the future, such cases—at least that was what was believed in 1941—should remain the exception and applications for such a ruling should be made only in special circumstances. In cases of minor damage above all the local authority was urged to offer speedy assistance for specific needs in the form of cash or materials, to enable those bombed to buy clothing and furniture.[190]

Two forms of cash payment were envisaged: the actual compensation payment received when the process was complete and an advance payment that depended on the urgency of the case. The issue of when the payment was made in particular caused repeated arguments. No one had a right to instant compensation and as the war went on more and more cases arose where the war damage offices, unable to gauge in advance the sums payable in the claims submitted, deferred making a decision.

Fast, generous, and unbureaucratic in their granting of compensation for 'national comrades'—that was what the war damage offices were supposed to be.[191] There was one exception, however: Jews were excluded from any form of compensation. They were not allowed to make claims and could not expect any restitution after the war. On the contrary: from the outset Jews' property was regarded by the local compensation offices as an important resource they controlled and that could be used in the interests of the 'national community' to provide victims of bombing with furniture, household goods, and living quarters. Whereas the racist character of the decree admitted of no ambiguity, in practice the war damage legislation produced a huge number of unsolved problems that forced the authorities almost daily into making new decisions and repeatedly overtaxed their competence.

Thus the air war gave rise not only to new legislation but also to new institutions such as the Reich War Damage Office (RSA), which from April 1941 onwards was the highest authority in all matters concerning war damage compensation.[192] The RSA supervised local offices and was also empowered, after confirmation from the Reich Ministry of the Interior, to issue binding guidelines on the implementation of the KSV. In the words of a leading government lawyer in the Reich Ministry of the Interior, this was 'a first in the history of government',[193] because for the first time the president of an administrative court would be responsible for supervising an administrative agency and thereby would be consciously contravening the principle of the separation of powers, albeit that the separation of powers was in fact merely a formality. The head of the RSA was to act as the 'active link between the court and the executive' and form part of a new Nazi symbiosis of public life and the executive realm that aimed to neutralize one of the evils of 'liberal thinking', the separation of powers.

The course of the air war set the pace for the war damage offices and created so many new problems in a very short time that local offices were in danger of drowning in the flood of issues that required regulation. Did thefts committed during air-raid warnings count as war damage? Did insurance companies have to put up the money to repair damaged houses?

Were wives of husbands serving in the war entitled to make claims on the latter's behalf?[194] This issue in particular caused numerous disputes, for the KSV stated that only the property owner was entitled to compensation. Wives could submit claims for compensation 'in their own right' only in so far as their personal property was affected.[195] The German civil code (BGB) did, however, entitle a wife 'to attend to her husband's affairs on his behalf and to represent him', within the bounds of her 'domestic sphere', and so wives could submit claims for war damage compensation and take legal action on their own authority, provided their power as persons entrusted with the household was involved. The RSA took that to mean principally everyday items, clothing, and household goods that were urgently needed after an air raid. The husband did in fact have to be interviewed before the war damage office could make a decision and no payment or advance could be made without the husband's permission. The offices were not, however, entirely happy with this, for in view of the distance between a bombed-out family back home and a soldier at the front it made much more sense if a wife could use her husband's authority even beyond the domestic sphere.

To the judges at the highest level of the war damages court the mainte-nance of male dominance in the compensation process was more important than this practical simplification of procedures to help wives, which would also have the effect of strengthening their legal status.[196] For, according to the senior judge, Rempel, the limited extent of a wife's power to represent her husband could be 'in the husband's interest', if he had had particular reasons for being unwilling to give his wife authority over his affairs before he was called up. The judge had every sympathy with this and, as the resti-tution of property lost through bombing was in general becoming increas-ingly difficult in any case owing to the problem of obtaining supplies, many issues to do with claims that went beyond acute problems were unlikely to be of great significance in practice.

There were further problems with compensation. What happened if premises used for trade were damaged or income from lettings ceased because of bombing? And who paid for damage caused in the course of rescue work or sustained by municipal buildings? At an early stage the RSA called on people to make inventories of their personal possessions including their value, which meant that nothing was considered safe any more and anything and everything on the home front could be lost. And only those who had prepared for this total loss could expect rapid help.

The heavy air raids from 1942 onwards revealed not only the weaknesses in air defence but also the limitations of compensation in practice. Although there was still talk of 'unbureaucratic' and rapid assistance, the level of compensation payments that the Reich had to fund exceeded with increasing frequency the financial estimates of local finance offices. After the first wave of payments resulting from the British raids on Cologne the Reich Finance Minister, Schwerin von Krosigk, as representative of the Reich's financial interests, complained about what he saw as lax checking of compensation payments.[197]

At the beginning of November 1943 Schwerin von Krosigk urged the relevant authorities in regions particularly affected by the air war to adopt a policy of restraint.[198] In his estimation expenditure on compensation in the previous months had reached 'extraordinary levels'. The Finance Minister was concerned about two things: first of all, that state transfers of money would create surplus purchasing power and thus threaten the stability of the currency, with the danger of inflation; secondly, that compensation payments would place too heavy a burden on the Reich budget. He considered the over-generous compensation payments made by some local authorities as one reason for this development.[199] In those areas the victims of bombing had evidently been given too much consideration, probably because officials were bearing in mind the demands of the Nazi Party. 'We must make every effort to ensure order, frugality and respect for even small sums of money': this was Schwerin von Krosigk's message to his civil servants and it meant: rein in the inflated expectations raised at the outbreak of war and examine more carefully than hitherto whether compensation, in the form of cash or material restitution, should or could be paid or might even be deferred to a later time, such as after the war.

According to the Reich Ministry of the Interior the level of compensation for war damage to property claimed by the end of September 1943 amounted to a total of 31.7 billion Reich marks. The prefecture [*Regierungsbezirk*] of Düsseldorf alone was responsible for the lion's share of claims, a good 15 billion Reich marks, comprising as it did large areas of the Ruhr which had been bombed early and frequently.[200] The costs arising from damage to dwellings and commercial property as well as for public property made up only a small part of this sum, as from the beginning of 1942, as Stuckart wrote to Himmler, there had been no reconstruction owing to the air war and many of those affected had not taken any action or rather were not in a position to determine the level of damage precisely. In many cases the task of giving an accurate assessment also went beyond the capabilities of the war damage offices.

They differentiated between various types of damage: first of all, damage to dwellings, which according to the information issued by the Reich Ministry of the Interior amounted by 1 November 1943 to some 325,000 buildings destroyed and not rebuilt, of which 58,000 buildings were in Hamburg alone. The assumption was that up to this point about 1.3 million homes plus contents had been damaged beyond repair. As the rebuilding costs for a home in the Reich were on average around 10,000 Reich marks and the costs of refurnishing and equipping it came to a similar sum, the Ministry of the Interior assumed an estimated total cost for replacing dwellings that were either destroyed or severely damaged and their contents of a good 26 billion Reich marks.

The cost of the second type of damage, damage to commercial and public buildings, was equally difficult to calculate accurately, but the total sum of 30 billion Reich marks was considered realistic. According to the calculations of the Finance Ministry the total damage up to the beginning of November 1943 was likely to be some 60 billion Reich marks. Moreover, the outlook for 1944 was no better. According to the first estimates Allied air operations between November 1943 and February 1944 targeted at Berlin in particular had caused 20 billion Reich marks' worth of additional damage.

In view of the scale of the problem, in August 1943 the Reich Ministry of the Interior had instructed all assessing authorities to pay strict attention to whether a compensation payment was actually economically justified, which in the Ministry's view applied to businesses important to the war effort that urgently needed capital to maintain or increase their production. It applied also in cases where those affected had debts to pay but were no longer able to after suffering bomb damage.

At the same time the Interior Ministry required that the term 'replacement' that the war damage legislation used for material compensation and provision of goods be more broadly interpreted than had often been the case. In future cash would be issued less and less often, it was predicted, because as the war progressed there was less and less opportunity to buy replacements. The Ministry pointed to another matter: although it must not appear that those who had suffered bomb damage were being dictated to, it was nevertheless more important than ever to rein in and reject 'unjustified demands', including those instigated by the offices of the NSDAP.[201]

The policy of symbolic and immediate material compensation for the burdens imposed by war played a key role in securing compliance with the Nazi dictatorship. For that reason it was the local branches of the Party above all that helped people to fill in claim forms, at the same time formulating the requests that those affected presented at the war damage offices.[202] In the minds of local Party functionaries there was no doubt that compensation in the form of replacement goods was crucial in persuading the population to accept mobilization in wartime and in giving their assent to the Nazi dictatorship. For as long as the Reich was capable of replacing property in sufficient quantities it could go on hoping for support in a war that implicated the mass of those affected by bombing as beneficiaries of a Europe-wide campaign of plundering. For that reason Nazi media went into detail about new decisions made by the war damage offices, for example on the question of whether the state was obliged to stump up for the loss of people's stamp collections.[203]

The answer was typical of the ambivalent compensation practice from 1942/3 onwards. The Reich War Damage Office stated that the Reich was in principle liable to compensate for the loss. At the same time it pointed out that in wartime conditions it was impossible to replace stamps or only at prices that significantly exceeded those of the pre-war period. The cost of replacements could not in other words determine the amount of compensation. The Reich's obligation to replace the stamps was therefore acknowledged 'in principle' in a preliminary assessment but the application of the war damage decree deferred until after the war. Thus those concerned were put off to an indefinite point in the future but at the same time their hope of restitution was bound up with future victory and with the political survival of National Socialism.

In a circular letter to the war damage offices at the end of September 1943 the Reich Ministry of the Interior gave strict instructions from now on to make decisions only in the most urgent cases. The Ministry did not subscribe to the illusion repeatedly created by propaganda that the 'national community' would be able to meet all demands for compensation thanks to its drive and solidarity, for it was evidently convinced that the war situation meant that for the foreseeable future furniture and household contents could not be replaced. That being the case, it seemed permissible to adapt cash compensation payments to the reduced opportunities for obtaining replacements—and that meant either deferral or limited pay-outs, varied according to the demands on the particular war damage office.[204] The consequence of this was that the assessment thresholds for direct compensation grew more and more stringent.

In July 1944 the newly appointed Reich Minister of the Interior, Heinrich Himmler, ruled that compensation payments should be reduced once again: to cover people's needs after an air raid they were to be reduced to 500 Reich marks for the first person in a household, 200 for the second, and 100 for each additional person.[205] Although Himmler, like Göring before him at the very start of the war, issued a warning about the threat to the population's 'mood' if compensation arrangements descended into 'pettiness', he none the less emphasized how dramatic the consequences would be for the currency and for retail prices if unwarranted cash pay-outs were made.

In practice this meant above all that to a great extent the compensation process was deferred.[206] In cases of substantial damage the instruction was to issue only a preliminary assessment. By contrast with the decisions of the Reich War Damage Office (RSA) this move was not, however, made public and every effort was made to maintain the impression of generosity. The war damage judge Bernhard Danckelmann was indignant when a senior civil servant in the higher administrative court allegedly claimed that the notion of making Germany's enemies pay for the costs of war would have to be dropped, leaving the Reich to shoulder its own debts.[207] Anyone who asserted that it was indefensible to compensate those affected for loss of use if they did not absolutely need assistance was, said Danckelmann, 'contradicting the wishes of the Reich government'. What was most feared was in other words the moment when the policy of putting people off would be plain for all to see and a compensation system based on plunder and murder collapsed. The claims of propaganda and the actual practice of compensation could not have been further removed from each other.

Once there were no more resources to distribute and the progress of the air war had made the problems of providing for people increasingly difficult, the regime turned more and more from 1943/4 onwards to repression to keep loyalty to, and what remained of confidence in, the regime alive. Offences related to claims were treated with increasing harshness and more and more frequently even minor infringements were dealt with under the Decree against Public Vermin. At the same time the regime set about prosecuting cases of fraud and publicly shaming those accused in order to create at least a sense of 'justice' being done in the spirit of the national community. For if the sums being paid out were getting smaller and smaller and preliminary assessments were making people wait more and more often until the war was over, it was at least important to maintain the appearance of bureaucratic normality and not to accelerate even more the erosion of confidence already observable in many quarters. When, however, the Reich's finances were largely exhausted and the property plundered from others distributed, the only response was a further escalation of violence.

Thus criminal and war compensation legislation were both part of the same battle on the home front to secure compliance with the dictatorship by means of bribery and repression. Offences against war damage laws could be tried under special wartime criminal law and thus punished not only with imprisonment but also with penal servitude and in particular cases with the death penalty. Anyone who harmed 'the community's aid organization', according to Thierack, the Reich Minister of Justice, with reference to war damage legislation, must be 'ruthlessly' punished because such people were exploiting the war situation and the helpfulness and trust of the authorities.[208] This was particularly true, he explained, of owners of businesses who attempted to enrich themselves by putting a very high price on the damage they were claiming for and he cited the case of a 30-year-old furniture dealer who was said to have set the value of his losses 40,000 Reich marks above their true level and was caught. In such a case the only punishment possible was a death sentence.

The crucial factor in sentencing in the case of offences against war damage laws was, as Thierack emphasized, the motive. If the special court judged that greed was the motive it was clear that the guilty parties had to be sentenced as 'vermin'; if they could credibly attest that the motive for giving false information had been a fear of possibly receiving less compensation than they were due then the court could sentence them 'merely' to imprisonment. In other words, much depended on the special court judges and their interpretation of *völkisch* norms of criminal justice. What this meant became apparent, for example, to a woman with several children who lived in a municipal women's hostel.[209] After an air raid she had applied to the war damage office for coupons to a value of 71 Reich marks for shoes for her children, even though she had not suffered any damage. The special court condemned her on the basis of the Decree against Public Vermin to two years' penal servitude and two years' loss of civil rights—quite rightly so, according to Thierack, who considered the heavy sentence appropriate because the accused woman had been an 'inferior person'. *Völkisch* racism and social disciplining went hand in hand when air-raid damage was being dealt with in practice: first of all when plundered property was being distributed and then in the regime's death throes when an ever-expanding number of groups of 'useless' people were subjected to public exclusion.

Even though compensation in practice was falling ever more short of what had been promised, in the public sphere at least no doubts were to be allowed to develop either with regard to the process or to the 'justice' of it as an expression of the 'national community'. Or, to put it another way, if the preliminary assessments of the war damage offices were no longer dependable, then at least the repressive nature of the regime was.

4

Cities at War

Preparations for War

Repression and compensation, administrative adaptation, and the control of information were all aspects of the attempt by Britain and Germany, albeit in different ways, to organize their societies under a state of emergency. This was particularly true of urban life. Thus this chapter examines the role of local government in overcoming the crisis created by the bombing campaigns, its importance for maintaining morale, and the strategies used and provisions made to help those who had been bombed out.

To begin with, the removal of damage and the provision of initial aid were urban problems and so local government had a particular responsibility. But how did it exercise this responsibility? What kinds of conflicts developed between central and local government? What role was played by the different British and German administrative traditions and what effect did the growth in power of the Nazi Party during the war have on the situation in Germany? Finally, the chapter deals with the notion of 'bombing as an opportunity', with the various plans discussed during the war for the postwar reorganization of urban life, plans in which the different visions of and social models for the 'national community' and the 'People's War' found expression.

Local government and the state in Britain

On paper, the city authorities and ministries in Britain made intensive preparations for the threat of aerial warfare. Long before the first bombs fell, central and local government had wrestled with the issue of how to organize civil defence to fit in with the existing British civilian administrative structures without too many clashes. This was in fact fraught with all kinds

of difficulties because local government possessed a complex structure of
rights and responsibilities, in some cases dating back centuries. The central
government, for example, could not delegate new responsibilities simply by
passing a law, let alone, as was the case in Nazi Germany, use a 'Führer decision' to abolish the federal system overnight.

The provincial decision-makers kept a jealous watch over their sovereign
rights. This was not only a question of their responsibilities and the growing fear of the expansion of central authority but also affected the financing
of the costs of the war. For the local authorities were not happy about having to pay for civil defence measures in addition to the increasing burden of
welfare payments they had to carry.[1] Local authorities from Land's End to
John O'Groats complained that this was the state's responsibility.

After much debate the two sides agreed on a procedure by which local
authorities were put in charge of civil defence but the costs were largely
borne by central government. The Air Raid Precaution Act of 1937 was
particularly notable in that for the first time it established a division of
labour in which civil defence became a core task for local authorities in an
emergency. The local authorities prepared the emergency plans, coordinated aid, recruited volunteers, and appointed air-raid wardens, while central government retained the right to inspect whether the preparations were
adequate and in order.

However, even before the air raids began a row developed over how seriously the cities were preparing for war. There were big regional differences,
which stemmed partly from the poorer northern cities' lack of money and
partly from the fact that Labour local authorities were fundamentally suspicious of the militarization of civilian life and therefore concentrated their
energies on other areas of local government. At a conference organized by
the Home Office in October 1938 the police complained about the, in
some cases, catastrophic state of the preparations. The chief constables criticized the lack of activity in almost all the large cities. The Manchester
police chief, John Maxwell, made no bones about his disgust. Civil defence
was a task of national importance and yet up to now the local authorities
had simply produced a lot of paper. But when it came to putting the plans
into action all initiatives came to nothing for reasons of cost.[2]

That may have been somewhat exaggerated, but nevertheless government representatives repeatedly complained about inefficiency and the
inadequate state of the preparations, which resulted from the difficulty of
reconciling the interests of local and central government. Leading members

of the cabinet were wary of announcing peremptory and authoritarian decisions for fear of jeopardizing the credit they would need when it came to mobilizing the nation for war. Thus laborious dialogue rather than control from above would have to be the way to achieve a settlement with local government.

Regional Commissioners acted as travelling mediation committees in the defence zones into which the country had been divided, tasked with the responsibility, in consultation with the local authorities, of reviewing the state of mobilization and of controlling operations in the event of a catastrophe. Originally created in 1926 as a mechanism for dealing with crises at the time of the general strike, they were now intended to act as an extended arm of the Home Office and to carry on the government in the provinces in the event of invasion and a total collapse of communications, if necessary wielding dictatorial powers. This exceptional position was controversial apart from anything else because it had not been clearly established under what concrete circumstances a state of emergency could be declared, and this was very much in the hands of the Regional Commissioners themselves.

However, so long as a crisis had not occurred they had no authority over local government. The Commissioners had a staff and were obliged to consult with representatives of the police and army and with experts from the administration and the aid services. Their main function was to mediate on a daily basis, to coordinate civil defence, and to control the flow of information between central government and the provinces.[3] As Britain, unlike Germany with its states [*Länder*], Gaus, or strong prefects [*Regierungspräsidenten*], had no intermediate level of coordination, the Commissioners soon became an indispensable link between Whitehall and the provinces.

They were in charge of the preparations for the air war. In the meantime the local authorities had also set up an organization to enable them to respond rapidly to air raids. An Emergency Committee was established to organize the clearing of the damage.

The set-up was entirely predicated on consensus and mutual control and on the conviction that above all aid must be organized on a local and quasi-neighbourly basis and should not come 'from above'. The Regional Commissioners derived their power from their control over the flow of information and not from the right to issue orders. Nevertheless, as a result of the growing threat from the air, the relationship between the central and local government had started to change. On the one hand, local government had begun to acquire increasing responsibility for air defence with its broad range of tasks; on the other hand, this meant that central government acquired more of a right to participate in decisions on local issues.

Thus the preparations for war were no longer the preserve of the city council but were now subject to regular inspection by government representatives. In this respect air defence matters were a sphere where a shift in the balance of power between the two authorities was occurring, even if this became apparent only gradually. The local authorities were extremely irritated by this new division of responsibilities, as well as by the ministries' elaborate attempts to regulate and control them. There were numerous complaints not only about the increase in work involved but also of administrative chaos and the duplication of activities. Thus, in addition to his traditional administrative tasks, the Town Clerk was now also responsible for the organization of civil defence, the housing of people who had been bombed out, looking after evacuees, and the provision of food supplies—a mammoth task for which the plans were often not worth the paper they were written on. Moreover, local government officials complained about over-regulation. Because there was no agency linking local and central government and coordination between the ministries was sometimes lacking, the local authorities claimed they were receiving contradictory instructions, which was particularly irritating when these involved financial commitments. However, it was the sheer weight of information that evidently made some of those involved feel like giving up. One official of a town in southern England reported to a Mass Observation observer that in the space of two weeks he had received over 500 memoranda, orders, and instructions.[4]

'The national community at war' and air defence

Whereas in Britain the idea that there could be a terrible bombing campaign was well understood and discussed in public, in Germany the Nazi authorities had initially emphasized Germany's desire for peace in their propaganda, thereby downplaying the likelihood of a threat. Although there had been air-raid exercises, people were generally vague about what might happen.[5] They were convinced that there would be sufficient capacity to house those who had been bombed out within the city boundaries and nobody contemplated large-scale evacuations, or if they did the plans of air defence experts rarely came to anything.[6] After all, defence was not a notion appropriate to the combative stance of a 'national community at war'. Thus the neglect of air defences was a logical consequence of their aggressive policy of expansion.

By the end of 1939 the city authorities had established new food offices and rationing offices, which were subsequently specially adapted to cope with the effects of war.[7] In Cologne, for example, the existing welfare office was restructured because the original plans had not envisaged how devastating the air raids would be and the resulting burden imposed on the city's welfare facilities.[8] Special departments were created to deal with emergency accommodation, the feeding of those affected by the bombing, the securing of household goods, and the provision of information about those who had been killed or were missing. Other offices were added: the War Damage Office, the War Welfare Agency, which looked after those who had been injured, as well as the Claims Office.[9]

Leipzig, like Nuremberg,[10] had concentrated all tasks to do with the war in one department: cooperation with the Wehrmacht, civil defence and the construction of bunkers, the Rationing and Food Offices, the provision of welfare for those affected by bombing, and the fire brigade.[11] Augsburg established a department with the title 'Reich Defence' directly subordinate to the Oberbürgermeister, which was tasked with preparing for emergencies in association with other city agencies.[12] In Duisburg and Essen the city authorities had also established crisis units focusing on air defences and the care of the victims of bombing.[13]

In Britain this kind of specialization never happened[14] because among other things, local government operated under a different legal system. For while the rights of local authorities in Britain were not substantially revised as a result of the outbreak of war and they resisted all attempts to erode these rights, the Local Government Law of 30 January 1935 had already removed the autonomy of local government in Germany, subjecting the local authorities to the will of the Nazi government and strengthening the position of the Nazi Party. And so when, on 29 August 1939, the local authorities were reduced by a 'Führer decree' to mere agencies of the Reich authorities this was hardly more than the conclusion of a process that had already begun with Hitler's appointment as Reich Chancellor on 30 January 1933.[15]

However, political reality could be very different from constitutional theory and it was above all the local Nazi Party organizations that ensured that, contrary to the legal position, the local authorities were by no means merely agents of the Reich authorities, but retained considerable freedom of action. For although their local autonomy had been progressively eroded, the fact that the centralization of the administration led to the cities and towns becoming agents of the regional and national state administration meant that they acquired numerous new tasks through the back door, so to speak. At the grass roots of the regime this 'totalitarian network'[16] of local authorities and local Party organizations acted as a seismograph for the national community's 'state of mind'; it had its ear to the ground listening to the population's aspirations and concerns and acted as the backbone of the home front, doing everything possible to keep the war machine oiled and running.

Its role in dealing with the effects of air raids was one reason for this paradox and that in a dual sense: it countered the threat that they posed and at the same time acted as a dynamo in this war of plunder and annihilation.[17] The Nazi city administrations adapted local government and administration to wartime conditions, backed the war up with propaganda, and thus through their administrative activities and by providing local support formed the central pillar upholding the Nazi war effort.

The city administrations were, for example, responsible for the organization of food supplies and the regulation of their consumption. The same was true as far as dealing with the effects of air raids was concerned: even before 1939 the demands on the cities had already begun to change in the light of the propaganda surrounding the preparations for aerial warfare. The construction of bunkers and air-raid shelters was the responsibility of the cities. However, given the lack of financial support from the Reich and the dominant view that the war would be fought mainly beyond the frontiers of the Reich, and also given the economic requirements of war, elaborate arrangements for air-raid protection appeared neither necessary nor financially sensible. People were later to pay dearly for this negligence.

Plunder and Aid

Apart from the problems of civil defence, local government became involved above all in the welfare of and compensation for those affected by bombing, which developed into a major focus of local administration.[18] While some other departments within city administrations had largely ceased to operate, the so-called registration authorities, which were responsible for dealing with war damage, were expanding their activities. They often took over personnel from other departments, but first they had to fight for their place within the administrative structures of local government.

The institutional solutions that were reached varied according to the size of the local authority and were dependent not least on the balance of power between the city administration and the local Nazi Party and also on the local impact of the war. There were no authoritative rules for how local authorities should deal with the administration of wartime crises. Instead there were frequent contacts between local government officials and the Local Government Association [*Deutsche Gemeindetag*], a professional organization representing local government, in which views and experiences were exchanged about how to deal with air raids. What were the most efficient administrative structures for dealing rapidly with war damage? What welfare measures were necessary? How could one cope best with damaged buildings? How could unnecessary administrative friction, chaos, bottlenecks, and duplication be avoided? And how could the administration be adapted to the conditions of aerial warfare in such a way that maximum effectiveness could be achieved?

For in the case of all the various attempts at solutions one thing was clear: popular support for the regime was also dependent on its bureaucratic efficiency. The Nazi state could be fairly sure that the home front would not be broken by a 'stab in the back', as it believed had happened in November 1918, only if it succeeded in fulfilling its propaganda boast that it could keep Allied pilots out of Germany. Or, to put it another way, the administrative handling of the emergency was an essential aspect of a successful war of conquest, for which local government officials were expected to prepare the ground. The first air raids on the Rhineland and Westphalia in 1940 had already demonstrated the vulnerability of Germany's borders and led local authorities to begin to investigate ways and means of responding to the threat both flexibly and efficiently. They focused on five issues in particular: the organization of the registration office, caring for those who had been bombed out, the recovery of furniture from bombed buildings, the repair, renovation, or rebuilding of flats and buildings that had been damaged or destroyed, as well as the replacement of lost household goods and other items.[19]

After the first air raids in the years 1940/1 the city of Düsseldorf created a special department for the removal of damage caused by air raids, which was directly subordinate to the Oberbürgermeister. The department covered every aspect of war damage. The city worked on the assumption that it was not a 'normal' city department, but was carrying out national functions and so could make use of the services of the police and of other city institutions. At the beginning of March 1942 around fifty personnel were working in three sections, which dealt with damage to property, buildings, and services.

Up to this point people in Düsseldorf who had suffered damage had put in around 32,000 claims; two-thirds of the claims for damage to buildings had been dealt with and in the case of damage to property, which mostly covered damage to personal effects such as clothing, household goods, or furniture, 84 per cent of the claims had already been processed.[20]

During this early phase of the air war it was still possible to settle claims for damage to property, which were often for no more than 500 Reich marks, on the day after an air raid. Claims that were higher than that were not processed immediately but were subject to further examination involving the police, who assessed the damage. Up to 5,000 Reich marks the Düsseldorf office, like the other war damage offices in the Reich, was permitted to act on its own authority, but for any claims above that the 'Reich representative' had to be consulted. The city was very careful to ensure that its own funds were not used to settle claims for damage. Once a month the city's buildings department prepared an account which was then agreed and paid by the Reich.

Hamburg had opted for a somewhat different organizational solution. Here the office was part of the buildings administration and made use of the infrastructure of other departments. Thus the first assessment of damage was in the hands of the office of the buildings police,[21] which by the spring of 1942 had already received some 180,000 claims and had paid more than 100 million Reich marks in compensation from the Reich finances. As in other cities, the Hamburg war damage experts set up a number of branch offices where those affected could submit their claims and which as a rule were housed in the premises of the local Nazi Party. There must therefore have been few Hamburgers who did not come into direct contact via this route with the NSDAP as a 'service provider' in the bombing war.

Hanover was no different. Here claims could be submitted to the municipal buildings department, the authority in charge of war damage, only through the local Nazi Party.[22] In addition, the local branch had the task of entering the cause of the damage on the claim form and if possible suggesting the cost. Where local Nazi functionaries were not in a position or were unwilling to give precise information, the war damage offices were responsible for pursuing the case. In Düsseldorf the war damage office and the local Nazi Party leadership agreed on a more elaborate arrangement: the offices handed the files of victims of bomb damage to the local Party branches and they checked the details of the bomb damage certificates once more. By doing this they were assuming prerogatives originally enjoyed by the administration in a major matter of policy relating to the national community.[23] The Nazi block leader had the job of checking claims, though he was sworn to secrecy, for this type of surveillance did not seem at all to be in line with the approachability that the regime was trying to project in its system of dealing with war damage. As in Hamburg, those who had been bombed received money for essential everyday items from the social services office and advance payments from the assessment office itself. The items that people who had been completely bombed out could claim were goods made of iron or steel such as saucepans, cutlery, tin openers, or bread knives. A two-person household could also claim plates, a meat dish or milk jug, a salt cellar, and a chamber pot as necessary items.[24]

Those staffing the offices were urged to treat 'national comrades' generously and obligingly as 'customers' not as supplicants. Staff should not be put out, even if those who had suffered damage were 'somewhat agitated',[25] as guidelines issued by the Hanover war damage office put it. For damage costing up to 1,000 Reich marks it was not normally necessary for the claimant concerned to attend in person, as long as the paperwork seemed in order. In the case of larger amounts the claimants had to be interviewed and the office might have to use its own investigators to check the damage on behalf of the war damage office.[26]

In Hanover a detailed procedure had been designed for Jews and people born of marriages of Jews and non-Jews (Mischehen), the first principle of which was as clear as it was simple: Jews could not make claims for damage. This applied also to businesses in Jewish hands, concerning the ownership of which the chambers of industry and commerce provided information. If a Jew was suspected of disguising himself as an 'Aryan' the claimant had to produce details of his family background going back to his four grandparents.[27] In cases of 'mixed marriage' the claimant's 'Aryan' background also had to be checked. In doubtful cases where it was difficult to decide whether the claimant was a 'Jew' or not the officials dealing with them had to refer the decision to a superior.

In contrast to smaller towns and cities that had as yet been less affected by bombing[28] local government in the west and north of the Reich had been forced from the middle of 1942 onwards to commit ever-increasing resources to coping with war damage.[29] To keep on top of the growing mountain of claims, procedures had already become more formalized. One of the main problems was checking the amount of compensation claimed. The war damage offices could draw on qualified staff from other municipal organizations or from the chamber of trades to make a precise assessment. The number of people affected and the severity of the damage grew from one month to the next and there was an awareness that shortages of staff because of the war and the growing number of cases must not lead to a drop in quality in the way they were dealt with. In the opinion of a senior civil servant in the Reich Ministry of the Interior, the administration must impart a sense of security to the population. Bomb damage had, he said, an 'absolutely huge' impact on people's daily lives and so, in the area of compensation in particular, 'special care' should be taken and those who had not yet been affected by the air war, above all in rural areas, should prepare especially carefully for the possibility of catastrophe.[30]

It was not therefore just blatant propaganda when the representative of the Reich Ministry of the Interior in discussion with local government experts insisted that the latter had to understand that they must spare victims lengthy journeys and treat them appropriately and generously, while helping them to receive their due. In other words the hardships of the air war had to be relieved through rapid compensation, thus ensuring that in the midst of catastrophe 'national comrades' gained an impression of peace and order in local administration.[31]

At least up to 1942, before the full force of the bombing was felt, most cities succeeded with just a few hiccups in organizing compensation fairly smoothly. That at least was indicated in the authorities' internal reviews. In Kiel by the end of May 1942 some 48,000 damage claims had been submitted, of which around 22,600 had been settled.[32] A mere 216 complaints had been made in connection with damage to property claims and 101 of them could be dealt with. The claimant had raised an objection in less than 1 per cent of the cases processed.

In practice, dealing with war damage varied from region to region and depended largely on the degree and timing of the damage. In Cologne, Essen, and Düsseldorf the authorities were confronted earlier than in the south or south-west with virtually insoluble problems in dealing with cases quickly because the amount of damage and the number of potential claimants consumed resources and the budget more and more rapidly. From 1943 at the latest the gap between making a claim and having it settled had become unbridgeable throughout Germany and the fulsome assurances were unmasked as empty propaganda. At the end of the war in Nuremberg barely one in three out of the approximately 123,000 compensation claims for damage to buildings or loss of use was settled, the majority of them having been submitted in the final twelve months of the war, when the bombing extended even to the 'city of the Party Rallies'. The backlog in cities that had been more heavily bombed or had been bombed from the beginning of the war, as in the Rhineland, was even larger.

In Düsseldorf complaints about long waiting times had been growing since 1943/4.[33] By May 1944 a good 430,000 cases of war damage had been reported there, of which a mere 167,400 had been settled. After every subsequent air raid the authorities reckoned with an additional 60,000 claims, though the Düsseldorf city administration knew full well that this number did not reflect all those who were entitled to claim, because the struggle of everyday existence meant that many were not yet able to submit a claim at all.

Where there was significant damage, finding replacement items was evidently hopeless; the destruction was too great and the supplies of replacement items too small. In spring 1944 the authorities in Berlin had decided in future to 'suspend' processing claims for damage to household goods in view of 'present circumstances', as the language of officialdom put it. The supply situation meant that a 'just' distribution could not be guaranteed until after the war.[34] In fact it was not at all the issue of the fairness of state welfare procedures that heralded the end of compensation payments but the critical situation pure and simple. Although the validity of claims was to continue being assessed 'in principle', there was no provision for any payment. The Berlin war damage office also decided to adopt so-called 'normative valuation procedures', which determined compensation with reference to average incomes and so abandoned individual assessments in favour of standard payments. Where the value of the damage clearly exceeded the norm there was to be a careful examination and assessment based on pre-war values.[35]

The administrative practice of the local authority offices was therefore not at all dependent only on the directives of the central Reich authorities.[36] At times the war damage offices had considerable discretion and were able to use it, much to the annoyance of the central authorities, in the interest of claimants.[37] At the same time, however, they could promote increased stringency in the procedural rules. In Nuremberg in March 1943 the war damage office proposed examining whether claimants were themselves partially responsible for their losses. After the air raids had provoked a 'mass flight on the part of residents', as the war damage office stated, damage to the 'city of Party rallies' had been particularly serious, because in fleeing many people had abandoned their duty as members of the national community to protect themselves by fighting fires. These people were therefore to some extent themselves to blame for the destruction, as the office suggested, and thus in many cases had forfeited the right to compensation.[38] Although it was hard to prove this in individual cases, 'for educative reasons alone something must be done', as the office insisted. For it seemed indefensible that rescue services should protect the homes of people who by fleeing from the city to relatives in the country had not been prepared to share the fate of the national community.

Thus the war damage offices were not simply an executive arm of the Reich during this crisis but could contribute to the escalating radicalization and, if their suspicions were raised, could prompt police to investigate claimants, though when these suspicions were unfounded the offices could come under fire from the police themselves, which happened in Düsseldorf.[39]

This specifically Nazi way in which local government coped with the crisis caused by the air war is demonstrated even more clearly by its attempts to 'obtain replacement furniture'. War damage compensation and 'replacement' were closely related to the plunder, persecution, and deportation of German Jews.[40] Anti-Jewish policies and local government attempts to tackle the air war went hand in hand.[41] The official removal of Jewish property was part of the remit of the Reich financial administration, which had been responsible for the 'administration and liquidation' of confiscated Jewish property since the start of the large-scale deportations in the autumn of 1941.[42] The possibility of using it to meet the needs of those affected by bombing had been considered at an early stage. The distribution of the property had, however, caused major power struggles between the financial authorities, the Reich Security Main Office, the NSDAP and its Gau headquarters, and local government.

Although local authorities had staked a claim to the vacant homes for bombing victims as soon as deportations began,[43] the financial authorities had secured priority access to moveable goods, intending to use the plundered items for their offices and convalescent homes and auction the rest for the state coffers. Although the Nazi welfare organization (NSV) and the municipalities were supposed to cooperate in the sale of all other items, they had no monopoly over them, for private dealers in second-hand goods could also be used by the finance authorities to secure the Reich a high price for the confiscated items, in fact a price they hoped would be higher than the municipalities, the Party, or the bombing victims themselves could pay at public auction. Given the unclear procedures, decisions about what share bombing victims were to receive of plundered Jewish possessions were often not made until they came to be liquidated, and how this was done varied greatly and was dependent to a considerable extent on the air war.

In dealing with the population some financial authorities were open about the connection between deportation and compensation. Internally the guideline was: 'first principle: comfort for the Reich financial adminis-tration. Make the offices luxurious.'[44] Conflicts were therefore inevitable. In Nuremberg representatives of the city and of the regional finance office had met immediately after the Reich Finance Minister's announcement that deportations were imminent in order to work out jointly a procedure for 'securing items from Jewish households for victims of bombing'.[45]

At that point it was not yet clear how extensive or how valuable the Jew-ish property was that now belonged to the Reich after the first major depor-tations of 1941.[46] Yet arguments over the distribution of cupboards, beds, and other furniture were already in full swing because the regional finance office's appointee at first insisted he needed them all for his own use. His view of what should be done was that he should satisfy his needs from the confiscated property and then estimate the value of the remainder, selling it to an intermediary, who would also deal with Jewish houses and flats and the storage of goods. Following the line taken by the Reich Minister of Finance, he insisted on making a profit from 'Jewish property' as quickly as possible and therefore on selling it to the highest bidder.

The representatives of the Nuremberg city administration did not agree with this procedure. As the assessing authority for war damage compensa-tion they insisted on assuming responsibility for the distribution of Jewish property and on passing it on to their own authorities and their staff to be shared out. The city refused to be fobbed off with the leftovers from the expropriations and instead wished to play an active role, after discussion with the Party, in directing the distribution.

From the start of the deportations the Nuremberg Gau's business adviser had tried to get control of Jewish property that had been confiscated or which Jews had wished to sell before their 'departure'. The city did not, however, want to auction the goods on the open market but rather to prompt selected firms to acquire them so that in the event of an air raid they could be distributed. No one envisaged that acquiring them would pose any financial problem and if necessary the city savings bank could step in with a loan to the local authority.[47] After some debate the city and finance office arrived at a compromise on how Jewish property was to be used in future. Experts from the city administration were to estimate the value of the furniture and homes that were not required by the finance office and removal firms were to bring the household goods to warehouses. From there they were to be distributed to victims of bombing.

The procedure for this followed more or less the same pattern everywhere: after reporting their losses and having their claim for war damage approved those affected received money or coupons with which to buy goods or obtain them at auction at the Reich's expense. The identification issued by the local Nazi Party branch when the claim was submitted allowed them to take part in regulated competition for Jewish property. The proceeds from the sales went directly to the coffers of the regional finance office.[48] The property of 299 Jews deported from Fürth brought in some 66,000 Reich marks to the municipal finance department, which was then sent on to the Reich finance office.[49] In Oldenburg between 1942 and 1944 the city was able to record around 467,000 Reich marks as 'General Administrative Income' from the sale of Jewish property.[50]

Finally, from June 1942 onwards the regional finance offices took on complete responsibility for the process of liquidating Jewish property, though only after there had been repeated arguments between the Berlin headquarters and the regional branches over the scope of their powers to deal with it. At the same time, the various administrations began to take stock of Jewish property they had already acquired and were expecting to acquire. In so doing they were consciously building the radicalization of anti-Jewish policy into their calculations of how local government would tackle emergencies.

At a meeting at the beginning of September 1942 attended by the head of the Nuremberg regional finance office, the Nuremberg-North finance office, and representatives of the city an agreement was reached in the light of the anticipated 'evacuation' of the 'remaining Jews' from Nuremberg and the resulting availability of sixty-nine homes: first the regional finance office was to take over the homes and all the remaining contents from the Gestapo[51] and separate out what was valuable such as paintings, carpets, or stamp collections.[52] The remaining contents stayed in the homes, which were then bought and managed by the city, acting for the Reich, at a price estimated by the finance administration.[53]

In the run-up to this the finance administration had established a precise procedure and established commissions made up of local government employees to set a value on the homes. Thus bombed-out families could rent or buy them and so move into them without long delays. The availability of new homes was to be advertised by public notice, though it applied only to families who had 'lost everything', as confirmed by the local Nazi Party branch. By January 1943, of the 645 Nuremberg families who had been rehoused 127 occupied 'Jewish homes', the owners of which had been deported. According to post-war estimates around 50 per cent of Jewish property in Bavaria had passed into private ownership, 34 per cent was in state hands, and around 10 per cent had been grabbed by the Nazi Party and its organizations.[54]

The victims of bombing were therefore in no way the only and not even the most significant links in the chain of 'property utilization'—in spite of all the attempts made through propaganda to present the deportations as a kind of socio-political redistribution for the benefit of German national comrades. Even though certain patterns recurred, there is evidence to suggest that, as far as victims of bombing were concerned, conflicts over the distribution of plundered property could have different outcomes in cities and in rural areas. In particular in places where the air war had already done great damage by late 1941 and early 1942, in the Rhineland and Westphalia, at least some finance offices evidently supported the distribution of Jewish property to victims of bombing more vigorously than their Bavarian colleagues, who had been much less affected by bombing.

In a letter to the president of the higher regional court immediately after the first deportations of Jews in October 1941 the regional head of finance for Cologne strongly advocated distributing Jews' household goods 'first and foremost' to victims of bombing.[55] In addition, before the heavy raids of May 1942 the district Nazi Party leadership had pressed for those who had lost their homes to be given anything usable via the Nazi welfare organization. They got their way and the usual large-scale auctions[56] did not take place.[57]

Hence the influence of the district leadership of the Nazi Party could have an impact on how the proceeds of 'Aryanization' were shared. Should, as was discussed in the case of Cologne, only those who could prove they were bombing victims by producing certification from the local Party branch be allowed to take part in auctions but not commercial bidders? Or should they be entitled to bid first? These matters were being discussed in the Rhineland from spring 1942 onwards and while the deportations lasted. But what attitude was taken by local authorities and finance offices in regions that in 1941/2 had only just begun to feel the impact of Allied raids?

In Trier the city's rationing office was very reluctant to accept the Cologne finance authorities' request for Jewish household goods, clothes, and linen to cope with the city's destruction. The national community's solidarity quickly ran out when people feared that the course of the war would soon make them the target of raids.[58] For this reason rationing offices in areas as yet less affected by bombing created their own stores of supplies, for example of Jewish crockery or cutlery, for future distribution. People seemed certain that the air war would continue and affect areas hitherto spared bombing—and so Jewish property would come in very useful.

At the same time, in the summer of 1942, the municipal rationing and welfare offices in many places were acquiring a new task. Up to this point public auctions of Jewish property at 'full value' had often been directly commissioned by the Reich financial administration. In many places these duties were now taken over by the municipal authorities, which from a fiscal point of view could only be advantageous, for the rationing and welfare offices paid the maximum price set by the pricing authority for the goods and as a result the Reich finance offices could save the costs of the auctions and pass the savings on to local government. This was particularly true given that especially valuable items could still be reserved by the Reich financial authorities to use themselves.

From the standpoint of the finance offices the matter was settled, for the best price had in the end been obtained for the confiscated goods and that had been the primary aim and more important than who finally received them. In some instances they referred to the needs of those who had been bombed out simply as a tactic in the negotiations with the various parties with an interest in Jewish property in order to achieve the best price for the exchequer.[59] For the city authorities, on the other hand, this matter in particular was of considerable importance, for now they could organize the distribution and disposal of Jewish property themselves via the Nazi welfare organization in large public spaces such as the Cologne trade fair premises in Deutz or the Düsseldorf stockyards and ensure that victims of bombing, who had often lost out at public auctions, were now given a fair crack of the whip under the Party's protection.

Thus, to the delight of the financial authorities, the city administrations took over the task of transporting and storing the items, which as a result incurred no further costs.[60] As the air war became more extensive the Reich Ministry of Finance searched for a solution to this conflict of aims, namely on the one hand to raise as much money as possible for the state coffers and on the other to provide victims of bombing with furnishings at a time of diminishing resources.[61] In the cities' view, however, the acute shortages were decisive, persuading them to agree to this division of responsibilities and to relieve the exchequer of the costs and the risk associated with administering and disposing of Jewish property.[62] In rural areas from the summer of 1942 it was the mayors and district rationing offices above all that took care of the distribution of Jewish property and responded to any enquiries about it—and there were a good number of these during and even before the start of the deportations.[63]

The 'liquidation' of Jewish property was therefore a public event that the population used as a huge bargain basement. The aim was, after all, as they said in Hamburg,[64] 'to get the goods out at suitable prices to as large a section of the population as possible'. Occasionally notice of the auctions was given in the press.[65] Sometimes press announcements were subject to the agreement of the head of the finance office who, as in Darmstadt, would give it only in exceptional cases. In rural areas auctions could be held at short notice by word of mouth in order to keep competition and too many rival bidders away.[66]

The market in 'Aryanized' goods for bombing victims was boosted from late 1941/early 1942 by another predatory initiative; prompted by Alfred Rosenberg, Hitler had agreed at the end of 1941 to the confiscation of Jewish property in the Netherlands, Luxembourg, Belgium, and France and its distribution to the population in areas hit by bombing under the stewardship of the 'Rosenberg task force'. The SS, finance authorities, customs offices, and city administrations worked closely together on distributing the plundered Jewish property. By the end of July 1944 the Western Office had 'registered' almost 70,000 Jewish houses and apartments and dispatched their contents to territories affected by the air war. Six hundred and seventy-four trains with some 27,000 wagons set off from Antwerp and Paris towards the west and north of Germany to the regions that had been most heavily bombed. In the first phase the Ruhr area, Münster, Düsseldorf, Osnabrück,

Hamburg, Lübeck, and Karlsruhe were the principal recipients of linen, crockery, cutlery, and toys and after that other cities, even in the south and south-west, benefited from the increasingly efficient authorities.

As the Allied air raids intensified the demand for goods grew, prompting in its turn another more extensive wave of 'registration' and deportation,[67] the culmination of which for most Jews was Auschwitz and for their furniture the railway stations of Cologne-Lindenthal, Essen-Borbeck, or Hamburg-Dammtor.[68] Between March 1942 and July 1943 Hamburg alone received 45 shiploads from Holland, containing 27,000 metric tons of furniture, household goods, and clothing that were intended primarily for the victims of bombing.[69] In total some 100,000 inhabitants of the city and the surrounding area are likely to have benefited between 1941 and 1945 from plundered Jewish property, which, in the words of one of the auctioneers speaking after the war, went 'for the most part for knockdown prices' without arousing significant moral qualms.[70]

In Hamburg, moreover, Karl Kaufmann, the Gauleiter, had requisitioned 3,000 to 4,000 shipments of property belonging to Jewish emigrants from Germany that had not been sent by the time war broke out and forwarded the proceeds of the sale to the Gestapo—7.2 million Reich marks by the beginning of 1943.[71] And after the 1,000-bomber raid on Cologne the Gauleiter Josef Grohé noted how smooth, considering the scale of destruction, the delivery of furniture and household goods from Belgium and northern France was, and how useful for coping with the crisis.[72] In order to make up for shortages in provision, the state's financial administration played a key role alongside the local authorities in this process of expropriation and transfer of 'Germanized' property to loyal national comrades; it was a policy propelled by a combination of racism and bureaucratic self-interest.

Local government and coping with crisis in Britain

This specifically German form of coping with crisis at local level had no equivalent in Britain. There was neither an agency that influenced the political landscape at local level and constantly fought to increase that influence, as did the Nazi Party, nor did racism play a role in policy concerning compensation and provisioning, precisely because, by contrast with Germany, 'administrative normality' was preserved.[73]

The British cities that had suffered bombing found themselves under considerable pressure precisely because they could not take advantage of this kind of plundering and were forced to tackle extraordinary circumstances with traditional means. It was a problem faced primarily by industrial cities and London. Since the start of German air raids, for example, Stepney and West Ham, which together had several hundred thousand inhabitants, were among the most heavily hit areas of London. Jewish and Irish immigrants had settled here in East London and given the Labour Party an unassailable majority on the local council. Even before the outbreak of war there had been considerable conflict between the council and Councillor Davis, who had been involved in corruption scandals, primarily because preparations for the air war on the part of the authorities were felt to have been inadequate.[74]

It was above all conditions in the large public shelters, particularly in Tilbury, that had caused an outcry in the press. The scandal kept on growing until the Prime Minister himself intervened and demanded that Davis be immediately replaced as controller of civil defence. Davis and the Civil Defence Committee protested vigorously against the Ministry of Home Security's plans to remove him, the Ministry being altogether conscious of the high-handedness of its intervention. Finally it was decided on the basis of the Civil Defence Regulation to intervene in the local authority and appoint Arnold James, town clerk of Islington, as controller, conferring on him full powers to act in civil defence matters.

This decision was regarded at first as extremely sweeping and positively dangerous. After all, the new appointee had powers that caused *The Times* to speak of a 'civil defence "dictator"'[75] and was quite out of line with the tradition of local autonomy. However conceivable the centralization of powers and the militarization of civil administration had become, the first steps towards the implementation of the Civil Defence Regulation showed how great was the resistance and how important the widest possible consensus was in legitimizing the war.

It was therefore hardly surprising that the reception James got from the local agencies was anything but warm and that in spite of his extensive powers he wore himself out reorganizing civil defence. Important areas of responsibility such as first aid or care of the wounded had already been transferred to the Ministry of Health. Calm did not return until the heavy bombing tailed off in summer 1941 and there had been some respite from air defence, clearing the rubble and housing the homeless, providing food, and constructing shelters.

The desk officer for health matters had repeatedly resisted being told what to do and openly pursued a policy of obstruction. Stepney Borough

Council was not given back responsibility for the homeless until November 1944, after earlier complaints about the local authority's lack of powers had grown so numerous that civil servants had taken over this area of responsibility. Often the controller and local authority failed to pull together to deal with issues such as reconstruction or the distribution of shelters, instead obstructing each other by duplicating work and not assigning tasks clearly.[76] It was probably only the decline in air raids that prevented the overlap in local and central bureaucracies from causing more damage.

In West Ham similar conflicts arose. The heavy bombing in September and October 1940 had hit the working-class area around the docks particularly hard and made thousands homeless. London County Council (LCC) was ill prepared for such a blow and in the period after the raids the administration disintegrated almost completely.[77] When the LCC finally decided to appoint Councillor Hall controller, thus putting him in charge of dealing with the state of emergency, the Regional Commissioner raised the alarm, for the 70-year-old Hall, a long-serving Labour councillor who had just been re-elected, was one of the people responsible for the problems. Finally the Home Security Minister, Herbert Morrison, intervened to appoint a younger candidate, but this was no solution because the new crisis expert rapidly turned out to be a bad appointment. While he was absent from his desk because his daughter was ill in Scotland there had been a further raid. And once again voices were raised in West Ham, accusing the authorities of failing to care for the homeless and put out the fires.

Yet again it looked as if the autonomy of local government would have to be violated, a step that could be averted only because Reverend Paton, who had been newly elected by the LCC, enjoyed enough authority and public support and could rely on the confidence of the Regional Commissioner. The fact that in the end and unlike in Stepney a controller could not be imposed from outside but came from the local community was regarded by many people as a 'victory for democracy', as Richi Calder enthusiastically put it in the *Daily Herald*.[78]

This did not of course make the problems disappear. As the Regional Commissioner reported in August 1941, there was still a lack of coordination and the emergency committee still did not have the powers it really needed.[79] As in Stepney the most urgent problem was looking after the victims of bombing, which was essentially a matter for the LCC and was covered by the 'Poor Law' administration. It gave help to and took responsibility for victims of bombing according to whether they came from the borough in question, in which case that borough was responsible for them, or whether they had sought help at the reception centres after fleeing from other areas. In the latter case central government or their home local authority took care of their needs.

In practice this policy of drawing narrow local boundaries created a great many problems and bureaucratic over-regulation, because every single case had to be dealt with individually and then settled between local government and central government.[80] The decisive factor in the issue of who was responsible for those who had been bombed out was money. Before the air raids began the Ministry of Health had limited payments for emergency accommodation in the Greater London area to £20 in each case. That had just been sufficient for a few beds but not nearly enough to cover larger groups.

At best there were facilities to hand out tea and biscuits but not to cope with thousands of hungry people who after the bombing no longer had anywhere to call home. The idea behind Poor Law provision was not that people would need considerable state support over a lengthy period, indeed that they would even have to be given somewhere else to live. There was provision for emergency aid but not for long-term support. Many working-class districts simply did not have the money and the technical expertise for this, for even staff at the rest centres, the emergency hostels, were not regarded as being particularly experienced in coping with crises. Although in Liverpool there was a growing number of volunteers, their working conditions and the furnishings and equipment supplied were so inadequate, even before the first bombs fell, that for many the burden was too great and the night shifts were not staffed.[81]

There was no comprehensive state network of provision in case of catastrophe but rather the plan was that after recovering for a few hours those affected by bombing would be accommodated by friends and relatives and thus the neighbourhood itself would solve some of the basic problems created by the air war. There had been little detailed consideration of possible ways of apportioning living space, let alone of compulsory state intervention in housing, something which was heavily criticized at the time by those who remembered the air-war experiences of the Spanish Civil War.[82] Even after the first few weeks of German air raids on London in 1940 it quickly became clear how dangerous the poor provision was: the number of homeless rose from week to week and by the end of September had reached around 25,900.[83] London County Council reacted by appointing Henry

Willink Special Commissioner for the Homeless. His principal task, for which he was given extensive powers, was to improve coordination between the LCC and the boroughs and rein in local self-interest.

Willink appointed new staff to the rest centres, organized accommodation for single men whose families had already left London and whose homes had now been destroyed, and saw to it that local authority workers were not primarily employed repairing the authority's buildings but were available to work on private houses too, so that those who needed housing could go back to their provisional accommodation more quickly. In fact the number of homeless steadily reduced in 1941 to some 6,700 by April, the result on the one hand of some let-up in the Luftwaffe's efforts and on the other of effective repair work. Acting on the instructions of the LCC, Willink now pressed hard for the right to requisition living quarters even in the face of resistance and to insist on help from numerous volunteer organizations such as the WVS, the Red Cross, or the Friends' Ambulance Unit.

Care of the homeless was an area of local government policy with huge explosive potential, for at its heart was the issue of how much municipalities and the state were prepared to do for those who were suffering most, the poorer sections of the population. This issue had concerned the government since before the outbreak of war. Initial projections were based on the assumption that the damage incurred in the first three weeks alone would run to the unimaginable sum of £550 million.[84] Half a million bombed-out houses and some one to two million significantly damaged ones—these were the figures the experts considered realistic. Compensation at whatever level would have to wait until after the war, in their view. Conflicts over war damage, insurance against, or compensation for the risks of war continued all the same, in part because it was plain that without some kind of compensation morale on the home front, as in Germany, would suffer. A first step in this direction was the ruling that more needy families could be reimbursed at least part of their outlay to replace furnishings.[85]

In the end the War Damage Act of 1941 regulated compensation for the destruction of homes, possessions, and commercial businesses. There was compensation for damage caused during a period specified by the government, either through the financing of repairs to restore property to its previous state or through direct payments. Before that there was an elaborate procedure for checking claims that stretched far into the post-war period and meant long delays for many claimants.[86] What was changed by the War Damage Act was above all the entitlement to make a claim, for now those affected by bombing could apply for material compensation irrespective of income and social circumstances.

To the homeless—and estimates assumed that some 2.5 million people in Britain fell into this category for a longer or shorter period, of which around two-thirds were in London and the surrounding area[87]—this was small comfort, for their immediate worry was getting hold of warm clothing and a few sticks of furniture. They were given immediate help after an air raid by the Assistance Board, which was part of the municipal social services department and assessed the claims for compensation.[88] Anyone whose household income did not exceed £400 received help; single people had to earn less than £250 and the local authority had the power to curtail payments for clothing and furniture until the tax authorities had conducted a means test.[89]

For those claiming compensation the requirement to go to these offices was very onerous in 1940/1 and resulted in vociferous complaints. In London in particular with its two-tier administration at borough and LCC level, the question of which Board was responsible for which victims of bombing caused much confusion and many visits to the offices in question. Moreover, the officials had up to this point normally dealt with the unemployed and were now responsible not only for implementing new legislation but for a new clientele composed of applicants from a variety of social backgrounds.

In addition to the Assistance Board there were further possible sources of public and private funds in case of need. The WVS provided small sums for linen and clothing in an unbureaucratic way. The Lord Mayor's Fund, which was made up of state and private funds, existed in most cities and was allocated by a working group at local government level. The basis on which payments were made could vary from one city to another. In some places those worst affected could apply directly for assistance as individuals while in others, such as Bristol, money was channelled towards civilian organizations such as the Rotary Club or the churches and they decided how it was to be distributed.[90]

However it was done, the distribution of these special resources was a political matter. Thus as early as September 1940 in Liverpool the unions and the Labour Party had put pressure on the Emergency Committee through an initiative demanding a more active approach to the allocation of vacant living accommodation, furniture, and clothing.[91] Their aim was to put an end to the reticence that in the view of the Labour Party and the unions manifestly shielded only those who already had sufficient resources and family networks at their disposal. In fact this was one of the arguments that the controller had used up to this point: as far as possible people were supposed to make use of their own resources. The scale of devastation had shown this approach now to be inadequate, as had become obvious since the winter of 1940 in Liverpool, which had been bombed from 20 to 22 December.

The local authorities were not obliged to shoulder the cost of accommodating the homeless, which fell to the Ministry of Health. By contrast with traditional poor relief, however, those receiving assistance were not to be treated as paupers. As the Ministry's letter to local authorities stated, they were to be treated as tenants. The accommodation temporarily requisitioned for them was to be made available at an appropriate rate and one that for the local authorities was commercial.[92]

This was, of course, far from simple, for some people had been given short-term accommodation that was clearly beyond their means. Those in power tended to shy away from coercion, preferring to use advertisements in newspapers to encourage people to offer vacant rooms rather than compelling them to rent out unoccupied, still less furnished, accommodation to strangers. Yet this had now become conceivable. Within a few months the provision of emergency accommodation had provoked an intensive debate about how the homeless might be housed in the longer term, if necessary.[93]

The raids the city suffered at the end of November 1940 exacerbated the problem posed by the housing shortage, one factor being, as the Emergency Committee complained to government representatives, that available space was being blocked by servicemen and internees.[94] For most of those bombed out, however, their problems began much earlier. There had already been complaints about the conditions in the reception camps and as a result an inspection was supposed to clarify arrangements and introduce improvements. As the Chief Billeting Officer, who was responsible for immediate assistance, reported, the result left much to be desired.[95] Apart from schools, church halls and meeting rooms staffed by volunteers were among the places where immediate relief was provided. A total of eighty-seven such centres had been inspected in Liverpool. Whereas the official found the infrastructure in schools generally satisfactory, his conclusion on the church halls and adapted public meeting rooms was extremely sobering. Often there were inadequate sanitary facilities; frequently there was only one toilet for men and women and even the provision of food was unsatisfactory. It was no wonder, therefore, that confidence in the competence of the city authorities was manifestly lacking and people voiced strong criticisms in private.[96]

Though the raids had not yet been particularly heavy, from the late autumn of 1940 onwards many cities had been seriously affected by them and had to rely on private initiatives and individual efforts at coping with the damage to make up for the deficiencies in preparation for air raids. It took months for the cities in the south-west and the north to adjust to the raids and to be organized after every wave of bombing to accommodate several thousand people who had not all immediately been taken in by relatives or friends. And yet many places were still way off their target. In Manchester, which was bombed heavily for the first time shortly before Christmas 1940, Mass Observation sources reported that there was particular outrage that provision for the victims was so inadequate, in spite of the fact that there was by now some experience in dealing with heavy bombing. Despite its protestations to the contrary the Emergency Committee had blatantly failed to learn from the first raids. There were no mattresses in the reception centres and even the forms those affected could use to claim support in money and goods and those evacuated needed to apply for a new home were in short supply. It was particularly frustrating that it had evidently taken almost a whole day for the victims to be given a cup of hot tea, and though there were two nurses to give first aid there were hardly any medical supplies.[97] All in all a disaster.

The Extent of Damage and Interregional Strategies for Dealing with Crisis

In August 1942 Liverpool's Emergency Committee took stock for the first time in response to a meeting of representatives of northern cities with the government about the problems of dealing with the crisis. The Ministry of Health feared that after the short period of respite from the summer of 1941 onwards the local authorities might lapse back into their old slapdash ways and neglect the air defence activities that had only just got under way. It did after all seem more than likely that the 1940 autumn of heavy air raids might be followed by an equally massive winter of bombing in 1942, after the Baedeker Raids in the spring had served as a reminder of the vulnerability of cities.[98]

In May 1941 in Liverpool the various local government offices had been consolidated into a special department that attempted to work cooperatively to organize help for the homeless. After initial problems this was a first step towards defining responsibilities and gaining a clear view of shortages in provision. Their primary concern was accommodating those who had been bombed out and so there was a team that inspected possible living quarters and began to gather information on how much capacity there was in private homes, empty schools, and boarding houses.

The city had some 11,600 beds, some 16,400 unfurnished spaces where in an emergency beds could be put up, and around 8,400 private lodgings offered by volunteers, to which people could bring their own furniture. These various types of accommodation were strictly regulated and inspected by a commission. Admittedly this was a long way off the target that the government had issued of emergency provision for some 3 per cent of the population, or in Liverpool's case 20,000 beds a day. A succession of massive raids would have quickly exhausted the available resources, and precisely this had been the city's experience at the end of November 1940 and in May 1941.

Thus it became clear that in view of the looming threat a separate policy for coping with the crisis for each local authority would create considerable costs and as a result from 1941/2 onwards numerous local authorities, facilitated by the Regional Commissioners, formed loose groups to cooperate on emergency plans, rescue services, and the distribution of resources. Bombed cities such as Sheffield, Manchester, and Liverpool exchanged experiences, passed on information about how they dealt with the homeless and provided accommodation, and agreed on the circumstances when mutual assistance would be necessary.

In Britain there was no organization like the German Local Government Association that could pass on knowledge about air defence on an intermediate level between local and central government. Thus it was the task of the Regional Commissioners to fill this gap and direct the exchange of information. At their prompting the responsible city controllers produced extensive reports that were made available to other cities and to the ministries so that conclusions could be drawn on how to improve safety. These reports provided an opportunity to formulate prudent changes of course within the complex of interests of local authorities, Regional Commissioners, and ministries, without immediately resorting to legal methods of demarcating areas of responsibility or to dictatorial powers.

After the raids on Norwich at the end of April 1942 the Commissioner responsible for the Eastern Civil Defence Region, G. H. G. Anderson, put together a wide-ranging catalogue of requirements that he immediately passed on to all mayors and those in charge of air defence in the region.[99] Some 15,000 buildings were damaged in the raids and 158 people were killed.[100] The infrastructure did not break down and safety procedures had, according to those responsible, largely functioned smoothly. This was possible, however, only because all institutions met soon after the raids to exchange information about the damage reported, to discuss the tasks needing to be done, and coordinate what should happen next. Central control was the necessary precondition for tackling the damage quickly.

In Anderson's view it was counterproductive to have a multitude of institutions with a complicated network of responsibilities. For that reason the Regional Commissioners should in future intervene more than in the past in crisis prevention, naturally not by an extension of their legislative powers but by means of their involvement in meetings, in establishing special offices, or in heading up crisis management teams. Anderson, for example, envisaged that the London Commissioner as intermediary would in future chair the committee responsible for the reconstruction of the city. This was a massive intervention in local government responsibilities as the committee would determine how in future the material and financial resources available to the city for repairs to housing were to be allocated. He intended at all costs to prevent local builders at a time of need from giving priority to private commissions over state projects. This move indicated a gradual change in function: although after the first raids the Regional Commissioners had also aimed to achieve a precise analysis of the damage, to make initial suggestions on reorganization, and to promote the dissemination of knowledge about air defence, they were reticent about making concrete demands and interventions.[101] The more cities and regions were affected by bombing the more vigorously did the Regional Commissioners attempt to intervene in the work of the local authorities, though without challenging their powers. In this respect the bombing of Coventry was a shocking experience.[102]

The raid on the city in the middle of November 1940 had inflicted severe damage and left a deep mark on the local infrastructure. Out of 75,000 buildings 60,000 had been destroyed or damaged overnight; 75 per cent of businesses were hit, the majority of them in the city centre; there was no water or telephone, power and gas supplies were interrupted, and the railway network had collapsed.[103] Emergency plans either made no impact or turned out to be completely inadequate. Although police and firemen were quickly sent from Birmingham to Coventry, it was already clear during the night that the manpower available would not be sufficient to bring the massive effect of the concentrated raid under control. Help came from the soldiers hurriedly summoned by the police chief, the first hundred of whom set to work within a few hours.[104]

When the Home Secretary Herbert Morrison visited the city forty-eight hours after the raid to discuss the situation with those in charge locally he found them totally overstretched in coping with the crisis. Although there was an Emergency Committee, as everywhere, many members had not made it to the meeting. The mayor could offer the minister whisky but not water, as the public supply had still not been restored; the head of the fire service fell asleep from exhaustion during the meeting, though only after he had sung the praises of his men; the rest of the members, most of them Labour councillors, blamed the minister severely for the fact that the city was so ill prepared for the air war and so little had been done for air and civil defence. The atmosphere was poisonous and while the Emergency Committee laid the blame for the disaster on Whitehall, Morrison accused those responsible of not clearing the rubble fast enough.[105] A combination of incompetence and a deep-rooted scepticism about the war on the part of the left-wing city administration seemed now to have culminated in this local catastrophe.

Yet although the minister suspected the committee of defeatism, after initial consideration he did not take the ultimate step of removing power from the local authority and transferring it to the Regional Commissioners, as he feared the consequences. His response was the same a short time later in Southampton, where local government appeared similarly unable to cope with the aftermath of German bombing raids, and yet in spite of criticism from the Regional Commissioner himself no changes were made.[106] The autonomy of the regions was considered so sacrosanct that even when those involved recognized that organizational structures were not fit for the purpose nothing was done to change them. Rather than centralizing power directly Morrison was forced to find a way of exercising power indirectly and call on the army and the Regional Commissioner to take a prominent role in matters surrounding reconstruction, thus sidelining the city administration at least informally.

This attempt to shape the administration to suit the conditions of war was the result of a recognition that local government could not fulfil its role as backbone of the nation unless the damage inflicted were precisely evaluated and local authorities subjected to close critical review. At the beginning of 1941, therefore, the General Inspector, who was responsible for air defence, considered it necessary to subject every level of the administration to continuous scrutiny to establish whether the existing organizational structure was still effective. The crucial factors for him were that the Regional Commissioners made full use of their powers and were ready to assume decision-making authority themselves if a catastrophe should occur. Military intervention was part of this plan. Given the experience of the air war in British coastal and industrial cities this seemed a real threat that was not confined to London. The aim had to be greater efficiency for cities had to be ready, for example, to organize the feeding of thousands of homeless overnight and to build up alternative methods of communication rapidly.[107]

Local authorities were called upon to re-examine their strategy for dealing with a crisis. Though this sounded innocuous it was in fact a slap in the face for local experts, who had evidently not done their homework and who would benefit, in the General Inspector's opinion, from new blood from outside to shake up outmoded structures. By far the most important task in his view was the rapid restoration of civic life and the reorganization of the administration and infrastructure. For this a 'strong man' was required, who combined in himself diverse powers and was ready to make decisions quickly in cooperation with industry and government representatives, without wasting time on who was responsible for what, as had been the case so far. In the following months there was hardly any area of air defence that escaped scrutiny. Fire services, air-raid wardens, shelters, food supplies, use of volunteers, public information—all were subjected to continuous examination, and experience from the raids, on London in particular, was turned into a handbook of practical guidance that was then sent out to cities and regions.[108]

This procedure was adhered to even when the German air raids abated in the course of 1941. Whether this type of institutionalized self-examination really had the desired educative effect is difficult to tell. On the one hand, there was evidence of considerable administrative sluggishness: the Special Commissioner for London in a statement to Parliament in June 1941, at the end of the Blitz, reported that neither he nor any of his team had been asked by any municipality in England, Scotland, or Northern Ireland about their experience in providing shelter for those bombed out or for any help. On the other hand it was evident that other cities, those that had not been bombed until the Baedeker Raids of spring 1942, had the benefit of more information and some inkling of what they would be faced with. They were thus in a position to design their plans with the realities of air war in mind.[109] Thus cities such as Exeter had access to the reports and organizational deliberations that neighbouring cities such as Plymouth and Bristol had on the whole produced only after they had been bombed. These could now be used as blueprints.[110]

How difficult this was in practice was, however, made clear by H. M. Medland, the Deputy Regional Commissioner, at a meeting of representatives of cities of the south-west in July 1942. Though other cities had supplied extensive information, this could not be applied directly to a new situation. The new series of raids, he said, had been aimed primarily at smaller cities which lacked specialist staff and financial resources. In addition, there were still no precise arrangements about the provision of inter-regional help.[111] The debate between Cornwall and Devon representatives showed that in spite of the seriousness of the situation no agreement had been reached about how help should be organized, whether in line with traditional county borders or focusing on regional centres in major cities such as Plymouth and Exeter.[112] Regional interests were therefore by no means obliterated by the national wartime spirit and were a serious obstacle to the organization of civil defence.

The attempt to learn lessons from what others had suffered was not restricted to British experience. To discover how the Germans coped with heavy bombing raids and what conclusions could be drawn for civil defence in Britain, the experts of the Research and Experiment Department studied the effects of their own raids.[113] The damage inflicted on Cologne in the raids at the end of 1942 was of particular significance, for the experts' view was that Cologne had been the 'first' mass raid, bringing a level of destruction not yet experienced in Britain, that the German authorities had had to deal with. Was there something to learn here from the Germans? What was the effect of such an overwhelming raid?[114] Admittedly the information available was sparse and was in effect limited to a series of articles that appeared shortly after the raid in the *Münchner Neueste Nachrichten*. Although the Cologne city administration's logistical problems and the chaotic distribution of powers between city and Party were not visible to the British analysts, even the material that was published pointed to inadequacies in air-raid protection. One point of reference for measuring the attitude of the population and wartime morale was the German raid on Plymouth in spring 1941. There seemed not to have been significant differences: in neither city were there signs of great panic and the people of Cologne, like those of the British port, took matters into their own hands by organizing their own evacuation. From the point of view of morale the cities thus seemed very comparable and the difference was above all in the tonnage of bombs dropped.

British local authorities had to focus on several aspects of the consequences of such a massive raid and revise their existing action plans. First of all, the raid on Cologne showed that mass bombardments could cause public communication systems to collapse and that this damage was not as easy to rectify as after smaller raids. Secondly, it was crucial to set up special control rooms where news could be gathered. These would be roughly similar to the ones established in Cologne by the Nazi Party to coordinate the work of the local Party branches. According to the report, local government infrastructure in parts of Britain appeared to have reached breaking point after the wave of German raids in 1940/1, and thus it was time to think again about how responsibilities for air-raid protection were distributed.

The staff of the Ministry of Home Security were at any rate convinced that the threat of air attack remained acute and that British cities were not properly prepared for the escalation of the air war from 1942/3 onwards. That also called for a review of how people and resources were being used. In none of their reports had the Germans paid extensive tribute to their emergency services, which could not be accidental, given that the British media highlighted the heroic actions of rescuers. Evidently the emergency services played no particularly prominent role after raids when seen in the light of other pressing problems. It therefore made sense to consider whether some volunteers could be transferred from the emergency services to strengthen other areas of public infrastructure such as gas and water.

Even though the air raids had become less intense, according to the experts the introduction of new weapons and techniques had moved the war to a new phase that made a thorough revision of local war preparations an absolute necessity, in fact a matter of survival. This was true even in spite of the shift in German war priorities, which as a result of Operation Barbarossa were focused completely on the eastern front. Göring's bold announcement that as soon as the east had been dealt with, Germany would turn its attention to Britain again, was considered a serious threat by the Ministry of Home Security. Thus it was all the more important for local government, in spite of the easing of air-raid warnings, not to become complacent and think the worst was over.

German cities under a 'state of emergency'

At the end of 1942/3 the majority of leading local government officers in Germany would have assumed that even worse was to come. Initially many cities had thought it possible to keep on top of the raids, using the means at their disposal hitherto to prepare for war. Increasingly overwhelmed by the severity and duration of the bombardments, local officials in the worst-hit regions in the north and the west began intensive discussions, at the latest from 1941 onwards, about their experiences of containing crises, agreeing strategies, comparing organizational structures, and adapting the administration to the changed circumstances of war. In many places the preparation of air defence had been lax, which was the result not only of the tide of enthusiasm for the war and the resulting lack of awareness of the problems but above all of mistaken priorities. The large-scale construction of shelters that Hitler set in motion in September 1940 proved not to have been conceived as a coherent whole, was inadequately resourced, and the logistics had not been thought through in advance.[115]

In addition, the 'Führer's Emergency Programme for Air Defence' abandoned the construction of expensive, if secure, bunkers and focused for reasons of economy on converting existing cellar space. Thus by November 1942 a mere 0.7 per cent of the German population was in the end able to take refuge in a bomb-proof bunker.[116] Many local city and Party officials were confronted daily with these problems and for a long period had had no misgivings about a policy of inadequate provision.[117] In 1940/1 the cities in the south and east of Germany were still looking westwards with a certain degree of equanimity, even while it was beginning to dawn on many people there what the impact of targeted bombing was really like.

From the middle of 1941 onwards, however, the cities of the Rhineland and Westphalia had begun to gather together municipal construction experts under the umbrella of the German Local Government Association in order to look for new ways of preventing damage.[118] This was a threefold process consisting of the assembling, interpreting, and storage of information. An obvious gap was opening up in local authorities' strategies for coping with crisis between what they claimed and what they could actually achieve and this gap revealed that traditional methods were no longer adequate in the face of the increasing severity of the raids. Local government officers were thus forced first to examine their notions of air warfare and recognize that how it was presented in propaganda coincided less and less with the realities of dealing with it on the ground. The conclusion they drew was based on the expectation that the air war would do an increasing amount of damage and that the only way to deal with this was for the regions affected to varying degrees to find new ways of sharing their experiences.

These were necessary to disseminate the formal information gathered by regions already bombed and distinguish between the important and unimportant material. The local government experts were to set new topics for discussion: the organization of the removal of rubble, the construction of shelters, the rebuilding of homes, support for victims of bombing, the management of labour, energy supply, and issues connected to the allocation of responsibilities across local government, the state, and the Party.[119]

Although these meetings were from the start strictly confidential they nevertheless created channels for information, at first regionally and later nationally, that ran in parallel with propaganda and enabled local officials to form a largely unadorned impression of the level of damage and the success of preventive measures. The cities' aim was to open up a new information channel that would assist them in preparing for future air raids and adapting their strategies accordingly. That meant above all learning by observing others, a strategy that was an attempt to compensate for the Nazi regime's polycratic form of government and therefore to create new bodies of knowledge.

That was also the reason why in the Nazi state the reports on the experiences of the first cities to be affected by the air war became a key element in the interregional exchange of information. These reports frequently gave very precise details about administrative shortcomings. For example, the municipal head of construction in Münster reported at a meeting organized by the German Local Government Association on the crucial problem of lack of staff; the first big raids in 1941 so exceeded what had been expected and prepared for that the crisis could be dealt with only with the help of specially recruited staff.[120]

In other areas of work also local government organization and administrative practice diverged considerably, continually provoking renewed debate.[121] How, for example, should a war damage office be organized? What roles should the departments for road and sewer construction play after a raid? Who was responsible for staffing? How could emergency plans

be organized and where were food and homes for evacuees and those
bombed out to come from after a large-scale raid? Were homes to be built,
repaired, or was the gap to be filled by private accommodation? And finally
who was to pay for the damage, what sums had to be planned for, what role
should the district trades organizations play, and where were materials and
labour to come from for the reconstruction, which people still believed in?
None of these problems had been dealt with on a national basis but had to
be negotiated between cities, ministries, and special agencies. The meetings
were thus also aimed at safeguarding local powers or blocking attempts by
new agencies to intervene in the management of the crisis.

The experts often had the opportunity to form a first-hand impression
of the situation in bombed cities. For an important element in the meetings
and visits consisted of tours of the cities conducted by the heads of the construction and welfare services, who in giving details of the damage done by
the Allies and the reconstruction work did not attempt to hide inadequacies. The year 1941 saw the beginning of 'bomb-site tourism', with devastated cities becoming primary objects of study for local government
administrative and fire experts. Strölin, the mayor of Stuttgart, for example,
prepared very carefully for such visits. Before he was due to go to Bremen
after it was bombed he read up on the city's infrastructure and had his
experts compile a set of detailed questions geared to the problems Stuttgart
was finding difficult to solve: How can those bombed out be housed? What
is the Party's role? Who gives assistance and in what form: cash, food, or
vouchers? How successful was the programme of building shelters in
Bremen?[122]

Just two months after Strölin had visited German cities in the north and
west he used their experiences to formulate an emergency plan for Stuttgart
specially designed for its needs; homeless 'national comrades' had to go to
specially created assembly points, details of which were given in leaflets and
posters in the city. The Party took responsibility for receiving people and
giving them food. At the assembly points the city set up special emergency
offices where staff from the welfare, food, rationing, housing, and settlement
departments took care of the homeless immediately after air raids.[123] This
decentralization and the concentration of municipal agencies directly at the
location of the bombing victims were in particular designed to prevent the
authorities being overwhelmed by requests for help and at the same time to
guarantee the quickest and most efficient handling of the consequences of
the bombing. The creation of these emergency offices derived above all

from the experiences of cities already bombed, where local government departments had at first taken some time, as for example in Münster, to cope with the unexpected volume of applications from those in need.[124] Stuttgart's plan also took into account the initial lack of clarity among the various authorities about the scope of their responsibilities. It was now established that the homeless were to be advised about compensation by the welfare office, provided with ration books and coupons by the food and rationing offices, found temporary accommodation by the accommodation office working with the Nazi Party, and allocated alternative housing by the housing and settlement office. The Stuttgart local authority had shown itself to be flexible and realistic in its acknowledgement of existing deficiencies and its ability to adapt its administration and its expectations of the progress of the war on the basis of the experiences of other cities.

The German Local Government Association developed from 1942 onwards at the latest into the interface for the exchange of knowledge and experience. The heavier the raids became and the more the problems and the costs of clearing the damage grew, the more important it became as an information exchange, local government wailing wall, and representative of the latter's interests in the process of negotiation between the centre and the periphery, between the state and local government. Cities such as Cologne, for example, complained about the increasing financial burden of maintaining public air-raid shelters, which between 1940 and 1942 had risen from 30,000 Reich marks at the outset to some 250,000 Reich marks.[125] War-related costs such as the loss of local authority buildings and the expense of clearing rubble from the streets or sewers added to this burden. Expenses regarded as insignificant before the war became more important and new costs such as the creation of fire watches, rent for auxiliary hospitals, and provision of accommodation for the homeless were added.

What the local authorities feared was above all being left with all these costs. The heavy air raids in the first six months of 1942 changed the priorities and the information needed by the municipalities. For financial issues gradually took a back seat in the face of acute problems and the immediate challenge of organizing air-raid protection and coping with the destruction became dominant. The raids sent a shock through the air-raid personnel in cities and led to considerable loss of confidence. They demonstrated plainly what dimensions the air war might reach.[126]

With 16,000 people bombed out, Lübeck, according to a report in September 1943 from those responsible for Hamburg's air-raid protection, had been a 'warning signal' to the city administration.[127] After the city centre and with it large parts of the local authority buildings and the social administration responsible for the care of bombing victims had been destroyed in the raids the decision had been taken to do away with any kind of centralized offices. Special emergency plans were developed in response to the fact that people had fled the city and many offices had ceased to function immediately after the raids. One measure was to reinforce the professional obligation of civil servants and white collar employees in local government not to 'sit in the cellar' if catastrophe should strike but to 'go above ground, when Tommy comes and drops phosphorus bombs' and 'look danger in the eye'. It was precisely those smaller cities such as Rostock and Lübeck that were assumed by air defence experts to have much greater problems reorganizing than a large city such as Cologne after the 1,000-bomber raid.[128]

After that heavy raid at the end of May 1942 the cathedral city became a favoured object of study. Following the raids much of the city administration had ceased to operate.[129] The Nazi welfare organization (NSV) had not managed to cover the needs of the population, the various offices had not done enough to agree what responsibilities they would take on, and it was more than a week before the city administration was able to provide adequate food supplies for the city.[130] The city's leaders, however, managed to distract the attention of the outside world from the tensions within and prevent the problems being faced from appearing to be the result of inadequate preparation.[131] As an observer from Stuttgart remarked, these problems included the breakdown of communications in the inner city and also the problems of 'finding new accommodation' or caring for those affected by bombing, many of whom, contrary to expectations, did not come to the assembly points but sought shelter with family or friends.

The most important finding that the Stuttgart official took away with him was the 'call to strengthen self-protection and make the population aware of how to respond in air raids, in particular how to deal with incendiaries'. Above all, he could now visualize what area bombing involved and what his city might have to face—and that was far beyond anything people there had experienced so far.

To ensure that the practical aspects of coping with crisis were continually being adjusted in line with the reality of the air war and the cities could fulfil their task of being 'the epitome of *völkisch* life',[132] the Reich Ministry of the Interior issued a decree a few days after the raids on Cologne giving the German Local Government Association a new objective: it was no longer only to advise the municipalities and local authorities about the air war but was called upon to give 'active assistance' in preventing damage.[133] What this meant in detail was not yet clear at this point, even to the municipalities themselves. Several proposals were on the table: the German Local Government Association encouraged its members to disseminate all forms of service instructions, legal rulings, information sheets, or service reports via state and provincial offices in order to give the municipalities easy access to a comprehensive view of institutional structures relevant to civil defence and to the clearing of war damage. The Association also considered it sensible to increase the frequency of meetings at which particularly badly hit cities presented their suggested solutions to problems; and, finally, the Association aimed to help cities to send their own observers to devastated areas so that they could find out about the strategy of raids, the size of bombs, and logistical matters.

A first step in this direction was the introduction of an information system designed for regions to exchange amongst themselves their experiences of air warfare. From the end of October 1942 onwards the German Local Government Association sent out circulars to all authorities with more than 20,000 inhabitants. These 'Special Bulletins' differed significantly from other official communications that came from the state or the Party by offering cities a forum in which to pass on their experiences of bombing raids, information about new techniques of bombing, and methods of controlling fires.[134] The information was not, however, restricted to successful defensive strategies but also reported failures and logistical problems, albeit to a very limited audience.[135] Thus the bulletins conveyed an impression of the growing problems and their pressures and the constant changes to which the local authorities, working in cooperation and competition with the local Nazi Party branches and the NSV, were subject. At the same time they offered an authentic picture of the situation in Germany, acting as an indicator to the authorities of the state of the constantly invoked loyalty of the national community and of possible sources of discontent. These were becoming evident in the wake of evacuations and the tensions between the Gaus evacuating people and those receiving them.[136]

The impression conveyed was of an administration in a permanent state of stress. Yet although the tools at its disposal were becoming less and less adequate to cope with the growing burdens of bombing, communication among local authorities had created an opportunity to compensate at least in a small way for shortcomings in the management of air-raid precautions produced by a polycratic regime and for the tendency of Reich agencies to over-regulate.[137] The organized exchange of experience, which included special conferences of leading mayors,[138] developed increasingly in the course of the war into a kind of polycratic clearing house, in which the decisions of various Reich ministries and special agencies were shared, interpreted, and their implications discussed.[139] At the same time a counterweight was being created at local government level that, in spite of all the competition among regions for resources, tried to put up a defence against external encroachments on traditional areas of responsibility and was successful to some extent in managing the effects of the air war.

Of course, as even the municipal leaders in Hamburg conceded, there was little that could be done in the face of major catastrophes such as Operation Gomorrah. The extent of the raid exceeded everyone's imagination. The fact that at meetings of local government representatives people on occasions spoke very candidly may well have contributed to a more realistic estimate of the seriousness of the situation (which had long been underestimated) and of the effects of possible 'fire storms' and to their prevention through the isolation of possible sources of fire, as in the case of Augsburg.[140] At the conference of the Party's head office for local government policy in September 1943 the leading mayors found out at first hand what had actually happened in Hamburg and what was neither printed in the newspapers nor available in official bulletins or reports. They heard the true story of the immense destructive force of the raid, about the need to set up 'dead zones' in the city that no one was allowed to enter and where thousands of bodies still lay, some 26,000 of which had been recovered thus far, with many thousands still to be added to the total.

Horrific news of this kind may well have motivated many in local government to take air-raid protection more seriously than before.[141] In spite of all inadequacies, the sharing of information among cities provided an opportunity of developing at least an initial conception of the possible destruction. This could be adjusted to reality after each new wave of bombing and so contribute at least to some extent to a more efficient organization of air-raid protection by the local authorities. This informal sharing of information arising from meetings painted the clearest possible picture of the cities in the midst of the air war: In the middle of July 1943 a Düsseldorf engineer responded to the enquiry of his colleague in Stuttgart about the results of the most recent air raid by saying that the inner city had been completely devastated: 300,000 people who had lost their homes had to be cared for. Though there had not been extensive use of phosphorus and the shelters had withstood the raid, there had been a problem getting water to put out the fires and the shelters had been over-full by a factor of ten. He advised his Stuttgart colleague against evacuating the old town in the event of a similar catastrophe, at least while there were still sufficient cellars.[142]

This sharing of experience and information among the local authorities also reflected the extreme situation of each. After a visit to Cologne in July 1943 Strölin, the mayor of Stuttgart, reported to the city council on its destruction. He summed it up saying it was just about as bad as it could be and that he was acutely aware how in a short time fact-finding visits had turned into visits to ruins: 'What is clear is that destroying homes is the simplest and most effective means of destroying the economy.'

There was no reduction in the exchange of information from the north to the south during 1943/4, although the focus and suggested solutions shifted. After visiting Kassel, the inner city of which was completely destroyed in a raid on 22 October 1943, Strölin identified the most important outcome: 'The population's will to resist must be maintained in all circumstances, even if raids become more intense.'[143] Evidently he recognized in the coincidence of increased bombing and indications of the dissolution of the national community one of the basic problems of defending cities in future. Though not yet acute, in his experience these problems were becoming increasingly prominent.[144]

In the meantime issues such as rapid reconstruction, financial compensation from the Reich, or the setting up of war damage offices were no longer important; now the problem was organizing survival in the ruins of the inner cities, which as in Mannheim more and more often presented a 'picture of desolate devastation'.[145] In view of the further large-scale raids now expected, the main focus was therefore on constructing a dense network of escape routes, on evacuating the crowded old town areas, and on making sure that the rationing and food offices kept going.[146] After all, the city administrations not only had to struggle with the increasing scarcity of resources but also had few staff with which to cope with the growing workload. However useful the sharing of information among cities was for working out emergency plans, in the end how they coped with acute catastrophes depended on the 'most flexible possible'[147] distribution of tasks among the staff of the cities and local authorities.

Local Authorities, Coping with Crisis, and the Mobilization of the Nazi Party

In Germany the power structure in local government was determined above all by one factor that fundamentally distinguished it from local politics in Britain: the relationship between the municipalities and the Nazi Party. There was no comparable mass organization in Britain and even party structures that continued to exist, for example those of the Conservatives and the Labour Party, were considerably weakened in many places by the war.[148] Local officials were neither sidelined and replaced, as they were in Germany by the Nazi movement, nor was there a political force that aimed for the total mobilization and control of the population and to which the air war offered the opportunity of proving what it could achieve.

In Germany up to the outbreak of war civil air defence had been a part of the general responsibilities of the administration and shared among police, Luftwaffe, and local authorities, the police being the dominant partner. After an air raid the city's head of air defence was expected to try to get public and commercial life 'started again as quickly as possible'.[149] He was to ensure that there was 'unified leadership', to coordinate fire-fighting, and to cooperate with the army and other agencies to deal with the damage. Frequently the mayor was 'director of emergency measures' and thus the central point of reference enabling the diverse tasks to be coordinated in a crisis and conflicts of interest over responsibilities and resources to be settled.

Even before the outbreak of war the Nazi Party and the Nazi welfare organization (NSV) had managed to extend their influence to civil air defence and, as the 'backbone of the home front', had voiced the Party's claim to guarantee mobilization for the coming war.[150] Air defence played a key role in this and as early as June 1939 Department M[obilization] of the Office of the Führer's Deputy, which was responsible for all issues of mobilization in the Party, had stated in a 'work plan'[151] that in future the NSV should take over 'care of national comrades affected by air raids'. What that meant in detail was still undecided for the NSV was at that point still primarily an organization of subscribers and less of social practice.[152]

In case of war the plans already envisaged the NSV being made available to the local Nazi Party functionaries and to the leaders of the district and town branches. When the first air raids began on the Rhineland these preliminary considerations turned into concrete plans that, in the absence of a clear ruling covering the whole Reich, formed part of the processes of local authority negotiations. What was evident was that the Nazi Party was taking over the task of 'leadership' (*Menschenführung*) and was charged with boosting the 'inner strength of all national comrades for the defence of the Reich'.[153]

Even before the start of bombing in April 1940 the Nazi Party in Cologne drafted a detailed deployment plan aimed in the event of air raids at a comprehensive mobilization of the Party and an extension of its areas of responsibility. Although the district Party leadership did not challenge the police's authority with regard to local air defence issues, it nevertheless emphasized strongly its growing claim to power. As, according to its estimation, the capacity of the fire service, technical emergency service, and police was inadequate to protect the home front it was now up to the Nazi Party with the help of the NSV and local Party branches to take over the feeding of victims of bombing and the recovery of their household goods.[154]

In many cities from 1940 onwards similar plans and agreements had been made involving the leaders of district Party branches, local government, and directors of local air defences to settle the matter of procedures and responsibilities after air raids.[155] The outcome was similar in most cases: the Nazi Party assumed responsibility for the care of victims of bombing and looked after food and accommodation, though leaving central control to the air defence directors.

By the outbreak of war a variety of air defence duties fell to the Nazi Party: the monitoring of the blackout and shelters, the 'psychological' care of the injured, the recruitment of air-raid wardens, the involvement of the population in evacuation procedures, and the use of propaganda to 'provide support' for the morale of the national community. In part this involved the local branches and the NSV in quasi-police functions, though the primary task was the immediate care of those affected by bombing and that meant providing them with food and living quarters. In both areas the city administration and the Party worked closely together[156] and were thus involved in a continuous process of negotiation and exchange that lasted almost until the end of the war and frequently incorporated the experience of earlier bombing raids.

Practice hardly varied from one city to the next. The local Party branches gathered the homeless together in their own reception camps if there was no more private accommodation available, and welfare workers from the Party and city supplied the victims with basic clothing and application forms.[157] With the agreement of the district Party leadership and the city administration the NSV took over the task of feeding them.[158] They used their own large-scale kitchens, also calling on the resources of the restaurant trade after more serious raids, and set up special supply contracts with the Wehrmacht, which in an emergency made field kitchens and stew available. In addition, Düsseldorf made use of the experiences of Dortmund and Essen, where the NSV had organized mobile kitchens and cooperated closely with works canteens. The food came from the stocks of the food offices, which drew the necessary batches of supplies from individual businesses and wholesalers.[159]

In fact the NSV and the food offices succeeded in the main very speedily in organizing food after air raids. There might be shortages at various times, primarily after heavy raids such as that on Hamburg, when the NSV had to take care of feeding and accommodating some 900,000 homeless, or when transport systems had been damaged and goods, which were become scarcer, could no longer be got to the central locations.[160] Yet through a mixture of improvisation, improved organization, mobilization of the Party, and inter-regional assistance things could mostly be sorted out.[161]

For the regime the rapid provision of food after raids had considerable importance, as Hamburg's mayor, Carl Vincent Krogmann, put it at a meeting of leading local government politicians in February 1944 with reference to his own experiences: 'When, after the terrors of the night, a national comrade holds a piece of bread and butter and a thick slice of sausage in his hands with a cup of coffee or a plate of pea soup the world immediately looks much rosier.'[162] Where the escalation of the air war made this less and less feasible and shortages turned into absolute want, as in the west of the Reich after the Battle of the Ruhr in spring 1943, in the face of diminishing resources the NSV pressed for access to aid to be regulated and distribution to be subject to strict controls. This was in order to exclude any unauthorized beneficiaries and to activate the population's efforts at 'self-protection'. Welfare, conformity, and surveillance therefore went hand in hand.[163]

The same was true of support for evacuations and the provision of living quarters for the homeless, a problem that from 1942/3 onwards increased in importance as part of the interface between local authorities and the Party.

The NSV and Nazi Party local branches had discovered in this an activity the significance of which kept on growing and extending its scope. The NSV took over the organization of evacuation transports from the Gaus sending to those receiving evacuees, was responsible for the 'rehousing' of women, the elderly, and the sick in the wake of the 'extended programme of child evacuation',[164] and finally also with defeat imminent for the 'evacuations' of 1944/5.

The NSV developed its power to exert discipline above all during discussions to decide who should have the right to be evacuated in the event of a catastrophe. What the Party and the city had agreed in Düsseldorf applied here: whether he or she was 'essential to the war effort' was the deciding factor in whether any individual was allowed to leave the locality and it was the job of the city and the Party to test this and reach a common verdict on the application according to 'personal impressions' made.[165] A similar procedure was adopted in the matter of repairing living accommodation. After the first heavy raids the cities in the west and north of the Reich had very quickly adjusted the organizational structure of their building departments and made them more flexible so that damage could be more rapidly assessed and repairs more quickly authorized.

Like the war damage offices the local authority building departments were decentralized and tasks passed on, for example to the district trades council.[166] In view of the extensive destruction of housing Cologne and Düsseldorf had formed special committees covering the area of a local Nazi Party branch in which the urgency of repairs was decided by representatives of the building department and the municipality together with a Party functionary.[167]

Thus a committee was created for each section of the city where decisions could be made about the scarce resources of the building trade. The Party representative acquired a dual role in the building departments: he was to act as a control preventing tradesmen and architects from creating more homes than was absolutely necessary and economically justified, and he was to act as a kind of 'lightning rod for the national community' by passing on decisions to the applicants and representing their interests. This gave the Party man considerable powers in the local construction committees and made him an important agent in the distribution of resources in a key area of local government.

The same was true of civil air defence. There too the local Party branches were able to extend their influence within the power complex operating among city administration, police, Wehrmacht, and Party.[168] This process could vary from region to region and was also dependent on the personal relationships among mayors, district leaders, and Gauleiters. In Hamburg it was the Gauleiter Karl Kaufmann rather than the Oberbürgermeister who was the strong man of the city[169] and this had an impact on responsibilities for air defence, whereas in Augsburg and Münster there was close cooperation between the Gauleiter and Oberbürgermeister that created a strong link between the Nazi Party and the city administration and its task of combating the effects of bombing.[170]

Forms of cooperation were therefore dependent on the development of the air war. In Munich, for example, at first the Gau leadership of Munich-Upper Bavaria had instructed the local Party branches in September 1941 in the event of an air raid only to make contact with local air-raid staff and to concern themselves at the end of the raids with the homeless.[171]

On the other hand, there were as yet no orders for the Party to intervene actively in air-raid protection. This changed only when the air war escalated. From 1942 according to an instruction from Wilhelm Frick, head of the Reich administration, Gauleiters were to take pains to ensure every local Party branch created an office for air defence.[172] Where the local office was located within the Party headquarters, as in Gau Munich-Upper Bavaria, the Bürgermeister, the local police officer responsible for air defence matters, a member of the NSV, a billeting officer, a representative of the Reich Air Defence League, and the member of the local Party branch responsible for emergency deployment should meet as a group. It should, however, be led by the Party and in particular by the local Nazi Party branch leader.

Although Göring had stuck to the view right up to the end of 1942 that civil air defence remained an area over which the state had sovereignty, in spite of the additional tasks taken on by the Nazi Party,[173] it became increasingly clear that the local Party branches' potential to mobilize and exert discipline was of considerable importance for local authorities coping with crisis. This expansion of responsibilities overlapped with various areas of municipal responsibility for the 'defence of the Reich'—and National Socialist 'leadership of and looking after people' (*Menschenführung/Menschenbetreuung*) went hand in hand with this. Local Party branches and district offices together with Nazi formations now not only took on the task of maintaining stability on the home front by means of propaganda but were now jointly responsible both for tackling immediate emergencies by, for example, digging ditches and air-raid shelters, removing rubble and retrieving bodies, or supervising the blackout, as well as for allocating living quarters and food to evacuees and those who had been bombed out.[174]

From 1942/3 onwards the Nazi Party therefore largely concentrated its activity in local politics on coping with the air war.[175] From its perspective at least two tasks were important: the Party's 'leadership' (in other words the mobilization of the population through propaganda for 'self-help' and active 'preparedness for air defence') as well as practical training in air defence, use of fire beaters, fire protection ponds, and other methods of fire-fighting.[176] At first 'self-protection' became the province of the Party only gradually and often in the wake of local shifts in power, then it was legalized throughout the Reich, and finally in August 1944 it came totally under the Party's control.[177]

In many places the local branches had already completed this move. They formed special 'air defence units' and mobile service commandos, which coordinated 'self-protection' under the leadership of local branches and district headquarters, came to detailed agreements about all air defence measures, and attempted to exert pressure on the municipal authorities in order to speed up reimbursement of war damage 'for psychological reasons'.[178] Other areas of activity, primarily practical fire-fighting and the extension of shelters, steadily increased in importance from 1943/4 onwards.[179] In special practice lofts the Party trained people in the use of gas masks and conducted courses on methods of fire-fighting, and a special 'lay support' programme was designed to inform women above all about the most important methods of assistance and to mobilize them for 'self-help'.[180]

This 'Party activation'[181] had a dual function. First of all, its aim was to train the population in air defence and prepare them for catastrophic situations such as were becoming increasingly frequent. Secondly, the Nazi Party was concerned to raise its profile in civic life and emphasize its drive as well as its efficiency and tight-knit organization. And in the end the air war led to an extension of the control and surveillance functions of the local Party branches. This was a development that in particular in the case of monitoring the blackout, which since 1940 had been the Party's central contribution to air-raid protection,[182] was to combine 'leadership' with social control.

For the 'air defence community' the blackout was obligatory.[183] It provided the police and local Party branches, using a considerable amount of propaganda combined with the constantly recurring call for 'total readiness for air defence',[184] with a further instrument with which to intervene in civic life. Those who had completed further training in fire-fighting and

knew how to use the equipment, who blacked out their windows and business premises carefully, and were prepared to report 'blackout offenders'
were considered to belong to the 'air defence community'. Since the start
of the air war the Party and the police had repeatedly complained about the
'lack of air raid discipline',[185] claiming it contributed to the damage done to
the property of the 'national community'. Infringements had therefore to
be punished. There was no consistent notion of sentencing underlying the
catalogue of penalties the police could impose at the prompting of the local
Party branches. Sometimes only a warning was given, and sometimes, as in
Frankfurt, fines of up to fifty Reich marks were handed out.[186] Blatant and
'malicious' offences against regulations could, however, lead to people being
reported to the Gestapo.[187]

The local Party branches invested a considerable amount of time in the
constant revision of the blackout regulations. At the same time they either
seized on events they had heard about as locals or from air-raid wardens or
from members of the public complaining about the state of the blackout
and referred them to the police,[188] or they took matters into their own
hands and organized veritable blackout crackdowns, intended to reveal
repeat offenders by means of a system of their own invention and report
them.[189] 'Blackout offenders' were summoned to the Party branch offices
and questioned; if the infringement was serious or repeated often enough
the district Party boss was to be brought in to determine the punishment.
Public stigmatization was a further important tool of repression used in
blackout policy.[190] One Munich branch, for example, affixed red posters to
buildings where flats were not properly blacked out with the text: 'A blackout offender lives in this building'.[191]

By such means local branches developed in many ways into an important
surveillance tool for the Party, while they, sometimes in very candid terms,
bemoaned existing shortcomings in air defence and tried, albeit mainly in
vain, given the hopelessness of the war situation, to improve things. In
autumn 1944, for example, complaints about the state of public air-raid
facilities came thick and fast from the Munich branches of the Party. The
verdict could hardly have been more devastating: none of the air-raid shelters, with a few exceptions, was up to standard and more and more often the
population was forced to endure air raids in severely substandard shelters;
shelters were jam-packed and lacked hygienic facilities.[192] In the centre of
Munich, for example, many apartment blocks had no water for extinguishing fires and hydrants for combating the threat of large-scale fires were also

scarce. The city and the Party were then reproached with making exaggerated promises and claims. 'As long as nothing serious was happening, people
could be calmed down by being told that bunkers and slit trenches were
unnecessary,' the head of the task force from the Munich-Freimann local
branch recorded in October 1944. 'Up to now people were always told that
in low-rise buildings a simple shelter in the cellar is adequate. Now, however, people are seeing with their own eyes what it means for 30 to 40 people or more to be in a shelter in a single-story building. [...] At the moment
we have no means of holding people back when their nerves are shattered.
Even the Gauleiter's ban on cars being driven away is ignored, especially by
the Wehrmacht. If you try to stop people fleeing you immediately get the
reply, "Give us bunkers and then we'll stay." '[193]

At this point there was little confidence in victory left. Local and regional
Party organizations tried to push their way through to the front line of crisis
management and set themselves up as the mouthpiece of the discontented,
using air-raid prevention in particular as a lever. They met comparatively
little resistance from the local authorities.[194] Naturally municipal officials
were extremely annoyed when for example Paul Giesler, the Gauleiter of
Munich, drew on the city's budget to finance what the Reich was supposed
to provide or when from the beginning of 1944 the post of head of air
defence came under the Party's authority.[195]

In practice the carefully formulated and repeatedly revised demarcations
of responsibility between the Nazi Party and city administrations did not
altogether prevent conflicts, for in the final analysis both were in competition for the trust of the 'national comrades' and were constantly trying to
create an impression of limitless efficiency and support in coping with crises, thus putting themselves in the most favourable light.[196] Yet on the whole
the relationship was determined more by cooperation and work-sharing
than by serious differences in objectives. Though in most local authorities
there was a noticeable tendency for the nexus of power on the 'internal
front' to shift in favour of the Party and its organizations that by no means
led to city administrations completely losing influence or the right to contribute to discussions; still less did they surrender all decision-making powers to the Party.

Departments important to the war effort such as the welfare and food
offices remained under the control of the city, even if the Party managed to
acquire increasing influence over local administration. The balance struck
could vary greatly from one authority to another and according to the

amount of overlap between Party and city functions, yet only in exceptional cases were the city administrations merely the obedient executors of instructions from Party offices. Key tasks such as support for those bombed out were carried out in close consultation with the city authorities. Sometimes, however, it did come about that in spite of the strains of the war situation the Party, with its organizations such as the NSV, German Labour Front, or Hitler Youth, had potential human and material resources at its disposal, whereas the local authorities in their reduced state were increasingly stretched beyond their capabilities by the force of the air raids.[197]

In spite of the erosion of bureaucratic power, for a short period in the air war this form of local government polycracy and of special agencies created for the 'defence of the Reich' was able to help compensate for the dysfunctionality and lack of strong management at the centre through the concentration of powers in the local authorities. This was true, for example, of the improvised emergency measures to remove rubble, in spite of dwindling building supplies and raw materials, and ensure a minimum of administrative activity. At the same time the accumulation of power by local and district Party leaders during the war supplied an essential element in the crisis and loss of legitimacy of the Nazi state.[198] For the radicalization of the air war

Figure 4. Members of the Hitler Youth with fire hose.

revealed that no amount of resources, however great, and no party, however apparently active, was capable of standing up to the superior power of the Allies. On the one hand the bureaucracy was wearing itself out and on the other the Party was increasing its powers in specific areas in accordance with its ideology. This combination linked strategies for solving local problems with the extension of the methods of internal terror.

One of the key areas in which this development can be seen was the rapid removal of rubble and reconstruction of homes. At an early stage, from spring 1941 onwards, special battalions of POWs captured by the Wehrmacht were created on the initiative of Albert Speer. These were deployed in Berlin, in the coastal cities of north Germany, and in the Rhine–Ruhr area and used in particular for roofing and glazing after air raids.[199] Gradually city administrations grew increasingly keen to find cheap labour to help clear the streets, remove the rubble, recover those lying dead under it, build houses, and get transport moving.

The removal of rubble was not just a logistical problem but a key element in winning the trust of the national community. For air raids demonstrated the vulnerability of the regime and scenes of devastation were, as it were, its visible wounds. Repairing buildings and removing rubble therefore had considerable potential to cause problems for local administrations, for their power to resolve crises was after all an indicator of how far the regime was still able in wartime to ensure the safety of the population.[200]

Thus a quiet home front was a concern of Heinrich Himmler when, at the end of a visit to the areas in the north-west affected by bombing in September 1942, he gave the order to sort out problems in dealing with damage and put great effort into recovering those buried.[201] He was clear that the raids would increase. Thus he saw it as vital for convicts and concentration camp inmates to be sent to cities to clear rubble and remove unexploded bombs, so that the 'courageous firemen' would not be put at risk but instead the 'thugs' who were 'sitting pretty in prison or in a concentration camp'.[202]

In consultation with Speer the SS's plans for using special construction units were becoming increasingly precise from September 1942 onwards.[203] As part of the 'Emergency Measures after Air Raids' concentration camp inmates were moved from Buchenwald, Neuengamme, or Sachsenhausen to areas affected by the air war and housed in new branch camps, often in the middle of the city, so that after air raids they could be set to work immediately. Cities on the Rhine and Ruhr, which had fought hard to get this cheap slave labour, now created special bureaucratic structures to integrate the work units into the system of air-raid protection and ensure that it worked smoothly.[204] Up to February 1943 Carl Haidn, the Oberbürgermeister of Düsseldorf, had 600 prisoners at his disposal, in Bremen in November 1942 some 750 prisoners belonging to SS Construction Brigade II from Neuengamme concentration camp were already housed in huts, and in summer 1943 Cologne had access to some 1,000 prisoners from Buchenwald.[205]

Increasingly local authorities, in close cooperation with the SS and the Reich Plenipotentiary for Construction, created branch camps in the middle of cities in order to have the quickest possible access to the prisoners' labour and be able to deploy them flexibly after air raids. The striped prisoners' uniforms soon became the most visible sign of the gradual merging of city and camp. The city administrations had more than enough tasks for them to do: equipped with picks and shovels, the columns of prisoners, under strict supervision and constantly rising work pressure, were forced to remove the rubble in the cities, lay rails, clear out cellars, and assist with the reconstruction of the water and energy infrastructure. In Hamburg SS Brigade II with up to 930 prisoners was detailed to work in the 'dead zone', those areas of Hamburg that had been worst hit in Operation Gomorrah and where under the weight of rubble and mounds of corpses life had come to a complete standstill.[206]

The prisoners worked there on recovering goods, stones and wood, roof tiles and metals; many were used in special units of craftsmen who carried out work ordered by the Reich Plenipotentiary for Construction under the supervision of firms of craftsmen. Further types of task were added: from time to time private firms of craftsmen made successful attempts to take advantage of the labour of prisoners[207] and parts of the brigades were used to build 'pre-fab homes for those affected by bombing'. Two types of work were especially feared by prisoners. One was the recovery of the dead and injured, because they were often forced to work to the point of exhaustion and beyond with inadequate equipment on sites particularly in danger of collapse and in conditions that from the point of view of hygiene were catastrophic. The other was work with one of the bomb disposal units.

As early as 1940 Hitler had instructed that unexploded bombs were to be made safe by convicts or concentration camp inmates and not by soldiers or firemen.[208] After his tour of the bombed areas Himmler himself exerted considerable pressure to ensure that this command was put into practice with suitable stringency after forming the opinion that it had been treated too casually. From 1943 onwards prisoners from the SS brigades were regularly sent off to join the Luftwaffe's demolition squads, which were responsible for bomb disposal. Sometimes, as in Düsseldorf or Wilhelmshaven, they became permanent members of the squads and, in fear of their lives, were deployed for particularly dangerous tasks, often with fatal results.[209]

From the outset the competition among local authorities for cheap labour was fierce and often it was the city that was able to use its influence within the Nazi bureaucracy most forcefully to get its way that ended up with a contingent of prisoners.[210] The cities also competed for SS resources and in the race for slave labour they had no compunction about squeezing the last ounce of work from the prisoners. At the same time the local authorities had to adjust to the regime's altered priorities as far as armaments were concerned, for from 1944 onwards at the latest it was downgrading the protection of cities and the policy of 'emergency measures' in favour of other projects, chiefly the relocation of armaments factories and the building of new types of aircraft. For the cities this meant above all growing interregional competition and after the gradual relocation of the SS construction units the need to look for other possibilities.

The problems of clearing rubble continued to grow and now some new competitors for resources, in particular from among cities in the south of Germany, arrived on the scene. From the point of view of the Nazi leadership strengthening local authorities' 'power of resistance' and community 'self-help' at a time of 'total war' meant above all getting the population to mobilize itself and exploiting local resources more relentlessly.[211] To put it another way: because little could be expected from the Reich government and the expansion of the armaments industry determined priorities the cities and local communities had to be creative and find their own solutions. As a rule, therefore, local authorities continued where the SS brigades had left off and looked for cheap substitutes. Increasing numbers of other forced labourers and prisoners were put to work. Thanks to its good political connections Bremen got new prisoners from Neuengamme, Osnabrück secured prisoners from the Emsland camp, and in Düsseldorf POWs occupied the huts of the construction brigades, which were now helping to build the Atlantic Wall and the 'miracle weapons'.[212]

Yet even the systematic exploitation of forced labour and concentration camp inmates could do nothing to alter the fact that after the Battle of the Ruhr in the middle of 1943 at the latest local authorities had reached the end of their ability to cope with the crisis.[213] In his monthly report for April

1943 the city treasurer of Essen recorded almost with resignation: 'The administration is [...] exhausted. We're just muddling along, with insufficient and inadequate staff and with no resources, for in the end homeless people who have already gone through a long and wearying process often have to be told that we cannot give them what they want.'[214] Resources were exhausted and shortages of everyday necessities such as fabrics and shoes, which up to 1942 had been obtained through a war of plunder and annihilation and distributed largely without difficulty via the coupon system used by the rationing and food offices grew more acute from one month to the next.

The Reich authorities responded to the widening gulf between the lack of basic commodities and growing demand for them by limiting entitlement to coupons, so that the shortages would be managed at an increasingly low level, though they were well aware that calling for 'self-help' and frugality could be a serious threat to the population's morale. Thus, for example, the Düsseldorf city administration was hardly pleased that the national coupon system favoured victims of bombing over normal consumers. This in turn raised expectations about access to commodities that were less and less likely to be met and so provoked considerable resentment in the population.[215] By now local authorities and the communities they administered were living from hand to mouth and could only stand by helplessly while their infrastructure was destroyed by Allied bombers.

The Air War as an Opportunity:
Planning and Reconstruction

British local authorities were also under pressure, even if their concerns and difficulties were a long way from being the life-and-death matters affecting their enemies in Germany. As air raids grew less intense they were able to begin planning the reconstruction, in many cases the day after the air raids, and thus focus priorities in local government policy on the 'future'.[216]

Whereas from 1942 onwards German towns and cities could hardly keep up with the most vital repairs, the end of bombing of British cities marked the beginning of a passionate debate about the British city of the future and about the opportunity the air war had created to, as the Left put it, build a 'New Jerusalem'. 'Planning', and its more concrete manifestation, 'town planning', were the new key concepts that would help to control unre-strained growth, urbanization, and the industrialization of conurbations, and change the face of Britain.

That at least was the challenge issued by the Royal Commission which back in January 1940 had presented a report advocating a massive extension of central government planning in order to correct failures in regional development from previous decades.[217] The debate about the 'proper' path urban development should take, about the relationship between traffic plan-ning, the construction of social housing, and the layout of new estates, had been in progress since the inter-war years, but it was not until the advent of war and the destruction it caused that the opportunity the planners had wished for arrived. Projects that had hit the buffers as a result of conflicts of local interests were now necessarily at the very top of the agenda in local and national policy-making.

By the end of 1943 there were at least 155 municipalities in England and Wales with more than 100 homes damaged by bombing, and in 41 of them more than 1,000 houses had been rendered uninhabitable. For local authorities this loss of housing was not simply a social problem but also an economic one, for the destruction of properties meant that the local author-ities lost a significant part of the revenue they received in rates.[218]

Illustrated magazines such as *Picture Post* had from the beginning of 1941 taken up the subject of reconstruction and linked it with the demand for a new and more just social order.[219] Under the heading 'A Plan for Britain' photos no longer showed only the usual signs of destruction, but rather people working to clear the rubble and find ways of starting afresh. What was this 'new Britain' to look like and on what foundations was it to be built? In features in the working-class press the 'little' people expressed their views and reinforced the demand that the needs of the workers and of the less well-off should be prominent in any national reconstruction. And reconstruction could not mean just 'homes fit for heroes', as after the First World War, and be confined to improving the quality of housing of the working class. This opportunity presented by the Blitz to local authorities and indeed to the whole country should, as much and as boldly as possible, be exploited to create a new, more equitable Britain.

Seeing the air war as an opportunity was, however, not peculiar to Britain, nor was the fact that even before the bombing architects and town planners believed their moment had come and that they could finally turn into reality the plans they had developed before the war to redesign cities.

But by contrast with Britain, in Nazi Germany a critical attitude to modernism was combined with a much more radical delusion about what was technically feasible and with racially motivated notions about the use of space. Boosted by the new opportunities that the Nazi regime seemed to be offering planners, these factors gave rise as early as 1933 to visions of towns and cities restructured on *völkisch* lines. These would be places, so it was claimed, that overcame the 'collectivism of the city' and the 'individualism of the village'.[220] The thinking of town and country planners and their architect colleagues was guided by the concepts of 'harmony' and 'internal order' and no project seemed too large nor any plan to 'Germanize' or resettle populations too ambitious.[221]

Victory in the west in the summer of 1940 also seemed to herald the time for considering what was possible and desirable 'after the war': large-scale building projects, pseudotechnocratic standardization, and the attempt, at best symbolic, to individualize housing and thus supposedly solve all the 'old' problems connected with the social organization of mass societies.

One of these was the notion of the 'city' as the root of many evils. It was to be replaced by a new, *völkisch* model: the 'townscape' or 'cityscape', a new organism with more space and with modern estates linked as neighbourhood communities and organized by the Nazi Party. Initial plans had already been drawn up to combine reconfiguring the space and extending the cities 'organically' with comprehensive control by the Party. Control by means of the organization of space had since the beginning of the war been one of the central categories in the field of town planning; 'organic structuring' was the term used but it meant controlling the population through modernizing the infrastructure. 'People's halls', which Hitler had dreamt of back in 1938 in a speech to the Party conference as the local focus of the 'national community', formed part of this programme of construction[222] and these were often found in numerous plans. Gigantomanic large-scale projects such as those of Speer that delighted the Führer and were meant to represent the power of the new, victorious Germany were only one aspect of town planning. At least as important were the plans formulated even before the air raids for the transformation of cities into a new kind of 'settlement community' along Nazi lines and it was these that were given impetus by the air raids.

The 'new city' in wartime united two expectations: it had to be 'able to defend itself' and it had to be 'spacious'.[223] Cities were to provide proof of their ability to defend themselves by evidence of more extensive air-raid precautions, bunkers, secure cellars, and anti-aircraft gun towers; the importance of 'spaciousness' was by contrast the conclusion drawn from the detailed analysis air strategists made of the bombing of Warsaw and the Battle of Britain: the effects of enemy attack were less severe the more spacious and uncrowded the city was as a whole.[224] The separation of business and residential areas and the 'introduction of space' between rows of houses were therefore two absolute requirements for new cities that could defend themselves in wartime.

Leading architects such as Konstanty Gutschow in Hamburg had been pondering for some time how to incorporate bomb-proof anti-aircraft towers into the new cityscape and came up with a vast number of plans, drawings, and models. These 'defence towers', which were also envisaged for Berlin and Vienna, seemed to be a sort of monumental display of power, a symbol suggesting something 'truly great', as the architect Friedrich Tamm said. In addition, for Hitler the 'severe law of architecture' was perceptible in the spare, almost 'masculine' structures.[225]

The reconstruction of the cities was an aspect of the attempt to cope with acute crisis and the province of those concerned with housing policy and with securing new locations,[226] while at the same time reflecting images of the projected 'national community' in the period after the expected final victory. The architect Richard Zorn had collected fifty-three photos of burnt-out Hamburg houses as a documentary record for the city's photographic department of the destruction of Hamburg's architectural features. In his postscript he alluded to this mixture of destruction and utopian projection: the photos were a reminder of traditional Hamburg architecture, of a time when there were neither the bad habits of 'the nasty kind of free enterprise' nor 'cheap profiteering'. The implication was that after the war the reconstruction would resume this tradition and so display the 'true' face of the Hanseatic city, free from capitalist distortions and the ugly manifestations of (Jewish) greed.[227]

In March 1943 Albert Speer, chief architect of the Reich capital, persuaded Hitler to accept his plans for the reconstruction of German cities and the result in October 1943 was a 'Führer Decree concerning the Reconstruction of Bombed Cities'. Hitler had already spoken with calculated cynicism to Goebbels about the British raids on certain towns, commenting that however cruel they might be they nevertheless had a positive aspect. 'He has studied the map of Cologne in great detail', Goebbels noted in April 1942 in his diary and had come to the conclusion that principally those streets of houses had been destroyed 'that should in fact have been demolished to create open spaces but had we demolished them this would have imposed very severe psychological strain on the population. The enemy has thus relieved us of having to do it.'[228]

In December 1943 Speer set out his plans in a letter to the Gauleiters. By contrast with his (and Hitler's) earlier dreams of an architecture suggesting imperial pretensions his tone was more subdued. Immediately after the war, according to Speer, reconstruction was to begin; that was the correct time because up to that point all construction workers would be concentrated in armaments and would not be available until later. Plans for the reconstruction (and this was a shift in priorities) did not consist in designing individual groups of artistic buildings, but rather the task in hand was to concentrate fully on restoring the extensive streets of houses and on rebuilding those areas of cities that had been particularly badly hit.[229] Thus Speer no longer used the term 'really large' but rather spoke of the need to save and to examine which areas could be rebuilt. In particular reconstruction was to be used to save cities from traffic gridlock, which was a danger in Germany as it was in London or New York, if the increase in overall traffic were not regulated and the roads significantly widened.

Pragmatic considerations were therefore a priority: the rapid building of estates of 'massive type construction', temporary housing of all kinds made of wood or precast concrete and the reconstruction of city centres, including shops needed by the population. Plans for coping with acute crisis and projects to reconfigure the inner cities were thus directly linked and yet had a markedly more defensive character even than in 1942. In view of the destruction caused by the Allies on the home front there was virtually no more talk of *völkisch* building projects. At the same time, the experts with whom Speer discussed his plans evidently sensed a growing crisis of confidence among the population. The top priority in reconstruction was therefore to be homes rather than gigantic, showy Nazi buildings. Homes also seemed an urgent priority because, as one representative at talks with Speer said in November 1943, the 'enemy', Britain, was constantly putting out reports about its post-war plans and this had already caused great concern among the German population. In highlighting huge home-building programmes for 'little people' and hence the welfare state as the alternative to fascism, British propaganda was having a marked effect.

From December 1943 onwards Speer's ministry had a 'working party for the planned reconstruction of bombed cities', which began work in February

1944 by first acquiring a detailed overview of the level of destruction.[230] The picture emerging from local feedback was grim and left no doubt about the devastation caused by the bombing. Yet at the same time great opportunities were created: by the beginning of 1945 the architects in Speer's ministry sketched, drew, and modelled as it were the exterior view of the 'national community', conducting a ceaseless argument about what it should be like with other ministries and Party organizations involved in the provision of homes. What was the 'right' sort of new building? How large should a national comrade's home be and, viewed from the perspective of racial and population policy, did it in any way conform to these require-ments and assumptions, however insane they might be?[231] And who, in the final analysis, was to decide on the allocation of resources in the polycratic power structure that was the Third Reich?

In his speech to the Gauleiters Speer had made it clear that his department had a purely advisory role and the real planning authority remained at local level. This was to calm the extremely sceptical Gauleiters, who rejected any attempt by Speer to encroach on their powers and were particularly unwilling to write a blank cheque for architects who came from outside to reconstruct their cities. In fact debates about the future of the city had been going on for years in local government. They ground for the most part to a halt as Allied raids expanded. At the Hamburg office for work important for the war effort directed by Gutschow all planning matters had been on hold since May 1941 because priorities had changed and new housing had to be created.[232]

In the first weeks and months after the city was severely damaged at the end of July 1943 the town planners' main task was to deal with the crisis. The struggle to obtain raw materials and labour, to establish areas of responsibility, and to create living quarters left no room for extravagant plans. But as early as December 1943 Gutschow had begun again to consider the reconstruc-tion and remodelling of the city, taking up again the work he had begun in 1941 as official 'architect for the remodelling of the Hanseatic city of Hamburg'. This time, however, he was in a position to do a more thorough job, working closely with the working party for the 'reconstruction of Ger-man cities'. At the end of 1943 Gutschow and his deputy, Rudolf Hillebracht, toured Germany, visiting cities such as Kassel and Berlin, Rostock and Lübeck, Dortmund, Essen, and Wuppertal and trying to obtain from Speer's working party reliable data about the severity and impact of Allied air raids that they could use in designing a 'new' Hamburg. Not only architects but doctors, statisticians, and sociologists were involved in the planning.[233]

The general development plan of 1944, the master plan for reconstruction, was thus imbued with the vision of a 'new Hamburg'. Most of the damaged buildings in Gutschow's view were no great loss.[234] The enemy bombs had destroyed many of the 'inferior areas of the city'. From the planners' point of view the destruction provided a unique opportunity and was a positive 'blessing'. Now there were no more tenements and low-grade housing. The Hamburg he and his colleagues dreamt of would be new and yet also 'be distinctively Hamburg'. *Völkisch* thinking and local patriotism were bound up together. There would be widened streets, open spaces, and 'Alster arteries' creating a network of waterways in the city. In future people would be able to live in small, integrated developments, on the edge of which would be crèches, hostels for the Hitler Youth, and play areas. Businesses were to be moved out of the residential areas and living and working to be separate. Even if at the outset, as Gutschow said, the primary object was to provide homes for bombed-out families, no city of the future could develop without large community buildings such as the Führer had spoken of, for it was these in particular that distinguished the city of the future from that of the past, from the soulless architecture characteristic of big cities. The upper parts of the banks of the Elbe were earmarked for the 'development of monumental buildings': a Strength through Joy* hotel, grand quay, and palace of the 'national community'.

The priorities for reconstruction were, however, a matter of dispute among the various authorities, local government districts, and architects. Even if architectural visions fired the imagination of men such as Gutschow, a good number of radical suggestions met with resistance. In Hanover, for example, the architect Gerhard Graubner, professor at the Technical University, had drawn up his own plan for the Gau capital at roughly the same time as Gutschow and presented it at the beginning of March 1944 to the city councillors. The focus was the city's 'ability to defend itself' and by this Graubner meant the fundamental reorientation of city planning to take account of the conditions of future air warfare.[235] In every instance the 'concept of defence' was more important than historical reminiscences of the architectural traditions of the past. Plans up to this point had in his view not paid sufficient attention to the new requirements.

---

* Translators' note: Strength through Joy (Kraft durch Freude) was the German Labour Front's leisure organization.

In concrete terms this meant that the city had to be protected from air attack and be organized in such a way that life could go on in spite of air raids. In his view there should be numerous 'tall, tower-like buildings' in the town, defensive structures where the population would take shelter and where anti-aircraft teams would be stationed. The plan envisaged moving many everyday activities underground and building in Hanover a unique system of tunnels and transport links so that if possible production could go on even during raids. His fellow architects regarded the plans with extreme scepticism, not because they considered the 'concept of defence' absurd, but because there was great reticence about, as it were, subordinating all matters to do with city planning to this one preoccupation and so ignoring the whole historical development of the city.

Detailed information about these discussions was rarely to be found in the newspapers and whenever there was talk of what was euphemistically known as the city of the future and enthusiastic reference was made to future Nazi buildings the reaction at the end of 1943/4 was very unexpected. The reconstruction of ruined cities was supposed to engender hope amid the destruction and also be an appeal to people's determination to keep going; but this message was not well received, as the SD recalled after an article was published in 1944 in the *Völkischer Beobachter* about the reconstruction. 'There is no question now', the article stated, 'that the terror of British-American bombing is creating a beneficial situation with regard to the difficult matter of restricted freedom of movement. It is freeing polluted spaces for the healthy, well-designed and attractive buildings of socialism.'

Many people considered it 'beyond comprehension' that the author could make a virtue of necessity by emphasizing the positive aspects of the devastation. The next thing, the SD reported numerous outraged people as saying, would be that the head of a rationing office would be glad that 'national comrades' had been killed in a raid because he had thereby saved meat and butter coupons.[236] The cynical logic of the city planners' modernization schemes therefore reached at this point the limits of what could be said in public; that did little to rein in their ambitions.

'Grand Designs' for the Modern British City

In Britain at this point the future of bomb-damaged cities was also on the agenda, though they were not burdened with damage on the same scale.

And this future was no less politically charged for after all the problems were of a similar kind to those in Germany: the future of densely populated industrial areas, the relationship between city and countryside, the state's promise of a better society, and some mitigation of the negative aspects of urban development. However, the response that emerged to these similar problems of modern industrial societies and the new options the air war had created were different.

Up to 1942 there were no central state planning authorities. Now, after increasingly intense debate about the future of the British nation and the welfare state, such an authority was created as the Ministry of Works and Planning with eleven regional offices.[237] The first high point was the Town and Country Planning Act of 1943, which subjected all land not already covered by regulations to a unified set of planning rules. Many Conservatives in particular were less than enthusiastic about this and the first battle lines began to emerge for future conflicts between many a euphoric town and country planner with ambitions for social reform on the one hand and landowners and entrepreneurs on the other.[238] The war and the Blitz had opened the floodgates for a new and heated debate about architecture and policies surrounding house-building that had already taken place among experts in the inter-war period but until now had not had the remotest chance of being turned into reality.[239]

From the end of 1940 and beginning of 1941 the climate of opinion had seemed to be changing, with the result that many city planners gained new impetus and plans that had in the main lain for years in a drawer had a chance of being implemented. The moment was favourable and a good many local government officials, for example in Bristol, Coventry, and Southampton, hoped that reconstruction could be financed from state funds.[240]

Plymouth was one of these cities. There the air war had made already existing problems critical: the city could not cope with the rise in the volume of traffic, the housing stock was old, and the increasing numbers of people moving there along with industrial expansion meant that the population density was more than twice the national average. These factors were apparent to the Minister of Works and Buildings, John Reith, when he visited Plymouth in early July 1941 and advised that an independent committee of experts should be formed to guide the reconstruction. From September 1941 therefore the leading city planners and architects Patrick Abercrombie and James Peter Watson worked on a 'Plan for Plymouth' that was to solve the acute problems caused by bombing as well as correcting the city's deficient infrastructure.[241]

The Blitz offered them the opportunity to build a city that promised to improve people's quality of life. Narrow Victorian streets were to be done away with. The air raids had, in their view, destroyed particularly ugly parts of the city such as the Victorian West Pier. Now there was space for the people and the city should be adapted to those people. This was the new concept of the 'modern' and was in complete contrast to all the collectivist German visions of a 'national community' entirely controlled and documented. Their plan envisaged that the old city centre would be cleared and a broad promenade and pedestrian way would run through the city. To the north there would be offices and government buildings, further south the shopping streets, hotels, and restaurants, in the west industry and a marine pavilion, and in the north the railway station and the central bus station. There was little left of the old city, apart from part of the port, and this would be named 'historic Plymouth'. The plan for the whole complex was a radical and deliberate break with the architecture of the nineteenth century and everything connected with Victorian values.

The time seemed right for a less densely populated city centre, built from the region's traditional limestone and the steel typical of the modern age. The model they presented to those who had commissioned them was supposed to reflect both the history and future of the nation in wartime: affluence, security, health for all—these were the aims of this new architecture, which promised a response to the search for national and local identity, for Britishness in wartime.[242] They moved seamlessly from Sir Francis Drake and the defeat of the Spanish Armada in 1588 to Plymouth's unbroken spirit in its fight against the Luftwaffe and to the reconstruction of a humane city. The remodelling of the city centre thus appeared to be a symbol of the rise of a nation that had gained supremacy over the seas with Drake and that now with victory over Hitler was to experience a new beginning. Yet however memorable the message and however much applause the planners garnered at first throughout the country, the plans were by no means universally accepted.

Soon there was vigorous resistance, for the plans envisaged shifting the traditional boundaries between city and countryside and locating new buildings outside the city limits that had existed up to that point. That meant not only huge costs for the purchase of land but also that numerous residents had to pay their rates to different local authorities, causing considerable reductions in expected revenues.[243] And there was a further problem: these ideas assumed there would be close regional cooperation, and yet even more than in the area of air-raid protection local authorities were extremely vigilant to prevent the 'tentacles' of the city from invading the autonomy of smaller towns and communities and even eventually burdening them with additional costs. It was in the neighbouring districts in Cornwall in particular that the plans were heavily criticized because they gave the impression of opening the door to the city's drive to dominate the region.

Planning and coordination were thus regarded as a means of removing regional autonomy by stealth in favour of central jurisdictions. On the other hand, Dunstan, the chairman of the Plymouth Conservatives, used all his eloquence at a meeting with neighbouring councils to persuade them to send a representative to the joint reconstruction committee. The purpose of this committee, as he assured people repeatedly, was not 'territorial aggression' but rather it had been created solely in order to reconstruct the city after its destruction by German bombers.[244] There was still resistance and the grand plans for the region were gradually cut down to size in the battles over responsibilities and by local authorities anxious about their interests. On the other hand, the redevelopment of the inner city, with a few adjustments, did in the end gain majority support in the city council and was a matter of lively national interest, embodying, as it seemed to do, that spirit of 'national renewal' whose time had come.

Among local leaders and in the press the mood was so euphoric that there was reluctance even in Whitehall to oppose some of the proposals, including a local 'Magna Carta', on the grounds that they were too extravagant and radical.[245] After all, Plymouth was the first city that in the wake of the Town and Country Planning Act 1944 applied for the state to take over the costs of the expensive reconstruction[246] and was finally able in 1947 in the presence of the royal family to open the first major intersection of this massive development project.

The Town and Country Planning Act was, however, by no means the consequence of exaggerated ambitions. On the contrary, after it was passed there was a storm of protest.[247] Many city administrations considered the regulations far from adequate. One example was that the state funds that could be applied for were available for only ten years. In view of the extensive plans this was clearly too short a period in which to deal with serious cases of war damage.

However often people appealed to the spirit of reform, in practice reconstruction told a different story. Reservations about 'experts' and socialist 'visions'
were not confined to the Conservative chairman of the Portsmouth planning
committee, who used a newspaper article to make fun of clueless technocrats
who produced grand schemes on the basis of no practical experience.[248] Left-
wing MPs were also unenthusiastic about the bolder plans for they were concerned less about long-term reconstruction than about short-term and
medium-term provision of housing and solutions to acute problems.

The raids on Hull, Britain's third largest port, in March and May 1941
had caused severe damage, exacerbating the existing housing shortages and
destroying much industrial plant around the port.[249] Urgently needed labour
had left the city, and as a result of the drop in population and the destruction
of the infrastructure the city's revenues had fallen, as in Portsmouth and
Southampton. Immediately after the raids ceased and the most pressing
emergencies had been dealt with the debate about reconstruction began.
The plans produced by Max Lock by invitation of the council and presented
in the city in 1942/3 were, like Plymouth, an attempt at a 'grand design': a
new city centre, wide new streets, parks, and separate areas for homes and
industry. The city was to lose its class structure and a new 'community' was
to emerge. The plans' starting point was the need for 32,000 homes, 15,000
of which were considered urgent and not to be postponed.

At the outset of the project Lock, supported by the Labour Party, had
managed to win widespread and enthusiastic acceptance for his plans among
the various parties and interest groups. Even Conservative local politicians
and publications signalled they were in favour. But from the middle of 1943
at the latest the tide turned. Whereas initially the planners could also count
on the Ministry's agreement, in October 1943 a ministerial scrutiny committee criticized the estimates for the planned housing provision as distinctly inflated. A lesser sum would be entirely adequate, they said, and
besides, the city's reconstruction should not be confined to housing but
there should be concern for its industrial future. That meant putting more
money into the reconstruction of the port and less into accommodation for
the workers. Now (the summer of 1944) was not the right time for 'beauty
spots and sports palaces', according to the *Daily Mail*, while local industry
ceaselessly thundered that Hull was 'a city and a port and not a cheap edition of Blackpool'.[250] While Labour stuck to its plans and strongly emphasized the importance of housing, Conservatives and business associations
rallied ever stronger forces to oppose them.

Throughout the country shop owners objected to proposals discussed in Hull and elsewhere to create new city centres with long shopping streets that threatened to destroy the traditional pattern of businesses.[251] At the same time more voices were heard in ministries, such as the Town and Country Planning Ministry, appealing for over-ambitious schemes to be rejected and for a stronger emphasis to be put on economic and commercial interests than hitherto.[252]

Coventry's ambitious plans for a socially more balanced redevelopment of the city centre, for new bypasses round the city and a pedestrian precinct in the shopping centre with new buildings for local government and culture,[253] had begun by attracting national attention, before the Ministry voiced its scepticism, claiming the plans were not fully thought through and too expensive. There was, however, reluctance to oppose them openly, for this was the city that was, as it were, the symbol of the war's destruction and thus its demands had particular moral legitimacy. What is more, on one of his visits in 1942 the King had voiced support for the plans, which, contrary to the Ministry's assumptions, had been widely welcomed in the city itself. Whitehall therefore put its faith in delaying tactics and on constant technical interventions, which could amend local plans and proposals, even if they could not actually block them.[254]

This policy of limited interventions reflected a change of priorities in British domestic politics. If Churchill and the War Cabinet had yielded at the beginning of 1940 to increasing public pressure and appointed Lord Reith, an acknowledged expert in the field, to head the new authority, the latter's support dwindled in the course of the war and finally led to his dismissal in February 1942. Churchill himself had been pressing for it and had barely disguised his attempts to rein in those ambitious planning proposals, for which his chief planning expert was held responsible. After a short period of euphoria and exuberant planning, from 1942 onwards at the latest the decisions of local politicians were taken in the shadow of absolute penury. Disillusionment and disappointment were felt by many who in the debates of the first two war years and in the 'Blitz spirit' had seen a cross-party consensus in favour of constructing a new Britain and had believed that the much-invoked solidarity of nights in the air-raid shelters would be the foundation on which to build the post-war society.[255]

At the beginning of October 1944 *Picture Post* published a long article on 'London's Bombed Homes: A Defeat on the Home Front'.[256] A few years earlier the magazine had reported on the generous support given to those who had been bombed out but now, the introduction said, it was forced to write about the tragic failure of the reconstruction. The cover photo showed one of the cramped temporary homes, where plaster was coming off the walls, the windows had only scraps of curtain, and people had hardly more than a few sheets and a bed. The defeat referred to was the defeat of the solidarity shown in the Battle of London, a rank injustice towards those who had courageously stood up to the enemy and had now been abandoned by the authorities.

The relevant committees of the LCC had already prepared in December 1940 for the challenge of rebuilding homes after the air raids. The assumption was that there would be 100,000 homeless families who would need rehousing as quickly as possible after the raids and not merely in temporary accommodation. On that basis 50,000 new dwellings were required. The aim was to produce rapid results. After all, house-building had stopped with the outbreak of war and with it all the initiatives that the LCC had taken since the 1930s to clear the slums in working-class areas.

The demand for quick results, however, also implied abandoning thoughts of long-term, expensive, though higher-quality building projects or at least putting them on the back burner, because in the opinion of the finance officers responsible both the labour and more especially the money were not there. But as in Plymouth leading architects and town planners had been working in London since the heavy raids on a 'grand design' that attempted to deal with the numerous social and infrastructure problems, though admittedly on a timescale stretching far into the post-war period that held out no hope of solutions for several years.[257]

The County of London Plan published in 1943, in which Patrick Abercrombie again played the leading role, envisaged a 'mixed structure' for the many boroughs, where families and other households settled around central amenities such as schools, shops, and businesses, and so created a new 'sense of community'. The destruction caused by the air war seemed to offer just the right opportunity to begin such a project. Even before the outbreak of war, the plan stated, London had been ripe for fundamental redevelopment: poor housing, too much industry in the inner city, unequal distribution of green spaces among the various boroughs, a transport system that had not kept pace with the growth of the city. These were all factors that fed the planners' imagination.

In addition, the plan was to take account of social change, which was a by-product of any war. Thus the town planners aimed to create new districts of small units of some 6,000 to 10,000 people. Their workplaces were to be separate from where they lived and everything they needed for living was to be close to hand. Green spaces were to mark the boundaries between neighbourhoods and at the same time offer somewhere to relax for the 'community', at the centre of which there would be public squares and buildings where people could meet and socialize.[258]

German and British town planners had much in common in their desire to remodel cities and in their vision of the spacious city as a response to the 'Moloch' of the past. Short distances, small districts, shops and businesses to hand, regulated traffic, and a concentration of community life in central locations—these were deliberations that in London, Coventry, Berlin, and Hanover were supported by the common hope that the air war had created the preconditions for the 'grand design' of the post-war world. But whereas in Germany the function of the city in wartime and the militarization of society played an increasing role, in Britain there were no such considerations.

What would have happened if German air raids had continued for longer and even more cities had been destroyed is a matter for speculation. It is altogether possible that the significance of air-raid precautions would also have been greater. What is clear is that in Britain there was sympathy neither for monumental, stately buildings nor the restrictive discipline and control of 'settlement communities'. However similar on both sides was the perception of the problems of 'the modern', British and German visions of a new society were very different. Both sides used the term 'community' but for one side it meant free individuals and for the other regimented national comrades.

Whereas in Britain virtually nothing was known about German plans and discussions after the end of 1943, in Hamburg Gutschow's architects evidently watched carefully what their colleagues in London were designing and discussing in professional publications such as the *Architect's Journal*. Articles were quickly translated and made available to the staff, though on the strict understanding that the contents were secret.[259] This was presumably unnecessary as wide-ranging plans in Britain were soon on the defensive, for they offered a solution only for the distant future, too late for many families needing somewhere to live now, while the war was going on. It was the boroughs and their administrations that took immediate responsibility for the reconstruction and repair of war damage and from 1941 onwards they had come together in special cross-boundary working parties in order to tackle the destruction jointly.

After air raids it was the task of Report Centres set up in every district to request help from the responsible regional and state organizations. Competition for resources was fierce, as it was for labour, experts, and materials, and tensions resulted. Even so, by 1 June 1944 more than 2.15 million people had been given 'first aid', while additional work had been done to some 1.32 million homes and about 1,075 million had to be repaired a second time.

The London boroughs therefore had their hands full, the more so because from the summer of 1944 onwards additional workers assigned to repair work were removed and redirected towards preparations for the invasion. Finally the situation became acute once more, when the city came under fire from V-1 rockets. At the end of June 1944, just two weeks after the first V-1 raids, the Metropolitan Borough Standing Joint Committee met to review the situation: some 337,000 homes had been damaged. The assumption was that up to 20,000 would be damaged every day and there was no telling when this spectre would pass. The worried representatives of the boroughs affected produced reports on the damage up to that point.[260] Only one week later the number of damaged homes had already risen to 443,000. Given the limited resources reconstruction could not keep pace with the growing number of homes destroyed. The V-1s and V-2s, contrary to what was implied by the eloquent silence of propaganda on the subject, had in fact created considerable problems for the London borough administrations. There was in the final analysis uncertainty about what the Germans might still throw at Britain, in spite or precisely because of the hopelessness of their situation. From late September 1944, at any rate, the London city authorities had been setting about reviewing their reconstruction arrangements. The newly created London Repairs Executive Committee now took over leadership of the reorganization.[261]

Equipped with extensive powers, it could override many sectional interests and at the same time direct aid towards particularly needy boroughs. For this to happen there first had to be a review of priorities. Top of the list were now essential repairs to damaged homes and shelters; the reconstruction of completely destroyed houses was postponed until the end of the war; state compensation payments were restricted, to prevent private individuals from investing money in the reconstruction of their own homes and thus tying up valuable labour that was more urgently needed elsewhere. Finally, the committee made efforts to compensate for the lack of materials and labour by seeking assistance from other parts of the country.

Yet however successful the reorganization was, by the time victory was assured in March 1945 and preparations for the post-war period were in high gear, the city still had a backlog of urgent repairs.[262] The last V-2 raids on London in March 1945, though they made no impact on the course of the war, nevertheless caused the greatest amount of damage since the beginning of the year: some 3,000 buildings were severely damaged, around 30,000 slightly damaged, and there was great concern that further raids would inflict even greater losses.

The acute crisis management that was still required left no room for grand plans for the future. Although the national 'Building Programme' had envisaged in 1944 that at least 60 per cent of all new buildings would be homes, these new buildings were still just plans, the money for which was still uncertain. By the middle of June 1947 at any rate a mere 1,500 of the 50,000 new homes planned had actually been built.[263] As in Germany, at the end of the war the cities had radically changed, which was favourable to those with a vision of totally reconfiguring their centuries-old layout. In practice, however, what was soon uppermost was the search for cheap and rapid solutions that left virtually no room for the great dream of new ways of structuring communities that would achieve social solidarity within a class-riven society.

Thus for local authorities the air war was an opportunity and a burden at the same time. Even though the threat of night raids had passed, the structural problems of cities were far from being solved. On the contrary, the legacy of the air war was to preoccupy cities for many years, keeping the memory of the Blitz alive. The role of the Christian message of reconciliation and resurrection in all this and the role of the churches as a whole in the Blitz is the subject of the next chapter.

5

The Churches and the Air War

A Just War, with Just Bombing?

There was no cry of jubilation to be heard from British churches, whether Anglican, nonconformist, or Catholic, when war was declared on the German Reich on 3 September 1939. The mood was more restrained and subdued than in 1914, when prominent bishops had called for a crusade against Germany.[1] The horrors of the Flanders battlefields were still deeply imprinted on people's minds in 1939 and shaped their expectations and interpretations of war.[2] Leading bishops were also aware that their church had taken part in propaganda for that 'holy war' and so had to bear some of the responsibility for the catastrophe.

In the inter-war period there had therefore been intensive efforts to achieve a new Protestant ecumenism in Europe, a Christian spirit that crossed national boundaries and would form the basis of a new partnership. A sizeable number of members of the ecumenical movement were also committed to pacifism in organizations such as the Peace Pledge Union (PPU) and engaged in radical criticism of war, seeing the real danger in war itself, rather in the rise of fascist movements.[3] Yet in spite of a rise in popularity this pacifism, which was often located in nonconformist churches, remained a minority view. Leading Anglican churchmen such as William Temple, who was Archbishop of York when war broke out, had condemned pacifism in their own ranks and regarded themselves as vindicated by the threat posed by National Socialism. Peace at any price in the conflict with Hitler would have meant putting at risk the Christian foundations of Europe, as Temple made clear on 3 October 1939.[4] The aggressor must be stopped. Nevertheless, the war was not to be waged against the German people as such, itself the victim of a brutal dictatorship, he said. Britain was not going to war to save Christianity.[5] But the conflict with Nazi Germany was a fight to preserve the possibility of leading any kind of Christian life in the world—and that was an existential challenge by any standards.[6] What, however, constituted justified means in a just war? The bombing of cities, the bombing of civilians? Where were the limits and what was permitted? And what contribution could the churches make to maintaining morale in wartime?

This chapter investigates the significance of the churches in the air war, the relationship between state and church, the attempts to give meaning to death and destruction, and the issue of what consequences bombing had for pastoral practice in Germany and Britain. In the process it is important to take into account the background from the First World War onwards, as well as the different political and administrative positions of the Christian churches during the war that enabled them to speak publicly about war, violence, and pastoral care. For a democracy and a dictatorship set very different limits.

In Britain the issue of the ethics of war had aroused serious misgivings even before its outbreak. In May 1939 Alan Don, secretary to the Archbishop of Canterbury, had to reply to a question from a troubled church member about the church's position on the moral justification for bombing. Don declared himself convinced that the RAF would avoid any strategy that targeted air raids on densely populated areas with the intention of causing panic among the civilian population.[7]

In June 1939 Cosmo Lang, Archbishop of Canterbury, told a meeting of bishops about his correspondence on this subject with the Secretary of State for Air, Sir Kingsley Wood.[8] In it Wood had sketched out the future limits of British operations: 'The intentional bombing of civilian populations is illegal.' Only targets of a clearly recognizable military kind were legitimate, and what was more, raids on military targets could be carried out only in such a way as to leave civilians unharmed.[9] The bishops could accept this line of argument and defend it actively against critics from their own ranks. When in June 1940 the Archbishops of Canterbury and York met representatives of Christian pacifist movements at Lambeth Palace, Temple assured his sceptical interlocutors that he would reject any war in which the bombing of 'open cities' and hence of defenceless civilians became a strategic aim.

From the point of view of the pacifists, however, the discussion had not delivered the desired result at all, namely a proscription of war. They were quick to observe how some bishops, as in 1914, seemed prepared to celebrate the victory of the Allies as the victory of Christianity. 'Although we were fighting totalitarianism there seemed to be an increase in our midst of that very evil,' as one of the downcast participants recorded after the meeting with Temple and Lang, and this, he felt, was a tendency that, if it continued, might lead to a schism within the church between the minority of pacifists and the majority of those in favour of the war.[10]

Even if this assessment was obviously exaggerated, the view taken of the air war and the morality of war as a whole touched a sensitive nerve in the Anglican church with regard to how it understood its tradition as a state church. What role should the church play in wartime? One similar to 1914, when it offered the right spiritual cues for war and was clearly subordinated to the state's aims? Never again, at least as far as the leaders of the pacifist movement such as Charles Raven were concerned, should the church be so closely linked with state authority.[11]

George Bell, Bishop of Chichester and later one of the most emphatic critics of Allied air raids, addressed this problem in November 1939.[12] The church in wartime—in future this must mean defining moral standards of judgement independently of national interests. For Bell Christian ethics were the central issue, not strategic military planning. Both sides, state and church, had different functions. The ethics of war should not take their lead from national priorities but must be guided by universal Christian values. Bell therefore demanded that his church should not ally itself with the lies and hatred propounded by propaganda but should seek reconciliation with the enemy. Such an understanding of the church, he said, positively requires its members to raise objections to the plans of one's own government, if, for example, these mean the bombing of civilians or the annihilation of the enemy.

Even if Bell's emphasis on a theology of peace was clearly distinct from that of other leading bishops, it nevertheless, despite all reservations, did not exclude the possibility of military conflict. As he attempted to explain in a diocesan letter, war appeared as a 'tragedy', an expression of human weakness and sin, and thus could never, as in 1914, be understood as a 'holy war'.[13] The assumption was that it would be a kind of warfare that, as Bishop David of Liverpool demanded in April 1940, remained 'decent', spared civilians, and was not prone to hasty retaliation.[14]

The issue of retaliation was soon in fact to be on the agenda, when in summer 1940 first London, then, from the autumn onwards, cities through the country were targeted by the Luftwaffe. Although at one of the funerals for those killed in the raids on Coventry in the middle of November 1940

Bishop Mervyn Haigh in his short address appealed to the power of for-giveness,[15] only a few weeks later (more churches had in the meantime been destroyed in air raids) Haigh made it clear in a speech to his diocesan con-ference that the German style of warfare could not be without conse-quences. The British government could not be condemned if it started to mount similar raids on cities, given that the Germans had been doing it for some time. In the final analysis this meant bombing the civilian population. Anyone who was not prepared to take this step should not have gone to war with the Nazi aggressor. In his view it was not fundamentally morally rep-rehensible to resort to such tactics, as long as these helped to avert greater dangers. In the end, Haigh said, it was not Britain that had started the war or desired it, but rather it had been forced to go to war by external forces.[16]

For justifying retaliation the Bishop of Coventry had to endure harsh criticism. To condemn atrocities while at the same time calling for fresh ones was inconsistent, as a reproachful commentary in the influential *Church Times* pointed out.[17] Yet there were also prominent advocates such as Bishop Arthur Headlam of Gloucester. Whereas up to that point, January 1941, Britain had confined itself to bombing dockyards such as in Hamburg the Germans had already killed 20,000 people in Rotterdam.[18] He could not see what moral standards were being contravened by the RAF's treating German cities as the Germans had treated Coventry.[19]

Basically Headlam had only taken to its logical conclusion what was already normal practice in the air war. Within a very short time retaliation had become an essential component in its strategy and propaganda. Quite a few leading Anglican bishops were thus on the horns of a dilemma. No one wanted to speak openly of 'retaliation' for this was too sharply in conflict with Christian ethics and the bitter lessons learned from the euphoria of the First World War.[20] At the same time it was also evident that the German bombing of British cities was bound to provoke a response. The boundary, as Cosmo Lang, the Archbishop of Canterbury, made clear at a meeting of bishops at the end of May 1941, was set at the point where unintentional collateral damage, such as was unavoidable when military targets were being bombed, turned into a policy aimed at taking human life.[21]

George Bell, on the other hand, became more and more convinced that the boundary to senseless violence had been crossed. At the end of Octo-ber 1940 in a letter to Britain's leading military strategist Liddell Hart he had characterized the tit-for-tat bombing of the German and British capitals as a 'calamitous mistake'.[22] Liddell Hart was a close personal friend of Bell's and the two were to have frequent discussions in the coming years about their reservations concerning the British air-war strategy. In addition, he had supported Bell's initiative to ban night bombing raids. This was a suggestion the bishop had made in *The Times* in April 1941, hoping it could bring Britain and Germany to the negotiating table.[23] Among the small pacifist groups in the nonconformist churches, from whom less and less had been heard during this period as a result of state censorship, Bell's suggestion, planned in the first instance as a unilateral British gesture to prevent a further escalation of the war, was much welcomed. He could not, however, gain the support of other bishops or politicians for his initiative.[24]

In his younger days Bell had been private secretary to Randall Davidson, predecessor of Cosmo Lang as Archbishop of Canterbury, and the former's pacifist teachings from the First World War had left their mark on him. By contrast with William Temple, who succeeded Lang as Archbishop of Canterbury in 1942, Bell did not believe the RAF's assurances that the expanded air war against German cities for which Arthur Harris was responsible was continuing to concentrate on industrial and military targets.[25] That was what the Air Minister, Archibald Sinclair, had assured Temple in a personal letter in July 1943.[26]

The background to Temple's enquiry was the growing number of letters of protest that had been landing on his desk since the end of 1942 criticizing the changes to the air-war strategy.[27] A group of Anglican theologians, for example, feared that a spiral of violence was being set in motion which in the end would lead only to ever greater misery. The raids on Cologne and Hamburg and the impending bombing of Rome were in their view evidence that Britain was on the way to jeopardizing its moral credibility, which lay in the fact that it was waging war for a 'higher' cause and in a 'Christian' manner.[28] As one of the group, Ashley Sampson, noted, it seemed as though the war had now entered a phase in which the motive of revenge was being raised to the level of a strategic necessity and so all the boundaries circumscribing a just war were disappearing.[29] As after the First World War, the church would therefore have to answer for how it responded to the growth of this dangerous mood. The solution proposed was not to desist from bombing in general but to return to a policy that did not pay back the enemy in kind, retaliating with atrocities for atrocities suffered, in order not to end up on the same level as the Nazi criminals.

Admittedly the critics did not come only from Britain but also from the international ecumenical movement. In a confidential letter to Temple its general secretary, Willem Visser't Hooft, spelled out the growing misgivings within the Protestant churches about 'such a brutal form of warfare', that 'in truth [would] obliterate whole cities' and by no means attack only military targets.[30] In the face of this policy even 'some of our best friends' (by which he meant above all sections of the German Protestant resistance, with which Visser't Hooft kept up close contact) were striking a 'tone of injured innocence and self-pity', thus forgetting most of what 'their nation has done to others'.

Evidently therefore, as Visser't Hooft observed, the tendency to cast themselves as victims and the emotional tone of innocence had affected even people who otherwise saw themselves as intellectually far removed from National Socialism. He alluded in his letter to Temple to the moral dilemma of the Allied conduct of the war: on the one hand to be waging a war, in his view, evidently as 'total' as that of the Nazis, if not even more comprehensive; on the other, he had been hearing an increasing number of voices from countries occupied by Germany saying with 'Schadenfreude' that the Germans were now getting what they deserved. Visser't Hooft and the ecumenical movement in no way intended to let itself be hijacked to support German foreign propaganda and to mount an international appeal by Christians for a halt to the air raids. At the same time he was alive to the moral dilemma posed by a method of waging war that was in danger of resembling that of the Nazis, and indeed of being worse, and thus forfeiting its credibility.[31]

Temple's response, like that of the large majority of Anglican and Catholic bishops, did not acknowledge this criticism of the bombing raids as atrocities. In the light of the information he had had from Sinclair he neither shared the judgement that the raids exceeded the boundaries established up to this point, nor did he believe that it made sense to pursue a war against Nazi Germany without using tough, at times terrible, military force. As Temple told one critic in December 1943, that meant accepting that the war had become a 'total war'.[32] Although he continued to maintain that the bombing of civilians was inadmissible, he nevertheless held fast to the assurance of the military leadership that, in spite of reports of the destruction of German cities, that position had not changed.

Temple and the majority of the other bishops had nothing to do with military triumphalism or the aggressive rhetoric of war, and this was very different from 1914. Yet in the final analysis they did not as churchmen consider themselves responsible for matters of military strategy. In the end, criticism of the details was less important than national solidarity, and the broad consensus that this war being fought for the future of Christianity demanded extraordinary force and extraordinary suffering and the church had to play its part.

How broad this consensus was, was something George Bell was forced to find out in his own diocese. In September 1943 the Dean of Chichester made it absolutely clear to him that after his strident criticism of the increasing brutality of the armed forces and their unrestrained bombard-ment of innocent civilians he was no longer welcome as a celebrant at a Battle of Britain memorial service to be held in the cathedral.[33] Bell was the bishop but the dean was in charge of the organization and liturgy of the cathedral.

Bell accepted this decision and, along with Bishop Headlam of Glouces-ter, who had also spoken out vigorously against area bombing as waging war against civilians,[34] he remained an outsider. This, however, did not prevent him from sparking a debate in the House of Lords on 9 February 1944 on the morality of British bombing tactics. To Bell the moment seemed to have arrived for him to make use of the forum provided by his position as a bishop to criticize the government and the military—a unique act of pro-test of this kind. Bell argued that the conflict with National Socialism was as much an ethical as a military one: Britain's credibility and moral superi-ority over the enemy were at stake.[35] He also indicated that military leaders must differentiate between the Nazi regime and the German people and employ military means accordingly.

The bishop had long been one of the Anglican church's experts on Germany. He knew it from his own experience, and as a result of his work in the ecumenical movement in the inter-war years he had numerous, close personal contacts. He supported the Confessing Church and saw himself as a kind of intermediary for the 'other Germany', whose activities were better known to him than to any other British bishop and frequently from first-hand experience. For example, after a meeting in Sweden in June 1942 with Dietrich Bonhoeffer the latter gave him an account of the German resist-ance and asked him to act as a secret courier to relay plans to the British government. Bell was convinced that there was broad commitment to resist-ance to the Nazi regime on the part of the Germans and this mistaken belief played an important role in causing him to reject the bombing campaign.

Emphasizing that even he considered the raids on industrial plant and armaments factories to be necessary, he nevertheless insisted on his view that an appropriate balance had to be found between strategic goals and what achieving them meant in practice. To bomb cities without taking into account many thousands of deaths was to his mind not justified.

Hamburg was just such an example, he felt. With its port installations and industries the city was a prime military target and yet at the same time even before 1933 the city had been one of the foremost bastions of democracy. According to his information there had been 28,000 fatalities—a death toll, as he concluded bitterly, hitherto unprecedented in the history of war. The bombs had not only killed human beings but had destroyed Germany's cultural heritage in the form of buildings, churches, and libraries and these were integral to the 'other Germany' and vitally necessary for post-war reconstruction. The destruction of Germany's cultural riches and the cities as innocent victims were his central critical points.[36] In addition, Bell questioned whether the raids were actually achieving the desired effect and demoralizing the German population. Everything that could be gathered about Germany, including information coming via neutral countries, indicated the opposite.

At first Bell's outrage made little impact in the House of Lords. It did not at any rate provoke the desired debate, not least because no other bishop took an active part. It was Lord Cranborne who had the task of defending the government strategy of area bombing. Without engaging with Bell's actual arguments, he insisted that targeted bombing of cities was the only way of halting the German war machine. Without these raids the war would be prolonged and with it the suffering in Europe.[37] Bell did receive support, however, from Cosmo Lang, the now retired Archbishop of Canterbury. While not sharing Bell's fundamental criticisms he was nevertheless impressed by his speech. He too regarded the recent raids on Hamburg, Frankfurt, and Berlin as crossing the line. He also regretted that some parts of the press had gloated over the raids, thus betraying the values for which the war was being fought.[38]

Bell's protest began to make an impact after newspapers and the BBC reported on his speech in detail. In Nazi Germany it was grist to the mill of the Propaganda Ministry, which cannibalized his criticisms while vaunting the fact that German morale was unbroken.[39] Goebbels suspected that the debate was being used as a cover and convenient moral alibi to pacify certain sections of the public.[40] Bell received a letter from Geneva from Visser't

Hooft about the response from the ecumenical movement: his speech had had great resonance and he could imagine that responses varied widely. At all events church representatives were grateful that Bell had broken the long silence.[41]

In Britain reactions varied and were by no means only negative. The *Daily Telegraph* reported that the RAF was furious and trusted that the head of Bomber Command, Arthur Harris, would give the required response. The *Daily Mail* similarly rejected Bell's views. A cartoon showed two bishops being hit by a German bomb during an air raid while holding up large peace placards saying, 'Let's not be nasty to the Germans' and 'Let's not bomb them once more'.[42] Other newspapers such as *The Times*, on the other hand, published sober reports of Bell's speech in the House of Lords and, as in the case of the *Spectator* and the *New Statesman*, conceded that his arguments had some persuasive power.[43]

His spirited appeal at the very least commanded respect even from his critics and every article in the Anglican church press paid tribute to Bell's courage. This was true also of Temple, the Archbishop of Canterbury, who at the same time regarded his assessment as wrong. The moral principles behind the conduct of the war had not shifted since Harris's appointment. Neither he nor the Bishop of Oxford,[44] Kenneth Escott Kirk, could discern any abandonment of the principles of a 'just war' in the bombings.[45] More support for Bell came from another quarter. Liddell Hart congratulated him on his courageous appeal,[46] saying that an RAF friend of his had let him know that a significant section of the 'silent public' shared his misgivings. That may well have been an exaggeration, for Bell had met with vigorous support neither in the House of Commons nor in the House of Lords. Yet among the responses to his speech there was a majority that felt it had been a courageous appeal to Christian conscience.[47]

Bell also received support from the Catholic church, albeit carefully formulated. The *Catholic Herald*, the most influential Catholic paper, paid tribute to Bell's brave protest, saying that though one might not agree with every detail it did touch on a sore point, namely the escalation of violence in 'total war'. The Catholic press came to his defence against critics, some in the Anglican church, who claimed Bell's protest had played into the Nazis' hands: the fact that Britain still had political debate was in itself a sign of the special quality and superiority of British democracy compared with the Axis countries. From a Catholic perspective the argument surrounding the morality of bombing was linked to the issue of the distinction between civilization and barbarism, as shown by the aims as well as by the manner of conducting the war. Discriminating between combatants and non-combatants was as much a part of this as was the appropriate treatment of prisoners of war.[48]

The *Catholic Herald* was by no means alone in this view. For Catholics the debate about the morality of the air war had long since crossed national boundaries, in particular as a result of the acute threat to Rome. In Catholic circles in the United States it was above all Vera Brittain's book condemning Allied air raids that caused a stir.[49] In it Brittain, a leading pacifist and founding member of the Bombing Restriction Committee, had criticized more sharply than Bell the British change of strategy under Harris and his deliberate targeting of the civilian population. The policy of bombing German cities and the destruction of cultural heritage built up over centuries were to her mind symptoms of the moral decline of the Empire in wartime. Extracts from the book were published the same year in the United States under the title 'Massacre by Bombing' and gave rise to vigorous debate.[50]

One reason why her criticisms attracted so much attention was because virtually simultaneously French and Belgian bishops had protested against the Allied bombing. Brittain's view was that the Americans and British now hardly distinguished between military and civilian targets, thus making themselves guilty of offending against one of the central pillars of a just war, namely the distinction between combatants and non-combatants. In a letter to Roosevelt and Churchill the primate of the Belgian Catholics, Cardinal Joseph van Roey, called on the Allies to put a halt to the bombing that had plunged almost the entire country into 'death and despair'. Many medieval cities had been destroyed, he wrote, and thousands of people killed. Yet contrary to the Allies' assurances that the raids concentrated on military targets the reality of the air war looked somewhat different: many bombs were dropped indiscriminately without any regard for the regions being hit and their populations.[51]

From the point of view of moral theology the radicalization of the air war from 1942 onwards clearly contravened Catholic teaching and the will of the Pope. That at any rate was the opinion of the American Jesuit John C. Ford in an article published in *Theological Studies*, the leading Jesuit theological journal in the USA.[52] Unlike Brittain Ford was not a pacifist. He had no problem with the tactical use of bombing. The deliberate targeting of civilians, however, as now practised by the British, was, he wrote, a different matter. For him one issue above all was central: what rights had non-combatants in modern warfare? As he saw it, natural law admitted no exceptions: protecting innocent human lives was an absolute obligation. Whereas soldiers who took part in unjust violence could themselves become the objects of violence and guilt, the same did not apply to the civilian population. Thus he rejected the argument that German cities had themselves turned into battlefields and that the killing of civilians, for example those who worked in industries, was thus morally justified, for a non-combatant was someone who did not bear arms. Ford saw his standpoint supported by the Pope, who, although issuing no direct statement on the bombing raids, had nevertheless given indirect warnings about the continuous radicalization of the war and about the 'instruments of destruction'[53] that by now were threatening the Holy City itself.

Concern about the Holy City had also caused Bell to act. Using his connections with the interim committee of the ecumenical movement in Geneva, which in 1948 was to become the World Council of Churches, he tried to create an international lobby for the strict regulation of air raids. Admittedly this was an initiative that was destined to fizzle out in view of the war situation at the time, as well as numerous other problems. Even so, Bell's efforts and in particular his speech in the House of Lords carried weight, more weight than the weak voices of the pacifists protesting outside Parliament, or, in the case of the two Labour MPs Alfred Salter and Richard Stokes, inside it, against the British bombing strategy.[54] For he was precisely not a radical opponent of war but someone who as a bishop and leading Anglican churchman could not simply be ignored. His speech was an event, touching as it did on the fundamental reasons why the Empire had gone to war.

The majority of Anglican clergy regarded themselves as representatives of a national church that was an essential component of Britishness and part of a Christian identity rooted in an established church. The war against Germany was a renewed defence of this identity. If, as in the case of Bell's criticisms, it was put in question the role of the Church of England seemed to be no longer clearly defined.

The question posed shortly after the outbreak of war by the Bishop of Chichester in his article on the churches' role in wartime was more topical than ever in 1944/5: if this method of waging war was given support, was the church in the final analysis really anything more than an arm of the secular powers? Or, on the other hand, was it indulging in a form of damaging moral rigorism that could only undermine the fight against National

Socialism? Most bishops tended to take a pragmatic view. In the first place this attitude was fully in line with their traditions of thinking as the established church, which were founded on the assumption that the state and the church had identical goals and interests and to a great extent sidelined questions of military strategy. In the second place, German raids on British cities and emerging information about German atrocities encouraged the view that this war was being fought against an enemy who had to be treated ruthlessly; better to incur some 'guilt' than lose the war. In the third place, ultimately people believed the assurances of the military leaders that the method of waging war against German cities had not changed at all. Bell did not and paid the price.

When on the death of William Temple on 26 October 1944 the bishops started jockeying for position, Bell's name was at first high on the list of those earmarked for leadership of the church. He was experienced, a circumspect administrator, and as a result of his work over decades in the ecumenical movement he was respected both at home and abroad. But at Number 10, which had the final word in the appointment of bishops, Bell's critical standpoint was considered 'sympathetic to Germany' and thus he was mistrusted and ruled out.[55] So it was the Bishop of London, Geoffrey Fisher, who succeeded Temple and not Bell, and when Fisher's successor as Bishop of London, the third most important church appointment after Canterbury and York, was named, Bell was once more passed over.

Thus the controversy over the relationship between church and state and the ethical boundaries of the conduct of the air war developed from being a theological debate within the church to a political conflict in wartime, the repercussions of which were to stretch far beyond 1945.

Why Us? The Theology of War and the Destruction of the 'Homeland'

There had been no comparable open controversy over the conduct of the war among German Catholic and Protestant bishops and in view of Nazi policy towards the churches such a thing could not happen. Indeed, at the beginning of the war the majority of German bishops would not have welcomed it. Whereas Anglicans, nonconformists, and Catholics in Britain were still able during the war to engage in vigorous debate about ethical and political issues, in Germany the debate on the air war had to remain primarily a theological one, for it was only within these narrowly defined limits that it was permissible to reflect on the war at all. At the end of 1939, however, this was not a serious problem for the majority of bishops, for duty to the nation, obedience, and willingness to make sacrifices were the precepts Christians of both churches took into the war with them. For this reason, as war approached they had refused offers from the international ecumenical community of prayers for peace.

At Whitsuntide 1939, only a few months before the outbreak of war, the right-wing nationalist bishop of the Lutheran state church in Hanover, August Marahrens, indignantly rejected on behalf of his church an invitation originating with the Archbishop of Canterbury, Cosmo Lang, to take part in an ecumenical prayer for peace. Many Germans had been 'alarmed', he said, to hear of Lang's support for cooperation with godless Bolshevism. Beside that, there was 'truly no reason to regard this peace as ordained by God and as a blessing for the world and to bewail its collapse as the destruction of the divine world order'. What purported to be a call for peace was promoting suspicions about the German nation and being used as a political weapon. 'In answer to that I am obliged to state that we Protestants, along with all sections of our nation, stand behind our Führer, whose historic project is putting right the injustice of Versailles. It is the destiny and duty of Christendom that Christians are part of their nations, feeling and acting with them. You are loyal to your nation and to what it regards as sacred, as I am to mine. I share your desire for peace to be preserved for the nations on the earth. I ardently wish that it might be a peace in which the nations relate to one another in a just and lasting manner. May the God of peace grant us such a peace and keep us in it!'[56] It was the last time that Marahrens sent a letter to Britain.

The Protestant church media sounded the same note in deploring that Britain was doing battle with the defenceless, with women and children, and claiming that the 'fundamental hypocrisy' of the 'British notion of religion' had been exposed. Shortly before Christmas, at the height of the Battle of Britain, the Protestant Press Association for Germany took stock for the first time and was satisfied: 'For more than three months our Luftwaffe has been striking almost daily at Britain. [...] Fires are showing the British what the German Luftwaffe can do.' But it was the British themselves who had caused this war and military conflict. 'We are, however, obliged to ask them: Don't you British remember that our Führer proposed to you and to the whole world not only to get rid of aerial warfare but even to outlaw it?'[57]

At this point the air war still posed no actual threat to everyday existence and the main focus was on allocating unequivocal blame for the escalation of the war as a way of making propaganda. But from 1942/3 onwards at the latest the consequences of the raids were far more than part of the propaganda battle; they provoked existential questions of religious meaning. How could such suffering be relieved and how could comfort be given in the face of increasing destruction?

At first the only help available was through traditional (Neo-scholastic) concepts and interpretations: air raids were an aspect of 'divine wrath', punishing people for turning away from God. The sufferings endured in the air war thus seemed part of a divine trial that Christians had to go through. For it was not war itself that was wicked but rather it was judged according to the methods by which and the authority on which it was waged.

In the Christian churches the idea of 'divine punishment' was a standard mode of interpretation based on the Old Testament, though it was also ambivalent. For divine intervention in the shape of the war could be provoked by a loss of religious faith but also by the godlessness of the regime that was calling people to war. Unlike in 1914 the Catholic bishops were reluctant to call the war just. Yet at the same time there was no doubt that, in spite of any reservations about the regime's policies regarding the churches and its strategy of repression, Christians should be committed to the war out of 'patriotism', as an act, as it were, of atonement in the service of Jesus Christ and the nation and as the ongoing consequence, as the Munich Cardinal Faulhaber believed, of the unjust peace of 1918/19.[58]

The challenge was to resolve the contradiction between the 'anti-Christian' policy of the Nazi state on the one hand and its natural authority as a state and the shared political and ideological values arising from its opposition to 'Bolshevism' on the other. Leading Protestants and Catholics were operating within these conflicting pressures. Active resistance, if even contemplated, seemed not only hopeless but to the overwhelming majority was inconceivable.[59] Words such as expiation, penance, 'divine punishment', and apocalyptic visitation were part of the semantic arsenal that Catholic and Protestant bishops drew on to create a language in which to speak about the bombing war and at the same time to reconcile a new way of experiencing violence with the traditional Augustinian doctrine of war, which as a rule was used to judge how others conducted warfare but not one's own side.

From 1942/3 onwards understanding the air war as part of a divine visitation on the 'national community' became a recurrent theme in cross-denominational thinking on the theology of war,[60] which attempted to respond to two central issues: the problem of theodicy, why God permits an evil such as aerial warfare with all the suffering and destruction it causes, and the search for appropriate forms of dealing with death, ways of giving spiritual comfort and counselling to the bereaved. The air raids were regarded in this context as cruel acts of destruction, arbitrary and unrestrained, an expression of how technical advances had got out of control, devastating objects of cultural value such as the German nation's churches and monuments.

German air raids were not part of this interpretation and virtually no German bishops seemed to find the bombing of Britain a significant moral problem. 'Total war' had produced destructive power of a new order, a 'frenzy of blind destruction', greater even than the Thirty Years War, as the Munich Cardinal Faulhaber commented to his congregation in a sermon at the reopening of the Munich Cathedral in the middle of August 1943.[61] In this respect the bombing was part of the history of human technical progress, whose temporary endpoint was marked by ruined churches and monasteries.

The bombing war as a sign of civilization losing its way and of people turning away from God—this was also the interpretation offered by the Bishop of Münster, Clemens August Count von Galen. During a pilgrimage to the shrine of Mary at Telgte in July 1943 and after the city of Münster had already been badly bombed, he reminded people that God had given human beings 'reason and free will'.[62] They had the opportunity to use their freedom and autonomy to decide for God and perform his will on earth. Yet for large sections of humanity it was the case that 'You have abandoned God, your father, and you have forgotten God, your creator.' Galen went on: 'Is there any country where God's sovereignty is still generally and publicly acknowledged and where He is honoured as he should be? People live happily enjoying the material things that God gave human beings to use, exploiting all the resources and riches of the natural world that God created.' As human beings had rebelled against God and like the 'sorcerer's apprentice' could no longer control the forces they had unleashed, they should not be surprised about God's response.

This theology was linked to familiar narratives from the First World War, when war was not part of a concrete historical process but was almost exclusively a transcendent religious experience that could be spoken about only in the abstract language of Neo-scholasticism.[63] According to this theology war was not a blind force or an event outside God's control; rather it reflected divine activity that was the beginning and end of history. God had permitted the air war, which was also a judgement on humanity for turning away from God, and thus at the same time a call to return, in a double sense: as a return to God and a reintegration into the community of the faithful.

The Protestant Bishop of Württemberg, Theophil Wurm, used a similar argument. He too interpreted the bombings as part of the history of moral decline, at the end of which all the western nations, even the Germans, had sinned against the Christian order and had become guilty of 'the unprecedented cruelty of total war'.[64] And yet in his publicly read pastoral message he went a clear step further than his Catholic counterparts. For whereas they also saw the rejection of God as being the fundamental reason for the evil in the world, Wurm regarded the bombing not only in a generalized way as a divine judgement that had to be endured. He was one of the few to make a direct and not purely theological connection between the bombing and Germany's conduct of the war. For in taking part in this violent contest Germany had brought 'great guilt' upon itself through 'the manner in which it had directed hostilities towards members of other races and nations before and during the war'. It had brought about destruction on a scale that members of the 'German Christians'* movement had attributed only to the 'bloodthirsty imaginings of the Jewish mind'.[65] Now many innocent people were having to suffer for this in the air war. And given the nature of this war, could anyone really be surprised 'if we are feeling the effects', Wurm asked his Protestant congregations, continuing what he had already stated openly in a letter to Lammers, the head of Reich Chancellery. For it was Wurm's belief that the population saw the air raids as 'retribution for what had been done to the Jews'.[66] He was thus interpreting the Allied bombing as a response to Germany's crimes, thereby not only indicating indirectly that the population was aware of the persecution of the Jews but also challenging that theology of war that regarded the conflict with the Allies as a kind of national self-defence which for that very reason required solidarity and self-sacrifice, as continuously preached by Marahrens.[67]

Wurm's interpretation was a very uncomfortable response to the problem of theodicy, one peculiar to him and not widely shared. The overwhelming

* Translators' note: The 'German Christians' (Deutsche Christen) were a strongly pro-Nazi group within the Protestant church.

majority of Catholic and Protestant bishops interpreted the air war as one of the human aberrations visible in 'modern' societies and further evidence of a turning away from God. Air warfare was a trial and a challenge that Christians had to face and that demanded sacrifices from them—sacrifices required not only from the soldiers fighting courageously at the front but also from those at home, even women and children. The removal of the boundary between soldiers and civilians had now been incorporated into a theology of the home front.

'Sacrifice' in this context denoted part of the expiation through which human beings as followers of Jesus had to suffer crucifixion vicariously. 'If a nation must atone, to propitiate God's judgement, then even innocent children must be among the sacrificial victims.'[68] This at any rate was how the Munich Cardinal Faulhaber in his sermon for the dead of two air raids in the summer of 1944 attempted to give deeper meaning to the deaths of many children and to bring comfort to their families. Human freedom was thus only one reason for the evil in the world and the suffering brought by the air war. This calamity was also part of divine providence, part of 'God's punishment', and was summed up in the cardinal's recurrent theme: 'He is Lord.' These were times of 'great judgement', times that gave people an opportunity to repent and commit themselves to God—'more than in many decades of tranquil and peaceful existence', as the Cologne Cardinal Frings emphasized at the funeral service for the victims of bombing from his home town of Neuss in September 1944.[69]

The rising levels of devastation created an apocalyptic mood, in which the war was felt to be part of the ultimate and decisive battle between 'good' and 'evil'; at the end of November 1944 Frings wrote in a letter to Pope Pius XII of an 'Advent mood'.[70] The crucifixion and redemption were the central, recurrent motifs referred to in sermons. The suffering and death of Christ on the cross set the pattern for human beings to accept their fate and submit to the divine plan for redemption, to providence, with all its trials. Thus Bishop Wurm of Württemberg in a letter of support to the Protestants in the Rhineland pointed to the fact that it was the particular power of Christ's message that helped the early Christians during the years of persecution to regard their earthly suffering both as a divine visitation and as progress towards the purification of their lives.[71]

Similar reasoning was used by Simon Schöffel, the former Protestant Bishop of Hamburg, who had resigned under pressure from the 'German Christians' in 1934. In his Christmas Day sermon in 1943, while reminding his congregation of the pain of their losses, he nevertheless comforted them by saying that in a way like the first Christians they could now raise their voices and bear witness to their faith as the Roman Christians had done at the time of persecution.[72] The 'purification' resulting from the experience of violence meant first and foremost turning to God again and contemplating the core values of Christianity—and this at the very least did not exclude a careful inner withdrawal from National Socialism.

The same sentiments could be found also in the sermon preached by the former Protestant Reich Bishop Friedrich von Bodelschwingh at a memorial service for victims of bombing in Hamburg on 7 November 1943. In speaking of the 'struggle against the powers of darkness', of a sea of blood and tears and the tribunal set up to judge human beings and in particular those beloved by God, he was echoing his fellow Protestant bishops. For him the 'catastrophe' was both a beginning and an end, part of 'world change', a new age in which old alliances would break up and defensive lines would crumble. New 'foundations' were needed so that something could be built up from the ruins. The apocalypse was therefore not at all the end of history but the precondition for a new beginning.[73] There was insufficient detail in this to allow definite conclusions to be drawn and yet it was clear enough for anyone who had ears to hear to detect a change in tone.

Such nuances left room for interpretation and yet the message of the Christian churches was essentially clear: endure, overcome doubts, remain confident, rebuild what has been destroyed, and be prayerful and humble, not acting vengefully towards the 'national community' but fighting to preserve it, while accepting God's testing. That was the religious interpretation of the concept of morale in wartime, which meant two things: carrying on in spite of all the losses and not losing faith. A combination of these defined the Christian in wartime, and it was the church's duty as a bringer of comfort to strengthen and sustain morale. For the church members in German society this interpretation offered an opportunity to combine a growing sense of estrangement from National Socialism as the war progressed with loyalty to the 'national community'—an important reason why in spite of the catastrophic war situation the 'Third Reich' did not implode but had to be defeated by external forces.

An essential part of the religious dimension of wartime morale was the central call, issued repeatedly by Protestant and Catholic bishops alike, to expiate guilt, both through the sacrifice of the mass and through the suffering of the air war.[74] For Faulhaber the fact that the righteous and the faithful also suffered as a result of the raids and were buried beneath the rubble could mean only one thing: 'Their deaths have been an expiation and have atoned in a small way for the great guilt of humanity and so shortened the period of visitation.' 'Visitation' had not only this apocalyptic dimension, however, but for Faulhaber it also meant going home to God the Father and thus the fulfilment of human beings in the next world with the Lord. This kind of attempt to bring comfort by giving meaning to suffering conformed entirely to traditional Catholic doctrine, familiar for generations to the faithful, and thus created continuity of interpretation in a world which the air war had reduced to rubble.

The same applied to the attempt to place the bombing of cities in the biblical tradition of the destruction of Jerusalem,[75] as in the Lamentations of Jeremiah, which, as Faulhaber commented, had acquired 'particular resonance'[76] in view of the bombed-out churches. Frings, the Archbishop of Cologne, spoke, for example, of his 'dead city'[77] and the Protestant Bishop Wurm included verses from the Old Testament in his interpretation of the air war, though using them as proof of the saving power of the divine message, which could not only topple walls but could save human beings. And just as the Lord stood by his people, so people in their hour of need should remain part of the 'whole nation' and, in spite of the war being interpreted as God's judgement and proof that people had turned from the true path, should summon up everything they could 'to protect their home towns, their homeland, their lives and their property'.[78]

Taking a distanced view of the conduct of the war on the one hand and bringing some stability to people's powers of endurance on the home front on the other hand were not therefore necessarily at odds with one another and they in turn had their roots in the power of prophetic lamentation. Thus it was no wonder that on receiving the terrifying news of the destruction of Hamburg at the beginning of August 1943 Wurm contacted the Oberbürgermeister of Stuttgart to ask how the churches could help to defend the country and what activities important to the war effort they could take on. After all, as Wurm knew, pastors were constantly being asked by their congregations for advice and so could relay instructions from the city authorities through what they said to their congregations in services.[79]

As far as the forces driving the destruction were concerned, it was, however, clear who had destroyed Jerusalem, the churches, and the cities and was responsible for the radicalization of the air war: the Allies.[80] They were the ones who destroyed culture and obliterated churches. 'Churches reduced to rubble are an accusation,' it said for example in a book issued by the Protestant Union documenting the extent of damage to churches and the determined Christian spirit of reconstruction among the Protestant churches.[81] According to this view, which was fully in line with Nazi propaganda, air raids were no longer 'chivalrous combat' but rather 'the satanic destruction of life and of everything sacred to it'.[82] Whereas the Wehrmacht had spared the French cathedrals this Anglo-American brutalization had taken the path towards barbarism, though the air raids had not succeeded in striking at the heart of Protestantism. The book, which was jointly financed by the propaganda ministry, was accompanied by a comprehensive documentation of the churches that had been destroyed, with eyewitness accounts by pastors and members of congregations who had experienced the bombing and had written reports about the churches' activities in the air war, the extent of the damage, and the pastoral care given. The reports, which came from the various regions in the Reich, read like an amalgamation of accusations and attempts to give sober, statistical overviews. The narrative strand emphasizing the destruction of German culture going back thousands of years by Allied 'murderous arsonists' and their 'degenerate air war' was the recurring theme.[83]

The documentary evidence laid particular stress on the loss of ecclesiastical and cultural buildings and other material items, and photos of damaged church interiors were published to demonstrate these losses. At the same time the written extracts attempted to locate the air raids in a historical continuum of nights of terror in the history of the city and thus to create a language for them and the possibility of making comparisons. From its *völkisch*, nationalist standpoint the documentation reminded readers that the heavy raid on Wuppertal in early summer 1943 was the worst event in the history of the city since the Great Fire at the end of the seventeenth century.[84]

By virtue of such attitudes the church was fully engaged in supporting the home front, spiritually but also in its charitable activities towards those who were involved as Christians in defending themselves.[85] This *völkisch*-Protestant perception of the war as a defence of the nation against barbaric and godless external forces represented a fusion of religious and Nazi interpretations of the air war, producing a rhetoric expressing both anger and defiance. Yet at the same time and in spite of general condemnation of the Allied raids the churches' terminology and the target of their criticisms varied considerably. For example, however much the Catholic bishops pointed to the Allies as the real force behind the air war and however clear it was that German soldiers in the east were fighting against godless Bolshevism,[86] there were still distinct differences in how the 'enemy' was described and the same was true of the German Protestant churches. Here it was the 'German Christians' who adopted the aggressive rhetoric of retaliation. By contrast, part of the church at least was hesitant about adopting Nazi terminology. There was mention of 'cruel' and 'brutal' air raids, of 'air ambushes' and of 'heedless cruelty',[87] but as a rule there was no reference to the bombings as acts of 'terror', whereas in Nazi propaganda this was a dominant theme.

The more important difference was, however, to be found elsewhere. Whereas the Nazi regime with its rhetoric of retaliation and of miracle weapons promised that final victory was near, bishops such as Faulhaber and von Galen rejected the logic of retaliation as a 'reversion to Mosaic–Jewish notions of justice'.[88] German soldiers were engaged in a war out of 'love for their nation and country'. In the spirit of the 'miles christianus' they were not motivated by Old Testament, and thus Jewish, vengefulness or hatred but were fighting courageously and chivalrously against Bolshevism. Thus conceived, their war was not, as in the case of other nations, powered by 'base vindictiveness' but was an expression of 'manly restraint' and was directed 'only at the armed enemy defending himself', as von Galen believed.[89] Hence the ban on air raids on non-military targets, as these contravened the notion of Christian warfare. In 1943/4 von Galen and Faulhaber quite openly and with undisguised criticism of Nazi propaganda promoted the idea of renouncing 'retaliation' and instead of directing all energies towards reconstructing the cities. Christian opposition to Judaism and to Bolshevism came together in this to sound a note of Christian steadfastness in suffering that was different from Goebbels's empty rhetoric of miracle weapons.

Churchmen's own experience of bombing may well have played an important role in making them sensitive to the sufferings inflicted by the air war and gentler towards those who were seen as the actual fireraisers. After all, as the Freiburg Archbishop Gröber stated after a heavy raid on Freiburg at the end of November 1944, the war had inflicted misery and death not only on Germany but on all the countries of Europe[90]—a clear indication that seeing the war as a just, defensive struggle against Bolshevism was wearing thin. It was striking how by this stage the narrative of legitimate retaliation in the Old Testament sense could evidently no longer be preached unreservedly either by the Catholic or the Protestant churches in Germany (with the exception of the German Christians) or in Britain, without losing credibility in the face of such comprehensive devastation; after all, both sides claimed to be fighting for a 'Christian cause'. This development could certainly be read as a transnational learning process, even though partial and fragile, in which the experiences of bombing had considerable significance.

Sermons in the final years of the war were full of biblical images of destruction and downfall rather than, as earlier, of those of the soldierly virtues of Christian warfare, while there was absolutely no talk of a 'just war' as there had been in 1914.[91] Now the talk was of mass graves, death and redemption through the cross, of cities turned into vast areas of rubble, and of 'human ruins',[92] the dead of the battlefield and at home. As a result of the continuing air raids the categories of front and homeland were now related to each other theologically and fitted into the theological interpretation of 'total war'. As von Galen said to the faithful in a sermon preached during a pilgrimage in 1943, the war reached 'beyond the frontlines and deep into the peace of the homeland'.[93] Prayers should therefore be said for soldiers who had fallen in battle as well as for those who had lost their lives in air raids.[94]

Yet the problems of a theology of the home front went further than this. For the bombing raised a question for the first time among the civilian population that had up to that time been resolved only for soldiers at the front, namely, how should Catholics behave in an air raid, when they could be killed any minute? Had they the right, like soldiers in mortal danger, to receive a general absolution without making an individual confession? This was not a theoretical matter but an existential religious concern that troubled the clergy and their congregations alike and recurred every time there was an air raid. In an emergency could priests forgive people's sins even without auricular confession? Was the air war such a precondition, similar to fighting at the front, where such an act was permissible? And to whom did such a general absolution apply, to all those present, all those whom the priest could see, or also those who, as they fled from the bombs, had had no time for repentance and penance and so were unprepared for the Last Judgement?

After the raids on Munich at the end of September 1942, Cardinal Faulhaber as probably one of the very first among the German bishops had issued special religious rules of conduct during air raids and formulated a solution to the issue of general absolution for his archbishopric.[95] In notices posted up in the churches in his diocese he called upon the faithful to prepare for an emergency: 'The commandment of the hour is: Be prepared. You know neither the day nor the hour. Blessed is he who has a clear conscience and is in a state of grace and at peace with God and so ready at any time to appear before the judgement seat of God.' It was repentance that Faulhaber demanded if people were to avoid meeting their Maker unprepared. Ten minutes after the air-raid warning—this was the time they had to find shelter and prepare for what fate had in store—the priests of the town along with their cardinal would pronounce the general absolution along with complete remission for sins.

This was certainly an unusual step to take, for Faulhaber had now declared towns and cities battle zones in a theological sense and in an important sacramental matter had attempted to adjust to the new reality of the air war—and without agreeing this with other bishops. In addition, in the public notices on the church doors of his diocese he had referred to a papal authority that did not exist in this form.[96] For in deciding in favour of a very generous extension of the regulations on absolution Faulhaber had taken his cue from a ruling by the Sacred Consistorial Congregation of December 1939, which made no direct reference to aerial warfare but simply alluded to particular 'danger zones in the homeland' in wartime legitimizing such a procedure.[97] There was no 'papal authority' in the sense of one designed especially for regions particularly affected by the air war, let alone for Munich itself. At any rate, Faulhaber's initiative was evidently controversial both among his own clerics and in other dioceses; Rottenburg-Stuttgart, much to Faulhaber's annoyance, made a direct enquiry to Rome about the Munich procedure and requested a 'final' decision.[98] None was forthcoming, however, for Rome wanted first to examine this matter and 'if possible' give a decision—which in the end never happened. Faulhaber interpreted this as supporting the argument that he was acting in complete harmony with the Pope.[99]

The main point at issue was whether the general absolution given before every bombing raid might lead to an abuse of the sacrament of penance and to people receiving forgiveness even if they had not prepared themselves at all for death through active contrition. Was there a possibility, therefore, that this absolution applied even to people who had not seen the priest at the end and had not heard his words at all or had been standing too far away from him? How close was it necessary to be to the priest for the words of contrition to be efficacious? And did the sacrament have force for those who had not repented at all, were unprepared for absolution, and yet were standing close to the priest or happened to have taken refuge in the air-raid shelter? That was not only a theoretical concern, for a number of bishops and theologians who had been involved in interpreting the 'Index facultatum' for army priests and chaplains took the view that believers could be pronounced forgiven all their sins only if they were no more than twenty to thirty metres from a priest. They held that a general absolution in the event of an air raid was not admissible for in that case the sacrament of penance had been administered without the 'dolorosa accusatio' of the believer.[100] Faulhaber, however, unlike his Cologne colleague Frings, took the view that the papal faculty was to be interpreted generously and that, as he remarked with irony, 'priestly authorities'[101] should be overridden. For such a petty interpretation was to his mind totally inappropriate in a war situation. In taking his initiative Faulhaber was guided by experiences of pastoral care at the front. The ruling that absolution was effective only if the believer was no more than thirty paces away was at best suited to the needs of peacetime but not to wartime and was not in the spirit of the Pope's decision. In taking this position the Munich cardinal had sought special support from moral theology.[102]

Only those 'who are not engaged themselves in pastoral care' could hold this restrictive view based on pre-war pastoral practice, Faulhaber told Frings at the end of December 1942.[103] In essence sacramental absolution was not, he said, a question of distance and lay in the 'legal prerogative of the Church' and thus within his powers as a bishop. In the light of this new kind of threat facing his diocese he did not consider it sensible 'to carry a ruler with him to demarcate distances'.[104] In this life-and-death matter pastoral practice should adjust to the new demands of the air war and not the other way round, a considered opinion that, after arousing evident scepticism initially, began gradually to be accepted. After the first bombing raids on Vienna in August 1943 Cardinal Innitzer likewise issued new pastoral instructions for the diocese of Vienna.[105] Priests were to make the faithful aware of the need to show contrition when in danger of death, such as during an air raid. Although sermons should not mention air raids directly but rather speak only in general terms of future dangers, it was nevertheless obvious to anyone what the focus of the sermons was, namely being ready to meet death even without confession. All the faithful were expected to offer up the prayer for absolution 'Jesus, have mercy' and, if possible, several quick prayers. Then if a raid followed the priests could pronounce all the faithful in the parish forgiven, and give the apostolic blessing and complete remission of their sins. This procedure was effective in so far as people had the intention of making the confession they had missed if they survived the raid.

Whereas hitherto the emphasis had been on interpreting the war theologically, from 1944 onwards at the latest the theme of the future peace emerged, a peace that was similarly part of divine providence and salvation and would put an end to the 'visitation'. For, as the consoling message ran, God had not created the world to be desolate but for life—and life would return as soon as nations stopped warring with each other. That vision therefore looked beyond the acute emergency; peace had become conceivable and was integrated as a point of reference into the wartime perspective. And it was not a 'victorious peace' but rather part of a return to God. The image of God projected was no longer that of a draconian disciplinarian imposing moral lessons and times of trial. Rather, unlike the First World War and most likely also as a result of the wartime bombing, God was a protective and consoling force and would help people to overcome earthly suffering.

Day-to-Day Religious and Pastoral Practice

When the bombing began it was not theological interpretations but quite different problems that were at first important. At the end of October 1940 the bishops received a letter from the Reich Minister for Church Affairs that caused a great uproar in the dioceses: the ministry informed the bishops about an instruction from the Führer that after air raids 'daily church services' were in future to be forbidden before ten in the morning.[106] The reason given was that people should be free to contribute to the clearing up after heavy raids and have time to recover from the rigours of nights spent in air-raid shelters and cellars. Any 'duty of conscience' imposed by the church, the requirement to attend mass every Sunday, must therefore cease.[107]

What at first sight appeared to be a normal measure to mobilize the home front and adjust to the air war seemed to the churches an outrageous intervention in religious life. For up to that point the Nazi state had not intervened in the structuring of church services, apart from the growing problems faced by the religious press in obtaining paper for parish newspapers. Now sub-prefects and police departments were giving priests instructions about when and in what form services were permitted—and when they were not. To many, including the Cologne Archbishop Schulte, this seemed like a 'special ban' affecting Catholic worship that would inevitably provoke considerable resentment among the population and opposition among the clergy.[108]

The chair of the Fulda Bishops' Conference, Cardinal Bertram of Breslau (Wrocław), struck a fairly moderate tone in his submission to Hitler, pointing to the fact that 'Catholic belief and all experience' confirmed that 'church worship and pastoral care' gave Catholics 'the most powerful and effective source of strength to fulfil faithfully and eagerly their duties as citizens and in their personal and professional lives, particularly in times such as the present, because they offer people not only natural spiritual exaltation but above all convey special supernatural help from God'. Catholics were therefore unable to understand why at this of all times, when people longed for 'sources of supernatural strength', church services and pastoral care were being curtailed more than was necessary. Bertram thus advocated a flexible interpretation of the 'Führer instruction', which left the decision about attending services after air raids in the hands of the priest.[109]

The Western German Bishops' Conference decided to wait and see what would come out of the negotiations following on from Bertram's letter. Admittedly, there was little optimism that the protest would actually be successful,[110] a view that soon turned out to be correct, when in a letter to the chair of the Fulda Bishops' Conference Lammers announced Hitler's decision to rule out any change to the decree; if they were in doubt about how to interpret it they should discuss the matter with the Reich Ministry for Churches.[111] The bishops were enraged by this unbending attitude. Cardinal Faulhaber from Munich protested against the decision in a furious letter, saying that this intervention in purely church matters was 'something new' and was not only a throwback to 'the Josephinian age' but contradicted the Concordat, which guaranteed the free and public practice of religion.[112] His Bamberg colleague, Archbishop Hauck, went even further and openly refused to obey the instruction.[113]

Meanwhile, numerous bishops had received news of how the instruction was being put into effect and of the growing number of conflicts between congregations and the police authorities. Occasionally, as in the diocese of Limburg, local rulings even went significantly beyond the contentious instruction: the sub-prefect for the Lower Westerwald, for example, issued a ban on all church gatherings between 8.30 in the morning and 8 in the evening, whether there were night-time air raids or not. In Frankfurt am Main the chief of police interpreted the passage concerning 'night-time air-raid warnings' as the basis for a wide-ranging ban on church services: any air-raid warning sounded after dusk was regarded as sufficient reason to ban services the following morning. In some places the ban was extended not only to public masses but also to those in monasteries—all in all a development that in the estimation of Göbel, the vicar-general of Limburg, severely restricted people's opportunity to participate in a Sunday service. In the view of many Catholics it was part of a strategy 'deliberately to offend the Catholic population' and was linked to Nazi plans for a final reckoning with Christianity in the period after the war.[114]

In fact the decree did increase the potential pressure that could be exerted on churches to make the timing of their services dependent on the dictates of the police authorities. In the months immediately following the 'Führer instruction' conflicts arose throughout the Reich, because many dioceses were failing to inform their priests about the new regulations, after at first assuming that an amicable solution would be found before the state authorities began to apply them strictly.[115]

Although there were attempts to circumvent the ban by means of 'silent masses' and independent local arrangements, this happened in a constant atmosphere of uncertainty and primarily in rural areas, which could evade checks by the authorities and were rarely affected by air raids. For many priests the restrictions imposed on services signified the most painful curtailment to date of their pastoral duties and thus of church life in the Nazi state in general. In the judgement of the town priest of Waldkirch im Breisgau, speaking for numerous unnamed clerics in the diocese of Freiburg, up to that point this 'Satanic movement' had been met purely with tactical methods and a certain 'pliability'.[116] Now this 'emergency law' had given rise to a new situation that was no more and no less than a 'dress rehearsal' for the imminent closure of all Catholic churches. He painted a true horror scenario: Easter services abandoned because of air-raid warnings, deliberate false alarms designed to disrupt day-to-day church activities, people giving up confession and the sacrament of penance, locked churches, from which people, 'unbelievably exhausted by the work imposed on them', were turned away, unable to receive Holy Communion. All of this seemed to him to point to a new period of Christian persecution, now that the Reich Ministry for Churches decided what God's commandments were. In the face of such a threat this priest did not even consider it an absolute duty to follow this regime loyally to war. 'Does the natural concern for the fatherland really commit us to this when compared with the demands of the supernatural world? The first Christians surely also had experience of obligations but they did not overestimate purely earthly ties but lived in their native countries as though they were strangers and every foreign place was home to them.' On the part of one section of the clergy, this assault on the autonomy of religious practice had led, as no other issue had done, to significant criticism not only of the regime but also of the compliance of church leaders.

The case of the Black Forest priests marked a clear boundary in Catholic loyalty to country and willingness to make sacrifices, which stopped at the point where the core of church life seemed threatened. Even so, the priests did not want to rebel openly. The refusal of individuals to comply served no purpose, they said, and a united stand was more necessary than ever before in these exceptionally difficult times. It was therefore necessary to live with this ruling, in spite of all protestations. Occasionally it was possible with support from Bürgermeisters to keep to the old arrangements for holding services, but often a considerable concession had to be made, namely the relaxation of the obligation to attend on Sundays.

Numerous parishes, in particular in the regions most at risk from bombing, now tried to find a balance between pastoral care, increased work pressure for the population, and regulation by the authorities by introducing new times for services and confession. As the Munich diocese informed its clergy, under the extreme conditions imposed by the air war evening masses could also be celebrated with Communion and the church's week adapted to the rhythm of the war.[117] This decision did not please all clergy, however, and was implemented in different ways in the individual dioceses. It was regarded at best as a 'concession to the needs of the time' and the short-term relaxation of the requirement to attend church on Sundays should not become the norm and should go on being limited to city parishes.[118]

The longer the Allied bombing continued the more pressing became the issue of church services. For the Reich Ministry for Churches maintained an inflexible stance and rejected all requests for change. In summer 1943 the bishops of the Rhineland and Westphalia, led by the Archbishop of Cologne, Joseph Frings, attempted a new initiative, taking it directly to Hitler.[119] From December 1940 onwards the situation, particularly for the dioceses, had changed radically. The air war had destroyed many churches and in the meantime, the bishops said, the population had endured 'huge psychological and growing nervous strain' while air raids were becoming increasingly heavy. Even so they left no doubt that in spite of all the suffering the 'homeland' was standing firm behind the soldiers at the front and that people were demonstrating 'a heroic attitude' in their loyalty to the fatherland. They therefore felt it was all the more regrettable that 'amidst our nation's unprecedented struggle' a ban should be in force that made it impossible for national comrades to attend church after the sorrow and destruction of an air raid.

By summer 1943 the air war had already completely changed church services. Not only were many churches no longer in use but working hours had in many cases been extended; work now began even earlier than usual, which made it clash directly with the ban. The increased employment of women, the bishops said, also meant that, caught between work and household duties, they no longer had time to go even to the evening service and thus were deprived for a long period of 'an emotional boost'. Thus the Rhineland and Westphalian bishops could exploit the vital role the church played in supporting morale on the home front in the war as an argument for their request that the problematic ruling be revoked. For, as the bishops emphasized, it was specifically the 'patriotic and religious national comrades' particularly affected by bombing in the west of the Reich who in view of the daily air raids were in special need of spiritual support.

The effect of the war was extremely ambivalent. At the end of 1944 the Archbishop of Cologne remarked in a letter to Pope Pius XII that on the one hand as the war situation worsened a growing number of people were again going to church and receiving the sacraments but on the other hand this revival within the Catholic milieu was matched by a considerable number of people who had no answer to the question of why God could permit this ordeal.[120] Thus in Frings's view it was hardly surprising that a 'kind of Advent mood' had arisen in which more and more often 'the Pardoned', self-appointed prophets, appeared who heard heavenly voices and made apocalyptic prophecies to people. The dioceses of Munich and Cologne, he wrote, were actually seeing an increasing number of apocalyptic and esoteric chain letters calling for 'repentance' and announcing the imminent destruction of the world.

As in earlier times of suffering people were officially encouraged to invoke the saints and the Virgin Mary in particular.[121] The veneration of Mary, an integral part of popular Catholic piety, was now experiencing a revival, meeting the religious needs of women in particular, who amid private loss sought consolation and support in their grief. Invoking Mary as the mother of God was supposed to save people from collective suffering and preserve them from war and violence, thus a mixture of invoking feminine virtues, spirituality, and protection from the future that was often entirely a response to the threat of the next air raid. Mary was held above all to give protection against bombing raids and this increased her popularity considerably during the war. Mary was an advocate with God and immediately understood anxieties and distress and the ordeals of wartime. She knew how to defy the bombing itself. Thus at the reopening of Munich Cathedral after the air raids of spring 1943 Cardinal Faulhaber reminded people that the Munich Madonna had survived the devastation of the city and that after the raids the statue of the mother of God had still been standing amid the ruins in defiance of all the destruction.[122]

The exceptional experience of air raids made it particularly necessary to seek religious meanings in being in unfamiliar places and suffering fear. Faulhaber himself composed a prayer designed to express the terrors of war in a suitable and up-to-date prayer to Mary, though it also drew on older models. As the patron saint of Bavaria, Mary was now to preserve the city and its population from the effects of war, as she had done during the last great period of terror, the Thirty Years War: 'Sweet heart of Mary, be my salvation! Mary, spread wide your cloak, make it into a shield and protection for us, let us shelter safely under it, until all storms have passed.'[123] Special illustrations depicting idyllic countryside and the heart of Mary adorned the manuscript of the text, which appeared under the heading 'Prayers to bring forth perfect contrition'. At the end of his sermon for All Saints' Day in 1943 Faulhaber added a further prayer that did not use the abstract image of Mary's protective cloak but rather referred directly to the experience of the city's population in the air-raid cellars. 'We beseech Thee, O Lord, to be present in this shelter and keep the enemy far from it! Let Thy holy angels dwell here to preserve us and may Thy blessing be ever upon us! Through Christ, our Lord.'[124]

The form and content of these prayers were an attempt to adapt rituals and beliefs to the changed experience of bombing, which the Protestant clergyman Johannes Mehrhoff of Wuppertal, for example, also tried to do. After the city was bombed in May 1943 and his congregation evacuated he quickly set about re-establishing contact with them. Letters and sermons were intended to help him overcome the physical separation by creating some proximity as a pastor, if only a virtual one. Mehrhoff kept church members informed about the fate of their church and the everyday activities of the congregation.[125] The loss of their home town, their houses, and possessions was one of the central experiences that Mehrhoff addressed in his sermons: the fire had taken from people what they held dear and yet the real horror of that night was not whether one's own house had been spared.[126] 'The hidden horror', Mehrhoff said in his sermon after the raids in June, was expressed in the words: 'You fool, this night will your soul be required of you. Where will you find shelter? Who will you be? (After such a night). This question reveals our lack of an external and internal home.'

Many people felt they had lost their home, felt empty and that they had only just escaped death. And yet—and this was the crucial message—the 'lack of an external home' was insignificant in the light of 'God's gift'. Even if they had lost all their savings, survivors at home and evacuees far from home were still children of God, confident that the world was finite but God was 'eternal'—words of comfort intended to help them over their loss. The air raids, as Mehrhoff said at a memorial service for those who had been killed, had demonstrated the 'transience of all earthly things [. . .] The advantage we have over those we now mourn is only a short span of time. God wishes to dwell with this little company of afflicted, transitory people. He wants to be their God. [. . .] And yet we can say of these haggard figures, these cowering specimens, these eyes red with weeping: God is with us. He releases the fixed stare of eyes that can weep no more and dries their tears. He takes from our frozen lips their cry of pain and teaches them everlasting worship.'[127] Even in a diaspora, his message went, church and congregation remained the focus of Christian life, the locus of worship and comfort, regardless of whether the walls were still standing.[128]

How convincing such exhortations and attempts to provide meaning were is difficult to judge. The reactions Mehrhoff received convey a strong sense of how much the members of the congregation felt 'far from home' and how glad they were about the contact with him. Others were simply pleased to have news from home and to be sure of what had happened to friends and acquaintances.[129] Even though few church members may have used the contact with their minister to discuss fundamental religious issues regarding their own faith, the lively correspondence was only superficially concerned with secular matters such as the pattern of life in a strange part of the country.[130] For there was no strict division between spiritual and social needs. It was in particular the experience that the church community could exist independently of a location and consisted of more than just neighbourliness that gave a special character to the church's day-to-day life and this could continue (at least minimally) far from home on a spiritual level.[131] This made the pastoral support given to evacuees, which could sustain the church in wartime, even in the absence of a social and physical milieu, all the more important.

This development could vary considerably from one region to the next. Reactions to attempts to give a theological explanation for the loss of home and homeland varied also. In September 1943 a pastor in Cologne commented that prayers in wartime repeatedly contained things that God was unwilling to grant, above all being preserved from air raids.[132] Every day people were confronted with the fact they were not receiving what they asked God for—a practice that required urgent reform because it ignored the reality of the air war. Evidently this clergyman from the Cologne suburb of Nippes did not believe that the bombing would stop and a sudden improvement occur through prayer. He was therefore unwilling to contribute further with his own prayers to his congregation's disappointment and intended instead to concentrate entirely on the 'crying spiritual need' of the times. He thus suggested that wartime prayers should concentrate on spiritual requests: the preservation of the faith, the loyalty and purity of young people, and divine justice for the fallen.

Thus it was very unclear whether the bishops' interpretation of suffering and sacrifice had the desired resonance or whether the experience of the air war had already left theological interpretations far behind. What was clear, at any rate, was that liturgical and pastoral practice were undergoing significant change. Presumably this change did not go as far as to offer a convincing answer to the one overriding question of theodicy. Yet even so the attempts to do so, when compared with the First World War, had become more varied.

For many believers the bombing had become a religious experience in which both the fear of death and divine omnipotence played a role.[133] A few months after the end of the war a Catholic told of the hours he spent in Freiburg Cathedral, where he was attending a service along with several dozen others when heavy bombing began.[134] Once again, in this apocalypse, it was Mary who was called on as the bombs detonated: 'Mary, spread wide your cloak.' This was a prayer for protection but also would help defeat the enemy in the 'divine battle'. It was the women, above all, who prayed aloud, their hands raised to heaven, and began singing the 'heavenly hymn' before the open tabernacle in order to strengthen the whole congregation—that at any rate was how this man in his distress recalled the event.

Clerics also reported that in the numerous prayer circles founded by lay people it was principally the women who led the saying of the rosary to ward off harm.[135] They tried by this means to dispose 'divine judgement' to be merciful and clung to the hope that they were able by praying for God's help to intervene themselves in the war. According to the assessment of the clergy the air raids had caused a significant number of people to pray once more. The bombs, as one priest on the outskirts of Munich noted, had achieved what missions and sermons had failed to do: 'The parishioners have started to pray again.'[136]

A Protestant district nurse from St Peter's in Hamburg reported something very similar in 1943. For the need for a sense of community manifested itself 'more strongly than before' and even 'otherwise such reticent people as Hamburg workmen' had felt the need to talk after the raids.[137] Yet as Protestant pastors in the city observed, this quest for consolation from the church evidently did not last for long. 'So much affliction, so little repentance': with these words the Hamburg state bishop Tügel admitted that hopes for a renewal of faith from the spirit of wartime destruction had been illusory.

This ambivalent development, with signs of renewal of faith and rejection of it, was not only a Protestant phenomenon, however. Even in good Catholic families, as a Munich priest reported, the war had left an 'unhappy scene'.[138] The men stayed away and increasingly the women, and from 1943 onwards more of the children, who were all members of the Hitler Youth and no longer took part as much in the life of the congregation. The congregation had in many places shrunk to a hard core, as some clerics ruefully stated. Many parishioners were unwilling to 'understand God's severe trials' and remained, as they had always been, 'indifferent and unreceptive to everything to do with religion'. In this context too the lamentations of Jeremiah provided the interpretative and semantic frame of reference in which what was inconceivable, the rejection of religion amid a homeland in ruins, could nevertheless be captured in words. 'Lord, thou hast stricken them, but they have not grieved; thou has consumed them, but they have refused to receive correction [...] they have refused to return' (Jeremiah 5: 3).

The theme of air raids as a 'chastisement' and 'ordeal' that had to be endured was one that recurred not only in bishops' sermons but also in the minds and imagination of large numbers of parish priests, even though they could now reach no more than a small section of their own parishioners.[139] A 'widespread conversion' as a result of the air raids was at any rate not something Heinrich Schmid, a member of the Augsburg Protestant Consistory, could detect;[140] he seemed sceptical about whether the large numbers attending services after 'Augsburg's night of terror' on 25/6 February 1944 were really an indication of the impact of 'God's call to repentance'. The state of emergency and the search for pastoral care were far from being sufficient reason for people to come back to the church, as so many Catholic and Protestant clergy dreamt they would.

Occasionally there were also those who not only attributed the growing difficulty in giving pastoral care to the direct effects of the war but observed a longer-term ebbing away of the influence of Christianity and 'a rejection by people of metaphysical values', as did the priest of an inner-city parish in Munich. The war seemed at best to reinforce this process but not to be the actual cause of a 'de-Christianization'.[141] The priest agreed about the catastrophic state of parish work. Parishes in regions particularly hit by bombing had had 'their very existence' threatened and had had 'very grave wounds' inflicted on them.[142] Religious life was thus determined principally by the rhythm of the air raids. For reasons of air-raid protection bells could not be rung as in the pre-war days, while catechism classes and youth work ceased or were severely limited. The possibility of attending a church service, above all, was reduced in view of the increasing danger from the air. The war had turned the parish, as this priest saw it, into a 'desert', a pile of rubble consisting of the wrecks of trams and ruined buildings. The Protestant bishop of Hanover, Marahrens, reported how much church life had suffered under the impact of the raids; the inner-city congregations had been almost wiped out and Hanover was now a 'city with hardly any churches'. Their loss seemed to bring with it the loss of 'church morals and order' and severe damage to the administration of pastoral work.[143]

In many cases clergy who had not been called up had been assigned to train as civil defence assistants, not least because the stepping up of the air war meant that more and more often churches, their buildings, and their administration were affected. For example, in Hamburg after Operation Gomorrah twenty-eight churches were destroyed, among them the main churches of St Nicholas and St Catherine. Services, funeral, and memorial services for the victims of the air war had to be held in makeshift and private premises for many months after it was judged that some seventy parsonage houses had been destroyed.[144]

The administrative infrastructure of numerous bishoprics and regional churches was significantly restricted, with the result that many congregations were left to sort themselves out and frequently turned in distress to the most senior church authorities for help over how to organize pastoral support at this time of 'God's judgement'.[145] One solution was the attempt to maintain pastoral care by means of circulars and support through missionary tracts.[146] Many congregations like those in Hamburg tried to keep their fellow Protestant Christians who had been evacuated informed about the state of affairs in the city, comforting them, and sending devotional texts that enabled them even far from home to retain the familiar forms of religious practice. Such circulars were however subject to strict controls and the longer the war lasted the more difficult it became to make copies of the news sheets and send them out.

All this often involved the attempt to adapt the normal church practice of giving comfort to what for the church also were the 'exceptional circumstances' of the air war. The church community and services were for many people one of the few spaces they could retreat to, where they could spend time with others, and where in addition to prayers information was exchanged, contact maintained, and practical help offered.[147] Pastoral care had to respond to the 'particular mentality' of people in bombed cities, as the Bochum priest Josef Riekes commented in autumn 1943.[148] Those who had remained in the city and had not yet been evacuated were often particularly emotionally vulnerable and sensitive, he said. In many cases he had observed that it was men over 30 who now comprised the core of the church communities. There were women too, though a large number had already left the cities with their children, which resulted in many Catholic congregations in the Rhineland and Westphalia having no children's or youth work. The changing pace of the daytime and night-time raids was causing immense health and mental health problems; some grew frailer, some increasingly highly strung. That necessarily had implications for the religious life of his Bochum congregation. Riekes too noted the ambivalent development observed by his Munich colleagues: alongside the core members of the congregation, who were faithful to their church and were preparing themselves for death and purifying their conscience, there was a sizeable number of people whose attitude to religion could only be deemed 'apathetic and indifferent'. The experience of massive raids and dramatic struggles for survival seemed to have provoked a crisis of faith and doubts about divine providence in many Catholics. There was at any rate no increase in his parish in those who came to confession and communion.

The air raids, the constant fear of death, and the comprehensive and compulsory mobilization of his congregation forced Riekes to make a decision about the central tasks for pastoral care in future in cities affected by war.[149] His answer was to concentrate on the essentials. First among those was the celebration of the mass. The liturgy, receiving the sacrament, and prayer should transmit a sense of being safe to people among the ruins. Thus services should be 'as beautiful and solemn as possible' and there should be particular emphasis on decorating the altar and on a dignified celebration of communion. Because of the severity of the 'divine visitations' the sermon had to be given a central role, for a purified concept of God had to be communicated to the faithful. That meant above all reminding them of childlike trust in the fatherly love of God, a love that would help those undergoing trials not to be crushed by them or to look to superstitious and 'foolish prophecies' for comfort. The congregation was also to be instructed to keep the Ten Commandments, for in Riekes's view the seventh commandment, 'not coveting one's neighbour's property', had not been respected since the most recent air raids.

Being told to trust in God had not just a disciplinary function but was also a means of immunizing people against utter despair and the promises of salvation peddled by apocalyptic prophets of doom on the margins of the church, as well as against the relaxation of moral standards brought about by the war. Riekes identified three further areas of pastoral practice: charity work, care of particular groups such as work with men, women, and young people, and finally home visits to bring comfort to those in the worst affected areas. Yet these efforts could reach only part of the congregation; the other part consisted of evacuees far from their home region and often living life, as Riekes reported, in difficult circumstances. Many of those from 'comfortable and respectable backgrounds' felt themselves to be 'beggars' in the regions where they had been settled and were humiliated by having to ask others constantly for help. And in cases where even generous hosts were unable to respond to excessive demands ingratitude and anger were soon the result.

Many priests in fact had stories to tell about social conflict between evacuees and the local population. A frequent claim was that peasants were niggardly, refusing to give milk or bread; often conflicts arose from the different cultures of city and country populations, who heaped reproaches on each other, the former being accused of laziness and of refusing to help with the harvest and the latter of being mean and exploiting the suffering of the city dwellers. These clashes were very similar to those in Britain; they were the locus for a negotiation not only of religious but also social and gender-specific differences which had been brought to a head by the rapid mobilization of wartime. Thus the rejection of rich 'city folk' included reservations about city women, who were held to behave 'in an undignified manner', wore revealing clothes, viewed their time in the country as a holiday, and created conflict in the village community through their 'city' manners.[150]

As the clergy reported, there were prejudices on both sides, with the result that they often saw their task as being to settle disputes and to pass on to evacuees a taste of their religious home. An important part of this was the instruction of evacuated children, who were also accused of being freer, less inhibited, and sometimes even 'arrogant and undisciplined' by comparison with the country population. In this instance Catholic clergy regarded evacuation not only as part of divine testing but as an opportunity to show the way and to do missionary work. The children lacked awe for life in the natural world and for plants and animals, an Essen priest reported of his experiences in Bavarian Swabia. 'Perhaps providence has brought these children into a country environment in order to teach them awe for the life going on in homes and in the fields.' Evacuations could thus be seen both as a time of probation and as a mission, for Christians in an unfamiliar world could return to their faith and also bear witness to it as messengers of Christ.[151]

Yet in many places treating this unfamiliar setting as a mission field turned out to be treacherous, for contrary to the priests' expectations it was by no means obvious that evacuees from Catholic regions were attending services while exiled. The numbers of those attending mass were frequently far less than chaplains and priests who had joined their evacuated congregations in the regions had anticipated. The cohesiveness of the core Catholic milieu evidently faced a significant challenge as a result of migration; the conditions reported by a priest from Essen after a visit to Saxony were at any rate worrying.[152]

For the church's administrative centres the pace of initiatives, both state organized and privately organized, to relocate people made it difficult to maintain a clear overview of the evacuations. In many cases the local priest and local parish team could not find out precisely where any particular member of the congregation had ended up.[153] Often the only things that were known were that the Gaus receiving evacuees from Cologne and Aachen were Lower Silesia and Saxony, parts of the dioceses of Breslau and Meissen; Catholics from the Düsseldorf area were evacuated to the dioceses of Würzburg, Fulda, Linz, and Berlin, while the Essen population was sent to the dioceses of Rottenburg, Vienna, St Pölten, Freiburg, and Augsburg. The immediate consequence for pastoral care was the need to adapt to this new dynamic that had been imposed.[154] Although the 'Church on the Move' supplied a network for this from the pre-war period, large-scale evacuations meant that this administrative structure providing 'continuing spiritual support' was facing an entirely new challenge.

This applied to the logistics of the problem, in particular to the attempt to maintain contact between old and new congregations far from their home and to the continuation of Catholic life in regions of the diaspora. To counteract the loss of the link between church and milieu, the archbishopric of Cologne, for example, planned to supply all evacuees with news from their parishes about church life at home and to continue, at a distance, to give instruction in matters of faith. Apart from sending news of practical things, the point was to stay in close spiritual contact. Evacuees were therefore to be incorporated in the daily worship of their home parishes and formally remembered. Finally, it was planned that where possible and if the local parish agreed priests from the home parish would go to join their parishioners in order to support them in their exile.[155] As the parish was a kind of 'parental home' and the parishioners now in a strange environment, Cardinal Frings of Cologne said, priests should devote particular care to those who were now far from home.[156] The home churches and those in other parts of the Reich should maintain lively contact with each other even beyond this time of testing.[157]

This shift in pastoral practice was reflected theologically in many sermons preached by the bishops from 1943/4 onwards, in which the war experience of 'losing one's homeland' was given new meaning. The eruption of war into people's 'peaceful home areas'—this was a central theme—had not only destroyed human life but had caused the German people to suffer a terrible 'loss of its homelands'. This metaphor of the 'lost homeland' had a dual sense: it referred not only to the loss of faith typical of the age and the 'longing for the Lord' in the hereafter but also to the attempt to come to terms with the damage inflicted by the war on the Catholic milieu. This was especially true of the way the war had led to the mobilization of families and of the use of women as war workers, which from a Catholic perspective had become a heavy burden imposed on the German nation. The very core of 'family life' seemed threatened by 'total war', by the deployment of men and women but also by the evacuations and the large number of homeless. Now it was the homeland, where home towns and churches had collapsed, that bled 'from a thousand wounds'.[158] The loss of one's homeland meant the loss of religious community, the loss of friends and one's own home—a fate suffered by Jesus Christ as no one else had and thus a source of comfort to others in their misfortune.[159]

Pastoral care in Britain

The sight of bombed-out churches made Protestants and Catholics in Britain realize from the start that the war would be a testing time for Christians.[160] The controversy over the 'just war' and the legitimacy of the bombing campaign was thus only part of a much more fundamental reassessment by the churches of their position. Since the outbreak of war bishops and Anglican intellectuals close to the church had not tired of describing the war as a fight for 'Christian civilization', the outcome of which would be a better, Christian world.

For many it was the very rejection of Christianity that was the cause of the war in Europe. The war against Hitler was part of a defensive battle to enable Christian life to continue. Yet even if Churchill at times used religious terms, such as in describing the Battle of Britain in June 1940 as a fight for the survival of Christian civilization,[161] both he and other leading figures in the War Cabinet like Eden, Attlee, Bevin, and Beaverbrook were hardly moved by religious enthusiasm. That a good society had necessarily to be a Christian one was something the writer J. B. Priestley refused to believe. Although the new world that was to emerge after the war needed religious values, he did not sense any great desire for crowded churches, constant prayer, and cries of Hallelujah.[162] And he was not alone in this.[163]

Even before the outbreak of war the Protestant churches had had to cope with immense problems. At the turn of the twentieth century one British person in six still went to communion at Easter, but by 1940 it was only one in nine. In a Mass Observation survey in London at the end of the war two-thirds of the men and some four-fifths of the women said they believed in God,[164] though 60 per cent of those questioned never went to church. In the cities in particular the Church of England suffered increasingly from organizational problems and a decreasing number of clergy, whereas the Catholic church grew by 400,000 to a total of almost four million in the 1940s as a result of immigration and a growing number of conversions and was able to extend its organizational structure, especially in the north of England.

As during the First World War, the Mass Observation researchers noted a growing search for meaning through esoteric beliefs and interest in astrological and spiritualist interpretations of present and future.[165] Yet in contrast to the Great War, when the focus was primarily on the terror of the Day of Judgement, the growing influence of liberal Protestant theology since the inter-war years meant that notions of divine judgement and the torments of hell had largely disappeared. With the air war the need for religious direction had grown in many places, even if this was not necessarily anchored in church attendance and did not imply that church membership had been revitalized.[166]

After an initial rise in church attendance following on the outbreak of war, euphoria over what was taken to be a growth in interest soon gave way to the sobering realization that, with the end of air raids and the growing confidence in victory from the middle of 1942 onwards, church attendance was declining again.[167] To a great extent people's minds were on their very immediate worries before and during air-raid warnings and on the need for divine aid.[168] A familiar saying heard again and again in air-raid shelters and expressing these thoughts went: 'God is our salvation. Have no fear. During the bombing He will be with us.'[169]

Many prayers called on God's mercy to spare homes and churches and asked for particular support for all those serving on the home front and suffering the bombing.[170] As a London vicar said, they committed themselves into God's hands with a peaceful heart, hoping that under his protection the danger would pass over.[171] The Catholic Truth Society produced a leaflet to help Catholics to behave appropriately in the air war—and that meant preparing themselves for death.[172] Everyone must be ready at any time to appear before God. Catholics should therefore take the opportunity of going to confession before the bombing raids, for after all it could be already too late to confess one's sins when the German bombers were already circling over the city. As soon as the air-raid sirens sounded they should sprinkle themselves with holy water, as this offered protection against the disaster threatening to descend on them.

This advice to believers did not, however, mention a general absolution of the kind discussed in Germany. People should and must make their confession, not during the air raids but rather beforehand. Each person should examine his or her conscience so that nobody was obliged in the end to depart this life without having confessed or having just managed to do so at the last minute in the air-raid shelter. Supporting believers there was one of the new tasks in urban pastoral care.

In some cities such as London and Bristol the various churches attempted to coordinate their work in this area, while in others such as Birmingham it was the responsibility of the local congregations and individual clergy who were particularly active in pastoral support in air-raid shelters.[173] For some the shelter was, as it were, a place of spiritual awakening and seen as an opportunity for people in extremis to learn to focus on God again. At least that was how it was interpreted by a London Methodist in a book about religious and national revival designed to win American support. He painted a picture of the role of the clergy and of religious belief in maintaining the stability of the home front. His message was that people who had turned their back on God were now praying again; people sought comfort in praying with others and at the moment of bitter personal loss clergy were at the side of those who were mourning to support them.[174]

That was in many respects probably an exaggeration, but at the same time this self-perception reflected the search for a role that had evidently been lost in an increasingly secular world and thus the hope of regaining ground through the war. There was little mention, however, of the war as a 'religious crisis' or of people becoming more distanced from religion. It seemed rather that the loyalty of those who even before 1939 had been faithful church members and had, for example, attended services regularly was strengthened—a development very similar to that in Germany.

In the parish magazines that many congregations produced each month with information about times of services and pastoral activities the image of the committed clergyman who engaged with people's concerns and also performed civil defence duties was not unusual. This was a possible pattern of behaviour in particular for those who after the experience of the First World War had become convinced pacifists and now watched with anxiety the military escalation, while at the same time wishing to serve their country. They too were able to play an active role in the fight against Nazi Germany and contribute to boosting morale. Here was an opportunity not simply to distribute hymn books and prayer cards but, where resources allowed, to care for the physical well-being of bombing victims and so provide evidence of Christian charity.[175]

The air war had created numerous new pastoral duties that went far beyond supporting people in the shelters. At the outbreak of war strict blackout regulations had been imposed that had a direct impact on the daily life of churches; the restrictions they brought with them, for example concerning the ringing of bells, were accepted with great reluctance. Thus at the end of September 1939 the Central Council for Church Care appealed for air-raid precautions to be applied to important military regions rather than to the country as a whole.[176] The fear of what might happen to the churches was based not least on the assumption that when the war got under way all sensitivity to the historical and architectural importance of buildings would be tossed aside and every consideration would be subordinated to the imperative of the war alone.

Worried letters from clergy in all parts of the country flooded into the office of the archbishops' War Committee. They complained that armed members of the Home Guard wanted to use church towers for their duties or that parades and exercises were timed for 11 on Sunday mornings at the same time as services, thus not only making attendance difficult but also challenging the sanctity of the Lord's Day. In Sheffield the bishop was indignant that because of a scheduled invasion exercise at the end of October 1941 a newspaper announcement called on everyone to stay at home on a particular Sunday and thus people were deprived of the opportunity to fulfil their obligation to attend church—and this had been done without any consultation with him at all.[177]

Church life was, however, affected in other ways by state interventions. In the winter months the times of services had to be altered or services moved to other premises that were easier to black out. Early communion services in particular now often took place in the dark. At best small candles were permitted so that the prayer book could be read.[178] Often the only light illuminating the church interior was the candle by the tabernacle or the altar, by means of which churchgoers could find their way from their pew to the altar rail at communion. The type of blackout could vary considerably from one church to another: in some it was limited to covering the light bulbs with a box, in others the congregations designed their own coverings for the windows and doors so that in spite of any blackout regulations they could still hold services.

This was particularly important for the main church feast days at Easter and Christmas, because services were held late at night or early in the morning and any disruption to, let alone any rescheduling of, the traditional sequence of events was felt by many to be a great loss that they remembered long into the future. Not only the temporal rhythm but also the atmosphere in the services was affected by the air raids. Congregations in Bristol, Southampton, and Plymouth, for example, adapted their services to the air war, holding them as close as possible to the shelters or directly inside them.[179]

As the fire service was overstretched in many places congregations organized their own teams of fire fighters, who kept watch at night to protect their churches. In St Paul's Cathedral there had, for example, been a twenty-four-hour fire watch from August 1939 that lasted to the end of the war, also putting out fires, clearing rubble, and doing everything possible to prevent German air raids from disrupting the planned services.[180] The protection of key church buildings was not just a matter for the congregations but, as the Dean of Exeter, Spencer Carpenter, made clear, a task shared between the nation and Christians. The motives behind people's investing time in it were therefore very varied. For quite a few the cathedral, which was more than a thousand years old, was the spiritual hub of the south-west and protecting it thus a Christian and a patriotic duty. Others joined in because they saw the cathedral as an integral part of the beauty of their city and its long history, and this was reason enough to spend nights on the cathedral roof.[181]

Apart from minor damage Exeter Cathedral survived the heavy bombing raids of May 1942 and in the spring of 1943, as Carpenter looked back on the events of the previous months, it towered up over the cityscape because it was one of the few buildings still intact in the centre. Smaller congregations on the other hand found it more difficult to organize effective teams of fire fighters from their own resources. In Plymouth in May 1941 the police authority appealed to the moral duty of congregations to form volunteer watches.[182] In the autumn and winter of 1940/1 in particular it was not unusual for church life to collapse for a short time under pressure from the raids, as happened in Portsmouth. A Mass Observation respondent who visited the city in January 1941 was shocked to find, as he stated in his report, that all eleven churches he had visited were closed and looked desolate.[183] It was no wonder therefore that reopened churches and services among the rubble drew a large public and were intended to demonstrate once more the determination of the city and the nation to survive.[184]

The presence of the church in local life grew more prominent, not least as a result of the hardships of rationing. Many of the parish magazines had their own series in which women were advised on how to run the household as economically as possible.[185] The church came to the people. In order to save oil for lighting, for example, the Church Times called on clergy in 1941 to approach church members and pray with them in the open air. In Methodist congregations services, known as 'cottage meetings', were moved through shortage of space to the homes of church members. It was not only the blackout that changed the use of churches for a short time. At least as important was the fact that city churches were used as aid centres for the local community, as hospitals, or as reception centres for victims of bombing and thus were open to a sizeable number of people.[186]

Necessity gave rise to another type of cooperation. The evacuations in autumn 1939 had led to different faith groups encountering each other, even if these encounters had not been entirely free of friction. For example, children of Catholic working-class families in Liverpool were sent to rural Anglican regions of Wales. The Catholic community realized with horror what a hostile environment their children had landed in and how they had to hold their own without any pastoral infrastructure. There were no Catholic churches and on Sundays their host families took the children with them to the Anglican service.[187] Ecumenical contact did not, however, arise solely out of the fear of air raids, as in the case of evacuations, but also as the immediate reaction to the destruction. The loss of church buildings and the gradual relocation of congregational activities below ground led to hitherto unknown points of contact among the churches. In Plymouth, for example, the Methodists offered their premises to the neighbouring Anglican church after its own building was bombed.[188]

In Bristol too such types of practical cooperation resulted in Anglicans, Methodists, Baptists, and other nonconformist churches forming their own ecumenical discussion groups, which at a time of external threat were supposed to create a sense of Christian solidarity and interfaith community and possibilities to give mutual support.[189] The Protestant churches could draw on the experiences of the ecumenical movement of the inter-war years, which reached a temporary high point with the war and the subsequent establishment in 1942 of a common platform in the British Council of Churches. Reconciliation across religious and national boundaries was a crucial legacy of the lessons drawn from the catastrophe of the First World War.

Catholics had always had difficulties with ecumenical discussion, for they always retained the feeling of being religious outsiders and not full members of British society, though the Archbishop of Westminster, Cardinal Hinsley, the leader of the Catholic church in Britain, was both a convinced patriot and open to ecumenical dialogue. He not only defended ecumenical initiatives against opposition in his own ranks but actively promoted them.

A year after the outbreak of war, in a hitherto unheard of act of ecumenical solidarity, the Anglican Archbishops Lang and Temple, together with Cardinal Hinsley and the chairman of the Free Church Federal Council, Walter H. Armstrong, wrote an open letter to *The Times* in support of the

Pope's appeal for peace.[190] Peace was possible, they said, if all the nations of Europe made Christianity the basis of their politics and in so doing respected national sovereignty. The message was less remarkable than the inter-confessional cooperation being shown in action, in particular the cooperation with British Catholics; with their large Irish immigrant membership, whose national reliability was a matter of some dispute in Britain,[191] they were regarded by some as being potential Nazi sympathizers.

Among the British Catholics a group of lay people joined together in summer 1940 under the banner 'The Sword of the Spirit' to defend democracy and common British values. They not only opposed the sympathy widespread among Catholics with authoritarian and dictatorial regimes such as in Vichy France, Italy, and Spain, but aimed to contribute to a defence of Christian values—one that transcended denominational differences—in the face of the challenge from totalitarianism. This initiative was directed inwards as well as outwards, inwards as an expression of British Catholics' commitment to democracy and outwards as an ecumenical signal to the Protestant churches that they wanted to join in fighting for the common British cause.

Given the experience of bombing, the common threat, this seemed entirely justified. On 10 May 1941, a Sunday immediately after a severe raid, the leaders of the Christian denominations met to discuss a new 'Christian International Order'. Thus for the first time and on the strength of a Catholic initiative an ecumenical platform had been created which allowed people to exchange ideas directly on the social and spiritual challenges of the time.[192] It was a platform that all parties wished to cooperate in forming and also underlined the central role of Christianity for the present and future of the Empire.

The air war therefore raised once more the question of the significance of the churches in a particular sense. For the destruction of churches and the public scars left by the Luftwaffe's bombs seemed to lend additional legitimacy to the Christian defensive struggle. The ruins not only pointed to Nazi barbarism, which destroyed culture, but they were also proof of the British nation's power to resist. Christianity and the 'People's War' fused together in a particular religious narrative of destruction and reconstruction. The ruins of the Gothic cathedral in Coventry were, as it were, the starting point for this interpretation.

The German raid in the night of 14/15 November 1940 had left hardly anything of the Parish Church Cathedral of St Michael standing, apart from the tower and the external walls. Yet the bombs had not wiped the city out, as German propaganda crowed. Coventry had survived and, as the *Birmingham Gazette* was the first to report, although the city had been left to bear the marks of the most savage raid in the history of modern warfare the proud spirit of the cathedral towered over all the grim scenes of devastation.[193] The article was entitled 'Coventry—our Guernica' and set the tone for the rest of the reports by its references to the horrors of the Spanish Civil War, pictures and reports of which had caused considerable alarm and shock in Britain.[194]

Immediately after Coventry British propaganda concentrated above all on the image of the Nazis as destroyers of churches and it was this message they targeted at the USA. Now the motto of the Ministry of Information was not to hush things up or talk them down, as in the case of earlier raids; instead, comprehensive reporting about the effects of the bombing was the order of the day and pictures, which had not previously been used, were included. The results of this change of strategy were not slow in coming: Among others the *New York Times* responded to the raid by talking of the 'madness' and 'barbarity' that were threatening western civilization, to which the ruins of the cathedral bore silent witness.[195] The pictures released by the British censors went round the world, giving a bird's eye view of the vista of rubble, which made clear the full extent of the devastation. Nothing had survived apart from the tower and the external walls and smoke from the bombing could still be seen rising from the interior of the cathedral.

At first propaganda concentrated on presenting the raid on the city as a crime against innocent civilians. Just a week after the raid the Ministry of Information sent the painter John Piper, who was an official 'war artist',[196] to Coventry to capture the moment of destruction in two oil paintings.[197] His painting 'Morning After' used naturalistic colours to show the tragic sight of the cathedral after the bombing. The walls still glowed, thick smoke and soot hung in the air and nothing seemed to have survived. Yet the scene did not convey a sense of total destruction, for clear bright light shone from above into the empty interior, breathing new life into the dead walls. And not far away another church had survived intact and stood defiantly against the German terror in a shining golden glow. For Piper 'Morning After' was a kind of preliminary study for numerous pictures of churches and monasteries he painted from late autumn 1940 onwards. They formed part of the war pictures commissioned by the Ministry of Information, which were exhibited during the war and published in book form in a special series.[198]

Figure 5. The interior of Coventry Cathedral after the air raids. 'The Morning after the Blitz', a painting by John Piper.

Churches in ruins, chancels with caved in roofs, charred crucifixes—all spoke of the tragedy of destruction and the loss of the past, but at the same time they were supposed, in line with the wishes of the Ministry, to suggest the ambivalence of architectural losses.[199] For tragedies also always opened up new possibilities for the future and indeed for the present too. The iconography of destruction therefore symbolized both tragedy and (spiritual) triumph in equal measure—mourning for the loss of things of cultural value but at the same time hope for reconstruction and the Christian spirit that would rise again from the material remains, if indeed it had ever been destroyed. Piper's painting was concerned less with crimes against humanity, let alone the loss of human life. His pictures remained abstract and distanced, focusing on the city's material, architectural, and cultural losses and not on individual suffering or the fear of the inhabitants. As a result they lacked the immediate accessibility needed for war propaganda.

Herbert Mason's photo of St Paul's Cathedral, on the other hand, was immediately striking and less ambivalent. It appeared on New Year's Eve

Figure 6. St. Paul's Cathedral after the air raid on 29 December 1940: a photo in the *Daily Mail* of 31 December 1940.

1940 in the *Daily Mail* and even during the war became an icon of British war photography on the home front. Taken on the roof of the newspaper's offices directly after the severe bombing raid on London on 29 December 1940, the photo showed the cathedral silhouetted among the smoke and flames. St Paul's (Old St Paul's) had last been damaged by fire during the Great Fire of London in 1666.

Now, in spite of two serious hits, the cathedral had miraculously survived—and thus what it embodied survived too, namely centuries of British culture and architecture, the imperial tradition, and not least the Christian heritage and Christian future.[200] It was precisely this combination of historical, imperial, and religious narratives that Mason's photo captured and that gave it such impact. The picture caption in the *Daily Mail* linked the various interpretative possibilities with the rhetoric of survival in the spirit of 'London can take it'. St Paul's thus symbolized endurance and resolve in the fight between good and evil[201] and gave Londoners hope and confidence. The Blitz had become a religious event transcending confessional differences, a divine test. And the most important thing was that St Paul's had survived.

Christian Iconography and Ecumenical Experience

Other churches, however, had been more seriously hit or damaged beyond repair. In Bristol, the City of Churches, more than thirty churches of all denominations were destroyed. The destruction of their places of worship seemed therefore a common ecumenical burden that the city's Christians had to bear but which also bound them together more closely than ever.[202] Shortly before the end of the war the Revd Paul Shipley and Howard Rankin published a richly illustrated volume of photos of the churches that had been particularly badly damaged. The Dean of Bristol, Harry W. Blackbourne, had contributed a supportive foreword, reminding readers of the fact that many of the churches documented could probably not be rebuilt and that it was therefore all the more important to put on record the riches of ecclesi-astical buildings.[203] The photos printed came mainly from the holdings of local newspapers and some of them had already been published. As a rule the accompanying text gave a sober account of the church's history up to the German air raid. Nowhere was there any detail about who had caused the damage. The Luftwaffe was not mentioned and no one considered it appropriate to present the air raids as part of a military conflict.

The Blitz appeared to be a divine 'visitation', a 'trial', yet it was precisely those 'supernatural' forces, the small 'miracles' spoken of in the reports and texts, that allowed glimpses of the beginnings of reconstruction and divine grace. On the morning after the bombing the congregation of Redcliffe Crescent Methodist Church could save only a Sunday School bible.[204] Already damaged, it was salvaged and dried by one of the oldest members and two weeks later the scriptures could again be read, though with an additional surprise: the bible always opened at a place in the book of Ezra concerning the rebuilding of the Temple after the Babylonian exile of God's people: 'Let the work of this house of God alone; let the governor of the Jews and the elders of the Jews build this house of God in his place.'[205] As in Germany, it was the Old Testament image of the Temple destroyed that pro-vided an explanation and offered hope by means of a transnational canon of images and interpretations that were fundamental to the church's tradition of giving comfort in times of distress.

The photographs in the volume showed the ruins from different per-spectives and with different figures. In some children were playing among the pillars lying on the ground; in others firemen were extinguishing blazes and rescuing people. The contrasting pictures before and after the bombing, with their comparison of the blameless splendour of the building with the violence of the attackers, made use of interpretative iconography, as did pictures showing packed services and people who were not deterred by the danger of walls collapsing bearing witness to their faith whether the church had a roof or not.[206] During the night of 2 December 1940 Tyndale Baptist Church had received a particularly bad hit during an air raid on Bristol. The photo showed charred beams, collapsed walls, and a chancel that was beyond recognition. What was left, as the commentary explained, had been destroyed by fire. Yet Tyndale Baptist Church was not just one of many churches destroyed, but was the first badly damaged one in which a baptism was held early in 1942.[207] The picture showed a little girl with a devout expression and head bowed receiving the sacrament of baptism and in order to do so she had clearly had to make her way through the ruins of the church. Innocence and new beginnings, faith, hope, and the towering ruins all came together in this picture, which was published in the press and underlined the unbroken will to survive in the City of Churches.

Whereas in Bristol and Exeter the cathedrals had survived the raids, Coventry Cathedral had not. Immediately after the bombing, however, the decision was taken to build a new cathedral in the same place. The official line promoted in Britain, that British bombing of German cities was in retaliation for Coventry, was rejected by the provost, Dick Howard, who gave a different interpretation of the fate of his church and the consequences of the air war. The bombing, he said in his Christmas Day sermon broadcast by the BBC to the whole country, was a merciless and wicked crime, and yet in spite of the destruction the cathedral had retained its beauty and dignity. Christ had been reborn in its heart and the Christian community should therefore try, however hard it might be for them, to banish all thoughts of retaliation and rebuild the cathedral.[208]

Central to this move towards Christian reconciliation was the message of the crucifixion and resurrection of Jesus, which Howard saw not only as a call to rebuild the cathedral but as a form of active work towards peace. This was admittedly not an easy task in the face of repeated bombing raids in the first half of 1941 and it was not reciprocated in Germany. Howard's aim and that of the new bishop appointed in 1942, Neville Gorton, was to make the new cathedral special in a variety of ways.[209] One of them was the idea, which ran counter to Anglican tradition, of positioning the altar in the centre of the nave, to make it 'an altar for the people', belonging not only to the clergy but to the congregation. The plan was that in the 'People's Church' they sat around the altar and the priest no longer stood facing them.[210] The Christian mission of reconciliation was to be reflected in the interior in a Chapel of Christian Unity, to be used by Anglican and nonconformist churches. These were unconventional and controversial ideas,[211] and yet at the same time they were in tune with a body of ecumenical experience that had been growing from the inter-war years onwards and regarded reconciliation as the crucial lesson to be drawn from the catastrophe of the First World War.

Ecumenical practice in Nazi Germany

At first the ecumenical experience of German Catholics and Protestants could in the main be summed up in one word: unwanted. It was the result of wartime mobilization and evacuation, which destroyed the boundaries of different milieus and at first provoked in many people a sense of being a stranger and under threat. Pastoral care had of course concentrated on keeping the milieu intact or on recreating it in the diaspora.[212] Yet at the same time the clergy responsible for the congregations of the diaspora were reliant on help from societies where another denomination formed the majority. First and foremost there were practical matters to deal with. Where could services be held in areas almost without Catholic or Protestant infrastrucure? Were Catholics allowed to enter Protestant parish halls and vice versa? And were people prepared to give help without hesitation, bearing in mind that the same could happen to them?

Since the outbreak of war and the founding of the 'Una Sancta' movement ecumenism had gained momentum. Protestant and Catholic theologians meeting to discuss the priesthood, guilt and retribution, and the form of the mass[213] could only rarely hope for support from the bishops for the latter, with few exceptions, were overwhelmingly reserved, openly sceptical, or, in the case of the Protestants, doubtful about finding a common Protestant position. Even so, in the face of the external threat posed by National Socialism this move towards ecumenism prepared the way for a gradual abandonment among the broad membership of the churches of rigidly opposed positions and for isolated efforts, for example in Munich, Augsburg, and Berlin, to work towards dialogue.[214]

Ecumenical experiences could vary considerably. In Thuringia, a stronghold of the German Christians, it had been forbidden since 1939 to hold

Catholic services in Protestant churches. Though individual pastors were evidently more than willing to put church premises at the disposal of Catholic evacuees, they were not prepared to decide these difficult issues without the approval of their Church President, Hugo Rönck.[215] In the summer of 1944, however, Rönck turned down the request of a Catholic priest for Catholic services for evacuees to be held in Protestant buildings. He justified his decision by saying he had concerns that, because of the large number of evacuees, Thuringia could become a mission field for Catholics precisely in rural areas and that many of those concerned would in the end settle in Thuringia, which he considered completely unacceptable. Finally he referred to the fact that up to that point there had been no consistent ruling on the matter of the use of premises by Catholics and he would therefore be obliged in any case to press for one before he could make a decision. This was not an absolute refusal but most probably an attempt to put the matter off.[216]

In view of Rönck's nationalist and *völkisch* outlook, this standpoint was not exactly a surprise. Since being elected President he had, after all, always projected an image of himself as a belligerent hardliner.[217] This section of the Protestant church, being more aligned than the others with the Nazi state, which it had welcomed and supported, had little sympathy with ecumenical concerns. It made no difference that the Catholic cleric pointed to decisions made by other Protestant regional churches, where from the start of the evacuations Catholics, for example in Prussia or in Württemberg, had been able to hold services in Protestant churches and church halls.[218]

In other regional churches and dioceses Protestant–Catholic cooperation was less fraught with conflict. In Württemberg or the Harz, for example, it was completely normal for Catholics to use Protestant premises for their Sunday services.[219] And in turn Catholic congregations, for example in Württemberg, supported Protestant clergy in the pastoral care of evacuated families by placing Catholic facilities at their disposal.[220]

Thus the air war had indirectly compelled the churches to arrange their pastoral work by agreement with their fellow Christians and to reach some kind of compromise with them. All of them were, after all, conscious of how difficult it was to give pastoral care to people who had lost their homes and possessions. But it was not only away from home that Catholics and Protestants encountered one another. With its tower and cellar air-raid shelters the air war had created new places where people came into contact with each other, places where both Protestants and Catholics underwent severe trials and where they prayed together or at least came into contact with each other's faith and liturgical forms. The results could vary considerably. For example, a pastor in Augsburg wrote of his unease when he encountered Catholicism. During an air raid a group of about sixty people were sitting in the shelter, the doors were locked, and the only light came from the candle burning on the improvised altar. Then someone called on the group to pray. While anti-aircraft fire and bombs detonated people began to say the rosary. 'When the danger was past', the pastor remembered immediately after the raid, '[...] many people expressed their gratitude. However shattering it is to hear the rosary being said by someone trembling with fear at a moment of serious danger, I was struck still by the poverty of a type of prayer that was confined to the traditional formulae of this rosary.'

One of the members of his congregation had a similar experience when evacuated to the country and living with a Catholic family. Though he had been made welcome, the pastor of St James reported, here also the rosary made a rather 'inadequate' impression, considering the extreme situation; it was therefore cheering to be reminded of the richness of the Protestant tradition and to be able to immerse oneself totally in prayer using 'hymn book and psalter'.[221] The air war did in fact have an impact on the practice of prayer. Circles linked to the 'Confessing Church' in Berlin produced 'prayers when in fear of death' designed to help people survive nights in the air-raid shelters.[222] These centred on the approaching apocalypse, on refuge and trust in God, and on salvation from the 'flames of Hell' encircling people and their children. There was little mention of life, of surviving, and even the war itself seemed a vast abstract idea of divine testing that had to be endured piously and with absolute trust in God. The mechanical repetition of the rosary may not have measured up to the Protestants' richer biblical language, but both Protestants and Catholics believed that focusing completely on God and persevering with humility in the air-raid shelters was the only attitude possible to the 'visitation' and the only way of meeting the obligation to maintain morale. As there was a limited number of shared religious expressions it was mainly the Lord's Prayer that was said together in cities like Augsburg, where the population was both Protestant and Catholic; for many Christians, whether Protestant or Catholic, it was their very first direct experience of ecumenical worship.[223]

Loss, Guilt, and Reconstruction

American sociologists from the United States Strategic Bombing Survey were also interested in 'wartime ecumenism', when shortly after the war they questioned a group of Protestant and Catholic clergy about their experiences of the air war.[224] Even allowing for the fact that people were unwilling to say negative things about other Christians in Germany, these discussions with the Americans provided confirmation that external pressures, Nazi repression, and intensified bombing had perforce led to some degree of rapprochement between the churches, though it is doubtful whether this was 'pronounced', as the Superintendent of the Cologne church circuit stated in July 1945.[225] While this was probably wishful thinking, virtually all those questioned mentioned that space had been made available to evacuees and that cooperation in coping with the aftermath of bombing raids had been good.

There was a strong consensus that the bombing had severely restricted church life and above all the possibility of attending church, though Albert David, the vicar-general of Cologne, did not see in this a rejection of the churches' interpretations of the catastrophe but rather a tendency for church members to intensify their 'individual spiritual commitment'.[226]

Catholic and Protestant clergy alike remembered that the air war had assumed a central role in sermons in the second half of the war, even if it had often been alluded to only indirectly and integrated into a theological interpretation. In the case of the archbishopric of Cologne David stated that Catholics had been 'uniformly instructed' to view the war as the consequence of rejecting God and his commandments. The targeted bombing raids were a 'constant admonition to be prepared for death'. Life could cease at any moment and people could find themselves facing God's judgement. They had to make themselves ready for death and this readiness to die had, it was claimed, created 'an exalted religious state of mind' comparable only with experiences at times of 'severe persecution'.

In addition to repentance, preparation for the hereafter, and a certain apocalyptic note in the prevailing mood, David's assessment included a further theme that linked wartime experience directly with the post-war period, namely the war as a time of double persecution for Christians, by the Nazis and by the Allies. It was the Christians who as a substitute for all had taken upon themselves the punishment for the world's rejection of God and whose sufferings, now that they had stood the test, conferred on them

a new authority in the period of reconstruction; once free of the new occupying power they would be morally intact and fortified by the years of trial.
Thus, in the opinion of a Catholic priest from Münster, the bombing raids
had not been the 'revenge of world Jewry', though he also referred to the
dissemination of this interpretation in the Münster area, which was Catholic, and hence to the enduring influence of Catholic anti-Semitism.[227]

The motif of 'God's punishment' could, however, be interpreted in two
other and very divergent ways. On the one hand there were evidently
Christians who saw God's judgement not as a spiritual trial but as a direct
response by God to the murder of the Jews and a punishment for the Germans' crimes.[228] The Cologne Superintendent clearly had little sympathy
for this interpretation, for he alluded to a second line of interpretation that
explicitly rejected the theme of 'God's punishment' and conceived the
bombing as the root cause of spiritual crisis and alienation. Bound up with
this was the conviction that in a 'total war' not only the Germans but also
the Allies had incurred guilt, and it was incomprehensible why God should
mete out such punishment only to the German nation. There was no more
mention of divine testing; rather there was incomprehension and anger
about the workings of providence and the punishment of the innocent.
What was paradoxical was that divesting oneself of guilt seemed positively a
precondition for a 'soft' theological landing in the post-war era, where it was
no longer possible to connect in the same way and with the same intensity
with the traditional, centuries-old theology of war.

During the war, therefore, the question of theodicy, the meaning of the
victims' suffering, remained the fatal flaw in the churches' attempts to make
sense of what was happening, a problem not faced in the same way by their
fellow Christians in Britain. There, in a country where church and state
were much more closely linked, it was considerably easier to regard the war
against Nazism as a fight for 'Christian civilization' than in Germany, where
the Nazi state was hostile to the churches. In spite of this, in both countries
the destruction of churches was expressly seen as synonymous with the
'barbarity and contempt for culture' of the other side and an expression of
the superiority of their own civilization. They were an important resource
through which the legitimacy of the war could be established and morale
thus maintained. Even during the war a part of the iconography of survival
and reconstruction familiar in the post-war period was being created
through the exploitation in propaganda and the stylization of the destruction of church buildings and this in particular was to form the self-image

of the Catholic church in Germany as the 'victor amid the rubble'. In Britain too this use of the destruction of churches was a vital element in the change to the ecumenical semantics of peace, Coventry being the prime example.

And yet none of this offered an answer to the question of theodicy. Responses changed in the course of the war, not least in the wake of news from the front. Though criticism was voiced of the Nazi rhetoric of retaliation, appeals for people patiently to endure their fate and prepare for the hereafter took the place of the themes familiar from the beginning of the war. These had invoked, albeit without passion or militant enthusiasm, the 'national community's' fight to defend itself and the national emergency. In 1943/4 less and less was heard about the 'nation'. Of course it was still important to do one's utmost to strengthen the home front and defend the Reich, but the focus was now the salvation of the individual through the Cross; the war had taken the churches back to this their central Christian message.

In the case of a narrow and highly integrated section of the religious milieu this was probably sufficient and led to renewed inwardness; yet to those who saw themselves as victims of the war, as refugees in their own country who had lost house and home, there seemed to be increasing difficulty in accepting the church's response to one of the fundamental questions at the heart of the Christian understanding of the world.

Even during the war the churches were aware of this tension. A number of attempts to adapt theology to the progress of the war can certainly be read as part of a learning process that was the starting point for a new theology of peace. This theology held that wars were not just part of the state's 'just actions' but an expression of the potential of the modern world to destroy civilization. The air war was a manifestation of this human destructiveness, which in future had to be controlled and prevented. 'Inwardness' was a possible response to this, while also being a rejection of 'modern' methods of warfare. But it took a long time to reach that point, and in the end the reality of being integrated into the national community's 'fight to defend itself' overshadowed those dissenting interpretations that raised the question of political responsibility and the moral legitimacy of the war.

While Germans were pondering guilt and responsibility, Coventry's Provost Howard was already working on the issue of how to escape from the theological cul-de-sac. Even during the war he was using the term reconciliation and making great efforts to establish Coventry as a special place of remembrance, thus giving the cathedral a significance it had not possessed before the air raids, and because it was the centre of a very young diocese (founded in 1918) this status was not granted it without opposition from other cathedrals and war-damaged cities. Thanks, however, to the Ministry of Information's Coventry campaign and the great resonance the bombing of the city had had in the United States, offers of help reached Howard in the summer of 1941 from overseas, where there were plans to raise money from donations for the reconstruction. Howard reported this to Fisher, Bishop of London and chair of the interdenominational War Damage Commission and responsible for all churches destroyed in the war.[229]

The sum needed to rebuild the cathedral was about £750,000. According to Howard, a third would be required from the War Damage Commission, the city would come up with another third, and the remainder could be covered by American donations. The matter was not so simple, however, for other bishops objected to Coventry's trying to turn its propaganda success into hard cash, thus depriving other bombed churches of it. What if Coventry were to receive the money but then no more donations were forthcoming for other churches? In Exeter, for example, people were not at all convinced of the special significance of Coventry. Their cathedral, they said, represented a thousand years of Christian and western culture in Britain and had defied the Normans and all other threats in the course of its history.[230] Neither St Michael's in Plymouth nor the markedly younger St Michael's Cathedral in Coventry could point to a comparable tradition, nor did they benefit from this unique blend of historical tradition and spiritual aura. These should be the criteria governing decisions on where the funds for reconstruction should flow.

The Bishop of Winchester spoke emphatically in favour of delaying any campaigns to raise donations until the church published a joint call for reconstruction.[231] Fisher and the members of the War Damage Commission, which consisted of representatives of the dioceses and independent finance and building experts and scrutinized the submissions from the parishes, supported this view.[232] He told Howard that there should be no discrete money-raising for Coventry. It was still not clear what the total costs of reconstruction would be and Coventry was not, after all, the only church damaged by the air war for churches in Exeter, London, Bristol, Plymouth, and Southampton had also suffered in the raids.[233]

Although the War Damage Act envisaged that the costs of repair or possible replacement of buildings would in general be met by the government,[234] some time was to pass until funds were made available as a result of limited wartime resources and the necessary architectural reports. The church's War Damage Commission estimated that in total at the end of the war some 15,000 church buildings were damaged by bombing and several thousand completely destroyed.[235] The Methodists, for example, reckoned there were 2,600 instances of severe damage to their churches and as yet there was no clear idea about the cost of rebuilding. The authorities responsible estimated the cost of the damage to St Paul's alone as being about £150,000.[236]

Meanwhile, since 1940 congregations and dioceses had been setting up their own commissions with the intention of keeping records of the loss of buildings and valuables and thus creating a basis for war damage claims. Regions that had been recognized by the church as special emergency areas in wartime as a result of the level of destruction or large fluctuations in population and evacuations took priority and they were now asking for money from the communal pot.[237]

Yet the question of finance was only one of the problems the Commission had to solve. It was also responsible for the creation of new pastoral units, which involved issues of power to the highest degree, providing ample scope for conflict and causing heated discussions in the dioceses. And a central issue had not yet been decided, namely whether all churches destroyed should be rebuilt at all. And if not, which ones? For many congregations the destruction offered an opportunity to adapt to new social and spatial conditions, taking account of the reduced membership and church attendance that were widely bemoaned. It was clear, at any rate, that the plans under discussion since 1941/2 to restructure cities would make some churches redundant and it therefore seemed advisable to consider whether from a pastoral point of view a different location made more sense.[238]

This was obviously not a possibility for damaged cathedrals. For, as the Dean of Exeter stressed, churches were not simply disposable quantities for town planning purposes. 'His' cathedral fulfilled at least a threefold function: It was a 'sign of God', which in view of the external threat had redoubled significance. It was a place of silent prayer, from which people could draw strength in times of danger, and finally it was a 'national institution', a historic place where in times of danger the nation had always gathered and therefore the nation would need its protection in future.[239]

The catharsis of the air war seemed therefore to have bound the nation and Christianity more closely together than ever, and nothing symbolized this closeness more strikingly than a newly renovated cathedral, resplendent in its former glory, that in the post-war world could once again be active as a spiritual and social centre of the south-west. Renovation thus meant not just simply being made ready for use again but was also an assertion of the claim to active participation in building the New Jerusalem. To speak about reconstruction also meant mapping out the social position of the Anglican church as the established church in a secularizing society and documenting the Christian claim to a leading role in the post-war era.

Whereas the damage to Exeter Cathedral was still financially manageable, the War Damage Commission was obliged to deal with many cases where simple renovation work was not enough. Of the 45 churches in the City of London, by spring 1945, in other words while the city was still within range of the V-2 rockets, 17 were so badly damaged that there had to be a decision whether to pull them down or to rebuild. What was clear was that bombed-out churches were more than just buildings and that was something everyone concerned agreed upon.

Besides rebuilding and new building a third suggestion for how to deal with bombed-out churches arose during the Blitz: the ruins could be memorials warning against war, places where the Blitz could be remembered and thus remain standing in the new plans for the cityscape as symbols of the city's will to survive and the violence of war. This type of plan was first discussed from autumn 1941 onwards in connection with Plymouth, when the city commissioned the leading town planners Patrick Abercrombie and Peter Watson to develop ideas for the reconstruction. Their 'Plan for Plymouth', published in April 1944, envisaged among other things that the remains of one of the bombed churches would be left standing and integrated into the new and radically altered cityscape. The church was to serve as a reminder that, as when the threat had come from the Spanish Armada in 1588, the city had survived this time too, withstood Hitler's bombs, and frustrated an invasion—and nothing would symbolize this more vividly than the remains of a ruined church in the centre of the city.[240]

These newly created city memorials were to give future generations an idea of the severity of the crisis and the scale of destruction the air war had brought the city and the nation. That at least was what the initiators, town planners, and church representatives had in mind,[241] warning that in a few decades nothing more would remind people of the wounds inflicted and the victims claimed by the war and thus the Blitz would 'disappear' from memory. The ruined churches were not simply to be left uncared for but to serve as places for tranquillity and meditation, giving people the chance to pause in the hectic life of the city and making it possible to hold church services regularly in the open air. Thus they were also a kind of substitute for the lack of space to withdraw to in modern cities, somewhere to linger for a few moments or spend a lunch break.

The proposal to preserve selected church ruins thus provided an answer to three problems. With towns and cities growing and the congregations that had kept the churches alive dwindling, the bombing had made even more pressing the question of whether the distribution of churches in large cities such as London was still appropriate to the times and whether it was not better to build new churches where they were needed, namely in the suburbs and housing estates on the periphery. Was the church not obliged to adapt to precisely these changed social structures and regard the destruction of churches as an opportunity to tackle these inadequacies, of which people had been aware since the inter-war years? That could not be avoided and yet one question remained open, namely what was to happen to the places of worship in the heart of the city. The ruined churches offered a compromise in this situation, for at least a small number of churches remained as places of thanksgiving and faith, as in London, so that their original function as places of worship was preserved into the present and thus created a link between past and future.[242] At the same time they were visible signs of spiritual depth in what seemed an all too materialistic world.

As 'open spaces' the church ruins also served as an oasis for meditation and a contrast to the bustle of the city. And finally the devastation gave a solemn and appropriate outer expression to mourning and remembrance and made the time of suffering continuously visible—in a way that could be shared by all the groups that had played a part in the war, each of which was to have its own church: the RAF crews that had been shot down, the women who had served the nation, the dead of the Royal Navy, and finally at least one church in the centre of London dedicated to the memory of the thousands who had lost their lives in the Blitz.[243]

None of these questions had been answered by the time the war ended, however. For the church this was an opportunity and a burden at the same time. In spite of state grants the financial burdens were considerable and at the same time the debate that had begun during the war about the future of city living put the Anglican church under significant pressure to reconsider the structure of its ministry to communities and face up to its constantly declining importance by reorganizing itself. At the same time ruined

churches and churches rescued were visible evidence of the Christian foundation of the nation's will to survive, and it was this that had made victory
over Hitler even possible in the first place. These churches could thus be
integrated positively into their surroundings, while offering also a Christian
message, albeit one that was still muted at this juncture, of transnational
reconciliation based on the rebirth of the Crucified One, with whose help
former wartime enemies could find a common language as survivors in the
ruins of a godless, totalitarian age. At the end of the war this was a line of
interpretation shared also by Catholics and Protestants in Germany.

6

Fear and Order: Life in Air-Raid Shelters

Security and Unrest

Air-raid shelters were the internal bulwark against the external threat. They were intended to provide protection against the weapons of modern warfare, against gas and bombs. But their propaganda significance went far beyond the provision of deep tunnels and solid cellars. Given that overcoming people's fear and maintaining public order were the basic preconditions for sustaining wartime morale and therefore the nation's fight for survival, it was not surprising that social relations within shelters were a particular subject of interest from the very beginning of the war.

However, their first experiences with German air raids had completely confounded the expectations of the British air defence experts.[1] For to begin with they had assumed that the raids would be brief and violent and above all would take place during the day, which appeared to make elaborate security arrangements for night-time unnecessary. Moreover, before the start of the war many city authorities had had reservations about building large shelters because they were afraid that they might become centres of social protest and disobedience for the working class. Thus the planners aimed to leave families to look after their own protection and encouraged the creation of protected spaces, which could be constructed in people's gardens or within their homes[2] and which in any case would be more economical than any other solutions.

What then was the importance of air-raid shelters as a new form of community during the war? How were they designed? How were they projected in propaganda and visually represented? What forms did social conflicts take? What specific gender norms were established? What methods of control were used? And how did people become personally engaged? What were the common features of and the differences between expert assessments of the behaviour of the population in shelters? And in what ways were changes in the significance of and the function performed by the notions of the 'national community' and the 'People's War' reflected in the controversies about air-raid shelters?

Fortress and national community

Although there had been a lot of talk about air-raid defences in Germany before the war, in practice there had been far less construction than the planners had anticipated. To begin with this was part of the logic of the way the war was being fought; they were prepared for anything except a long bombing campaign. However, the first British air raids had caused some uncertainty, making it clear to those in Berlin that in the long run the loyalty of the 'national comrades' could be guaranteed only if people were permanently protected from raids. A few months after the inauguration of the 'Führer's Emergency Programme' for the construction of secure air-raid shelters on 10 October 1940 the head of civil defence in the Reich Air Ministry, Kurt Knipfer, set out the following vision of a future air-raid shelter programme.[3] Right from the start the construction programme was highly ambitious. Women and children were to be taken care of and at the same time workers in the armaments industry were to be protected, with their work during the day being exchanged for security at night.

By the winter of 1940/1, however, it was clear that this over-ambitious programme was going to be a complete fiasco. This was all the more dangerous because for various reasons shelters had a major role in sustaining popular morale and thus for the self-image of the 'national community'. For in the final analysis the internal and external design of the shelters was meant to reflect the nation's military strength and warlike spirit. These were spaces in which the structure of Nazi society was given its military expression as a struggle for membership of the 'community', as a promise of protection by the 'Third Reich', and as the model for a new Nazi society.[4]

'In past centuries', the General Plenipotentiary for Construction stated in 1942, 'in many cases fortresses and castles did not simply serve the purely material function of defence, but gave the builder the opportunity to find an appropriate form with which to express their defensive purpose, and in many cases they have remained cultural monuments with an importance far beyond their original material function.'[5] Thus function was not the only consideration in the designing of air-raid shelters. They were supposed to represent much more: the history and presence of the 'national community'. As architectural showpieces they were to be symbols of its overwhelming determination to survive. At the end of the war the tall, undamaged towers would not only stand for the success of the 'national community' but also for its future and its creative strength and so be part of a new, militarily strong Nazi city.

From the end of 1940 plans were already being drawn up in city building departments to integrate the air-raid tower shelters into the city's future planning and to adapt them to the urban environment. In many cases, as in Brunswick, Frankfurt am Main, Berlin, Hamburg, or Emden, tower shelters were erected on spaces where, up until 1938, Jewish synagogues had been standing, which after being plundered and confiscated had been taken over by the city. Anti-Jewish violence and the security of the 'national community' were two sides of the same coin.

In the city of Hamm in Westphalia from spring 1941 onwards the city planners had begun to integrate preparations for the construction of air-raid shelters into an overall concept of urban development, which as in other cities consciously referenced its medieval past.[6] Nine tower shelters along the old city wall, which surrounded the city centre, were intended to turn the city into an impregnable fortress and its inhabitants into fighting citizens ready to defend themselves against the 'robber barons of the air'. Soon, however, and at the latest by the autumn of 1943, it became clear that these ambitious plans had come to nothing in the face of inadequate resources and the force of Allied air raids on Europe's largest marshalling yards and that only a small proportion of the population was being protected. Instead of towers the authorities now concentrated on extending private shelters and constructing protected spaces underground.

In Hanover the city planners contemplated relocating large sections of the urban infrastructure underground. The aim was to create a 'sheltered' ('verbunkerte') city, combining the vision of a well-fortified medieval city with the modern plans for large-scale reconstruction typical of Nazi architecture and redolent of the spirit of Albert Speer.[7] Especially during the first two years of construction the shelters and their large building sites became central locations through which the Nazi state could reassure itself and the population of the legitimacy of its claim to be providing protection.[8] Nothing, it seemed, could go wrong if, on the initiative of the 'Führer', the population was being protected and shelters were being energetically provided. At the same time, this staging of security was a double-edged sword. For, on the one hand, such public rituals documented the determination of the 'national community' to defend itself, but, on the other hand, as the war went on they became a reflection of its vulnerability. And thus it was not surprising that from 1942 onwards pictures showing ground breaking ceremonies for shelters disappeared from public view.

Underground

In Britain there was no comparable programme of shelter construction, either at the beginning of the war or later, when the focus continued to be on the mass production of individual shelters and less on large underground or tower shelters. This was not without risk. For with the first major air raids on London in September 1940 the situation became much more critical. To begin with the anticipated casualties did not occur, but it was soon clear that the existing capacity of the shelters was insufficient, even when a large number of Londoners were not taking advantage of them and only a minority were seeking mass shelter accommodation.

There was not yet talk of it being the nation's fate to spend its life in a shelter. At the start of the raids many sought shelter in public buildings, in churches and schools, but not in the London Underground, which at the beginning of the war was not seen as a place of refuge. On the contrary, ministerial officials were convinced that, as a major means of transport, the tube must under no circumstances be besieged, let alone blocked, by masses of people.[9] It was after all the heart of the public transport infrastructure and thus particularly vulnerable. That changed when, as a result of the increase in raids, the amount of damage and the population's discontent kept growing. People complained that the government was incapable of providing adequate protection. After considerable pressure from the public the tube stations were opened.[10] The construction of shelters, hygienic conditions for mass accommodation, security measures and escape routes, the provision of food and water, opening times, and air warning systems—at the latest by the late summer of 1940 all these had become sources of political conflict, with the spotlight on the government's competence at dealing with the crisis.

Thus, in the final analysis, it did not matter so much how many people actually went to the shelters; what was important was that they were at the interface of various conflicts whose origins lay in the pre-war period but which had significantly intensified during and as a result of the war. They included fears concerning the political reliability of the working class as well as the conflicts of British class society, which had already become apparent during the evacuation programme. The squalid living conditions of the working class in the major cities had long been the subject of vigorous polemic. Again and again reporters and writers had complained about these conditions. But now, following the conflicts over evacuation, air-raid shelters threatened to be another area of social controversy.

From 1940 onwards, life underground, the provision of shelter, essential services, welfare, and help from the government increasingly formed part of an intense debate about the state of the nation, about the point of the conflict with fascist Germany and the hope of a 'New Jerusalem'[11] that would at last deliver to the working class the material freedom it had been denied for so long. The conditions in the air-raid shelters were in this respect the outward expression of the need for reform and a canvas for social conflicts and, as a result, an acid test of the willingness to carry out significant improvements.

From the end of 1940 readers of the *Daily Herald* and the *New Statesman* could follow in the reports of Richard Calders what life underground was like. Full of empathy, his stories told of the poor souls who under the threat of bombing had sought a new place in which to survive. His key sources were clergy who took him with them on their visits to the shelter communities or characters like 'Micky the midget', a slightly hunchbacked and grumpy former optician, who had now become head of a large shelter in Stepney. In the depths of the underworld, according to Calders, he encountered old men sleeping alone on stone coffins during cold nights; he saw women and children in the cold and overcrowded tunnels warming themselves with hot tea and looking frightened and ill;[12] they were stories reminiscent of Charles Dickens.

The most notorious of all the public air-raid shelters was Tilbury. Calder noted that here people were sleeping on cardboard boxes. It was hardly possible to get through the overcrowded tunnels; everywhere people were standing and lying around, coughing and slumped—all without any sanitary arrangements, toilets, or washing facilities. These were conditions with which Calder was not familiar in Britain and whose images were more reminiscent of the Orient, of Cairo and far-away bazaars. He adopted the style of popular travel reporting from the 1920s and 1930s[13] and its images of the Orient reflected the perceptions and images of the period. The fact that this exotic place should now be on people's front doorstep was what made Calder's stories and the reports he published during the war such a sensation.[14] His reports re-imported analogies already familiar to his readers about that exotic oriental world back to London and as a result turned them into a political scandal.

An important element in this orientalization of the underground shelters was his description of the ethnic composition of their inhabitants. For the whole country could now read what was going on in the darkest corners of London. Together with Micky, his informant, he descended further and saw not only the dark eyes of black children, but also a large Bengali asleep who looked like 'a breathing monument of an ancient crusader'. He did not believe what he was seeing could possibly have existed in the western world. Everywhere there were people with different features and skin colour: 'People of every type and condition, every colour and creed found their way there—black and white, brown and yellow; men from the Levant and Slavs from Eastern Europe; Jew, Gentile, Moslem and Hindu. [...] Scotland Yard knew where to look for criminals bombed out of Hell's Kitchen. Prostitutes paraded there. Hawkers peddled greasy, cold, fried fish which cloyed the already foul atmosphere. Free fights had to be broken up by the police. Couples courted. Children slept. Soldiers and sailors and airmen spent part of their leaves there.'[15]

The shock produced by the conditions, concern about the influence of 'the other' on the state of morals, the tradition of urban underground reporting on the shady side of big cities—all this was only part of what made Calder's reporting so special. For what he believed he had observed in the shelters was not a world that represented the opposite of what a nation needed in order to defeat fascism. What he had seen was a form of self-organization that had not been recognized hitherto, a new form of democratic community that had made a virtue of necessity and had created the nation anew.

Calder observed that on their own initiative people had developed their own rules, elected democratic bodies, and created an entertainment programme for the nights when bombing was taking place. In fact new forms of urban space had emerged in the shelters, initially out of pure necessity and against the will of the government. The first occasion when the underground was opened the government had been forced into it by infuriated locals. The communist *Daily Worker* celebrated this as a victory for the working class. Together with the Communist Party, the paper had for some time been acting as the spokesman of a class-conscious civil defence policy and its criticism of the lack of concern for workers' protection had met with some measure of support.[16]

Thus, in September 1940, after the forced opening, the police and the Ministry of Health watched with some scepticism how people began to settle into the shelters, even, as an official noted with astonishment, taking their bedding with them.[17] That appeared to be anything but a reassuring scenario. Thus the police and Health Ministry debated among themselves how, instead of heading for the morally dubious and unhealthy tube, people could be persuaded to go to private or smaller shelters in their immediate neighbourhood, where the threat of passing on diseases was less acute and which in general did not pose the same risks as the overcrowded conditions of mass accommodation.

The Organization of Fear

What, however, should be the rules governing this underground space? Who was to be allowed to enter? These were questions that preoccupied both Britain and Nazi Germany. At the end of May 1941—the Nazi shelter construction programme had been going for only six months and hardly a single tower shelter had been built—the Reich Air Ministry issued instructions intended to regulate the use, servicing, and supervision of these shelters.[18] Right from the start it was clear that the Nazi Party was going to have an important say in the matter. The police chief, who was the person in charge of all aspects of civil defence, was expected to reach his decisions on the allocation of shelter space to families and individuals in all cases 'in agreement' with the Party.

The criterion used was the potential risk involved. If the inhabitants had shelters in their houses of sufficient quality then they were put at the back of the queue. What was decisive was the police's assessment rather than any individual claim to security. Those who received permission to access one of the shelters were allowed to go there every night but were duty bound to be there during an air-raid warning. Those who were not could lose their place. However, passers-by who were suddenly caught out by a raid were permitted to go only to the general shelters.

The shelters represented the attempt to transfer social and neighbourly links underground and so to stabilize social relationships in an emergency situation. In addition, shelters were part of a society that had been forced to become mobile during aerial warfare[19] in which people from different backgrounds and with different life experiences were thrown together and had to get through the nights. The local police appointed an air-raid shelter warden from the regular shelter users from the neighbourhood whose task it was to secure order and Nazi control. He appointed marshals, usually the air-raid wardens of the nearby houses, who controlled life in the shelters. He determined who served as doorman and as members of the guard controlling access to the tower shelters. Their task was 'self-protection', to patrol the neighbouring streets, to observe and report bomb damage, and, when necessary, to put out incendiaries.

Normally the shelter wardens were involved in the Nazi Party, in one of its ancillary organizations,[20] in the Reich Air Defence League, or were police pensioners. While the shelter wardens were responsible for internal security, shelter administrators dealt with the technical infrastructure, ventilation and other equipment, the provision of water and electricity.[21] They were also responsible in an emergency for opening the shelter for the neighbourhood and giving the all clear when the situation allowed. Although the shelter wardens had no authority over the shelter administrators, they were the local functionaries of the regime responsible for maintaining order and all offences had to be reported to them. Thus, it was by no means unusual when in December 1944 the Nazi Party's Vienna district headquarters instructed one of its local functionaries to take over command of the air-raid shelter. It justified its request by claiming that 'recently there have been an increasing number of unpleasant incidents and disturbances, evidently encouraged by political opponents, in public air-raid shelters and anti-aircraft towers'. Thus the public shelters should be taken over by 'suitable political leaders' in order 'to calm people down and enlighten them politically'. This activity was not a normal 'public order duty, which falls to the police, but a political task' and that was a matter for the Party.[22]

The shelter wardens, who were issued by the police with a service card, wielded considerable power and could determine admission to and exclusion from the 'shelter community'. The key to their exercise of authority was the list compiled and authorized by the Party's local branches, the Reich Air Defence League, and the air defence police, which contained the names of all those 'national comrades' permitted to enter and who, after a careful check, had qualified for a shelter card. These individually issued entry cards assigned places in the shelter and regulated the admission to the cubicles equipped with beds for families, mothers with children, and whole house-holds; it was a procedure that operated without any great problems until 1942.

However, the shelter card did not represent a definite obligation to pro-vide protection. It could be, as was stated in bold print, withdrawn for mis-behaviour, and 'misbehaviour' could mean many things: shouting, a joke or a public complaint, illness or infirmity. From the end of 1942/beginning of 1943 inadequate provision and increasing destruction led to changes in the criteria. The evacuations beginning in autumn 1940 had already repre-sented a response to the lack of shelters.

The regime concentrated more and more on restricting scarce resources to small sections of the population. There was no room in the shelters for men between the ages of 16 and 60 years of age. In the middle of June 1943 Göring officially confirmed this practice, which had already been in opera-tion in regions that were particularly badly affected by air raids. In view of the limited number of places in shelters and the general absence of men from the 'air defence communities' male 'national comrades' were to be forbidden access to the shelters.[23] In a number of cities such as Essen that had been particularly badly bombed this regulation was already being extended to all 16- to 70-year-olds because of the increasing shortage of space and continual breaches of it. It applied above all to members of the Wehrmacht on leave and to front line soldiers, with contraventions being severely punished.[24]

Such regulations of the 'shelter question' caused considerable discontent not least because, as in Rostock, the few new underground shelters that had been built were being reserved not for the general population but for the district leadership of the Nazi Party and this produced considerable resent-ment. Were the Party bosses trying to preserve their privileges at the expense of the 'little man'? Such at any rate were the rumours being picked up by the SD.[25] Similar stories were circulating in other areas and their basic truth was being officially confirmed. Thus in the middle of November 1944 the Hanover police chief reported the results of an investigation into the city's shelters. Among the people who had sought refuge in the air-raid shelters even before the warning had been given were numerous civil servants and white collar public sector employees from the neighbourhood. This behav-iour greatly annoyed the blue collar workforce who did not have time to leave their work. He intended in future to bring all those who continued to behave in this offensive manner 'to account'.[26]

The 'Jewish question' produced problems for the authorities. In October 1940 the Reich Air Ministry had pointed out that Jews could not be totally banned from admission to public air-raid shelters because otherwise it would be liable to have 'detrimental effects' that 'could also be disadvantageous for the members of the population with German blood'. Göring did not make it clear what was meant by 'detrimental effects', but it was certainly not so much a sense of solidarity with Jewish fellow citizens as people's anti-Semitic concern not to be robbed by Jews during the time when they themselves were in a shelter and so were unable to keep an eye on their property. Göring, therefore, pressed for Jews to be accommodated in separate shelters and if necessary for the existing shelters to be divided so that Germans and Jews did not have to be in the same space.[27]

The Nazi Party's local branches were a driving force in the exclusion of Jews. In March 1944, for example, the Munich-Keuslingstrasse Nazi local branch ordered the 'half-Jew' Adolf Franck to desist from using the 'apartment block community's' air-raid shelter. The residents could 'not be expected to tolerate' this. In future he was to seek refuge in the cellar.[28] Victor Klemperer reported a very similar experience. On 20 January 1945, during a raid on Dresden, he had quietly and secretly sought refuge in the block's 'Aryan' shelter and hidden in a corner only for a woman to shout: 'You're not allowed to stay here!' Another resident of the block demanded: 'What are you doing here?' His embarrassed response was that he had simply come down to the cellar to fetch some coal and that he just wanted to rest for a moment. But the 'block community' did not allow him to enter and so he had to drag himself back up the stairs to his flat.[29]

With the deportations the government regarded the problem as finally solved, while another problem acquired increasing importance: how to deal with the growing millions of foreign workers? The Air Raid Shelter Regulations of 18 September 1942 laid down that prisoners of war and so-called Eastern workers were on principle banned from entry to air-raid shelters. The shelters should be opened for other foreigners, for example Italians or French, only if there was sufficient room for them. In any case their needs had to be subordinated to those of the 'national community'. Instead of secure shelters they had to put up with draughty and cost-effective covered ditches, which they were expected to dig for themselves.

The few arrangements for air-raid protection in factories often beggared description. At the end of August 1944 a Belgian clergyman, who had to carry out forced labour in Essen, noted in his diary: 'The siren sounds the preliminary alarm, then the full alarm and we have to run to what they portentously call a "shelter"! A ditch which is one metre wide, 1.50 metres deep and 30 metres long, including the corners and the entrance, and 350 people were squeezed into it in rows of three. Our heads hit the ceiling, which is covered with 60 cm of earth. With all the body odours of the forced labourers who never change their clothing, who wear it for work, during their free time and at night.'[30]

In such spaces the air was limited and the supports were only provisionally secured. By the morning of 23 October 1944 during the night raid on the Ruhr 62 of the 350 foreign workers had been killed, 5 were missing under the rubble and a further 45 were wounded. From his ditch Alphonse Come could hear how in the separate concrete shelter for German workers the radio was announcing the impending raids, raids which were threatening both his life and those of his comrades in their insecure shelter and making 'our lords and masters ever more ill-humoured', as he drily noted. At the same time the bombs were also harbingers of approaching liberation and provided a ray of hope in the bleak conditions of brutal forced labour.

The practice of admission could vary from city to city and from plant to plant.[31] Sometimes the forced workers from Western Europe were permitted to use the factory shelter or large public shelters[32] or, as in Bremen, they tried to force their way in. The shelter wardens were also allowed a certain amount of flexibility which could be used on behalf of the foreign workers. That was probably the reason why, for example, at the beginning of January 1944 the shelter wardens in Bremen were reminded by the police that POWs, eastern workers, and Poles were forbidden to use public air-raid shelters and that they could be admitted only if there was already sufficient space for the local population.[33] Normally, however, they had no other option than to seek refuge in the covered ditches or other insecure places, with the result that often a disproportionate number of casualties of the raids were eastern workers, who came last of all in the list of safety concerns and consequently were 'victims in a dual sense', victims of German exploitation and of the air war.

There was, however, a direct conflict as regards this issue between racial exclusion and economic exploitation. Evidently as a result of a radicalization in the practice of admission to shelters by the local authorities, in the middle of August 1943 the Reich Air Ministry felt obliged to remind them that there was not in fact a Reich-wide ban on foreign workers seeking refuge in air-raid shelters.[34] And, in January 1945, the Ministry was still having to point out in a circular that foreign workers who were deployed in the German economy should as far as possible be protected. Göring's circular was a response to the practice by numerous air defence directors of flatly denying foreign workers access to public air-raid shelters. In view of the importance of their labour this should in future be avoided and, if necessary, given the shortage of space and contrary to the practice of previous years, there should no longer be separate accommodation for 'western workers' and Germans.[35]

Races, Classes, and Genders

Such conflicts involving race and ideas of social utility were a quintessential feature of wartime Nazi society and they came to a head in air-raid shelters. Britain did not adopt such a brutal approach. However, the tunnels, tube stations, and air-raid shelters in Britain were also by no means the harmonious democratic laboratory on which Calder had lavished so much praise. The different ways in which the problems were perceived and the conflicts resolved reveal crucial differences between the two wartime societies.

In fact in Britain too during the first few weeks it was unclear in many places who was responsible for what and how arrangements were to be made for people to live together under the new conditions of war. For many people found themselves plunged overnight, as it were, into a new social order in which there was great insecurity about norms and laws and about 'correct' and 'incorrect' behaviour. The police were responsible for law and order. They, however, transferred a large part of their functions to specially installed shelter wardens, who in an emergency were supposed to mediate, to look after people, and to deal with admission to the mass shelters.[36]

According to the reporters of Mass Observation, after a few weeks rules emerged, unwritten laws which people were obliged to obey if they did not wish to risk provoking conflicts. Passages had to be kept free, and nobody must get in the way or sleep there. It was a crime to touch someone's blanket or take someone else's place.[37] Someone's reserved place was holy ground and the same was true for the immediate surroundings, for where there was no more privacy there had to be a small protected zone. The loss of privacy was one of the quintessential features of shelter life. Shelters made what was part of the intimacy of family life public. Society began, literally, to observe itself and that was by no means purely a pleasant thing.[38]

Apart from anything else there were pragmatic reasons for this. For the majority of those who sought refuge in tube stations at night were workers and low-grade white collar employees, only a minority of whom had access to a private shelter or an Anderson shelter in the garden. If there was any social interaction between different social classes in shelters the class barriers remained intact.[39] While they lived together, were polite to each other, and each showed their best side to the other, the 'simple' people separated themselves off from 'their betters'. Clothing was an important distinguishing feature.

In February 1942 the police noted in a report for the Regional Commissioner that there were three types of people who, despite the declining threat, were still using shelters. The first were 'respectable middle class people', who were so frightened of bombs that they were even prepared to put up with the stigma of spending the night in a public air-raid shelter.[40] This group, however, intentionally separated themselves off from other social classes and tended to form their own small shelter communities. A second group saw shelters as places offering social warmth with food, medical care, and adequate light, all things that in daily life had to be paid for. Around 40 per cent, the police estimated, were there for these economic reasons. And then there was a third group, who sought refuge in shelters every night because they did not want to give up their social privileges: a fixed place, a little bunk, or a spot on a tube platform, with the danger of then not having anywhere to stay in an emergency.

In view of these social tensions, organizing and directing this life spent in tube stations and so being able to control this new social space was by no means easy. London's City and Metropolitan police forces put up large posters on the entrances to the tube stations establishing a new code of behaviour for life underground. Any attempt to protect one's own berth from prying eyes by putting up a blanket was banned, as was throwing away bottles, tins, and newspapers.[41]

After their initial experiences those responsible for civil defence developed a comprehensive set of rules aimed particularly at housewives.[42] Women were expected to plan in advance what they had to take with them and what could be dispensed with. A change of clothing and warm socks for the winter nights should be put ready every evening. They should carry their most important documents with them: identity card, rent book, building society savings book, old bills, and—very important—their gas mask. Remaining calm and following instructions were the two main rules of behaviour which had to be followed under all circumstances. The disciplining of emotions and behaviour affected all areas: women who were afraid should distract themselves by knitting and should not show their fear. Women also had a duty to try and 'look beautiful' in shelters.

There were strict rules against disturbing other people, not least to try and stop people snoring. Snoring was considered a clear breach of the code of behaviour and prompted a further catalogue of suggestions. The author Creswick Atkinson advocated that potential offenders should on no account lie on their backs or keep turning over; it would best if they lay on their side.[43] After a certain amount of toing and froing, the Ministry of Health provided affected cities with regulations trying to cover all aspects of the new social order from admission to the shelter to waste disposal, regulations that were quickly adopted.[44]

Concern about air raids had prompted the local authorities into frenzied activity, not least because cities such as Plymouth, Liverpool, and Bristol quickly became aware that the existing strategy, which had been entirely based on the private provision of shelter, was clearly inadequate to cope with the needs of those sections of the population who lacked resources. In Bristol, for example, from November 1940 onwards there was a working party which focused on the organization of life in shelters: on financing their construction, on the provision of food, leisure, and health facilities.[45] Its agenda covered not only the fight against bacteria and infections but the whole issue of maintaining morale. In April 1943, when only a few people were still gathering in shelters at night, city officials were complaining about immoral behaviour. To make it more difficult to indulge in sexual activity dubious parts of the shelters were to be placed under special observation and if necessary cleared by the police.[46]

The shelter wardens and shelter marshals were in charge of the shelters. According to Calder and 'Micky the midget', some of them were official and some were self-appointed supervisors of the shelters. Often small shopkeepers from the neighbourhood,[47] during the war they had already achieved literary fame as local heroes of self-government. They were portrayed as uniformed officials who were always cheerful, helpful, concerned to sort things out, and able to settle a quarrel, but who were not too full of themselves to serve a cup of tea or open the door for a lady and who were always ready for a chat. The metropolitan police commissioner had instructed the responsible district superintendents to be considerate to people and not to wield a big stick.[48] The view was that by simply using pressure and imposing strict rules they would never be able to establish their legitimacy and respond to criticism of the conditions. People must be won over and convinced about the war and not forced to conform. Adopting a polite tone seemed the right way to proceed.

Some time passed, however, before these informal posts acquired formal tasks. In Bristol, for example, in November 1940 the shelter committee determined what exactly a shelter warden had to do. He was responsible for the heating and the provision of drinking water; he had to deal with matters of hygiene and cleanliness and ensure adherence to the shelter rules.[49] Formally he was subordinate to the city engineer, a member of the city administration to whom he had to report breaches of the rules. This was the theory. In practice, however, the shelter wardens exercised considerable power.

What appeared to Calder a small-scale republic could in reality reveal itself to be an authoritarian regime. At any rate, a Mass Observation reporter in Tilbury noted: the shelter 'presents a huge opportunity for Little Hitlering'. While the police and the supervisory staff dealt with people appropriately, in his view it was above all soldiers and the shelter marshals who used their power to tyrannize over other people.[50]

There could also be senseless rules, people could be shouted at, and there was strict social control for newcomers who, for example, settled down in particular parts of the shelter, thereby upsetting the informal allocation of space and challenging the privileges of those who were already there by right of continuous occupation. This was in a certain sense the early version of the self-organization that could be observed in some, though by no means all, of the mass shelters in London. These were shelter organizations that were initially outside state control and, as freely elected committees, grasped the initiative by pressing for improved hygienic conditions. From the late autumn of 1940 onwards some of them published their own journals: The *Subway Companion,* the *Holborn Shelter,* or the *Station Searchlight.* These were small magazines distributed in the shelters and intended to increase political pressure on the government and on the administration of the London Passenger Transport Board and also to encourage a positive 'shelter mentality'.

The *Swiss Cottager,* named after the tube station, for example, not only criticized the government strongly for its inactivity but also talked of a common struggle against the 'shameful apathy' of bureaucrats who were hiding behind regulations and not doing enough to provide for the most basic needs of people who were in distress.[51]

These small but in some cases very self-confident pressure groups caused some concern to the authorities because they were suspected of being communist front organizations that could destabilize the home front.[52] This self-mobilization in the underworld combined the self-confident representation of interests with social and ethnic demarcation. Thus creating a community involved adapting to the patterns of behaviour that were 'required' for civilians on the home front and involved resisting the fear of loss and destruction as well as expressing anger at the fact that to begin with they were having to spend their nights in miserable conditions while others were continuing to live in security.

At the same time this self-mobilization could also lead to violence against those who were regarded as not belonging to the nation: blacks, Indians, and above all Jews. They seemed to be responsible for everything: for the chaos that often occurred at the entrances to tube stations; for brawls and the decline in morals, and not least for the overcrowding in tube stations. The *Catholic Herald* described Tilbury as a 'brothel' where the Jews and their families had made themselves at home and had not only spread disease but also tried to distribute communist propaganda to the people there.[53]

In October 1940 a policeman told a Mass Observation reporter with total conviction that the refugee German Jews who were in the city in large numbers were responsible for the catastrophic conditions and overcrowding in the Oxford Circus shelter. Ninety-five per cent of those who sought refuge in the shelter were German Jews.[54] In another case a woman complained about the alleged omnipresence of foreigners and Jews, rich Jews above all, who were drawing attention to themselves, smoking fat cigars, and taking other people's places.[55] In any case priority in the provision of shelter should be given to British people and not 'dirty foreigners'. And the *Swiss Cottager* also reported that the majority who were seeking shelter at night were foreigners.[56]

In September the Mayor of Stepney, Frank Lewey, reported that many people were suspicious of British Jews and believed that their characters were not up to coping with the demands of modern warfare.[57] Jewish householders were accused of not doing enough to protect their houses, Jewish civil defence groups were denounced as a security risk, and there were continual rumours in the East End that it was above all Jewish shop owners who were benefiting from the German raids. The Communist Party in the East End was also a target since it was vociferously demanding improved air-raid protection and secure shelters for the working class. It was suspected not only of being loyal to Moscow but also of being controlled by Jews.

It was not only elements of Oswald Mosley's fascist movement who were responsible for this. Mosley and other members of the leadership cadre of the British Union of Fascists had been in prison since May 1940. According to Mass Observation surveys, anti-Semitic sentiments were evidently far more widespread than this and were linked to traditional prejudice against British Jews and 'foreigners'. It is not easy to say how dominant this kind of thinking was.[58] The fact that, as is testified by a number of observers, it increased in the course of the war and was based on traditional racial concerns indicates its relevance. And yet the differences between it and Nazi racial anti-Semitism are very clear. For nobody talked of racial exclusion by force and no leading British politicians contemplated banning refugees from accessing secure air-raid shelters or separating them off from 'true' British people. That was out of the question.

The policy of creating a sense of community focused primarily on the positive, 'British' behaviour that was being shown in the shelters and that meant, according to The Times, people who through it all remained calm and good humoured, did not become fatalistic but took matters in hand and founded 'a new kind of community'.[59] And Jews too could belong if, as it was put, they were prepared to fit in and integrate into British society.[60] Moreover, this corresponded to what Calder had been seeking in his reporting. The social mixture of refugees, foreigners, and old established East Enders was capable of creating something which the nation lacked. He saw a new sense of citizenship emerging in the shelters, among the core elements of which were democracy and a sense of community.

This 'citizenship' came from 'below', spontaneous and organized from necessity. This reflected the astonishment and in many cases the wishful thinking of middle-class left-wing intellectuals, who saw in the solidarity of the social structures of the shelters which had been organized from below a contrast to British class society and a kind of model for the reform of the state. Calder was by no means alone in this wishful thinking. Shelters appeared as 'a topsy-turvy world'[61] in which the existing social order had been turned upside down. That was true in a dual sense: the mass shelters were reminiscent of the bleak descriptions of London in the 1880s and these were now being reproduced 'under ground'. At the same time the 'topsy-turvy world' existed not only in a spatial sense but also in terms of the turning upside down of social relationships.

What authors such as Calder were observing was that as a result of the blackout many a male middle-class citizen was becoming aware of a relaxation of sexual norms, an Afro-Asiatic exoticism that appeared simultaneously seductive and dangerous. What seemed special about this civil society was its facility for self-regulation, its ability to prevent the shelter from becoming a place of libertine anarchy, but instead to develop rules to restrain the putative debauchery and limit the dangers arising from the war and the nights of bombing. But the world was also 'topsy-turvy' because the shelters were part of a class society whose boundaries appeared to be becoming more fluid. This at any rate was the view of those who accompanied Calder on his trips through the shelter world, most of whom were members of the middle class. It was miraculous and disturbing to see how out of the inhabitants of the most dingy corners of the East End there were emerging heroes of the underworld who took on responsibilities, saved lives, organized meals, and through their calmness and patience were enabling the nation to survive at all.

But even during the war this image was becoming disfigured. Thus by April 1943 the Mass Observation reporters, who themselves were playing an important role in this social self-observation, were by no means so sure any more what features of the new socially harmonious, self-created social order of the underworld would last. In the meantime the raids on London and other cities had become infrequent and it seemed as if with the passage of time there was an increasing danger that the extraordinary spirit that had been created during the Blitz could fade. That at any rate was the concern of some Mass Observation reporters as they once more embarked on an investigation of the lives of those who, despite the decline in the threat of raids, every night continued to seek refuge in tube stations.[62] In their view the new life in the tube stations had not simply been marked by deprivation but had offered the chance of social mobility and of a new social prestige. Independently of their social status some people had managed through sheer strength of personality and irrespective of their origins and education to take responsibility for themselves and for others and had done so in a particularly dangerous situation. Now with the normalization of daily life in wartime there was the threat of a return to social distinctions.

It had not yet come to that. But the social researchers thought they could recognize the signs. Fear of disorder in shelters and the continually increasing costs were in any case reason enough for both the War Cabinet under Winston Churchill and the Ministry of Home Security to have considerable reservations about building very large-scale shelters. Right at the start of the planning process it had been established that not everybody should have access but that it would depend on the individual's contribution to the war effort. It was considered that just being afraid would not by itself entitle anyone to protection in a shelter. Thus in Britain too having the 'right' war morale had some influence on the degree of protection granted by the state to the individual. An important criterion was the individual's commitment to 'total war', which was to be rewarded with superior protection.[63]

When in summer 1943 the committee that was intended to administer the new shelters met Herbert Morrison, the responsible minister, in order to discuss financial and logistical support with him, he responded coldly[64] that the shelters had originally been planned at the height of the Blitz and so under different circumstances. In the meantime the threat had changed. The cabinet was concerned that the shelters would create a kind of fear complex and that even the building of such large constructions might lead to disproportionate panic reactions on the part of the population.[65] Moreover, the minister declared he was concerned about current developments, about the fact that some Londoners were exploiting the favourable social conditions, the free food and accommodation, and making a pleasant life for themselves in the tube stations. Here there was no talk of a 'new community' but rather of excessive social benefits and of people who were enriching themselves at the expense of the community. Finally, according to the minister, in wartime people had to put up with difficult situations and by that he presumably meant the loss of housing.

The shelter committee was furious and pressed for the shelters to be opened as soon as possible. This seemed to them a necessary response not only to the horrors of the Blitz but also to the disaster that had shocked the whole of Britain only a few weeks earlier. In March 1943, 173 people had been killed as a result of a mass panic in front of Bethnal Green tube station. Bethnal Green tube station was one of the largest air-raid shelters in London and was used mainly by local workers. Like many other shelters Bethnal Green had not been planned as a mass shelter and to begin with had only been a makeshift solution. It was not surprising, therefore, that the safety procedures were inadequate. There was only one entrance; the staircase was narrow; there were no hand rails on the walls and the ventilation was poor.[66] It was a disaster that many had earlier predicted.

A commission of investigation was set up to look into the background to the catastrophe, which had caused considerable anxiety and anger among the population. Should not the government have made more provision and spent more money to protect people?[67] There were waves of protest and the ministry was deluged with letters of complaint, not least in response to Morrison's decision not to publish the report.[68] He feared that the Bethnal Green case might give the Germans an insight into British morale and the nation's psyche. Panic, fear, and stress were feelings that if, as in this case, they could not be controlled should at least not be allowed to become visible to the outside world.[69]

This was also the reason why the observations of the chairman of the commission of investigation, Laurence R. Dunne, on the source of these feelings could also not be published. After the British raids on Berlin and their propaganda exploitation by the press many people were evidently fearing German retaliation.[70] The introduction of the strategy of 'morale bombing', the new character of the war with the expansion of the combat zone and the intensification of raids on German cities and the civilian population, could not, it was felt, be without consequences. That meant that after the air-raid warning people had little time to get to the shelters. In the spring of 1943 it was considered quite conceivable that there would be a return to large-scale destruction and death. In this event panic might well break out.

A few days after the catastrophe rumours were flying around: apart from administrative chaos might there not be other causes of the disaster? The Home Secretary received numerous letters in which people provided the results of their own 'researches' and reported what they had heard: Bethnal Green was a 'Jewish shelter' and it was Jews and above all the 'foreign Jews' who, as a result of their lack of discipline, now had those people on their consciences and who, unlike the British, had lost their heads in a difficult situation. Other people maintained that it was the 'wrong', in other words Jewish, civil defence officials who had failed to size up the situation. Moreover, and this fitted in with the conspiracy theory, these civil defence experts were communists.[71]

Xenophobic and anti-Semitic finger-pointing was by no means a marginal phenomenon and formed part of the discourse in which people tried to reassure themselves about their national identity. Thus even the chairman of the investigation commission felt obliged to remove all doubt about alleged Jewish misbehaviour in order to put a stop to the wild rumours.[72] The Jews were not, however, the only scapegoat for people's fears; criminals and 'Fascists' were also cited by anonymous letter writers as responsible for the disaster, as were youths roaming around and up to no good.[73]

Finally, in summer 1944, after several delays, a number of large shelters were finished[74] and thus at last some adequate protection was available and it was no longer necessary to fall back on improvised tube stations, but in the meantime aerial warfare had taken on a very different shape with the arrival of the V-1s and V-2s. For now the time between the air-raid warning and the impact of the explosives was much shorter and so the surprise effect on the population was much greater and there was often insufficient time to reach the shelters. Although at the end of 1944/beginning of 1945 there were still a few thousand people who regularly sought refuge in shelters, they had become a very small minority.[75] During the peaceful months since 1943 numerous public shelters had been closed, although the city authorities, anxious to answer the citizens' need for protection, preferred to use the term 'vacated' rather than 'closed'.[76] After all, nobody should be allowed to gain the impression that the reduction in shelter personnel and the partial closure of shelters that had been built with state funds represented a saving at the expense of London's inhabitants.

In other cities the issue of shelters had already completely disappeared from the agenda. Hardly anybody in Bristol, Liverpool, or Hull reckoned any longer with the possibility of again having to suffer such massive bombing.[77] There no longer seemed any point in investing more money than was necessary. Unlike in 1940/1 there were no more pictures of people seeking refuge in shelters after the air-raid warnings of the 'miracle weapons' and then making a comfortable life for themselves there. The topic had almost completely disappeared from the pictorial agenda. The aim was under no circumstances to play into the hands of the enemy by providing them with information about the effectiveness of the new weapons.

There was great concern, therefore, when initial reports on the effects of the V-1 raids in 1944 provided a more than worrying picture of the population's morale; it appeared that because the risk was incalculable people were more fearful of death and destruction than at the start of the air war. At any rate there was no more talk during this last phase of the war of a 'new community' in the shelters that had been reopened in the tube stations.[78]

Despite the rules, despite censorship and the 'state of emergency', British society had access to public spaces in which debates could take place about ways of and strategies for dealing with social conflict, and official decisions were subject to public appraisal and required justification. That could be in the form of the reports and picture series in *Picture Post* or through questions in Parliament or, as in the case of Bethnal Green, via a special commission of investigation, which could oversee the work of the authorities and require them to answer for their actions to the public. In other words war as a 'social condition' did not make everything permissible. In this respect sorting issues out through consensus was part of the solution not part of the problem, which was not the case with Nazism.

Sites of protection, control, and violence

The Nazi state had in fact intentionally suspended such democratic mechanisms, thereby providing the basis for an ever more radical policy of exclusion and inequality. Tower shelters (*Bunker*) and cellar shelters were, therefore, simultaneously sites of protection and sites of violence, allowing the boundaries between normality and emergency increasingly to disappear and leaving no doubt about how great the discrepancy between the promise of security and the threat of death actually was.

While the privatization of the effects of aerial warfare and the minimal equipment of shelters in Britain may have been a long way from the dreams of a New Jerusalem, nevertheless the discursive context in which shelters and tube stations were embedded as part of the People's War was something very different. In response to anti-Semitic undertones and expressions of overt racism the British authorities, far from opening the floodgates to them through changes in legislation, publicly refuted the rumours and held firm to the legal traditions that had operated before the war. And the utopian notions associated with British shelters could hardly have been more different from the huge concrete sites of control that the Nazis built by exploiting millions of slave workers.

Norms of behaviour and the maintenance of social discipline were comprehensively imposed in the shelters. This began at the entrances. Behaving in an orderly fashion was the most important duty[79] and this was rigorously enforced by the shelter wardens and their assistants. Pushing and shoving to get a better place in the cellar was contrary to Nazi wartime norms. Rules of behaviour printed in large type were posted on the walls. Smoking was strictly forbidden. The stairways had to be kept clear and people had to make sure they did not stand around getting in the way of the civil defence personnel. In the passages and in the rooms where people were spending the night police posters containing the civil defence regulations reminded them of the purpose of the shelters. Shelters, they were told, had the task of protecting the civilian population. Thus everyone was expected to follow the instructions of the air defence police and to make sure that they did not behave in any way that might undermine the 'shelter community'.[80] Old people and mothers with children had priority and they had their own specially designated areas.

The notion of the 'air defence community' as the smallest cell in the defensive struggle, which had originated when people were engaged in active 'self-protection' in their blocks of flats (for example, dealing with incendiaries), was supposed to continue to guide behaviour in the tower and cellar shelters.[81] Entry was restricted to those who had a valid shelter pass or who had been surprised by a raid. Animals were banned, as were people carrying infectious diseases. Whereas in Britain people soon began to do their own thing inside the shelters and tube stations and, although the shelter wardens also insisted on orderly behaviour, they could not use police powers to enforce their instructions, in Germany, by contrast, the use of shelters required the observance of strict norms of behaviour. People were reminded by the posters to be considerate in the interests of the 'national community'. Anyone who contravened this instruction was threatened not only with the withdrawal of his or her shelter pass, but 'troublemakers' were to be 'ruthlessly' removed and handed over to the police.[82]

Children, therefore, were not allowed simply to run around. People were permitted to play music only in specially designated rooms and the same was true of cooking and the use of electrical equipment. The fact that forms of self-organization (let alone a public sphere particular to the shelters, as developed in some tube stations) were not explicitly forbidden was presumably only because they were inconceivable and did not fit into the notion of an 'orderly' shelter community.

Even before they reached the shelters the population from Berlin to Vienna had the appropriate behaviour drummed into them by posters on the advertising pillars in city streets.[83] Before reaching the security of the shelters they had to make sure that the greatest danger of the air war, fires, had as far as possible been put out. Thus attics had to be cleared, sacks of sand prepared, buckets and baths filled with water, and not just when the warning had been given but beforehand. As soon as the sirens sounded the inhabitants had to assemble immediately with the air-raid wardens of their block of flats to prevent individuals from causing chaos by following their own escape route.[84] 'Self-protection' was the duty of 'national comrades' and that meant that everybody should have their air defence pack always to hand and not have to look for it after the air-raid siren had sounded.

There were also clear regulations for the air defence pack: a few pieces of clothing, a toothbrush, dishes, cutlery, and important documents from savings book to ration book. Water was required, as were blankets. Finally, the poster stated that it was not certain how long people might have to stay in the shelter. To prevent panic in an emergency all shelter users should work out how they might escape, where there were gaps in walls and exits.

By the end of 1942/beginning of 1943 the poster's final call—to be ready for anything—implied that people might find not only protection in the shelter but also death. Propaganda, however, was saying something very different. It portrayed the tower shelters as a defiant expression of the will to live, a place which, according to the emergency edition of the *Hamburger Zeitung* after Operation Gomorrah at the beginning of August 1943, had acquired a personal note: The shelter 'has now become my house, my guardian, a friend, this huge concrete block in the midst of rubble'.[85] In the midst of the rubble shelters became transformed into 'sites of the national community'.[86] 'A sense of solidarity and unity has emerged that previously one would never have believed possible.' Such was the *Hamburger Zeitung*'s assessment a week after the Allied raid. 'Daily life is dominated by a single spirit and a single will. Perhaps the most typical example of this are the evenings in and outside the air raid shelters [...] Here neighbours are sitting together to discuss the day's events; there acquaintances who have lost touch are getting together again; over there sits a married couple feeling that this crisis has brought them even closer together.'[87] The report could be interpreted as suggesting that this purification of the 'national community' had been necessary in order to overcome faint-heartedness and quarrels with neighbours.

Air-raid shelters were increasingly regarded as transforming the 'national community' into a genuine *völkisch* community. The Nazi vision of a 'new' society never appeared closer to realization than in the anti-aircraft tower on the Berlin Humboldthain or in the deep shelter on Hamburg's Spielbudenplatz. This transformation was reflected in the regime's pictorial language expressed in the drawings and photographs being published since 1942 by daily newspapers or journals such as the *Sirene*. These showed shelters as the contrast to the urban landscape of destruction that many people had been experiencing day after day since 1942/3. It was a vibrant society of young and old, who had come together in the shelters, a pact formed by different generations and by neighbours, a pact which appeared to have overcome all conflicts. In one picture people are sitting calmly at a table with a vase of flowers; the grandparents are playing with their grandchildren in spacious, cool, and airy rooms and in the background hangs a picture of the prophet and saviour, Adolf Hitler, who appears to be stretching out his arms to shield those under threat from the Anglo-American 'terror from the skies'. Here was time to study the current air-war situation and in the meantime to sew, to knit, and to prepare calmly for the coming raid.[88]

The propaganda literature of the Reich Air Defence League (RLB) liked publishing pictures of well-organized air-raid shelters in which people were sitting in rows on the shelter benches waiting for the all clear, while the shelter wardens, simultaneously showing caring concern and policing the shelter, were making sure that everything was in order, reassuring the women while at the same time warning people not to panic.

This male dominance in the shelters was manifested in the attempt to repress any expression of female feelings and any deviation from correct behaviour by imposing strict discipline.[89] The actual practices of air-raid protection and preparations for periods in the shelters, on the other hand, were considered a matter for women and in several respects. Under male guidance it was even possible for women with little technical training to learn how to deal with incendiaries. This was at any rate the line taken in the pictures of the RLB training courses in 'self-protection' published regularly in the Sirene.[90] It was men who showed them where the main water cock was and who became het up about the fact that hitherto nobody had really known this vital piece of information. Women got stuck in and, as members of the RLB or the Nazi women's organization, helped prepare for the bombing. They fought fires and helped with the removal of rubble and providing the population with food and clothing.

Male comradeship at the front had an iconographic equivalent in the female air defence community of the militarized home front. Women were part of the defensive battle and of the 'fighting national community', important actors in the conduct of the domestic side of the war, replacing men and helping the older men. Yet, despite their helmets and uniforms, they remained women, who did not lose their femininity. They formed part of the natural order of society and that order had not changed in the shelters.[91]

The image of the militant female air defence activist that had been dominant at the beginning did not disappear during the course of the war and yet the focus was increasingly on female comradeship and motherly care, virtues which now, in the context of 'total war', appeared essential for organizing the survival of the family.[92] RLB women were indispensable for tasks such as sorting out washing, packing up household goods, helping the neighbours, cleaning the cellar, and preparing for the next air raid.[93] However, the authority to organize the shelter society remained in the hands of the shelter warden.[94]

While working-class women evidently behaved impeccably, it appeared as if the threat to the shelter community came mainly from those middle-class and affluent women who considered themselves superior to other people instead of simply mucking in.[95] The 'German girl engaged in self-protection' made much of in RLB propaganda was different: she looked a bit dreamy as if she was thinking of her Führer, but neither the helmet on her head nor her uniform had the effect of changing her kind nature. But the picture of 'our Ursel' shown in the Sirene was misleading. 'Ursel' was anything but 'dreamy' when it really mattered. Trained in numerous RLB courses the 15-year-old had taken on responsibility at an early stage and had been prepared for the coming war. She attended the training course every evening, reported the Sirene, and when things got serious it was she who kept her head, raised her voice, and took control of the self-protection measures. She fought the flames bravely, rescued people from the rubble, gritted her teeth, and did not allow herself to be shocked by terrible sights, however awful they might be. Off to the factory in the morning; in the evening fighting on the home front, in the shelter, and on the streets—this was how the RLB saw its 'girls'.[96]

Despite this selfless commitment, however, which was continually invoked by Nazi propaganda until the end of the war, with the expansion of air raids it soon became clear that the shelters in which 'Ursel' was risking her life for young and old were not only sites of self- protection but also places of fear and danger. Their external architectural appearance had already been designed to demonstrate the national community's 'military determination', at any rate in places where there were any such tower shelters. Numerous regions, above all in the south, in the Tyrol or Carinthia, for example, had no adequate air-raid shelters let alone secure tower shelters, despite the increasing number of raids. As a result, at the latest from autumn 1944 onwards, their populations became increasingly concerned that from having been the Reich's 'air-raid shelter' they would become its 'coffin'.[97]

Inside the shelters the regime used other methods of maintaining morale. In Hamburg, for example, in 1941 the city commissioned the artist Max Ullmann to decorate the Wiesendamm tower shelter with drawings of folklore scenes evoking its Hansa past. On the walls there were pictures of Hummel, the water carrier, or the 'Zitronenjette'* designed to amuse and entertain, as were scenes from daily life, of fishmongers and peasants from past centuries.[98] In the Landwehr shelter drawings from Wilhelm Busch's *Die fromme Helene* (Pious Helen) were intended to amuse people; in the tower shelter on Dänenweg and in the Reeperbahn underground shelter those seeking refuge could view wall paintings on the staircases and in the common rooms which depicted the peaceful and successful Hanseatic life of the mid-seventeenth century: peasants, citizens, merchants, and musicians.[99]

In terms of iconography most of these paintings by second-rate artists revived narratives of the 'old', innocent city where citizens could go about their business in peace without threats from outside and where the old social order based on status was not threatened by 'terror bombing'. The homely shelter world was thus a kind of contrast to the increasing destruction, which the people who were fleeing left behind at the entrance, so that in the peace radiated by the past they could gather new strength for coping with the effects of war. The few surviving semi-official photographs which, though approved by the shelter warden, were not designed for publication but for family albums, are at first sight dominated by similar attempts to convey an impression of peacefulness and the creation of order in the midst of the prevailing insecurity.[100]

Private photos from the shelter in Elsassstrasse in Cologne from Christmas 1944 show a traditional ritual of Rhenish-Catholic piety and the continuation of ordinary life in the extraordinary situation of war. In the centre of the picture there is a Father Christmas figure wearing a mitre and carrying a crozier. This dignified-looking gentleman is surrounded on the one side by men and women, civilians and nurses, and on the other by other persons in authority, all separated by gender and rank. Further back, on the staircase and barely visible, are the other occupants. The civil defence and shelter officials in the front of the picture are all looking straight at the camera with serious expressions on their faces. Nothing, it seemed, should be allowed to detract from the impression that here was a group of men ready to fight to ensure the survival of the old and the weak and of mothers with children. And, when it came to it, they would prevent anything from happening of the kind that Goebbels was complaining about in a diary entry in 1944.

---

* Translators' note: Henriette Johanne Marie Müller (1841–1916) (the Zitronenjette) was a lemon seller, who became a popular figure in Hamburg about whom plays were written.

Goebbels reported that the 'careless and undisciplined behaviour of a woman' in a shelter in Berlin's Hermannplatz had caused a mass panic leading to numerous fatalities, an incident with which the shelter supervisors had evidently been unable to cope.[101]

Their presence ensured that shelters were secure places, spaces in which the 'national community' gave protection to those whom it considered in need of protection: mothers with children and old people. Yet however obvious the set of priorities frozen in this picture may have appeared at first sight, it was not in fact unchallenged. Thus from the beginning of 1944 the SD noted an increasing number of complaints from members of the public about the priority still being given to women and children in shelters. A growing number of people who were in work were expressing the view 'that women not in employment, children and the elderly and infirm have no business to be living in areas threatened by terror bombing. Particularly on crowded public transport', the report noted, 'people are increasingly saying that women with small children should no longer be given priority because they simply take away seats from those who are working. Above all women in work are increasingly complaining about mothers and children being given priority in shelters.'[102]

Security was thus not simply linked to the need for protection but was part of the self-mobilization of the 'national community'. In this connection official views about who should receive priority in the provision of protection evidently clashed with the self-interest of the members of the 'national community'. The radicalization of the policy of exclusion was thus not simply the result of state or Party decrees but could sometimes run counter to official views and represent a form of 'action from below' which went too far even for the authorities and unsettled the SD reporters. Moreover, the views reported by the SD were evidently not held merely by a small minority.[103]

The struggle for access to shelters, for the safe and favoured places, for places to sleep, or simply for seats on a bench was in full swing[104] and no decisions had been made about how the scarce resources were going to be distributed and what the priorities would be. Should women working in the armaments industry come first or should it be those with children to look after? However, the photograph of the Cologne 'shelter community' and its careful separation of the sexes told another story. While the shelter warden and his officials were staring straight at the camera, the Father Christmas figure had turned to his neighbour, who was smiling at him while filling his glass, thereby introducing an element of pure joy into the serious scene that was being portrayed. Although we lack information on the background to and motives for the photographs, it is clear that the real world of shelters could not be confined within propaganda slogans and that there was room within the 'shelter community' for people to give vent to their own feelings and wishes and that it was precisely these individual strategies that in many cases made the tension bearable.

It was probably at the beginning of 1940/1, before the first serious bombing raids, that a number of private photos were taken in the main room and in a number of 'cells' of the deep shelter in Cologne's Berliner Strasse, where occupants of the flats and neighbours took refuge whenever the air-raid warning sounded and always sat in the same places. They knew each other, knew who spent the night with whom, who worked where, whom they were related to, and whom they were acquainted with.[105] At this early stage of the air war there were still some men of military age in the shelters, many of whom worked in the nearby armaments plants, and the majority of them like their wives had specially done themselves up for the photographs. They spent the time listening to music; it looked more as if they were on an outing than at risk of being killed. They could crack jokes and sing and do a bit of flirting. There was hardly any sign of fear yet. And on the wall there was a large picture of Hitler to calm and reassure them, simultaneously offering protection and comfort and the prospect of revenge.

The social practice of this new life style was based on a whole variety of experiences. How far away from the shelter did people live? With whom did they share the 'cells'? How heavy were the air raids? Had people lost relatives and had they already had to struggle to survive? In reality shelters were places where people both hoped to survive and feared for their lives.

The Swedish correspondent Arvid Freborg commented on his experiences: 'In shelters one notices how little people know about their neighbours. Aha, so that's what she looks like when she hasn't had time to get herself dolled up. The mood is tense but not to an unpleasant degree. The children have made friends with each other and play around on the floor. The parents try to pass the time, which is the biggest problem in an air-raid shelter. Simply having to sit around and wait is quite an effort. It's much better to do something, however trivial. Usually I have my typewriter on my lap and type away at something that's going to be sent off to the paper the following day. [...] The elderly women never stop talking, concentrating on not losing the thread of what they're saying. They prefer talking about people who were hit in the last raid and egg each other on.'[106]

While the private photos from the early phase of the war documented the calm and lack of concern that made the trip to the shelter something that was required but not risky, from 1942 onwards illustrations and descriptions by individuals both changed. In the first instance that was true of shelters as space. Now people were packed together and frequently there were no more places to sit down, space was tight, and there was a continual crush. Even at the entrances there were long queues, pushing through the narrow doorways and causing fear and anxiety.[107] The entrances were the dangerous bottleneck into the underworld of the 'national community', outside which there were frequent fights and outbursts of anger and panic, sometimes exacerbated by the strict control of the police.[108] In many places from mid-1943 onwards entrance to the shelters ceased to be regulated. By mid-July 1943 the authorities responsible for the shelters in Oberhausen had to admit laconically that their carefully worked out system of allocating places had broken down under the mass of bombs and so the shelter cards had 'become illusory'.[109]

In Stuttgart, for example, in October 1944 there occurred what a city councillor called a 'life-threatening situation'. The station square (Bahnhofsplatz) was overcrowded and people kept pouring in from the trains that were arriving, trying to find a safe place in which to escape an air raid. But even in cities like Stuttgart that had so far been less affected there was no longer sufficient capacity to cope with a large number of people in an emergency. In many cases those seeking refuge, including many women and children, were running from door to door and kept being turned away. The assessment was that, in view of the threat, the decision to clear the Bahnhofsplatz had been a mistake because the population had simply been sent from one danger to the next. In any event, such acute crises could no longer be dealt with given the means currently available.[110]

In many places the struggle for a seat or a place to lie down and thus for access to a shelter had begun. The groups who had celebrated their peaceful communities in photographs for friends or to preserve as memories for the future could now defend their small 'cell communities' aggressively against 'external enemies'. They kept a jealous watch to make sure that 'a foreigner' or a 'newcomer' did not slip in and represent a challenge to the established 'cell community' by their mere presence.[111]

Immediately after the end of the war a soldier reported on the defence of his shelter space as follows: 'I wanted to put a stop to the panic-stricken toing and froing in the cubicle because it looked as though it was going to pose a threat to us. I discussed it briefly with my comrades and, because the other people didn't agree, we used force, pushed some of them out and shut the door. We had to hold it shut from the inside.'[112] At the end of March 1945 Irmgard W. from Bremen described a similar situation in a letter to her husband, only from the other side of the door: in recent months she had learnt to use her elbows in the shelter because reticence and modesty 'get you nowhere'.[113] Carola Reissner from Essen found this 'struggle in shelters' a 'real trial'.[114]

In view of the tough (male) competition, this search for a safe place in one of the big city shelters appeared increasingly dangerous, especially for women with children. And, as the war went on, the sense of national (völkisch) solidarity with war invalids, granting them priority in the shelters, increasingly ceased to be the norm.[115] The Nazi Party played an important role in the climate of violence emerging in the shelter communities as they developed their own culture. It sought vigorously to maintain law and order by taking tough measures against alleged 'troublemakers' and trying to intimidate the crowd. This was a task that involved numerous Party functionaries increasingly taking on (air defence) police functions and continually expanding their claim to control the shelters.[116]

The 'shelter community' portrayed in imagery and described in post-war memories always represented in practice a form of inclusion and exclusion. It was the active participation in and membership of a group achieved through rights 'acquired by occupation' and by the exclusion of others, who had only sought refuge later or who hitherto had not suffered raids and now still had to find their place in a 'völkisch' shelter.

The regime regarded this form of self-mobilization with mixed feelings. For from the point of view of the authorities shelters were not quiet places, exemplars of stoic discipline, but more a source of continual disturbance and danger. For example, according to a police report on conditions in an Innsbruck shelter at the end of October 1944 people were undisciplined and lacking solidarity and as a result the shelter was dirty. There were insufficient supervisors 'to maintain law and order'.[117]

It was precisely those groups who, either out of necessity or for convenience, stayed in shelters for days on end and began to create, as it were, parallel social structures who appeared a serious threat. For not only were they blocking shelter places that were vitally important without having the right to do so but they were also shirking their duties to the 'national community'. As far as the authorities were concerned this kind of behaviour was the equivalent of 'creating communist cells', prompting them to take tough measures.[118]

The local authorities considered the numbers of those who continued to stay in the shelters on the morning after air raids and after the all clear to be an important indicator of the state's loss of control. Various numbers were quoted by the authorities who were concerned to try and retain an overview. Evidently there were significant differences between the individual parts of cities and the social structure of the shelters. Occupants of the shelters who were members of families who lived in the neighbourhood or who had been bombed out and whose menfolk were already looking for accommodation were considered acceptable. According to the assessment of the Stuttgart authorities, these were predominantly people in employment or women and children who could not be evacuated and came from 'orderly' families. It was a different matter in the case of the occupants of the Wagenburg tunnel, a large shelter between the railway station and the eastern part of the city which accommodated around 15,000 people. Here the social circumstances were definitely more primitive and here there were 'elements' who came from 'a less orderly social environment'.[119] It appeared all the more important to quantify the size of the problem by counting and identifying those involved.

The practice of being physically close together could also prove problematic. For example, shortly before the end of the war, the *Neue Volksblätter* of Osnabrück requested national comrades to show more consideration in shelters and warned people not to take advantage of the needs of others. Those who stole other people's defence packs were enemies of the 'national community'. But the same was true of those who took too much luggage into the shelter, blocking the passages and jeopardizing other people's safety, and of women with children who had only their own fate and their own property in mind. They were all contravening the shelter community's rules.[120]

According to the regime's reports, in many cases it was women who were prominent and who took the lead in complaining about conditions in the shelters. At the end of 1944 the higher regional court in Düsseldorf reported to the Reich Ministry of Justice that 'defeatist' remarks were increasingly being made in public shelters and that even judges in their role as representatives

Figure 7. German civilians with luggage on their way to an air-raid shelter.

of state authority were not objecting to them.[121] At the same time, at the end of November 1943, the judges of the Cologne higher regional court were complaining about the fact that the limited space in the shelters was giving rise to social conflict. According to the judicial authorities in Cologne, which had been particularly badly hit, the destruction of housing and the fact that people were being forced to live cheek by jowl was causing a marked increase in the number of insults and assaults. In the heat and close confines of an air-raid shelter even minor matters such as the use of the staircase or the toilet could cause a row.[122]

The authorities considered it a gross breach of the air defence rules for women, as happened in Berlin, to stand at the entrances to the shelters even before the air-raid warning had been given in order to get in as quickly as possible with their children, or as 'shelter aunties' with their children and large quantities of luggage to block public transport at rush hour.[123] This behaviour could, however, be interpreted as an attempt to protect themselves and as a vote of no confidence in the air defence authorities. Their warning systems had long been regarded as inadequate. Some of the female shelter occupants had started working out their own ways of securing their safety.[124] That also appeared necessary because towards the end of the war they were increasingly having to assert themselves against other 'competitors', namely against an increasing number of men, more and more of whom, from 1944/5 onwards, were seeking refuge in shelters and who, contrary to regulations, were finding places at the expense of women and children.[125]

Although there have been no investigations of the social structure of public air-raid shelters, there is evidence to suggest that 'encounters' between different social groups, if they happened at all, were felt by some middle-class people to be rather disturbing—shelters were a 'topsy-turvy' world in which their ideas of the social order were turned upside down. 'It's all very confused,' noted the journalist Ursula von Kardorff in her diary entry for 25 January 1944.[126] The shelter in the Berlin Zoo district was already over-crowded when she arrived there seeking refuge following an air-raid warning. What she saw there was 'a herd of people behaving like animals', who were pushing through entrances that were far too narrow. 'When people switch on torches everyone shouts "put that light out!" Then people push and shove to get inside and it's surprising that in the end things turn out reasonably all right.'

Around her Kardorff observed a chaotic and brutal scene: masses of people distributed on various floors, 'frightened rich people, tired women, scruffy foreigners lugging their possessions along in huge sacks and soldiers looking really rather embarrassed. I thought to myself: God help us if panic breaks out here.' The concrete walls of the shelter reminded her of the stage setting for the prison scene in Beethoven's *Fidelio*; the whole scenario was like the Surrealist poetics that Ernst Jünger had sketched out in his book *Das abenteuerliche Herz, Figuren und Capriccios* (The Adventurous Heart, Figures and Capriccios). The shelter was a place without faces, the mass of people driven to seek refuge, obeying the instructions of the wardens in their desperate need for help and following the crowd in an almost slavish manner. Anyone in his right mind could see how these people underground were beginning to be transformed into an explosive crowd, a human volcano capable of erupting at any moment.

This applied not only to the structure of social but also of gender relationships in the shelters. The 'embarrassed soldiers' mentioned by Kardorff referred to something that many members of the Wehrmacht talked about after the war, namely the fact that their fear of being in shelters was greater than that of being at the front and that while they were home on leave they found it difficult to get used to this form of passive suffering. It went against their self-image as soldiers, particularly when they found themselves in shelters together with large numbers of women and children instead of taking an active part in air defence activities. In this perspective the home front and the front line seemed to have been transformed: it was not simply the fact that they had got 'closer together', it was rather that the soldiers' experience of staying in a shelter had brought home to them the existential threat—a fear for their lives that seemed even greater than when they were on the front line.

And there was an additional point: in her observations in the Zoo shelter Kardorff noted the young lovers who had withdrawn up the spiral staircases. Filled with a combination of curiosity and disgust, she called it 'a travesty of a fancy dress party'. A 22-year-old female Luftwaffe aide was even more shocked by her experiences in a tower shelter in Krefeld in what was probably the most disturbing night she had ever spent. She was passing through when she was surprised by an air raid. The young woman now found herself in a room where, as she recorded some weeks later, men and women of all ages were 'indulging' in schnapps. Shrieking women and prattling men and in addition a leaden fug of tobacco smoke made it impossible to sleep. Everywhere smelt of sweat and dirty clothes, a stink that made it difficult to breathe.[127]

Towards the end of the war Wehrmacht officers noted this increasing deterioration in conditions in their reports. Above all, as one report from Berlin put it at the beginning of 1945, 'young "ladies"' were behaving badly. They should take a tough line with such women so that they got the message that the places allocated to the wounded were not meant for them.[128] Shelters intensified the problems for the regime arising from everyday life in wartime in another respect. Above all they posed a threat as places where breaches of the regulations governing communication took place,[129] for rumours could be exchanged and news passed on and the regime's monopoly of communication undermined by individuals exchanging information.

On 18 January 1945 Victor Klemperer noted in his diary: 'everything is kept secret, one is entirely dependent on rumours, on what is passed on by word of mouth, on what cannot be controlled.' At this point Dresden had experienced the air war as 'rumour', through other people's stories. Nights spent in bunkers and air-raid shelters had not yet become the norm. This made the news from Berlin and Leipzig appear all the more ominous and the fear that the people of Dresden would not escape the misfortunes that had affected other cities appear all the greater. In the light of the stories that had been heard and passed on by friends and neighbours, staying in a shelter now appeared risky, an impression that was reinforced by reports about victims and fire storms. Shelters offered those seeking refuge the opportunity of talking to other people, including strangers, of considering their own personal situation, and acquiring information about the destruction of other places and parts of the city that had not been officially approved for release by the Party.

Often these rumours had local significance: which part of the city had survived? Was it true that the neighbouring towns were already on fire? Had the Allies begun to use phosphorus or even poison gas? And was it really the case that the Nazi bigwigs were having it cosy in the comfortable shelters of posh hotels and that more and more resources were being expended on their safety while 'ordinary people' were having to spend the night in the dark and the dirt?[130] Access to and the privileged use of public air-raid shelters was a regular topic of conversation. People talked about the fact that in Berlin shelters the spaces allocated to women and children were being occupied by the wife of the responsible police chief, their cleaning lady, family members, and other Party functionaries or that art works were being stored in shelters to which the public were not being admitted.[131]

In many cases the passing on of such rumours was influenced by people's social class and could help to channel their discontent and fear and at the same time strengthen the impression that they were 'not alone'. That was all the more important because the hours spent in the bunker represented a period of extreme threat. References to having to wait a long time for the raid to happen and to the disturbing silence in the dark cellars kept recurring in contemporary accounts as did memories of the walls shaking when the bombs crashed down, the suffocating heat, the tiredness and the racing heartbeat, fear of dying, and the loss of a sense of time. From one moment to the next shelters could be transformed from places of safety into death traps. Who should leave the shelter first in the event of fire? Women and children or men? And was it safer outside or inside, in an air-raid shelter or out on the streets?

People's individual behaviour could vary a great deal depending on the range of different experiences that they might have had of previous raids, on the timing of the raid, on their experience of personal loss, on their access to resources, and also on rumours, such as, for example, the one circulating in Darmstadt in autumn 1944 to the effect that their city would be spared. The result was that the shock was all the greater when the destruction that then occurred turned out to be particularly severe.[132] Even before the end of the war individuals were recording their memories of the terrible destruction, the loss of security, and the challenge to existing notions of good order they had experienced in the inhospitable conditions existing within the oppressive walls of air-raid shelters.

At these moments it was as if supernatural forces were at work. Life and death were the product of chance: some survived, others chose the wrong route out of the shelter and the following morning were never seen again. It was the encounter with death, with the fear of suffocating, that dominated people's thoughts when, immediately after a heavy raid, they tried to put into words what in reality was indescribable.[133]

The fear mentioned by so many people could be expressed in very different ways. Some people shivered the whole time they were in a bunker during a raid, with goose pimples covering their whole body; others reported in conversations with psychologists in the middle of 1945 how despite the heat they felt freezing cold, how their teeth chattered and they lost control of themselves and of their bodies.[134] Autonomic symptoms were not infrequent: people's legs gave way, their stomachs went haywire, they went weak at the knees, and their limbs hurt so much that leaving the shelter could become a form of torture requiring assistance. In the case of severe bomb blasts many of the shelter occupants were thrown into the air, lost consciousness and came to in a pile of dust and rubble out of which they could extricate themselves only with difficulty or with the help of others.[135] There were repeated reports of people who, on hearing the noise of engines and through fear of what was to come, screamed and cowered in corners because they had discovered that bunkers did not necessarily guarantee protection.[136] From this perspective trips to air-raid shelters were not something people simply got used to, with fear becoming reduced by routine, but rather the sense of threat intensified.

At the same time, there were other ways in which the bunker experience was being articulated. Male medical or police functionaries in particular emphasized emotional self-discipline, the need to overcome fear and remain completely calm despite or precisely because of the chaotic situation with which they were having to cope. Thus, a policeman from Kassel reporting on his experience in an air-raid shelter during the raid in October 1943 noted that, while all those around him were screaming and in their fear had almost torn his uniform off him, he had remained calm, tightened his belt, and in the end had managed to lead numerous national comrades through the flames to safety.[137]

Doing one's duty meant controlling one's fear.[138] That could take the form of projecting a heroic male self-image in wartime,[139] but it could also lead to a form of apathetic deadening such as was described by a 43-year-old architect who had experienced a raid in the middle of March 1945. There were dead bodies lying everywhere, he recalled: 'To begin with I was reluctant to try to rescue people because I didn't want to touch the numerous corpses. I began to touch them and then stopped. I kept hesitating until my moral sense told me: "You must do it". Two comrades were more hard bitten and simply tore at the corpses. I couldn't bear to see them dragging them around and we tried to sort the bodies calmly and deliberately. In the process I noticed that, although I'm generally not particularly tough, I was now unusually strong. I could easily lift up the corpse of a child with one hand. I was emotionally uninvolved. But my thoughts were completely clear [...] I had the feeling that I had spent two hours in the shelter. But, in reality it was already light when I left the bunker.' The man had lost all sense of time.

A short time later he felt guilty because he had seen one of his colleagues trying to rob a corpse and because they had prevented other people from entering their cubicle in the shelter. Above all he could not get over the sight of all the corpses. He was tortured by thoughts of suicide and feelings of indifference towards his family.[140]

Iconography of the Underworld

Neither in Germany nor in Britain was it possible to publish accounts of such violent experiences. Popular British magazines such as *Picture Post* published other kinds of pictures. With a circulation of nearly two million copies *Picture Post*, edited by a Socialist, Tom Hopkinson, was one of the most influential mass magazines in Britain.[141] It had the best photographers in the country documenting life in the shelters in a series of major reports.

The photographs developed a distinct iconography suggesting high morale and normality in the midst of an emergency. People who had made themselves at home in the tunnels and were enjoying a cup of tea, who were laughing and dancing and gave no sign of being stressed by the threat of bombing.[142] Nights in air-raid shelters appeared as modern big city adventures, as a kind of extended Saturday night out. The only people showing fear were some of the children clinging to their mothers. Shelters were depicted as places where there were brave women or, to be more precise, brave working-class women, who were given a lot of space in these reports. Unlike in some of the reports on evacuation in the early phase of the war, working-class women and their families were no longer viewed as a threat. On the contrary, they radiated calmness and imperturbability; they appeared both self-confident and responsible, indeed cheerful, and they conveyed a sense of dignity. They cooked and sewed, passed the time with other women, and looked after their children in exemplary fashion. In a sense the pictures represented a visual retort to the complaints made during the early days of evacuation.[143]

Although some photographs, for example the ones taken by the well-known photographer Bert Hardy for *Picture Post*,[144] showed the overcrowded tube stations, the cramped and sparse conditions, the darkness and uncertainty, nevertheless his view of the situation suggested that a certain order prevailed. Contrary to what the government and the Conservatives had feared, the people whom Hardy photographed did not pose a threat. There were queues for food and protests against cases of unjust distribution but he never showed a disturbance. The expressions on people's faces were serious; sometimes they appeared exhausted, but were never hardened.[145] Young and old supported each other as a matter of course, slept in the cellars, seeking refuge; some prayed and sang songs together. There was time for love and friendship, for fathers to tell bedtime stories, for cleanliness and clean linen, for which mothers were responsible. Their children were shown either playing in the shelters or as vulnerable creatures in the arms of their caring parents and thus as the embodiment of national innocence and the reason why the war had to be fought—as a struggle for the future of British children, as a battle for the fate of the Empire.[146]

Concern for their fate and the ordering of social relationships were directly linked and this involved the attempt to achieve normality in a state of emergency. Thus the photographs showed girls who found time to put on make-up and do their hair. Boys played cards and put out their clothes ready for going to work or to school the following morning. Where people were frightened there were those ready to come to their aid, helping hands supporting the old and the weak.

The generations were coming together and providing each other with mutual support. The packing cases on which they slept each night may have been hard and uncomfortable, but the walls provided protection and some people showed surprising ingenuity in making themselves a place to sleep in the cramped conditions. People's attempt to assert their individuality in the mass was also a key priority and a response to the loss of privacy. This was a frequent complaint for privacy was, it was claimed, an essential British characteristic, which people used creative means to try and recapture.[147]

This visual harmonization, normative imposition of gender specific roles, and integration of the working class was accompanied by other photographic reports showing the other side of shelter society: the life of the rich and wealthy in the more upmarket parts of the city, the people who smoked fat cigars, who had money for wine and expensive whisky, and who passed the time with people like them. Hardly a single photograph showed the classes encountering each other; their accommodation remained socially distinct. There was, however, a cautious criticism of the luxury, of the privileged accommodation and its opulent furnishings, which was at the cost of the working class.

The iconography of the underworld could, however, have other discourses, detached and ambivalent attempts to describe shelter life. In addition to George Rodger and Bert Hardy, Bill Brandt was one of the most influential wartime photographers. Born in Hamburg, he had been living in London since the early 1930s and had followed in the footsteps of J. B. Priestley.[148] Like Priestley's *English Journey*, in the mid-1930s Brandt had travelled through Britain from north to south trying to provide a photographic portrait of its class society and to explore the essence of the British nation. The title of his first documentary was 'The English at Home'. It appeared in 1936 and provided the blueprint for the pictures he produced for the Ministry of Information from 1940s onwards, which achieved a wide distribution.[149]

Brandt's pictures from the late 1930s of London as a moloch show that he was fascinated by the gloomy and inhospitable tube, which had now been taken over by the people. His photographs used strong black and white contrasts and tried to show the everyday existence of the masses, mothers with their children, labyrinthine places which at night were brought to life by those seeking refuge. His photographs told the story of order in chaos: overcrowded tube tunnels, which despite the cramped conditions were not about to collapse; people who although living cheek by jowl had nevertheless kept their personal identities by securing a piece of private living space and giving it a personal touch. Although the silence of the tunnels had something threatening about it and one could sense people's fear of air raids, they appeared able to master the situation, this external threat, through their inner strength.

Brandt's quasi-surrealistic version of the home front was soon adopted by contemporary publications and accounts of the nation's shelter life, which included the stark contrast between the world of the simple worker in the tube and the life of luxury lived by rich Londoners in expensive hotels. This was a contrast that the 'national community' did not recognize and of which therefore there were no pictures. Nazism had no room for such ambivalent visual messages.

Henry Moore's shelter drawings were produced at the same time as Brandt's photographic reconstruction of shelter life and were at least as influential, receiving much attention not only in Britain but also in the United States.[150] By this time already a well-known artist, Moore had produced around 300 drawings and paintings between autumn 1940 and the summer of 1941 for the War Artist Advisory Committee (WAAC). At this point Moore was in a difficult financial situation. The war had significantly reduced his earnings as an artist and art teacher so that the chance of selling his shelter drawings to the WAAC was timely, although he had little enthusiasm for working as a war artist. Thus he was not prepared to produce simple propaganda pictures. His paintings were the product of intensive research in the tube.

Moore's paintings were not intended to be purely documentary. They were the product of several processes of abstraction and alienation and were not created 'overnight' but in several stages, often as the result of different drafts and initial drawings. The subjects of his paintings differed radically from those of other artists and photographers. Although he complained in letters to friends about the poor conditions of the working class which he had come across, the categories of class and nation did not play a prominent role in his work. Instead, his pictures had a kind of monumental quality. His human sculptures in the uncompleted tube tunnels appeared more like spectres, faceless beings, who were stoically enduring their suffering.[151]

His figures often appeared more dead than alive, their bodies disappearing into the mass. The poor air made breathing difficult and people ill. Some of the faces were a yellowish-green and their clothes were bathed in a blue and red light; these were sick and anxious creatures, fearing for their lives. This was not how heroes looked. This was also true of the motif of sleepers, which continually preoccupied him: skinny people lying side by side on cold floors covered in thin blankets. Their sleep was uneasy; some had their eyes open and were staring into the distance. The air was thin and many were struggling to breathe.

Like Brandt, he was interested in the women. In their physical alienation Moore too accorded them a special dignity. Leaning on the walls of the tube, although appearing somewhat resigned and tired, they were calm and had the necessary strength to survive what was to come. Mothers holding their children in their arms were not shown as belonging to a specific class.

Figure 8. Henry Moore, 'Tube Shelter perspective', 1941.

Rather their portrayal was reminiscent of Madonna figures and enabled the shelter experience to be given existential religious interpretations. The suffering of women and their children was one of the main reasons for fighting this war and their salvation was thus the nation's war aim.

At the same time, Moore's paintings had another dimension, which was vital for their reception post-1945 and also responsible for his success abroad. Moore was not primarily concerned with portraying London's Underground tunnels. By decontextualizing it, he made the experience of the men and women of London universal. His subject was no longer the sufferings of the Blitz but humanitarian catastrophe, the tragedy of war, which London and its inhabitants were having to bear on behalf of the remainder of the free world. In his pictures fear of the coming air raid, lack of sleep, and people's concern for their children had become experiences transcending time and bursting the bounds of locality.[152]

However, the response to Moore's pictures in Britain was less positive than the post-war praise of his work in the light of the mythologizing of the Blitz suggests. The poet Sheila Shannon, for one, did not consider the shelter pictures a triumph of humanitarian vision; she rather saw them as 'soulless megaliths'.[153] And the response of the public when his drawings were shown in the National Gallery was also very varied. Some visitors were disturbed and found the shelter pictures too morbid. This 'topsy-turvy world' that Moore had portrayed had little in common with their own experience,[154] which may have had something to do with the fact that his pictures could not be used as an easy way of evoking a sense of community.

Sickness and Health

Moore had left no doubt about his hopes that the working class would be able to cope calmly with the air raids. The government and leading psychologists and medical experts were not, however, convinced by mere appearances. While Moore was doing his studies in Tilbury and Liverpool Street station, they visited air-raid shelters in order to examine carefully the population's response to stress, noise, confined space, and fear. In their view a dangerous 'shelter mentality' threatened internal security and thus the nation's ability to continue the war.

Concern about the effects of the disorderly conditions was sufficient reason for academics from various disciplines to cooperate on a variety of levels in order to acquire as 'objective' a picture as possible of the situation in air-raid shelters. The research was intended to provide an unvarnished view of the situation. It was based on the verifiable methods of statistical investigation and recorded interviews, which were endlessly discussed until finally a series of substantial reports were sent to the Home Office and the War Cabinet. The sources were interviews with those in charge of the shelters, conversations with ministerial officials, as well as the analysis of extensive questionnaires. Moreover those responsible used the method of personal observation, sending their experts into the shelters.

'Good', which meant disciplined, behaviour, as one report summed up the crucial point in November 1941, depended on certain essential preconditions, which the government must ensure.[155] Shelters must have sufficient room. Smells, overcrowding, inadequate sanitary facilities had in a number of cases produced considerable discontent and should, therefore, be avoided. A sense of security appeared to be a state of mind that was difficult to assess and, according to the psychologists, depended on a number of factors: on an 'objective dimension', on the shelter's condition and type of construction, on the public mood, and on rumours.

Thus many in Bristol who had sought refuge in the railway tunnels believed that they were particularly safe there because the tunnels were so deep and when inside one could hardly hear the bombs. In spite of the fact that, as one of the responsible engineers explained, this was only a feeling of security that did not, however, reflect the real security situation, this railway accommodation was for many their first port of call and filled up quickly every night.[156] The same was true of churches, many of whose interiors had been transformed into air-raid shelters in the autumn of 1940. And although it was clear how little security they would be able to offer in an emergency these places of religious worship had a great attraction. In fact psycho-social factors played a considerable role in determining whether or not people felt fear. Many pieces of research carried out in the field concluded that shelters with many distractions, with regular routines, with their own programmes for children and families, helped people to find their feet in the new order and through active participation to come to identify with the new surroundings.[157]

One of the leading experts was P. E. Vernon, head of the Department of Psychology at the University of Glasgow, who at the end of July 1940 had already put on paper his first impressions of behaviour in air-raid shelters. He produced an extensive code of behaviour designed to prevent the feared shell shock and at the same time to help air-raid wardens and those seeking refuge deal appropriately with the new kinds of problems being thrown up and with symptoms of illness.[158] According to Vernon, nobody should be ashamed of their fear and of their feelings when in shelters. After all, air raids were life-threatening. But excessive fear, let alone cowardice, would lead to people losing control of their feelings. In his analysis Vernon pointed out that fear could express itself in a variety of forms of behaviour and therefore must be closely observed. Fear could cause apathy or nervous disorders as well as physical illnesses.

Vernon advised people to put on warm clothing and to make themselves as comfortable as possible in shelters and thereby create an atmosphere in which together they could overcome their fear. For him the most important thing was to distract people from thinking about the threat: playing cards or darts, knitting, reading, occupying the children, having a cup of tea together, listening to music and singing with the other people. People who made themselves conspicuous and had evidently panicked should initially be separated from the others and then calmed down. They should be reassured that they were safe and that the enemy aircraft were still a long way off. If that did not help then more drastic measures such as a slap were legitimate. If the person's fear had turned to anger and they could no longer be controlled and represented a threat to others then they would have to be isolated from the group. This was, however, a response which in Vernon's view would not often prove necessary because the majority of people would calm down again after a short time. In any case, he considered the example set by the supervisors and assistants in the shelters to be more helpful than all forms of compulsion or force. Even before the major air raids on London from September 1940 onwards he was prophesying that people would quickly adapt to the exceptional circumstances. In Vernon's view, therefore, citizens in air-raid shelters had become 'civilians on the front line', adaptable and tough civilians who like soldiers were capable of putting up with suffering.

This reinterpretation of civilian life made comprehensible what in reality was a real surprise: contrary to what had been expected, the majority of medical experts and psychologists diagnosed hardly any serious damage to people's nerves or panic attacks among the occupants of shelters. People did not collapse; clinics had remained almost empty; hardly anything that had been expected had actually happened. But why was that? At the end of 1940 numerous researchers, among them Vernon himself, endeavoured to answer this question. For his study, among other things, he had assessed the findings of thirty British psychologists, medical experts, and civil defence specialists, who had been looking after people who had suffered from air raids in various parts of the country and had provided him with information about their work.[159]

Contrary to pre-war fears of what would happen, people's shelter experiences did not lead to new forms of neurotic illnesses. There was nothing that differed from the illnesses of the First World War. Being careful not to draw too far-reaching conclusions, Vernon gave a number of reasons why shell shock type neurosis had not occurred. To begin with there was the population's particularly stoical attitude, a pattern of social behaviour the importance of which could not be overestimated and which sprang from the spirit of 'Britain can take it'.[160] Thus every city wanted to follow London's example and match the great capital's readiness to defend itself and to suffer the consequences.

At the same time, Vernon believed he had recognized a characteristic feature of the Empire, in that the nation always showed its true face in difficult situations. What Vernon and others saw as the reason for the courageous 'shelter mentality' was basically a self-fulfilling prophecy. The phrase 'Britain can take it' was thus simultaneously the reason for and the consequence of a community that bridged the classes and the reason why people simply could not become ill. Forms of deviant behaviour did not fit into this interpretation. Thus psychologists tried to provide empirical evidence for this phenomenon of 'standing alone', which had been conjured up by the current discourse.

According to Vernon religion appeared to help people put up with their fate as did, not least, a specifically civilian pattern of behaviour in wartime. For while on the one hand civilians were at a disadvantage vis-à-vis soldiers, in that they lacked any kind of military discipline or sense of a specific group solidarity, on the other hand, civilians possessed something that soldiers at the front lacked and which helped to compensate for these deficiencies: the state of their mental health was better. To put it another way, while soldiers had to fight far from home, without their family or social environment, civilians had more freedom to determine and adapt their own behaviour. The prevailing code of social behaviour allowed them to show weakness and they did not always have to be ready to fight. Moreover, they knew they were defending not only their lives, but above all their own houses. As Vernon explained, this was why nobody wanted to go to hospital unless it was absolutely necessary. Whereas in the case of some soldiers this had the effect of saving their lives, for civilians it meant leaving their houses without protection and this was reason enough for making sure that when they left the shelter they were still in good shape.[161]

Thus mental breakdown was prevented by a combination of a 'civilian mentality' and solidarity based on group dynamics. Shell shock and war morale were to some extent behind this notion of how civilians on the home front of the air war should behave and also guided the thinking of the medical diagnosticians who suddenly began explaining a reduction in the number specifically of female psychiatric patients in terms of the effects of the Blitz. However, in 1942 contemporary psychologists such as Edward Glover were already warning against attributing the absence of mass neurosis that had been predicted before the war solely to the effects of the air war. They had both been myths,[162] and a Coventry psychiatrist noted in the light of his experience with patients that the number of neuroses was significantly larger than had been admitted hitherto and that many of these cases were not receiving the proper treatment and had also not disappeared again overnight.[163] The search for normality and the burden of having to clear up after raids did not leave much room for deviant behaviour and presumably kept a considerable number of those affected from visiting a doctor.

However, this did not alter the general conclusion, namely that the effects of air raids had not turned out to be as bad as had been feared. One factor that had no doubt contributed to this and which had been the subject of discussion since the end of 1939, above all by medical experts, was the hygienic conditions in the mass shelters. Concern about the possibility of epidemics and the spread of sexual diseases had been prevalent among planners during the pre-war period. The reports sent in by the Mass Observation and Health Ministry observers from Tilbury, Liverpool, and Manchester, particularly in the first few months of the war, gave cause for concern. A government commission set up by the Ministry of Health and the Home Office in autumn 1940 had already investigated conditions in the public shelters. Its conclusions made for sobering reading in every respect. The mass shelters in London, but not only there, were overcrowded and poorly ventilated. There was the threat of disease, medical provision was inadequate, and the personnel in the shelters were insufficiently prepared for dealing with the problems that were arising.[164]

On the initiative of the Health Ministry, the War Cabinet had also been involved in these issues and had discussed in detail the proposals for the introduction of more health controls in the shelters.[165] In a report for the Ministry of Home Security an official of the Women's Voluntary Service noted that the most serious deficiency was the lack of water and nothing, wrote the infuriated woman in September 1940, had been done to improve this situation. She was concerned as well because the station that she had visited was also a refuge for people who were well off and better dressed. She evidently assumed that the poor might possibly have got used to these conditions, but to subject the upper classes to them was simply unacceptable.[166]

A more professional approach was required and that was one of the responses to the crisis. More personnel were appointed with responsibility for the administration and provision of health facilities for shelters, tasks that up until then had often been performed by volunteers. Regular inspection by state agencies to prevent the spread of infection and above all to deal with the problems of ventilation was also important.[167] Hectic activity now ensued with the aim of rebuilding the mass shelters at least provisionally so that an albeit small section of the population could stay there for longer than was originally envisaged. Health officials began to organize the disinfection of the tube tunnels, the cleansing of the lavatories, and the creation of washing facilities.[168] The aim was to prevent epidemics and so more attention was paid to the spread of lice, bugs, and rats.[169]

From the point of view of the medical experts air-raid shelters represented a first-class area for research into health education, an opportunity they had hitherto been lacking in peacetime. Suddenly it became strikingly apparent how much poor people in particular were suffering from a lack of health information, poor diet, and inadequate protection from disease.[170] Thus shelters had become not only places of refuge but a field for action on health policy. The people who had to spend their nights on tube platforms were now no longer, as some doctors believed, being diverted by amusements such as sport or the pub. By removing any distractions the war and their life in shelters increased the chances that they could be convinced of the need to look after their health.

The existential experience of shelter life appeared to have opened the doors to fundamental changes in behaviour, for a new understanding of 'motherhood', of a proper diet, of adequate rest breaks at work, and a healthy adjustment in the rhythm of people's daily lives. Protection of the individual, health education, healthy eating—these were the concerns of the reformers, who saw the, in their view, intolerable conditions in the shelters as an opportunity to remove longstanding defects. This could succeed, however, only if women, above all working-class women, once more devoted themselves with renewed energy to their role of looking after their children. Talk of a new understanding of 'motherhood' implied education and introducing norms of behaviour, recalling working women to their function as caring mothers. Their cooperation was necessary, indeed an absolute precondition, for a new Britain for the post-war period to emerge out of the tube tunnels, so to speak.

In 1941 this approach was already determining medical discussion about the protection of health in public air-raid shelters, which was soon no longer confined to specialist journals but was turning up in mass circulation newspapers. They were illustrating their reports on shelters with large photos in which committed doctors and nurses were carrying out medical inspections, prescribing medicines, and explaining the rules for healthy living and the minimum standards of hygiene for children. What was remarkable about this was not only that health protection had now become part of the fight on the home front, but the iconographic 'sense of community' of the many volunteer helpers appeared to prove that here a 'new' Britain was emerging, a more healthy Britain marked by social solidarity, whose backbone was conscientious working-class women enlightened about health issues.

Shelter illnesses

Nazi medical experts and psychologists were also particularly interested in the behaviour of women in air-raid shelters for their emotional make-up was considered a potential security risk for the shelters. Thus control over shelters had a socio-sanitary function, namely to prevent 'female illnesses' such as 'shelter rage' or 'hysteria' and any expression of undisciplined feelings. The Nazi regime did everything possible to control the scope for individual expressions of feeling and to interpret shelter experiences in pathological terms. Since the beginning of 1941 psychologists, doctors, and health policy-makers had already detected shelters as a source of danger for the 'national body'. With the extension of the air war from 1942/3 onwards there was an increasing number of reports from civil defence paramedics and doctors on the growing threat of epidemics, on the lack of hygiene, and the increasing dilapidation of some shelters.[171]

Shortly before the end of the war a doctor from Hamm reported to the local health office in a shocked tone what he had observed during the previous months. After spending only a few days in a shelter, he concluded, people became lethargic, rude, and indifferent. 'After initially being over-wrought they become grumpy and monosyllabic. They misappropriate other people's things, don't look after their wives and children; all sense of order and cleanliness disappears. People who were previously very careful of their appearance don't wash themselves or comb their hair for days on end. Men no longer shave and they neglect their clothing; they come to their appointments dirty and smelly. In the shelters they no longer go and look for the lavatory but relieve themselves in dark corners. The mothers neglect their children. Men push their way through women seeking shelter using brute force. [...] Around seventy per cent of the permanent residents of the shelters have the so-called shelter illness (scabies) and there is no water, poor heating, and no chance whatever of delousing. I shudder when I keep see-ing children with scarlet fever and diphtheria in the shelter rooms wrapped in blankets and towels. I hope we can avoid typhus. [...] I can name you shelter doctors who are watching with horror the gradual brutalization of otherwise orderly people who suddenly, after the loss or destruction of their belongings, have become cave dwellers and to save their lives are spending days and nights in shelters and in the process gradually becoming bestialized and brutalized.'[172]

The exceptionally poor hygienic conditions and psychosocial situation reported by this doctor were of course simply a snapshot taken at the end of the war, when in western cities such as Hamm that had been heavily bombed the infrastructure and medical provision had completely col-lapsed.[173] At the same time, however, his call for help was more than a merely local phenomenon. At any rate, the doctor claimed the right to speak not only for himself but for a large percentage of his colleagues, who were looking after a similar clientele and had been making the same dis-turbing observations over a period of months. They were seeing rampant infection, national comrades who were psychologically unstable and liable to let themselves go and no longer respect property.[174] Thus shelters no longer provided security; during the course of the war they had increasingly become breeding grounds for bacteria and centres of infection that were difficult to control and, even with the strictest health regulations, were less and less capable of being protected, thereby constituting a major threat.

At the latest from 1942 onwards the pressing question of the policing of health in large shelters was being discussed with growing concern by experts in public health. They drafted a wide spectrum of disciplinary regulations: strict entry controls, the quarantining of sick men and women, hospital shelters with extra security and high standards of hygiene, regulations to prevent the spread of infectious diseases, and new methods of removing swarms of gnats. All of this was dominated by fear of the further spread of tuberculosis, for which shelters provided optimum conditions and which had to be combated with every means at their disposal.[175]

Whereas in Britain the focus in the campaigns dealing with civil defence was on the care and education of the individual, the German proposals were dominated primarily by the need to protect the 'national body'. 'Correct' hygienic behaviour was, however, only one side of the coin. In addition, there was the question of proper behaviour in shelters, the need for people to discipline their own feelings. The question of how to treat soldiers suffering from 'war neurosis', 'acute reactions of shock', 'hysteria', and 'psychopathy' had been intensively discussed by military psychologists since the beginning of the war with reference to earlier research from the First World War.[176] But how should one deal with psychological 'weakness' on the home front shown by civilians in air-raid shelters? And what forms of 'abnormal behaviour' were acceptable and what, conversely, were indications of an unstable character?

From roughly 1943 onwards this was being discussed often by the same leading psychologists who were already working for the Wehrmacht in hospitals, university clinics, and mental hospitals trying to cure mentally ill soldiers and gathering experience in the use of electric shock treatment and other methods for making people who were mentally damaged fit to fight or work again. The senior physician in the neurological department of the Augusta Hospital in Düsseldorf, Professor Voss, noted that there were at least two major differences between the front and the home front, between soldiers and civilians. In the first place, in his view in terms of health soldiers represented the more robust section of the population.[177] Secondly, civilian responses to air raids differed markedly from the situation on the battlefield. 'Soldiers confront the enemy with a weapon in their hands and thus are as well or better armed than their opponents. The knowledge that they can defend themselves is inextricably bound up with the idea of surrendering their own life in the moment of danger. In the case of civilians the situation is quite different. They are not armed and thus lack the mental attitude that goes with bearing arms, a matter of justified pride.' In the event of danger they must flee and hide; that alone weakens their position. But whereas after battle the soldier always remains a soldier, after bombing and the night spent in a shelter the civilian once more becomes a private person, who has to deal with his daily worries and see around him the many women and children who are incapable of suppressing their 'raw fear'.

In propaganda terms the front and the home front were one, but in medical practice the idea of civilians fighting in the war proved problematic. In the view of the Nazi physicians the reason for this was, first, that the home front was feminine and therefore less stable and, secondly, the national comrades who were being threatened lacked the possibility of fighting back against the enemy. They had to give in to their fate and were in many cases defenceless participants in the war, whose sole and therefore strongest resource was to adopt a 'good bearing'. Contrary to all expectations, however, their observations did not confirm the fears that bombing and people's stay in shelters, particularly in the case of women, but also of men, would lead to psychological damage, speech disorders, or other 'hysterical responses'. This medical diagnosis was based either on conversations that, like Voss, they had had with patients, or the doctors analysed the medical files produced after the patients' admission.[178]

In the case of Düsseldorf the head of the neurological department of the Augusta hospital came to the conclusion that the number of psychologically damaged patients who had to be treated was relatively small. In his view that was all the more remarkable given the fact that air raids had provided the preconditions for serious illness and, moreover, at home unlike at the front there was 'no military law' punishing desertion or lack of discipline. His diagnosis was that the absence of large numbers of examples of abnormal behaviour, neurosis, or panic attacks had nothing to do with the threat of punishment, police action, or the identification of those with inherited criminal tendencies, but rather had primarily to do with the 'inner strength' of the 'national community'. While he had seen numerous cases of patients complaining about headaches, sleeplessness, being agitated, and afraid, hardly any of them, Voss noted with satisfaction, wanted to use the fact that their illness might be caused by the air war as an excuse to stop working for the war effort. Despite bad experiences, the majority had not lost their courage and were trying to keep going. On the one hand, given his expectations, women had shown themselves to be astonishingly robust and less vulnerable than anticipated; on the other hand, they were still more unstable than men and so particularly at risk.

Generally, he estimated, a few sedatives were sufficient to overcome the acute state of shock and then, depending on the degree of distress, a few days of rest and recuperation in another environment would restore their ability to return to work. Being afraid in a shelter or the experience of having been buried in an air raid were in any case no justification for evading service to the 'national community'. Moreover, the experience of bombing showed the extent to which in peacetime and in the midst of far less serious events people used their alleged mental state as an excuse to go to court and make insurance claims.

The bombing war taught that 'hysterical reactions' had been attributed all too readily to accidents and this had led to compensation claims. As a result of psychological research conducted during the air war in future they could put a stop to 'professional neurotics' and ruthlessly expose their 'defective characters'. Yes, shocks and terrible things had happened in the Reich's shelters but the 'national community' had proved sufficiently strong to cope with them. There was no room for the few who had not done so and certainly no willingness to compensate them for their weakness. In 1943 Voss was evidently already thinking that after the war the question of compensation would be likely to come up again and not just on a small scale but as a problem that would have to be taken seriously. They would have to put a stop to this during the war in order to ensure that the 'strong' did not find themselves paying for the 'weak'.[179]

This utilitarian diagnosis interpreted 'shelter illness' as a phenomenon characteristic of the 'sick' elements of the 'national community'. It was not the 'anxiety' or acute shock, which made people lose control of themselves, that counted as deviant behaviour. They were considered understandable responses to the exceptionally dangerous situation. But they by no means justified people in becoming 'ill', let alone giving up work. For after all the 'bearing' of the overwhelming majority of the population showed impeccable 'character', which was evident above all in the remarkably small number of psychoses. The physicians' and psychologists' diagnoses were in their view proof of the national community's record of success in demonstrating its 'robust' health during the air war. It was only in the case of children that doctors noted an increasing number of bed-wetters, which evidently had to do with their fear of air-raid warnings.[180] But the behaviour of even the youngest was considered satisfactory. Male national comrades and, even more so, female national comrades were permitted to feel moments of despair but shelter medicine was not prepared to tolerate any more than that.

7

Experiences of the Air War

Wartime Morale as an Object of Research

Contrary to expectations, British psychologists and medics looking for a nation in trauma during the Second World War found very little evidence of it. The population seemed better able to cope with the threat from the air than experts had expected.[1] But how did those experts acquire their knowledge about the population's experience of the war?

This chapter will not only investigate this process of turning social experiences into objects of academic study, it will also present a variety of ways in which individuals survived, how they absorbed and coped with the experience of physical and psychological violence by means of language and found a way of expressing this in diaries, letters, reports, and interviews immediately after the war. This chapter thus links together various dimensions of the history of the air war as people experienced it, focusing both on contemporary academic observations and on how individuals responded to bombing and in their different ways managed to survive it. Finally, it will also take into account the first, if not entirely voluntary, instances of reflection on the effects of the air raids, which arose during the summer of 1945 and formed part of the extensive project of interviews conducted by the United States Strategic Bombing Survey. Even while the war was still being fought, this survey had begun to draw initial conclusions about the bombing.

The quest to discover people's experience of the war had taken psychologists not only into the air-raid shelters but also into the homes of workers in industries related to armaments production. Between November 1941 and March 1942 psychologists and social workers commissioned by the Research and Experiment Department interviewed some 900 workers in Hull and their wives, an experiment, unique in its scale during wartime, concentrating on morale in a particularly severely bombed city.

Those questioned were supposed to give information as individuals and in small-group discussions about their experiences during the heavy bombing of spring 1941. But the investigation went further, for the experts were interested in the family's experience too, in such things as previous illnesses and possible personality disorders. The end result was to be the most comprehensive picture possible of the consequences of air raids. The research group aimed to discover under what circumstances bombing led to neurotic illnesses. When did raids diminish people's capacity to work and how long was there a risk of the experience of bombing still having a damaging effect? Attention focused on possible sleep and eating disorders, weight loss, and absences from work, which were regarded by the psychologists as indications of a neurotic illness linked to the air war.

They identified different levels of bomb damage and separated the respondents into groups according to whether they lived around the city's dockyards in particularly badly affected areas or in those only lightly bombed. The results were very much as predicted on the basis of preliminary findings from other cities. While the number of those suffering from nervous illnesses was higher than in peacetime and workers from heavily bombed areas of the city suffered more frequently from psychosomatic disorders than workers in less severely bombed areas,[2] in general the frequency of longer-term illnesses was lower than expected and in only up to 3 per cent of those affected did the disorders continue for longer than five months. In the heavily bombed areas women became ill significantly more often than their husbands: 20.7 per cent of the men showed evidence of mild to moderate complaints, though these disappeared after a short time. In the case of women in particularly heavily bombed areas of the city the percentage was 53.3 and in areas less badly bombed it was 32.9.[3] The survey revealed that in the weeks following raids women went more frequently than men to the doctor and were more prone to feelings of anxiety. The sound of bombs dropping above all caused stress, while mortal fear was also felt by many of the respondents during nights of heavy bombing.

This fear diagnosed by the psychologists did not, however, in itself constitute a nervous illness. For that diagnosis several factors had to be present, principally an immediate, individual experience of destruction or of personal loss. In most cases it was not 'hysterical' reactions but rather a mixture of depression and dread that could lead to illness. A further finding was noteworthy: the calmer a woman remained at home, the more she kept a grip on herself, the calmer was the reaction of the men to a raid and to moving to the air-raid shelter. At all events the family situation played a key role as far as the psychologists were concerned in people's ability to cope with the danger. There was manifestly also a connection between earlier illnesses and those triggered by the bombardments; the investigation produced evidence that 76 per cent of all men whose health was 'stable' showed no signs of anything amiss after air raids. Evidently the power of the air raids to endanger health and morale was not linked to the efficiency with which help was provided after the raids. What seemed decisive was rather what experiences of war those concerned had already had to come to terms with and what sex they were.

The researchers concluded that in order to make a serious impact on the enemy and on enemy morale it was necessary to increase the level of threat to the individual by intensifying the raids. In this respect the raids on Hull were particularly instructive because they demonstrated how massive air raids had to be in order to achieve the desired effect and thus they served as an object lesson in how much devastating force was necessary to break the Germans' morale.[4] Certainly the amount of bombs that had fallen on Hull was insufficient. All in all, from the point of view of the experts it seemed that it was at most a question of quantity and of applying this finding to the bombing of Germany. However, what lay behind the terms fear and dread, used in the concluding report, and what it might mean to live for weeks and months with the fear of death, how people attempted to maintain daily routines and developed individual strategies for survival—these were matters on which the investigation's statistics gave little information.

The interviews themselves had certainly given some indications. The psychologists had noted severe anxiety attacks resulting from an air raid suffered by a 56-year-old dock worker, even though before the bombing he had been regarded as a stable character.[5] He had served in the First World War, when after a U-boat attack he had spent an hour in icy water and was later wounded once again. The psychologists described him as a reliable worker with a calm disposition. In spite of serving as a civil defence assistant he continued to sleep well and though he smoked more than before the air raids he did not drink more alcohol than previously. He had experienced the air raid at the dockyard. An aerial mine had exploded not far from his house, killing two policemen. He had heard it falling and tried to save his family. When it finally exploded he was thrown to the ground, his stomach hurt, and for a brief moment he felt he could not breathe. Everywhere he smelt a pungent odour of burning that stayed with him for weeks. When he could get to his feet again he first of all saw that his house had caved in and that only the walls of the room where he had taken cover were still standing. He heard cries but at first could not see anything and finally called to his wife and children. That was the moment, he said in his statement, when he almost went mad. Then he saw his wife, who lay seemingly rigid, called for an ambulance, and finally fainted. When he came round he felt terrible. Next to him his wife was calling out, his whole body was in pain, and he vomited for two days.

Six days later he left hospital, still exhausted and marked by the sense of once again having only just escaped with his life. At the same time he was tormented for months by a guilty conscience because he had not gone to one of the air-raid shelters with his family but had hoped to survive the raid in his home. In doing so he had endangered the lives of his family, or at least that is how he saw it himself. Returning home he concentrated on trying to forget his pain through work and everyday routine. In the meantime he had lost a considerable amount of weight. In the end it took two months before he returned to his former work and the acute symptoms of what was iden-tified as a bombing neurosis abated.

Many of the workers living in the heavily bombed areas round the docks reported suffering from insomnia; some felt less and less able to leave the house, suffered constant panic attacks, lost weight, and found it difficult to speak about the experiences of the nights of bombing. Quite a few believed they needed to apologize for their weakness: it had been a terrible night (in May 1941), as one dock worker explained, and one that would weigh everyone down, not just him.[6] He too had lost weight, felt weak, and needed to vomit repeatedly over a period of weeks. Many of those who complained about longer-term symptoms had lost all they had, including, in the worst cases, their families. A 41-year-old worker had lost several relatives in the May raids: his mother and three nieces had been killed and it had taken four days before the bodies were recovered.[7]

Such testimonies were particularly noteworthy precisely because the line 'Britain can take it' was so dominant as a public slogan, for they revealed the shock experienced by at least some of the workers from the industrial and dock areas. It was compounded by worry about wives and children that receded only when the latter had found somewhere to stay in secure areas in the country. Only then, one man recounted, could he sleep peacefully again and take things as they came. Even so, the feeling remained 'that life is not worth living'.

The loss of family members, the destruction of their homes, panic attacks, the worry that they could no longer fulfil their role as breadwinner and thus were emasculated and a burden to others—a combination of all these things contributed to the fact that a proportion of workers, though that proportion was only small and difficult to determine precisely, found it difficult to continue as previously. Only a very few had seen a doctor in any case, so that the symptoms virtually went untreated and could not be recognized as significant problems. And if medical help was sought it did not appear to be money well spent, for the interviewers did not note any precise diagnoses after a visit to the doctor, still less progress towards recovery.

This was true not only of workers but also of their wives, whom the psychologists assumed to suffer more frequently from nervous ailments than their husbands. Central to discussions were two questions: the effects of bombing on family life and the state of health of women. Mrs S. from Hull was one woman who had displayed severe depression and anxiety attacks as a result of the air raids.[8] She was married and she and her husband had a 19-year-old son who had also been ill since the raids and was confined to bed. Mrs S., however, blamed not the bombing for his slow recovery but the punishing shifts and amount of overtime that young workers like her son had to put in; these contributed to his not getting back his strength more rapidly. Their 25-year-old daughter was also ill and had been suffering for some time from sleep disturbances that her mother attributed to the air raids. During the May 1941 raids the family had been bombed out and lost virtually everything. What made an even greater impact was that in one raid her sister, who had always given her refuge, had been killed. When she finally came back to the city in November 1941 and saw her ruined home again she felt like giving up, as she said herself.

Her memory and concentration began to suffer; darkness and light both caused her anxiety and every alarm that sounded caused the feeling of panic to overwhelm her again. She was afraid of the blackout and could hardly sleep any more. At the same time the interviewers observed that Mrs S. was evidently neglecting her housework—something that on the one hand pointed to the fact that interviews were conditioned by accepted gender norms and the labelling of women on the home front as 'good' and 'bad', and on the other might also be an indicator of the increasing difficulties women had in organizing their lives. Like other women from families with higher incomes Mrs S. was not at any rate receiving medical treatment. To give a concrete example of these difficulties, a woman from a more prosperous family was also suffering from panic attacks months after the raids. After the raid in May 1941 some members of her family had been badly injured and she herself lived in constant fear of the next air-raid warning. The sound of the sirens made her start and, even though her health had improved in the meantime, during the interview she repeatedly broke down in tears as soon as she talked about those nights in May.[9] Six months later she still did not feel able to apply for compensation because she was too upset by having to list the things she had lost.

Those who had sought refuge outside the city, staying with friends or in public accommodation, often suffered as a result of being separated from friends, and from the uncertainty of whether they would see them or their homes again. At all events, the tendency to leave the city brought only superficial relief and many, like Mrs M., were forced after the closure of public accommodation to decide whether, in spite of their fear of the next warning, they felt able to return to the city or were instead going to look for lodgings in the surrounding area, as a result of which they had no money left over for going to the doctor.[10] The range of noises and the wailing of the sirens were clearly part of the totality of people's experience of violence during the air war and taken together with other experiences these had an immense impact on daily routines.

Being confronted with death—in an air-raid shelter, in a collapsing building, or in one's own Anderson shelter as it shook from the explosions— was an existential experience, though little account was taken of it publicly. That was very probably one of the reasons why even those who had suffered particularly badly as a result of the raids and, as it were, bore the scars adopted an attitude of disciplined endurance, an individual stance of 'I can take it,' as their model.

War and illness in Germany

'Endurance' was a recurring theme also in the SD's reports on the mood in Germany. As the correspondents noted, from 1941/2 the air raids had become one of the main topics of conversation.[11] The Reich as a whole and its inhabitants were not of course all equally affected and there continued to be great differences between city and country, north and south, that made it difficult, as it did in Britain, to make general statements about 'the' population. Yet the

SD correspondents recorded more and more frequently signs of insecurity and growing anxiety, including in regions where people feared they would be the victims of future air raids. There was even talk of an increase in anxiety psychoses, reflecting the sense of being a defenceless target as raids intensified. Although the SD repeatedly thought that fluctuations in the nation's mood and quite a lot of trepidation were discernible, from 1943 onwards the SD reports showed evidence of the fine semantic distinction that in March 1943 Goebbels had told the Nazi press to make, namely between a 'negative mood', a growing sense of war-weariness and a 'proper bearing', as shown in particular by the industrial workers of the Ruhr.[12]

The few foreign observers who reported over a longer period on the 'mood' and 'bearing' of the Germans were no more optimistic in their estimation of things.[13] The view of the Italian consul general in Cologne was that up to the summer of 1942 the mood of the city's inhabitants was robust and stable. The population had regarded losses as 'misfortunes' that could be coped with and got over by means of a resolute 'bearing'. 'Mood' and 'bearing' were thus also the categories used by a fellow fascist when reporting from Germany. What was crucial, he said, was that those who had suffered in the air war had quickly received replacements for goods they had lost and been allocated new living accommodation. After July 1943, however, the mood throughout the city had changed, the consul reported: 'In view of the permanent tension caused by the bombing the great mass of the population of this city [Cologne] is palpably and visibly completely exhausted. This mood is exacerbated by the lack of military success.'[14] With cities destroyed and many fatalities most inhabitants lived in 'constant fear' and tried as soon as night fell to secure a place in one of the shelters. The pressure on places was so great that the police had had to impose considerable restrictions on access to them. People who had been bombed out, women, children, and the elderly had priority; foreigners were not allowed in and outsize luggage had to be left outside. After the raids there was a mood of 'bitterness' and 'dispirited and pointed comments' could be heard, sometimes even 'tirades'. Such moments, the consul said, were clear evidence of the general pessimism, even if up to now there had been only sporadic incidents. The authorities were generally tolerant, though in serious cases they took immediate repressive action. He had learnt from a confidential source that during the first raid on Cologne a troublemaker had been immediately 'done in'. The situation had a particularly negative effect on soldiers home on leave.

His Swiss colleague, Consul General Franz-Rudolf von Weiss, who sent reports throughout the war from Cologne to the Foreign Ministry in Berne and had an efficient information network at his disposal, arrived at very similar conclusions. Since the raid on Cologne in May 1942 he had observed how depressed the mood was in the city and that it was getting increasingly so.[15] In his view, the lack of provisions and the devastation resulting from the air war had the effect of causing people stress, reducing confidence in the regime, and intensifying war-weariness. From the beginning of 1943 in particular 'passive resignation' was accompanied by a growing anxiety about the use of gas, though, as Weiss stated in May 1944 in a report,[16] that did not mean that the population was deserting the regime, contrary to the Allies' hopes. Although in his view the Nazi Party was held in low regard, particularly by soldiers, a rebellion was nevertheless inconceivable, nor was there any desire for the war to end badly for Germany. From what he could observe, the explanation for this lay less in any strong attachment on the part of soldiers and civilian population to the Nazi state but was rather attributable to practical material interests. For who would foot the bill for bomb damage at the end of the war? Only victory seemed to guarantee that the costs of the war would be refunded, whereas defeat would mean sitting on a pile of rubble. As long as the War Damage Compensation Offices provided goods and coupons and did not, as in many places in the Rhineland from 1943 onwards, rely on empty words of comfort and unsecured promises to pay in the future the regime could be sure of support from broad sections of the population. Once the basis of their material existence was destroyed, Weiss believed, an essential material pledge upholding the Third Reich was gone. Now, he thought, people were 'simply waiting and hoping for some happy change of fortune'. 'They do not want defeat but they no longer want to contribute to victory through their own efforts. They want only to survive the war.'[17]

The strength of the survival instinct in wartime, the population's actions during air raids, and the precise effects of the raids, were all matters that also preoccupied the Propaganda Minister. Though in his estimation the air raids were leading to a 'proletarianization' of the German nation, they were not leading to its 'Bolshevization'. The air war certainly did exacerbate social inequalities but Goebbels did not seem unduly concerned about this. He was at any rate certain, as he noted at the beginning of January 1944, that those bombed out remained 'loyal to our hopes of victory', if only because without the 'national community' they could not imagine being compensated for the loss of their property. 'As a result, those hopes our enemies had of grinding down our morale by means of bombing have been refuted by the facts.'[18]

Germany's opponents came to similar conclusions. At the end of 1943 US Air Force General Henry H. Arnold had commissioned a group of American historians of Europe to evaluate the effects of air raids on the war economy and on morale in Germany and to produce as 'objective' a picture as possible.[19] Their analysis, 'Germany's War Potential, December 1943', aimed to examine not only the strategic effects but also the consequences for the political system of National Socialism and the experiences of those who had been bombed. They had to complete their task under great time pressure, however, and contrary to their hopes they did not get the access they wanted to all the existing documents. Finally, and this was particularly serious, the experts made it clear that the effects of bombing could not be reduced to simple formulae from which instant strategic rules of thumb could be derived.

The Germans' 'morale', it seemed, could by no means be ascertained, let alone measured, as clearly as the leadership of the Allied air war wished. Regarding the Germans' relationship with their leaders, after evaluating interviews with prisoners of war, secret service reports, and newspaper articles by

Figure 9. German airmen write jokes on bombs to be dropped on England.

journalists from neutral countries,[20] the group of researchers commented that British–American bombing raids on German cities had so far not significantly shaken the population's support for the Nazi regime.[21] All the same, they took the view that there was something to be said for continuing the battle to lower 'morale'. The example of Hamburg in the summer of 1943 had at any rate shown that such massive bombing created a situation where fear of the war continuing became greater than the fear of the consequences of defeat.

While the British and American experts could therefore do little more than speculate about 'morale' young German psychologists and medical experts were primarily interested in the psycho-social consequences of the air raids. Since the First World War and with increasing intensity from 1939 onwards, leading military psychologists had been investigating what fear in wartime actually consisted in.[22] The factors determining how people typically reacted in air-raid shelters were even more applicable to the question of how the national comrades behaved before and during raids, what they thought about, what concerned them, and what might lower their resistance. For example, in a dissertation begun during the war the young doctor Peter Feudell had posed the question of the 'psychological and nervous reactions of the civilian population in wartime'.[23] His attention as a psychiatrist was directed primarily at pathological cases and at those in which, during the period between January and October 1944, the patterns of behaviour displayed had required in-patient treatment at the Leipzig city polyclinic. These were patients who had been referred, or who themselves attributed their symptoms, to the consequences of air raids.

Feudell examined his patients at a time when the majority of symptoms had subsided and based his diagnosis on patients' notes as well as on interviews with them. The former in particular gave him information about their precise experience during the 'terror attack', the patient's work situation, attitude to work, neurological illnesses, and especially background information on his or her family and personal history. The ratio of 15 men to 25 women corresponded in his view roughly to the composition of the city's population[24] rather than indicating particular susceptibilities. The interviews evidently centred at first on the patient's emotional state at that moment, on whether there had been any improvement and on whether that might lead to the patient's being able to work again. The symptoms spanned a broad spectrum: paralysis, panic attacks, 'nervous' reactions. Some reported losing control, grief at the death of family members or the loss of their homes, and the growing sense, in men in particular, of not being one's own 'master' any more. Those who had been buried under rubble, the study concluded, had had particularly shocking experiences; blackouts, distorted sensory perceptions, the nightmarish sense of mortal fear, 'psychogenic paralysis', or acute speech problems were only some of the symptoms arising from, as he put it, 'traumatizing' experiences.[25]

A 50-year-old businessman, who, as his notes stated, up to that point had never been ill apart from a thigh injury sustained in 1915, spoke about his experience of bombing. He had rescued his mother from the flames and when a bomb detonated he lost consciousness. While he was coming to, he realized his mouth was full of cement, his false teeth had been blown out by the force of the blast and he was holding the legs of the man next to him, who was dead. A little over a week later the first speech problems emerged. 'It's as though I had a lump in my throat,' the minutes of the interview record. 'I find it particularly difficult to get out words that begin with a vowel and I have to force them out or else I would be completely unable to speak. When you're a fifty-year-old businessman you don't want to make a fool of yourself.' For him the sound of the air-raid warnings was the worst thing. He would then feel 'blood rushing to his head, heart pains and trembling. The alarms that followed 7 July really finished me off.'[26] Reactions similar to his can be found in the case notes in other cities affected by the air war: that the 'terror' was caused above all by the sounds of the air war, the wailing of the sirens, the 'whistling and hissing of the bombs, the anti-aircraft fire', and the detonations.

The patients' first experience had caused them particular distress—a distress that, as the psychologist diagnosed, for civilians was a kind of 'ordeal by fire'[27] similar to what soldiers experience. Those who survived the ordeal were able as 'robust people' to discipline their feelings and control their inner agitation. And, according to his observation, it was those 'robust individuals' who had at their disposal especially strong mechanisms for regulating their emotions and were thus able to turn their extraordinary experience into a trial they had come through.

Feudell identified five different types of reaction. In the first people became apathetic in the days after the raids and fell silent. He assumed there were many more people in that category than the medical records suggested. Similar cases were known from the First World War and they would get to the stage of medical observation only if an additional psychological or physical ailment arose. Secondly, there were cases where reactions to the 'experience of terror' manifested themselves after some time. Thirdly, there were illnesses where heightened nervous reactions were interpreted by the patients as chronic after-effects. Fourthly, there were experiences that were intensified by any new raid and anything that provoked overwhelming fear. Finally, he distinguished a type into which the largest number of patients, fifteen, fitted and in which he observed 'chronic changes of personality, tearful depressions, a sense of inadequacy, nightmares, pessimism'. By comparison with the First World War, he concluded, civilian reactions were manifestly more uniform and by comparison with 1918, in Leipzig at least, there were in particular no 'hysterical reactions', whereas it was reasonable to conclude there had been an increase in chronic symptoms. Taken as a whole, Feudell judged that the air raids amounted to a 'mass experiment in people's ability to endure psychological stress'.[28] In his estimation it was particularly those who had been nervy and fragile before the war and whose family histories indicated mental disturbances who showed an 'abnormal reaction'. While it was only understandable if individuals had an emotional reaction to the loss of their possessions and to death and destruction, in the end how they reacted always depended, in addition to the extremity of the event itself, on the 'dissociability of their personality'.[29]

From the doctor's point of view psychological illnesses caused by the air war always had to be defined in relation to people's actual function, in relation to whether the patient could work and thus make a contribution to the community: 'The demands of the community must take precedence over subjective suffering.'[30] That meant, he wrote, that in spite of the great sensitivity among the population about questions of heredity and 'inferiority' family medical history should be of central importance. There was, after all, a tendency to attribute all illnesses to the war. To reach an evaluation of abnormal behaviour it was therefore absolutely crucial to clarify 'whether in many cases the nature of the unusual reaction was determined by an inability to come to terms rationally with the experience'.[31] Feudell nevertheless came to the, from his point of view, surprising conclusion that the number of 'hysterical' people and hypochondriacs had reduced by comparison with the First World War. He assumed that the 'impetus given by a *völkisch* attitude' also had a positive effect 'on the individual's determination to be healthy and his or her conscience regarding health matters'. War not only consumed a nation's strength but also mobilized it in much greater measure.[32]

Patients' experience of 'traumatization' appeared to be something that began primarily through the act of reflection. Many symptoms seemingly became evident, according to Feudell's interpretation, only at the point when patients began to think about the dangers they had just survived or to which others had fallen victim. Feelings and images following the event were thus a central reason for neurotic illnesses connected to the air war, and those most affected were people who in a 'spiral of fear' continued to dwell on their feelings and their experiences. Imagination and reflection on the part of 'primitive types' were particularly dangerous if, stoked by the 'irresponsible passing on of horror stories and exaggerated statistics', by which he meant numbers of fatalities, these gave rise to nervousness and anxiety. Doctors and psychotherapists therefore had the task, as he saw it, of curbing such developments. Speaking and thinking about feelings and various experiences of the air war were thus the first sign of an attitude and type of behaviour damaging to the national community and could lead ultimately to depression and fear. This conclusion marked a central difference from British psychologists' interpretation of air-war experience. Though the latter's research had produced similar results, different conclusions had been drawn and patients were positively encouraged to speak about their experiences. German psychologists saw the danger not as being in the 'terror' but in speaking about and discussing it with others. Thus silence, it was implied, was the best response to what had been experienced and the best strategy for dealing with it.

A study carried out in Erlangen at the same time had a rather different emphasis, however. It was also concerned with psychological 'disturbances following on air raids' and aimed to investigate whether the 'bombing terror' caused a variety of 'mental illnesses' and whether civilians behaved differently from soldiers.[33] The study also used patients' medical notes, such as those of a Hamburg woman who had been evacuated to Franconia. During the rail journey to Bayreuth the woman suddenly felt her arms and legs getting heavy. Up to that point, according to her statement, she had been healthy. Now she was also finding it difficult to speak, could not walk properly, and had lost her concentration. In January 1944 she finally had a breakdown. A 'rest cure' gave her only temporary relief, her legs continued to be painful, and even after several months her writing was shaky—all in all one of the 'typical', if not very common, cases of a direct psychological reaction to the air war.

Another woman in the Erlangen hospital with a similar diagnosis had, as the young doctor stated, been hurled into the air by an explosion after the raid on Hamburg and had hit the ground so hard that she lost consciousness.

At first, immediately after the raid, she could walk again, but after some time her condition deteriorated. When she walked her left leg always gave way and the pains increased. Even weeks later the numbness had still not gone from her legs, although there had been a slight improvement. Other patients, such as the postman Mr K., had shown 'paranoid reactions' after the raids, as the study stated. During a raid in November 1941 this man had fractured the base of his skull, after which his memory had perceptibly declined, he became increasingly restless, spoke in a confused manner, and felt persecuted. 'All of a sudden', as the doctor treating him observed, the patient was 'strikingly calm after a number of electric shock treatments'.[34]

Over all, however, the conclusion was different from what was expected and coincided with the results from other regions, as well as with those of British studies. Its verdict was that the enemy had not succeeded in breaking the civilian population's morale; overall, soldiers and civilians hardly differed in their behaviour. People who were already psychologically not robust were susceptible to being traumatized and that was equally true of soldiers as of civilians. In Erlangen at any rate there was no rise in the number of cases in which psychological, schizophrenic, or manic responses could be interpreted as the results of the air war. There were not even indications of a marked increase in cases of anxiety, nor could the assumption that women were more susceptible to this than men be confirmed. It could therefore be concluded that 'disturbances in psychological equilibrium' at home and at the front had evened themselves out since the First World War, a finding which furthermore, as the author emphasized, was in line with research in Britain.

For his study Fuchs had taken account of the work of the British psychologist P. E. Vernon published in 1941 in the *Journal of Abnormal and Social Psychology*, which had elicited a widespread response. According to his summary of the results, in Britain as in Germany the heavy bombing raids had caused people to get used to the air war. What was even more important, the number of cases of neurosis and psychosis had similarly been lower than feared. In the case of illnesses that could be attributed to the air war there had been, as in Germany, an 'unfavourable family history'. When psychological reactions did arise, these did not necessarily have to be taken as the result of the immediate 'terror' but could be attributable to exhaustion and other psychological disturbances caused by 'normal conditions of life'.

The results of the study showed that people in exceptional circumstances such as the air war could draw on extraordinary powers of resistance, with 'foreigners' and 'Jews' being the ones, if any, in Britain whose resistance was below average.[35] These results confirmed Fuchs in his thinking that the psyche has protective mechanisms at its disposal that help it to weather even the most punishing 'shocks to the mind'. Another important finding, central to the diagnosis of civilian behaviour during air raids, was linked to this. In the light of such a small number of documented cases and given similar results in enemy countries it was not valid to talk about a 'bombing neurosis' or 'bombing psychosis'. The air war had not created an illness of its own, there were no types of disorder that were specific to a bombing war, and in healthy people the consequences of their terrifying experiences would soon fade. There was at best justification for claiming that bombing had an impact on actions prompted by emotion but in the final analysis it did not cause them, nor did it give rise to any kind of abnormality that was not already familiar in 'normal society'. Everything supported the assumption that the civilian population 'grew' as the raids continued, growing stronger and refusing, whether in Britain or in Germany, to be crushed by external pressure. Thus British findings served as a neutral confirmation of German arguments, above all that 'abnormal behaviour' was an intensification of predispositions in the existing personality, a finding that had had no special significance in the British study.

Speaking and Remaining Silent

While the medical realm was pathologizing the experience of the air war, individuals found a great variety of ways of coping with nights of bombing. Numerous contemporary sketches, notes, and diaries in Germany and in Britain revolved around the paradoxical feeling of not being able to put the experience into words and of not having any terms adequate for the experiences of war and yet feeling compelled to write about them.[36] Various themes and narrative patterns emerge, but they resist any single explanation from which generalizations can be made, being ambivalent, multi-layered, and determined by a wide variety of earlier experiences, locations, and phases of the air war.[37] The same is true of the question (one that in view of the sources can have no definite answer) of how far experiences of the air war varied according to social class.

One of these narrative patterns is the distinction between 'inside' and 'outside', between those who had experience of the air war and friends and family who were assumed to be unfamiliar with any comparable form of violence. An important factor was not only when but also where air raids were experienced. To put it another way: something that had the force of an urban catastrophe in the city left people outside the city, in the country or in other parts of Germany, untouched. For that reason, it is not appropriate to speak of *the* experience of the air war, for the social and geographical contexts that made the experiences distinctive were too varied, as were the types and the intensity of the violence suffered. An aspect of this was its physical nature; people could be buried or burned and felt defenceless against the anonymous bombs falling from the sky. Medical studies had, of course, shown that although the Nazi state condemned the 'terror from the air' as a 'barbaric' act of violence perpetrated by uncivilized nations and attempted to nationalize mourning, it simultaneously pathologized individual suffering and illnesses and aimed, quite literally, to silence them.

Not all forms of violence were necessarily directly physical but could extend their impact to affect feelings, sense perceptions, imaginings, or rumours.[38] With the growing fear of the bombs the air war as a purveyor of future death obliterated the boundaries between city and country and removed spatial boundaries from the violence. People processed this violence internally and came to terms with it by employing very varied strategies. It may sound paradoxical, but observed from a distance air raids could definitely have a sort of calming effect, after it was clear to people that the neighbouring town and not their own district had been the target of the raid.

The Swiss Consul General, for example, reported from Cologne that a growing number of people there were of the opinion that the Berliners should finally have 'a taste of what the bigwigs there have brought upon us'.[39] The SD repeatedly heard comments from the population expressing relief that the bombs had once again passed over and fallen on a neighbouring town. In that situation the air war could look like a huge spectacle or 'magic fire', something that on the one hand instilled fear and yet on the other had the power to fascinate, appearing in the sky as an expressive, aesthetically pleasing painting full of dazzling colours, unreal, distant, and destructive in only a very abstract sense.

From 1940 onwards Jakob Felder watched from the village of Koslar, situated between Aachen and Cologne, how the British and later the American bombers flew in regularly towards the Rhine and Ruhr areas. Felder had been born in 1891, had completed his education at the elementary school, and then spent ten years working in the local parchment paper factory. After being unemployed for a number of years, in 1934 he found work with the local authority in Koslar and was responsible during air-raid warnings for protecting the mayor's office from fire. Every day he noted something about the news he had picked up from newspapers and conversations, reporting on people's mood, events, and celebrations, Party mobilization, everyday farming life in the village, the weather and the harvest, and, last but not least, the air war. Like many living outside the towns and cities Felder experienced the air war at first only in the form of newspaper reports and nightly air-raid warnings and not as an immediate threat. The Allied bomber squadrons caused the air-raid warning to sound every night but it was clear that Koslar was not their target. As a rule he knew nothing more than that there had been 'heavy bombing' in Cologne, Düsseldorf, or the Ruhr. If anything, he heard only rumours about the level of destruction, as they reached the little village in the days after the raids via relatives and travellers and then caused a great stir.[40] The air war remained for him something he heard and saw: the bomber squadrons flying over and the bombs that detonated for the most part at some distance and, on particularly bad nights, the glow of the fires caused by the raids. On clear nights Felder could make out a 'blood-red sky'[41] followed by flashes and bangs; in his view even in the 'theatre such a violent spectacle could not be staged more vividly'.[42]

Keeping notes about the air war provided people with an opportunity to express their fears and to do so frankly, in a way that was impossible in public. It could be a way of relieving one's mind and helped people to create categories for what until then had been unimaginable.[43] It was not easy, though, to write about the air war, simply because it was evidently difficult for 'outsiders' and even for close family members to understand the cares and fear that had to be coped with on a daily basis. That at any rate was the firm belief of Anna Schmitz, born in 1891, a homeworker and seamstress from Cologne, a Catholic, and mother of one son.

After the first air raids she wrote to her son, Rudolf, a soldier in Norway, on 19 June 1940: 'Last night we had had the worst bombardment so far here in Dünnwald. It was awful. The British seem now to be going all out to inflict as much damage on us and make us as fearful as possible. [. . .] You say in your letter, "What can those few planes do to us? You're far away from the bombing and can't hear anything." But everyone gets in a state about it! When evening comes fear comes too. The nights are so clear as well. What will we have to put up with next? May God help us. Now you see what things are like here! People have lost interest in everything. I hope, I really hope it will end soon!'[44]

God and the 'Führer': Anna Schmitz put her trust in them during those hours in the early stages of the war that she spent sitting fearfully in the air-raid shelter, hoping that the constant noise of the sirens, the edginess and tension, the terrible waiting and the short, sleepless nights would soon be over. She realized at the same time that the air battle over Britain and the bombing of London, which the Nazi press had crowed about so loudly, had hugely increased the threat to her own life and she braced herself now more than before for raids by the British. What she reported to her son as early as the middle of 1940 was far from being a confidence-inspiring picture of the home front. The fact that the war made her homeland a war front was something she felt every day and, showing some annoyance at his ignorance, she left her son in no doubt about this reversal of how war should be, that is seemingly worse at home than for soldiers in the field. More and more often people were getting ill from the cold in the shelters, more and more often essential items were lacking, and more and more girls, she was appalled to say, were being put to work in the armaments industry.[45]

With every new raid her fear increased. There could be no question of her getting used to this life-threatening situation, rather she seemed to feel more and more jittery. And while her son, now stationed on the eastern front, attempted to calm her down from afar, giving her accounts of the great successes of the war, she spoke of new raids at home, fatalities among the neighbours, and houses destroyed. In her letters to the front she hardly mentioned 'final victory' any more but rather spoke of the sense that this war might destroy more than it created. Her 'faith in the Führer' at any rate, which at the beginning of the war had given her so much hope and confidence, had been fading from 1942 onwards, even before the 1,000-bomber raid, to be replaced by entreaties for divine consolation: 'If I didn't have the Lord, I might despair', she wrote to Rudolf in Norway in April 1942. 'What would life be to us now without our faith? Without religion? It is the strongest support in any situation.'[46] The air war seemed increasingly to leave Anna Schmitz with a sense of powerlessness and an ominous defence-lessness that she could endure only with the help of her faith.

She was therefore altogether prepared for the severe British air raids on Cologne at the end of May 1942; nights in the air-raid shelter had become a frightening routine and she had already experienced death and destruc-tion. On 31 May, evidently on the same day as the raid, her son had sent a letter to the Rhineland, having heard in an army bulletin of massive raids on his native city.[47] If such a raid was mentioned officially and his mother had already written repeatedly about heavy bombing then there really was a possibility that something out of the ordinary had happened. Up to that point Rudolf had been in the habit of responding to his mother's worried news by pointing to the strength of the 'Führer' and the National Socialist determination to gain victory. Now something more serious had evidently occurred. Private communication about the air war could to a considerable extent undermine the propaganda slogans that had attached themselves to the terms 'front' and 'home'.

Through letters from home the air war moved closer and closer to the front and to the soldiers, many of whom could hardly believe what was going on back home. Rumours about the number of fatalities, devastated cities in the Ruhr, refugees and evacuees, a visible breakdown in the social order in towns and cities were passed on by the women at home to their brothers and husbands at the front and were very disturbing.[48] For example, Rosalie Schüttler from Cologne described with bewilderment to her boy-friend the news she had received from nearby Wuppertal, where people 'on fire and fleeing from the heat' had 'jumped into the river'.[49]

After a night of bombing the first and most important thing people tried to do was to let family members know what had happened to them. On the very evening of the raid on her home city Anna Schmitz from Cologne put pen to paper. That she had survived was the first thing she noted humbly and almost with disbelief, as much for herself as for her son. Her home had survived too. But she felt the terror in her bones. Death and destruction were all around. The trains were not running, everywhere there were sounds of anti-aircraft fire and exploding bombs, everywhere there was uncertainty about the numbers of dead, the state of the infrastructure, about all the things that might still lie ahead. The city had never experienced such a raid, she told her son. 'Cologne, our beautiful city! No, this air war is just too awful. Everyone is still very worked up. They can't thank God enough that they have been spared.'[50]

She was still reliant on eyewitness accounts that described the appalling scenes created by the raid. Her accounts were so accurate not least because no other information was getting through to her and she had to rely on what others told her, had experienced, and had heard themselves. She felt that the air war had not only turned night into day and swept away the proper structures that ordered the world but had pitched people into a dangerous chaos from which only God could save them. 'Our lovely old Cologne. I wept when I saw it. Aunt Fintchen was with me. It's indescribable. You'll see it when you're here. It can't be worse in the war zone. There are still fires everywhere. Rubble and ashes, glass and all sorts of things are just lying around.'[51] The loss of her native city, the sight of it in ruins—after the shock of the heavy raid these were the first impressions she recorded for herself and her son. For Anna Schmitz the scale of the destruction was beyond imagining and that is presumably why she repeatedly spoke in letters of how unimaginable it must be for outsiders to hear of the devastation when even to eyewitnesses it was almost unreal. The bombing raids of late May/early June 1942 were the prelude to a constant effort to escape being herself a victim of the air war, though this was hardly possible in any city in western Germany.

Early in 1943 the situation was so threatening and the supremacy of the Allied bomber squadrons so obvious to her that after a raid at the end of January she recorded: 'There was another raid tonight of a kind we haven't seen for a long time. The sky is still lit up and red and in Mülheim or Cologne there seem to be large fires. A lot of bombs were dropped. And flares such as we haven't seen before, in every colour, bunches of them. And something silvery fell, like in a firework display. What a lot of people have lost their lives again and what a lot of pain and suffering are caused by such events. Today I was so frightened it was eerie. The light went out. And there's nothing you can do, only pray.'[52]

As time went on the raids drove her 'insane' for there was never a break and life had become a permanent state of emergency, with no real escape except through prayer and God's mercy. Nazi terms, even the word 'Führer', receded more and more as points of reference, and even if on rare occasions she wanted to retaliate because of her own suffering 'revenge' was far from being the dominant feeling she wrote to her son about. Instead it was the growing terror and the helplessness of being exposed and defenceless against danger and being forced to fear for her life once again every time the siren went off. At the same time the air raids and the now publicly visible signs of destruction, migration, and evacuation undermined her previous confidence in the state and its organization. She felt she had lost her homeland. From the summer of 1943 onwards Cologne was full of refugees who wheeled their possessions, their suitcases, and their household goods in handcarts through the city, looking for a safe place, something in increasingly short supply. Cologne, at any rate, would, as she wrote to her son, become 'a dead city'.[53] At best, she wrote at the beginning of December 1943, the 'newly born saviour' would rescue them and bring peace and joy back to this 'dark world, full of hatred'.[54]

A Time for Feelings

The feeling of having survived, the almost incomprehensible loss of one's possessions, the lack of faith in one's ability to communicate one's own experience of catastrophe to 'bystanders' and make them aware of the burden of suffering—these were some of the elements in narratives constructed to attempt to integrate the air war into people's daily experience of war. Another strategy for describing the unimaginable was to make comparisons with other bombings experienced at first hand by friends and acquaintances or at least known to them by word of mouth. This way of explaining things was used with increasing frequency in the last phase of the war from late 1943/4 onwards. Three days after the raid on Darmstadt on 11 September 1944 Margaret Werner wrote (presumably to her daughter): 'People say the raid was even worse than the one on Frankfurt am Main.' It was being said that no other city had been so badly hit as Darmstadt, and as though the comment that many eyewitnesses confirmed this were not enough she added that everywhere bodies were lying in the streets and buried under rubble. Rescue teams had to cart them away and bury them in mass graves.[55]

There was a variety of forms in which the air raids could be spoken about. One of them was the attempt through sarcasm to reduce the daily terror, to be ironical about it and so domesticate it. Those who had suffered bombing, like a woman from Bremen writing to her son at the front towards the end of the war, might speak of having come through 'another nice raid'.[56] Others, like Carola Reissner from Essen on 15 June 1944, had experienced 'a bit of magic' again the previous night.[57] Being laconic in the face of terror was capable of calming people's own nerves as well as those of the people they were writing to.

Everyday alarms

It is difficult to tell how typical these kinds of reaction were. Such examples can simply be merely individual approaches to the history of the air war as an experience. There is, however, some evidence of similar strategies for coping being adopted by individuals in some parts of the British population too, even if there the air war was not a state of emergency lasting years with the continual threat of death on an almost daily basis, as in Germany from 1943 onwards. In the days and hours after the first air raids, when hardly anyone had any stock of experiences of aerial warfare to draw on, speaking about what they had seen, exchanging stories and rumours, was part of the first phase of people's regaining confidence through language amid the unknown.

Comparing one's own story with that of others and recounting it repeatedly had a dual function. It helped people to set their experience in context and make their survival comprehensible. At the same time the stories gained significance by the fact that the individual could use them to exercise some control over what was uncertain. Jokes about the air war, laconic witticisms, and ironic distance were thus more than just a specific form of British humour often referred to in propaganda and frequently used by researchers into morale as an indicator of the stability of the home front.

A day after the raid on London on 7 September 1940 a young girl described the night of bombing she had gone through with her boyfriend:

Suddenly a swishing noise came creeping along to the left of us, increasing in force and sound as it came. The noise seemed parallel to the ground. C. threw me on to the ground and covered my head. As I fell, triangular spurts of flame seemed all around; the whole effect was like a gigantic jumping cracker. I seemed quite numb, my mouth was full of grit and dirt. All was quiet, and pieces of earth showered on to us. We both got up. Laughed a little—we were both terribly dirty. Clouds of smoke were all around and a very strong smell of earth. We both walked down the road towards home. I felt very excited, flushed and warm. Ready to laugh a lot, and probably talking a great deal [...][58]

Laughter drove away terror and writing about it helped to capture the immediate impression of numbness, dirt, and noise. Even people who had not suffered any direct damage recounted how the bombs fell closer and closer to their homes.[59] Thus individual lives gained significance because they were now in the enemy's line of fire and so contributed to the national effort: 'We're living in the front line! My own home—it's in the Front Line', as an elderly Londoner summed it up as he stood looking at the ruins of his house in the East End.[60]

'Pride' was mentioned in another connection too. After the heavy raids on London in September 1940 even those who had not yet been bombed spoke ever more frequently about their 'experiences' in the air war for the first horror scenarios were playing out in their heads and they now insisted on telling their 'heroic' stories of survival.[61] In this respect London, in contrast to Berlin, became a kind of yardstick of exemplary conduct by which the inhabitants of other cities attempted to measure themselves. 'If London can take it, we can take it too',[62] was a popular saying that pollsters were constantly registering from autumn 1940 onwards, and they were happy to do so for in their view it reflected a sort of defiance and spirit of resistance that was necessary if people were to hold up in the raids. Many people in Dundee were said to wish they would finally be bombed so that London would have a night's respite.[63] Three days after a raid on Bristol a woman noted in her diary: 'All the big papers on Sunday have given us a good write-up; they say we have had the worst raid outside of London so far, and Bristol is the worst blitzed city of the lot.'[64]

There was an element of pride in this but also relief. For the knowledge that they had acquitted themselves well and borne a degree of suffering greater than that of other cities or one at least as great as the capital's made their own fate easier to bear. After a visit by the Regional Commissioner to Barrow one of the women who kept a diary for Mass Observation, Nella Last, wrote down with a certain satisfaction his comment about the destruction of the town: Barrow had been every bit as badly hit as many other places in Britain, including Bristol and London.[65] Thus many of the local accounts of the bombing chose their own criteria in order to have the right to bear the title of a community subjected to a particularly heavy ordeal: Coventry, which had received the first blow and lost the most beautiful church; Sheffield, which had the most impressive ruins, or Hull, which could show the highest degree of destruction per inhabitant.[66]

At all events London was the notional point of reference and the air battle of world importance. This could be a source of pride even to those in the 'provinces'. For a number of decision-makers in local authorities reference to London was very likely a cheap line employed to demonstrate their own importance or divert attention from their failures. Yet people's attempts to link the city's tragic fate to their own lives were more than just propaganda, for the air raids acquired something like a deeper meaning if they involved enduring suffering that was as least as great as that borne by the heart of the Empire. Where German propaganda reported on air raids it had never aimed to create a comparable focal point and the various testimonies mentioning Berlin never make it representative of the fate of the nation. The regionalization and universalization of memories of the air war was probably a product not only of the different propaganda strategy but above all of the development and dimensions of Allied bombing. For in relation to other cities Berlin was not especially badly hit. Widely repeated jokes indicated that in some of the badly hit regions in the west people were hoping for a short respite, while those who had got everyone into this mess, namely the Berliners, would finally get what was coming to them. A popular rhyme picked up by the SD in the Ruhr area went: 'Lieber Tommy, fliege weiter, wir sind alle Bergarbeiter. Fliege weiter nach Berlin, die haben alle "Ja" geschrien' (Dear Tommy, fly on past. We're all miners. Fly on to Berlin. They're the ones who shouted 'Yes!'*).[67]

The boom in Britain in stories of local success and survival had an additional dimension: it reflected the attempt to remove from one's own life anything that was beyond the everyday and to take control again of one's own fate. Routine had to be restored and established family rituals that had been suspended during nights spent in air-raid shelters and frequent warnings were to be resumed. A London woman who kept a diary for Mass Observation complained in the middle of November 1940 about how the nightly raids disrupted her plans for the evening. She had been playing chess with her husband when suddenly loud noises could be heard. A bomb exploded nearby, the blast shook the building, and she threw herself on top of her son to protect him. Then, after a short time, when the danger was past, she looked about her: everyone had survived. Only her husband's spectacles and her knitting had gone.

There was no more time for chess now, she noted laconically a day later. Rather they waited for an interval in the bombing in order finally to make themselves a cup of tea.[68] When that had been drunk they first of all went outside, looked around, took in the damage, and spoke to neighbours. The following morning the work of cleaning and clearing up began. Debris was removed, the carpet cleaned, plates and cups were put back, lampshades secured and pictures put up again. If necessary, they went up on the roof to mend the holes and make the house rainproof. These were acts of private reconstruction that also helped to prevent the fear of being killed from dominating one's life, for at this stage many people could not tell when any compensation might arrive and what form it might take. A young London woman reported how she and her family had waited with bated breath for

* Translators' note: an allusion to Propaganda Minister Goebbels's speech in the Sports Palace in Berlin on 18 February 1943, in which he asked the audience, 'Do you want total war?'

an official from the city administration to come and assess the damage. Though he had come as arranged, he had, to the horror of her mother, done nothing more than tell them that at that point there were no more roof tiles to be had. Then the first aid group had left without repairing anything or saying how the family was supposed to survive the coming weeks.[69] In the end they managed to repair the holes in the roof and the burst water pipes themselves. When the young woman went to bed, images of the raid and the fear she had felt came back to her: the roof collapsing and the falling tiles that buried her. Then, she recalled, she finally fell asleep from sheer exhaustion.

The attempt to bring renewed order into their lives in a state of emergency was thus one of the main motives driving the predominantly female diarists writing for Mass Observation. At first, in the early autumn of 1940, the bombs came as a shock to many people. Fear was dominant, also shock at the level of destruction, and even for those who were not directly affected, the sound of 'screaming bombs' created a profound fear of the unknown terror approaching, as Nella Last confided to her diary.[70] What air-raid practices and ministerial simulations could not convey was what many Londoners were experiencing at first hand: the smell of burning that spread and got into everyone's clothes; the first pictures of the injured, which presaged worse to come; the unnerving beams of the searchlights, which spelt danger as well as protection.

In London, offices and factories had adjusted the start of work to the circumstances of the air war. Many businesses and administrative offices had been opening at least half an hour later since the heavy raids and closing an hour earlier. Lunchtimes grew shorter, with lunch breaks often being spent at work; in many offices the pace of work increased and for many the working day did not end until they had done their stint in air-raid protection. Anxiety was caused not only by the direct damage inflicted but also by the numerous alarms that interrupted the working day. Offices moved their premises to neighbouring cafés for fear of finding windows blown out again and files and documents in disarray the morning after a raid.[71]

Even though the burden of work increased, in particular for women (who were drafted into jobs in war production, both on the shop floor and in administration, much more than in 1914[72]), even though getting to work and the obstacles created by the blackout were burdensome, nevertheless the attempt to maintain or re-establish the daily routine was an integral part of adapting to the air war. As a response to it many people longed for diversion and their daily work routine, as one report on the mood on the home front said.[73] Even though many people complained about lack of sleep, wherever possible people got up the next morning, set off, waited for the bus or the tube, and hoped to arrive more or less on time at the office or factory.

In spite of the air-raid warning many businesses stayed open until the owners themselves thought it was time to go to the cellar. Cinemas and pubs could stay open and quite a few people did not let the air-raid warnings stop them from seeing the end of the film.[74] This attitude may well have been caused in part by a certain degree of habituation to the new danger, but contributing to it also was certainly an awareness of how faulty the system had been up to that point, sending out warnings too early, too late, or not at all.

The issue of whether people should carry on working in factories, and in particular in the armaments industry, after the siren sounded and if so for how long provoked considerable conflict among employees, unions, the government, and employers. In view of backlogs in armaments production and the threat of work time being lost through the bombing the government in Whitehall made every effort to keep interruptions to a minimum. The unions for their part were concerned to reconcile the matter of working time with the protection of employees and their families and to push for improvements in safety measures in factories, which had been felt to be deficient. By the late summer of 1940, when the air raids began, there was still no set of agreed regulations, with the result that practice could vary markedly from one firm to another.

Many firms operated with their own air-raid wardens, who were stationed on the roof to monitor the situation and warn employees only when the plant was in immediate danger. This practice became increasingly prevalent in the course of the war. Although Whitehall tried to initiate a single set of guidelines, it was in the final analysis for firms to negotiate how they would decide the level of risk and provide financial compensation. For the unions at any rate the conflict over working times was both material and symbolic, for from their point of view safety in the air war should not be a matter of social class. Their basic willingness to compromise in the negotiations with the employers led, however, to workers in cities such as Manchester, Salford, and Leeds rejecting their guidance and refusing to continue working when the siren sounded. After all, as they said, they could not otherwise look after their own families. And there was another reason: many workers evidently mistrusted the government's claim that if they were injured they would receive appropriate compensation.[75]

Although the employers had pressed for permission to operate the machines for as long as possible, the point at which it was time to go to the shelter and how long employees were permitted to stay there was a bone of contention between the workforce and the management. What happened if a raid was looming during the lunch break, when the workers were not paid anyway? And what was the situation with piece-work, given that production was much lower in the night shifts because of the air-raid warnings? Should the firm pick up the tab for this? A managing director whose firm produced fighter aircraft commissioned by the RAF did not accept this, his view being that if, for political reasons, it was impossible to withhold payment completely for the time employees were in the shelters, they should at least be paid no more than the rate for unemployment benefit.

The air war had made daily life increasingly burdensome. In those parts of cities particularly badly hit—and many of these were working-class areas built around industries, such as in Hull,[76] Coventry, or Portsmouth[77]—the distances to travel had increased. Rubble was lying on the roads, businesses were destroyed, and buses were no longer running. From time to time reports suggested how much the consequences of air raids were felt to be a continuation of unjust class structures; when, for example, 'little people' waited at the bus stop in Portsmouth for public transport, while middle-class car owners drove past them into the city without thinking of offering their empty seats, that, for Mass Observation respondents, most certainly gave grounds for complaint.[78]

People were agreed that the raids would continue. That seemed certain, even though there were persistent rumours that the Germans would never bomb the same place over and over. But that was really a form of superstitious wishful thinking that expanded rapidly with the raids for it offered some element of certainty in predicting the future.[79]

After the terror came the attempt to adjust, even if this was far from easy. After the first, admittedly still light, air raids Tom Harrisson summed up the findings of Mass Observation as follows: People had expected and feared bombing for a long time. But now, after the initial experiences, it turned out that many of the horror scenarios had in fact been exaggerated and thus the opposite effect to that in Germany became evident. For although many people there also tried to adjust to a state of emergency and to align their imagined terror with reality, with the expansion of the raids year on year the consequences of this state of emergency became more and more grave, affecting ever broader sections of the population. Moreover, increasingly the ultimate catastrophe, as in Hamburg, seemed possible.

As far as Britain was concerned, the observers recorded how surprising it was that the bombs actually affected people so little. Their conclusion was that the raids had become a daily routine in a very short time.[80] While that may perhaps have been a slight exaggeration and an example of wishful thinking as well, there was certainly supporting evidence. Thus at the end of October 1940 Nella Last noted: 'If anyone had told me I could have felt so unconcerned when an alert—or guns—sounded, I would not have believed it possible. The first bomb dropped made me choke with palpitation, and for a few days I jumped at the least bump or slam of a door. I can tell my feeling is shared by many women I speak to, and those very nervy people who liked to have a fuss made over them are beginning to get used to things.'[81] And a teacher from Kent who had seen the 'Nazi hordes' flying night after night towards London said at the end of 1940 that, although she could not explain it, the air-raid sirens no longer stirred any emotion in her. It was routine.[82] 'Getting used to air raids' was one of the constant topoi of the reports and analyses commissioned by Mass Observation. Similar turns of phrase also appeared in the Ministry of Information's reports on the national mood. At the end of November 1940 the morale experts thought they detected a 'toughness of spirit'[83] and of the mood at Christmas 1940 they noted that in the last few weeks the British had become increasingly accustomed to the dangers and everyday worries of the air war.[84]

On the basis of psychological studies[85] the experts believed that those who had already gone through several raids and thus knew that the danger of being killed was much less than originally assumed behaved in a particularly stoical and level-headed manner. As the raids had continued, the yardsticks for what was regarded as safe and what dangerous had changed. At any rate, psychologists observed the phenomenon that over time the wailing of the sirens no longer made such a dramatic impact and became one of the sounds of everyday life. The danger had not disappeared but it had become calculable, in particular because, in contrast to Germany, the number of raids and thus the potential threat was constantly reducing from the early summer of 1941 onwards.

The narrative of 'getting used to raids' comprised a variety of overlapping levels of meaning. In the articles in the daily newspapers it served as proof of the heroic 'character' of the nation. 'Londoners Hear the Music of Guns and Rejoice' was the headline in the *Daily Herald* on 13 September 1940,[86] thus changing the air battles from being precursors of death into a musical act of liberation. This type of behaviour seemed at the same time to demonstrate the nation's powers of resistance, taking its destiny into its own hands again after the initial shock and not allowing itself to be terrorized by Germany. The various testimonies that were produced for Mass Observation also reveal another, individual behaviour strategy, that of disciplining the emotions.

Shortly after the end of the war John Sweetland, by then 18, wrote a history, using as a basis his own notes and diaries, of growing up in wartime. In it he recalled how he and his family tried to get through the night during the raids. His mother had been anxious and had been the most worried. He, on the other hand, had tried to control his feelings and his fear by listening regularly to classical music and reading *Picture Post*.[87] Fear in such circumstances was at best a 'female' reaction, while lads and men, though they were certainly permitted to feel some unease, were obliged at the same time to fight this feeling and suppress it.

Many accounts of the air war therefore turned stories of fear and danger into adventures displaying youthful and masculine heroism. After assessing the diary entries in December 1940 the experts of Mass Observation came to the conclusion that after the long phase of waiting and anxiety many people regarded the raids with anticipation. In their view what one correspondent noted about the behaviour of his neighbours was not unusual: 'I don't think I'm exaggerating when I say most people enjoyed it.'[88] That meant above all looking up to the sky with excitement to see the dog fights, walking through the streets in the blackout, taking cover and waiting, and then, at the end of the raid, seeing that things were not so bad after all and the chances of survival had been greater than assumed earlier.

Such reports were not on the whole written immediately after the raids but after a certain interval, and it was principally men who chose this narrative survival strategy. The air battles thus seemed to be more a game and an adventure for big boys for whom the greatest pleasure consisted in being able to identify the enemy aircraft. Jerry had been so close that he had almost been able to make out if it had been a Dornier 17 or 215, Richard Brown, an Ipswich engineer, noted in his diary—an encounter which, as he stated with pride, he had 'enjoyed very much'.[89] To compete with the dangerous German planes and their bombs and to survive the conflict with them could thus be an important element in masculine identity formation.

Fascination with the technical side of war, war without bloodshed, with aircraft types, machine guns, and the depth of bomb craters, took precedence over all other emotions, Brown asserted. Though he had been glad to know that during this dramatic air battle his family had been safe under the table he had not felt any fear himself. The most he would admit to was 'slight agitation' when shortly before Christmas 1940 German bombers again bombed the city. Caring father, dispassionate observer, a man with a passion for war—this is how Richard Brown saw himself. Round about him he heard the neighbours shouting. A house had been hit, but he did not panic or allow himself to be overwhelmed by emotion. On the contrary, he listened and watched the searchlights picking up the enemy aircraft's vapour trails and the pursuit in the air.[90]

The adventure going on in the air was, however, not always such an 'interesting' spectacle, interesting because of its technical aspects. In April 1941 Brown experienced a raid with his mother. The sound of the enemy engines, the whistling of bombs falling ever faster, and the uncertainty about where and how the fatal cargo of explosives had fallen made him feel fear in his bones 'a little'. One 'poor chap', an air-raid warden, had been killed in the raid and there had been eight casualties. But there was little time for grief, for after all the next raid was imminent[91] and every air-raid warning in the night was followed by a new day when people had to work.

The threat from miracle weapons

When from the middle of 1944 German 'miracle weapons' were dropped on London, these 'flying bombs' did not allow for lengthy warning periods, so that, unlike at the beginning of the war, sirens no longer alerted people to the danger. The ominous rockets could strike anyone at any time. Learnt behaviours did not kick in in this situation. The unexpected in wartime created fear; what was more, for a time in the summer of 1944 it seemed as though the intensity of the raids would equal that of 1940/1, or even exceed it. A Gallup poll in August 1944 found that half of the population felt the impact of the 'flying bomb' raids to be worse than the Blitz. Only 31 per cent believed the 'miracle weapons' would have less effect than the raids by the Luftwaffe.[92] After five years of war, as the Home Secretary Herbert Morrison said, the population was certainly less resilient than during the months of the Blitz.[93]

The reports reaching him from the Ministry of Information were unsettling, the more so because there was no public forum where the effects of the raids could be discussed.[94] The strict press embargo was still in force, even up to the point where tens of thousands of homes in London had already been reduced to rubble and queues were forming again outside aid stations. At the same time the reports of Mass Observation contained an increasing number of mentions of renewed class division in London. Why, an interviewee said angrily, were only the Presbyterians named in the reports about the V-2 raid on Battersea but not the many poor people who were also victims.[95]

The rumours spreading in the city alarmed political leaders. More and more often there were complaints about the government's lack of provision, about the numerous elderly people who had suffered heart attacks from fear of the V-weapons, and about new weapons Hitler and Germany had at their disposal that were capable of inflicting even greater damage.[96] Vivienne Hall, a secretary in Putney, noted in her diary: 'We now live, sleep (when we can), eat and think of nothing but flying bombs. They are always with us—at the office we listen for our warning overhead bell and dash to the store cupboard many times a day as the beauties fly over; the all-clears and alerts follow one another all day long, sometimes as many as fourteen times, and at night I lie and listen as the approaching bomb gets nearer, and as it passes overhead I draw up my knees and cover my head with bedclothes until it has gone or bursts with a sickening thud.'[97] By contrast with the months of the first German air offensive in 1940/1 the population's insecurity had hardly diminished.[98]

From summer 1944 onwards London experienced a new wave of departures by those desperate to get out of the city and out of the West End, which had been particularly massively bombed. Between July and September 1944 alone some 1.1 million Londoners gave the Post Office forwarding addresses, many of them in safe outer suburbs or in the north.[99] London's stations were packed and queues formed at all the ticket offices. More than a million Londoners, some with official permission, others on their own initiative, left the city and sought shelter in the outlying areas. Some of those who remained experienced the rocket bombardment as a renewed crisis, one that rekindled the old class conflicts that seemed to disappear for a short, historic moment during the Blitz.

Asked by Mass Observation about his experiences during the raids by the 'miracle weapons' one Londoner recorded that back in 1940 the eyes of the whole world were on London. Now, on the other hand, when the city was under renewed attack by the Germans, conditions in the city had radically changed. People were now wrapped up in themselves and the kindness and solidarity that had grown up during the Blitz had dissipated. Death now lay in wait every moment on every street corner. There was no room for collective resistance. In the final analysis everyone looked after himself or herself, everyone was reduced to the level of a personal battle with fate.[100]

Rumours spoke of up to 250 victims of the rocket attacks.[101] Everyone knew how dangerous they were but talking about it did not seem the right thing to do, indeed seemed unpatriotic. But what if it got to the stage where the Germans went over to the ultimate weapon—gas bombs?[102] That was a worry that at that moment seemed more real than at any time during the war. It had a direct effect on the policy of Bomber Command and was partly responsible for the fact that there was virtually no scope for alternatives to the strategy of area bombing.

For at the same time as anxiety was growing about increasingly destructive weapons there was a rise in the summer and autumn of 1944 in the number of those in favour of large-scale retaliation. That meant, as one observer put it, 'taking off the kid gloves' and attacking German cities harder than hitherto.[103] Tottenham council called on the government to go on destroying German cities until the raids finally ceased and Londoners could live in peace again.[104] 'Are we never to be free of damage and death?' moaned Vivienne Hall a week after the first V-2s fell on London. 'How much longer does this go on, I wonder? Surely five years is long enough for any town to have to suffer?'[105] The last V-2 finally landed on British soil on 27 March 1945 and then it was to take a little more than a month for the call for retaliation to be drowned out by the sigh of relief at once more being able to live life without a fear of bombing, rockets, and gas attacks, a life without the shadow of Hitler and National Socialism.

Habituation and violence

In Britain and Germany there was frequent talk of the population being able to get used to the bombing. But was it really possible to accommodate oneself to a state of emergency? And what did this depend on? For some of those being bombed the raids were a source of hope—hope, namely, of rescue from continued forced labour and extermination. Thus the sounds of approaching bomber squadrons might herald liberation and so give rise to some satisfaction. Mirjam Levi, a Dutch Jew deported by the Germans to Bergen-Belsen, noted after her journey to the concentration camp through the ruins of Germany: 'We passed a deserted heap of rubble [Bremen, D.S.]. Deserted of course because it was night. But in big, big areas of the city— the train travelled past them for minutes—the rubble in the streets was piled as high as buildings and there were collapsed houses, houses without roofs, buildings with only one or two storeys [...] Bremen made the whole journey worthwhile.'[106]

Levi observed the devastation of Bremen from a passing train. In the bombed cities, however, many inhabitants struggled to find words to describe what they were experiencing with the normal conventions of speech. For example, on 1 August 1943 Gustav Schmidt, a headmaster, wrote to his son Dieter, who at this point was serving with the army in Holland, about his first attempt to go to his old place of work after the air raids. 'The walk along Lerchenfeld, Wartenau, Landwehr, Mittelstrasse is something I'll never forget. The most grisly experience I have ever had. Even in Flanders it wasn't so gruesome! The clouds of smoke made my eyes sting, ash was whirling through the air, my nose was affected. I took off my glasses and set out with a big, wet cloth clamped over my mouth and nose. From Land-wehr onwards the path was lit up by the headlights of army lorries; I stumbled on over the rubble of collapsing buildings, dangling tram wires, constantly at risk of being crushed by the toppling remains of walls. All the buildings were still on fire, some ablaze, some slowly burning out [...] Mittelstrasse yawned like a dark hole, perhaps something like the mental pictures people had in mediaeval times of the jaws of hell.'[107]

In these first days and weeks people continually spoke of doom, and for many the only comparison that seemed fitting was with the apocalyptic atmosphere of the New Testament's vision of the last days. In the vestry book of the congregation of St Mark's in Hamburg someone recorded this sombre mood immediately after the raids of 25 July: 'The sun no longer shines and the congregation wanders aimlessly among the burning houses.'[108] 'Who', as the Protestant Hamburg pastor Ernst Bauer pondered three months after the raid, 'could even have imagined such a "devilish catastrophe"?'[109] One of those caught up in the bombing of Darmstadt noted: 'Priam's fortress has fallen, Troy lies in dust and ruins.* Since I saw the first

* Translators' note: Quotation from Friedrich Schiller's poem 'Das Siegesfest' (The victory celebration).

bombed buildings I have not been able to get these lines out of my head, and I keep thinking of them every time I go through Darmstadt.'[110] The event was unimaginable, so also were its consequences and the impressions it made, which went beyond anything people had experienced before and so were difficult to put into words.[111] How dominant were the biblical analogies, which gave a historical dimension to the inner and outer devastation and so, as it were, made them comprehensible, is hard to say.

There is considerable evidence that, in addition to this religious vocabulary and tendency to interpret events in terms of catastrophe, there were other multi-layered attempts to find words to capture what was happening. Among them, for example, were the extensive descriptions of streets destroyed, of bomb craters that people had to negotiate in order to get home, of rows of burning houses, of buildings familiar from childhood or as places of work now gone; also of the altered sense of time, for in the chaos of the air war distances that were easily covered in peacetime now took four times as long or else the route was now impassable. Again and again such attempts by people to come to terms with the terror they had experienced were linked to dark visions of downfall and destruction, of hell and 'witches' sabbaths'.[112]

Yet the history of loss could also give rise to a different narrative—that of individual loss involving, in particular for many housewives, shattered sideboards, collapsed roofs, broken vases, and lost documents. As Margaret Werner reported on 14 September 1944 after the raid on Darmstadt, not only was the house a charred ruin from top to bottom, even the silver had melted and every ornament, bust, picture, piece of linen or upholstery down to the stores of jam and preserved fruit were gone in an instant. All their documents were gone, both business and private ones. Coats and suits were burnt and the only things remaining were some suitcases from the laundry containing a few bits of clothing. As she told her daughter, she sat 'in silence' looking at the burning ruins, unable to speak. Although after four weeks her speechlessness had gone, or at least the unimaginable had in the meantime become very real and describable, at the same time Margaret Werner became ever more conscious of the pain of what she had lost. Just four weeks after the raids on Darmstadt she described her own process of absorbing the shock: 'The more days pass since this appalling catastrophe, the more I realise the seriousness of the situation we're suddenly in. At first I was numb with pain and sadness over the loss of so many tangible and intangible things. Now I'm beginning to wonder what will become of me.'[113]

After the heavy raids on Augsburg in February 1944 Anni L. wrote to her brother Otto, who was in Neubrandenburg with his unit: 'The first shock is over but now we have the bleak reality. I'm writing to you above all about the effects of the war on A., because I'm hoping that will make me forget more quickly what I saw.'[114] That was another possible way of taking on board what had happened. The bombs seemed an event positively outside time, a bolt from the blue that plunged the supposedly peaceful family idyll into darkness in the blink of an eye, extinguishing it and sweeping away the old house and children's toys—a narrative repeated in numerous British accounts as well. Some people would just be sitting with their families in the front room having supper,[115] others would be writing letters unsuspectingly to friends and relatives when the bombs began to fall. People often began their attempts to explain what happened by recalling the summery weather that day,[116] the innocent pursuits in the hours before the bombs exploded, the everyday events, the day's normal routine, so different from what was to come. Nature's contrast between the sunshine of the day and the grim darkness of night created a linguistic and temporal distance between the before and after of people's individual experience of war, giving their accounts an arc that began with an idyll, moved on to the destruction of their home, and could preserve some vestige of hope by reaching a final conclusion by way of endurance and resurrection.

Such an ending seemed particularly vital if air raids were destroying overnight all that people had, as it were, and bringing about a new form of social inequality by dividing city dwellers into those who had been bombed out and those who were still able to live in their own homes and were now defending their possessions against claims from outside. Certainly for the Hamburg lawyer Friedrich Ruppel, who had lost his home at the end of July 1943 and lived with his wife in a room in the house of an elderly lady in the suburb of Bergedorf, the shock of living in very restricted quarters after being a prosperous professional and of being forced to apply for help from others at government offices must have been considerable. In a letter to his siblings just three months after Operation Gomorrah he described his situation: he now had accommodation in a pleasant house but they had only one room in which to live, sleep, and receive visitors. He could not call this emergency accommodation an 'apartment', but rather a 'place to stay' that they wished to leave as soon as possible. All the same, they had had good fortune amid the misfortune and had proper beds, and they could not complain about the neighbours on the same corridor. On the other hand, dealing with the bureaucracy, waiting for hours at the Rations Office in order finally to be given coupons for items they needed to survive, was much more of a trial.

As Ruppel described it to his siblings, the further the bombing lay in the past, the more people relapsed into their 'normal state of indifference and brutality'. Those bombed out of their homes had, he said, become objects of curiosity whom people could stare at to their hearts' content. 'We have had numerous visitors to our accommodation. I'm sure they just wanted to see how those who had lost their homes actually manage to live in such quarters, what sleeping arrangements they have, how they cook and eat and so forth. When this type of public exhibition had lost its novelty value I'm glad to say these visits grew increasingly rare, only to be replaced by visits arranged so that people could profit in some way from the advantages enjoyed by those who had been bombed out. On the other hand, there were others who felt it was right to withdraw completely and avoid any contact if at all possible, viewing us as the ones who have been unlucky.'[117]

Thus overnight members of the prosperous middle classes could become impoverished supplicants to the 'national community'. For many, such as Anni L. from Augsburg, the process of enumerating her losses and, in her distress, communicating them to her brother Otto represented also a personal statement of what the war had cost her: intangible losses such as the family's past and things of sentimental value but also very tangible, material losses that made it clear that now the Nazi state, friends, or family had to step in and help.[118] Others were simply conscious of the 'incomprehensibility' of what had happened, the moments when they felt deep distress that they could not readily put into words but were simply overwhelmed by the miracle of having survived.[119]

Guided memory

The impetus for people to speak of how they had conducted themselves during the air war could, of course, come from outside as contributions to a Nazi initiative to establish 'air-war archives' such as those in Vienna, Munich, Hagen, or Hamburg, where collections of memories specific to a particular place could be created for the post-war era to draw on. These would then ultimately provide a resource for the prosecution of Allied war crimes and document the national community's will to survive. In Hamburg, for example, the authorities planned to establish an archive, open also to the general public, containing not only reports from Party and government offices but also individual experiences as well as artistic, photographic, and pictorial evidence of the Allied 'bombing terror'. This was to create a location in which grief and grievance on account of the losses suffered could be concentrated and attributions of guilt could be immediately established.[120]

A few months after the heavy raid on Kassel on 22 October 1943 the missing persons bureau had called upon citizens affected to make statements about their experiences. The authorities encouraged those concerned to express their feelings in recording their personal suffering. This procedure blurred the boundaries between private loss and public shows of mourning, while the opportunities to speak about the air war were dependent on very diverse demands. The interviews offered the possibility of fitting individual experiences into a composite Nazi display of the national community's will to survive. The air war was not over, nor was it clear whether the city would be subjected to such a severe attack again, when the director of the missing persons bureau, Kurt Paetow, conducted more than a hundred interviews with survivors and recorded their stories.[121] The aim was to document the 'bombing terror' for posterity and create fragments of memory that would convey to future generations something of the heroism with which people had fought to defend themselves.

Even so, the reports told of very different experiences. The sense that only a 'miracle' had kept people alive in such an intense raid was in many cases combined with something approaching a guilty conscience for having survived and, unlike other people in the same building or neighbourhood, for having found a way to escape the 'fire storm'. Getting out of the air-raid shelter through the ruins and mounds of corpses had saved individuals but the price was high: friends and relatives were dead and, even worse, many people were missing and there was no news of them. People did not know where their children were and asked themselves if they had left them in the lurch. Or was there still hope that one's child had made it through the burning city and was now perhaps being looked after on a farm outside the city and nobody had had a chance to let the authorities know?[122]

One reason therefore why people responded to the call from the authorities to tell their story was so that they could tell their own tragic history to an official representative of the state and thus be able to see a meaning that transcended the fate of their own family. They spoke, therefore, in order not to be forgotten. Though some, like constable Ludwig B. from Kassel, had been able to recover the bodies of neighbouring families, they could find no trace of their own family.[123]

Among respondents to the missing persons bureau were several people holding responsible positions in the police and air defence, who in, as it were, semi-private, semi-official monologues justified their actions during the air war both to themselves and to the bureau and thus crossed the line separating direct war experience and the politics of memory. These were not isolated cases. Georg Ahrens, a close colleague of Karl Kaufmann, the Gauleiter of Hamburg, described in a familiar tone in a letter to family members how the police and rescue services in the city had battled against the 'terror attack' and had vanquished the sea of flames.[124] Although the letter had not been intended for publication it was much more than a private communication to close family. Ahrens gave a detailed account of the heroic battle fought by the local officials responsible for defending the city.

The picture he painted showed Hamburg reeling under the impact of the blow but it was far from being a dead city, in the way that Anna Schmitz had described her native Cologne. It was a catastrophe beyond anything imaginable and yet nobody had been forced to go hungry, for the supply lines and assistance from neighbouring Gaus had been effective. The 'miracle' Ahrens wrote about was not just the miracle of survival but of the national community's energy, its tireless will to survive, and the backbone that people had demonstrated. The 'bleeding city' had come through and the acute state of shock felt in the first moments after the raids had only a few weeks later turned into a triumph over adversity.

Masculine and feminine emotions

The way in which the air war was perceived had already begun to become distorted during the course of the war, as it moved from being a lived experience to being a memory, and the regime's functionaries played a central role in this. After all, it was those actively involved in air defence who as rule told the story of their own (masculine) success during the 'terror bombing'. These were stories great and small of survival, discipline, and joint effort, helping hands, and decisive leadership. Many of these accounts spoke of what allegedly did not exist: panic and fear, stress and chaos. They thus combined two functions: disciplining the national comrades and raising the profile of the individual and his office.

Yet these accounts, as collected amongst others by the Kassel missing persons bureau, could be deeply fractured and full of contradictions. Franz Aschemann, sergeant in charge of a Kassel police station, reported in March 1944, for example, that in the moment of danger he had done his duty as a policeman and searched for an old man who had been left behind, had struggled through the heat and the blaze and led a group of people asking for help through the streets to safety. The people had remained calm and 'well-behaved'. He, however, had had to bear a bitter personal blow, for contrary to what he had hoped, his family had been engulfed by the fire and perished. In an almost laconic account he records: 'It seems they ran in the wrong direction, up Jägerstrasse. Their remains were found in numbers 3 and 5. It must have been too late to go up this street.'[125] As he said himself in his statement, Aschemann had done his duty, had kept a level head, and had intervened at a critical moment when his task was to safeguard the lives of those entrusted to him. At the same time, this responsibility meant leaving his own family in the lurch. He did not, at any rate, speak of heroic deaths; rather his family met their end abruptly and even months afterwards this event had something unreal about it.

The self-discipline exercised by men over their feelings could be a possible guide to other air defence workers on how to cope with extraordinary situations, about which by virtue of their jobs they were forced to give information. It was Operation Gomorrah above all that changed the range of people's experience and imagination, and not only that of those involved but also of those who learnt in the course of their work of what up to that point had been inconceivable experiences. For example, air defence experts and city councillors from various cities in the south and south-west of Germany were given information first hand about the experiences of their Hamburg air defence colleagues—and even for tried and tested professionals these experiences were altogether harrowing.[126] It seemed that after Hamburg nothing was as it had been. Everything imaginable up to that point had to be jettisoned. The shattering power of the bombs, it was said, had 'terrified' the air defence workers to such an extent that they were frequently 'completely incapable of extinguishing fires'. Hamburg was a scene of horror. The Hamburg air defence expert testified in unvarnished terms to his South German colleagues to 'gruesome scenes', to many dead, particularly women, whose summer dresses were shredded by the fire.

By contrast with Nazi propaganda, which after only a few weeks had once again conjured up the unswerving resolve of the 'national community', in his mind's eye he could still see the images of those first hours after the bombing in their full horror: 'It is the most nightmarish thing to behold, when you can walk for an hour through and over ruins, without encountering a living thing.' Yet while he was trying to find words to express his own devastation, he was concerned in the same breath to draw an imaginary line between a terrified population and his own, professional approach. Panic, he told his South German colleagues, could be controlled only by discipline and instruction, delivered in a 'clear and businesslike' manner.

Women looking after the welfare of evacuees also spoke retrospectively, in a way very similar to the male air defence experts, of unbroken morale, when immediately after the war in the summer of 1945 they were questioned by Allied social scientists from the United States Strategic Bombing Survey (USSBS) about their experiences of the air war and the attitude of the population to Nazism. What interested the interviewers was above all the issue of whether the air war had been crucial in weakening the German war effort and the daily routine of the home front and how closely the (female) population had been attached to the Third Reich. The people selected had to give information about their profession, membership of the NSDAP, age, and marital status. The majority, 60 per cent, had been educated to a basic level, 35 per cent had had more advanced schooling, and some 5 per cent had been to university.[127]

Whereas the American researchers set out to find the 'essence' of German 'wartime morale', the majority of women interviewed regarded the process of answering questions as a mixture of testimony and confirmation of their effectiveness and the success of their war work—which explains why the majority painted a rosy picture of the situation. One woman, who had worked in the local authority department for personal injury and dealt with the care and provisioning of those bombed out, provided her applicants, victims of bomb damage, with a more than satisfactory report overall.[128] There had been no 'revolutions or agitation'. Everything was handled in a disciplined fashion, even if reactions to what had been provided had varied 'according to personality and speed of provision'. The work of the welfare centres began when people were still in hospital and, she said with conviction, it helped people overcome 'the psychological stress and powerful shock' that the air raids on Hanover had left behind them. In her view help in the form of money and material goods, care of the sick, and local authority support were an important psychological means of reassuring the population. As long as it seemed certain that the 'national community' was there for each individual, as long as there was the guarantee that it would step in in an emergency and look after the injured or, in the worst case, the dead and their families, then cracks were not to be found in the community. Particularly striking were her observations concerning the sexes' diverging experiences of violence.[129] For as she saw it, the air raids were an assault above all on female emotions, and in a dual sense. Of the roughly 25,000 injured in Hanover at least half were women. In the estimation of Frau Zierach, one of the employees interviewed who dealt with claims submitted to the department for personal injury compensation, overall women were dejected, 'despairing and very embittered' more often than men.

Her view was that it was not so much the psychological pressures, the lack of sleep, or the air-raid warnings that affected women's susceptibilities. Rather their responses were linked to the physical dimension of the violence, which had not been known before then. She at any rate observed that it was the charred bodies and physical disfigurement that threatened to destroy women's sense of identity and their aspirations. To lose a limb or have one's skin disfigured by deep scarring was something that had acquired a new and hitherto unknown significance as a result of the bombing. Physical injuries made women afraid that they would no longer be perceived as such. It was evidently not uncommon for injured women to fear they would no longer have a chance of getting married. Whereas men focused on ensuring that the 'national community' acknowledged the injuries they had suffered, for the most part in the line of duty, and compensated them, women did not have comparable expectations. By comparison with men, women therefore saw themselves as exposed to a threefold risk. They were physically injured in air raids as frequently as men, if not more so; they had to take care not only of themselves but also of their children; on top of that, even the physical consequences of the bombing were unevenly distributed. For men, injuries were part of their work; for women, on the other hand, according to the observations of the personal injury claims employee, injuries had a significantly more profound impact on their lives, for they regarded themselves as physically maimed as women and thus deprived of an important 'role' as caring mothers in the 'national community'.

Keeping on working

What particularly interested the Allied social researchers was the issue of the 'morale' of male and female workers and the impact of the bombing on their ability to do their work in the German armaments industry. This was, after all, at the heart of Allied bombing strategy, for the assumption was that an important indicator of the success of 'morale bombing' would be reduced enthusiasm for work and a higher level of absenteeism.[130]

According to the industrialists and labour experts interviewed in the summer of 1945 by the USSBS, one of the key objectives had not been fulfilled: German workers had not fled in massive numbers under the impact of the bombing. The extent of their absences had clearly been limited. But could absenteeism be used as an indicator of a rejection of Nazism, in any case? Did going to work signify support for the regime or was it not likely that a whole series of diverse motives lay behind it?

A furniture manufacturer in Freiburg gave four explanations for absences by his staff after a heavy raid in 1944: a number stayed away from work in the first days after the raid either because they had to move their families to safety, or because they were helping in their neighbourhood, or because the whole transport system had broken down, or because they were desperately searching for their relatives. In the first few days about 15 per cent of the male staff members were absent, whereas the proportion of female absentees was around 70 per cent. It took about a week for normal working to be resumed and the vast majority of staff to be back.[131] Not least among the reasons for the high number of female absentees was most likely the fact that they shouldered the main burden of caring for the family and thus were forced to see that it survived by organizing food and shelter. The Freiburg manufacturer concluded that air-raid warnings had caused a 'considerable' increase in his staff's tiredness and tension; these had reached a level where productivity had dropped by half. He did not see in his staff obvious signs of collapse, let alone of resistance or opposition, though the grumbling of the foreign workers was suppressed by means of a 'strict regime'.

Often it was above all the indirect consequences of the raids that determined everyday life at the workplace, as was the case with the Ford works in Cologne.[132] Along with the air raids the management had noticed a drop in 'workplace discipline', and yet the number of workers, an estimated 5 per cent, who were absent because they 'couldn't be bothered' was still at a level that could be absorbed, in particular because apart from some grumbling there were evidently no traces of genuine opposition. A more serious problem was the fact that the constant warnings were a significant disruption to the rhythm of work; the quality of production in 1944 had clearly dropped by comparison with the pre-war years.[133] Overall it appears most likely that in the vast majority of large firms, in spite of short-term lapses, industrial workers' loyalty to their firms was hardly affected by the air raids.

But why did people go on working at all? Why, in view of the level of destruction did industrial workers not rise up against the regime? A particularly important factor in this, especially with regard to the final phase of the war, was the extent to which large firms were vital to survival. Works canteens provided guaranteed meals during the working week and distributed additional rations that went beyond the meagre diet provided by the rationing offices. Many firms also had their own advisory offices that helped people find replacement goods and made sure that employees did not have to travel long distances in order to submit a claim to the war damage office. Some lucky people could also get hold of inexpensive shoes or a few lamps via their employer or might even be able to organize replacement glass for shattered windows. The work routine could be a means of keeping going and not giving way to despair. According to an SD report, one miner from the Ruhr put it this way: 'The thought of the evening terrifies me. While I'm at work I can ignore everything, but when I get home, I'm back to the horror.'[134]

Returning to work after a raid could therefore, in a way similar to letter-writing, be a restoration of normality, of order within disorder.[135] Both for the observers of the SD and for the researchers of the USSBS this was taken as evidence of the integrating force of the 'national community'. Surveys conducted among former forced workers in summer 1945, however, already indicate other possible motives. From their standpoint the reason for the relatively small number of absentees was primarily fear of state terror. This was supplemented by a further, very down-to-earth reason, namely that compensation payments were made only after workers had reported back to their firm.

What option did most employees actually have, other than to return to work? Even if the burden of work was constantly increasing, not least as a result of the many tasks associated with air defence and defence of the workplace, the alternatives were very limited. Thus a paradoxical situation could often arise: the progressive erosion of the regime's legitimacy as a result of the bombing, the growing crisis of confidence in the regime's capacity to solve the nation's problems, and the dissolution of social ties were linked to the obligation to 'self-mobilize'. The NSDAP and its organizations created a platform for self-mobilization and thus could present people with something like a social network in which the boundaries between political power and society dissolved. This in turn was the precondition for the fact that, in spite, or precisely because, of the devastation, the bombing, and the evacuations during the war, the national community was turned into a Nazi 'community of downfall' where individual survival strategies went hand in hand with the excesses of a politics of exclusion based on criteria of social utility.

Children in the Air War

The fact that innocent children were the ones most affected by the air war was already one of the topoi of war propaganda even in the First World War. Instead of pictures of grieving parents, however, those that were passed by the British censors were more often of boys and girls merrily singing or travelling in long trains to secure regions in the country or playing on the platforms of tube stations under the watchful gaze of their mothers. The picture of a little girl who has just survived a V-1 attack on London and is screaming in the arms of an air-raid auxiliary became an iconic image only after 1945.

It was a different matter in the years up to 1942, when the suggestion was that the war could not touch children and if it did then these were acts of barbarous terrorism that once again underlined the bloodthirsty nature of German warfare. Such propaganda slogans revealed nothing about how children saw themselves. This was the assumption behind the work of British researchers who from the beginning of 1940 onwards examined the lives of evacuated children and finally, at the request of the government, from the autumn of 1941 set about exploring the experiences of schoolchildren in Birmingham and Hull of night-time bombing.[136] The members of the ministerial research group, who had already organized the survey of bombing victims in Hull, selected pupils from a variety of classes and schools and asked them to write as accurately as possible about how they had felt. The accounts they produced were intended not for teachers and parents but for academics, though the large quantity of 2,000 essays and changing research priorities meant that the latter did not in fact evaluate the material.

The descriptions repeatedly adopted the same pattern: the moment of the first warning, going into the shelter or into the Anderson shelter in the garden, the sound of the bombs detonating, going back home. As a rule the stories were written about six months after the raids, time enough, in other words, to talk about those terrible nights with parents and school friends and give the accounts a certain uniformity. It is therefore unsurprising that many accounts began with roughly the same words: in April Birmingham suffered terrible bombing, during which, as a girl from Bloomsbury Secondary Girls' School recalled, her school was badly hit. The majority of the children spent the nights of bombing with their mothers and grandmothers, while their fathers were out controlling fires and so were separated from their families. Yet in contrast to the official version of events given by adults, who claimed to see the shelter as a place of safety and companionship, for many children the nights in the shelter seemed to be times of profound anxiety and threat and only rarely coincided with the stories of adventure during the raids that circulated after 1945.

The experience of her first night of bombing was something that deeply affected young Barbara Kendall: she would never forget it all, she noted at the beginning of her essay.[137] She had been frightened, frightened of the bombs that kept on landing all around her. The sound of the impact was terrible. She could remember shouting and a neighbour knocking on the door of the shelter and tearfully telling of the two people she had just seen dead. For children too the experience of death had become real as never before. The shelter was the place that offered protection but it was also a place where news was shared about the terror of the raids, where rumours circulated and became an important source of information, because only they, and not, for example, the censored newspaper accounts, could help people imagine what had happened and what might happen.

Death and injury, loss and grief were manifestly part of the experience of the home front that children and young people spoke about. Joan Ray,[138] who was in the same class as Barbara Kendall, experienced the raid in a shelter in her own garden. A bomb dropped directly beside her home and she saw how her father was buried under the rubble and her mother searched in vain for him. The shelter gave them protection and although she did not give precise information about her father's fate it was clear that even if he was not dead he was severely injured at the very least. The day after the raid (mother and daughter were unscathed) neighbours came, surprised that they had not been killed, as everyone in the neighbourhood had feared they had been. And yet they had escaped with their lives. Other children wrote how family members had been injured or killed and they had been confronted with death directly.[139] Ten-year-old Peter Bell, a pupil at Constable Street Boys' School in Hull, told how he had been gripped by terrible fear after a bomb exploded right next to his shelter and he had lost his hearing for a few minutes on account of the blast and thought he had gone deaf.[140] Not only the threat of physical pain provoked fear but also the knowledge that private shelters hardly provided adequate protection and were in danger of collapsing. Then one had to run for one's life to the public air-raid shelters.

Once in the shelter the children often found the atmosphere unfamiliar and unsettling. Pauline Day, a pupil at Chapman Street Girls' School in Hull, remembered how she and her parents stood in front of the heavy iron door of the public air-raid shelter and went down into the cellar, where she was confronted eventually by a large number of strange men standing smoking near the entrance and making a slightly sinister impression.[141] The way to the lower levels of the cellar led through another heavy iron door and finally down some dark steps. But even down there she did not feel safe. On the contrary, even underground she could hear the impact of the bombs close by, a sound that made her tremble.

Whereas some of the children recalled that occasionally there was singing in the shelters, it was the silence above all that stuck in Pauline Day's memory—a threatening silence because, as she knew, those were the moments just before the bombs landed. They sat there for hours and when she finally came into the daylight, she saw not only the ruined houses and the dirt and the dust that covered their home but also many people weeping as they stood looking at the rubble to which their lives had been reduced. Barbara Kendall's narrative and that of other girls ended with the hope that there would be no more nights like that.

The experiences the children wrote down coincided only partially with the observations recorded by Mass Observation correspondents and teachers about the behaviour and responses of children during the raids. One primary school teacher from Sheffield remembered how after one of the heavy raids on the city he was late arriving to teach and the class was already waiting for him. The pupils greeted him cheerfully with a joke about the bombing, before quickly getting back to business. The children from the areas of the city that had been badly bombed did not strike him as being on edge but had adapted happily to the new situation.[142] London children were on the whole calm and courageous, according to the conclusion of a Mass Observation report in 1940.[143] They carried on playing as before, both in the street and in the shelters. The only thing that had changed were the names of the games. They were no longer 'cops and robbers' but 'rescue party', a game in which the pursuers no longer caught the pursued but 'rescued' them. Those

reporting did not recognize signs of fear or sleeplessness or indications of
nervous problems. Rather, the report stated, one boy proudly pointed out to
a policeman where his home had stood before the Germans had destroyed it.
In the eyes of the adults he was a 'little hero' of the home front, facing up to
the raids with a good helping of cheek as well as courage.

Exactly what happened to city children after air raids, evacuation, and
separation from their families was something Anna Freud, daughter of Sig-
mund, and her colleague Dorothy Burlingham wanted to know. They had
established their own home for children affected by air raids and observed
their behaviour there over the course of a year.[144] In their view there was no
doubt that children over the age of 2 had some conception of how dangerous air raids could be. According to their observations such children could
sense the dangers and distinguish between the sounds of bombs dropping
and machine-gun fire. Children were aware of what it meant in the days
after the raids for streets in London or Liverpool to be blocked and the
smell of fires to hang in the air. They were conscious that going to the shelters with their parents was not for recreation and the psychologists were
convinced that, in spite of the efforts of their parents to protect them, children were confronted with the horror of war, the fighting and destruction,
the injuries and death itself. Even so, in their estimation there were no indications of lasting trauma being caused by evacuation or air raids. As long as
children were under the protection of their parents or in the care of other
adults they survived the consequences of the air war largely unscathed. This
conclusion was supported by the experience of other London psychologists.
Neither Britain nor Germany could identify any specific illness caused by
the air war. Children coming into the cities' initial aid centres along with
their parents certainly did not show any particular behavioural symptoms.
They slept, ate, and played normally, in contrast to those children who had
been separated from their parents during the raids.

Fear and discipline

The fact that children were killed in the air war as the 'innocent victims' of
'barbaric terror' had been a key message of Nazi propaganda from the start
of the bombing onwards and was designed as a political move to undermine
the legitimacy of British air raids internally and abroad. Admittedly, children
and young people were not merely propaganda tools but had their own
realm of experience. The state's paternalism was fully geared to children and

young people playing their part and taking responsibility themselves, while conversely being able to rely on being protected and cared for by their parents. Thus it was not surprising that the relationship between parents and children was, for example, one of the central themes of a series of school essays written in autumn 1943 by students born between 1926 and 1929 in vocational training in Cologne.[145] As the majority of the fathers were at the front, it was usually the mothers who woke their children when the warning was sounded and hurried with them to the shelters. They then spent the hours of a large-scale raid with them, as on 28 July 1943.

The students were supposed to record their experiences just three months after the events themselves, three months during which the Nazi regime had continued to denounce the 'terror bombers' and life for the young people had moved on, even if for some it did so under different auspices. A number of them, such as 15-year-old Gertrud L., had experienced the raid along with her mother and sister.[146] They had taken refuge in the cellar, where she remembered how everyone was shouting or praying. Their house was hit and they found it difficult to make a hole in the wall in order to escape the threat of choking to death. Gertrud ran as fast as she could; she had ripped up her petticoat and held a piece of the material to her mouth. They ran and finally reached a packed public air-raid shelter. There too the smoke was getting denser all the time. In the end she 'fell asleep', lost consciousness, and was no longer aware of how she was rescued from suffocation by auxiliaries who carried her to safety.

She finally came to in a reception camp. She could not remember anything and realized her family had disappeared. She searched and searched the whole day but with no success. 'On the Thursday morning I started searching again. Suddenly a man told me that my mother, my sister and her child were dead. I could not believe it. Then a man showed me where my mother was lying. She lay on her stomach and her hair was in one hand. She was lying next to several others who were headless and some of them charred. But my sister was not there. Then another man told me that as he was bringing my sister out on the Tuesday her child had drawn its last breaths. [...] I put a label on my mother with her name. When she was moved it got lost. So they were buried as unidentified. Many people have gone into the next world. I shall never forget that night as long as I live.' By the time she was writing, the burial had taken place a number of weeks before and the daily routine of school had returned at least in part. Presumably she had been taken in by relatives. Her consolation was evidently to remember the past and to know that her mother, sister, and nephew had 'gone into the next world' and thus were still alive and she would see them all again one day. The desire to speak about what had happened sprang therefore from the sense that it brought her closer to her dead relatives and made her feel less alone.

Just after surviving an air raid on her native city of Berlin, 15-year-old Liselotte Günzel confided to her diary at the end of December 1943: 'We have one advantage over earlier generations because we have got to know the fear of death. It makes everything fall away from people, all the glossy exterior, and even what was most sacred to me next to God left me when the finger of death was pointing at me. [...] The only comfort left to me in my mortal fear was the everlasting love of God in my heart. That did not forsake me.'[147] Since the first raids she had felt constant fear, and though she fought against it with God's power, it was continually overwhelming her again, at first only at night during the raids and later in the daytime as well. At the end of November, when she first began to write down her experiences of the air war, she had not yet been directly affected herself. But now, after the RAF's raid on Berlin, her father's office had been destroyed, her school burnt out, and a number of her relatives bombed out.

The fear of destruction grew from week to week. When the sirens suddenly went off on Christmas Eve and the bombs dropping on her district, Friedrichshain, kept coming closer, she took shelter in the nick of time in the cellar, before a bomb landed close by. When the raid was over she finally noted that evening that death had never come so close and she had never before been so frightened. The sight of her street went far beyond her worst fears. Everywhere there were ruined houses and shattered windows. In her own home there was debris and glass. Hardly anything was in its old place and there was chaos and destruction wherever she looked. Yet that was not the worst for her. The fear kept returning in the days and weeks that followed, at first only when she went into the cellar or at night but then in the end in the daytime too and in her dreams. Death was trying to lay hold of her and it must be fought off every day that the bombs fell. There was only one thing she must not do in this situation, namely break down. Her nerves were raw and yet she knew what was expected of her. On 3 January 1944 she wrote in her diary: 'You have only one thought: "If only it would stop." But it doesn't stop. You think your nerves must shatter the next moment. You must call out, but you can't, you must remain composed and not become weak, for Frau L. [her German teacher] told me so.'

'Remain composed' was the watchword Klaus Seidel, a 16-year-old anti-aircraft auxiliary from Hamburg, used to help him survive and describe his duties on the home front and in air-raid prevention.[148] As he wrote to his mother in Darmstadt, after the raids on Hamburg at the end of July 1943 he was continuously on duty, putting out fires and manning the anti-aircraft guns the whole night long. The following morning he set off to search for his grandparents; their house had been bombed and when he could not find them anywhere he dug his way through the rubble of the house but to no avail. Klaus did not wish to pass on his fears to his mother, or only indirectly, by quoting other, experienced military men from his anti-aircraft unit who were of the opinion that Hamburg had been much worse than anything they had experienced in Poland or France. In so doing he could give his mother an inkling of what he would not or could not write about, namely about fatalities and charred bodies, corpses and destruction. Yet while he remained completely 'composed' and very guarded about revealing his feelings, he was still a boy, one who loved to go swimming in the park and dreamt of the model aeroplane he was building at school until the bombs put an abrupt stop to it. Self-discipline and the experience of death went hand in hand with youthful games and the search for normality; for many children and young people these were part of a complex and tangled emotional situation that defined their everyday experience of war.

There was not much talk of revenge, nor of the 'English terror bombers', as Agnes, a classmate of Gertrud's a year younger than she, described them.[149] Viewed through the eyes of children and young people the solidarity of the national community could result in very different types of behaviour. Seventeen-year-old Hilde from Cologne wrote altogether in the language of Nazi air-war propaganda when reporting on the many helping hands, the untiring commitment to help strangers and save their property, and on her own self-control in making herself stop regretting the loss of her own possessions. Self-discipline had instead helped her to regain her composure after a few moments of weakness and to remember that everyone around her had emerged unscathed and, in spite of losses back home, life went on.[150]

Though her classmate Agnes, born in 1929, also referred to the enemy attackers as 'English terror bombers', she evidently did not experience the air-raid shelter as a bastion of national solidarity. Once in the shelter she managed to get a place in the upper part of the complex. As the bombs approached and the air became ever thinner, Agnes wanted to move with her family to the lower area of the shelter, but the other occupants were unwilling to let them. The door remained locked, at least until it was forced open. Having finally got there, they again felt afraid and helpless. There was no room for them, as more and more people were pushing their way into the space. There was hardly any air and no possibility of sitting down. Then she keeled over with exhaustion and fainted. When she came round a man led her through narrow breaches in the walls. They struggled on through a burning building, past people lying dead and unconscious, until they could finally get their breath back in the opera restaurant.[151]

Children and their teachers

It is difficult to say what impact such experiences had and how representative they were. From the standpoint of the teachers who were prepared to give information immediately after the war to the USSBS workers and were questioned for the final report, the air raids had considerable consequences for schools and pupils. When there were morning raids, teaching was usually abandoned and in any case from 1942/3 onwards regular classes were often virtually out of the question, as the example of Bremen demonstrated.

From 1941 onwards complaints from school heads had been growing that after nights spent in the shelters many children gave the impression of being irritable and lacking in concentration and that these disturbed nights clearly left their mark on them.[152] 'Fear and depression' were not evident, however, according to one teacher who gave information to the American social researchers of USSBS immediately after the end of the war. Possible psychological repercussions, he said, had disappeared at the latest by the time of the programme to evacuate children. If any undisciplined behaviour at all had been displayed then his view was that in the end it could be attributed only to an inadequate upbringing by the mother. Summing up, he said that the raids had not succeeded in destroying family relationships; there had been many instances among children over 13 of 'courage and a strengthened will to resist', in particular on the part of boys. In his view German children had coped well with the war and the constant warnings, had adapted to the exceptional circumstances, and even played 'very happily' outside the shelters in the short pauses between two air raids.

An employee at the Bremen school authority denied that experiences of the air war had provoked oppositional attitudes among teenagers. If any criticism at all had been heard in the final months of the war of the Party or the Hitler Youth, then it presumably came from some adults encouraging their children, he said.[153] Like the German nation as a whole, the children had at all events proved themselves, showing toughness, courage, and commitment, and where this had not been the case it had not been the result, for example, of the increasing danger of the raids, the varying levels of fear or risk of death, but simply of the fact that their mothers (their fathers were away fighting) had not looked after them well enough.

The majority of teachers in elementary, middle, and vocational schools in Bremen took the view that although the air war had had a strong impact on the rhythm of teaching it had in no way contributed to a 'moral debility' in the students. Interviewees understood the question concerning morality in two ways. In the 'sexual realm' there had been no licentious behaviour, let alone significant infringements of the rules.[154] Even co-educational classes, which were born of necessity, created no irregularities but rather led to respect and a competitive spirit to serve on the home front, as people assured themselves afterwards. The conclusion reached was that boys and girls had put much effort into air defence activities out of a 'sense of duty', and if there had been moments when relations between the sexes had taken an unfortunate course this was in no way a consequence of the air raids. In the shelters it had been possible to observe young people's 'tender concern' for their relatives. Often boys and girls had carried their grandparents' heavy suitcases into the shelter or collected their mothers and grandmothers from their homes and accompanied them to the shelter.

A teacher from Bremen noted that he remembered two boys of 5 or 6 remaining completely calm during the air raids and also three girls of between 14 and 16 and a boy of a similar age whom he observed as showing 'no fear or psychological disturbance' during the 'heaviest raids'. On the contrary, while numerous adults were afraid, they used the gaps between raids to make voluntary checks on their building and thus showed a courage that, according to the teacher, was confirmed by other girls.[155] On the basis of these data the American social researchers came to the conclusion that the raids, the destruction of schools, and disruption of teaching had not achieved any real or immediate weakening in morale.[156]

This was one side of the story, which teachers interviewed in other regions readily confirmed. At the same time some teachers had in fact observed other developments that had also been apparent to the USSBS team. For example, there was no unanimous response to the question of how the raids had affected the relationship between children and adults.

Some teachers spoke of how touchingly mothers had taken care of their children and tried to calm their fears as much as possible.[157] Others on the other hand mentioned an 'unfortunate influence', supporting this by alluding to mothers having too little time to attend to their children and, for example, to provide them with a hot meal. In addition, children suffered as a result of the deteriorating living conditions in cold and often overcrowded spaces, which caused many to become ill and more prone to illness. Children lost an ordered structure to life, could not relax, and were under psychological and physical pressure. There were also indications from a number of districts in Bremen that the closure of schools, coupled with a lack of authority figures at home, the absence of fathers and the need for mothers to work, had led to many children being left to their own devices. The American personnel were particularly struck by the report of a Bremen teacher who had been evacuated with his class to Meissen, returned after a time to Bremen, and gave a comparison of the Bremen and Saxon children. Whereas the children in Meissen worked undisturbed and drew little attention to themselves, it was impossible to ignore how tired and washed out the Bremen children were.[158]

In July 1945 one teacher from Bonn made a statement that was markedly more critical than those of his North German colleagues. In his estimation the air raids had led to a constant reduction in the children's concentration.[159] From the middle of 1944 at the latest, he claimed, the physical robustness of children and young people had been undermined and children under the age of 10 had had to live since August 1943 with the constant fear of air raids. Whereas older children from about 14 upwards became used to the danger and learned to live with it, it was the younger children above all who suffered as a result of the raids and whose progress at school 'rapidly' declined.

In his view the consequences were serious. The 'moral attitude' of the young was affected by the raids. That was less true of 'moral', or to be more precise sexual, 'lapses' than of the fundamental relationship between teacher and pupil. 'Respect for authority' was declining and 'teachers felt more and more that their words no longer had the impact and the credibility that are essential preconditions for their work'. In particular an additional factor making things worse was that in families that had been separated for lengthy periods as a result of the war the relationship between parents and children demonstrated a distinct 'inner alienation'.[160] A health care worker from Bremen had the appropriate explanation for this. The splitting up of fami-

lies could have a variety of consequences. Whereas in 'good, socially valuable families' evacuation, though painful, was nevertheless accepted as a
necessary evil, there was an apparent tendency to grow apart in 'socially less
valuable' families, where the programme to evacuate children was experienced as a positive 'burden lifted'.[161]

In other words the evacuation was clearly being transformed into a character test of fitness for the national community. At least—and this was some
small consolation—parents knew that their children were more or less safe
'in a strange place' or at least they were not in such immediate danger as in
the city centres, places where 'death from the skies' was a real and constant
threat.

8

Death in the Air War

Simulations

Even before the outbreak of war the British authorities had been worried about the prospect of civilian fatalities in future air raids. Experts estimated around 200,000 deaths during the first raid on London alone, while in Portsmouth, for example, the projection was for 500 to 550 fatalities per day.[1] Whitehall was convinced that the Luftwaffe had the power and the will to put all its eggs in one basket and create widespread destruction through mass bombing, which appeared likely to be even more devastating than the bloody battles of the First World War. How could the expected legions of dead be coped with? Was there a danger that the 'funeral front' would collapse? This matter troubled both the British and German authorities, for massive fatalities and the administrative and religious challenges connected with them would threaten morale. How many deaths could the 'home front' stand? What place should the dead occupy in the nation's memory, indeed how were civilian deaths to be honoured? How should they be commemorated and mourned? And how could fatalities be 'administered' in a situation of total war? All of these were new questions for which the First World War provided no precedents.

In Britain all administrative issues were to be put in the hands of the Ministry of Health.[2] Two problems were of central importance. First, a collapse of the 'funeral front' had to be prevented at all costs, for otherwise British health experts feared catastrophic consequences for morale in cities hit by the air war. At the same time it was also vital to keep funeral costs to a minimum and burden the public purse with them as little as possible—a concern familiar also to the German authorities.

Whereas Whitehall set overall policy and was responsible for dealing with nationwide crisis situations, the task of coping with acute crises fell to the particular city councils involved. The Ministry urged them to make emergency plans and to prepare to mobilize their resources in the event of a catastrophe. This involved resolving the issue of how to transport corpses as well as the search for further burial grounds and careful coordination among all other agencies who played a part in the burial of the dead. This affected first and foremost the churches but also local funeral directors.

In the event of a catastrophe the local authorities were now empowered to call on all available resources to bury the dead and prevent any mass panic or outbreak of disease. From the early summer of 1939 at the latest, municipalities throughout the country were preparing for the risk of raids. In London there were many boroughs where cemeteries were not the direct financial responsibility of the local authority. Although the Defence Regulations gave the city councils extensive powers to intervene, in view of the complicated organizational structure for burials and the threat of massive fatalities it seemed necessary for the boroughs to come to an agreement among themselves and make common emergency plans, even if sometimes this was manifestly done with great reluctance.[3]

In Exeter the Public Health Department put thought into the types of fatality that an air war made it necessary to prepare for. How did they intend to deal with mass deaths and, if the Germans used gas attacks, with contaminated corpses that would then have to be buried?[4] In Plymouth, Bristol, and Coventry the authorities checked what buildings were available to store the dead bodies. They had to be centrally located, within easy reach, and, as in the case of Coventry, provide space for at least 800 bodies.[5] In the City of Westminster there had also been discussion about how the dead could be most speedily transferred to the mortuaries. Part of this calculation was based on the authorities' assumption that a number of the dead would have been contaminated by German gas attacks and would thus need specialist treatment. Several information centres were planned to coordinate information about the number of dead and the availability of burial sites in the city.[6]

The planning and objectives set were anything but uniform, however, and the Ministry's specifications had in many respects raised more questions than they had provided answers. This was true of a wide variety of different areas. For example, it remained unclear who was responsible for registering the dead and what were the powers of those involved, from the police to the local authorities. In addition, it was still an open question who was responsible for financing these new duties and would bear the cost of recovering and burying bodies. There was therefore a power struggle going on between local and central government that was reflected in the clashes over responsibilities. Central to these controversies were also the issues of this unaccustomed manner of dealing with dead bodies, the relationship between the individual and the state, the right to a private burial, and the need to decide whether the dead would be buried or cremated.[7]

In the view of the National Association of Cemetery and Crematorium Superintendents (NACCS), which organized the state and local officials, there was no real alternative to burial, even if some authorities and private funeral directors took a different view.[8] The most important reason was that the capacity of the existing crematoria was insufficient to cope with the expected number of dead. And what would happen if the air raids destroyed the crematoria's infrastructure by cutting off electricity and gas supplies? This seemed too great a risk to take.[9] Even if the impending destruction made it impossible to give every person killed his or her own grave, it was still important to give each one an individual coffin and to ensure that the graves of those killed in the raids were not somehow in an out of the way place but were easily accessible. This could be best achieved by locating them on sites that were still unconsecrated, in order to avoid religious conflicts that could arise if, for example, Catholics were buried in Anglican ground.

Above all, in the event of massive loss of life the Ministry of Health was pressing for burials to take place in large mass graves. If necessary, shrouds should replace coffins, if the dead could not be identified quickly enough and swift action were needed to avert a public health crisis. That, it must be said, was controversial, for cost effectiveness and bureaucratic pragmatism collided with the powerful resistance felt by large sections of British society to the idea of mass burials. For, unlike in Germany, they raised the spectre of the paupers' funerals of the nineteenth century. Burial in a mass grave not only meant bereavement for relatives but epitomized loss of social status. But it was not simply a question of the status of the deceased who could not afford a proper burial and so had to be buried at public expense. Publicly funded burials were so unpopular, not least among the working classes, because they also involved indignities in the manner in which they were conducted: coffins with holes in them through which the deceased was visible, restricted access to the cemetery for poor people assumed to be 'dangerous', dismissive clergy, who skipped the burial service or kept it to a bare minimum. All these things left little scope for the relatives to mourn.

The dead person was removed from the protection of the family group and in a final act of social exclusion was turned into a nameless number in an anonymous grave.[10] A year before the outbreak of war the MPs Arnold Wilson and Herman Levy had emphasized in their study of funeral practices how crucial a fitting burial was for social integration, above all for the working class. Common burials, they stated, were still tainted not only with the 'disgrace of poverty' but with a lack of respect towards the dead and with social exclusion, in that the identity of the dead was extinguished and they were abandoned to the authorities.[11] Funeral directors pushed up the price of 'dignity' even more by behaving as if there was a direct relation between the money spent on funerals and the respect the family had for their dead relative—a vicious circle that could be broken only if the state assumed control over this area, as Wilson and Levy demanded.

Before the outbreak of war these costs had not been debated with anything like the same intensity in Germany, a result in large measure of the different traditions and responsibilities of the cities and churches with regard to the upkeep of cemeteries, which led to the costs being clearly distributed. Although the authorities responsible for air-raid protection had already made projections of possible losses resulting from air raids and in particular gas attacks,[12] by contrast with Britain the German authorities did not in the final analysis seem particularly nervous about the course the war might take. They trusted the responsible institutions to handle the administration of future wartime fatalities successfully, which meant above all discreetly and without risk to the home front. The Reich Air Ministry and the head of public health decreed that the recovery and burial of bodies should be a matter for city councils and they were to make all preparations necessary for an emergency. In big cities such as Munich it was the chief of police who as local head of air-raid protection distributed the various tasks at the beginning of January 1940.[13] The funerals office and transport services were responsible for making staff available to recover and transfer corpses, organize lorries, and get cemeteries ready for rapid burials. The guiding principle was that the population should be made aware as little as possible of the loss of life. The way in which death was handled was the product of the extraordinary tension between, on the one hand, the discreet removal of corpses and, on the other, the publicly staged acts of remembrance. This tension was not at all easy to disguise by use of the set phrases of propaganda. On the contrary, as a result of the expansion of the air war from 1942 onwards and the growing number of fatalities it was this fundamental contradiction in the Nazi regime's practice at local level that was to become a key element in wartime morale. To put it another way: for the regime massive fatalities were both an opportunity and a threat. They were an opportunity because ritual displays of mourning could be a powerful instrument with which to bind the community together. They were a threat because every new fatality called into question the ability of the Nazi state to cope with crisis and the adequacy of its provision for the national community.

Recovering the Dead

The relationship between the death of individuals and state control was therefore far from being clarified, either in Britain or in Germany, when the air war began, and for both countries this was to become a crucial issue in maintaining morale.

Even before the first bombs fell, the British Ministry of Health had stressed that normal burial practices should be maintained as far as possible and that deviations from the norm should be allowed only in an emergency. But with the first air raids and fatalities these arrangements seemed quickly stretched to their limits. In November 1940 the Ministry, while instructing the local authorities to maintain the burial practices used hitherto, nevertheless indicated at the same time that they should make arrangements for future mass burials after air raids and check on the progress achieved towards that goal.[14] If they had not yet been formulated, this was the last possible moment for making emergency plans—and the term emergency implied also that alternatives to traditional wooden coffins would have to be considered. After all, it now seemed more than likely that in the event of a raid all available resources could be destroyed. The provision of coffins and a fitting and traditional burial, in spite of external threat, were in the view of the Ministry of Health absolutely necessary not only for public health reasons but above all for reasons of morale.

For the expansion of the air war meant increasing restrictions on the amount of consultation with families concerning the kind of funeral that would take place and its timing. In view of the military situation and the pressure on resources, it was, after all, unacceptable for the burial wishes of individuals to take precedence over the need to cope quickly with the crisis. What was at stake in this attempt by the bureaucracy to make adjustments to burial practice was the authority of the city council and the question of who had power over corpses. After the first, still light, raids on Coventry the Town Clerk was outraged by clinicians from a neighbouring hospital taking it upon themselves to issue death certificates, hand them out to relatives, and, to cap it all, to enter as the cause of death 'war operations'. He alone, he claimed, had the responsibility for doing this.[15] It was likewise his responsibility to identify the dead, determine the cause of death, and also the point at which the dead would be released to their relatives for private burial. It was not long before local authorities found themselves confronted with death not only in simulations but in real life and they found it difficult to see their way through the tangle of competing jurisdictions.

The heavy German raid of 14/15 November 1940 on Coventry had left more than 500 dead, more than after any previous bombing raid. Amid the shock of the raid, however, confusion about responsibilities led to those involved—Town Clerk's office, health authorities, treasury department, and the newly appointed superintendent of cemeteries—being unable to cope and the emergency plans had to be quickly abandoned.[16] The dead were brought first to a swimming baths that had been turned into a temporary mortuary. There they and their religious affiliation were identified as far as possible on the basis of their documents and of any visible religious symbols.[17] They were given a number and finally, after transfer to the funeral director, they were registered by the responsible officials. Even that process was a sensitive matter before the actual burial. For dealing with the corpses and severed body parts, sorting the various limbs, and providing pastoral care to the relatives proved an almost overwhelming burden for the funeral staff and one hard to bear without the help of alcohol.[18]

Things became even more confused if, in the chaos of the first hours, people failed to note the precise place where the bodies had been found or other personal information and the dead were then delivered to various centres in the city and thus were hard to identify. In Belfast, where on Easter Tuesday 1941 a heavy raid left behind several hundred victims, volunteers were constantly faced with the problem of coffins being delivered without precise labelling. While distraught relatives searching for family members were queuing outside, they were obliged to open each shroud individually and certify the mangled remains.[19]

The air war had thus created at least three substantial new problems. First, there was a considerable number of dead whose identity was initially unknown. The First World War had also created the phenomenon of a mass of anonymous corpses, but there the soldiers were mainly buried in distant mass graves. Now nameless death had come to the home countries and had to be accommodated within the familiar rituals of death.

Secondly, the bombs changed the physical aspect of death itself. For many victims who had been buried under the rubble of buildings or struck by flying objects had lost their physical integrity. They had been decapitated or lost limbs or become unrecognizable. Death on the home front, as a Belfast nurse commented, had acquired a new and savage form. She had treated soldiers in the First World War, but the sight of the injuries and mutilated bodies after air raids went beyond the horror of what she had seen then and so it was hard for her to hide her revulsion. During the First World War, she remembered, soldiers had died on the battlefield or in hospital with their eyes closed and their arms folded over their chest. Death was both tragic and dignified. But dying in bombed buildings and air-raid shelters made death into something grotesque, ghastly, and horrific, for nobody could be with those people as they died to close their eyes or lay their hands on their chest if their limbs had been torn off and lost.[20]

What was the appropriate way of dealing with corpses that had suffered this degree of trauma? It was clear that in such an extreme situation there was even less scope for private arrangements or individualized rituals. The authorities had power over the disposal of dead bodies, not only for reasons of hygiene that were entirely in line with the traditions of public health established in the nineteenth century, but at least as much because British authorities like German ones were concerned as far as possible to remove the dead from public and private 'display' and make them 'disappear' as quickly as possible to prevent them from becoming symbols of national vulnerability. That was an important reason why in Coventry even before the war detailed discussions were initiated between the city council and private funeral directors to ensure that sufficient wooden coffins were held in reserve. As those responsible could announce at the time of the first mass burials at the end of November 1940, no one had to be laid to rest in a shroud or in a cheap coffin made of papier mâché.[21]

Thirdly, the air war brought about changes to the topography of mourning itself, to the architecture and underlying coherence of cemeteries. It began in the course of 1939 with the creation of special areas in cemeteries for the future civilian victims of war. These areas were to be set a little apart so that after the war they could become places of remembrance with war memorials. Individual gravestones that gave the dead an identity and a name and provided family members with a place for remembrance could not be accommodated in these spaces, which were subject to strict public regulation. With their mounds of earth and pits, these burial sites were the visible expression of the danger threatening and in addition represented an invasion of the culture of the graveyard, which tried to generate an idyllic environment in cemeteries as 'holy' places where society found reassurance about itself.[22] In the end in Coventry the coffins were buried in long pits dug immediately after the raids or, as in the case of a second mass burial, up to thirty coffins were placed in a large grave split into a number of chambers.[23]

It was the sheer numbers of dead that created the greatest problems. Private funeral directors were largely overwhelmed by the task, not least because many had themselves lost property in the raids and were not immediately able to work. Another factor was damage to the transport system, leaving few usable vehicles with which to move the dead from the holding centres to the cemeteries. Where the city no longer had sufficient resources, private firms stepped in, though they had of course to be paid. Negotiations had taken place even before the first air raids. After some toing and froing the Ministry of Health had decided that all costs connected with public burials, including coffins and transport, would be borne by the city, which would be reimbursed by the state.[24]

In the case of private burials the family was still expected to pay; compensation payments to families were planned only for cases where someone was killed while serving as a civil defence volunteer. Even then the relatives did not receive the money directly from the city but had to apply to the Ministry for Social Security and Pensions, which made a decision based on the individual case.[25] This ruling mystified large parts of the population. For however much the city councils tried to make the public funerals a dignified occasion families still wished to bury their relatives in private and not be obliged to mourn in public. Thus city councils received many requests from citizens who had at first forgone help from the authorities and organized the funerals themselves and nevertheless expected financial assistance from the city. On principle, these requests met with a negative response.[26]

The experiences of Coventry in coping with death on a massive scale quickly developed into an important repository of information when it came to the Blitz. From all over came questions about the city's view of how to deal with catastrophes on this scale, how bodies could be buried, graves set out, and mass burials conducted.[27] Should women also be enlisted to help in an emergency?

How were the various tasks coordinated with the central agencies in London? And how was public information regarding the number of fatalities to be handled? At the beginning the municipalities largely made their own decisions about the latter issue, until in the end Churchill himself put a stop to it. The need to give information to the public seemed to him in every case less important than the possible negative consequences he feared might ensue if the Germans could draw conclusions from the number of hits. He therefore rejected the idea of publishing names in the local press, instead advocating the practice adopted hitherto of posting up a list of the victims in council offices.[28]

At this point there was no functioning interregional agency that coordinated and directed the dissemination of information. Either city councils sought guidance directly from Town Clerks and their offices or the ministries themselves attempted by means of questionnaires to elicit information and to develop offers of help and directives on that basis. The Regional Commissioners served as a kind of interface for the exchange of information and experience, though at the height of the Blitz they were hardly up to this task. In many cases the local authorities did not begin until the second half of 1942, after renewed air raids by the Luftwaffe, to step up the exchange of information and discuss their various strategies for dealing with sudden mass deaths.[29] Thus at this early stage it was above all the responsibility of local government officials to gain an overview of the experiences of cities affected by bombing.

Coventry was the preferred example of how to deal with death. It had taken a little more than a week there for all the victims of the bombing to be recovered, identified, and removed from the mortuaries to the cemeteries, so that preparations for the first public burial could be completed. That in itself was a tricky business. As officials from Plymouth reported with regard to their own experiences, dealing with relatives in particular required special tact. Essential matters for the authorities to take on board were the need to show sympathy and to avoid making family members identify their relatives in the large mortuary so as to spare them the sight of so many corpses. As an observer from the Ministry of Home Security Research and Experiments Department commented after a tour of inspection of the London mortuaries at the end of December 1943, it was important if possible at least to place a cross or some flowers in the places where bodies were identified, this being a mark of respect such as was normal in hospitals. It was even better if someone were specially assigned to take care of the relatives.

The long waiting times that had become usual before people saw their deceased relatives for the last time were, he said, to be avoided at all costs, the more so because the formalities for burial had to be organized in the same place.[30]

Learning from catastrophe

The German local administrations knew nothing of the problems confronting the British local authorities in the air war. They were equally unaware of how little time remained to consider how to honour the dead or even provide enough wreaths for them. Only gradually, and completely in ignorance of the conditions in Britain, did they begin from 1941 onwards to discuss their strategy for a future crisis, the cardinal principle of which was initially to remove the dead as discreetly as possible and with the minimum of fuss.[31] Personnel from the Security and Aid Service formed a special unit that was charged with recovering bodies from the rubble and transferring them to secure spaces until they were finally moved to the cemeteries. The police authorities particularly emphasized that all relatives were to be kept away from the corpses and that they were not allowed to accompany their dead family members in the hearses. Thus, when fatalities occurred, the air defence authorities and a 'corpse recovery service' took responsibility for the bodies of the 'fallen', with the aim not only of preventing families from claiming them but also of protecting them from 'desecrators'. Confidence in the 'national community' was not very great in this latter regard and thus the police authorities gave special instructions to city employees to protect the bodies as far as possible from looters.

Once bodies had been recovered, doctors from the air defence medical service were to establish the cause of death and sign the label that identified the dead body. Unlike in peacetime, after air raids it was no longer necessary to obtain permission for burial from the prosecutor's office. This could be issued after the event. Nothing was more important in this situation than to remove as soon as possible all public signs of destruction and to keep control over the dead bodies. Just as in Britain, these plans did not meet with universal approval. Local authority officials took exception, among other things, to the fact that the police authorities and not the municipal experts on the spot had control over the removal of corpses.[32]

At the beginning of 1940 these plans had yet to stand up to any real test in practice and the organizational details could vary from one local authority to another. In Berlin, for example, there had been initial plans since the outbreak of war for collection points in the city for the dead, where they could be identified and then moved to the cemeteries. Families had forty-eight hours in which to bury their dead themselves; after that the plan was to bury the bodies in mass graves for public health reasons.[33]

In order to gain an overview of the state of preparations the German Local Government Association began in May 1941 to collect information from all the major cities in the Reich about their arrangements for dealing with the burial of 'aircraft victims'.[34] How were burial grounds selected? Were there plans for commemorative cemeteries for the 'fallen'? What kind of space was planned for the dead, several graves or one large single grave? How far should the influence of families and their claim on the victim's body extend? And who in the end should pay for the funerals? The responses varied according to how massive the effects of bombing had been on the cities at this early stage of the air war. In Kiel the city paid burial costs up to 260 Reich marks; the city did not set additional insurance pay-outs on death against the cost of any burial that it had commissioned from one of the local funeral directors.[35] The city of Kiel also covered additional expenses for the public memorial services. Other cities gave no subsidy but rather sent a bill that the relatives could send to the family insurance companies for payment. The level of subsidy varied from place to place; in Hamburg the social services department covered the costs up to 350 Reich marks, whereas in Berlin at this stage only in cases of particular hardship was the pay-out more than 210 Reich marks.

The authorities had been particularly 'generous' in how they dealt with the first victims of the air war in August 1940 and paid the whole costs of burial. By the middle of 1941 there were deviations from this practice and in order to lower the costs agreement was reached to adopt a procedure in which death was no longer something that concerned the 'national community' but rather the costs were increasingly privatized, at least in cases where the dead were to be given a special, individual memorial in the form of a gravestone.[36] The problems of reimbursement lay in the detail, and it rapidly became clear that solidarity within the national community and local authority budgeting priorities did not necessarily coincide. After the first raids on Kiel, for example, the city had taken responsibility for paying death benefit for those who had died as a result of the delayed consequences of air raids. The family support office, which was in charge of processing death benefit, became increasingly doubtful, however, about whether this form of compensation was valid. As a result they were considering whether payments should be made only where the victim's death had been 'directly brought about by the enemy'.[37]

Many other cities, in particular in the east and south of the Reich, had not yet given any serious thought to such matters, as the number of victims at that point had not exceeded expectations. The graves of victims of the air war—at least this was the thinking at this time in Stuttgart, Berlin, and other cities—should be located near the 'field of honour for the fallen'. The costs of the few fatalities up to that point were borne by the city, which was also responsible for the planning of any monuments, though decisions about these would not be made until after the war.[38] The funeral offices were in many cases still very uncertain about how to proceed for the best. They therefore shared ideas and useful local experience in dealing with air-war fatalities, which was coordinated by the Local Government Association. For most local authorities seemed conscious of one thing: what had been planned so far would not be adequate for what was to come.[39]

The municipal cemetery administrations were among the first to revise their provisions, for they were obliged to be on the spot immediately in any emergency and had to see to it that bodies were buried as quickly as possible and continued to be buried as long as was viable in individual graves rather than in a soulless mass grave. In view of this they extended their grounds, got ready for an increased number of dead, and made space in the 'groves of honour', where the dead of the First World War were buried. At first it was regarded as unrealistic to claim that graveyards needed something like a new design and layout. Graves could be set out in rows, but the norm still seemed to be burial in the traditional family grave. The authorities did make ready to keep an adequate number of coffins in reserve; these were produced after discussion with local coffin retail cooperatives and were an important indicator of the kind of damage that was expected. In Duisburg, which by July 1942 had already suffered a number of heavy raids, the city's craftsmen were working on the assumption that 210 coffins for adults and 74 for children were sufficient to ensure the smooth burial of bombing victims, even if casualties were to be quite heavy.[40] One year later projections in Duisburg as in other cities of the Ruhr had been thrown to the winds and the demand for coffins had risen dramatically. The hope was that at least 800 coffins could be produced by the firm responsible if it came to the crunch. Some were already in secure storage, others would be made in the near future. In addition, efforts were being made to get assistance from other cities and so contacts had been established with outside firms.[41] Local government officials considered up to 1,000 dead as entirely realistic at this point. Particular attention was paid to the quality of the coffins. They were to be made of wood of reasonable quality, though their fittings were an important factor in keeping possible criticism of state subsidy in check.

From the beginning of 1943 onwards there was hardly a major city in which the production of coffins kept up with the increased demands, and as a result the authorities revised their estimates upwards almost on a monthly basis. The 'dignified' burial of the dead was the highest priority for the local authorities, for in addition to considering the risk of disease, particularly in the summer months and in hot weather, it was important to honour not only the living but also the dead as essential contributors to the 'national community'.[42] The Berlin War Damages Office bemoaned the fact in April 1944 that mutilated corpses were repeatedly to be found lying for days hardly covered. This was dangerous not only for reasons of hygiene but had a 'repellent and injurious' effect on the living.[43] For the local authorities the message was to retain the traditional rituals of burial for as long as possible, to take the wishes of individuals into account, and above all to avoid using mass graves. In spite of the larger scale of the damage, this was a policy not very different from that of Britain.

For example, the city administration of Duisburg was outraged by a request for information circulated by the Munich funerals office about how the western and northern parts of the Reich were organizing the recovery and burial of bombing victims.[44] In Munich efforts had been made for a considerable time to adjust to the altered air-war situation. People there wanted to know if there had been burials in which the corpses had had to be buried without coffins, indeed without any kind of shroud. In the light of Munich's initial experiences and reports that had come in from other regions this was altogether conceivable and a problem that people intended to be prepared for. In Duisburg, however, the very question seemed an insult to the efficiency of the 'national community'. At the end of July 1943 a member of the Duisburg city council replied that up to that point there had been no mass burials. The victims of bombing had been buried in the proper manner and as the relatives had wished. That was also, in his view, an answer to the question about shrouds: in Duisburg, at any rate, the authorities had been ready for anything and that meant that there had been enough coffins and enough space in the graveyards. Apart from anything else, the circulation of such questions, the councillor added, was 'hardly pleasant' and left 'a bad impression', in particular when they came from the 'capital of the [Nazi] movement'.[45] The Munich funerals office had doubtless touched a nerve, for it was being open about what the Reich might have to face in the future, and in some places this was no longer far removed from their everyday experience of clearing up after air raids.

Düsseldorf was only one of many examples of this.[46] At the beginning of June 1943, according to the estimates of the authorities, a good 1,200 people had been killed in air raids. The local emergency teams were overwhelmed by the scale of the transports of corpses, which within a short time were twice what had been anticipated. Emergency plans were ineffectual. The cemetery buildings were quickly full to overflowing, so that even the space for garaging vehicles belonging to the cemetery administration was required to accommodate all the dead.[47] In spite of this, the available capacity was rapidly exhausted and it was the sheer mass of bodies that made an ordered identification process virtually impossible—and thus made the mass of fatalities visible to anyone and hence a threat to the regime.[48] The dead first had to be brought into the open and identified there because there was no space anywhere else. Yet even outside it was almost impossible to organize burials effectively. In many cases information about the dead was missing, where their bodies had been recovered or objects belonging to them. Names were illegible or obviously false and so identities were hard to reconstruct.

Special criminal police identification units were working under pressure.[49] Often they had no more than a scrap of clothing or a ring as a clue and in the worst cases not even that.[50] The identification of the dead was an important part of the 'internal battle' on the home front. Without names the dead were of no value to the 'national community', because access to them and their past as victims of bombing was lost. For that reason the Party placed its own announcements in newspapers, parallel to the death notices placed by families, describing the dead as the victims of 'British bombing raids', 'terrorist violence', and 'murderous attacks' and attempting thereby to absorb individual tragedies into the solidarity of the national community. Only in cases where a collective notice for the 'fallen' was published was it permitted (and this not until 1942, after some hesitation in the early stages of the air war) to use the 'Iron Cross' for civilians killed in bombing raids.[51] This was not permitted in private death notices.

These collective notices were noteworthy because both men and women were mentioned. Thus dying a 'hero's death' was no longer reserved exclusively for men but could apply to women too—and in view of the Nazi cult of the heroic this was a remarkable transformation. Moreover, from 1943 onwards being designated as 'fallen' was no longer a male prerogative,[52] after there had been complaints from the population about how inexplicable it was to 'female national comrades' that symbolic distinctions were to be made between male and female dead. In the end it made no sense, people said, that a man 'should have the Iron Cross conferred on him in the newspaper notice, whereas his wife as victim of the same bomb received no honour'.[53]

This was of course possible only where the dead had a name at all and were not missing for weeks or so mutilated that their identity could no longer be established beyond doubt. Families searching for the remains of their relatives were therefore a heart-rending sign of the hollowness of propaganda and the vulnerability of the 'wartime community', if the enemy was capable of erasing the identity of victims. Anonymous mass graves were the cruel backdrop against which the Nazi liturgy of death, with its rhetoric of survival and standing the test, was enacted. Unless there was certainty about the loss it was impossible to mourn. It was therefore not surprising that, as after the heavy raid on Kassel in the autumn of 1943, the burial of the unidentified dead was delayed as long as could be justified. Thus 'respect', in the view of the authorities, was forced to take second place to the demand for identification.[54] The regime was thus compelled on the one hand to take seriously the concern of survivors about the identification of their relatives, but on the other hand it was prepared to subordinate individual needs to the requirements of the 'national body'. As the employees at the Kassel cemetery administration surmised, the warning about the danger of infectious diseases and the instruction to bury people without prior identification were possibly more the product of anxiety about the erosion of morale than of genuine public health considerations.[55]

Thus the ink was hardly dry on many emergency rescue plans when, after the start of area bombing from spring 1942, they were overtaken by the reality of the air war. In Munich, for example, which at this stage had got off relatively lightly, the report produced by the funerals office in October 1942 excoriated practices surrounding the recovery of bodies, the chief of police being responsible for the administrative framework within which they operated. After the last raid, now some weeks back, there had been numerous problems. In the case of a good number of bodies the cause of death could not be established because the accompanying cards from the doctors were missing and there had been neither the time nor the staff to examine the corpses. The director of the funerals office feared that because of this people who were unconscious might be pronounced dead, placed in coffins, and taken away.

There were a number of instances where various Party and police agencies had seen themselves simultaneously as responsible and had requisitioned vehicles to remove the bodies.[56] This was a problem that grew more acute as the air war intensified, until finally in the middle of 1944 the funerals office and the police accused each other of incompetence and of failure in recovering and housing air-raid fatalities, blaming each other for the fiasco resulting from their inability to cope with the crisis and for a lack of foresight in acquiring sufficient coffins or adequate transport for the bodies. Not only organizational failures were highlighted but also whether the bodies had been transported to cemeteries in a 'respectful manner' or like 'animals for slaughter'.[57] In this Munich was not an isolated case.[58] At the beginning of August 1943 the Oberbürgermeisters in the Düsseldorf area complained 'that when they have been recovered from the rubble the fallen are left lying in the street, because the police and the city administration cannot agree on who is responsible for their removal'.[59]

In order to clarify responsibilities once and for all the Reichsführer-SS and the Reich Ministry of the Interior issued a ruling in June 1944 that provided for the recovery and housing of the 'fallen' to be the task of the police or the air defence police and for the transportation of the dead from collection points to the cemeteries to be the responsibility of the local authority.[60] Admittedly, that was not much different from what had been agreed already,[61] nor was the instruction new that the operation as a whole should be directed by the air defence police.[62] Since in an extreme emergency it was impossible to abide by a strict division of responsibilities, all those involved should cooperate in a 'considerate' manner. In the final analysis that was an admission that everything should remain as it was and the local decision-makers should be left to their own power struggles. The latter promptly led to complaints that the police, ignoring their proper duty, were also putting the burden of the 'dirty work' of recovering bodies on to the funeral offices and thus making the whole process more difficult.[63]

Inefficiencies as a result of friction were thus the order of the day and were exacerbated by the lack of staff at the funeral offices. Although they had enough coffins in reserve they did not have enough staff with experience of coping with the 'very particular, unpleasant and psychologically stressful work' of recovering bodies.[64] Funeral offices and graveyard administrations therefore requested forced labour at an early stage to make up for this staff-ing shortage, equipping them with schnapps and cigarettes before setting them the task of recovering bodies. After the heavy raid at the end of July 1943 the chief of the Hamburg police had requested 450 concentration camp prisoners because the air defence police had objected to being made to work among the piles of corpses.[65]

The police authorities proceeded with extreme brutality in forcing pris-oners to work in the 'dead zones' of Hamburg. A number were shot—as a 'deterrent', as it was put—for refusing to pull the dead of Hamburg from the rubble in the searing heat with little equipment.[66] 'Dead zones' were the areas of the city that had been particularly devastated and where the massive fires had raged. Prisoners from the SS Construction Brigade II scrabbled through the ruins in these cordoned-off 'dead zones'. Dressed only in their prisoners' uniforms, without masks or gloves they worked their way through the mountains of burnt out cellars and walls, searching for body parts, which they pulled out of buildings that were still hot, col-lecting them in washtubs and finally piling them up in schoolyards and preparing them for removal. Almost six months after the raid the 57 recov-ery units were still at work. Up to 80 prisoners were working immediately after the raid at the Hamburg-Ohlsdorf cemetery alone. Their task was exclusively transporting the corpses or digging mass graves and burying the many thousands of dead and this took months.

Forced workers and convicts were in fact a 'scarce commodity'. Thus there were disputes over the extent to which they could, for example, be used to recover bodies. In Munich and other cities the SS commanders refused to make prisoners available because they were needed in the muni-tions industry and were indispensable. Funeral offices and local authorities made great efforts to recruit new workers who could be forced to do this highly unpleasant work. Whether British prisoners of war could be used was an open question. The Oberbürgermeister of Munich, Karl Fiehler, had presented such a proposal in August 1944 but immediate reservations were voiced about whether using prisoners of war for this type of work was in fact covered by the Geneva Convention, or whether this was even still valid and so the Reich could use them at will.[67]

The raids on Hamburg had been a powerful shock. It was the sheer num-bers of dead that turned the city, which up to then had had 'only' 1,400 fatalities, into a charnel house. Other local authorities anxiously took note of Hamburg's experiences and took pains to learn from the collapse of the local infrastructure and to adapt their own organizations to the threat of area bombing of dimensions unknown up to that point, whereas conversely the Hamburg city administration, Kehrl the police chief, and Kaufmann the Gauleiter projected an image of being experts at coping with catastrophe and neglected no opportunity of giving information to other cities in order to emphasize not only the fate they had suffered but also their own towering achievements.

The air war forced the local authorities constantly to engage afresh in a process of learning and adaptation, an element of which was a system of observation that was continually being renewed. They had to examine themselves and check the existing arrangements for recovering bodies but they also had to look outwards, at the cities in the west and north in particular, which were the first to be forced to cope with mass death and whose experiences people in other regions wanted to learn from. What happened, for example, if during air raids such as those on Düsseldorf or Duisburg whole funeral complexes were hit? Where were resources to come from if the collection points for bodies had reached full capacity? How could people be identified and the dead distributed quickly to the various cemeteries? And what had the procedure to be after 'fire storms', if an immense number of people had been killed and even recovering the bodies was extremely dangerous for the air defence teams?

In Stuttgart the reports from Hamburg radically changed the terms in which the consequences of air raids were discussed and did so within days, as at this early stage many regions of Germany were assuming that the raid had left between 100,000 and 150,000 dead. Now there was no longer talk of only a few hundred coffins but of space being needed for mass graves in the main cemetery. These were intended to accommodate so many people that after a raid the dead could be buried without coffins in three layers if necessary. At the city cemeteries office 50,000 bodies was now the number being mentioned for which the necessary provisions were to be made.[68] The local authority officials were evidently so deeply shocked that they deviated from the line they had previously taken and considered mass graves as well as rows of graves to be necessary; the pits for them in the cemetery could also be used in an emergency for cremations.[69]

In less than two weeks further news of the consequences of the Hamburg raid spread via the German Local Government Association or through direct exchanges between the authorities, giving those cities not yet affected by 'fire storms' an inkling of the immense destructive force of Allied bombing.

This impacted on very different spheres, for up to then most local authorities had been more or less successful in dealing with the effects of the raids and burying the dead quickly with no significant problems. The raids on Hamburg and a little later on Kassel were something hitherto unknown, as many experts were quick to comment. A new problem arose, for example, when bodies found dead in shelters had been exposed to temperatures of over 70 degrees centigrade over a long period and were now mummified. For this kind of work rubber gloves and work clothing were adequate, as reported by the Hamburgers. More dangerous for the recovery units, however, were often the bodies lying in the street and beginning to decompose, for they could burst open after recovery and release fluids. For this kind of work, in addition to rum and brandy, people urgently needed anti-gas protective clothing, and after the Hamburg experiences it was particularly necessary in the summer months to protect the recovery teams against insect bites to reduce the danger of infectious diseases.[70] This, however, involved taking precautions that as a rule applied to the Security and Rescue Service and employees of the cemeteries offices but not to prisoners. With the increasing intensity of the air war from 1943/4 onwards the authorities, no matter how well prepared, and even though they tried to recognize their staff's efforts by means of awards,[71] were more and more often overwhelmed by the task of recovering bodies. Bodies could no longer be given name tags; personal items belonging to the dead were lost and thus it became virtually impossible to identify mutilated corpses and restore them to their families. Body parts were left lying in hallways and were simply forgotten, while relatives had to keep scurrying from one authority to another if they were finally to get information about the whereabouts of their close family.[72] All in all, it was, in other words, a catastrophic situation and the British authorities could have had no idea how serious it was.

Death and Mourning

For both British and German local administrations the physical integrity of the dead was one of the most pressing concerns. In the first instance it was a matter of coping with death itself. People had burnt to death, been suffocated by dust, crushed by beams and buried under rubble, or killed by the force of the explosions. The medical diagnoses noted ruptured lungs, severe shock, damage to intestines. Many, above all after major bombing raids such as in Hamburg, had been killed in cellars or in the streets by the heat of the fire, though fewer died from lack of oxygen.[73]

It was the sheer quantity of bodies that made it difficult if not impossible to look for the dead without coming to public notice. The columns of prisoners' work details, whose task it was to do the searching, were from 1942 onwards part of the street scene in German cities. They were an invariable sign that there were not enough home-grown workers to clear away the after-effects of the raids. It was therefore all the more important for families, after searching often for days and waiting in anguish for a sign of life, to be able to bury their dead relatives with dignity and as quickly as possible. It was already unsatisfactory if, as a result of poor communication between authorities, members of the same family were taken to different cemeteries and their relatives then had to chase from one office to another to find out if their spouse or children were still missing, had been rescued, or were lying dead in a mortuary on the other side of the city.

From the point of view of local authority officials, losing track of information about people's whereabouts could significantly impair the city's efficiency in dealing with the crisis and damage citizens' confidence in it; it was therefore, in the opinion of a Düsseldorf expert, to be avoided at all costs.[74] Funerals themselves were a particularly sensitive issue, for it was important to many families that the funeral was not organized by any old funeral director but rather that they took care of things and chose a firm they trusted. In particular in regions with a very marked denominational identity there were strong reservations about memorial services staged by the city and the Party. Thus, for example, in the summer of 1940 plans for a lying in state and burial of victims of the air war to be jointly organized by the district Nazi Party leadership and the city administration came to nothing as a result of the 'special wishes' and reluctance of the relatives.[75]

Up to the end of the war there were reports of similar conflicts, such as in the small Catholic town of Stadtlohn in the diocese of Münster, which was finally bombed on 11 March 1945, leaving 142 dead. There the Nazi Party district leadership had intended once more to exploit the funeral service to inspire the town to stand firm to the last and to promote 'confidence'. The response of the mourners was undisguised resentment, which was finally expressed through audible prayers, thereby enabling the relatives and members of the congregation to save their funeral rites from being turned into a Nazi quasi-religious event.[76] Even though it is difficult to be sure how typical such cases were,[77] at the end of the war in particular the erosion of the cohesive force exerted by the national community was clearly visible, and it was evident that neither the local authority nor the Party could simply ignore people's wishes and rituals without arousing serious discontent. In addition to this, people wanted to restrict funeral services to close family members and to decide themselves where in the cemetery their relatives were to be buried, in the 'graveyard of honour' and the 'field of honour' specially created for bombing victims or, as a 'not inconsiderable number' of relatives demanded, in their own family graves.[78]

That was a wish that had been difficult to fulfil from the middle of 1943 onwards; after Operation Gomorrah it had been impossible in Hamburg. Thus many relatives looked for a way of making up for the absence of a grave that would have allowed them to take leave of family members whose lives had been cut off overnight and to come to terms with their grief gradually by means of their own rituals and symbols. Immediately after the mass burials many Hamburgers therefore made the pilgrimage to the cemetery in Ohlsdorf, bringing photos of their dead relatives, leaving flowers, lighting candles, and trying to give the dead an individual face—something that caused the authorities considerable unease.[79] In Würzburg, for example, there was much dispute over whether the authorities were allowing private citizens to bury their relatives in individual graves after the severe bombing of 16 March 1945. It was allowed on condition that they dug the graves themselves, placed the dead in them, and covered them again. While families insisted on their right to decide on the form the funeral was to take, the authorities, mindful of the need for rapid burial and the threat of disease, imposed restrictions.[80]

Often the shock experienced by survivors was etched into their faces. As they gazed at the devastated city they were seeing not only burning buildings. While the fires were raging many people had seen others burnt to death and after the raids had watched the coffins being brought through the town and the remains of their relatives collected. Mass death was visible, upsetting, an experience that people mostly tried to grasp using terms such as 'horror' and 'terror'.[81] Things were particularly bad in Pforzheim, where people were not dug out but rather incinerated with flamethrowers because in the meantime the stench had become unbearable.[82]

There was scope for speaking about the immediate experience of death in the Nazi-controlled public sphere only if individual suffering could be given 'meaning' by being integrated into the story of the 'national community's' survival and thereby acquiring a broader significance. In private jottings made immediately after the raids people employed a variety of narrative strategies to integrate the experience of death into their personal biography. As well as expressing pain at the destruction of the city and the foundations of their own existence they also conveyed the positive sense of having survived, in spite of all the horror. Thus the raids had 'meaning' only if one was a survivor.

Immediately after the raid on Kassel a poem entitled 'Thus my home town of Kassel died' was circulating. It was an attempt to give distinctive formal expression in language to the night of the air raid.[83] These were the opening lines:

> In sorrow Chasalla* wears mourning dress
> Her walls contain unspeakable sorrow.
> All that the human mind has invented,
> That hardworking hands once created,
> That began a thousand years ago,
> Was destroyed in a single night.

The poem spoke of a double death. The lament for the city, the 'destruction' of the homeland, was an established part of the cultural canon and harked back to the Old Testament lament of Jeremiah at the destruction of Jerusalem and rupture of historical continuity.[84] At the same time the deaths were immediate and caused suffering: 'Thousands knew great suffering. | Thousands were killed by the flames. | Thousands for whom there was no escape | Were laid to rest for ever beneath the rubble.'[85] Though the poem mentioned 'war crimes' and many private letters alluded to 'terror attacks', the strident rhetoric of Nazi propaganda was very rarely dominant.

That was true even in cases where the Nazis, as they did in Kassel, conducted interviews during the war with victims of bombing in order to gather documentation concerning the 'Allied terror' for the post-war period and where the interviewees must have been aware of the expectations attached to the discussion. People gave accounts of solidarity and effective action to cope with crises. They demonstrated something else too, however, namely that their experience of a hitherto unimaginable destructive force demanded a safety valve, so that amid the silence and the 'ban on mourning' they were permitted to lament as individuals and thus find some consolation for the loss of family and property. Many listed in their letters what the

---

* Translators' note: The original form of the name Kassel.

air war had robbed them of: trunks and linen, clothing and documents, the inventory of their business, coats, and briefcases with old letters. Mothers wrote to tell their sons at the front what had happened to the house, what was destroyed, and what could be saved. By contrast with the 'proud mourning' imposed by the Nazi funeral liturgy and which, as Victor Klemperer observed,[86] was repeated in the death notices in the newspapers, there were sudden eruptions of emotion, such as when someone admitted, 'I can't think clearly any more, it's so awful. It was as though I had died when I came away from the ruins.'[87]

Such a comment, made after the raid on Darmstadt, was by no means rare, not was it unusual for the letter-writer to try to reassure the recipient that she and her family had survived all the same and that her son at the front should not worry about them on top of everything else. For many people one of the main difficulties was to grasp mentally what had happened and find words in which to speak about it that got away from the metaphors the Nazis used for the air war. One possibility was for people to invoke the power of fate and to interpret their own survival as a 'miracle from God'. If family or the writer had survived it must have been through divine intercession.[88]

Yet survival could also be a burden, as one woman reported in March 1944 about the raid on Kassel:

All the others were killed, including my husband. I didn't want to hear anything about it. I was the only person saved as if by a miracle. It was because a voice inside me said: 'Bend down, bend down, bend down' and I vomited twice. That was my good luck. But my husband and relations are all dead [...]. I didn't want to know or believe any of it.[89]

To have survived did not therefore bring only a sense of happiness but possibly a sense of guilt for not having been killed like the others. And another issue was bound up with the sense of guilt, namely how much others could be expected to bear in hearing about the horror. What the individual could articulate and how far he or she was capable of finding words to express the images of destruction was not therefore the only important thing. Some experiences were so terrible that they could not only not be spoken about but others should be spared this experience too and not be made to share in these images of death.

The tensions between private mourning and the national community's cult of the dead could lead to serious conflicts. In July 1944 in Munich families of victims of bombing complained vociferously to the funerals office because their dead spouses and siblings had been carted off before their interment from the mortuaries in the city cemeteries through half the city in order to boost a Nazi burial ritual being performed at a cemetery on the other side of the city.[90] This procedure not only increased the risk of infections but the relatives complained that it disturbed the peace of the dead, quite apart from the fact that the hearses presented the city with a frightening image of its own vulnerability.

The Nazis' insistence on controlling the rituals of death allowed little room for public displays of individual mourning. They put much time and effort into collectivizing the experience of death and reinterpreting individual pain as an expression of the spirit of self-sacrifice on the part of the national community. This reached a stage where, for example in Hamburg-Ohlsdorf, the local authority employees were urged to remove private tokens of mourning such as letters, crosses, or flowers, and to replace them with monumental wooden panels. 'Mourning' thus conceived was not only a proud activity but also a silent one. The important thing was to 'maintain composure', to show no emotion, still less to weep, at the graveside. Pain and personal loss were to be 'overcome'. Sacrifices had a purpose if they resulted in the living being toughened up and given strength to fight on. Outpourings of emotion were inappropriate and regarded as manifestations of 'womanly' weakness.

Understood in this way, death was part of a selection process in which the individual submitted to the laws of transience and death acquired meaning above all as the individual sacrificing himself for the survival of the 'national community'. 'Standing the test—Community—Reconstruction': this Nazi triad summing up the home front allowed no room for the fate of the individual. There was comfort only for those who were convinced that death was part of a new *völkisch* order; the need for it to survive prescribed the rhythm of life—and of death.

Death and mourning in Britain

Unlike in the First World War, the propaganda of the Second World War and the potent idea of the People's War did not lead to any comparable collectivization of dying. The battles of the First World War had left behind a vacuum of ritual mourning only inadequately filled by state-orchestrated remembrance, solemn large-scale ceremonies, and strident nationalist confidence in victory. There was no convincing language that would give them meaning. Whereas the fatal effects of the air war had confronted British and German administrations with similar problems, all of which related to the core issues of the relationship between the state and the individual, between legitimacy and confidence, wartime morale and public health, and to some extent produced very similar administrative instruments for coping with crisis, socially agreed norms regarding the acceptability of mourning and its public acknowledgement diverged considerably. Discreetly was how both societies were supposed to mourn and even in Britain the authorities attempted to curtail the amount of scope individuals had to mourn as they wished. Dictatorship and democracy equally confronted the problem of how far the state's prerogative to control the sensitive area of honouring the dead, burdened as it was with religious significance, could be restricted and regulated.

Yet 'quiet mourning' did not necessarily mean the same thing in Britain and Germany. One of the ways this could be seen was in how the popular mass media dealt with the topic of death and tried to create a new aesthetic, iconography, and language of death all of their own. One of the best-known examples was Richard Hillary's autobiographical novel *The Last Enemy*.[91] Hillary had fought as a spitfire pilot in the Battle of Britain in 1940, was shot down, and severely wounded. Though he survived, he was at first unable to continue flying. His narrative, which quickly became one of the most famous and frequently bought books of the war period, arose when he was on a tour of the USA for the Ministry of Information to recruit young pilots. *The Last Enemy* told of a pilot for whom the war initially was above all a personal adventure and individual quest for meaning.[92] His decision to join the RAF was in no way an act of heroism to defend the civilized world. Flying was what mattered to him, along with the emotional 'kick' he got from combat and the risk of death, which as a pilot he confronted on a daily basis. Hillary did not believe there was a religious, Christian meaning to the struggle.

He described the deaths of his friends, killed in air battles, in an equally sympathetic but unsentimental manner. It was not until he himself was wounded and had to undergo painful operations that a process of inner transformation began, at the end of which he was prepared to leave egoism behind and to submit to the external demands of modern warfare. Now he understood what his friends had died for: humanity and civilization. This way of interpreting the war was particularly persuasive in the case of those who had been committed to pacifism after the First World War.[93]

Hillary's own death a year after his US trip during an exercise in preparation for his return as a fighter pilot lent his memoirs an additional spiritual
dimension that significantly boosted the book's success, for this after all was
someone who, disenchanted with individualism, had died after committing
himself totally to the war. *The Last Enemy* marked so to speak the interface
of individual and collective narratives about the meaning of war, death, and
the necessity of violence. To bear pain and deny oneself was thus the fulfilment of a higher political purpose. And the scars visible on his face after he
had been shot down were evidence of the price exacted by war.

Beyond war and death, according to Hillary, was a new British nation,[94]
a harmonious blend of the ruling elites and the rest of the population. Pilots
like Hillary were the embodiment of this new, ambivalent type of person,
who had placed himself in the service of the state and yet retained his individuality. As such they were not unlike the modern heroic Nazi pilots.[95]

Yet even though the book had many aspects that chimed in with British
wartime propaganda and in its final section, which extolled national values
over an exaggerated individualism, demonstrated clear similarities to the
völkisch cult of heroes and airmen of the war period, contemporary reception
of the book was by no means unequivocal and it was precisely that that distinguished the British and the Nazi ways of dealing with death. Immediately
after the book's publication, for example, Arthur Koestler spoke out against
surrounding heroic death with an unproblematic mystique.[96] For him Hillary
was less a victim of war than someone who had attempted to keep on fighting, at times by desperate means, and so was finally killed not by Hitler's
soldiers but by his own actions. It was above all the external expectations he
struggled with and less the search for himself, as he deceived himself it was,
that in Koestler's view constituted his life and in the end the mythic quality
of his death. Characters such as Hillary, he believed, were helpless victims of
the violence of war and the mythicization of death. That too was one price
of war and reason enough to remain sceptical in the face of pretensions to
heroism. Precisely in this matter it was evident that public responses and
propaganda diverged considerably. In the public sphere there was most certainly still scope—in a way similar to the controversies that had raged since
the inter-war years—to criticize the heroicization of pain and death and to
make clear the ambivalences and dangers of exploiting them for 'higher'
ends. This had nothing to do with sympathy for National Socialism but
much to do with a basic scepticism in the face of exaggerated nationalist
rhetoric, about which the Left in particular had considerable reservations.

Just how ambivalent was the attitude to death and pain, damaged men, and physical infirmities among the heroes of the RAF during the war, was something Hillary experienced personally during his tour of the USA.[97] Although he was permitted to talk about the Battle of Britain, contrary to the original plans he was not given the task of recruiting young pilots. The Ministry of Information feared that young men eager to fly and their parents might be put off by Hillary's scarred face rather than encouraged to opt for a career in the Air Force.[98] Disfigured bodies were not meant to be displayed in public.

It was the same with 'quiet mourning', which, by contrast with the risk of death that went with the air war, was the province of women. *Millions like us*, along with *The Gentle Sex*, was one of the greatest war propaganda films and central to it was the role of women on the home front.[99] It focused on a group of young women called up to work in a factory. Their service in the munitions industry was their contribution to the nation's victory and was no less valuable than the military service performed by their soldier husbands. *Millions like us* tells the story of female war mobilization and social change in a digestible way, though without entirely excluding death and loss. One of the women loses her husband, a pilot shot down over Germany, only a short time after the wedding. She is mourning, feels alone, and misses her relatives and so does not feel like letting her hair down and singing like the other factory women after the lunch break. Yet through the solidarity and optimism of her new fellow workers she eventually succeeds in forgetting her own grief and joins in the gaiety of those around her. In the end she has become part of the new war community, which helps people forget private loss and individual pain.

The 'People's War' was thus also a response to the loss of meaning that many had felt in relation to death after the First World War and which was exacerbated by the decline of belief in Christian eschatology.[100] The British air-war strategy had been based on a dual assumption: on the one hand, it was believed, German air raids strengthened British morale, but, on the other, Allied raids on the German Reich undermined morale in the population there. This illogical argument required that death and losses on the British side had to be made, as it were, invisible or, as in the case of mourning, at least 'silent' and 'subdued'.

The Way to the Stars, which was made in the last weeks of the war, was the story of RAF pilots and their families, their worries and tribulations. For the bomber crews death was ever present and yet their attitude to it was, to outward appearances, serene, often laconic. 'The less said the better'—words written in one of the poems that a pilot gives his fiancée to remind her that death might soon overtake him too. Again we find a tendency not to waste words, to be quiet. The film ends with a plane crash, the pilot sacrificing his life in order to avoid coming down in a village with a group of children. Here too the messages are ambiguous, as is the role of the church, which has difficulty in giving death a religious meaning and touching the hearts of those affected. What we are left with, regardless of all ambivalence and debates about the morality of war, is the knowledge that in spite of all the sacrifices the battle against Nazism has been worth it, both at the front and on the home front. That, one might say, is the only meaning, though one that individuals have to find for themselves and which is not really imparted by communal rituals of mourning.

The relationship between the individual and the state, between death and mourning, was not, however, purely a media or propaganda issue but one that raised numerous problems after each new air raid. As in the case of evacuations, this was true, for example, of denominational conflicts in cemeteries. After a heavy raid, was it permissible for Protestants, Catholics, and members of free churches to be buried together in mass graves? This was a dilemma that caused considerable uncertainty in London and elsewhere.[101] Cemeteries designated areas for different denominations, consecrated areas and non-consecrated ones. People's religious identity was thus expressed through spatial separation and the iconography relating to various types of memorial.

In Coventry an attempt had been made to solve this problem by creating special non-consecrated areas for the victims of air raids that would be available to all Christian denominations, to other faiths, and to the growing number of people with no faith. Denominational tensions, familiar from the beginning of the century, when the Burial Act of 1880 prevented Catholics, for example, from being buried in Anglican soil, were to be avoided at all costs in view of the external threat.[102]

Burials following smaller air raids (Coventry had already experienced a number before 14/15 November 1940 and several followed in 1941 and 1942) were clearly structured on confessional lines and according to arrangements agreed before the war: Catholic and Anglican dead were buried together in the 'war cemetery', though each had their distinct areas where the service and interment took place.[103] It was agreed that the Catholic funeral would be held first, followed by the Anglican one, but while the ceremonies were separate there was an unwritten law that the Catholic mourners would attend the Anglican burial.

Ecumenical funerals were avoided as far as possible, though this did not apply to mass burials. For in such a case not only was the religious affiliation of the dead sometimes unclear, but simply for reasons of public order hundreds of dead had to be buried together, as on 23 November 1940. There had been no clear plans for such an eventuality, but on the basis of the established practice of earlier burials both churches agreed to bless their dead in a common ceremony. Thus the two communities stood side by side at the start on a platform above the burial site. Yet ecumenism had its limits, for at the planning stage the Catholic priest had pressed to be allowed to stand alone on the platform when the dead were blessed and address his Catholic flock. The Anglican clergyman therefore accommodated this by going to the end of the platform to begin his service in conjunction with the nonconformist churches after the brief Catholic one. This very limited form of cooperation was the result of the acute threat. Both churches would have preferred to go on conducting funerals in separate spaces with separate liturgies and in a private context, but they were compelled to agree to large-scale wartime burials and had no choice.[104]

In spite of transport difficulties private funerals of victims of the air war were still allowed after the raid, though this applied only to those who wished to bury their dead relatives outside the city and were able to engage a funeral director from outside who would collect the deceased from the mortuary and remove him or her in a coffin. That involved significant financial outlay and logistical problems for the relatives, because all the Coventry funeral directors were engaged by the city.[105]

Whereas private funerals were the rule after less severe air raids, the example of Coventry had revealed all the problems connected with mass death in the air war. In view of the destruction and the high number of fatalities the city had decided to bury the majority of victims in two successive mass burials. This procedure angered the families, but they were not given any opportunity to say what kind of funeral they wanted.[106] The city's policy was not, however, focused exclusively on the pragmatic challenges of coping with the catastrophe. The issue of how much the population could be expected to accept before their support was lost and before this burial policy reminded people too much of paupers' funerals was central to the process of coping with the acute crisis and arose from public expectations of the sympathy and respect due to the dead. In London the responsible

Regional Officer for Civil Defence got into difficulties explaining why no official representative of the city administration had been present at the burial of several civil defence workers who had been killed in raids at the beginning of October 1940 and why there had been a delay in informing the families about the funeral.[107] Appealing to the fact that the administration was overstretched by the acute crisis did not, in the event, seem very convincing.[108]

Many decision-makers in the local authorities were, however, fully conscious of their special responsibility. For that reason the General Superintendent of Funeral Services in Coventry resisted moves, prompted by the huge number of victims of bombing and the logistical problems arising from them, to identify new ways of storing bodies. He rejected the proposal to establish temporary mortuaries at the cemeteries themselves, pointing out that that might give rise to rumours that the dead were being buried with indecent haste and without observation of the proper forms. That impression had to be avoided at all costs, as did relatives attending funerals being confronted with the sight of lorries carrying fresh corpses, and for that reason space should be found outside the boundaries of the cemeteries.[109]

Yet even though mourning was, so to speak, to be outsourced, the burials were still public demonstrations of sympathy attended by city dignitaries and leading churchmen. The cemetery was thus both a spatially separate area for private mourning, where the families, secluded from the gaze of outsiders, could stand at the graves of their relatives, lay flowers, and remember their dead in their individual ways, and at the same time part of the public sphere regulated by state control, where the relationship between personal grief and public displays of sympathy was ambivalent. No wonder, therefore, that the kind of public staging of air-war burials that had become usual was by no means universally welcomed.

After the heavy raids of April 1941, when a further 475 people in Coventry were killed, their families and members of the clergy were outraged by the large number of those attending the funeral who were unconnected with the victims. This, it was felt, was a distraction from the service and led to the relatives not having enough space and the burial being turned into a public spectacle.[110] Instead of this the relatives ought to be allowed to be on their own to a great extent and remember their family members in peace. For this reason tickets should in future be issued for the burial services so that access was regulated. This suggestion did not meet with much support, however, for, much as the mourners wanted quiet, it was also clear that the mass burials had to be public ceremonies, if only because a considerable number of the dead could not be identified and the relatives of those missing had as much right to public sympathy as all those who wished to mourn their own work colleagues, acquaintances, and friends.[111] In Manchester, for example, several hundred people stood at the graveside of the seventy-two victims of the air war who were buried at the end of December 1940 in the city's southern cemetery. In its report the *Manchester Guardian* commented with approval that, in addition to the relatives, the Civil Defence Service lined up to pay their last respects and that the funeral had not been disturbed by the inappropriate behaviour of any idle spectators.[112] Even though the dead had no individual graves or gravestones this public leave-taking was the penultimate act of mourning for the unknown victims, the ultimate one being to remember them, to tend their graves, and to erect war memorials.

Rituals of Death

The organization of mourning caused conflict in the city among relatives, the city council, health and funeral authorities, but from it arose an important impetus to establish a new, central regulator during wartime. The Coventry Emergency Repairs and Co-ordinating Committee was created by the mayor as a response to the failures of the first weeks and given extensive powers to deal with crises, so that problems similar to those arising during the first Blitz of mid-November 1940 would not have to be confronted again. From the beginning of 1941 onwards the working group got ready for the next serious raids, taking pains to learn from the mistakes of the past. In addition to the issue of public access and suitable rites of mourning, this involved trying to prepare in as much detail as possible for mass death, including the creation of even larger burial sites.[113]

The faster the raids spread and the more civilian victims cities had to bewail, the more vigorously the central authorities attempted to intervene in the everyday business of coping with crisis and to 'nationalize' private mourning. In November 1940 the Ministry of Health's directive was that only in exceptional cases should there be any deviation from the original plans to entrust private organizations in the main with the task of burying the dead.[114] With German raids on the increase and resources coming under pressure it changed its position on this, however. In March 1941 the authorities took the view that private burials were no longer advisable in situations where there was the threat of heavy raids or they had already caused extensive damage. Finally, in June 1942 the Ministry of Health instructed city councils in the north-east that, in view of recent German bombing, private burials would lead to 'labour difficulties' and were thus no longer practicable. The Baedeker Raids had thus accelerated a development in which private mourning was increasingly subordinated to the imperative of saving resources and funerals were increasingly 'nationalized'. As there were objections to this, however, the controversy about the financing and form of funerals was accompanied by an attempt to distribute the costs of the war in a new way, both semantically and symbolically. The reactions of cities that up to that point had not yet suffered heavy bombing were at first anything but enthusiastic. In Hull and York, for example, the intention was to stick as far as possible to private funerals for victims of bombing, in spite of the growing pressure.

In Whitehall this stance was viewed with scepticism, for in addition to the difficulties that could arise from inadequate preparation for large-scale raids it was above all money that was the bone of contention between central and local government and functioned as a lever with which to secure their respective interests. In view of the experiences of other cities the Ministry of Health was no longer prepared to take on the costs of digging graves that, as in Hull, were not suitable for mass burials and which were big enough for only a few coffins. Yet the authorities tried to dispel reservations about mass burials not only through financial pressure but also with financial inducements. In a circular to all city councils in August 1941 the Ministry pointed out how important it was for those responsible in the funerals offices to urge relatives to accept the form of burial made necessary by the war and above all to assure them of a dignified ritual.[115] And the National Council of Social Service, which had edited a handbook for local authorities on dealing with the aftermath of air raids, impressed on those responsible under no circumstances to fail to explain to those concerned that funerals provided free of charge by the city were in no way connected with burials of those dependent on city handouts. Everything was included—the coffin and pall bearers, the hearse, and other funeral costs.[116]

Added to the material bonus was the symbolic one designed to remove the social stigma from local authority burials. At public funerals the dead were therefore to be treated with 'proper reverence and respect'.[117] They were to be buried by a representative of the city council, in accordance with the Ministry's instructions, but the interment was to be carried out in a manner as dignified as was usual in the case of servicemen, and that meant that the Union Jack should be laid over the coffin. Admittedly, this rule could not be observed at the first mass funeral in Coventry as the city had not kept a large enough supply of flags, though it had sufficient coffins.[118]

This demonstration of the symbolic equality in rank of combatants and non-combatants was striking in a number of respects. The merging of front and home front found its most visible expression in the common flag that enveloped the dead bodies. At the same time differences in procedures for dealing with death in the military and civilian spheres had been eroded by the air raids. In the First World War the funerals of fallen soldiers had already been passed to the state, just as the funerals of paupers had in the nineteenth century.[119] In the case of paupers and soldiers killed in war the aim was to organize the funerals with as much speed, economy, and hygiene as was decent. A further factor came into play: it was impossible for grieving families to project their feelings onto a dead body lying in a mass grave either in a public cemetery or in a grave for an 'unknown soldier' on the First World War battlefields. The air war strengthened this tendency to level social differences in death and mourning, for now not only soldiers and paupers but also civilians from different social classes were buried in mass graves rather than in family burial plots, thus losing their genealogical identity.[120]

In Britain too the heroicization of death was an attempt to fill the void that existed for the mourning families with symbols, though in Britain the tone and ceremonial of these attempts were much more muted than in Germany. The first element in this process was the notification of the death, which was the Town Clerk's responsibility. His letter of condolence always had the same wording: 'The Minister of Health asks me to express the deep sympathy of His Majesty's Government with you in your loss.'[121] This terse letter made no mention of 'sacrifice' nor of 'the national good', for which the individual had given his life. It gave only the date of the burial. The burial, which was announced over loudspeakers and through posters, was designed as a whole to be a large-scale ritual embracing all classes and denominations in 'quiet mourning'. A prominent place was given to short addresses by senior local clergymen. In Liverpool David, the Anglican bishop, set the tone for the ceremony in May 1941, at which unnamed and unidentifiable fatalities of the air war were laid to rest: 'The enemy may break our bodies, but they will never break our spirit.'[122] He did not, however, attempt to give a comprehensive theological account of the meaning of suffering, death, and pain and confined himself to honouring the dead men, women, and children as the fallen in a battle against evil.

Surviving and being steadfast in spite of all life's imponderables—these were the principles that David commended to people. They were very similar to those commended by German churchmen and were indications of both nations' shared but at the same time limited fund of theological and political concepts. But unlike the majority of Catholic bishops in Germany their fellow Catholic, Archbishop Downey of Liverpool, found it much easier to portray the war against Hitler's Germany as a struggle for survival between good and evil. The situation seemed too plain and obvious to everyone for dispute. And thus, as Downey declared in few words, the living owed it to the dead to fight on until ultimate victory against Nazi Germany had been achieved.

Another important difference was evident in the structure of the ceremony itself. In Germany under the Third Reich state, Party and churches usually held separate memorial services. It was precisely the structure and sequence of memorial services that had repeatedly led to conflict, for from the perspective of the Nazis some sections of the church threatened their prerogative to control the meanings given to life and death. British funerals were in the main free from such suppressed and at times quite open conflicts, for church and state stood side by side in public and even the various religious denominations laid more emphasis on what they all had in common that went beyond death, rather than on denominational differences.

Not all worries were dispelled, for, after all, fear of mass dying, such as in the First World War, was still the key experience hovering in the background to the funerals, and in view of the omnipresent threat of apocalyptic scenarios the problem of how to give 'death from the skies' its own meaning, beyond grandiose phrases like the battle between good and evil, was far from being solved. In Liverpool the first large-scale funeral for victims of the air war had taken place as early as 6 December 1940. The burial was overshadowed by the shock of the heavy raid. No one in Liverpool had ever experienced such destructive force, nor such a death toll. It was therefore not surprising that the search for words of comfort was given more weight than strident exhortations to keep going. Bishop David therefore made a point first of all of reassuring relatives that the air war did not cause people to lose their lives in a particularly painful way[123] and telling them that they had departed this life quickly and had been received into God's kingdom.

This in no way made their deaths meaningless, for they all—children, women, and the elderly—had died on the battlefield and that made their deaths particularly honourable. There could be no distinctions between soldiers and civilians in this respect and certainly not as far as God's grace was concerned. There was consolation in the knowledge not only that the deceased had been received into God's kingdom but that their deaths had brought redemption and that they had played an active role in defending the nation. What for the most part was lacking, however, was the sacralization of death in which a direct link was made between dying on the battlefield at the front or on the home front and the Christian doctrine of sacrificial death.[124]

Although the Catholic Archbishop of Westminster, Cardinal Hinsley, was a prominent representative of a kind of Christian nationalism that glorified soldiers as courageous Christian knights,[125] on the whole the tone adopted by leading Anglican churchmen, particularly William Temple, was distinctly more restrained and they avoided any oversimplified identification of the nation's war and the Christian cause. The horrors of the First World War were still too deeply imprinted on many for that to happen. When in December 1940 260 fatalities from an air raid were buried in Sheffield, the official history of the Blitz, published before the end of the war, commented: 'These ceremonies had nothing of the "pauper burial" about them, so dreaded by many relatives. The provost arranged for clergy representing all denominations to be present, the Lord Mayor and representatives of the Civil Defence Service acted as mourners, and simple military honours ensured that the bereaved should have such consolation as may be derived from the dignity of death on active service.'[126]

In Hull, according to a report in the *Daily Mail* of a mass burial on 13 May 1941, the mourners held back their tears at the sight of the mounds of earth and went home in silence.[127] The *Times* reporter described how the families of thirty-one London children killed in an air raid at the end of 1943 hugged each other as they stood before their children's coffins and yet were composed.[128] The occasion was characterized above all by 'quiet mourning', which was also a response to what a Home Office civil servant had observed in November 1941, namely that the majority of those bereaved by the air war were unhappy that the deaths of their relatives had been linked to the war. More than anything they wanted to forget those circumstances, something that was 'understandable' in the light of what was often a horrible death. Beyond that, he said, everything pointed to the fact that the authorities' concern to honour the dead of the air war as heroes and to commemorate them like fallen soldiers aroused 'little enthusiasm' in those directly affected.[129]

This observation may well have applied also to the relatives of victims whose identities could not be established beyond doubt and for whom there could therefore be no private funeral services. Mass death, anonymity in death, and the loss of their relatives' physical bodies had led to a semiotic vacuum after the First World War[130] that the funerals for the total of some 60,000 dead from the air war could hardly fill. More than that: the funerals themselves were the expression of a search for meaning that veered between mobilizing people for war and 'quiet mourning' and had insufficient symbolic capital at its disposal to produce a relatively conclusive answer to the question of the meaning of death on the home front.

'Völkisch' rituals of death

For the Nazi regime the answer was at first very simple, for the burial rite for the dead of the air war was not in the first instance aimed at the relatives of those who had died. The dead remained objects within a staged performance, silent, anonymous witnesses, of whose fate as individuals the funeral took little note. What mattered were the duties of the living as members of the 'national community at war'. Death was supposed to bestow on national comrades a special dignity beyond class and status. Where supplies of textiles permitted, the wooden coffins were wrapped in swastika flags. The larger the number of dead, the more frequently the Nazi Party had to make do with plain coffins without flags. The Party was at the heart of the event.

In the run-up to each funeral the Nazi Party decided on the road that it and its organizations should march along en route to the cemetery. The Party dictated the order of the procession of mourners, chose the music, ordered the Hitler Youth to line the streets, sent out the invitations, and expressed sympathy to the relatives in the name of the Führer. It was also the Party that showed the representatives of the city administration and of the army and not least the mourners themselves to their seats for the ceremony. This organizational straitjacket left little space for the relatives because the venues were often cramped and so, once the majority of seats had been reserved for leading members of the Party, municipality, and army, there were seats left only for close family members.

The ritual of honouring the dead followed strict rules and was timed to the minute. First of all, employees from the funerals office and the Party decorated the 'grove of honour', where the dead were to be buried. At the same time a vantage point was chosen for the photographer who was to take photos for the newspaper, so that he had time to think about the best angle. A loudspeaker was set up so that those who had not been invited could hear the speeches by Party representatives. Finally, the burial site was cordoned off by the police and the Party detailed two men to keep order, while the army supplied four soldiers for the guard of honour. It was also the army's job to provide the pall bearers, all wearing helmets. At the same time the massed flag bearers of the SA and a column of infantry gathered, ready for the salute. Just before the commencement the guard of honour, standard bearers, and quite often the Hitler Youth and League of German Girls (BDM) took up their positions.[131]

When the funeral began the Party took over the direction of events. At the stroke of 12 a representative of the Gauleiter or the Gauleiter himself took his seat, which, chosen with photographers in mind, was immediately behind the bereaved relatives. Then there was a brief silence, until the ceremony began with the playing of the funeral march from Beethoven's piano sonata no. 12 in A flat major by the army band. After a short address—'words of commemoration'—from the Gauleiter or district Party leader the coffins were lowered into the 'grove of honour' to the strains of the presentation march and the 'Song of the Good Comrade'. A military salute and finally the national anthem and the 'Horst Wessel Song' and the ritual of mourning was already at an end. The podium guests and the massed standard bearers moved off, leaving a priest to bless the graves in the absence of the Party bigwigs.

Depending on the number of victims, the speakers took time to read out the individual names, while a rhythmic, muted drumbeat was maintained in the background. At the first big funerals of 1940/1 this was still the normal procedure, for those present knew who was being buried. In July 1941, when four victims of an air raid on Warnemünde were buried, the district Nazi Party leader, Otto Dettmann, took time to name the victims of a 'devilish British raid', two men, one woman, and a child, whose funeral took place a short way out of the town on Sedan Meadow.[132] The Party particularly emphasized the 'criminal' nature of the raid when children were among the victims. Although on such occasions there was mention of 'sacrifices' for the 'national community', in view of the families' distress words such as 'belonging' (to the national community) and 'sympathy' were used more frequently than usual.[133]

It was more difficult to adapt the ceremony at mass burials, when bodies had been impossible to identify and there had been no time to inform family members. Although as a rule families sat in the front row and local dignitaries sat with them, the addresses avoided any reference to individuals and the victims were not mentioned by name. Reports in the media were no different. Whenever newspapers reported the funerals they showed the sea of SA troops with flags lowered in a 'final salute'. Readers could see a large crowd but no individual mourners or at best the backs of their heads. What they could see were the Party bigwigs and the local Wehrmacht commanders, occasionally the pall bearers, friends of the families, or members of the Nazi Party's affiliated organizations, who accompanied the dead to the actual burial site in the cemetery.

The coffins draped with flags were merely props in the scenery for a *völkisch* death ritual rather than integral to a funeral involving loss and pain.[134] The addresses given by Party functionaries were similar; the 'Song of the Good Comrade' set the tone in musical terms for the transformation of the bombing victims into 'fallen' soldiers of the home front, who had died in battle. The front was now the homeland and here too people were fighting for the survival of the 'national community'. At the same time—and this was the paradox—the dead of the air war were civilians, 'innocent victims' of 'Anglo-American air terror tactics' and thus not in fact soldiers but blameless human beings who had been torn by chance from their working lives to be victims of ruthless murderers who did not flinch from killing children or destroying churches and thus devastated lives at will.

The dead in their coffins in the 'grove of honour' had the same rights to have their graves tended as Wehrmacht soldiers[135] and hence were both 'home front soldiers' and the civilian victims of Allied war crimes. This manner of presenting them had begun to be accepted from 1942 onwards and its duality was useful and flexible as a way of fitting the rising tally of victims into the story of the destruction and heroic survival of the German cities. It was not uncommon to hear the sentiment expressed by Haidn, the Oberbürgermeister of Düsseldorf, during a memorial service for members of the city administration, namely that 'his' city and region had lived up to Hitler's expectations and their 'toughness' had equalled that shown on the eastern front. Death in the air war, he said, thus appeared to be a form of purification and a test of endurance that compelled people to abandon their normal lives as civilians. The heavy damage suffered by the city was in the final analysis what the Führer had required—to take part in the battle, bid farewell to a cosy existence as a sign that everyone, and not only soldiers in uniform, was prepared to fight his/her own battle and defend his/her position, wherever that happened to be: in the office or the shelter, at home or at work, among the family or out in the fields.[136]

Life—or death—on the home front was thus no different from life or death at the front, apart from the fact that soldiers carried weapons they could use, whereas civilians were at the mercy of the aggressors' whim. For Haidn mourning was an act of quiet contemplation and commemoration and at the same time a commitment to put aside all war-weariness and play a part in the nation's defence with new and defiant energy. Otherwise, if those left behind gave up and the Allied murderers and their Jewish string-pullers achieved their goal, the dead would have died in vain. Thus the air war had become an anti-Semitic battle, not a war between machines but between races, in which the Allies had become criminals and cultural vandals with innocent children and the elderly on their consciences.

Commemorating the dead was thus functional in character. It was an appeal to the living to carry on, to endure and to get the city back on its feet. The dead had to live on in the memory of the 'national community'. The Nazi ritual of mourning admitted a moment of reflection but this moment of spiritual awareness of death was also a ritual to establish a common identity among all those who had survived. The ritual of death was thus extremely ambiguous. On the one hand the funerals formed part of the growing state takeover of mourning, in which the attempt was made to prescribe the meaning, language, and images of death and thus to control reactions to loss. On the other hand, this new ritualization of death allowed little scope for individuals to respond to and accept what was being prescribed, for the bodies of the deceased had passed into the control of the Party and public health authorities, their identity had been absorbed into the 'national community', and their families were given only a moment of 'quiet mourning' to take their leave.

There was room only for something different, for a particular form of lament familiar to the Christian churches as well as to the Nazi state and one that had a tradition stretching back over thousands of years, namely the lament for the downfall of the city, the destruction of the homeland, and the loss of local history and culture. In this regard death and regeneration went hand in hand and provided a secular reinterpretation of the Christian

doctrine of the resurrection. This involved interpreting the deaths of contemporaries as part of the process by which the nation fulfils its destiny as a
chosen people. Reports in the *Essener Nationalzeitung*, for example, made a
particular point of establishing the precise number of fatalities, not only to
counter wildly exaggerated rumours of the number of dead but also to
document the 'outstanding' civil defence achievements; after all, a total of
even several hundred dead was 'amazingly small', given the brutality of the
Allied terror raids and was not greater only because the 'national community' had proved to be an air defence community.[137]

The precise numbering of the dead was designed to give death an additional meaning, because those who had 'sacrificed' themselves in the air war
were, as it were, a precondition for, a sort of national down-payment on, the
rebuilding of the city. Their deaths were the 'price' the city and the nation
were obliged to pay for 'security' and 'freedom' at the end of the air war.

The Nazis' deliberate staging of death as the link between the dimensions of space and time under their rule was given its most vivid expression
in the dates chosen for the ceremonies in Kassel and Hamburg, which took
place on 9 November, the anniversary of Hitler's Munich putsch, the march
on the Feldherrnhalle on 9 November 1923.[138] The dead of the air war were
thus not merely anonymous 'civilian soldiers' but, like the early heroes of
the movement, they had died for the 'national community'. They had thus
not died in vain, for their deaths pointed to a future of hope, which, although
it came at a price, would finally end in victory.

Thus the Hamburg dead became the 'advance guard of revenge', as the
Nazi press put it, on whose graves the city would be rebuilt to be more
beautiful than ever before. Not only that, the dead were a pledge that terror
would be followed by retribution and that the air raids, no matter how
heavy, could not strike at the core, the essence of the nation; although terror
from the skies caused fatalities it only made the 'national community'
tougher.[139] In Hamburg at the same time preparations were under way for
a further memorial event that attempted to integrate the deaths into the
everyday rhythm of the year and thus 'normalize' them. The large-scale
ceremony was planned for 21 November, 'Totensonntag', the annual day of
mourning for the dead, which up to that point had been reserved for front
line soldiers and for fallen soldiers who were members of the Party and now
acquired new significance through the massive number of dead. It was to be
the act of mourning for the 'summer's bombing victims',[140] and Party, city
administration, and the Wehrmacht all geared up for it. To be more precise,

the public event was announced not as an act of mourning but as an act of commemoration, which attempted to interpret the thousands of deaths as part of the life cycle of the 'national community'. Thus it was to be a ritual focusing not on mourning but on self-sacrifice, not on loss but on 'composure' and 'dignity'.

Rather than Beethoven it was Gerhard Schumann's poem 'Immortality' that formed the prelude to the mourning. Delivered in a deep voice by a Hamburg actor, it reminded people that 'birth requires death and dying means bringing forth. | You must mourn now but do not despair.'[141] That the ritual of mourning was accompanied by trained speakers was by no means uncommon and was designed to strike the right note of heightened emotion and courageous determination to survive.[142] These were the minutes reserved for 'quiet mourning' and provided space for individual pain at the loss of friends and relatives. Yet that was not the actual leitmotif of the occasion. After the act of mourning there was a change of tone. The actors' voices, now reciting 'Our dead', were to ring out and help transform mourning into a profession of commitment to the nation. Finally, the first part of the mourning ritual was brought to a close by the 'Song of the Good Comrade'. After pain and consolation came new hope and encouragement.

The SA standards, lowered thus far, were raised and all flags fully unfurled. Finally Kaufmann, the Gauleiter, spoke. His key term was 'testing' and he reminded people again of the terrible nights the city and its inhabitants had suffered. Kaufmann spoke of the city's proud history and the resilience of the Hamburg people. Regime officials in the Rhineland and Westphalia, in Frankfurt, Kassel, Berlin, and Munich, took a similar line when attempting to interpret the violence of the air war and the determination to rebuild as integral to local identity and the special task of the German homeland. Extinguishing fires was thus, as in Rostock, part of the battle of culture with 'barbarism' and a continuation of the defensive battles the 'proud cog ships'* had fought since the earliest times.[143] Reconstruction was the most important task but it was not an end in itself, for it demanded that national comrades take on new duties: 'fighting—work—sacrifice'. Reconstruction in this sense meant not only building new houses; it meant the total mobilization of all resources, complete commitment to work for the war economy and the end of all holding back.[144]

---

* Translators' note: 'Koggen' were sailing ships used for trade in the Baltic in the Middle Ages and particularly associated with the Hanseatic League.

Nazi functionaries made use of their own particular semantics of death in order to give dying a meaning relevant to the national community. 'Commemorating with respect' was one part of it, as was the 'elevating' and 'dignified' ceremony, which the newspapers reported the following day, giving the whole event a quasi-religious hue with its Party leader as high priest, its 'heavenly' symbols in the form of the standard bearers, the altar-like location where the victims' coffins were placed, the Wehrmacht's 'death watch', the 'lowering' of the coffins, the prayer-like singing, and the death knell of the SA's drums. The dead had left a 'legacy': the 'national community's' will to survive, resting on courage, determination, and an unlimited confidence in ultimate victory.

The Führer had a variety of roles to play in the memorial ceremonies as a source of consolation and as a 'redeemer'. A wreath with his name was always placed on the graves and the Party speakers repeatedly tried to allude to him as a saviour in their addresses and to boost by means of symbolism people's attachment to the dictator. At the beginning this was done aggressively; the air war was presented as a test that the Führer had wished for in order to emphasize his toughness and powers of endurance. Even so, many Nazi district leaders were uneasy about whether people were actually receptive to the comfort Hitler was supposed to impart, given that they were standing in the midst of ruins.

After the devastating raid on Darmstadt on the night of 11/12 September 1944, when more than 12,000 people were presumed to have died, the local Party leader appealed to the population's determination to survive. His rallying speech sounded more beseeching than confident: 'Our confidence in the Führer, who rescued Germany from the depths of distress, is our rock even in this hour when we take leave of the dear departed and we ask God to preserve the Führer who guarantees our victory.'[145]

The reference to God was rather an unusual one and probably an indication of the catastrophic juncture, when the Nazi interpretation of events was felt to be inadequate even by its own leading players. Death in the air war was at any rate not an occurrence in which Hitler took a personal interest, particularly not from the summer of 1943 onwards, when Party and city dignitaries were forced to gather with increasing frequency at mass burial sites and 'groves of honour'.

The memorial ceremonies were presented in the press as signs of the interdependence in the national community of Party, army, state, and 'Volk'. What the papers did not report were the conflicts that had arisen over the exploitation of the 'dead body'. This applied in particular to the relationship between the Party and the churches. While there was much agreement and while it was not just in Hamburg that sermons about testing and endurance were a leitmotif of Protestant interpretations of events, competition over interpretative authority and ritualization led to serious disagreements.[146]

During their New Year conference, for example, the Bavarian Catholic bishops discussed the growing number of cases in which burials and issues surrounding them had ended in conflict between priests and the Nazi Party because agreement could not be reached about who was responsible for which part of the burial and at what time.[147] In the case of the funerals of bombing victims, where there might be competing rituals, unnecessary friction was to be avoided by prior discussion without the church giving ground over fundamental beliefs. Among these were the insistence that the burial must be in consecrated ground, prayers must be said, and the mass celebrated. These were key requirements and everyone who wanted to be buried according to the Catholic rite had to comply, even if the Party was present at the ceremony or had even organized it. A possible compromise could, for example, take the following form: the Party held its ceremony outside the church with the church burial following on immediately from it or the other way round: first the Catholic burial service followed by the Nazi ceremony at the graveside. What the bishops ruled out was the attempt by district Party leaders and Gauleiters to exclude them completely from the ritual and to curtail their religious authority, to the extent that priests would have been responsible only for blessing the body, without any mass being said. A burial in which the church was excluded from the ceremonial in this manner could not be acceptable to Catholics and in that case no supplementary 'religious service' could take place.

In practice conflicts continually arose and as a rule the funerals were not given a church blessing. On 'Totensonntag' 1943, while in Hamburg the Party was commemorating the victims of bombing in Adolf Hitler Square, a simultaneous service was being held for them in St Peter's. This competition was probably a reason why attendance was only moderate. Even before this there was a ban on religious services being conducted during that day at the actual burial sites. And the authorities did their utmost to impede church memorial services afterwards, as well as the churches' own attempts to document the damage. Thus in October 1943 the chief of police in Hamburg withdrew the permission already granted to the Protestant state church to take its own photographs of bombed-out churches and collapsed walls and

roofs. Power over the pictorial record of the destruction, as part of the process of monopolizing both ritual and memory, was to remain with one
authority—the Nazi state. As the war went on, however, it became clear how
fragile its authority over the religious sphere could become, at any rate if
competing strategies for solving the crisis collided, something that could be
observed much more frequently in Catholic cities and regions than in Protestant ones.[148]

Whereas in spite of the rising toll of victims and mounting logistical
problems the Reich Propaganda Ministry wanted to stick to the form the
ceremonies had taken up to then, in the funeral offices, particularly as a
result of their close contact with those affected, there was growing scepticism and discussion about whether in view of the rising death toll the
memorial ceremony should be shortened, given a more strongly symbolic
character, and not held as regularly as had become usual.[149] After all, as those
with reservations suggested, the more ceremonies there were the less special
they became and the less propaganda impact they had. To put it another
way, the 'memorial ceremonies' were losing the ability to make sense of the
destruction.

What the usually well-informed Swiss consul in Cologne, Franz-Rudolf
von Weiss, noted after the massive raid on the city in the summer of 1943
points to the same thing: the funeral that the Party and the city had organized for the population had met with very limited approval. 'To put it mildly,
the overwhelming majority of the Cologne population felt it was tasteless
in the extreme to conjure up once again in the minds of an unutterably
battered population, who loved the "holy city of Cologne" with every fibre
of their being, images of the ruins they had been walking about in for days.
As various reliable people confirmed to me, it was almost exclusively Party
members, army and suchlike that took part in this event.'[150]

There are no comparable reports from other places and what exactly the
pictures in the Nazi press tell us about well-attended mass gatherings is also
not unambiguous. What is certain, however, is that specifically during the
final phase of the war in 1944/5, when there was a massive toll of bombing
victims, the numbers of dead rose so steeply that there was virtually no time
or energy for events staged for propaganda purposes, however they were
received. In the hours following raids the streets were on fire, communications broke down, and the last vestiges of bureaucratic order collapsed,
though the recovery and identification of the dead was one of the first
things the authorities attempted to do when the bombing was over, for after

all the very survival of the city was at stake. In Berlin, for example, the raids beginning early in February 1945 had largely destroyed funeral arrangements, for now there were shortages of everything: coffins and fuel for the vehicles, materials, and personnel. Coordination had broken down and the dead had to be kept out in the open because there was no other space for them, in particular, as the authorities let it be known, because the private funerals business had completely collapsed.[151]

After raids such as those on Darmstadt in September 1944 the number of unidentifiable bodies rose. It was to take days and weeks before the last of the dead were recovered from cellars and shelters. There were more and more question marks on the lists of fatalities after names and details of occupation, while dwindling supplies of petrol and vehicles made recovering bodies a race against time.[152] A very short time after the heavy raids on Dresden on 13/14 February 1945 a sickly-sweet smell covered the city, the smell of decomposing corpses, almost obliterating the pungent smell of burnt flesh.

This mixture of odours was the herald of an impending catastrophe: epidemics. In the first few days the recovery teams dealt with up to 1,000 corpses a day, often no more than disfigured remains of bodies, limbs, shredded torsos. By 10 March 1945 some 35,000 had been reported missing, while the recovery teams were repeatedly finding remains of charred bodies in the cellars and in the ruins of the main station. The staff coping with burials were hopelessly overloaded, there was no transport, and many of them had themselves lost relatives or their homes. As in Hamburg, the chief of police declared particularly devastated areas of the city 'dead zones', to which access was forbidden for fear of the growing danger of epidemics. A last resort as far as civil defence leaders were concerned was to burn the bodies. Ten days after the raid the flames burned brightly on the old market square. Horse-drawn carts brought bodies from all areas of the city to the centre. Long rows of corpses stretched round the square, now cordoned off. If possible the corpses were identified and registered. Soldiers piled them onto a metal grid, petrol was poured over them, set alight and—in a final gesture of Nazi 'dignity'—their ashes were interred in a mass grave.[153] There was no room here for mourning.

After the raid on Würzburg on 16 March 1945 the chaplain Fritz Bauer reported meeting a man and a woman, both of whom had lost their partner during the bombing. Now they were carrying their remains, recovered from the rubble, in a sack and a large preserving pot. They wanted the priest to bury the two of them as quickly as possible. They dug two holes, the priest said the burial prayers, and then, as he noted in his diary, 'we sealed up the graves'.[154]

Is it really the case that the Christian rituals of death were marginalized at the end of the Nazi dictatorship by competing rituals and did the Nazi cult of honouring the fallen create a vacuum from which mourning had been abolished, one that held sway into the post-war era?[155] The Würzburg example can arguably be read differently: precisely at moments of extreme pain the authority and an awareness of the Christian tradition regained their meaning, in spite of the bans on clerics having access to mass graves to bless the dead there or say mass. In Würzburg there was such a need for spiritual support that the cathedral chapter positioned chaplains in the mornings and afternoons in the cemetery specifically to be ready to pray with those mourning someone who had had an individual burial.[156]

Not a great deal is known about such conflicts over the dead at the end of the war,[157] and it is completely impossible to give precise statistics about funerals and burial ceremonies.[158] This is primarily because from the end of 1944 at the latest the central records of the Reich Office of Statistics became increasingly unreliable, as clearing rubble and recovering bodies were becoming ever more costly and the authorities sent in their data often months late. Announcements about the state of the air war made by the chief of the order police, who passed on the information as accurately as possible, formed the basis for their estimates. By the beginning of 1945 some 200,000 people had probably lost their lives as a result of air raids, a total that coincided with the information given by the Reich Propaganda Minister.[159] There is much evidence that in the months of January to April 1945 up to 200,000 more people were killed by bombing, principally in cities such as Dresden, Würzburg, Pforzheim, Magdeburg, and Dortmund.[160]

Presenting a clear survey of the background and social position of the victims of the air war is even more difficult than arriving at a precise total, for such details were recorded only in exceptional cases. Neither the Reich Office of Statistics nor the Allies were able to give precise information. In particular, reports sent in during the last months of the war were too vague and the information that could be collected about the victims too uncertain. Thus, for example, reports on the air raids of July 1943 on Hamburg were not received in Berlin until the beginning of 1945, and even if regional headquarters, such as for the criminal police in Dortmund, were still returning precise figures for the fatalities at the end of 1944, the details given were at best surname, Christian name, sex, and town or city, with nothing about family background or occupation.

It was frequently even more difficult to obtain information about forced workers. The criminal police assumed that fatalities exceeded the numbers actually notified because they were hard to identify and fewer pains were taken to find out who they were.[161] Of the 34,000 fatalities resulting from Operation Gomorrah around 50 per cent were women and 12 per cent children.[162] Whether a higher than average number of women fell victim to bombing is difficult to tell, because the demographic structure of cities could alter several times during the war and, as the Cologne authorities stated after the war, the 'ratio of the sexes was all over the place'.[163]

In the case of those killed in air raids in Kiel there are particular details. Almost 59 per cent of fatalities were men, though this number includes the category of 'non-residents and foreigners', in other words forced workers. The cause of death was essentially the same as for women: some 28 per cent had been buried, almost 17 per cent were killed by collapsing buildings or shelters, and about 8 per cent died in the extensive fires. There was a significant number of dead (around 14.7 per cent of the male fatalities[164]) whose identity and cause of death were unknown. The majority of the women killed in the air raids were housewives (55.6 per cent), a much higher percentage than for workers, domestic staff, and those employed in businesses, at around 5 per cent. Although information of this kind cannot furnish the basis for generalizations, there is nevertheless some indication that social inequality played a significant role in the air war. Working-class areas close to industrial plant were on the whole more severely hit than affluent residential areas in the leafy suburbs on the periphery. This is, admittedly, hardly surprising and was established by the Allies themselves in their final estimate of the damage inflicted.

The root of the problem is the lack of statistical information. Mass mobilization, evacuation, labour conscription, and conscription to the forces made it extremely difficult for the local authorities to give precise information about the population and thus about the distribution of fatalities according to age and sex. Bearing in mind all caveats, in Cologne, for which there are reasonably reliable records, the following picture emerges: of the 20,000 dead 10,032 were men and 9,968 women, a ratio therefore of almost 1:1.[165] There is, however, insufficient information about the gender-specific breakdown of the population for conclusions to be drawn about whether men and women were exposed to an equal risk of falling victim to bombing.

How radically this could change in the course of the war is shown by an analysis of the individual phases of the war: Up to the end of 1942 54.2 per cent of the dead were men and 45.8 per cent women; in 1944, however, the balance had been reversed (44.1 per cent were men, 55.9 per cent women), with the same proportion of dead of both sexes being made up of the age group born between 1881 and 1930. What was remarkable was that from 1944 onwards the majority of them died in what was presumed to be the safest place in the city, namely the air-raid shelters.

9

Memories of the Air War
in the Early Post-War Period

The Guilt of the Victors

On the day of the German surrender *The Times* published a series of pictures giving a compact survey of the final months of the war. The five shots showed British marines landing in the Pacific, the Royal Navy firing at Japanese gun emplacements, and pictures of the destruction of Cologne in enlarged format.[1] Whereas the war was still raging in Asia, in Europe the battle was over and tanks were rolling through the city. The photo, which linked the two theatres of war, showed Cologne Cathedral still standing. The towers rose up 'majestically', as the picture caption read, from the landscape of ruins and breathed new life into the dead city, into which the Allies were advancing.

It thus seemed that not everything had been destroyed. The cathedral stood as a sacred symbol, evidence of the fact that unlike Nazi Germany the British had retained some vestige of respect for cultural artefacts. The violence of the destruction and the military power of the victors were one part of the story told by the picture; at the same time the sheer size of the cathedral suggested that the war had been won by a power that had not set out to destroy the German population.

Up to this point the British public had not seen many pictures of the destruction of German cities. On the whole they were reconnaissance photos, which did not convey much about the impact of the bombing,[2] and before 1945 it was rare for (mostly hazy) pictures to find their way into the British press. As the Allied troops advanced, this changed. Immediately after the bombing of Dresden in the middle of February a picture was published of the destruction of the Lower Rhine city of Cleves taken by low-flying

British pilots. In the centre there was hardly a building still standing and everywhere there were craters and ruins.[3] Only a few weeks later the major newspapers published an aerial photo of Cologne that gave a clear impression of the effectiveness of Bomber Command; there was hardly one stone left upon another and only the cathedral remained, towering over everything.[4]

The photos of ruins told the British who had also suffered air raids something about their superior power and presented the craters in an aesthetic light, thus making them into a sort of show of military strength. The *Daily Mirror* reporter David Walker wrote that the pictures of urban 'skeletons' were a demonstration of power and at the same time a warning: evidence of the RAF's 'triumph', an admonition to future generations in Germany, and the result of Hitler's madness.[5]

That area bombing had been necessary and in the final analysis the price the Germans had to pay for the war was the consensus on which most comment and reports were based. When finally the first British reporters saw for themselves the destruction of the cities most of their reports expressed above all a mixture of horror at the extent of the damage and the view that the Germans had brought their misfortune upon themselves.

The British–German argument over the legitimacy of the air raids and memories of the bombing were by no means over when the war ended; on the contrary, under different auguries the effects of the raids were to become an important reference point in national and local commemoration, being part of the history of British–German relations and German–German relations. This and the following chapter focus on boom periods and continuities of commemoration, the politics of history and memory, and mediatization. They attempt to establish the protagonists and areas of conflict in post-catastrophe memory of the air war up to the present and thus investigate the cities as spaces for commemoration, the churches as key players in the culture of remembrance, the media, monuments, and forms the musealization of the air war has taken.

The British public learnt next to nothing about the conflicts surrounding the development and impact of the Allied air-war strategy, to which the picture in *The Times* pointed. For months little had appeared in the press about the issue of German morale and the need for area bombing;[6] instead, shortly before the end of the war the emerging question was what overall conclusion could be drawn about the air war from a historical perspective. British–American air force commanders thus issued a communiqué concluding that their bombing strategy had been successful. The air war had smoothed the path to victory, massively hampered German oil production, destroyed transport networks, prepared the way for ground forces, and eliminated the Luftwaffe. There was no mention of 'morale bombing' but only of targeted and successful strikes against the German military machine.[7] The air war against Germany quickly disappeared from illustrated reports in the British newspapers, not least because the novelty value of information about the condition of the cities was exhausted.[8] Other topics dominated the news from Germany, for example the Allies' plans for a new order and more particularly the shocking news from the concentration camps about German atrocities.[9]

The disappearance of pictures of the air war against Germany from the Allied media in the immediate post-war period was linked to the controversy over how to present the pilots of Bomber Command, Arthur Harris, and the legitimacy of carpet bombing. This had in no way become a taboo subject or fallen victim to a 'spiral of silence'.[10] At the end of the war the emphasis was on the victors' authority. For how could the moral legitimacy of the occupation be maintained if the Allies put themselves in the dock— the place where, according to Nazi propaganda, Harris and Churchill in any case belonged? Was it possible to be victorious over fascism and a criminal at the same time? Were air raids and the Holocaust in the final analysis the same, as Hitler's former Vice-Chancellor, Franz von Papen, put it cynically while in British captivity?[11]

The propaganda battles of the Second World War most certainly did not come to an end in 1945 but were destined to leave their mark on post-war controversies, though they used different language and were conducted under different auguries. After the bombing of Dresden Churchill gradually distanced himself from the air-war strategy he had himself ordered and this process continued after the war. Even in his victory speech he had failed to acknowledge Bomber Command. He ranged widely, from the heroic battle of 'the few' against the Luftwaffe, to the Blitz and the Royal Navy, the German V-weapons, and the daring D-Day invasion, but there was no word about Bomber Command, only a brief mention of the heavy damage the bombers had inflicted on Berlin.[12] Whether this can be attributed to Churchill having a guilty conscience is, however, speculation.[13] It is entirely possible that a different intention lay behind his victory speech and failure to mention Bomber Command, namely to avoid heaping further humiliation on Germany by commending the bombing as a just punishment. He did, after all, wish to avoid driving the Germans into the arms of the Soviet Union and thereby putting the victory so dearly bought at risk.[14] Whatever the explanation, this omission provoked indignation and may well have been one reason why only a little later Churchill thanked Harris and Bomber Command effusively for their historic contribution and spoke of the 'duty nobly done' by the pilots.[15]

Weeks later and in spite of these partial amends Harris still felt deeply wounded. He was also annoyed that the Air Ministry had vetoed a special decoration for Bomber Command on the strength of, in his view, various purely formal pretexts and instead had merely honoured the airmen with the Home Defence Medal, which, as Harris indignantly commented, was in no way commensurate with what Bomber Command had achieved. Even the name was wrong, he said, for after all Bomber Command had played an offensive role and fought on enemy territory. To refuse the pilots their own campaign medal was to demean their outstanding achievement in the war.[16] A short time later Harris's name cropped up again in the newspapers and once again the subject was the role of Bomber Command in the war. When the Prime Minister, Clement Atlee, published the New Year's Honours List in 1946 almost all the names of the military leaders were there apart from Arthur Harris's. This provoked wild speculation in the Conservative press. Was Harris's awkward personality to blame? A headstrong man who was no longer right for the times? Was Harris in the final analysis not politically acceptable, particularly in view of German reconstruction?[17]

In fact Harris had clearly been on the list of nominations compiled by the Labour government that had come into office the previous summer.[18] Yet there are a number of indications that Harris himself had refused a seat in the Lords, just as he had shown no interest in becoming military governor in the British zone of occupation after leaving the RAF. In spite of this there were persistent rumours at an early stage that his former rivals in the Air Ministry had been responsible for sabotaging Harris's honour. Harris himself preferred not to let those around him know why he had made his decisions and thus gave the persistent rumours free rein. The rumours were in any case convenient to him, for he was sceptical not only about the new government but also about the new faces in the Air Ministry and did not mind them being regarded by the public as responsible for intriguing against him and Bomber Command.

Something else was most likely at the bottom of this conflict. Removing Bomber Command from public consciousness was certainly not the primary motive.[19] Much more important was the issue of which part of its history was considered worthy of commemoration and essential to its identity and which not. The battle over interpretation had already begun during the war, unnoticed by the public. For the discussion already taking place in 1943/4 in various sections of the military was to continue after 1945. Quite apart from any ethical issues, had the strategy of 'morale bombing' been successful or did the turning point in the air war not come at the moment when, from the autumn of 1944 onwards, the British and Americans took the joint decision to concentrate their raids more on the German transport network and the oil industry?

Whereas from the middle of 1944 onwards American forces had begun to test the success of their bombing strategy by means of the United States Strategic Bombing Survey and to draft statistical models for investigating German morale,[20] in Britain, though there was a formal equivalent in the shape of the British Bombing Survey Unit (BBSU), in practice the group of academics led by the scientist Solly Zuckerman[21] was no more than a dozen strong. Their independent report met with considerable resistance and, unlike the report produced by the Americans, was not based on primary sources, namely interviews with Germans.

Their *Overall Report* was a first, if as yet unpublished, history of the air war against Germany. The roles of hero and incompetent were clearly allocated and it was a history that focused more on economic and strategic matters and less on the precise analysis of German morale.[22] Without addressing the subject head on, the study came to the conclusion that it was not in fact area bombing that had smoothed the path to victory, for in the final analysis this mode of warfare had not decisively weakened German armaments production. An important source for this conclusion was above all the information the Allies elicited from Albert Speer, now in custody. He willingly expounded his view of the 'armaments miracle'[23] in order to bolster his own historical role as an independent and successful military expert.[24] According to this account Bomber Command acquired decisive strategic importance only in the final phase of the war, when the raids were concentrating on German transport and communications networks and doubts had increasingly been voiced in many quarters about whether 'German morale' could in fact be broken. In the authors' view it was this change of strategy that ultimately represented Bomber Command's crucial contribution to the outcome of the war and not the impact of area bombing on armaments production or on morale. Even while the BBSU was still working on its report Harris was

busy giving his own take on things, though this became less and less convincing in the institutional memory of the Air Ministry and the new
government.

In his memoirs, published in 1947, and his unpublished final report as
Commander in Chief Harris advanced the argument that, first of all, the
raids of 1943 had succeeded in pinning down the Luftwaffe over Germany,
thus hampering the war in the east. Secondly, the German army had been
forced to move resources from the front to Germany in order to protect
industry. Thirdly, the bombing of towns and cities led to a decrease in armaments production and thus in the long run prevented retaliatory weapons
from being dropped on British soil. Fourthly, air raids created the conditions
for a successful invasion by ground forces.[25] Even though the assumption that
German morale had collapsed had not turned out to be true, the population's low spirits as a result of the air raids had been a reason for declining
productivity and on those grounds alone a highly significant achievement.[26]

Nothing Harris wrote was at all new. Up to the time he took over as
Commander in Chief, exactly five years previously, the notion that victory
in 'total war' could be won by attacking enemy morale had been dominant
since the inter-war period and was now regarded as a matter of common
sense by military leaders. Harris may have put forward this view particularly
vigorously, but he was anything but the exception or an eccentric figure.
The reason why his standpoint so quickly lost ground and Bomber Command had to fight for military recognition was to a great extent bound up
with the new priorities in British policy towards Germany and towards the
armed forces; after the end of the war it became increasingly difficult to
integrate into this new policy an approach that had given outspoken support to area bombing and which in so doing, in the view of some Allied
experts at the end of the war, had set the wrong priorities. At the same time,
Labour's victory in the 1945 election had also contributed to a change in
priorities and Churchill's former loyal followers were coming under pressure. How could support for European reconstruction follow on from a
strategy of 'total war', the consequences of which had not been made clear
to the British public and the ethical and strategic dilemmas of which had
been hard to cover up even during the war?[27]

It would, however, be an exaggeration to assume that Harris had become
something of a pariah as a result of the guilty consciences of others. That
was true neither of him nor of Bomber Command. After all, almost no one
in the British military command or in the new Labour government had

strong feelings about the legitimacy of the air raids, which were completely overshadowed by the images emerging from Bergen-Belsen and Auschwitz. There was an overwhelming consensus that the Germans had simply got what was coming to them.

Harris's autobiography *Bomber Offensive*,[28] published in 1947, was therefore given decidedly favourable reviews in the press. The author had not conceived the book in any way as an angry self-justification but rather as a sober account of his assessment of matters and had cleared critical passages with the people involved, such as Churchill. At the same time, the public was told nothing about the dispute over bombing targets that Harris had had with his opponent, Portal, in the winter of 1944/5, focusing on the question of whether area bombing or raids on infrastructure and oil refineries should be the priority for Bomber Command. Some readers may well have been surprised at how small a role morale bombing played in his book; the bombing of Dresden was not mentioned at all. As *The Spectator*'s reviewer noted, in the final analysis Harris had delivered what the British public wanted.[29]

After retiring from the RAF in 1948 Harris retreated, a disappointed man, to his native South Africa. Though he may have regarded himself as something of a scapegoat, he was given support and recognition when he retired, from, among others, Herbert Morrison, Deputy Prime Minister in the Labour government. Writing to Harris he said he was 'a great admirer of your work and of the men who served under you' and wished he had known sooner of his personal difficulties.[30] When, shortly after, in March 1949, the former pilots and members of Bomber Command were reunited for the first time since the end of the war by invitation of the *Evening News* Harris was the acknowledged hero of the night,[31] even though he was not there in person. In his speech Lord Tedder, Chief of the Air Staff, alluded to the historic achievements of Bomber Command in defending the nation. Although there was no mention of the bombing of Germany and the dangerous sorties over enemy territory, tribute was paid to the remarkable spirit that had distinguished the work done by all the crews. The country, Tedder said, needed just this commitment shown by the bomber pilots to overcome the economic challenges of the present. Britain had paid a very high price for victory, the state was deeply in debt, resources were scarce, and food rationing made everyday life difficult.[32] What Bomber Command had achieved during the war in defending the country was thus directly linked to coping with the Herculean tasks of the present.

462 MEMORIES OF THE AIR WAR IN THE EARLY POST-WAR PERIOD

The bombing of Germany was thus viewed as a necessary evil but not as what had really distinguished Bomber Command, namely the tireless commitment, hard work, and the composure with which the pilots and ground staff had defended the Empire and helped to bring victory. This part of the story of Bomber Command was easier to integrate into the narrative of the People's War and the Battle of Britain, which now after 1945 was achieving widespread fame a second time. This narrative centred not on death and destruction but on national solidarity and reconstruction, on the surmounting of class barriers, and on the courageous resistance to the threat from fascism.

When on 15 September 1945 London first celebrated Battle of Britain Day in peacetime RAF planes led by former heroes such as Douglas Bader flew over the city as a reminder of the great battle fought to defend it, a battle which, as Attlee put it in a memorandum, immortalized Fighter Command and preserved the freedom of all human beings.[33] The pilots were thus more than just heroic airmen. They were at the head of a national movement and the second part of the ceremony showed what was at the heart of it: in the procession that marched the following Sunday into Westminster Abbey they were joined by members of the Home Guard and aerospace industry workers.[34] Thus victory in the air war was not only the achievement of 'The Few', as in the first two years of the war,[35] but tribute was paid to those who had bolted the engines together and had gone out at night on patrol. This democratization of the commemoration of war heroes had already taken place in 1943/4 and was continued by the Labour government. Such an act of cross-class integration was certainly less liable to provoke conflict than the difficult issue of the bombing of Germany. By contrast with the history of Bomber Command, the commemoration of the Battle of Britain made it easier to make use of the Christian symbolism of sacrifice and resurrection and thus forge a direct link between the war and the post-war period.

In July 1947 the Royal Airforce Chapel with the Battle of Britain window was unveiled by the King, with Queen Mary and the Prime Minister also in attendance. Plans for such a chapel in Westminster Abbey began during the war.[36] The location had great symbolic significance and seemed to be appropriate for such a place of commemoration because it already contained the grave of the Unknown Soldier.[37] The chapel was financed through donations and at its centre there were large, brightly coloured stained glass windows commemorating various RAF formations. A hole in the wall was a reminder of bombing by the German Luftwaffe and several panels showed the RAF's and the nation's suffering and redemption: a squadron leader rests his head in the hand of Jesus, who blesses him with his hands outstretched to heaven; a second scene shows Mary as Mater Dolorosa, the dead Christ in her lap after he has been taken down from the cross, who serves as a reminder, as the official explanation states, of all the widows and women who mourn the death of their sons; finally, two pilots bow their head before the crucified one and thus indicate their own experience of sacrifice and above them is another RAF pilot witnessing the resurrection of Christ. Below the central window was the quotation from Shakespeare's *Henry V* that gave meaning to suffering and death: 'We few, we happy few, we band of brothers.'[38]

These 'happy few', as the Archbishop of Canterbury, Geoffrey Fisher, stressed in his address to relatives, were the ones who had stood 'between us and the abyss'. To lose one's life fighting for one's country and for the right was, he said, a significant action and only God knew what it really meant. It should be noted that Fisher had not spoken only of dying for one's country but also of 'the right', for which the pilots had died and for which they were being commemorated now in a Roll of Honour. The archbishop therefore did not present their deaths only as a sacrifice for the nation but also alluded to the purpose of fighting the war. There was no specific mention of Germany during the ceremony but only of 'evil' and the 'abyss' the nation had been facing and from which the pilots had saved it.

With the consecration of the Battle of Britain Chapel the mixture of Christian and military iconography employed to express the theme of national renewal continued the use of images that had already become established during the air battle over London. St Paul's had been only one example of it, becoming a unifying Christian symbol of British determination to survive. The plans for the chapel and its windows intensified this imagery of a crusade, making a link back to the visual traditions of the First World War. This interpretation, which made a connection between national revival, martyrdom, and the Christian notion of a 'just war', probably had its greatest impact in the last phase of the war and in the weeks immediately following victory over National Socialism. The inauguration of the chapel and the great interest it aroused therefore marked the end rather than the beginning of a new phase of commemoration, attempting as it did to find an answer to the question of how and indeed whether the dead of the Second World War could be memorialized.

When, in September 1960, the Air Minister presented to his cabinet colleagues a proposal to create a national monument to the Battle of Britain,
the response of the Conservative Prime Minister Harold Macmillan was at
first reserved. Prompting the Air Ministry's proposal was the concern that
the air battle over Britain was becoming less something people remembered
and more a historical event. Though, it was claimed, the dead were commemorated in the chapel in Westminster Abbey, there was no place where
the events themselves were memorialized. Yet it was important that they
should be because this battle more than any other was central to how people remembered the war and for that reason the government and Parliament
should take joint action.[39] The cabinet began by postponing any decision
and called for information about whether it was politically advisable to pay
tribute to one particular group of victims of the war from among the many.[40]
Less than a year later the issue was again on the agenda. Although in his
report the Defence Minister saw no particular public interest in a monument to the war dead, the Battle of Britain was, he said, perceived by most
people as something special. There would, however, be some point in putting
up such a monument only if everyone involved in the battle were honoured, in other words not simply the pilots but also the air-raid personnel,
aviation workers, and the civilian population as a whole. Thus even the story
of the one-time heroic airmen, 'The Few', had been democratized and
assimilated into the People's War.

In order to gauge whether such a monument would really meet with
majority approval the Air Ministry was to go public with it and float the idea
in *The Times*, though most of the cabinet was sceptical about whether the
project was really a wise move for, after all, in the end only particular people
among the dead would be honoured. In addition, the financing of the project
was still an open question; it was conceivable that such a place of commemoration might be paid for from private funds but it did not seem advisable to
spend public money, thus distinguishing between the dead of different classes
and periods.[41] Precisely because the fatalities of the Second World War, in
contrast to the First, resisted any single type of commemoration and conflicts
over precedence and prestige were bound to emerge, Macmillan regarded
such a project as wrong and dangerous. The post-war consensus seemed to
be a turning away from extravagant religious interpretations of death such as
found expression immediately after the war in the Battle of Britain Chapel.

Commemoration of the Battle of Britain thus had developed early on
into something that could be assimilated in a multitude of ways; indeed its

multiple uses were part of the attraction. Apart from the religiously based complex of interpretations there was from the start another, more dominant secular and political complex and this was demonstrated by the use of analogies with the 'battle' against the economic crisis, scarce resources, and food shortages. From being the struggle of the 'few', the triumph of heroic individualism, the Battle of Britain had thus become the common struggle for survival, a continuation of the People's War and one that in view of the acute crisis was by no means over. Reference to the experience of the Battle of Britain was designed to give hope, for it promised escape from a desperate situation and appealed to the wartime experience of a solidarity that overrode class differences as the foundation on which to build post-war society. What was written or said about the battle of 'The Few' therefore always had multiple meanings, being an interpretation of the war, an analysis of the present, and a projection into the future.

The history of Bomber Command, by contrast, lacked a utopian dimension to give it integrative force, not least because the outcome was so laden with contradictions, as was universally apparent by this time. The policy might have been the right one but it was hardly possible to use the rubble of Germany as the legitimization for a new political beginning. But how, in spite of this, could a form of commemoration be found that included the war dead? Depictions of sacrifice and the crucifixion clearly no longer provided the range of meanings suitable for memorials designed to commemorate the Second World War.

In November 1944 Mass Observation had asked members of the middle classes what forms of commemoration they considered appropriate.[42] There was huge scepticism with regard to forms of commemoration that expressed themselves in monumental obelisks or statues, for the hope that attached to them after 1918 had not been fulfilled. In this regard the Battle of Britain Chapel was an anachronism. Those interviewed instead suggested looking for new modes of representation or using the money right away for something useful—and there were many such things after the bombing. The fact that in Kirkby Stephen the Second World War was commemorated by the installation of electric lighting in the parish church and the names of the dead recorded on a plaque or that in Salford the victims were commemorated by the renewal of the balustrade in the local cemetery was in no way intended as disrespectful.[43]

During the war itself artists and intellectuals such as T. S. Eliot and John Maynard Keynes had encouraged people to conserve some of the bombed churches as permanent ruins and thus to create a distinctive idiom through which to express the terrors of the attacks on the British homeland, an idiom that the heroicizing war memorials of the First World War did not and could not use because they reflected front line experience rather than a war waged against the civilian population. These memorials also rested on the assumption that the Great War had been a war to end all wars.[44] This hope had not been fulfilled and this made it difficult to continue to use older forms of commemoration, at least where the focus was on warning against the next war and mourning the anonymous dead. Because of the cost, in many places communities and cities made do with simply adding a mention of the dead of the Second World War to the old First World War memorials and left it at that.

Yet that did not make the war disappear. On the contrary, the more time passed the greater seemed the need to reconnect with it, or at least with a specific part of the history of the air war, 'virtually'. The best known and most successful of these early post-war productions was the film *The Dam Busters*, the story of Operation Chastise and air squadron 617, which in a spectacular mission in mid-May 1943 had bombed the Möhne, Eder, and Sorpe dams.[45] The raid had been celebrated as a huge success even during the war. The film could take up this success story and gave extensive coverage to the painstaking planning, frustrations and obstacles, and finally to the bold execution of the idea of directing specially constructed bouncing bombs across the water at the walls of the dams. *The Dam Busters* was a story that fitted how Britain imagined the air war and the policy of Bomber Command and blended seamlessly with the present. It was the battle of fearless young pilots who, as it were, found themselves through service and dealt the enemy a significant blow. Air raids were purely a matter of (male) nerve and the result of bold technical planning. The targets were carefully selected and this was in no way mindless 'terror bombing'.

At the very start of the film the director, Michael Anderson, has one of his central characters muse on the purpose of the air war. While the engineer, Barnes Wallis, who despite others' scepticism is working in the Air Ministry on the development of the new bomb, is conversing with a neighbour, British bombers heading for Germany fly over. Wallis's interlocutor is totally convinced that the Germans will not be able to withstand the raids for long. Wallis is much more pessimistic, fearing that the air raids will have little lasting impact. It is like trying to fell a giant by firing at his arms and legs with thousands of peashooters rather than at his heart. Wallis then recalls the raids on London: 'Well, you know what happened when they tried to wipe out London!' Nothing.

The film was a success at the box office and featured a number of spectacular scenes with aircraft, for which Anderson won an Oscar in 1956. The incorporation of some original sound and images was designed to emphasize the 'authentic' nature of the film and thus the special significance of one of the most spectacular British wartime operations.[46] The raid on the dams did after all take place at a point when considerable losses had been inflicted on Bomber Command and it was far from being in a position to paralyse Germany's armaments industry.

The RAF had supported the film and named it the year's best public representation of the RAF.[47] It was a war film totally to their taste and caused a number of cinema owners to open special recruitment offices in the cinema. The reviews were enthusiastic precisely because the film gave such detail about the inner lives of the pilots, their tragedies, and their strength of character and strove to be 'just' to the protagonists. As a notable film critic commented, these young men had certainly not thrown their lives away heedlessly.[48] The pilots were fulfilling the mission of a lifetime and through this the film showed the story of a nation at war refusing in spite of all setbacks to be deterred from delivering a decisive blow to the enemy and thus combining individual action with a sense of community. Death acquired true meaning in this battle between the Teutonic giant and the British underdog, for the pilots who died in it had not been sacrificed for some pointless operation but had taken part in precision bombing aimed at the enemy's heartland.

Dramatic quality and special effects raised *The Dam Busters* above the mass of war films of the 1950s. But there was something else that distinguished the film from others such as *Appointment in London* (1952), which also told the story of the RAF at almost the same time. In this movie too the pilots' everyday experience was marked by failure, frustration, and stress. Yet it flopped at the box office, unlike *The Dam Busters*, for the latter showed an air war fought with purely strategic goals, targeting reservoirs and industrial centres rather than human beings, and thus turned its back on giving an interpretation of 'total war', at the heart of which had been the population's morale.

In 1954 this part of the history of Bomber Command was eventually commemorated, with some delay and with much less use of the rhetoric of Christian redemption than in the story of The Few, in a small memorial in

Lincoln Cathedral. Lincolnshire was regarded as the 'Bomber County' and the heart of Bomber Command, and thus immediately after the end of the war numerous memorial events and tributes to crews of Bomber Command who had been killed had taken place. In this region their deaths were more than just one aspect of a controversial strategic decision but meant the personal loss of family members and comrades and thus were an example of how the memory of the Second World War could be fragmented and regionalized.

How contentious and awkward the story of Bomber Command was became clear when in 1961 the four-volume history of the *Strategic Air Offensive against Germany*, commissioned by the government, was published.[49] The authors were Charles Webster, a diplomatic historian and expert on international relations, who taught at the London School of Economics, and Noble Frankland, a military historian who himself had worked in the Air Historical Branch of the Air Ministry. Instigated by the Air Ministry, the project had been in progress for ten years. Conflicts were inevitable and not only with regard to free access to files. Almost all the crucial participants were still alive: Portal, the Chief of Staff, Arthur Harris, and Winston Churchill all wanted tribute to be paid, though in vastly different ways, to their roles in the bombing war against Germany.

Since the end of the war Churchill had been working on his history of the Second World War, which had appeared in six volumes between 1948 and 1954 and caused a worldwide sensation. Bomber Command was hardly mentioned. Churchill devoted just two pages to the actual climax of the air war in 1944/5. There was not a word about Harris, nor about the conflict over the strategic direction the bombing should take, for which he after all bore political responsibility. With regard to Dresden, Churchill spoke of a 'heavy raid' directed against the communications hub in the eastern sections of the front.[50] His summing up of the air war as a whole was similarly brief and unequivocal: though Britain had underestimated the toughness of the German armaments industry, as the war went on Germany had been forced to refocus its war economy on dealing with the consequences of the air war. The message was clear: in the end British and American bomber crews made a decisive contribution to victory over Nazi Germany. Churchill had approved these passages of his memoirs, in which a whole group of experts and advisers had had a hand, without significant cuts or revisions and had merely added the words 'courageous' and 'disciplined' to describe the German civilian population.[51] On the subject of Dresden he either would not

or could not say more. When the historians writing the official history of
Bomber Command put questions to him he gave the curt reply that he
could not remember. He thought the Americans had done it![52]

Thus in the mid-1950s Churchill had already given the world his version
of the air war: the bombing had been justified and decisive for the outcome
of the war. Yet at the same time, with regard to the effects of area bombing
of urban targets he kept a low profile, almost as though he had had nothing
to do with the decisions. It was therefore hardly surprising that both
Churchill and Harris watched the progress of Webster's and Frankland's
volumes with some unease. At first Harris had supported the project but he
became increasingly sceptical about the direction the publication would in
fact take and refused to have anything further to do with it.

In fact before Webster and Frankland published their multi-volume work
they had many obstacles to overcome. Were they really allowed to quote
from Churchill's papers? What was to remain secret and what could be published? In the end the Conservative Prime Minister, Macmillan, had to
make a decision before the work could appear.[53] Both authors had done an
impressive job, as most reviewers agreed.[54] What made the book a political
issue was not so much excessive scholarly detail and scrupulousness as two
other things: first, the historians published the till then virtually unknown
correspondence between Portal and Harris, which revealed quite unmistak-
ably how contentious an issue area bombing had been, even among military
leaders; secondly and even more importantly, their final judgement on the
British bombing strategy was hardly enthusiastic. Mismanagement, dissatis-
faction, unclear decisions: their history gave a certain authority to matters
that hitherto had been discussed at the most behind closed doors. The planning and strategic execution of night raids had, they claimed, been far less
efficient than had long been asserted; the concentrated raids on German
industrial concerns had been much less effective than hoped and the ability
of the German war economy to adjust had been underestimated. The crucial aim of gaining air supremacy over Germany had not been pursued
consistently enough. Finally, German morale did not collapse under the
force of the raids. They did not, it is true, condemn Bomber Command
entirely, for they held to the view that its contribution to victory over
Germany, especially in the final phase of the war, had been considerable.
Webster (who did not live to see publication) and Frankland were far from
being polemicists and were at pains to present a balanced argument. For that
reason, during the controversy that followed Frankland emphatically refused to

adopt the language of Nazi propaganda and refer to the purpose of area bombing as 'simply to strike terror into the German people'.[55]

Area bombing was therefore in no way a taboo subject. What was new was that 'official' historians, to whom a certain authority attached, no longer viewed the work of Bomber Command as a massive and unqualified success that justified the killing of civilians. Did that mean that the 55,000 British pilots killed were in the end the victims of a strategic error on the part of the British leaders? Could victory have been won at less cost? And was it really the case that 'Now it is officially admitted we killed 180,000 German Civilians in vain', to quote the title of an article that appeared in *The People* newspaper on the history's publication?[56] Had the air war against Germany been a 'costly failure'?[57]

That the work caused such a stir may well have had something to do with the time it was published. Since the end of the 1950s the Campaign for Nuclear Disarmament (CND) had turned the fear of nuclear war and an escalation of the Cold War into an important internal political issue and was gaining increased support. In 1960 between 60,000 and 100,000 people took part in a demonstration in Trafalgar Square to press home their demand for nuclear disarmament.[58] The backbone of the movement was composed of parts of the political Left and pacifist nonconformist groups such as the Quakers, who even during the war had belonged to the small band of opponents of British area bombing and now feared a renewed spiral of violence.

They defined the essence of the nation as being a 'peaceful Britain' and neither carpet bombing nor a policy of nuclear rearmament was compatible with this notion of British identity. After the Suez crisis criticism of strategic planning and of the extension of the nuclear weapons arsenal formed part of the now heated debate concerning the nature of 'Britishness' in the post-war, postcolonial era and judgements of the air war and area bombing were included in this. Thus what was taking place was by no means a 'historical' argument about facts and strategies but the search for an answer to the question of what lessons were to be drawn from the Second World War and what they signified with regard to the tarnished moral position of Britain in the world.

Thus, even though the interpretation of sources was the primary focus, a number of other issues were at stake in this controversy, such as Britain's integrity as the victor and the nature of the sacrifice made by the servicemen killed. Members of Bomber Command also protested loudly at the suggestion that the deaths of their comrades had been a 'costly failure'. They complained that Frankland and Webster had not given sufficient weight to the importance of area bombing for the outcome of the war. As early as 1942, when Arthur Harris took up his post, and not just from 1944 onwards, the groundwork had been done towards massively curtailing Germany's war capability.

In spite of criticism, however, there was hardly anyone who doubted that the bombing of Germany had been necessary and at least an indirect success. Publication of the book had contributed to the re-examination of this problematic part of wartime history and to a revival, sixteen years after the end of the war, of the debate that during the war was held behind closed doors. That such a debate had taken place at all necessarily seemed dubious to large sections of the British public, particularly at a juncture when the full extent of the raids had become plain for all to see. But this was in no way a lasting 'shock',[59] for in the end the consensus of society about the reason for and purpose of the war was too strong, while in Harris a scapegoat was available to exculpate others in the case of difficult moral issues, even though Webster and Frankland had not intended this. At the same time the government of the day could draw a dividing line, consigning area bombing to 'history', from which the necessary conclusions for future military conflicts could be drawn.

Victims of the Air War

Britain's relationship with the new Germany was only a side issue in this controversy, even if occasionally there was mention of the suffering of the German civilian population as victims of the war. By contrast, there was all the more talk in Germany about its own bombing victims and also about its relationship with Britain and the meaning of the Second World War. *Der Spiegel* reported with obvious satisfaction on the controversy unleashed in Britain by Webster and Frankland's book,[60] adopting its phrase 'costly failure': area bombing had neither brought about a collapse in German morale, nor had it had any direct effect. The journalist remarked on the fact that the work had been commissioned by the British government and thus had official status. The article also reproduced criticisms by numerous leading members of Bomber Command who had come to the aid of the RAF. According to *Der Spiegel*, they were particularly angry because they assumed that the publication was an attempt by the government to push responsibility for area bombing onto supposedly unscrupulous military leaders. Thus the article particularly emphasized Churchill's role and that of other leading members of the government, all of whom had advocated the bombing of German cities.

Der Spiegel and other sections of the German media clearly intended to put the British Prime Minister in the dock of history. Webster and Frankland's account had given them the ammunition finally to be able to confirm what German military experts had been repeatedly proclaiming since the war, namely that British military strategy against Germany had failed, that the bombing had been senseless, and thus that the Allies were guilty of crimes under international law. The report in *Der Spiegel* was accompanied by an illustration, a drawing of Dresden after the bombing in 1945, to make clear once again what the aim of this policy of bombing had been: death and the destruction of Germany as a nation of culture.

This article was fully in line with a report *Der Spiegel* had published earlier the same year on a book written by Hans Rumpf, the former Major General of the Fire Protection Police and a leading Nazi air defence expert. Entitled *That was the Bombing War*, it also appeared in 1961 and told the story of the 'war of fire storms' waged against German cities and of unbroken German morale.[61] It was a story of British failure and made clear who was responsible for the bombing war: 'On top of the guilt that already weighs heavily on us and which we justly bear, Germany is not also obliged to take upon itself the immense burden of having unleashed total air war.'[62] The stepping up from the later 1950s onwards of the German judiciary's research into German war crimes and increased media attention gave the debate about the alleged crimes of the air war an entirely new significance, for it enabled Germans to set these crimes of the Allies at least indirectly against their own, now undeniable, responsibility for the murder of the Jews and thus to remain morally on the same level.

Thus it was altogether comprehensible that in 1961, shortly after the trial of the SS Einsatzgruppen in Ulm and during the Eichmann trial, Rumpf's book struck such a chord with a substantial part of the German public. In it Harris, an almost pathological war criminal, as *Der Spiegel* suggested, was the villain who had been the first to call for German cities to be burned, something the Germans had not done to British cities. There was therefore a certain logic in the fact that fifteen years after the end of the war the air war was still the event that divided the two nations and made reconciliation difficult, reconciliation in this context meaning that it was the Germans who had something to forgive.

Unlike in Britain it was not historians but former Nazi air defence activists who had been writing the history of the bombing war since the 1950s and so were perpetuating what had been begun by Nazi propaganda. They were united by a twofold criticism of what they termed the 'Anglo-American bombing war'. The 'terror raids' had been criminal and had made no military sense, thus being in the end 'mass murder'. Churchill and Harris, they claimed, had been motivated by hatred of Germany. 'Terror bombing' was contrary to international law, whereas from the first the German conduct of the air war had been 'humane and chivalrous'. These were topoi used in the First World War and they were used again here to assert a fundamental distinction between Anglo-American and 'continental' strategy: Whereas 'continental' strategy confined itself to using the air force as a support, the British and Americans had identified the civilian population as a target at an early stage, thus signalling the beginning of the end for moral scruples. By contrast, the German Luftwaffe had been more or less immune to Nazi ideology and had made constant efforts to exercise restraint towards innocent civilians.

For that reason Rumpf and others also placed such great emphasis on the qualitative difference between the supposedly justified bombing of 'fortified' cities such as Warsaw and Rotterdam and on identifying the Allies as initiators of the indiscriminate bombing war. On the one side the 'spotless', heroic Luftwaffe and on the other the grubby, morally indifferent RAF with its mediocre leaders: this was a line of argument that in its essentials had already found expression in the collection of documents published in 1943 by the German Foreign Office,[63] in order to emphasize in a supposedly sober and neutral tone the sole responsibility of the British Empire for the barbaric escalation.

There was a particular fondness, as in the article in Der Spiegel, for quotations from British authors such as Webster and Frankland to underline the moral dubiousness of Germany's former enemy.[64] In a way this was a special variant in the history of transnational relations: the former enemy served as the principal witness for Germany's innocence. As early as 1950 the German public had had the chance to read in Der Spiegel that the works written by the influential though by no means uncontroversial military theorist J. F. C. Fuller were precise and scholarly and evidence 'that it was Churchill who lit the fuse that led to the explosion of a war of devastation and terror never seen since the fall of the Seljuq Empire'.[65]

This extremely influential take on the air war, which existed in a number of variations, was first put forward in an official publication, *Documents of German War Damage*,[66] the first of several volumes of which appeared in 1958.[67] Like the large-scale project on expellees, this also emerged from the publishing house Thomas Oberländer,[68] although the initiative for it came not from the Ministry for Expellees but from the central association of victims of bombing.[69] Lobbyists for those bombed out and evacuated were concerned about two issues: on the one hand they wanted their own status as victims to be acknowledged and on the other they wished to acquire a lever to enable them to pursue legal claims for compensation for the loss of property more effectively. The selection and compilation of the documents as well as their editing and organization lay to a great extent with the central association, which produced the series in close consultation with the relevant departments in the ministry.

Central to the edition were documents relating to the equalization of burdens, regulations for compensation payments for 'victims of currency reform', and various kinds of legal assistance for evacuees. The ministry produced two volumes of analysis of the historical background as an introduction to the work, and that meant a history of the air war and the damage suffered by Germany's cultural heritage that was largely based on the data that the German Foreign Office had collected during the war as evidence against Britain, which could now be given in extended form. However dry the descriptive section for the most part was, it was nevertheless unmistakable who was being blamed for the escalation:

The essential turning point came on the night of 10/11 May 1940. The previous day the Germans had started the western campaign; the war situation had intensified. The first air raids on open cities now began. For a long time the beginning of the 'use of terror against the civilian population' was regarded as being a raid mounted in error by German planes on a German city, Freiburg im Breisgau. [...] In fact it was the less effective British bombing of cities in the Ruhr area that night that marked the first deliberate transition to raids on non-military targets.[70]

That the war itself and technical advances were responsible for the escalation is, we read later, 'most probably true, but equally it cannot be denied that the escalation began and was pushed to the furthest extremes of brutality by those who considered themselves to be, or were, superior to the enemy'.[71]

In those words the question of guilt from the German perspective was answered and the German people had become victims of the war. The document collection went further than this statement. Reports in the foreign press about the air war were published in a special volume, its purpose being to act as something of an objective counterweight and underline the unrestrained barbarity of the air war; these reports had already served the Foreign Office well under Ribbentrop.[72] A further volume contained accounts by those affected, Party offices and various official bodies, who all confirmed the image of a community at war, bound by one fate in solidarity and self-sacrifice. A recurring theme was that of personal loss and suffering as documented in the numerous accounts of people's experiences of nights in the shelters and in individual stories of destruction, pain, and death. Another theme that also emerged in numerous later publications on the history of the air war was the heroic struggle by local officials to defend communities against the external threat.[73] Taking as an example the shared 'baptism of fire' as it was known, namely the struggle against incendiaries, those who had been responsible described the immense efforts of city administrations to limit the damage. This gave rise to a certain confidence, even pride in a shared achievement, that was now being continued in the post-war reconstruction.[74]

At the same time this heroic story of communities being defended allowed people to distance themselves from and criticize Nazism, which was held responsible for failings and inadequacies in civil defence. In general, however, Nazism played at most a peripheral role in *Documents of German War Damage*, as in other contemporary publications, and when it did it was as the cause of administrative chaos, in which the 'German nation' stood on one side and Hitler, and occasionally Goebbels, on the other. Thus Nazism disappeared from the history of the air war, while accounts were dominated by the narrative of loss and victimhood, in which the bombing raids became instances of the British and Americans crossing a line in committing actions that were not only essentially barbaric but also unsuccessful within the fight to the death that was 'total war'.

Psychological Damage, Psychiatry, and the Experience of War

One of the ambivalent aspects of this national master narrative was that in cases of tangible suffering and loss in the air war there was virtually nobody who actually took the real experience of violence seriously, at least not if it cost money and those affected were unable to work because of what they had been through. In spite of shortcomings and differences in detail there had been a broad parliamentary majority in the Federal Republic in favour of war victims being able to make claims for material provision. But what was the position with regard to psychological damage, which might have unforeseeable consequences? And were the nights of bombing, being buried under rubble, or being disfigured genuine examples of war damage in the form of war neuroses?[75]

There had already been heated debate in Britain and Germany about the meaning of the term after the First World War. Victims of shell shock, as the Reich insurance board had laid down in a policy decision of 1926, had no legitimate claim to state pension payments. As the judgment stated, a 'previous mishap might still not be an essential cause of an inability to earn a living, if as a result of the mishap the insured person had nurtured the idea in his mind that he was ill, or if his mind was dominated by the wish to obtain compensation for the mishap or if the damage to his mind had been intensified by negative influences deriving from the compensation procedure'.[76]

The studies of leading psychiatrists such as Karl Bonhoeffer and Ewald Stier formed the basis for this judgement. They had investigated neuroses following accidents and vigorously rejected 'traumatic neurosis' as a syndrome.[77] The board's decision endorsed their thinking. In their eyes state funds simply prolonged the illness, which in many cases could be put down purely to the desire for a pension.

After the Second World War this debate, with similar participants, was to start up again, though this time it was not about soldiers but about the civilian population. In the face of nights of bombing and panic attacks was it now necessary to speak of neurotic illnesses arising from a mishap or more precisely an air raid? Were these experiences not the cause of serious damage to the nervous constitution? Once again it was Bonhoeffer who in an initial, influential publication compared the 'psychopathological experiences' of the two world wars and in doing so was able to base his work on the research and observations of his medical and psychiatric colleagues from the war period. Among them was first of all the assumption that the effects of war had in no way contributed to a serious rise in psychosomatic or autonomic disturbances. 'Hysterical reactions', a few cases of which were observed by a number of doctors after air raids, were regarded by the majority with general suspicion and were not looked on as an injury relevant for social insurance purposes.[78] Bonhoeffer was prepared to recognize only a 'vasomotor complex' as an effect of 'fear and terror'. But precisely because there was no compensation for such complaints, he argued, there was no point in those affected 'taking refuge in illness'. Unlike after the First World War, he wrote, the cities of post-war Germany were not full of 'shell-shocked people standing in weird poses in trains or on the streets and trying to provoke sympathy'.[79]

His assumption was that the air war had hardened people and forced them to find 'a proper yardstick for gauging the effect of shattering experiences', so that, unlike in the 1920s, they had 'become more economical with their sympathy'. To put it another way, never did morale seem better and people's fortitude greater than during the night-time air raids—and thus there could be no valid claim for compensation. The first negotiations concerning the federal pensions law, which was to give a unified ruling to cover the provision individual states would make for their own war victims and in the formulation of which the various interest groups had had an important hand, concluded by linking the level of basic pensions and pension top-ups to the level of injury suffered. Unlike earlier rulings concerning the federal pensions law it did not concern only provision for the armed forces and their families but included also civilians who had been injured in the war.[80] Only physical injury was assessed, however, not the psychological consequences of war, for which even the interest groups had not pressed.

An extensive study written by Friedrich Panse, Karl Bonhoeffer's former colleague at the Berlin Charité hospital, reached the conclusion that there was as a rule no 'experience' of the air war with long-term consequences and that serious abnormal reactions were often the result of an individual predisposition established in the pre-war period. Panse had been working since 1936 as the medical director of the Rheinland Institute for neurological and psychiatric genetic research and from 1937 onwards had held a post as lecturer in psychiatry, neurology, and racial hygiene at the University of Bonn. A 'euthanasia' assessor, from the start of the war he was also a Wehrmacht medical officer and advisory psychiatrist to military district VI. He had treated 'war neurotics' with electric shocks and attempted to distinguish the 'genuinely' ill from 'malingerers'.[81] While his (subsequently successful) case for reinstatement as a university teacher was still in progress, it having at first been rejected by the state of North Rhine–Westphalia in 1952,[82] Panse published a study in the Ministry of Labour series that was soon to become a standard work in the psychiatric literature on 'traumas' and on the 'process of coping with the results of war'. It was called *Fear and Terror* and central to it, as Panse's introduction explained, was the issue of 'mass experience' of the most serious 'emotional traumas' suffered during the air war.

The study was based on interviews with ninety-five men and women he had questioned about their experiences and their fear during air raids. It dealt with fear in air-raid shelters, fear of the next raids, physical reactions during and after raids, sweating and heart palpitations, loss of muscle tone to the point at which fear becomes uncontrollable and takes over the entire body, or even emotional paralyses, moments when those interviewed evidently switched off their feelings and in spite of their fear continued to function. 'Abnormal reactions' were thus by no means the exception, but they depended in the final analysis on the personality structure and on the 'intelligence' of the person affected, in other words on that person's psychological make-up and 'moral' constitution. At the same time, even in serious cases, breathlessness, raised heart rate, and anxiety attacks were not 'illnesses' but occasional disturbances that were reversible and thus of short duration.[83] If there should be any longer-term effects, Panse said, these were observable in less intelligent people and came under the heading of 'inappropriate reactions deriving from the individual personality'.[84] No claim for compensation could be based on such 'abnormal reactions'. Hence Panse noted 'that we have no occasion, and that includes our capacity as medical officers for the pensions office, to change our attitude as psychiatrists with regard to abnormal reactions ensuing after fear and terror'.[85] In practice this meant that patients presenting with problems they attributed to air raids could have little hope of a benevolent assessment of their claims.[86]

Panse was one of the influential assessors in traditional psychiatry who spoke out stridently against even tentative tendencies within their tainted discipline of attributing the development of illnesses to psychosomatic causes.[87] Nothing, in Panse's judgement, seemed to be contributing more to the 'loss of the clinical approach' than attempts 'to make almost everything physical comprehensible as a psychological phenomenon'.[88] The uncompromising rejection of psychoanalysis cannot have been the result purely of a 'scholarly' dispute among medical officers deriving from the discipline's own inner logic, for it was only too evident that the critical attitude to psychosomatic approaches and to psychoanalysis was also part of a post-war political controversy concerning the past position of psychiatry in the Third Reich. That at any rate was the view of important participants such as Alexander Mitscherlich.[89]

As long as it seemed clear that the 'abnormal reactions' disappeared in time and it was only already vulnerable types who were liable to suffer from them for a more substantial period, the prevailing view was that the pension providers' problem was solved. There was therefore no amendment to the federal pensions law. Panse's research was well received among psychiatrists and doctors specializing in social medicine.[90] In the course of the 1950s it was quickly adopted by German textbooks and guidelines for assessors and in addition supplied arguments for why not only soldiers and expellees but also Jewish victims of persecution had for the time being no grounds for making claims on the basis of psychological damage.[91] It was not until 18 May 1960 that the federal court issued a landmark decision conceding the possibility of victims of persecution making a claim for compensation for 'psychological damage' arising from oppression and violence suffered while under arrest or interned.[92] This was a decision that would turn out to be extremely problematic in practice, because, unlike in the United States, the majority of German psychiatrists remained sceptical about diagnoses of 'traumatic neuroses' and psychosomatic illnesses, and it took considerable time for a new psychiatric approach to begin to be accepted.[93]

The issue of compensation for psychological damage had not been very significant for the organizations representing evacuees and victims of bombing. Although there was still repeated reference to suffering and loss, not least in the *Documents of German War Damage* (numerous accounts by contemporaries, including extracts from Panse's study, left no doubt about the immense shock and huge tension from which the population had suffered during the air raids), demands were restricted primarily to material restitution and with it the symbolic acknowledgement that people had been victims of the war. The fact that the evacuees' organizations and the Ministry for Expellees relied on the findings of the study indicated that the various interest groups also judged the long-term psychological consequences to be slight. What was much more important was to be successful in the competition with other war victims in securing social and political resources. For success in this seemed to be the basic precondition for being in a position to cope with the 'terror of the air war'.[94] Psychological damage, if acknowledged at all, was regarded as an individual and time-limited misfortune, whereas material restitution was regarded as a collective responsibility and a 'price' that had to be exacted for the suffering endured.

Britain

Though organizations representing various interests were not active to the same extent, in Britain the issue of material compensation and acknowledgement of psychological damage as a result of the (air) war also played a significant role. As early as 1941 the National Union of Seamen had put considerable pressure on the government to give financial compensation to four sailors for their experiences during a torpedo attack.

The case broke new ground as it deviated from the ruling in force at the start of the war, namely that servicemen should not receive financial compensation but should be given medical treatment so that it did not occur to any of the patients to settle into long-term illness or to become ill as a result, as it were, of being diagnosed with 'war neurosis' and thus incapable of work and entitled to make a claim.[95] Rather than the initial event in itself, it appeared that secondary factors such as the desire for compensation could make a decisive contribution to the development of illness. Whereas in Germany Panse's studies had renewed the rejection of 'traumatic neurosis', in Britain there had been no general departure from the dogmatism of prewar diagnoses but a certain flexibility had been introduced. Hence the Lord President of the Council, Sir John Anderson, had stated clearly in 1943 that in the assessment of servicemen their psychological make-up at the start of the war was crucial and any changes must be judged in the light of that. In every instance, he said, it must be evident that the person affected should not be the one to bear the difficulties associated with the diagnosis of illness and that the patient should be given the benefit of the doubt.[96] In practice, however, by 1944 no serviceman had received a pension on the grounds of illness diagnosed as resulting from trauma, and even after 1945 the number remained small.

Thus the civilian casualties of the air war did not represent a significant source of worry for the state's limited pension and compensation funds, for their numbers were after all far fewer than had been feared. According to information given by doctors at the EMS Hospital, Mill Hill, studies of neuroses caused by the war and service in it among London firemen showed how seldom serious illnesses had ultimately developed. The majority of patients with depression were people who were already ill before they worked for the Fire Service; thus it was not primarily the air war or the negative impact of the work itself but the pre-existing problems that were contributory factors when a fireman was unable to carry on with his work up to the end.[97]

The results of a study published in 1949 in one of the leading professional journals in Britain and involving 212 psychologically affected wartime children also seemed to indicate something similar.[98] The study was based on investigations drawing on cases at a London children's hospital between 1942 and 1946. It focused on the relationship between trauma, how the symptoms presented themselves, family background, and clinical prognosis. The parents had been prompted by a variety of symptoms to bring their children to the hospital. In the main it was 'behavioural abnormalities'; children appeared particularly aggressive or 'nervy'. More than half were regarded as anxious, while just less than a quarter complained of difficulty sleeping. Some children having problems at school were included. According to the study, it could be shown that bombing raids and evacuations were responsible to a significant degree for the behavioural problems in many of the children. The experience of evacuation in particular had long-term effects, above all in children who had been only 5 or younger at the time they were evacuated. They were the ones who showed the most marked psychological abnormalities. After having been evacuated, many were now particularly sensitive and nervous and had difficulty in adjusting to being at home again. Above all the children suffered as a result of the changes to the family in wartime, from the results of conscription and the absence of a parent. In all, as the study's summing up read, the bombing raids had been responsible for a sizeable part of the behavioural problems and 'abnormal reactions', though the children's anxiety and nervousness receded with time.

The study named two factors that were crucial for the development of illness in the children: first, the attitude of the mothers. The medical notes and interviews had, it was claimed, demonstrated that children of 'neurotic' and 'nervous' mothers were more prone to neurotic and psychosomatic illnesses. Secondly, the proportion of children who had already shown abnormal behaviour before the war was high among those who developed problems as a result of the air war. Although morale was not one of the topics of the study, it was nevertheless clear that 'deviant' behaviour was interpreted as stemming from what was passed on from one family member to another and from individual character. The study also implicitly suggested that abnormal behaviour might also have something to do with nationality.[99] In addition, it seemed beyond question to the interviewers that 'neurotic' behaviour was passed on primarily from women to their children and there was not a single case where fathers were mentioned.

Another thing noted by the interviewers in their records of the interviews was not only what the children and their parents said but how they said it. This removed the distinction between medical history and diagnosis. Thus the records repeatedly referred to the presumed 'neurotic' behaviour of quite a few of the mothers, their agitated frame of mind, and their attempt to put the blame on the war for psychological instability—and this in turn was put down as inadmissible and an indicator of 'neurotic' behaviour.[100] Numerous psychiatric studies in Britain from the early post-war period were marked by a fundamental scepticism with regard to illness developing from the (air) war and its consequences.[101] Yet unlike the majority of their German colleagues British psychiatrists and even the Ministry of Pensions did not generally exclude traumatic 'war neuroses' as a possible phenomenon resulting from the war after 1945. The framework within which debates about neurosis and 'normality', about various types of 'morale' and the effects of war, were conducted had widened at least a little, in particular because—not least as a result of the expansion of the NHS—a new generation of doctors with a different academic background and expectations took up their posts and they were much more open to psychoanalytic and psychosomatic methods than their teachers.[102] There was also a further factor: British doctors reacted with a great deal more interest and much less suspicion to American debates, which even during the war had focused on the psychological toll being taken by it (in the first instance among US servicemen)[103] and thus medics and psychologists developed a sense much sooner than in Germany of what the long-term effects of imprisonment and extermination camps were.[104]

In Germany empirical research on psychosomatic illnesses had at first hardly registered and had then been acknowledged only with deep reservations. As late as 1960 leading German psychiatrists, among them Friedrich Panse, noted in an expert appraisal for the Ministry of Labour on the significance for social medicine and pensions of 'neurosis' that forms of lasting neurotic reaction, the cause of which, as in the case of concentration camp inmates, lay in the conditions of their imprisonment and in being treated with constant 'contempt', did in fact exist. In these rare (as it was claimed) cases there was justification for speaking of a 'lasting change resulting from experiences suffered'.[105] At the same time they referred to possible objections to any too broad interpretation and made it clear that it was not always easy to make a distinction between this and 'biased reactions deliberately willed or manipulated' by the subjects. The experts placed in this latter category the types of cases that had been labelled 'pension neurotics' in the 1920s and 1930s, that is neurotic types who were trying to claim compensation so that they could press for social security benefits. They therefore categorically excluded the possibility that war experiences such as being bombed or imprisoned could be the cause of lasting damage. These were rather 'reactions deliberately willed or manipulated' and could not lead to any legal claims on the state, for these conditions were not 'neuroses' in the 'true' sense.[106]

Church, Cities, and a Fresh Start

The aftermath of the air war in Germany was concerned with damage in another sense, namely with material and cultural damage, the loss and reconstruction of local identity. In the 1940s and 1950s the consequences of the air war were linked to a variety of controversies and it was above all in the microcosm of the city or town that the effects of the bombing had to be tackled and interpreted.[107] A mere glance at the streets of Hamburg and Würzburg showed clearly that the air war had not finished when the bombs stopped falling. That was true at least of the search for some meaning in individual pain and for the reasons for the destruction.

The commemoration of the air war was to a great extent, though not exclusively, part of a local history of coping with the consequences of war, and this process was by no means confined to national self-justification or self-victimization, but also played a role in the social conflicts of a deeply divided post-war society and fitted into a range of urban traditions.[108]

In Würzburg, for example, 90 per cent of the centre of which was destroyed in a raid in the middle of March 1945, an attempt was initiated the same year to find a language and form of remembrance for the experience of catastrophe. At the end of November 1945 the city council decided to establish the day of the bombing, 16 March 1945, 'as an everlasting commemoration'.[109] The first year after the end of the war the date of the bombing was central to the city's contemplation of the war experience. The city had been remembering the destruction at central commemorative events since 1946 but as in other German cities there were soon plans for memorials to the air war, many of which were set up in the course of the 1950s. In Würzburg the sculptor Fritz Heuler had created a monument in front of which the annual act of remembrance and wreath-laying had taken place in the presence of all local dignitaries since it was inaugurated in 1954. On this day flags were flown at half-mast on all public buildings and at the moment the raid began all the churches in the city rang their bells.[110]

Such commemorations were communal acts that transcended political parties, creating a consensus even among those who adopted very different political positions in the deeply divided post-war society.[111] In this respect death in the air war took no account of party affiliation or Nazi past and thus was a crucial local means of integrating people precisely in the immediate post-war period, helping to bridge the gap between widely varying experiences of war and violence. Unlike the anonymity of the battlefield for soldiers, the air war offered a concrete space and visible locations where people gathered for commemoration and that could become a visible point of reference for all sections of the city's population, for returning servicemen as well as for those who had stayed at home. A Social Democrat may have spoken a different language from a Catholic bishop but they were united in their demand that the Allied occupying powers should allow them to hold memorial services on the day of the worst bombing raids for those who had died. And where, as in Heilbronn, the Allies rejected the Social Democrats' proposal to declare 4 December a 'day of mourning', there was in the end a communal service and an act of worship at the graves of those who had died in the air war.[112]

It was precisely the fact that it was a kind of natural catastrophe with a supernatural quality about it that had characterized the air war and seemed to distinguish 'civilian' death from the 'soldier's' death and dying on the battlefield. Nuremberg's Social Democrat Oberbürgermeister Otto Bärnreuther reminded his audience in 1955 on the tenth anniversary of the destruction of the old city that the citizens who had died had in no way died a 'normal' death: many men, women, and children had been forced to fight for their lives for many hours as they lay buried beneath the rubble or they suffered the agony of suffocation or were burnt alive at the end of a cruel martyrdom.[113]

Until well into the 1950s memorial services for the dead of the air raids struggled to find a language for the indescribable, for an event for which there were no models and parallels in the city's history. The term 'terror raid' with its Nazi associations still suggested itself to describe the air raids and was, so to speak, the lowest common denominator that transcended political camps and religious differences. Yet it no longer had the same power to convince and explain. The issue of guilt and punishment, meaning and responsibility, was now more complicated. Just why did so many people have to die? The exalted language of the Nazi cult of heroism had been exhausted and could not be revived.

Instead it was at first the major Christian denominations that re-Christianized death in the air war and with it the fate of the whole nation, by locating the bombing war within the history of peoples that had turned away from God. In doing so they were picking up again the thread of interpretation they had already developed during the first nights of bombing. Language and terminology were, however, anything but consistent and themselves evidence of the fragility of the theological foundation on which an understanding of the nation's fate in the air war rested.

At the end of September 1947 Protestant Christians from Bremen could read a story in their church magazine, which had recently begun to appear, that was designed to offer comfort for all the terrible things they had experienced in the war years. It was the story of a night in the shelter which the (anonymous) author remembered because of its being the feast of St Michael.[114] The archangel Michael, patron saint of the Holy Roman Empire and of soldiers and warriors, had, according to the story, once defeated the devil in the form of demons and led the heavenly host. It was one of the terrible nights of bombing. The bombs were exploding, everyone was afraid, mortal fear spread among people. The anti-aircraft fire became a 'lashing and roaring infernal concert'. 'Tortured humanity', holed up in the shelter and taking upon itself, as it were, the sufferings of all, wore a distraught expression for destruction seemed imminent. One man only, who had found refuge with his daughter, radiated calm, in spite of the 'hellish fortissimo'. Then, as the noise of the bombs falling to earth was all around, his daughter asked him: 'Father, what does this all mean?' And the father answered the frightened girl: 'The demons have been let out.' 'And who can bind the demons?' asked the girl. 'Well, only God's angels could do that.' Finally the man took hold of the child's hand again as she looked steadily up at him.

This story was so important to the author because faced with danger the father did not tell the child some fairy tale or other but imparted 'something of his faith'. According to his gloomy interpretation, humanity had forgotten for too long this treasure trove of stories. Now it was time to remember them. It was good that the archangel was stronger than all the demons, so that human beings might not feel 'helpless' but protected by God. That, in the author's interpretation, was evidence of how fundamental Christian faith was at times of greatest distress. The demons seemed to be the bombers who were putting people in danger. Not the Nazis but the Allies were evil personified; that was what the story was saying or at least that was a possible meaning, one that made it easier to understand who was threatening the lives of 'innocent' people in the shelters and who in the end saved them.

The parable left room for manoeuvre, all the same. St Michael was also the one who kept a record of human beings' good and bad deeds and placed these before God on the Day of Judgement. As the 'weigher of souls' he wore the colour red, a mixture of blood, fire, and warmth, and the shelter seemed to be the place where it was time to face the final reckoning with oneself and one's life. As this father reminded his daughter of the power of the demons and promised salvation from them, so people in their distress were encouraged not to be tortured by demons but to dismiss them, remain steadfast, and return to their faith. The air war and the nights of bombing thus had two meanings, as the demonic, devilish activity of the forces of evil in human existence and also a metaphor for the final balance sheet of people's lives and their faith in God, as strictly and relentlessly recorded by St Michael—something of which everyone should be aware.

This type of interpretation made evident the fluid (and thus easily assimilated) boundaries between talk of terror bombers and apocalyptic visions of death and destruction and so avoided a sharp distinction that might have made the connection between the reason for the suffering of the air war and culpable behaviour on the part of the Germans. But the link to St Michael equally allowed scope for an interpretation that focused less on the Allied demons and more on their being overcome through the power of faith, thus providing the foundation for a new spiritual beginning.

Victory over demons was, however, not the only (nor even the predominant) possibility of reminding people of Christian martyrdom and spiritual renewal. During the bombing there had been no lack of iconography depicting victory over death. In 1950 Protestant Christians between Kassel and Frankfurt were able to read a startling story in their church magazine that reminded them of their own distress while being at the same time intended as a source of comfort.

The subject was a burning cross as a symbol of salvation and resurrection and an air raid on the city of Essen. Much of the city had gone up in flames, including the church. People ran about in panic until they noticed that the steel cross on the church tower was glowing brightly in the dark night and lighting up the darkness and thus was a sign of hope beyond all destruction and scenes of devastation.[115] After all (and this Old Testament interpretation was common to the war period and the post-war era), even Jerusalem had crumbled to dust and ashes, empires collapsed, and countries had been ravaged by wars. At the end of it all the cross was still standing, overarching everything, just as on that occasion on 27 August 1950, when people walked through Essen following the steel cross that had withstood the fire and bore witness to their faith in Jesus Christ. Death in the air war and the devastation of the city had some meaning, in spite of the immense toll, because it had demonstrated, so to speak in the form of a purifying trial and act of redemption, who had died for them and who alone represented salvation.

That had also been demonstrated by the Mainz Sisters of the Eternal Worship of God in a substitutionary act of martyrdom; according to the bishop's office, during a night-time air raid they had 'offered' themselves as sacrifices to God for the peace of the world. In spite of air-raid warnings they carried on with their ritual of 'partaking together of the Blessed Sacrament' and praying for the forgiveness of sins. As the Catholics of the diocese could read in their magazine in 1946, the Mother Superior had just placed the Sacrament on the altar when the city and the convent became the victims of a heavy air raid. Many nuns were killed in the raid and overnight, as the bishop announced at a solemn requiem, they became guardian angels of the city and diocese of Mainz.[116] In this instance it was no longer the demons who were at work but real Christian martyrs who had died as a sacrifice for the sins of the world. The protagonists of the air war had no role in this and no direct attribution of guilt was laid at the Allies' door. In the end the horror of war had its origin in people's comprehensive rejection of God and failure to acknowledge their sinfulness, the burden of which had, at least in small measure, been removed by the Catholic nuns.

Thus, in spite of a common stock of concepts and rituals, Catholics and Protestants could at times vary greatly in the language and strands of tradition they used. In numerous memorial services, which began immediately after the end of the war but from the early 1950s onwards had turned into centralized mass demonstrations led by local and church authorities, bishops of both churches reminded people of the apocalyptic downfall of their homeland, the immense forces of nature that had swept over innocent women and children, and the comfort that came from the resurrection of Jesus Christ. There was no more talk of demonic power. In every ending there was a new beginning, one that meant returning to God.

The remembrance of the air war was integrated into calls for the re-Christianization of a society that had turned away from God. The Christian churches offered a dual interpretation. On the one hand there was reference to the innocent victims and to the grief felt by their families, whose quiet worship produced the strength to go on living after the catastrophe. On the other hand, an explanation was offered for the misfortune suffered by individuals and the city that had to do with their own behaviour and relationship with God. The destruction was thus in no way 'inexplicable' but rather part of a rejection of God. As a rule this pastoral message to those who mourned remained abstract and made no historical reference. Incidents such as occurred in Kassel in 1953 were rare: there a Catholic priest, while blessing a new cemetery for victims of the air war, reminded the mourners of their own shared responsibility for the war and the air war and asked the rhetorical question, 'Were we not part of this wretched crowd that once shouted "yes" when asked, "Do you want total war"?'[117] But such references, which associated the sin with a concrete action and interpreted the air war as divine punishment for Nazi crimes, were the exception. Another change had taken place in the meantime. However prevalent it was to claim that the air war indicated a turning away from God, among Catholic clerics in particular there ceased to be much explicit reference to 'divine punishment' in the face of the suffering of the German population. As the chair of the German Bishops Conference and Archbishop of Cologne Joseph Frings explained in his first pastoral letter at the end of May 1945, people had suffered enough for the wrong done by Germany and had atoned for it.[118] The suffering of the nights of bombing had erased their guilt and made people ready for a new start. For Frings, looking into causes was less important than the lessons that should be drawn from such a radical experience. And those were to mourn with dignity the dead, to reconstruct Germany under Christian leadership, and to seek reconciliation in God's name. The Christian vocabulary of death and resurrection applied to the air war provided a connection with immediate war experiences and also offered people the opportunity to free themselves linguistically from the Nazi regime and, as it were, to denazify themselves.

At the same time the Christian language of reconciliation was universal and transnational and an essential precondition for gathering at the altar with fellow Christians who had once been enemies and to revive discontinued ecumenical relations such as those that before 1933 connected Hamburg's Protestants with Britain.[119] In a sermon broadcast on the radio at Christmas in 1946 Michael Howard, the Anglican Dean of Coventry, addressed himself to a priest in the devastated city of Hamburg, repeating his offer of reconciliation from the wartime period. Whenever he looked at the Christ Child, Howard said in his message to the Hamburg Christians, he thought of two things he would like to say to his opposite number: 'I think I see between us at our feet, the Christ Child lying in His crib. Across the Child I stretch out my hand and put it into yours, my brother. [...] Looking down into the face of the infant Jesus—God in human flesh—two words spring to my lips to say to you. The first word is "Forgiveness". [...] The second word is this—"New Birth". Here in Coventry we have 20,000 new homes to build, a whole new city centre and a Cathedral to restore. Your task is even greater. But more important still, there is a new spirit to be born—new courage, new faith, new unselfishness, new pity for each other's suffering, new family love and purity.'[120]

Only two years later Britain's most important churchman, the Archbishop of Canterbury, Geoffrey Fisher, visited Hamburg in order to take part in a joint German–British memorial service. As Bishop of London during the Blitz Fisher knew what it meant to live 'under the bombs'.[121] Fisher presided together with the *Land* bishop Schöffel at the crowded service, which was designed to mark an end and a beginning: the end of the war and the beginning of a new era of communion of all those who met at the Lord's table and broke bread. A confession of sin spoken by all was followed by the absolution pronounced by Fisher and broadcast on the radio, which, as the German newspapers commented, was a handshake signifying 'brotherhood beyond national boundaries and German–British unity'.[122] This was on the whole more wishful thinking than reality and the product of the Protestants' claim to be, like the British Christians, victims of the war. In Britain at any rate the gesture was hardly noticed because it was but one incident during Fisher's almost two-week visit to Germany to gain an impression of the situation in the British zone of occupation. Meetings with representatives of Germany's churches were of little importance to the public back home.[123]

If the search for an appropriate language through which to express consolation and mourning had been central to the first memorial services in the middle and at the end of the 1940s, from the beginning of the 1950s the emphasis was increasingly on reconciliation and reconstruction as lessons to be learnt from the experience of catastrophe. In many places reconstruction meant in very concrete terms the rebuilding of bombed churches. Many church magazines began their first editions after the war with a special series devoted at first to loss and then to rebuilding.

In Cologne and Mainz it was the stories of the survival and reconstruction of the cathedral that the diocese focused on and for which they collected donations. The survival of these buildings was taken as a sign of Christian steadfastness, as a 'memorial to warn people and point them to heaven', and as evidence of how new life blossomed from the ruins of the air war.[124] In this respect the cathedral was not just one of many church buildings but rather represented those 'ancient sites of culture' in which the peoples of Europe were reflected and its reconstruction, as the Cologne Cardinal Frings suggested, gave a signal from the thirteenth century for the old Christian west to draw closer together to resist the advance of forces from the east.[125] The 700th anniversary of the laying of the foundation stone of Cologne Cathedral in the middle of August 1948 was not only a celebration of the restoration of the choir and transepts but a proof of Christian energy and the fortitude that had grown out of the ruins of the air war.[126]

In Berlin immediately after the war congregations set about rebuilding their churches. The notion of rebuilding was, however, by no means as obvious as it at first sounded, for what was it in fact that was to be rebuilt? What could congregations afford and in what form should the building be recreated—as it was before the air raids or as the architectural expression of a new era?[127] In the autumn of 1945 Berlin's Protestants asked congregations for donations for the rebuilding of the Church of St Nicholas. It was after all not just any old church but rather the core of Brandenburg Protestantism, the soul of the city, and a refuge for people in distress. It was the duty of the church community to rebuild this place of worship but also a duty that 'every' German must respond to.[128]

When Hamburg's landmark church of St Michael was reopened in 1952 the whole city celebrated and it was a ceremonial act of urban and religious resurrection. The Federal Minister of the Interior, Robert Lehr, saw in 'Michel's' history a metaphor for the 'storms of the age that had swept over Germany'.[129] The restoration of the city skyline with its church towers and buildings chimed in exactly with the process of overcoming the past war and with a city community that even amid the fire storms and conflagrations of the past had not been destroyed. Destruction and resurrection were part of the shared story of Christian hope that had sustained the city over centuries. As Hamburg's *Land* bishop Volmar Herntrich suggested on the occasion of the reopening of a church in the Hamm district of the city, in the end the 250-year-old parish had resisted all external threats. After the 'cruel years of annihilation' the parish had 'risen like a phoenix from the ashes'. The Catholics of Würzburg also spoke of a 'phoenix from the ashes', when in 1952 they commemorated their patron saint, St Kilian, in a week of celebrations.[130] It had been 1,200 years since his remains had been accorded the status of relics and now, seven years after the war, the city and the church could look back on having cleared the worst of the devastation and the new flourishing of the Christian community. During the concluding service the nuncio reminded people of the history of the city, which he had visited for the first time before the outbreak of the war; it had been a wonderful, graceful city. But a 'sense of pain' had come over him the first time he saw it after the bombing, he said; 'Old' Würzburg had gone, its culture destroyed, lives cut short and the city had been confronted with the 'horror of death'. Now, however, he was delighted to witness the overwhelming 'spirit of reconstruction'.[131]

At the beginning of March 1949 *The Times* reported a very unusual act of resurrection and reconstruction.[132] In Düsseldorf, as the report read, there was a special project to effect a wondrous transformation: a church was being built from a former air-raid shelter by the hands of the members of the parish and encouraged by the church's animating spirit, the priest Carl Klinkhammer. This 'bunker church' was not far from the Rhine in an area on the border between Neuss and Düsseldorf that had suffered heavy damage. The tower shelter had originally been established by the Nazi authorities without the consent of the parish, which had planned to convert the existing temporary church building into a new church. After the war, although the plot belonged to the parish, the tower shelter had passed into the hands of the occupying authorities. The driving force behind this project was the 'Ruhr chaplain' Carl Klinkhammer, a man known beyond the borders of the Rhineland and a cleric who had come into conflict with the Nazis at an early stage; after 1945 he was among the most strident guardians of the Catholic faith with regard to the battle against 'filth and trash', against the 'moral decline' of the age, and against communism. In the eyes of this vigorous pastor and writer resurrection and Christian renewal, in a literal sense, went hand in hand.[133] For that reason it was not at all contradictory that Klinkhammer protested with stink bombs against showings of *The Sinner** in the afternoon[134] and in the evening and at week-ends laboured with his own hands to advance the shelter conversion.

In the process numerous legal issues had to be settled. In particular the consent of the occupation authorities had been required and also that of the curacy of the archdiocese, which finally made a considerable sum available

---

* Translators' note: *Die Sünderin*, a controversial film of 1951 starring Hildegard Knef.

for the purchase of the shelter and for the conversion. This demilitarization of a war structure was in fact unique in the post-war period and was soon to attract visitors from Germany and abroad. Windows were blasted in the thick external walls of the tower, intermediate ceilings were removed, and new internal walls created. In the end there arose a huge, oblong nave, 9 metres high, 20 metres wide, and 35 metres long.[135] Light now penetrated the previously dark building through the windows at the front. The interior was fitted in a simple and solid fashion and the concrete reminded visitors at every step that the church's foundation was an air-raid shelter. A larger than life-size crucifix of steel beaten then welded together was displayed prominently above the altar. This crucifix, a Baroque Madonna, and a Pietà searching for her lost son on the battlefield were the only pictorial representations in the church. Part of the church was composed of a cylindrical structure, to which was added a newly created bell tower.

When the bunker church was consecrated on 30 October 1949 there was great public interest. The Archbishop of Cologne Cardinal Frings celebrated the Pontifical Mass and focused on the verse from Isaiah: 'They shall beat their swords into ploughshares and their spears into pruning hooks.'[136] Frings reminded the congregation what a special act of transformation they were witnessing at that moment. A 'bulwark of war' had been turned into a 'place of blessing' that spoke of another life. For him the bunker church was both an admonition and an example of a better, more Christian era, for the 'dark, hulking tower shelter' reminded him, he said, of the state of the souls of people in these days who turned their back on the world outside and their neighbour and looked after only themselves and their own interests. Frings did not, in other words, take up the theme of the solidarity of the shelter community in their experiences during the nights of bombing. Rather, as he said, it was time to blow up the past's 'bunkers of the soul' and, like the early church, people should force windows into the walls of their inner selves. Taking on the 'easy yoke of Christ' was one part of this act of spiritual renewal and the other was to break out of 'the bunker of arrogant national pride and racial hatred'. This demand for spiritual renewal under the banner of the Cross, which was couched in militant language and legitimized by the moral ruins of Nazism and Nazi air-raid prevention, thus found in the bunker church not only a symbol but a location. Faith in Jesus Christ had not only survived the terror of the Third Reich but was even stronger than all the reinforced concrete that the church members had broken up with their own hands and on the remains of which they had built a tiny part of this new society.

The bunker church was more than just a new church building. For the Catholic church in the Rhineland it was representative of the integrity and dignity of its own history within the Nazi state, of the selfless urge to reconstruct and renew in a spirit of reconciliation and peace. Its position at Düsseldorf Handweiser seemed ideally suited to this for, as Klinkhammer liked to proclaim, it had itself been an expression of this religious war between a dispossessed church and the godless Nazis. Where better than here could the war-filled past and the Christian future be reconciled and where better could people speak about distress, mourning, and loss as much as about renewal and resurrection than in a bunker church? Thus, even in the early 1950s the tower shelter's history became increasingly detached from the air war and hence Nazism itself, and the building's past and present became more and more strongly absorbed into the story of Catholic resistance during Nazi rule, so reinforcing Catholic claims to leadership after the 'catastrophe' of the Third Reich.

10

Lessons of the Air War

The Politics of Reconciliation

Among the lessons to be drawn from the 'catastrophe' were reconciliation and the question of guilt and forgiveness. In this respect the air war was part of the 'comprehensive Last Judgement' in which no one was free from 'guilt'. Thus everyone could engage in dialogue with each other on an equal basis, both victors and vanquished. In Hamburg, for example, in the course of the late 1950s the provincial church (*Landeskirche*) had increasingly gained control of the content of memorial services for the dead of the air war, after the influence of welfare organizations and evacuee associations, who had organized these events in the immediate post-war period, continued to diminish.

On the occasion of the 20th anniversary of Operation Gomorrah citizens were invited to a service of repentance at St Peter's in order to commemorate the 'catastrophic days of 1943'.[1] In his sermon to a packed church Hamburg's bishop Karl Witte looked back to the nights of the raids, making a distinction between those who, like him, had 'experienced' them and those who knew them only through hearsay. 'We' meant all the Hamburg citizens who knew what was implied by the term 'conflagration'; 'we' meant the community of citizens of the Hanseatic city who shared one destiny and who had experienced something that would mark them out from other generations and cities.

But what was the reason for all this suffering, for the misery, and for this 'policy of annihilation' towards Germany? The bishop's view was that it had been 'humanity's general confusion' that had caused the catastrophe. 'All those involved' had made themselves guilty, Witte pronounced, Germans as well as the British. The 'scales of guilt' were in equilibrium. Who in the end would be prepared to accuse whom? He interpreted the bombing as God's judgement on the depths of human wickedness. It signified for him guilt and sin but also hope of moral regeneration through an act of purification. For those who had committed the 'crime' twenty years before were now the friends and comrades of today.

The concept of reconciliation could thus be absorbed into an overarching narrative in which the Germans were victims and this made it possible to speak not only about their own guilt but also that of others, and to do it in a tone of moral outrage at the suffering endured in the air war. At the same time it opened up the possibility of new forms of encounter and of the former enemies finding a new semantic field that allowed them to speak about their individual suffering and at the same time about a new future, thus turning the focus away from cause and effect. The Christian concept of reconciliation accommodated a whole series of very diverse historical interpretations and allowed people to extend the hand of friendship while consigning the argument about the causes of the war to the unknowable depths of the Christian faith, where they finally became an unfathomable 'mystery', as the Hamburg bishop had put it.

Reconciliation was also central to the dialogue between British and German Christians, which had been increasing since the 1950s, above all in connection with the rebuilding of Coventry Cathedral. Even after the war the ruins of the bombed cathedral, pictures of which had gone round the world, had lost nothing of their importance as a symbol of Britain's will to survive. On the contrary, in Britain's understanding of itself the city, after all, was regarded as the first in history to fall victim to modern aerial warfare and Hitler's barbarism. From 1945 onwards groups of visitors from all over the world were coming with increasing frequency to Coventry to see the ruins and gain an impression of the violence of the destruction the Germans had inflicted on Britain and how valiantly and courageously it had defied the forces of evil.

But after the war what was to become of the ruins and this place of particular significance for the British? Even during the war the provost, Dick Howard, had made it his special concern to ensure that Coventry should send out a distinctive message and he had won episcopal support for this plan. One of the earliest projects for reconstruction from 1944[2] envisaged creating a special Christian centre and a Chapel of Unity as a place for ecumenical dialogue that would offer Anglicans and nonconformists a shared place for prayer. Admittedly this project came under fire at an early stage from both Anglicans and nonconformists, for of course it seemed to cross denominational boundaries and water down differences in a completely inadmissible manner.

In 1947 Howard had accepted an invitation from the city of Kiel and had taken as a gift a small cross of nails, which was a miniature of the cross that stood on the altar in Coventry and had been put together from the nails from the collapsed roof vaulting. His concern, he explained, was for mutual 'forgiveness' and this cross was a symbol of it. The next day, Howard recalled, his Protestant host had taken him to see his own bombed church and at the end had presented him with a stone from the rubble[3] that was then given a special place in the Chapel of Unity as the 'Kiel Stone of Forgiveness' and so laid the foundation for the affectionate partnership that was to develop in the coming decades between Kiel and Coventry.

The strife that grew up around the rebuilding of the cathedral was even more serious than the interdenominational conflicts over the Chapel of Unity. The first stage was the issue of architectural form: should there be a new building or should the existing one be restored? Should the traditional English Gothic style be adopted or a modern style of church be tried? How in any case should a church look if it is a place of remembrance, yet one where dying for one's country, unlike after the First World War, could no longer be glorified and presented as an action with meaning for future generations?

The decision was made at a time when Britain as a whole was struggling to find a new architectural style in which to express the present. The Festival of Britain in 1951 had provided an opportunity to search for new and 'modern' forms in art, architecture, and design, which up to then had had hardly any impact in Britain.[4] The winning design by Basil Spence was in this respect a compromise. Condemned by conservatives as an unchristian 'mausoleum', many younger architects saw the building as an opportunity missed to blend Christianity and the modern. Spence's design envisaged that the ruins would remain as a 'Garden of Rest' and create a close spiritual link with the new cathedral, which was only a stone's throw away and built of sandstone. It was to be a church that focused on reconciliation and rejected any aura of heroism or superiority.[5] It was a design without exaggeration or extravagance and quite a few people would have preferred a more complex interaction of dynamic and static elements. Yet the building was full of symbols and allusions, integrated the historical location, and created a dignified atmosphere that, according to the majority of critics, did not break with the tradition of sacred buildings but had nevertheless captured a new and modern spirit.[6]

Until this view came to dominate in the course of the 1950s there was considerable conflict, not just over the design and structure but also over the liturgical arrangement of the new cathedral, because, contrary to the Anglican tradition, the high altar was at first supposed to be positioned in the centre of the nave in the midst of the congregation, as Spence explained. In the end, however, the protests from the reconstruction committee were so overwhelming that this idea and other proposals contained in the original design were dropped.

Criticism came finally from another quarter, for in view of the scarcity of resources and its own plans for building homes the Labour-dominated Coventry City Council had been keeping a very watchful eye on the extent of the works occasioned by the building of the cathedral.[7] In 1954 the councillors in a resolution finally protested against the start of building work. Shops, shopping centres, offices, and health centres were what the money should be spent on and not on new places of worship.[8] Opponents of the project exploited the conflict between the city and the church leaders to sound off against the building. A delegation from the city council travelled to London in order to secure a hearing for their views, but finally the minister responsible gave a ruling in favour of beginning work on the building. For as he made clear in a letter to the Lord Mayor of Coventry, the building of the cathedral was not a matter for the city alone. The echo of the bombs had been heard throughout the world and people had waited for the signal that British tradition and history had survived the bombing of Coventry and that the city had risen again. The reconstruction was, he said, an act of faith, and in view of the external threat it was more important than ever before.[9] That put an end to the matter and the city council, which had come in for public criticism, gave up fighting it. However appealing the message of reconciliation may have sounded, the subliminal reservations nevertheless continued. Disagreement arose, for example, over Spence's plans for the 'Chapel of Unity', a part of the church under the control not of the cathedral chapter but of the Joint Council of Anglican and Free Churches. Ecumenism seemed in this instance to be carried to extremes and the established and traditional rights of the church swept aside. The provost appealed worldwide for donations for his project for a Chapel of Unity, and that included Germany, where his request was welcomed. Yet when the German President Theodor Heuss donated money in 1958 for the windows of the chapel and the Chancellor Konrad Adenauer contributed to the reconstruction, there were one or two isolated voices in the conservative press critical of Germany that described the German donations as 'blood money'.[10]

Admittedly, this political barrage could hardly do damage to the relations that had by now developed between the two countries, particularly among churches. On the contrary, from the beginning of the 1950s onwards not only had services in Coventry regularly been held in German but there had been visits from young Protestant Christians. The links leading to the visit arose through Aktion Sühnezeichen (Operation Reconciliation)[11] and in the international office of the EKD (Protestant Churches of Germany), which coordinated the project and had been making efforts for some time to create closer ties with Britain. First of all, students from the Church University in Berlin travelled to London, Cambridge, and Coventry in order to gain an impression of pastoral work and theological studies there. Coventry was the diplomatic high point of the journey because it was there that the German party was on uncertain ground.

While they were still in the coach, as members of the group recalled shortly after the visit, the atmosphere had been tense and edgy. They were, after all, on their way to a city that Germany had destroyed and in Coventry they would be directly confronted with the issue of war guilt. Their nervousness made them feel queasy[12] and this apprehension melted away only after the first meeting, when the young students sensed how warmly they were welcomed to Coventry by Provost Howard and his congregation. Political issues were in any case not part of the visit. The services and worship were focused on pastoral matters, for example on pastoral care in industrial areas.

The past and the war were not on the agenda but instead the role of young people in the future. The young participants spoke at most indirectly about the war and if they did it was in the, for them, new language of reconciliation, which many had still to learn and the meaning of which they had still to grasp. The young theology students returned contented to Berlin, impressed by the warmth of their British hosts, if somewhat sceptical about the, by comparison with Germany, somewhat unsystematic character of their theology.

For Howard and his successor Bill Williams international youth work, in particular with the Germans, had a very special significance in his project of reconciliation. In 1960, even before the official opening of the cathedral, an International Centre of Reconciliation was created with extensive international support. German young people contributed to setting it up and it was inaugurated by the chair of the council of the EKD, Otto Dibelius. At the opening ceremony he first prayed for reconciliation and reminded the congregation that Germany had changed since the war. At the time when 'satanic' powers were destroying the church and the cathedral, even the church had been forbidden to speak. Here in Coventry therefore two sets of victims were meeting: the citizens and Christians of Coventry and the maltreated Protestant Christians of Germany, both equally victims of Hitler's dictatorship.

It was precisely this line of interpretation that enabled Dibelius to speak about reconciliation and parity, as both groups had been victims of a violent power they could not influence in any way and for which no one took direct responsibility, not even German Christians. Dibelius then made a further point. Britain and Germany stood on the threshold of a new era. The churches of Europe, not only the German ones, had freed themselves from their secular bonds and now, borne up by a spirit of love and hope, they had rediscovered their calling. The battle against hatred was the church's mission, and throughout the continent, he said, Coventry should be the new name and new symbol for Christian reconciliation.[13] Dibelius had paid tribute to Coventry's towering significance as the symbol of a crime and had also acknowledged the suffering that the city and the British nation had had inflicted on them. That was an important step. Yet at the same time he could speak in Coventry without being part of this 'satanic' country, the church itself having, in his own words, been silenced. In these circumstances reconciliation could gain a foothold much more easily, because this narrative did not involve the Germans in acknowledging their own or the nation's participation in this history of the air war and the military escalation; being open to reconciliation went hand in hand with styling themselves as victims.

For Williams and the Anglican church this was not an affront because their own idea of reconciliation was not too far removed from this. In August 1960, in a letter to Lothar Kreyssig, the initiator of Aktion Sühnezeichen, Williams had explained the motives behind his support for a British–German young people's exchange. The point was not to make a gesture of forgiveness but to bring about an act of reconciliation, for after all the war had been the result of human sin and everyone had incurred guilt.[14] He felt that too much German self-condemnation was damaging.

Then a year later as part of this Christian movement for reconciliation young Protestant Christians set off for the Midlands to help in the reconstruction of the cathedral's severely damaged sacristy.[15] At the same time plans for the official opening ceremony were in full swing and it was a major political issue who would take part from the German side and who would not. From the point of view of the German embassy in London German participation was absolutely necessary. This would be fully consonant with the symbolic acts of the West German President and government.[16]

Whereas the Catholic church had declined to take part, the director of the international office of the EKD, Gerhard Stratenwerth, travelled on behalf of the Protestant church to Coventry in place of Dibelius, who was unable to attend.[17] For some considerable time Stratenwerth had worked consistently for British–German dialogue and had been invited to Coventry in 1956 as a Protestant representative. It was not yet clear in the run-up whether a German was to speak at this occasion but Stratenwerth took great pains to be prepared for the eventuality. In the draft of his short speech he said much about reconciliation and friendship, about the war and the new experiences both sides had had since 1945, of which the newly constructed cathedral was a living symbol.

Stratenwerth, it must be said, explained to a close colleague what precisely he meant by the term reconciliation.[18] He had consciously spoken not of Germany's but of Europe's 'darkest hour'. His message was that the Germans were not solely responsible for the air war for the British were at least as responsible. His second argument and a view he strongly advocated fitted, he felt, into this historical understanding of reconciliation, namely that all nations should ask for forgiveness in Coventry. 'For this is the only legitimate thing to ask. What is not legitimate is the sentence that is written up in Coventry, albeit strongly felt but with little biblical justification: "Father, forgive them, for they know not what they do."' According to this view, reconciliation was not without preconditions but part of a politics conducted among equals involving an acknowledgement that the Germans were not the only 'guilty' ones in respect of the air war. Seen in this light, although the politics of reconciliation had more than an exculpatory function, it did attempt to go for the supposed vulnerable spot in Germany's former enemy, the 'morality of the bombing war'.

Stratenwerth had no opportunity to make his speech, however, because his British hosts changed their plans and did not ask for a German contribution. When the cathedral was finally consecrated on 25 May 1962 and opened by the Queen in a moving ceremony, the conflicts that had arisen

along the way had been largely forgotten and the press comment was full
of praise for this bold but at the same time not revolutionary new church
building that seemed to combine the traditional and the modern with
such imagination.[19] The Archbishop of Canterbury, Michael Ramsey,
restated clearly what in his view this church ultimately stood for, namely
the blending of art and craft, for the meeting of church with workers, and
a place—and he regarded this as particularly important—where nations
that were formerly enemies could sense the greatness of God and his
power for forgiveness and create a new bond of friendship on the strength
of this faith. This was a prophetic calling for a place that had been scarred
by war but where finally, from the ashes of the bombing, a new world of
reconciliation would grow up. That, according to Ramsey, was the meaning of Coventry![20]

Coventry and Dresden

As a result of the controversy surrounding the air war and the passionate
country-wide debate about the meaning and shape of the new cathedral,
within a bare twenty years Coventry had become a national, indeed an
international, place of commemoration of the war. The bombing of the city
was now one of the 'great' destructive events of world history and at the
same time Coventry was a symbol of Christian reconciliation and world
renewal—a transformation in which the historical link to the air war was
disappearing ever more from view. One of the core convictions of Provost
Williams was that reconciliation was a task for young people and was demonstrated first and foremost in a mixture of prayer and action. This conviction made him respond with great enthusiasm to a completely new form of
British–German dialogue, which was to make headlines in the years to
come.

David Irving's book *The Destruction of Dresden*, first published in English
in 1963 and a year later in German, had already hit the headlines.[21] The
book made such an impact because it appeared to provide documentary
proof of what an immense number of civilian victims of the bombing there
had been and how huge the damage suffered by this city on the Elbe, which
was as 'peaceful' as it was culturally important. For Irving it was apparently
certain that 135,000 people had lost their lives in the Allied raid.[22] These
deaths, he claimed, had been pointless so soon before the end of the war and

the victims had suffered as a result of a mistaken, indeed 'murderous' air-war strategy. One man was chiefly responsible, namely Winston Churchill.

The publication of this book had caused a stir both in Germany and in Britain. Richard Crossman, the Labour politician and a specialist in psychological warfare who even during the war had protested against area bombing and defended the studies of Frankland and Webster, reviewed the book in the *New Statesman*. His verdict on the bombing was that it was a 'war crime' and he praised the book as an impressive piece of historical research.[23] Other people, on the other hand, pointed to the necessity of the air-war strategy and its contribution to victory over fascism and particularly emphasized the way Dresden had been exploited for propaganda purposes.[24]

In most of the reviews in West Germany there was evident relief that Dresden's special status had been acknowledged and the 'truth' now plainly stated. The review in *Der Spiegel* appeared under the heading 'Sodom in Saxony'[25] and its report gave strong support to Irving's use of the term 'senseless terror' as a description of the Allied bombing. On the basis of the documents *Die Zeit* regarded it as proven that the raid had represented 'probably the largest mass murder in the whole of human history'.[26] The review had been written for an American readership by a former Dresden resident, who now lived in the USA. She reported in detail on the burning funeral pyres and the pungent smell of burnt corpses. The authenticity of the eyewitness account gave the review additional authority and reinforced its conclusion: 'Dresden', even more than Hiroshima and Nagasaki, stood for the total senselessness of modern warfare and was proof of its barbaric consequences.[27]

The Nazis' propaganda success had continued after 1945 and had left its mark on foreign reporting on Dresden as the symbol of the murderousness of the air war as a whole. In British and American newspapers there was repeated talk of 200,000 and even 300,000 victims[28] of the raids on this 'innocent', 'defenceless', and 'unique' city, three terms that were to remain constants in the many and varied narratives over more than six decades.

The German Democratic Republic (GDR) could also adopt these interpretations intact and follow on seamlessly from Nazi propaganda. In its early period, the years 1946 and 1947, leading functionaries of the Communist Party (KPD/SED) had spoken of the Germans' shared guilt in the air war and only then had bewailed the loss of 'innocent' lives in the city. From 1948 onwards, with the increasing rivalry between the two political systems in Germany, the answer to the question about the guilty parties changed. Now once more there was mention in public of the raids having hit women, children, and the old in particular and of the pointlessness of the bombing at that stage in the war.[29] In language redolent of the Nazis, reference was made to the 'Anglo-American' air war, the 'defenceless' city, and the crimes of the Allies.

When the Cold War escalated from the beginning of the 1950s onwards the note of self-criticism faded away and church-led ceremonies of remembrance were appropriated and reshaped by the mass demonstrations of the SED, which distorted them into public protests against the 'American warmongers'. In the run-up to the fifth anniversary of the bombing the SED *Politbüro* determined the line to be taken and the language to be used in the memorial ceremonies. Remembrance of the air war was to be an occasion for stoking 'national hatred for the Anglo-American warmongers' and protesting stridently against West Germany's alliance with these criminal states.[30] The bombing of the defenceless city of Dresden, as it was claimed at the mass gathering on 13 February 1950, was therefore also an expression of a conscious British and American strategy to lay waste to the Red Army's future territory and the Soviet zone of occupation and so to undermine progress towards establishing socialism in Germany. In this respect Dresden had not been the 'victim' of senseless bombing but had been quite deliberately 'executed', an interpretation that at least appeared to lend the death and suffering caused some kind of meaning distinct from that offered by Christian interpretations and incorporated the city's tragedy in a heroic narrative of socialist reconstruction.[31]

Five years later the national council of the GDR *Nationale Front* published precise instructions on how the coming memorial celebration for the tenth anniversary of the bombing was to commemorate it and what was to be said: Dresden was one link in the chain of great crimes against humanity and the endpoint of a sequence of violent events that, with its origins in German militarists and imperialists, had begun with the invasion of Poland and the bombing of Warsaw.[32] It had ended with Dresden and the attempt to reduce future existence in the guiltless city to rubble. And now, in 1955, there was a new threat, it was claimed, for the same murderers who had destroyed Coventry and Warsaw and were responsible for Oradour and Lidice were pressing for rearmament and German membership of NATO. Thus it was only logical that at the memorial ceremonies in the former concentration camp of Sachsenhausen in 1955 the Committee of Anti-Fascist Resistance Fighters was allowed to put not only the murderous SS in the dock but also the Allied 'air gangsters'.[33] The British media had responded with restraint to the growing vociferousness of the accusations. As *The Times* noted, they were part and parcel of the collected fables of communist propaganda, an attempt to misuse the city's fate in order to criticize the Allies and the plans for West German rearmament.[34]

At all events, from the 1950s onwards remembrance of the air war had become part of the fight against western imperialism. In addition, from the beginning of the 1960s there was more and more reference at memorial ceremonies to fascist German militarism, the roots of which stretched into the Bonn republic and were still influencing what was happening in West Germany. Laments over the 'air terror' increasingly blended into criticism of the Federal Republic's conservative tendency to restore old ways, which allegedly continued to pose a great danger to the citizens of the GDR. Thus, from 1965 onwards, SED propaganda put the story of a possible nuclear attack by the Allies on Dresden into circulation. In view of the tensions between the two blocks at that time it conjured up a new scenario that posed a very immediate threat.[35]

The political potential of the aftermath of the air war seemed important to the SED leadership in another connection. The year 1965 was that in which Christians were supposed to travel from Coventry to Dresden in order to place a special symbol of reconciliation there and to take part in rebuilding the Deaconess Hospital, which had been destroyed in the bombing of 13/14 February 1945. The initiative for a British symbol of reconciliation in Dresden came originally from David Irving. Irving had thanked Richard Crossman for reviewing his book favourably and had asked whether, in view of the initiatives in Coventry, it was not appropriate for Britain to reciprocate by donating a long overdue token of reparation to Dresden.[36] Crossman took up this proposal and forwarded it to Coventry's Provost Williams, who greeted it with enthusiasm. A joint venture with Dresden seemed to him to give precisely the right signal to the German people of the east as well as the west. He was quick to pull out all the diplomatic stops and sought support among church leaders and politicians for, after all, a bridge was to be built to a country with which there were no official relations.

In the months following Williams and Crossman worked closely together, Williams as the link to the church community and a man who could absorb the initiative into his international work for Christian reconciliation and Crossman as the quiet diplomat with informal connections to British and German government departments. That was important if only as a means of reassuring the West Germans, who had little interest in seeing the prestige of the GDR boosted through new, non-governmental connections and thus viewed the project with scepticism.[37]

For the GDR this dialogue was also not without risk, for in Aktion Sühnezeichen a difficult partner was involved. In addition, the GDR leaders had watched the reconciliation initiative in Coventry warily, if only because close contacts with West Germany had been created at an early stage and leading politicians had committed themselves to the rebuilding of the cathedral.[38] But the opportunity to cooperate with a foreign church, to put its own Protestant church on the defensive and at the same time to speed up the dialogue between Christians and Marxists on an international level, a particular goal of Ulbricht's, led to all diplomatic hurdles being overcome, though at a high price, for Gottfried Noth, the Dresden bishop regarded as critical of the regime, had to be excluded and the delegation from Aktion Sühnezeichen was subjected to significant restrictions.

On Remembrance Sunday 1964 Williams called upon church and society to contribute symbolically and materially to the reconstruction of Dresden. Two hundred thousand dead in twelve hours—that, in Williams's words, was the outcome of that notorious raid that had extinguished the city. Williams's wish was to provide a symbol of British–German reconciliation and hoped that £25,000 in donations would eventually be available. Coventry, as Williams reminded people in his appeal, had been rebuilt with German help. Dresden, which meant so much to people in East and West Germany, still bore heavy scars, he said, in particular the baroque Church of Our Lady (Frauenkirche).[39] Williams's figures were based on Irving's estimates, which in the meantime had grown.

The high death toll seemed one more reason to offer a token of expiation. For after all, as Williams recalled, more people died in Dresden than in Hiroshima. This token, Operation Reconciliation, was planned as a visit to Dresden by a group of British young people to take part in the reconstruction of the Deaconess Hospital destroyed by Allied bombers. On 14 March Provost Williams finally bade farewell in a service to the twenty-five students and reminded the congregation of the special service the Christian young people were to perform for the British nation in the months from March to September 1965.[40] Clearing rubble, mixing concrete, all these were important signs of reconciliation. As Williams had already said in the run-up, reconstruction was an 'act of faith', faith in the reconciling power of Christianity that can heal the wounds of the past. This spirit of the Christian religion was capable, he said, of bridging the chasm between nations, races, and historical traditions.[41] The British media reacted mainly positively to the journey, even if not with overwhelming interest.[42] It was rounded off by a visit from the provost, who received the city of Dresden into the community of cross of nails churches and thus provided a reminder of its special commitment to reconciliation.

Yet in Coventry reconciliation was not the prerogative of the church alone, but rather it was in direct competition with other agents of remembrance.[43] For apart from the cathedral, the Coventry Committee for International Understanding, created by local left-wing Labour politicians, was pursuing a similar project, the origins of which went back to 1956, when pacifists on the fringes of the Labour Party had founded the Coventry–Dresden Friendship Society. As in the case of contacts with the Anglican church, the SED leaders saw in British–German dialogue the possibility of breaking out of their international isolation and at first gave the project strong support. It was opposition to fascism that provided the glue that held this type of partnership between cities together, caused the visitors from Britain to grit their teeth from time to time as a result of the Germans' solipsism, and gave the SED an opportunity to tell their story about the common fate of the Germans and the British as victims, victims of capitalist air terror.

By the mid-1960s a forum had been created in Coventry as a result of its partnerships with cities and the international youth centres in which reconciliation and suffering could be discussed, though admittedly without the need to focus more precisely on guilt and responsibility. Thus aerial war seemed to have become the writing on the wall for the modern world and a threat to all humanity—to Christians and pacifists, left-wingers and workers in the east and the west—while Coventry was the place where it could be talked about without reference to religious or territorial boundaries.

Monumentalization and Witnesses to History

While international ecumenical organizations for reconciliation did not get properly to work until the late 1960s and were extending their field of interest far beyond their original parameters, the political map of the Federal Republic, into which the air war was integrated in the collective memory, was beginning to change. In many places the first political initiatives that in the immediate post-war period had exploited the war for socio-political purposes to level accusations and had bewailed the fate of evacuees and of those who had suffered as a result of bombing had run out of steam.

Reconstruction was over, the lack of housing dealt with, and new city centres had been built, and though these were reminders of the 'old' culture they had given people's 'home towns' a new and 'modern' aspect in the meantime. Numerous cities now combined the special memorial events for the dead of the air war, which had been the norm for many years, with the national day of mourning and thus the anonymous fatalities of bombing were taken up into the totality of the horrors of war in general and became part of the commemoration of the controversy surrounding the end of the war and the new beginning. Attendance at these ceremonies had consistently declined and, even for Oberbürgermeisters, what in the early years had been an absolute commitment in their diaries was now losing much of its importance. Even in Hamburg, where remembrance of Operation Gomorrah was an essential reference point in the politics of commemoration, in 1974 the Senate, without much resistance, decided to absorb commemoration of the air war into the general remembrance ceremonies.

Munich was no different, though remembrance of the air war had not faded out of the city administration's memory. On the contrary, the controversy surrounding the modernization and architectural redesigning of the city following on from its application to host the Olympics gave renewed prominence to the imprint made on the city by the air war, both in relation to physical space and the culture of commemoration, and also to the issue of how the ruins of the past should be dealt with. How, in other words, could the rubble of the past be incorporated into the design of a 'modern', urban cityscape? This matter had national importance because the architectural controversies surrounding the new face of 'modern Germany' similarly involved a negotiation between the past and present of the youthful Federal Republic, and how the legacy of the air war was handled played a central role in this.

More than 6,000 people had been killed as a result of bombing raids on the Bavarian capital and since the early 1950s there had been initiatives in the city to memorialize the dead.[44] In 1954 the city council had decided to gather together all the civilian victims of the air war who had been buried in 'groves of honour' in the various city cemeteries into one place and give them a central memorial, so creating a communal place of remembrance.

Thus in 1954 the city commissioned a memorial stone some seven metres high with a cross on top. It was placed among the gravestones marking the last resting place of more than 2,000 Munich citizens. A variety of iconographies was used to commemorate the apocalyptic quality of the war but the stone referred only indirectly to the bombing. Grieving family members could read the verse from the Letter to the Romans engraved on it: 'O the depth of the riches both of the wisdom and knowledge of God! How unsearchable are his judgments, and his ways past finding out! Amen.'[45] What happened in the air war was, in other words, a mystery to human beings. God alone was able to understand its meaning and the fate of human beings was contained within his wisdom alone. Thus it was precisely the unfathomable quality of the events that was meant to give consolation, the Christian mystery of death and resurrection. This was consonant with the predominant iconography of the Catholic city, which focused on the Resurrection and eternal life and in so doing offered people the defining interpretation of the 1950s. It was an explanation whose persuasive force consisted in the fact that it required nothing to be said about the war. At the same time, the war was evoked and a location was provided where people could mourn.[46]

In Munich there was an additional factor that was also to characterize the controversy later in the 1970s in other cities.[47] In several places in the city the work to clear the ruins after 1945 had produced sizeable mounds of rubble, which like the burial sites in the cemeteries were public evidence of what had been lost. In the summer of 1949 a group of local residents had put up a wooden cross in the Luitpold Park in Schwabing: 'Pray and remember all the dead buried under mounds of rubble,' were the words written on it.[48]

The wooden cross prompted the Bavarian Party once again to bemoan the fate of evacuees and victims of bombing and to demand a lasting memorial to the sufferings of the dead of the air war. The dispute that was brewing among the parties at local government level flared up particularly over the issue of what name to give this location in the topography of Munich. Should the term 'rubble mountain' (*Schuttberg*) be retained and thus a term be used that made direct reference to the ruins on which the cross had been erected? That was the Social Democratic Party's proposal. Or, to be fully in harmony with the Christian liturgy of redemption, should the mound in the end even be called 'Kreuzberg' (Mount of the Cross), as the Bavarian Party and the Christian Social Union had demanded in the debate? This name would refer not only to the place but to the fate of the nation as a whole, which was obliged to bear 'its' cross during the war. But in the end the majority of the city council decided in favour of retaining the name 'Schwabinger Schuttberg,' as it had by then come to be accepted.

In 1958, again as a response to agitation by the Bavarian Party and the Association of Evacuees and Victims of Bombing, which cooperated closely with it, the city council placed a fountain along with a pavilion on the rubble mountain at Neuhofen, which was designed to be a reminder of the history of this artificial hill and all the people who were buried under it. But it was to take until 1968 for the city finally to put up a memorial plaque explaining the significance of the fountain and commemorating the 6,000 citizens of Munich who died in the air war.[49] As previously, it was again the Bavarian Party and its council representative, Brentano-Hommeyer, who in his dual function as city councillor and functionary on behalf of the evacuees' association took up the cause, at the same time bemoaning the fact that in the meantime fewer and fewer young people had any idea of the story behind the rubble mountains. Yet in the thick of the Olympic bid and large-scale city projects not only young people but also many members of the council showed little interest in the initiatives of the association, the membership of which was in any case shrinking.

That was only one aspect of the development, however. The other concerned the interpretation and functionalization of the rubble mountains themselves. In 1966 the Munich trade union federation took the initiative to set up its own symbol of peace on the other large rubble mountain in the city, the Oberwiesenfeld, future site of the Olympic games, as a commemoration of the dropping of the atom bomb on Hiroshima.[50] The rubble mountain was especially suitable for this, the trade unionists argued, because it was a reminder of the terrors of the last war and was thus a warning of what war could lead to—total destruction. Thus the rubble of the air war had become a pacifist admonition and part of the still youthful peace movement, which feared that the air war had been the precursor of the present-day nuclear threat.[51]

The city council and the committee for culture and monuments discussed the project intensively, though in the end it was absorbed into Munich's Olympic bid and the architectural development as a whole of the restructured Olympic site. How did Munich, how did the 'new' Germany wish to present itself? And how did such a symbol fit into this new and 'modern' face represented in the winning design by Günter Behnisch?

A warning monument to Hiroshima gained majority support neither among those responsible for the city's culture nor among the party leaders, though there was support for the idea of creating a special 'symbol of peace' on the Oberwiesenfeld that would be the equivalent of the cross that had been erected on another hill on the site in 1960 during the World Eucharistic Congress. The commission was given to the expressionistic sculptor Rudolf Belling, whose abstract sculpture in bronze entitled 'Rubble flower' gave rise in the end to lively debate.

Belling's idea was to find a form that allowed something new and peaceful to grow from the metal waste of the rubble mountain, something that was connected by its roots to the past, while also stretching up into the present and future. The main criticism came from the building firm responsible for the Olympic site and from the architect Günter Behnisch, who adamantly rejected 'Rubble flower', deeming the sculpture to be a foreign body in the total work of art that was 'his' Olympic site. In addition, he was extremely sceptical about whether memorials of this kind were a suitable way to treat history. His view was that it was not appropriate for the Germans to be seen by the world as 'exhorting people to peace'.[52] His concept was for a more abstract form, a sort of 'negative sculpture' such as the American Land Art artist Walter de Maria had designed with his 'Thought Hole'. But if such a symbol should be required then, Behnisch said, could it please not be placed on an exposed site as planned. The opposition Behnisch organized was in the end so great that the city positioned 'Rubble flower' elsewhere, in a place among the trees seldom frequented by the public, and thus caused it to disappear from the view of people attending the Olympics.

When the Games were over the debate came to life again briefly when the Munich Free Democratic Party (FDP) put forward a motion to move the sculpture to the position originally planned for it, that is at the highest point of the site. This project dragged on and resistance began to grow among Catholic lay organizations, who feared that the sculpture would replace the cross that had been placed there during the World Eucharistic Congress. The Christian Social Union party (CSU) took up the cause and argued for everything being left as it was.[53] The FDP's motion did finally have majority support but the administrative costs of the move were so high that on the day of the city council's decision in 1976 it was already predictable that the scheme would collapse. So 'Rubble flower' was a monument to world peace that remained largely unnoticed by the public.

By this point the air war had lost its immediate historical location in cities. Even so, that did not mean that it disappeared as a powerful restraining influence in the 'atomic age'. On the contrary, from the early 1980s onwards it was the churches and the peace movement, Social Democrats and Greens, who, under the influence of the NATO Twin-Track Decision, were concerned about 'atomic holocaust' and based their concern among other things on the 'experience' of the air war and its 'mass killing'. Hans Eichel, the young Oberbürgermeister of Kassel, for example, recalled on the fortieth anniversary of the bombing of the city: 'The view that limited wars could be fought with atomic weapons forces us [...] to look back at the unbelievable, incomprehensible suffering of women, children and old men in October 1943.' His fellow SPD member, the Bürgermeister of Hamburg, Klaus Dohnanyi, warned of the threat of 'atomic holocaust' while deploring the 'mass murder' of the air war.[54]

The air war was thus integrated into the horrors of war, which, in the light of the arms race, had to be prevented. It was precisely this common refrain of 'No more war—no more fascism' in the 1980s that revived and catalysed local commemoration of the bombing and caused a straight line to be drawn from the book burnings of 1933, via the 'fire storm', to Auschwitz and Hiroshima. In this interpretative context, whether intentionally or unintentionally, concentration camp victims and bombing victims seemed to have died as a result of one enormous, violent mass crime, while their particular historical circumstances no longer seemed to be of interest. Warnings about the arms race were the logical conclusion of the fire storms and the experiences of the Third Reich. Such diverse groups spoke about the 'meaning' of the air war not in terms of achieving some kind of 'liberation' but rather because they were enmeshed in the guilt of the wider effects of the war, for which, they claimed, only a few people were responsible and in which most people were defenceless victims. The air war as a prelude to the apocalypse could thus be integrated into popular horror scenarios from the past and present of warfare and seemed to demand and legitimize protest against the NATO Twin-Track Decision and to be sufficient reason to try to revive memories of the air raids.

This search for indications of the archetypes of war was given a double boost from the 1980s onwards, both from the quest for 'objective' historical documentation and from the musealization of the experience of the air war.[55] In many cases it was the generation who had lived through it who now produced an 'objective' and detailed documentary account of the history of the air war in their home area. City archives or leading local historians promoted initiatives in cities such as Hagen, Würzburg, Darmstadt, or Kassel to engage with the history of the air war and incorporate it into the narrative of the destruction and reconstruction of their home town (*Heimat*). It was a history of devastation they had experienced at close quarters and now they were prepared to give an account of its terrors. While eyewitness reports were important and in most instances the history ended with some diary extracts or retrospective comments, what was new was the fact that the suffering of those caught up in the bombing was now integrated into an account of the city's destruction, and this covered much more than the sufferings of the population.

In 1978 Hans Brunswig brought out a study of this kind for Hamburg, of which there were many reprints.[56] It gave significant space to issues of air-raid protection and the Allied air-war strategies and strove for an 'objective' form of presentation without obvious apologetics. For the first time British documents were included in local accounts, holding out the hope of enlightenment about the 'why', the ominous decision-making process. But these documents were rarely analysed or put into historical context. As the local Kassel historian Werner Dettmar put it in 1983 in his history of the destruction of Kassel in October 1943, the documents should, after all, speak 'for themselves' and convey an impression of the all-encompassing war machine to which the city and its citizens had fallen victim.[57]

Most of these accounts were reticent about making judgements, let alone voicing reproaches or accusations. Instead, they turned the spotlight increasingly on military strategy in the air war and on how it was coped with administratively, something of which they, the generation of anti-aircraft auxiliaries, had direct experience. There was mention of British night raids and their orders, also of flight paths, tonnage, and strategic discussions about bombing this city and not others. The British bomber crews themselves seemed more like instruments of a dark and mysterious power who could not be held responsible for their actions, for like the Germans they were after all part of a struggle that had sucked them into the morass of 'total war'. The British pilots, as Dettmar made clear, had also felt the fear of death as they flew over night after night and in the end they had only carried out the orders that had come down from the highest level.[58] The British bomber pilots thus seemed to have more in common with the German anti-aircraft personnel than might be obvious at first sight. Both were involved in a war for which they were not responsible and both were young daredevils, for whom war meant adventure as much as danger. There was, however, no mention of motives or war aims, nor of any connection between bombing and the Nazi war of annihilation, just as Nazism, the Nazi Party, and its protagonists hardly played any role in the majority of these early local air-war histories and if they did then they were simply troublemakers meddling in anti-aircraft defences that were in all other respects organized competently and conscientiously.[59]

Despite being opened up to 'objective' and 'documentary' examination, the air war had lost little of its power, indeed its mystical quality. It had swept through the 'old', 'lovely' city like a hurricane and pictures, etchings, and photos in these books illustrated the lost heritage. It had overwhelmed the city and its citizens with its massive raids, simultaneously destroying its cultural and physical landscape.[60] Thus it seemed no more than logical to document recollections of the events and, as in 1979 in Hagen, for example, to create a special air-war archive to form the basis of local collective memory. This initiative took up ideas from the Nazi period of archiving and documenting the terror and now, more than a generation later, was designed to pass on to a supposedly indifferent younger generation some impression of the terror endured by the generation that lived through the war.[61]

From the 1980s onwards it was exhibitions more than such rigid ideas of establishing archives and putting on solemn ceremonies of remembrance that generated public awareness and developed into centres at local level for the recovery of the history of the air war.[62] In many places the fortieth anniversary of the heavy air raids was reason enough to experiment with new forms of presentation and to make use of the opportunity that arose from the plasticity of the process of putting things on show and setting them up to be viewed. Photos had already played a central role in early displays and publications, but now some displays acquired iconic status as a result of the way items were positioned and of the fact that they were constantly being reproduced. At the centre of the exhibition devoted to the bombing of Kassel in October 1943 there was a photo of two distraught young women who had been bombed out and were stopping briefly to get their breath back among the smoking ruins. Despairing and almost rigid with shock, they sat by the few possessions left to them. A short breather after the catastrophe, a moment of hopelessness. There was no trace of the spirit of reconstruction and hardly any indication of the actual place, Kassel, that had been destroyed. It was a photo that looked as if it could have been taken anywhere after an air raid. Everywhere the devastation was the same, everywhere the same distraught people, all with their own story of loss and suffering, who deserved the pity and empathy of those who came after them.

For the spectators this visual representation of the human tragedy of war provided sufficient scope for identification and at the same time the picture was non-specific enough to include the sacrifice made by the British bomber pilots who had been killed over Germany. And so the accompanying written texts did not fail to make reference to the bomber crews and the 55,000 men who had been killed in raids over Germany. Technical advance, the newest weapons of destruction, had caused this war and visitors to the exhibition could actually touch some of the instruments of destruction. Apart from bombs and photos of the devastation the creators of the city's exhibition presented the bombing of Kassel as the epitome of military escalation involving anti-aircraft guns and bombers, which in miniature form conveyed something of the terror and violence of the destruction.

The focus was not on guilt, in other words, but on war in its unrestrained violence, on the weight of hundreds of thousands of bombs that devastated the urban landscape.[63] It was not only in Kassel that such exhibitions, situating the destruction of people's home town within a universal story of the suffering inflicted by war and, in the light of the arms race, projecting them as apocalyptic visions of the end of the world, drew tens of thousands of visitors, more than any ceremony of remembrance in the previous decades. One of the many possible explanations was undoubtedly that exhibitions about the air war were always participatory. Their creators used newspaper advertisements to urge people to record their own experiences and make them available to all. As 'witnesses to contemporary history' those whose experiences could no longer be shared by a younger generation were explicitly encouraged to pass them on and thus 'rescue' them from being forgotten.

The creators of the exhibitions were therefore continuing what from the late 1970s onwards had first attracted the attention of the media, namely the eyewitness account as a new genre poised between history and remembrance. For up to that point individual life stories had actually often been no more than illustrative supplements prompted by the anniversaries of the bombing. Now it was noticeable that newspaper stories about the period of the air war set new store by the special impact achieved by individual accounts of survival—as a reaction to a clearly perceived generational divide between those who had experienced the air war and those who had not.[64] For now it could no longer be taken for granted that all readers would know what 'chaff' and 'Christmas trees' (parachute flares) were, what the inside of air-raid shelters looked like, or what the heat of a fire storm felt like. At the same time there seemed to be a battle going on between how individuals remembered and understood events and the public remembrance and interpretation of them, within which the media had a catalysing and reinforcing role because they legitimized the 'false' politics of remembrance with its failure to pay adequate tribute to 'individual' experience and thus turned the history of the air war into a political battlefield.

In Hamburg, for example, the Senate also planned an exhibition in the same year for the fortieth anniversary of Operation Gomorrah, but, unlike in Kassel, in Hamburg professional historians worked on the idea and were at pains to go beyond any pacifist parables about the horrors of war and be frank about the causes of the war and those responsible for starting it. This was an explicit decision to reject a process of universalizing the war that would result in its being decontextualized. The exhibition as conceived in the initial plans was to situate the history of the air raids within a history of the city in wartime and thus make it part of an account of the Nazi regime. On the one hand the suffering of human beings in wartime, on the other Nazi crimes—the creators of the exhibition wanted to address both aspects. But the very title and the picture advertising it revealed how difficult such a project was. The exhibition was titled 'Ashes and Rubble' and the poster for it showed, as in Kassel, total destruction in an anonymous location. With its scarred cityscape and smoke still rising from its gutted buildings, 'Hamburg 40 years ago', as the subtitle read, could have been anywhere on the map of destruction caused by the war.

It was precisely not what was particular to Hamburg but rather the universal quality of the 'bombing terror' that wove the title and the picture into a story that was hard to reconcile with an attempt to contextualize the Nazi regime. The opening ceremony showed how resistant the culture of public remembrance (still) remained to historiographical concerns. Thus the speeches of the Hamburg dignitaries revolved around the ubiquitous theme of 'No more war', which could be incorporated seamlessly into the existing narrative of the 'innocent' city and a war unleashed by 'those' Nazis, which of course the 'normal' civilian population had had little to do with.[65]

The NATO Twin-Track Decision and the debate about the arms race in the 1980s had determined the controversies over interpretation arising from commemoration of the air war as much as the new prominence of eyewitness accounts and the musealization of the war. Even before the Gulf War of 1991 and the conflict in Yugoslavia, which for many people concentrated the various strands of the discussion in the 1990s, the debate about war and peace was one of the central axes around which commemoration of the air war repeatedly revolved.

The often invoked 'spirit of reconciliation' arising from these experiences was also responsible for breathing new life into the existing twinnings, established as a response to the air war, of British and German towns and cities. In January 1990, for example, the city of Kiel, together with its twin city Coventry, opened an exhibition devoted to the history of the reconstruction and to urban planning after 1945, which emphasized shared difficulties and problems in shaping industrial communities.[66] There was no more talk of the 'burden' of the past but rather of traffic flow, social housing, and the improvement of the infrastructure.

A further dimension was added in the 1990s, namely concern about the stability of democracy in the light of a growing number of right-wing radical assaults and arson attacks. Remembrance of the war and the air war were not just a parable of peace but also an object lesson in the collapse of democracy and the consequences of the Nazis' politics of violence. It thus seemed all the more urgent to sound warnings about the dangers of totalitarian dictatorships by no longer commemorating a single air raid but by explaining what led up to it and integrating it into the history of Nazism.

For this purpose small exhibition displays or poster stands were no longer adequate. There was a recognizable trend to professionalize commemoration by involving archivists, historians, and exhibition organizers, who incorporated a variety of new directions in historiography, the media, and the museum world.[67] In March 1995, for example, the city of Würzburg opened an exhibition about the bombing with the somewhat artificial title 'Würzburg—16 March 1945. Re-vision. Background. Destruction. Reconstruction'.[68] What was striking was less the semantic symmetry of destruction and reconstruction, which was a theme permeating the whole iconography of the air war, but rather that there was now a triad of prior history, event, and impact and thus it was no longer a picture of city in ruins that opened the exhibition but rather a photo from 30 January 1933 of the first cabinet presided over by Adolf Hitler as German Chancellor. In other words, the exhibition spanned a lengthy period, from the 'seizure of power' and the Nazi takeover of Würzburg's city hall, via political persecution and anti-Semitic violence, to air defence practices, mobilization through propaganda, and finally the bombing of the city. Yet it was not the burnt-out buildings that formed the final part of the exhibition but the rebuilding, the return to normality, and Würzburg's transformation into a 'European City'. The motif of the 'phoenix from the ashes' that attached itself to the city immediately after the war continued to restrict the scope of interpretation of events and the term 'fateful day' was repeatedly used in relation to 16 March 1945.

The day of the bombing retained a central place in the exhibition but there was now a plurality of narratives. One large screen presented the day both from the standpoint of the residents and from that of the British bomber crews in the air. In addition, the eyewitnesses' perspective had been given a higher profile within the exhibition and had become an oral history project spanning the generations. Würzburg schoolchildren had interviewed elderly Würzburg residents and made video recordings. Visitors to the exhibition could share in stories and conversations recorded and played back on various 'time pillars' and thus gain an 'authentic' impression of the fears and distress of the war period. It was these contemporary witnesses in particular who brought the exhibition to life, in order 'to demonstrate to present and future generations' the dire consequences of war, which was the organizers' stated aim.[69]

Although many interpretations fitted into the traditional narratives that had grown up since the war, there were nevertheless differences and ambivalences that distinguished the exhibition from previous projects. This was evident even from the picture on the cover of the catalogue. Vistas of smoking ruins, burning churches, and collapsed buildings no longer served as a timeless reminder of the horrors of war, as would have been shown up to the mid-1980s. At the centre was now a collage of various pictures showing scenes from the city from 1933 onwards: Nazi brownshirts, Wehrmacht soldiers, newspaper advertisements, and, in smaller format, pictures of the destruction and reconstruction. In the middle was the city's logo, the Residenz (Prince-Bishop's palace), and the awkward title 'Re-vision', which was supposed to refer to visual presentation and to the connection between looking back and looking forward.

This pluralization of perspectives and protagonists in the process of remembrance did not, however, move at a uniform pace and could be very different from one place to another. Exhibitions were not always as politically charged or as clearly supported by professionals as in Hamburg, where in 1993 the Research Centre for Contemporary History and its director Ulrich Herbert weighed in to the debate. His intention, he said, was to

counter 'positively folkloristic ceremonies of remembrance' with 'something that sought to engage in a scholarly and dispassionate way with the air
war'.[70] This involved lectures, conferences, and guided tours of the exhibition, an exhibition that, like the one in Würzburg, tried to give a comprehensive contextualization of the story of the air war but in a more consistent
manner, integrating groups of air-war victims hitherto neglected, such as
concentration camp prisoners, slave workers, and POWs, into the 'story of
suffering'. Thus the experience of the air war acquired a new dimension and
no longer revolved solely around the dead of the 'national community'.[71]

'Taboos' and 'Traumatization'

This was all the more remarkable, because from the mid-1990s onwards a
new term appeared in the media and in the readers' letter columns in the
newspapers, which later, after the publication of Jörg Friedrich's *The Fire*,
was to become a buzzword, namely referring to the air war as a 'taboo'. One
of the first to use it in public was Horst Eberhard Richter in an address in
the St Peter's church in Hamburg, when he formulated the bold thesis that
only 'those who through resistance or persecution had earned the right' to
speak about the air war had been permitted to do so. 'The rest, those who,
however unwillingly, carried out duties on the side of the perpetrators,
sensed they were under an obligation to be silent. Their own sacrifices, such
as the loss of family members, possessions and perhaps even their homeland,
did not count.'[72] After the war there had been discrimination between the
'good' and the 'bad' dead: it was permitted to remember the former, while
the fate of the latter, as a result of some informal ban, could not be spoken
about. There had, according to Richter, been no public space for the tragic
stories of suffering and loss in the air war.

The official politics of remembrance appeared to many as a positively
obscene gesture on the part of unauthorized people, speaking thoughtlessly
about things they had no experience of themselves and so could not judge.
Numerous letters were sent to Hamburg's newspapers and the Senate offices
from people who, in spite of the immense commemoration industry, quite
clearly no longer related to the form and language of the gestures and
speeches and bemoaned the irreverent way of dealing with the dead of the
air war. Talk of a 'taboo' was an attempt to fill this gap left behind by changes
in the politics of history, for exhibitions and commemorative occasions no

longer placed the innocent suffering of the 'community sharing one fate' in the foreground, as they had done in the 1950s. Also, war had not just 'burst in upon' the city but had been the result of German aggression.

Now not even the status of victim in the air war remained exclusive, once the sufferings of the 'others', concentration camp inmates and slave labourers, were being highlighted ever more frequently. This change and shift of focus in the 1990s must in actual fact have been hard to bear for quite a few of the generation that went through the war. It certainly helped to prepare the ground for the passionate debate that occurred some years later over W. G. Sebald's *On the Natural History of Destruction* and Friedrich's bestseller of 2002.

Contrary to public perception the controversy over *The Fire* by no means erupted overnight but rather was part of a boom in publications, both literary and journalistic, that from the mid-1990s onwards explored with new intensity the perspective of the Germans as victims in the Second World War, examining experiences and paradigms for coming to terms with the air war, flight, and expulsion.[73] Finally, it seemed, people were now permitted to speak without misplaced shame about German suffering and a new German historical consciousness.[74]

Friedrich's book was wide-ranging and described in bold colours the military escalation of the war as well as stories of individual loss among the German air-war victims. 'Traumatization' and 'taboo' were the key terms in this new 'sense of history',[75] over which there was angry debate, to which, above all, the generation of anti-aircraft auxiliaries contributed their experiences. The impression was created that it had taken sixty years before it was possible to speak publicly about the air war and Friedrich seemed to be the first person to put an end to this protracted pain.

The controversy over *The Fire* made the air war suitable material for prime-time television and promised good viewing figures. One effect of this shift in the culture of remembrance, or perhaps more accurately this reflection on the past, was to reanimate an older theme in the interpretation of the air war, which had originated in Nazi and GDR propaganda but now acquired new topicality. The air war was now referred to in public, and not only in extreme right-wing circles with their anti-Semitic and anti-American polemics against the Allied bombing Holocaust, as a 'war crime'. Even during the war Nazi propagandists had tried every means of using the term 'war criminals' against the Allies. In the new version of this controversy following on from *The Fire* legal or historical and political issues did not loom large.

Like the German crimes in the east, Allied area bombing raids could now be branded as 'war crimes' and they could be denied any legitimacy. In February 2005, for example, the Thuringian newspaper the *Neue Nordhäuser Zeitung* began a survey in its web portal entitled 'What is your opinion of the air raid on Nordhausen in April 1945?' Some 8,800 people were presumed to have died in the Allied raids towards the end of the war. The editors provided three possible responses, which combined the specific terminology used in SED propaganda in relation to the culture of commemoration with the topical debate surrounding the air war as a war crime. Forty-eight per cent out of a total of 173 respondents agreed with the proposition that the raids had been 'retaliation for the Nazi war'. The majority (50.9 per cent), however, opted for the statement that the air raids had been a 'war crime'.[76] This may not necessarily have been representative but it had a considerable impact all the same. Hence in January 2007 the *Bild* newspaper carried a report on page one with the heading 'The first British war researcher to admit that the bombing of German cities was a war crime!'[77] It was referring to the book by A. C. Grayling, the British philosopher, who in a kind of historical show trial had put the Allied conduct of the air war on trial.[78]

If even the British themselves now admitted it, then what doubt could there be about the 'criminal' nature of the Allied conduct of the war? Such comments were reminiscent of what was being said in the early 1960s. What was noteworthy was not only the new tactic of instrumentalizing British critics of the air war as witnesses for the prosecution to support the idea of German victimhood, but also the striking tone: all restraint had gone and the verdict 'war crime' was proclaimed in an almost triumphant manner, as if it were the result of well-founded research. At the same time German history was interpreted as a warning example of the violent excesses of military force in the twentieth century.[79]

The fact that from the late 1990s onwards Dresden could become a favourite location for marches by the extreme Right and the anniversary of the bombing on 13 February the excuse for a march to honour the dead of the 'bombing holocaust' is connected with this change in the environment in which the culture of commemoration resonated. In the Saxon state assembly the extreme right-wing NPD had been using its parliamentary platform repeatedly since 2004 for intense provocations and tried every means available to exploit the remembrance of the dead. Meanwhile the political battle about how the dead should be 'properly' commemorated is in fact anything but over and remains the subject of vigorous argument.

In many cases rejection of the neo-Nazi demonstrations was the limit of what people had in common on this issue as citizens and members of civil society. How they responded to counter-demonstrations, to art installations, and religious acts of reconciliation provoked conflicts over 'appropriate' historical representation; these reveal how different people's vested interests and aims were when it came to remembrance and how contentious the issue of the 'historical context' of the air war still is, whether it is seen as an allegory of pure 'catastrophe' and 'symbolic' of the violence that people inflict on one another or part of a success story in which the citizens of Dresden achieve 'reconciliation' or as an example of how a city should deal with its Nazi past.[80]

In order to provide a scholarly answer to the persistent Nazi myths, a special panel of historians was established, which from 2004 onwards investigated on behalf of the city the exact death toll resulting from the air raids. This may well have reflected the city authorities' deep concern when faced with the ferocity of the political disagreements. Working with extraordinary energy and at great expense the panel finally published its report in February 2010. It put the number of dead at between 18,000 and 25,000, though it is not certain how far this will draw a line under the discussion. Most probably it will not, given that myths are hard to eradicate.

The present-day shifts in the culture of remembrance that seemed to make such painstaking documentation of the dead necessary to democracy as a means of countering the stereotypes of Nazi and SED propaganda become all the more evident if one again looks back a few years. In 1995 numerous German cities had made efforts to ensure that state and church representatives from the UK would take part in memorial events, not to inform them about the precise number of air-war fatalities but to use the language of Christian reconciliation to emphasize not guilt and responsibility but restored harmony and new beginnings in a meeting of equals.

In the special commemorative year of 1995 in Dresden Federal President Roman Herzog took on the task of putting into words the state's idea of what a culture of commemoration should be: not a list of grievances or an occasion to accuse but rather remembrance should be characterized by 'pure mourning'. It should be remembrance linked to a critical attitude to 'war as such', even though Herzog did not attempt any historical contextualization of the air war.[81]

Lamentation, the liturgy of mourning, and a message of peace for the present day formed a triad in which historical responsibility, though important, was just one part of 'general human' failure and thus allowed broad scope for a wide variety of expressions of commemoration and reconciliation. In Hamburg Prince Charles took part in person in the Senate ceremony on 3 May 1995, following an invitation from Hennig Voscherau, Erster Bürgermeister (Senior Mayor) of Hamburg.[82] In the run-up the Prince had let the Senate know that he was more concerned about the countries' common future than about looking back to mourn, let alone to accuse. Reconciliation and the 'old friendship' between Britain and Hamburg were at the heart of the ceremonies and public appearances that captured the city's attention in early May. In the presence of the Mayor of Hamburg, the Foreign Secretary, Douglas Hurd, and the Minister for the Armed Forces, Nicholas Soames, Prince Charles laid two wreaths, at the British military cemetery and at the memorial to the dead of the bombing of Hamburg. At last, as many German newspapers said with pleasure, even the British were honouring the dead of the air war. 'White and red flowers for the fallen', as the headline in the *Hamburger Abendblatt* read on 4 May, referring to the British soldiers and the German air-war fatalities, who, fifty years after the end of the war, had almost unnoticed become 'the fallen' again and thus civilian 'soldiers at war', exactly as Nazi propaganda had styled them.[83]

The End of the 'Good War'

In Britain the visit attracted widespread attention but unlike in Germany it did not cause a surge in the spirit of reconciliation. This was unsurprising in view of the prevalent scepticism regarding reunification and the critical noises heard about Germany in the British press. In Britain there was less mention of the dead than of the living, such as survivors of the Blitz and, more and more often from the 1980s onwards, the RAF pilots, who, stepping out from the shadow cast by their father figure Arthur Harris, attempted to give literary shape to their experiences and recounted their story in numerous memoirs.[84] It was, however, not at all a story of senseless bombing, of which the leader of Bomber Command had been accused in the wake of the *Official History*. While Webster and Frankland had concentrated entirely on the 'top brass' and their strategies, it was the stories of the youthful heroes of the bomber crews that were now reaching a mass audience and conveying a dual impression of the danger but also of the romance and adventure in the skies above Germany, making a link in their manner of presentation in many cases back to the legendary heroes of the Battle of Britain.[85] These were stories that did not conform at all to the bloodthirsty fantasies of destruction that parts of the British and larger parts of the German public connected with the name of Arthur Harris.[86] The fact that the 'history of those low down' in the hierarchy conquered the history of the war in the skies was in large measure due to the fact that academic history in Britain was increasingly opening up, becoming more diverse, and no longer concentrating exclusively on high politics and great war heroes but was beginning to research everyday life and social experiences seriously, and this trend applied even to aspects of military history.

As a result the history of the RAF could be told afresh and with even more confidence by those who had been involved in it. It was now easier for former pilots and their veteran associations to go on the offensive with regard to the politics of history. In 1983 a special RAF museum was finally opened in Hendon, north London, in which the pilots and aircraft of Bomber Command were highlighted and visitors could, for example, view Lancasters and Wellingtons in the Bomber Hall.

The role of 'Bomber Harris', admittedly, continued to be controversial. In 1989, five years after his death, the BBC broadcast a detailed profile of his life, which attempted to penetrate his difficult personality and provided dramatic reconstructions of the motives of and conflicts involving Bomber Command, thereby prompting once again a lively debate about the advantages and drawbacks of area bombing. The film played an important role in encouraging the RAF veterans' association, the Bomber Harris Trust, to pursue an idea it had had for some time to put up a memorial to Arthur Harris and—something that was soon to be forgotten—to the dead of Bomber Command.

The chosen location was prominent, the square in front of St Clement Danes, the RAF church in central London, and Queen Elizabeth, the Queen Mother, agreed to unveil it. In Germany news of the impending unveiling prompted strong protests. The mayors of Pforzheim and Dresden wrote angry letters, reminding people of the misery that attached to the name of Harris in their cities,[87] and the Oberbürgermeister of Cologne even called on the Queen Mother not to take part as planned, as the date set was 31 May, the same date as the 1,000-bomber raid and thus a particularly unfortunate choice.[88]

In Britain there was also considerable public agitation, even if it was less univocal and one-sided. The memorial was discussed in television forums and dozens of articles and readers' letters debated the question of whether Harris was a hero or a murderer. *The Independent*,[89] *The Guardian*,[90] and *The Times*[91] were the principal newspapers to issue a warning about the symbolism of the memorial and the delayed honouring of Harris and reminded readers of the fatal consequences of area bombing. In view of this stain on Britain's war record the papers considered it advisable not to proceed with the project. It was, on the other hand, mainly the conservative press, *The Daily Telegraph*[92] and *The Daily Mail*, that supported it, recalling once more the high death toll among British pilots and the huge responsibility they shouldered in the fight against Hitler's Germany. It was not just a rehearsal of the old arguments, however. In view of the Gulf War and the massive protests of the British peace movement, controversy over the purpose of military air interventions had immediate and topical significance. The proportionality of military means was once again the subject of debate and this time the legitimacy of Britain's current interventions, such as in Iraq, was under scrutiny.[93]

The unwelcome public response[94] caused by the unveiling was, at all events, somewhat uncomfortable for the Conservative government under John Major. Contrary to the usual practice at occasions involving members of the royal family, no member of the government was present at the unveiling, nor was the Anglican church represented by a bishop.[95] On the other hand, much-decorated veterans and public figures such as Margaret Thatcher, who had recently been forced out of office, were there to pay their respects to Harris and the RAF. They had the experience of hearing the Queen Mother's speech being loudly interrupted by a group of protesters.[96] After a short break she resumed her speech and once again explained what in her eyes the figure of Harris stood for. Harris, Bomber Command, and its young pilots had risked their lives to give hope to an embattled nation and had contributed to its survival in those 'dark years'. Thus it was with gratitude and pride that she wished to commemorate them and Harris, their wonderful leader, though without forgetting the victims of all (the emphasis lay on this word) nations who had suffered in the Second World War. With that this contentious part of the history of the air war had been commemorated and reached a temporary close, temporary because once again almost twenty years were to pass until in spring 2010 Westminster City Council approved the monument to the pilots of Bomber Command that had been demanded for so long by veterans' groups. The monument had the support of the new Conservative government and of the Prime Minister, David Cameron, personally and had acquired in Robin Gibb, the former Bee Gee, a high-profile and popular sponsor.[97]

The privately financed memorial in Green Park was dedicated by the Queen on 28 June 2012. In Gibb the former pilots' campaign gained a new face from the realm of (slightly vintage) pop culture. His fund-raising concerts gave the campaign for a memorial publicity and turned it into a project that spanned the generations, from those who experienced the war and came through it to their (now adult) children. This aspect too was consonant with the rhetoric of political renewal used by the Conservative–Lib Dem coalition government. However, there can hardly be said to be a consensus about whether such an isolated and individual memorial is even necessary or whether monuments of any kind can still be regarded as an appropriate form of remembrance.[98]

Less controversial at the moment but at least as significant in media terms is another aspect of the history of the war, namely remembrance of the Blitz.[99] The term usually refers to London and less to the other cities bombed in the air war, and in the war years it was pictures of London that defined the iconography of destruction and reconstruction and would continue to do so after 1945. The political conflict over the legacy of the war, its representation in the media, was therefore all the more rooted in fundamental controversies over the post-colonial role of the Empire, the present and future of the welfare state, and what was at the heart of being 'British' in the post-war order. When in the late 1960s criticism from both Left and Right of the culture of the post-war political consensus grew louder and in view of falling growth rates and rising unemployment there was increasing talk of the 'English disease', the existing interpretations of the war also started to appear less credible.[100]

Yet while this criticism was aimed at Labour governments' failure to press forward with welfare reforms, for Conservatives, and, from the end of the 1970s onwards, for Margaret Thatcher above all, what was important was to reinterpret the experiences of the Battle of Britain and the Blitz in order to legitimize her wholesale attack on post-war consensus politics, 'consensus' in her view meaning about the same as a 'socialist Labour state'.[101] The welfare state and state planning, once praised as positive outcomes learnt from the experience of war, were moral and economic evils in her eyes and responsible for the crisis of the British state. Britain must therefore fight a second Battle of Britain.[102] That in 1940 had been about fighting German tyranny, defending the right to freedom, and the independence of nations, not about introducing socialist state bureaucracy. This line of interpretation was to become a leitmotif of Thatcher's historically informed political outlook and it made a significant contribution to undermining the political Left's historical legitimacy and moral claim to lead the country. Memories of the People's War provided a suitable vocabulary for her confrontation with Labour and her vision of Britain's future,[103] and she used it to attempt to cast doubt on the historical legitimacy of the politics of the welfare state. She pressed even the Falklands War of 1982 against the Argentinian military junta into this mould. After all, as in 1940, the object was to liberate the free world from dictators.[104]

As the war receded into the past, it and the Blitz, understood as British experiences that crossed class boundaries and created the foundation for a 'new' state, became more contested and yet more popular than ever. From the late 1960s it was no longer only stories of heroic survival that were seen on television but also the first comedy series that focused on the home front. The most successful one, which was never shown in Germany, was *Dad's Army*, featuring a group of Home Guard volunteers in the fictitious southern English town of Walmington-on-Sea. The little provincial town in the crucial year of 1940 is under threat less from German bombs than from German invaders and yet the series treated with great wit and irony the essential characteristics of a society at war: the class structure and mobilization, shortages and British shrewdness, the victory of the underdogs against the Prussian–German love of order. This story, the tale of a small town and its eccentric heroes in a hopeless struggle against the military might across the Channel, was in miniature the story of the whole nation, as it most liked to see itself.[105]

The series played with many images and tunes that even during the war had established themselves as part of the British public's visual and auditory canon, parodying them and giving them contemporary relevance. This applied to the title song ('Who do you think you are kidding, Mr Hitler?') and to the individual characterizations, with their speech and clothing, which treated traditional British stereotypes with gentle irony and wove them into a history of 1940 that was nostalgic and 'authentic' in equal measure and at least as cheeky and anarchic as it was heroic. Patriotism, humour, and self-irony: the combination of these three qualities produced a very particular form of 'Britishness' and taken together suggested a contrast in character with the humourless, constantly buttoned-up Germans. The creators of the programme, Jimmy Perry and David Croft, who were in the

Home Guard themselves when young, showed their protagonists as every-day people—clumsy and at times helpless and vain—who were nevertheless all pulling together to defend their town against fascism. Thus, although the series was gently critical of military authority and obedience, the characters were by no means defeatists and none of them had any doubts that what they were doing in the Home Guard, pointless and boring though it some-times was, contributed to a national cause that was essentially good.[106]

The issue of class was central to the more than eighty episodes shown between 1968 and 1977, making it one of the most successful series in the entire history of the BBC. At the head of the unit is the stiff and uptight Captain Mainwaring, whose life consists above all in clarifying matters of status and prestige with regard to his military authority and in complaining about the stupidity and ignorance of his subordinates. Yet it is precisely his authority that is repeatedly shown being subverted and that is what makes war service in the Home Guard a 'People's War'. The village idiot is as much part of it as the naive communist sympathizer, the shopkeeper, and the Oxbridge graduate. Only women are largely absent and have a role in the country's defence at best as wives or girlfriends. It is no accident that the action is set in a provincial seaside town, where the planes heading for London can be heard and the famous White Cliffs of Dover can be seen: Churchill had spoken of them, summoning up visions of the heroism of the Battle of Britain.

Viewers and the media reacted very positively to this presentation of a community with a common cause. After the first episode was broadcast *The Daily Mail* felt reminded of that wonderful summer of 1940 when the 'heart of England beat to a single pulse';[107] and in view of the overwhelming political and economic problems of the present day it seemed to the left-inclined *New Society*[108] distinctly more pleasant to dwell on rosy memories of the past than on the difficulties of the present.[109] The publication gave a wide-ranging appraisal, from the honourable war of the little man to the RAF as a killing machine, an interpretation already formulated during the war by the pacifist Left.

The Guardian saw in *Dad's Army* the embodiment of that particular British characteristic of making a wonderfully enjoyable adventure even out of the biggest mistakes and failures (as, for example, the inadequate preparation for a conflict with Hitler) and thus celebrated the British 'amateur' thirty years after the war.[110] In the face of economic crises and growing social tensions in the present day, looking back to the past seemed to offer some clue as to how the nation had at one time and in spite of class differences committed itself to a single common purpose and defied the German bombers.

The fact that this series worked at all and as the years went by was to become *the* sitcom about the Second World War can probably be best explained by two factors: the slightly ambiguous mixture of idealization and ironic portrayal of military authority on the one hand and on the other the viewers' knowledge that this story would end well, in spite of, and even because of, the vanity, clumsiness, and incompetence of its protagonists. However low morale was, however quirky the people were, at the end of it was victory over Germany. That was probably one of the reasons why the public broadcasters in Germany never made an effort to show this series on German television, because for the Germans as the side that lost the war this kind of humour was not only difficult to translate but more than anything else was almost unbearable.

More accessible was the re-creation of the Blitz by the Imperial War Museum in a large-scale exhibition entitled 'Blitz Experience', which drew national attention when it opened in 1989. It conveyed very vividly the experience of the air war using exclusively the language and environment of the working class of London's East End. The entrance to the exhibition led first through a journey in time back to that period of national threat, when the nation was taking refuge in the underground tunnels. Penned up in a dark space, the visitors first heard the voice of George, the Air Raid Warden, whose cockney accent immediately betrayed his social origins. He told them what was happening when they heard loud noises, shouts, and finally the bombs falling ever closer. The seats began to shake and the room simulated the effects of a nearby explosion. After a few minutes of uncertainty 'George' led the visitors with a steady hand and voice out into the darkness of night in the East End.

Everywhere buildings are on fire but the heroic fire brigade is fighting the flames from the German bombs. Everywhere voices can be heard telling their stories of how they survived. There are injured and houses have been destroyed but there is no mention of death and violence. This is a clinical, sanitized version of the home front. Finally George led visitors past a diorama of London, giving them a last glance at St Paul's and the burning 'wounds' of the city. Then he guided them out of the world of war and explained once more how it came about that the war ended well, namely because everyone had pulled together.[111] This finale could be interpreted as being as much a response to the growing fragmentation of the British welfare state as a historical interpretation of the People's War. For at the height of the Thatcher era 'pulling together' was an expression that had not been heard for a long time, and more powerfully than *Dad's Army* and other series the exhibition engendered a longing for peace to be restored and for social conflicts to be removed that was evidently kept alive only by the past and the memory of the war.

The plans for 'Blitz Experience' had in fact been purged of a number of extremely awkward issues: death rates and overcrowding; poor hygiene and social conflicts among the shelter communities. It was no wonder, therefore, that in spite of immigration and ethnic change the East End was still regarded as the domain of a white, male working class, which, like George, seemed to look back nostalgically at the good old days of the war. Although during wartime the People's War was synonymous with the promise of social reform, from the 1970s and 1980s onwards it had mutated into a socially and ethnically static model for the beleaguered white working class,[112] which, beset by fears of decline in the present, sought both hope and salvation by looking back in history to the New Jerusalem once promised it. It was precisely that promise that continually gave the memory fresh relevance and made it so politically significant—even at the beginning of the twenty-first century.

Conclusion

Present-day wars are conducted using the blueprint of the past and this applies also to the history of European aerial warfare in the twentieth century, with the qualification that at the outbreak of the Second World War there were at best horror scenarios and test runs but as yet there was no well-founded knowledge about the effects of bombing. That made it all the more important to ensure that the population's morale did not collapse under the pressure of attack from the skies.

The term 'morale' and ideas about the 'mood' and 'bearing' or 'attitude' (*Haltung*) of the population were reflections of debates that dated back to the end of the First World War about the 'correct' and 'incorrect' type of behaviour in war, about loyalty and commitment, belonging and preparedness for war. The notion of morale touched the very heart of the legitimization of war and mobilization for it and provided information about the underlying condition of democracy and dictatorship. During the Second World War, therefore, in both Germany and Britain, morale was at the centre of politics. It was an important factor in 'total war' and was both contested and contradictory.

The history of how it was 'invented' has been central to this study, which has examined a range of issues: 'war as a condition of society', methods of coping with crisis employed by the state and by cities and the organization of a state of emergency, ways of dealing with death and mourning, the relationship between war and the public sphere, individual and collective ways of socializing violence and the memorialization of destruction, and reconstruction as part of British–German post-war history. The comparative dimension of this study and a time-span that takes us up to the present day have opened up a social and cultural history of the air war that no longer consists only of exhaustive examination of contemporary discussions about whether the air war was a 'war crime'. Rather than reproducing the old battles of erstwhile enemies, the approach used here of comparing countries and political systems has resulted in a challenge to assumptions about the distinctive national directions taken by modern societies at war.

In Britain as well as in Germany the 'state of emergency' created by the air war invested the experience of war with a mythic dimension, that of the nation bound together by one fate, while at the same time civilian behaviour was increasingly subject to the imposition of norms. Research into and monitoring of morale were an integral part of defining who belonged to the people and the nation and were thus a crucial focus of social conflict. Thus 'total war' from the air and the process of coping with it in no way proceeded with an autonomous, as it were self-fulfilling, logic of destruction. 'Total war' was not an active subject but an analysis put forward and an operational procedure adopted by two advanced industrial nations in order to secure political control and mobilize society. Thus 'war as a condition of society' describes a mutable state, depending on the period and political framework.

For Britain this change from a peacetime society to a wartime one was at first more abrupt than for the Nazi dictatorship. In Germany the coming of war had been signalled far in advance and racism, policies of economic exploitation, and the persecution of political opponents were already part of everyday life. For Britain, by contrast, the declaration of war against Germany in September 1939 signified a profound break with what had gone before because it entailed Parliament's relinquishing some of its power for a limited period, the transfer of extensive powers to the Prime Minister, and comprehensive economic and social mobilization. Censorship and control of public opinion were important but only reluctantly accepted norms of the new wartime society. Unlike in Germany, however, the key legal and administrative controls had already been put in place at the beginning of the war and were not to undergo any significant change.

War was the true elixir of life to the Nazi regime. It had been born out of war and was sustained by the violence of war. The attack on Poland in September 1939 offered it the radical option of cleansing society by means of wars of plunder and annihilation, and this had been its aim since 1933. It was precisely the coincidence of bureaucratic tradition with the utopian vision of the national community in a new, racially defined state that radicalized Nazi policy in the course of the war. The Nazi wartime brand of socialism resulted in the paradox of a permanent state of emergency, in which special commissioners and those acting on orders

directly from the Führer were increasingly superimposed on the traditional administrative structures.

By contrast, Britain largely retained the structures and distribution of
powers that had come into force at the beginning of the war. There was no
majority support for special, extra-legal authorities with extensive powers,
and as a result any discussions tending in that direction quickly fizzled out.
The degree and speed of the administrative transformation from a peacetime to a wartime society differed considerably in Germany and Britain and
so also did notions of what constituted 'war as a condition of society', what
it made possible, and what, even in a 'state of emergency', was ruled out.

War and Order

In both nations, therefore, the impact of bombing was of decisive importance. The bombs of the Second World War changed the spatial organization of both wartime societies. In Germany the air war deeply disfigured
many cities and confronted local officials with ever-increasing problems. At
the beginning of the war air raids had been a localized occurrence that
could be tackled on the spot with existing resources. From 1942/3 at the
latest, however, the destruction was visible everywhere and the local authorities affected had been forced to cooperate and to share their experiences of
the problems they faced.

As a result, communication networks developed to carry knowledge
about the threat posed from the air, for example through the German Local
Government Association. Not all cities were affected in the same way, to the
same extent, and at the same time, but the exchange of information and
experience among the various local authorities and the evacuation of those
who had been bombed out caused the distance between city and countryside and between regions that had suffered bombing and those that had not
to shrink. For both Germany and Britain the consequences were paradoxical, for the removal of spatial barriers on the one hand and political centralization on the other were not mutually exclusive but rather mutually
determining. The crucial factor in this process was, of course, the fact that
the bombing was concentrated in particular phases. Whereas bombing
reached its height in Britain in 1940/1, Allied raids on Germany were at
their most destructive only at the end of the war, in 1944/5. Like no other
event before it, the Blitz elevated London in its battle with Hitler to the

iconographic focus of the Empire, indeed of the whole democratic world. Pictures of the city ablaze and reports of its heroic resistance to Nazism went round the world. The photos of St Paul's surrounded by flames, of firemen in action, and of the ever cheerful, undaunted Londoners pulling together made a significant contribution towards winning over the American public for intervention.

Morale in the British capital was regarded by propaganda experts as the essence of 'good' behaviour, a narrative that New York's mayor, Rudi Giuliani, made use of shortly after the 9/11 attacks on the city, when he compared the resilience and heroism of its citizens with the historical example of London. 'London can take it' was by no means only the title of a successful propaganda film but an incentive for other cities to keep to the normative pattern of 'good spirits' and desist from criticism of the war.

In both countries evacuation as part of the wartime mobilization of society led, though at different points in time, to a growing number of social and cultural conflicts between refugees and hosts who came from different backgrounds and religious denominations. These clashes were a part of fundamental conflicts about the essential nature of the nation, about the rights of citizens, solidarity with others as one community, and Britishness. Reports on the evacuations in Britain followed on from a variety of often contradictory discourses from the pre-war period. Among them were the romanticization of country life. Nowhere did England seem more English than in the countryside. The increased attention given since the outbreak of war to life outside the cities as zones secure from German air raids was a particular aspect of this romantic idealization of the pristine quality of the countryside.

The arrival of large numbers of working-class families in the countryside was considered by many, it must be said, as an invasion by the dispossessed urban masses. The conflict surrounding evacuations thus not only touched on the search for the geographical heart of the nation, but was also part of the controversy over state provision, which grew more strident during the war and involved disputes over differing notions of poverty and social inequality. It was a controversy dating back as far as the nineteenth century and concerned the relationship of the individual and the state. The war had by no means given rise to a surge of charity or persuaded the state authorities to reform provision for the poor, and yet the effects of bombing had provoked an increasingly urgent debate about the causes of poverty and social problems that, together with other factors, prepared the ground for the creation of the welfare state after 1945.

No comparable open debate about the state of society could be conducted in Nazi Germany. Even so, the constant calls for people to show solidarity with evacuees and the many complaints received by local authorities and the Nazi Party can be interpreted as evidence of very similar difficulties in solving the problems arising from these movements of population resulting from war. These problems increased in particular towards the end of the war and as bombing raids grew more extensive. The night-time exodus from the cities to relatives and friends in the country and with it the attempt to utilize family networks that would provide a lifeline were, from the point of view of the authorities, not part of the solution but part of the problem, for now in many places there were not enough people to ensure the black-out and organize fire prevention. At the same time such family connections lay outside the control of mass mobilizations organized by Party offices and this alone sufficed to make them both a threat and an irritant.

Cities stood at the centre of this conflict and it was there that even during the war discussions began about whether the destruction might not also provide an opportunity for a large-scale clean-up. In cities such as London and Plymouth, Coventry and Southampton, local politicians and city planners had been arguing since 1941 about the city of the future. What should the new Britain look like? For the political Left in particular the time had come to make use of reconstruction to push through radical reforms, clear slums, create homes for workers, and make a brisk start on constructing a new and socially cohesive community. But in many places a more sober mood set in. Even in 1942/3 there was little left of the 'finest hour' and 'Blitz spirit' attested by Churchill. In many cases ambitious plans came to grief because of lack of public funds and local conflicts of interest. The 'New Britain' certainly did not command a consensus.

As in Britain, in Germany the project of rebuilding cities was simultaneously an aspect of coping with acute crisis and a canvas on which to paint a vision of a time after the anticipated ultimate victory. The level of destruction in Germany of course meant that the pressure there was considerably greater. For experts and propagandists the air war presented an immense opportunity to begin at last the architectural transformation of the German Reich, after the Allies had taken the work of demolition off them and had created space for expansive building projects. That at any rate is how Hitler, Goebbels, and Speer saw it. Unlike in Britain, however, the German city of the future was to be a fortress, a home, and a military defence base all at the same time. One feature of a future Nazi Reich that was constantly prepared for war would be massive squares for ritual expressions of community as well as anti-aircraft towers and underground shelters designed to make it possible to survive in a state of constant war.

Shelter Society and Coping with Crisis

The temporary removal of society underground had, however, already begun during the war and represented a huge upheaval in and mobilization of everyday urban life. In the shelters and bunkers 'war as a condition of society' was manifest in concentrated form. Shelters were spaces in which both dictatorship and democracy held sway and regulated behaviour. They were the subject of propaganda, places that promised protection and ones where gender roles were subject to imposed norms.

Both societies made vigorous attempts to control access to them and saw in the microcosm of society there the prefiguring of a new order, in which the state guaranteed safety but also imposed discipline, cleanliness, and obedience as a form of social hygiene. Even though the state's instruments of repression in Britain were a great deal less prominent than in Germany, there are many indications that the strategies in both countries for dealing with crisis were clearly not solely the product of differing political systems but to a certain extent also part of the dynamic of collectivization typical of industrial warfare.

A fundamental reason for this was most probably to be found in the idea of total war, which developed in the inter-war period. In Britain and in Germany this notion rested on the assumption that total war required total mobilization and could no longer be conducted merely on distant battle-fields but had to be fought on the home front and with the help of civilians. The transformation of the civilian population into soldiers on the home front provided both the precondition and opportunity for an air war directed against the enemy's interior, while also creating the latter's most vulnerable spot, for the homeland seemed particularly at risk from fickle workers and women.

Thus morale in wartime was the subject of academic study and political propaganda, an aspect of society's observation of itself and at the root of administrative conflicts over the organization of society under a state of emergency. A variety of institutions was involved in this process of observing patterns of social behaviour and subjecting them to norms imposed by war conditions. Their effects stretched far beyond 1945. In post-war Germany, for example, medics and psychiatrists ensured that 'traumatization' was not recognized as an illness and could thus not be grounds for financial compensation. The law in such cases did not finally change until the 1960s and as a result of pressure from British and American psychiatrists and numerous groups of Jewish victims of persecution, who had particularly suffered from the decisions of German social courts.

During the war there was little scope for academic exchange among nations at war; in so far as this was possible to a very limited extent, medics and psychologists took cognizance of each other's research findings. Both German and British experts believed that morale could be measured and they included in their studies pointers to how strong the inner cohesiveness of the nation actually was. The investigation of morale covered more than selective analysis of mood and bearing but was the subject of conflicts of interpretation concerning the internal organization of both societies at war.

The pathologization of deviant behaviour was one of the essential characteristics of German medical and psychological research, and though it was much more radical in language and types of sanctions proposed than research in Britain, it nevertheless shared a similar approach. In Britain estimations of the consequences of bombing varied greatly between one generation of medics and another. There was, for example, no agreement about whether air raids had any long-term 'traumatizing' effect at all and whether special clinics for nervous disorders would have to be created for sufferers, as in the case of First World War soldiers. Iconographic representations, the attribution of male and female characteristics, and also the application of political stereotypes revealed clear points of contact between Germany and Britain. The 'invention' of wartime morale was thus not specific to democracy or dictatorship. It was not a distinctive national trend but rather the necessary precondition for modern societies to conduct a 'total war', for total war largely abolished the distinction between combatants and non-combatants. This conclusion suggests the existence of forms of wartime collectivization that were common to differing political systems and of similarities in the internal processes of wartime mobilization.

At the same time, this should not obscure crucial differences in practice in the way the two societies coped with wartime crises. By contrast with Nazi Germany Britain, in spite of censorship, continued to enjoy a public sphere such as Parliament, in which state decisions were subject to scrutiny and government actions had to be legitimized. Although even in Germany the air war had created new types of (partially) public space, in which the effects of bombing could be discussed, this took place, as in the case of rumours, in defiance of Party controls and as an attempt to establish alternative forms of communication. It was no substitute for public debate.

Even Britain was not free from the growing anti-Semitism and xenophobia engendered by wartime mobilization. In contrast to Nazi Germany, however, the war did not open the floodgates; it did not lead to anti-Semitic violence or to the exclusion of particular social groups from the social security net. Traditional procedures followed since the nineteenth century continued to determine that consensual decisions were reached in Britain, whereas the Nazi state at war increasingly abandoned set procedures for decision-making, creating special administrative authorities and pursuing vigorously a policy of increasingly brutal marginalization of 'community aliens'.

In the bunkers and air-raid shelters protection and violence were connected more directly than in any other location in wartime society and it was precisely here that the specifically Nazi mixture of racially biased mechanisms to cope with crisis, stabilize control, and marginalize groups in society was evident. In Britain it was state officials who stood up to anti-Semitic rumours and insisted on established procedures being adhered to. The extent of the difference between the way the internal politics of setting boundaries operated in the two societies is demonstrated particularly clearly by how local government dealt with crises. However different the demands made, specifically in the final phase of the war, on city administrations in Germany and Britain, from the beginning of the air war onwards there was no doubt what the central axes of Nazi local government policy in wartime should be: violence, active anti-Semitism, and an increasingly radical policy of discriminating against specific groups on the basis of racial criteria.

An important factor in ensuring that the Nazi regime did not need to fear unrest on the home front was the fact that the provision of supplies of replacement goods—furniture, textiles, and household items—was largely problem free until some time in 1943. The war damage offices set up during the war were responsible for this and they performed a key role, hitherto largely unknown, in ensuring that the domestic needs of the national community were met. The regime was so afraid that citizens might protest that war damage offices were urged to take account in all circumstances of the difficult situation of those affected by bombing and to do everything

conceivable to deal quickly with applications for compensation, for which
the state intended to foot the entire bill. Up to the end of the war the solutions to crises were determined by anxiety about a new 'November 1918'
and the regime's fear of its own population, and these fears defined the
policy of war compensation.

At first the offices worked very efficiently, not just as instruments fulfilling administrative requirements but as independent institutions. From the
outset they pursued a policy of excluding Jews from any kind of help. In this
way the war damage offices managed to sustain into the second half of the
war the illusion entertained by many of those who had been bombed out
that the national community was ensuring that material losses would be
compensated.

This was to change from some time in 1943 onwards, when a growing
number of cities were bombed and the costs of the damage became unquan-
tifiable. More and more members of the national community put in applications and more and more frequently the regime had to put them off with
promises of payment after the war. This policy of postponement was an
important reason for the crisis of confidence in the regime amongst those
in cities that had been especially heavily bombed. As applications went
unprocessed not only did the piles of paper grow in the offices but so also
did people's doubts about whether the regime was in fact capable of guaranteeing safety and compensation.

Alongside that was an expansion of domestic terror, which was demonstrated in particular by the brutal use of prisoners and slave workers to clear
the rubble. Local authorities competed greedily to be allocated them. City
administrations were thus important perpetrators of repression, instruments
of terror and dictatorship, and worked closely with the Nazi Party. Up to
the end of the war city administrations as the 'backbone of the home front'
had used all means at their disposal to support the war on the eastern and
western front. That meant learning from the air war, increasing bureaucratic
efficiency, and exploiting systematically all available resources, starting with
Jewish homes and possessions and including forced labour, convicts, and
concentration camp inmates.

The air war offered the regime a welcome excuse to radicalize mechanisms at local authority level to exclude people from the national community. City administrations were central as perpetrators of this persecution,
helping to compensate for fundamental failures on the part of central government to exercise direction and control. These were in turn the result of

the polycratic rivalry of Reich authorities and the increasing shortages produced by the war. For a long time it was precisely this ability of local government to stabilize control from below that served as a central support to the regime. But in the end even this system, combining domestic terror and bureaucratic adaptability, was incapable of withstanding Allied air superiority.

Excessive demands, inadequate preparation, poor crisis management—these reproaches were also hurled at British local government during the bombing raids, but they remained confined to particular instances. In addition, with the exception of London, no British city was subjected to raids as heavy as those on Essen, Hamburg, Berlin, or Munich. City councils were still concerned that the air war might return, however, even after 1942, and in particular in 1944 the V-1 and V-2 raids seemed to confirm once again that they had little cause to regard themselves as safe.

Local authority infrastructure remained largely unchanged. There were no new offices or any special authorities. The office of Regional Commissioner represented the only instance in which the government created a jurisdiction that in the event of an actual invasion would have taken over command and formed a bridge between local authorities and Whitehall. That was significant if only for the reason that it represented a new communication channel that could quickly pass on information about deficiencies in air defence or new potential threats and was able to help to find consensual solutions to conflicts between local and Whitehall interests. In Britain too the War Damage Act of 1941 had been an attempt to insure the population against the consequences of war. In the case of Britain, however, far more than in Germany, insurance against risk was financed by private contributions, the consequence of a lack of state funds. Thus individuals were forced to shoulder much more of the burden up front than in Germany, on the assumption that, in spite of all apocalyptic visions of doom, the consequences of bombing would be limited and in the end the legitimacy of the war would not be eroded by financial issues.

People's experiences of violence that found expression in the applications made to the war damage offices were very diverse and it is risky to make generalizations about *the* air-war experience. The intensity, duration, and scale of losses were too varied. Experiences could differ greatly according to age, gender, location, and time. Being burnt and being buried under rubble were among those experiences, as well as physical disfigurement or the loss of family and possessions. However varied individual cases may have been, the experience of physical violence was one of the essential features of the new 'condition of society' that distinguished wartime fundamentally from peacetime, not only for soldiers but also for the civilian population and in particular for women.

The history of the experience of the air war was thus in significant measure a history of fear and of the attempt in the face of an uncertain future to search for ways of expressing what was beyond everyday experience in familiar language and thus making it accessible to friends and relatives who had not shared in it. In spite of the far greater intensity and destructive power of the bombing of German cities, clear similarities are observable in the way people in Germany and Britain internalized the threat to their lives.

In contemporary jottings and letters the air war often appeared as a supernatural incursion into a peaceful idyll, as the destruction of the 'innocent' homeland. People mentioned the miracle of survival, the feeling of bewilderment at having come through the nights of bombing. For many it was important to compare their suffering with that of other cities—in Britain with London in particular—and to derive their own local pride from having suffered losses and demonstrated the strength of their resistance. Speaking about and sharing experiences of the nights of destruction could help people to comprehend what had happened to them and allay some of the terror of their experience. In addition, many reports indicated how important it was in the struggle for survival for people to discipline their own feelings and how much men above all saw in this a key difference between them and the way women coped with crisis and maintained morale.

A further important narrative in Britain and Germany, which had continuing influence beyond 1945, centred on the concept of 'habituation'. Thus, for example, the Ministry of Information had stated in 1940 that it was those who were frequently bombed who had been able to get used more easily to the exceptional circumstances. Sirens lost their terror and the sounds of war acquired a predictable quality. This process of habituation seemed to be the expression of a 'healthy' personality. Goebbels and the SD had reported similar findings about acclimatization to terror and decided that it was in the end a good indicator of the state of the home front. How far the process of habituation actually went is difficult to say. What is important, however, is the extent to which the concept of 'habituation' imposed a set of norms that also affected medical diagnoses and propaganda exercises. It was an indication that behind this term lay an assertion of what was 'correct' morale as much as individual experience.

Death, Mourning, Faith

Everything in this new language of air-war experience was orientated towards survival in the air war. Both countries found it markedly more difficult to deal with death, for there was a difficult balance to be struck between individuals' experience of death, 'dignity' in death, and state control over the dead body. For the Nazi regime dealing with death was not only a question of public show and the ritualized cult of death, for it claimed the right to control the living and the dead and this meant that there was no more scope for the expression of individual mourning beyond the parameters set by the Party. The deceased was the property not of his or her family nor of the church but of the 'national community'. But the assertion of this claim gave rise to numerous conflicts. For on the one hand the cult of death was designed to be an impressive demonstration of Nazi collectivization, while on the other, from the point of view of the regime, every new air war fatality signified a threat to morale.

From 1943 onwards there was hardly a German city capable of producing sufficient coffins and in the face of Allied air superiority every month the projections were once again evidently obsolete. Local authorities in Germany persisted for as long as possible in trying to give the dead a 'dignified' burial, in other words one in an individual, rather than in a mass, grave. But before that they had been forced to solve another problem. For many of the dead were hard to identify and physically disfigured. Their official identification was part of the battle to maintain confidence and an attempt not to exacerbate the conflicts between individual mourning and the state's cult of death by burying the dead anonymously.

As the war progressed, the Nazi state's attempt to reinterpret personal loss as part of people's duty as members of the national community became less and less convincing. From the middle of 1943, at any rate, in some places the power of the cult of death seemed to be waning, with the result that funeral authorities, for example, pressed for Party ceremonial to be scaled down. In addition, in strongly Catholic regions in the west and south of Germany in particular, burial rites repeatedly provoked conflicts between the Party and the church over the location and form of the ceremonies. This was an indication that Nazi attempts to appropriate and reinvent religious rites in wartime had distinct limits. Dealing with mass death in the air war showed precisely that the church's authority over life and death could not simply be replaced by the 'national community's' rituals and that it retained its essential significance in spite of suffering many hostile measures and attempts at regimentation.

In Britain, as in Germany, dealing with death touched the sensitive relationship between the state and the individual citizen. Though faced with less extensive destruction and fewer deaths the local authorities in Britain were also confronted with considerable administrative problems. Even before the outbreak of war discussions were in full swing about how, in the face of the threat of mass fatalities, to prevent funerals from collapsing into chaos and so undermining morale and to keep them respectful and appropriate to the individual. Concerns about the anonymity of mass graves were markedly more acute in the UK than in Germany because they reminded people of paupers' funerals in the nineteenth century and thus epitomized loss of social status.

There was considerable scope for conflict to arise, on the one hand from the wish to provide individual and respectful burial and from state control over the dead body and the supervision necessary to safeguard public health on the other. The reduction in bombing from late 1941/2 onwards, however, meant that this potential conflict did not develop with full force. But even though the death toll from the air war in Britain was markedly lower than in Germany, coping with it was a top priority for Churchill's government, for their ability to cope with crisis was being put to the test.

Despite the similarities between the administrative mechanisms and the perception of the problem in Britain and Germany, the differences in norms and in the culture of mourning and ritual display were very considerable. Whereas Nazi propaganda promoting the national community presented death as a sacrifice for the nation, in Britain people found it much more difficult to turn death into something heroic. The battlefields of the First World War had discredited emotionally charged public celebrations of death and rituals reinforcing collective identity. Thus memorial ceremonies for the dead of the air war remained more restrained in language and display, less grandiose, and more circumspect in their attempt at collectivizing mourning. 'Quiet mourning' was the watchword at memorial occasions and the individual's fate and the significance of the family were the focus; unlike in Germany there was no appeal to the 'nation's struggle for survival'.

By contrast with the First World War Anglican clergymen did not interpret the deaths as Christian sacrifices nor did they invest the loss of life with religious meaning, not least because the ceremonies were themselves part of an ambivalent search for new words and forms of expression that recognized the need to give meaning while at the same time treating with reserve any continuation of a type of state mourning that failed to acknowledge the individual. 'Quiet mourning' in this context meant not making a public display of one's own grief or physical pain but keeping them private as far as possible. Paradoxically the public funeral ceremonies also served this purpose.

In this difficult quest for language and meaning the role of the churches was far from clear. For the Anglican church as the state church the war created hope that it would be able to emphasize its central importance in an increasingly secularized British society, though without repeating the mistakes of the First World War and subordinating itself unconditionally to state control. The dispute over the ethical legitimacy of the air war, which found its most eloquent critic in George Bell, Bishop of Chichester, was thus not only a conflict over the appropriate and, from a Christian point of view, defensible choice of weapons, but also part of the conflict about the balance of power between church and state.

The churches tried hard to give the 'People's War' a religious dimension, not by turning it into a crusade but by using it as a fixed point of reference in the construction of a new post-war order with a Christian basis, and they intended to make substantial contributions to discussions on this subject. It was thus no accident that it was St Paul's Cathedral that became *the* symbol of the resistance of the home front, a symbol combining both a secular as well as a religious message about the British will to withstand attack and appealing precisely for this reason. Unlike their German co-religionists British Christians did not have to fear imprisonment as a punishment for their dissent, with the result that, in spite of state censorship, an intensive debate arose within the various Christian denominations about the position of Christianity and new forms of ecumenical cooperation, which arose not least from the acute hardship caused by the bombing and the destruction of places of worship.

Church boards of management and clerics of all denominations in Germany were exercised by the question of whether the experiences of violence and death connected to the air war had brought the German population closer to the churches. Initially, it seemed that the bombing had made people return to the church with renewed faith. But this hope faded even during the first phase of the war. While there were many reasons for this, compulsory evacuations were an important factor contributing to the fragmentation of confessional milieus and the loosening of ties to the church. And in the course of the war a further problem became increasingly urgent for German Catholics and Protestants, namely how to make sense of the violent experiences of the air war and explain them in theological terms. In the face of huge devastation as in Hamburg some clergy were at first literally speechless.

In their sermons after air raids the majority of Catholic and Protestant bishops drew on a common stock of terms to make the hitherto unimaginable violence comprehensible. There was mention of repentance and apocalyptic visitation, of expiation and the theme of 'God's punishment' as explanations for the world's suffering. The bombing raids were seen as a divine visitation on the national community, an opportunity to show Christian steadfastness, as an act of destruction, an aberration of 'modern' warfare leading to barbarism and thus proof of how human beings had turned away from God; a judgement accompanied by a call to repentance. Only exceptionally did church leaders and representatives draw political lessons from the history of decline of the west that they bemoaned, let alone direct criticism at the Nazi state. The overwhelming majority of Protestants gave no cause to doubt their loyalty to the Nazi regime and they were obedient in much greater measure than their Catholic fellow Christians to the Nazi rallying cries to stick it out during the air war.

The churches' interpretations were by no means rigid, however. Although at the beginning of the war there had been no talk of a 'just war', there had been reference to the fight against the evil forces of godlessness. From about 1943 onwards it was evident that sermons used apocalyptic language with increasing frequency to talk about death and destruction and about spiritual and material ruins. Front and homeland now became theologically interwoven and part of a theology for an era of 'total war' that was manifestly searching for a new language in which to make the incomprehensible capable of being grasped. This was a very gradual process, which affected regions and bishops to varying extents and the 'German Christians' not at all. And it was as yet uncertain what its final conclusion would be. The call to reflect on the core beliefs of Christianity, on the earliest forms of the Christian faith, which were often spoken of while destruction was all around, could most definitely be interpreted as a rejection of Nazi propaganda's emphasis on retaliation. Yet at the same time church leaders provided a religious underpinning for wartime morale: carry on, persevere, remain steadfast in faith. The church saw its role as that of comforter on the home front and was an important source of psychological support sustaining people's wartime morale.

One answer to the question of the nature of the 'national community' in wartime most likely lay precisely in this paradox: although the air raids led to a growing crisis of confidence in the Nazi regime, at the same time the consequences of the destruction increased the pressure for people to mobilize themselves within the remaining structures sustaining the Party, the family, and organizations specific to various milieus. One aspect of this story was the growing brutalization of wartime society, the use of terror by the Nazi regime against a widening range of groups in the population. The social researchers of the United States Strategic Bombing Survey pointed to another aspect, when in the spring of 1945 they travelled through the devastated German cities and questioned officials, victims of persecution, and church representatives about the cohesive forces of Nazism. Their conclusion was that its cohesive power had been distinctly stronger than they had originally assumed.

Although Hitler's charisma may have been exhausted towards the end of the war and the Nazi state's lies about the war exposed, the combination of the threat of violence, Nazi horror scenarios of impending downfall, and ambivalent religious slogans calling for endurance had had some effect. This complex and contradictory set of circumstances played its part in turning the Nazi 'national community' into a German 'community of destruction' that was able to combine growing alienation from the Nazi system with the hope of Christian redemption and a will to survive in a situation where survival was all people could hope for.

Memory Contests after 1945

At the end of the war the churches were to come into the spotlight once again, but this time as 'victors amidst the rubble' and forerunners of a new theology of peace, focusing on the experiences of bombing and the idea of reconciliation. In Britain early initiatives had begun even during the war. As early as the 1950s a new, transnational place of remembrance of the air war developed in Coventry. The cathedral's history was part of Britain's difficult internal quest for a new way of dealing with the aftermath of war, a quest linked to the issue of how the air raids and RAF policy should be judged.

At the same time Coventry developed into a place of encounter for British and German Christians that aimed to draw a line under the hostilities of the past. The focus was on reconciliation, though this term could mean different things. Specifically in the early days of Protestant 'work for reconciliation' and of Aktion Sühnezeichen reconciliation meant above all the mutual forgiveness of equals and not some kind of confession of guilt by Germany or an act of repentance. For reconciliation meant that it was not the Germans alone who were guilty but that all combatants had contributed to the escalation of the war. By this process the Second World War seemed to have become not simply a 'German' but a European catastrophe, in which all nations had turned away from God.

Remembrance of the air war thus remained alive after the end of the war. It was part of the history of urban life after the catastrophe. Narratives of the air war were part of this search for answers and downplaying of conflict and they were repeatedly adapted in various ways to fit contemporary concerns: as the story of the 'rebirth' of German cities after 1945; as part of the conflict between east and west over 'Allied air terror'; as the history of Christian survival; as a pacifist parable for the peace movement; as the 'search for security' (Conze); as part of international reconciliation or as the story of the German 'taboo' (a phenomenon observable from the middle of the 1990s onwards). With the publication of Jörg Friedrich's book *The Fire* in 2002 this form of 'feeling for history' reached a temporary high point, which included the lament for the 'forgotten' victims of the war as much as the resulting condemnation of Allied (and no longer only German) war crimes, past and present.

In Britain the book also attracted attention because it was understood in some sections of the media as a challenge to the 'greatest Briton of all time', Winston Churchill, and fitted into the heated political argument about British involvement in the Iraq War and Britain's role as a war combatant in the twentieth century. Apart from 'morale bombing', this included Britain's use of military force in the colonial period, which had been attracting increasing attention since the start of the new century and had called into question Britain's traditional understanding of itself as a 'good' and non-violent colonial power.

Thus the reference points of war commemoration had shifted. Up to the 1970s the Battle of Britain and the Blitz were pivotal in legitimizing the young welfare state and provided a stock of memories of a heroic era, in which the nation had stood alone and defied fascism with courage and ingenuity and which was a substitute, so to speak, for the loss of the colonies. The loss of the Empire and the mythologization of the air war were closely connected elements in a continuous search for the significance and position of Britain in the global post-war order. It was a process that situated the experience of bombing in an entirely different historical context from that in which the air war was seen in Germany after the war. There the history of 'morale bombing' was much harder to integrate into the heroic story of ordinary men and women. The air war against Germany had exacted too high a price in death and injury to be remembered without also recalling the permanent debate about its ethical justification. The 'People's War' and the Blitz on the other hand told a tale of proud survival, the spirit of which was invoked after the 7/7 suicide bomb attacks in central London by British politicians and the media, who, drawing on the example of history, saw proof of the unbroken will of the nation:[1] London had not collapsed in the face of Hitler and his 'miracle weapons', nor would the nation be brought to its knees by cowardly terrorist attacks. 'We Britons never will be defeated,' was the commentary in the *Daily Express*. There was repeated talk of 'endurance' and the 'lesson' of the Blitz.

What had changed, however, was detectable in Tony Blair's speech to Parliament a few days after the attacks. Since the war, according to Blair, the face of London had changed. It had become more colourful and culturally and religiously diverse, and yet it had this wonderful community 'spirit' that helped it to bear misfortune: 'So different and yet, in the face of this attack, there is something wonderfully familiar in the confident spirit which moves through the city, enabling it to take the blow but still not flinch from reasserting its will to triumph over adversity. Britain may be different today but the coming together is still the same.' In view of the large number of British Muslims the Blitz rhetoric alluded to Britain's 'national' and 'multicultural' identity at the same time and was thus responding to the fear that the 'war against terror' in Iraq might give rise to a 'civil and religious war' threatening the country from within.

The history and remembrance of the air war are thus always linked to the present—and the history of the 'invention' of civilian morale in wartime a part of past and future controversies about the nature of military conflicts in which armed forces spread fear and terror through bombs. The comparison of two political systems has, in spite of all the differences, made clear that the process of involving civilians was based on similar presuppositions of what would be important in a 'total war' if the extraordinary threat posed by aerial warfare were to be tackled. One aspect of this was that the erosion of the principle of non-combatants applied not only to the war being fought on foreign soil but to coping with crisis internally. This justified a policy of militarizing the civilian sphere, though admittedly this had begun in Germany with the Nazi 'seizure of power' in 1933.

Whether democracies or dictatorships are better at solving crises is not a question that can be easily answered. What measure should be applied? Yet there is some evidence to suggest that the pressure from ritualized collectivization and the imposition of norms of social behaviour are equally an essential characteristic of dictatorship and democracy and their politics of sustaining morale in a situation of 'total war'. The decisive difference lay in the Nazi movement's willingness to use violence to radical and racist ends and the notion of the 'national community', which was increasingly decoupled from any moral framework.

The dissolving of the boundaries between combatants and non-combatants is part of the legacy of 'total war' and marks the smooth transition to those new wars of the present day, where military force has long since ceased to be the monopoly of the state. A willingness to include the destruction of enemy cities and the deaths of their inhabitants in calculations was also a stock feature of Cold War thinking after 1945 and of the theory of aerial warfare, in which the simulated use of atomic weapons made the enemy increasingly depersonalized. For that reason it is only superficially good news to hear heavily armed military air forces at the beginning of the twenty-first century publicize their 'clinically clean' operations.

The reality of aerial warfare looks different, however, from the seductive pictures produced by digital computer animations, in which towns and cities such as Baghdad or Kunduz are no more than grey patches and human beings tiny, mobile dots. At least the grim visions of destruction foreseen by H. G. Wells more than a hundred years ago in his novel *War in the Air* have not (yet) turned into reality. At the end of the book civilization has been reduced to rubble. After the war no victors have emerged but only barbarity and annihilation and no one can remember any more why it was fought.

Abbreviations Used in the Notes

AEK	Historisches Archiv des Erzbistums Köln
AEM	Archiv des Erzbistums München und Freising
AfS	Archiv für Sozialgeschichte
AP	Associated Press
ARP	Air Raid Precautions
ARPC	Air Raid Precaution Committee
BA	Bundesarchiv
BA-MA	Bundesarchiv-Militärarchiv
BBSU	British Bombing Survey Unit
BGB	Bürgerliches Gesetzbuch
BGNS	Beiträge zur Geschichte des Nationalsozialismus
BP	Bayernpartei
CBS	Columbia Broadcasting System
CHC	Coventry History Centre
Cmd.	Command Paper (1919–56)
CND	Campaign for Nuclear Disarmament
CSU	Christlich-Soziale Union
DAF	Deutsche Arbeitsfront
DDR	Deutsche Demokratische Republik
DGT	Deutscher Gemeindetag (German Local Government Association)
DLS	Deutscher Luftschutz
DNVP	Deutsch-Nationale Volkspartei
EAF	Erzbischöfliches Archiv Freiburg
EKD	Evangelische Kirchen in Deutschland
EKiR	Archiv der Evangelischen Kirche im Rheinland, Düsseldorf
EZA	Evangelisches Zentralarchiv
FDP	Freie Demokratische Partei
GB-Bau	Generalbevollmächtigter Bau (Plenipotentiary for Construction)
HASK	Historisches Archiv der Stadt Köln

HoC	House of Commons
HStA	Hauptstaatsarchiv
HStAD	Hauptstaatsarchiv Düsseldorf
HStAM	Hauptstaatsarchiv München
IfZ	Institut für Zeitgeschichte
ILA	Interministerieller Luftkriegsschädenausschuss
KdF	Kraft durch Freude (Strength Through Joy)
KPD	Kommunistische Partei Deutschlands
KSA	Kriegsschädenamt (War Damage Office)
KSR	Kriegsschädenrecht
KSV	Kriegsschädenverordnung
KZ	Konzentrationslager
LAELKB	Landesarchiv der Evangelisch-Lutherischen Kirche in Bayern
LCC	London County Council
LEA	Local Education Authorities
LMU	Ludwig-Maximilians-Universität München
LPTB	London Passenger Transport Board
MBliV	Ministeral-Blatt für die Preußische innere Verwaltung
MOH	Medical Officers of Health
MoI	Ministry of Information
NACCS	National Association of Cemetery and Crematorium Superintendents
NARA II	National Archives and Records Administration, College Park, Maryland
NCSS	National Council of Social Service
NRW	Nordrhein-Westfalen
NSDAP	Nationalsozialistische Deutsche Arbeiterpartei
NSV	Nationalsozialistische Volkswohlfahrt
OB	Oberbürgermeister
OFP	Oberfinanzpräsident
OKH	Oberkommando des Heeres
OKW	Oberkommando der Wehrmacht
OLG	Oberlandesgericht
OT	Organisation Todt
PPU	Peace Pledge Union
PRO	Public Record Office, London
RGBl.	Reichsgesetzblatt
RJM	Reichsjustizministerium (Reich Ministry of Justice)
RLB	Reichsluftschutzbund (Reich Air Defence League)

RLM	Reichsluftfahrtministerium (Reich Air Ministry)
RMVP	Reichsministerium für Volksaufklärung und Propaganda (Reich Ministry of Propaganda)
RSA	Reichskriegsschädenamt (Reich War Damage Office)
SD	Sicherheitsdienst (Security Service)
SED	Sozialistische Einheitspartei Deutschlands
SHD	Sicherheits- und Hilfsdienst
SMO	School Medical Officers
SPD	Sozialdemokratische Partei Deutschlands
StA	Staatsarchiv
SZ	Solly Zuckerman Archive
TH	Technische Hochschule
UEA	University of East Anglia Library
UP	United Press
USSBS	United States Strategic Bombing Survey
VfZ	Vierteljahrshefte für Zeitgeschichte
WAAC	War Artist Advisory Committee
WVS	Women's Voluntary Service

Notes

INTRODUCTION

1. Quoted in Thiessen, 'Feuersturm', 320; the interviews on which the article is based have been anonymized.
2. For a balanced overview see Müller, *Bombenkrieg*; recently also Hansen, *Allied Bombing* and Primoratz (ed.), *Terror*; Neitzel, 'Misserfolg', provides a comparison of the air-war strategy in both world wars.
3. On the crisis year 1940/1 see Kershaw, *Wendepunkte*, 25–75.
4. On Rotterdam see Strupp, 'Stadt'.
5. On this see, among others, Ray, *Night Blitz*.
6. For recent literature on the 'Battle of Britain' see Addison and Crang (eds), *Burning Blue*; Campion, *Good Fight*.
7. Compare Maier, 'Luftschlacht um England', 390ff.
8. See Overy, *Wurzeln des Sieges*, 148f.; for the following see *Wurzeln des Sieges*, 136–74.
9. For a detailed account see Boog, 'Luftkrieg über Europa'.
10. Overy, *Wurzeln des Sieges*, 151.
11. For detail see also Overy, *Air War*.
12. On American strategy see among others Sherry, *Rise of American Air Power*.
13. On this see among others Lowe, *Inferno*.
14. On the Ruhr area see Blank, 'Kriegsendphase'; Groehler, *Bombenkrieg*, 371.
15. See Overy, *Wurzeln des Sieges*, 172.
16. On the number of dead see the report of the independent Dresden historical commission: <http://www.dresden.de/media/pdf/presseamt/Erklaerung_Historikerkommission.pdf>; Müller, Schönherr, and Widera (eds), *Zerstörung Dresdens*.
17. Sperling, 'Luftkriegsverluste im Zweiten Weltkrieg'.
18. United States Strategic Bombing Survey, No. 65, Medical Branch: The Effect of Bombing on Health and Medical Care in Germany, IfZ-Archiv, MA 1566, Roll 5.
19. See the estimates in Schnatz, 'Zerstörung'; Groehler, 'Der strategische Luftkrieg', 343, reaches a similar conclusion.
20. Dear (ed.), *Oxford Companion*, 1135.
21. For a controversial overview see Boog, 'Bombenkrieg'.

22. IMT, xxxiv. 145. On this see in detail Toppe, *Militär*, 261.
23. Reemtsma, in *Krieg ist ein Gesellschaftszustand*, 8 and 10f.
24. On this see also Echternkamp, 'Kampf an der inneren und äußeren Front', 4.
25. Entry for 30 November 1943, in Fröhlich, *Tagebücher von Joseph Goebbels*, part II, x. 386.
26. Strachan, 'Total War', 35.
27. See also Noakes, 'Germany'; and Thorpe, 'Britain'.
28. Thus Mackay, *Half the Battle*, 2f.
29. Addison, *The Road to 1945*, 121; see also Aly, 'Demoskopie', 13ff.
30. Kehrt, *Moderne Krieger*, is now outstanding on Germany; on Britain see Francis, *Flyer*.
31. Patel, *Soldaten an der Arbeit* points in a similar direction.
32. See Echternkamp, 'Gewalterfahrung'.
33. From the multiplicity of theoretical reflections on comparative history see, as an overview, Haupt and Kocka, *Geschichte und Vergleich*. Kroll, *Kommunistische Intellektuelle*, is particularly stimulating.
34. For an empirical comparative study that has been seminal for research on fascism see Reichardt, *Faschistische Kampfbünde*.
35. On this see now Fitzpatrick and Geyer (eds), *Beyond Totalitarianism*.
36. See, for example, Winkler (ed.), *Krise in Amerika*; Patel, '"All of This Helps Us in Planning"', 252.
37. See, above all with reference to the crisis of the inter-war years, Wirsching, *Weltkrieg*. With reference to the potential for violence in democratic societies see in particular Mann, *Die dunkle Seite der Demokratie*.
38. On the First World War see Levsen, *Elite*.
39. For a critical view of the 'new' military and cultural history of the war see Neitzel, 'Standortbestimmung'.
40. See also Müller, 'Bomben und Legenden'.
41. Bernd Lemke's study, dealing with the topic of air defence, represents such an attempt: Lemke, *Luftschutz*; also Kressel, *Evakuierungen*; with reference to the pilots' assessments see Dines and Knoch, 'Deutsche und britische Erfahrungen'.
42. For a reference to similar forms of community solidarity during the war see Gregor, 'A Schicksalsgemeinschaft?', 1051ff.
43. See in detail Gestrich, 'Jürgen Habermas' Konzept der bürgerlichen Öffentlichkeit'; for a discussion of the recent research literature see in detail Schildt, 'Aufklärung'; Schildt, Führer, and Hickethier, *Öffentlichkeit—Medien—Geschichte*.
44. For research on communism see Rittersporn, Behrends, and Rolf, 'Öffentlichkeit', 10; for a summary see also Sabrow, 'Politischer Skandal', 19–23.
45. On the concept see von Saldern, 'Öffentlichkeiten in Diktaturen', 451f.
46. See Weisbrod, 'Öffentlichkeit', 24.
47. Popitz, *Phänomene der Macht*, 44.
48. See von Trotha, 'Soziologie der Gewalt', 26.

49. For an overview see MacIsaac, *Strategic Bombing*; United States Strategic Bombing Survey, IfZ-Archiv MA 1566; a selection of the reports in the United States Strategic Bombing Survey; an initial use of the material in Reuband, 'NS-Regime'.

50. See in detail Benda-Beckmann, 'Eine deutsch–deutsche Katastrophe?'; on the controversy see Boog (ed.), *Luftkriegsführung*.

51. For one of the first comprehensive regional histories see Beer, *Kriegsalltag*; see also Brinkhus, *Luftschutz und Versorgungspolitik*.

52. Gregor, 'A Schicksalsgemeinschaft?'

53. Mecking and Wirsching (eds), *Stadtverwaltung*; Bajohr, 'Hamburg'; Gotto, *Nationalsozialistische Kommunalpolitik*; Blank, *Hagen im Zweiten Weltkrieg*.

54. See among others Herbst, *Das nationalsozialistische Deutschland*.

55. For an introduction see the contributions in Süss and Süss (eds), *Das 'Dritte Reich'*; for an overview of the older research see Geyer, 'Krieg als Gesellschaftspolitik'.

56. See above all Süss, 'Volkskörper'.

57. On this compare the recent accounts in Bessel, *Nazism at War*, 163–5; Evans, *Third Reich at War*, 435–66; Fritzsche, *Life and Death in the Third Reich*, 286–9; Caplan (ed.), *Nazi Germany*; but see also Frei, *Führerstaat*, 193f. and 203.

58. See Echternkamp, *Das Deutsche Reich und der Zweite Weltkrieg*.

59. Overy, *Air War*; Boog, 'Luftkrieg über Europa'; Boog, 'Strategischer Luftkrieg in Europa und die Reichsluftverteidigung 1943–1944'; Boog, 'Bomberoffensive der Alliierten gegen Deutschland'; Müller, *Bombenkrieg*; Groehler, *Bombenkrieg*.

60. Jeremy Noakes in *Nazism 1919–1945*, vol. iv; the same point is made in Echternkamp, 'Gewalterfahrung'. See also Overy, Baldoli, and Knapp (eds), *Bombing, States and Peoples in Western Europe*.

61. For an introduction see Wildt and Bajohr (eds), *Volksgemeinschaft*; Wildt, *Geschichte des Nationalsozialismus*, 14f. Also Kramer, *Volksgenossinnen*; Stephenson, *Home Front*.

62. Frei, 'Volksgemeinschaft', 128.

63. For a critique see among others Mommsen, 'Forschungskontroversen', 20; and Mommsen, 'Amoklauf der "Volksgemeinschaft"?'.

64. See Süss and Süss, *Volksgemeinschaft*.

65. See among others Götz, *Ungleiche Schwestern*.

66. See also Gregor, *Nuremberg*, 1050ff.

67. See in detail Leonhard, 'Nationalisierung des Krieges', 97–101; Leonhard, *Bellizismus und Nation*, 813–18; also Heidekind, '"People's War or Standing Army"?'.

68. See among others Fielding, 'The Good War'.

69. See, for example, *The Times*, 24 April 1942: 'Lord Halifax on the New England'.

70. Crossick, 'And what should they know about England?'; Brüggemeier, *Geschichte Großbritanniens* provides a new comprehensive account, see especially pp. 191–220.

71. See the comprehensive bibliography: British History Compared, A Biblio-graphy. Compiled by Christiane Eisenberg, Humboldt-Universität, Berlin, August 2008 <http://www2.hu-berlin.de/gbz/index1024.html>, 10 March 2009; Stephenson, 'The Home Front in "Total War"', is an exception for the war period.

72. Webster and Frankland, *Strategic Air Offensive*, i–iv.

73. See among others Overy, *The Battle of Britain*.

74. For a comprehensive overview of the most recent literature see Süss, 'Krieg'.

75. See Jefferys, 'British Politics'; Lowe, 'Second World War'.

76. Addison and Crang, *Burning Blue* provides a recent overview; see also Titmuss, *Social Policy*.

77. Taylor, *English History*.

78. Calder, *The People's War*.

79. See above all Summerfield, *Women Workers*; Summerfield, *Reconstructing Women's Wartime Lives*; important on this is Hinton, *Women, Social Leadership, and the Second World War*.

80. For an overview see Harris, 'War and Social History'. The most important recent books are Robert Mackay's *Half the Battle*, Helen Jones's *Civilians in the Front Line*, and Sonya O. Rose, *Which People's War?*, which explores the issue of the gender-specific construction of citizenship during the war.

81. Sokoloff, 'Home Front', also argues along these lines; Thorpe, *Parties*, is impor-tant for the link between the national and local levels.

82. See most recently Stansky, *First Day of the Blitz*.

83. Excellent here is Arnold, *Urban Memory*, and Thiessen, *Gedächtnis*. For Britain, see Clapson and Larkham, *The Blitz and its Legacy*; Calder, *Myth*; Smith, *Britain and 1940*; Crawford, 'Constructing National Memory'; Addison, 'National Identity'; for a recent overview see Arnold, Süss, and Thiessen (eds), *Luftkrieg*; on Britain see Connelly and Goebel, 'Erinnerungspolitik'.

CHAPTER 1

1. Wells, *War in the Air*.

2. On this see Müller, *Bombenkrieg*, 15–20.

3. Memorandum on Bombing Operations for the Supreme War Council, January 1918, PRO, AIR 1/463/15/312/137.

4. See in detail Hanson, *The First Blitz*; Hyde, *The First Blitz*.

5. Geinitz, 'The First Air War' provides an overview.

6. Major Genth, 'Der operative Luftkrieg im Weltkriege, insbesondere gegen Eng-land', *Die Luftwaffe. Militärwissenschaftliche Aufsatzsammlung*, 2 (1937), 2, 10, quoted in Müller, *Bombenkrieg*, 19. On this see in detail Parton, 'The Develop-ment of Early RAF Doctrine'.

7. Quoted in Terraine, 'Theorie und Praxis des Luftkrieges', 539.

8. Rawlinson, *The Defence of London*, 4f.; see also Goebel, 'School', 222–6.

9. e.g. Bourke, *Fear*, 64ff.

10. On this see among others Le Bon, *Psychology*.
11. Konvitz, 'Représentations urbaines', 826f.
12. Colonel Louis Jackson, 'The Defence of Localities Against Aerial Attack', *Journal of the Royal Service Institute* (June 1914), 713, quoted in Bourke, *Fear*, 224.
13. 'Air Raid Psychology', *The Lancet*, 190, 14 July 1917, 55f.; 'Air-Raid Psychology and Air-Raid Perils', *The Lancet*, 190, 6 October 1917, 540f.
14. On this see in detail Jones, *Origins of Strategic Bombing*.
15. *The Times*, 15 October 1917: 'Political Bombing'.
16. *The Times*, 16 June 1917: 'Child Victims of the Enemy'.
17. On the borrowing of medieval symbols and images see Goebel, *Great War*.
18. *The Times*, 16 June 1917: 'Child Victims of the Enemy'.
19. *The Times*, 15 October 1917: 'Political Bombing'.
20. Chief of the Air Staff, Review of Air Situation and Strategy, 27 June 1918, PRO, AIR 9/8; see Overy, 'Bombing', 280; For the following see Overy, 'Bombing', 280.
21. On this see in detail Smith, *British Air Strategy*.
22. Quoted in Meilinger, 'Trenchard', 52f.
23. Hugh Trenchard, 'The War Object of an Air Force', 2 May 1928, PRO, AIR 9/8.
24. Goebel, *Great War*, 223–30.
25. Castan, *Der Rote Baron*, 277.
26. Kehrt, *Moderne Krieger*.
27. Goebel, *Great War*, 229.
28. On this see Fritzsche, *Nation*, 96ff.
29. Jünger (ed.), *Luftfahrt ist not!*, 9–13.
30. On this see in detail Gat, *Fascist and Liberal Vision of War*, 52–63.
31. Douhet, *Luftschlacht*; a partial translation of the Italian original into French was published for the first time in 1932 and was the basis for the British reception of the book.
32. Baumann, 'Entgrenzung', 226.
33. Baumann, 'Entgrenzung', 256.
34. Meilinger, 'Trenchard'.
35. Killingray, 'A Swift Agent of Government'; for the following see Killingray, 'A Swift Agent of Government'.
36. Killingray, 'A Swift Agent of Government', 443.
37. Killingray, 'A Swift Agent of Government', 440.
38. *Hansard, HoC*, vol. 280, 5 July 1933, 353f.
39. See Danchev, 'Liddell Hart'; Searle, 'Fuller and Liddell Hart'.
40. Quoted in Groehler, *Geschichte*, 118.
41. Lemke, *Luftschutz*, 205.
42. On this see above all Nebelin, *Ludendorff* and Hippler, 'Krieg', 414–22.
43. Ludendorff, *Der Totale Krieg*, 6.
44. Russell, 'Speaking of Annihilation'.

45. On this compare Lynch, *Beyond Appeasement*.

46. ARPC-Meeting of 20 January 1925, PRO, CAB 46/1; see in detail Lemke, *Luftschutz*, 170–86.

47. See Overy, *Morbid Age*, 175–218.

48. Smith, 'Luftbedrohung', 716. For the following see Smith, 'Luftbedrohung', 716.

49. Saint-Amour, 'Air War Prophecy'.

50. Lemke, *Luftschutz*, 180; For the following see Lemke, *Luftschutz*, 180.

51. See Chickering, *Freiburg im Ersten Weltkrieg*, 96–108.

52. See in detail Lemke, *Luftschutz*, 105ff.

53. On this see Kramer, *Volksgenossinnen*, 128–36.

54. Lemke, *Luftschutz*, 129, For the following see Lemke, *Luftschutz*, 129.

55. On this see in detail Schütz, 'Wahn-Europa'; see among others Helders, *Luftkrieg 1936*; Helders was the pseudonym for Robert Knauss, for a short time director of Deutsche Lufthansa and an official of the Reich Air Ministry, who was one of the most radical 'Douhetists' in Germany; on this see Boog, 'Robert Knauss'.

56. Zimmer, *Gas*, 143.

57. Gobsch, *Wahn-Europa*, 195.

58. Schütz, 'Wahn-Europa', 139.

59. Alexander, *Schlacht über Berlin*.

60. Von Leers, '*Bomben auf Hamburg*'; also e.g. Lemke, *Luftschutz*, 148f.

61. *Bayerische Staatszeitung*, 3 March 1933.

62. Lemke, *Luftschutz*, 240ff.

63. Lemke, *Luftschutz*, 308, 486.

64. Air Defence Law of 26 June 1935, in *RGBl.* 1935, part I, 827.

65. With the 'Anschluss' of Austria on 12 March 1938 the Austrian Air Defence League was integrated into the RLB and its structures were, at least formally, taken over.

66. Bauer, *Fliegeralarm*, 9; Süss, 'Krieg, Kommune, Katastrophe', 109f.

67. On this see also Hippler, 'Krieg', 421.

68. *5 Jahre Reichsluftschutzbund*, 19.

69. Reibel, *Fundament*, 159–228; Kramer, 'Mobilisierung', 80f.

70. See also among others Metzner (ed.), *Luftfahrt*.

71. Grundwaldt, 'Jugendpsyche', 219f.

72. Bauer, *Fliegeralarm*, 12.

73. Kramer, *Volksgenossinnen*, 136–143.

74. Ohliger, *Bomben auf Kohlenstadt*.

75. Ohliger, *Bomben auf Kohlenstadt*, 42f.

76. Kramer, 'Mobilisierung', 82ff.

77. First Decree for the Implementation of the Air Defence Law of 4 May 1937, in *RGBl.* 1937, part I, 559ff.

78. See now in detail Schüler-Springorum, *Krieg und Fliegen*.

79. Mattioli, *Experimentierfeld der Gewalt*; Mattioli, 'Entgrenzte Kriegsgewalt'.
80. Müller, 'Gaskriegsvorbereitungen'.
81. Luftwaffendienstvorschrift 'Luftkriegsführung' (Lv.Dv. 16), in Völker (ed.), *Dokumente und Dokumentarfotos*, 469.
82. On this see briefly Murray, *Luftkrieg*, 97–106.
83. Kantorowicz, *Spanisches Tagebuch*, 95; For the following see Schüler-Springorum, 'Mythos Guernica', 90f.
84. See in detail Stradling, *Your Children Will Be Next*, 215–46.
85. Schüler-Springorum, 'Mythos Guernica', 85–9.
86. Comprehensive coverage in van Hensbergen, *Guernica*.
87. *The Times*, 28 April 1937: 'The Tragedy of Guernica'; Steer, *The Tree of Gernika*.
88. Overy, 'Bombing', 287.
89. Labour Party, *A.R.P.: Labour's Policy*, 10; on this see also Meisel, 'Air Raid Shelter Policy', 306.
90. On the following see also Lemke, *Luftschutz*, 426f.
91. See Haldane, *ARP*, 100ff.; on the following see Haldane, *ARP*, 100ff.

CHAPTER 2

1. Churchill, *Reden*, i. 319f.
2. Kershaw, *Wendepunkte*, 40ff.
3. See also Woller, 'Churchill und Mussolini'.
4. See Herbst, *Das nationalsozialistische Deutschland*, 322f.
5. See Alter, *Winston Churchill*, 136–45.
6. Winston Churchill, War Situation, *Hansard, HoC*, vol. 361, 4 June 1940, 776–98.
7. See also Mackay, *Half the Battle*, 2ff.
8. Stephen Taylor, Memorandum, 1 October 1941, PRO, INF 1/292.
9. Morale in Glasgow (March 1941), Mass-Observation File Report Series, 600; see also Morale and the future (February 1940), Mass-Observation File Report Series, 27.
10. On the history and methods of Mass-Observation see Hubble, *Mass Observation and Everyday Life*; Calder, 'Mass-Observation'.
11. For an introduction to its history see Jeffery, *Mass Observation*.
12. See Süss, 'Kannibalen im eigenen Land'.
13. On this see among others Hinton, 'The "Class Complex"'; on its methods see in detail Stanley, 'The Extra Dimension'.
14. See Calder and Sheridan (eds), *Speak for Yourself*.
15. For the following see Summerfield, 'Mass-Observation'.
16. Mira, 'Psychiatric Experience'.
17. Reports from HMS *Capetown* on Japanese raids on Nanking, 2 August 1937, PRO, ADM 116/4174.
18. Air Operation during Sino-Japanese Hostilities, November 1938, PRO, AIR 2/3558.

19. See among others Jones and Wessely, *Impact of Total War*, Shephard, *War of Nerves*.
20. On this concept see in detail Chickering and Förster, *Introduction*, 8ff.
21. Ministry of Information Weekly Reports, No. 53, 8 October 1943, Stephen Taylor: Home morale and public opinion, PRO, INF 1/292.
22. Preliminary Report on Morale in Glasgow (7 March 1941), Mass-Observation File Report Series, 600.
23. See in detail McLaine, *Ministry of Morale*.
24. Tom Clarke to Deputy Director General, 10 September 1939, PRO, INF 1/185.
25. McLaine, *Ministry of Morale*, 36ff.
26. Memorandum on Press Censorship in the UK, PRO, INF 1/75.
27. See in detail Nicholas, *The Echo of War*.
28. Nicholas, '"Sly Demagogues"and Wartime Radio', 253.
29. Home Morale Emergency Committee, 22 May 1940, PRO, INF 1/257; see McLaine, *Ministry of Morale*, 78.
30. On the history of its establishment and the disagreements about its staffing and organization see PRO, HO 199/462.
31. Home Intelligence Daily Report, 20 May 1940, PRO, INF 1/264.
32. Note on rumour by Mass-Observation (n.d., around1940), PRO, INF 1/251.
33. Connelly,'The British People', 44.
34. Policy Committee minutes, 5 July 1940, PRO, INF 1/849; for the following see McLaine, *Ministry of Morale*, 81ff.
35. McLaine, *Ministry of Morale*, 86ff.
36. Home Intelligence Daily Report, 16 July 1940, PRO, INF 1/264.
37. Maier,'Luftschlacht um England'.
38. Boelcke (ed.), *'Wollt Ihr den totalen Krieg?'*, entry for 24 October 1940, 151.
39. Boelcke (ed.), *'Wollt Ihr den totalen Krieg?'*, entry for 24 July 1940, 108.
40. Boelcke (ed.), *'Wollt Ihr den totalen Krieg?'*, entry for 13 June 1940, 83.
41. Boelcke (ed.), *'Wollt Ihr den totalen Krieg?'*, entry for 31 August 1940, 123.
42. *National-Zeitung*, 5 June 1940:'Bomben auf Wälder, Felder und Wohnviertel'.
43. *National-Zeitung*, 3 October 1940: 'Neuer Anschlag Churchills gegen Frauen und Kinder'.
44. Joseph Goebbels,'Die Moral als kriegsentscheidender Faktor', *Der steile Aufstieg* (Munich, 1943), 406–13, article of 7 August 1943.
45. Goebbels, *Tagebücher*, part II, vol. v, 30 July 1942, 213.
46. Goebbels, *Tagebücher*, part II, vol. iv, 14 April 1942, 95.
47. *National-Zeitung*, 20 June 1940: 'Wie bekämpft man Brandbomben und Entstehungsbrände?'
48. See Bauer, *Fliegeralarm*, 10.
49. On this see in detail Groehler, *Bombenkrieg*, 230–7.
50. *Meldungen aus dem Reich*, 20 May 1940, vol. iv, 1152; 16 May, 1040, 1140f.
51. Beer, *Kriegsalltag*, 102.
52. See also Reibel, *Fundament*, 360f.

53. *National-Zeitung*, 17 May 1940: 'Herr Meier meint: Da klappt was nicht!'
54. On the language used in the weekly newsreels see Zehender, 'Tarnsprache'.
55. Announcement by the Chief of Police in Stuttgart of 25 August 1940: 'Aufbewahren, bei Fliegeralarm in den Luftschutzraum mitnehmen!', *Dokumente deutscher Kriegsschäden*, ii/1. 28f.
56. Police Chief Kehrl to the population of Hamburg, 21 May 1940, in *Dokumente deutscher Kriegsschäden*, vol. ii/1. 253; similar instructions have survived for Essen, Dortmund, Düsseldorf, Munich, and Stuttgart.
57. 'Vorläufige Anordnung über die Aufgaben der Dienststellen für Familienunterhalt bei Eintritt von Personen- und Sachschäden': instructions for Stuttgart, 6 September 1940, in *Dokumente deutscher Kriegsschäden*, vol. ii/1. 32f.
58. With reference to communist dictatorships see above all Behrends, 'Soll und Haben'.
59. *National-Zeitung*, 17 May 1940: 'Herr Meier meint: Da klappt was nicht!'
60. *Meldungen aus dem Reich*, vol. v, 4 July 1940, 1335f.; for the following see *Meldungen aus dem Reich*, vol. 5, 4 July 1940, 1335f.
61. *Meldungen aus dem Reich*, vol. v, 11 July 1940, 1365.
62. *Archiv der Gegenwart*, 1939–40, 4166; Groehler, *Bombenkrieg*, 240f.
63. *Meldungen aus dem Reich*, vol. v, 4 July 1940, 1339.
64. *Meldungen aus dem Reich*, vol. iv, 10 June 1940, 1236; see also Arnold, 'Bombenkrieg', 37.
65. *Meldungen aus dem Reich*, vol. iv, 27 May 1940, 1176.
66. Dröge, *Widerstand*, 127.
67. See Klee, 'Luftschutzkeller', 44–70; Kock, *Der Führer*.
68. *Meldungen aus dem Reich*, vol. v, 30 September 1940, 1622.
69. On this see Dröge, *Widerstand*, 127; compare among others *Meldungen aus dem Reich*, vol. viii, 13 November 1941, 2963.
70. *Meldungen aus dem Reich*, vol. vi, 6 March 1941, 2075.
71. Goebbels, *Tagebücher*, part II, vol. i, 5 September 1941, 359.
72. *Meldungen aus dem Reich*, vol. x, 2 April 1942, 3567.
73. *Meldungen aus dem Reich*, vol. x, 4 June 1942, 3787f.
74. See among others *Meldungen aus dem Reich*, vol. xi, 3 July 1942, 4016.
75. Goebbels, *Tagebücher*, part II, vol. v, 30 September 1942, 607.
76. Goebbels, *Tagebücher*, part II, vol. v, 13 September 1942, 492.
77. Kershaw, *Hitler-Mythos*, 259f.
78. See in detail Kershaw, *Hitler-Mythos*, 247–54.
79. See also Kallis, 'Niedergang der Deutungsmacht', 235f.
80. Goebbels, *Tagebücher*, part II, vol. ix, 25 July 1943, 160.
81. OLG-Munich report to the RJM, 3 August 1943, IfZ-Archiv, MA 430/1.
82. *'Wollt Ihr den totalen Krieg?'*, entry for 30 March 1942, 294.
83. See among others *Lübecker-General-Anzeiger*, 1 April 1942: 'Dokumente der Schande Englands'; *Kölnische Zeitung*, 5 June 1942: 'Gemeinschaftsgeist und Nachbarshilfe'.

84. *National-Zeitung*, 15 February 1942: 'Britenbomben auf Städtische Kinderklinik'.
85. See also *National-Zeitung*, 18 March 1943: 'Kulturbilanz nach den Terroran-griffen. Was wir verloren—und was uns blieb'.
86. *National-Zeitung*, 6 April 1943: 'Not- und Kampfgemeinschaft der Essener'.
87. Quoted in Rüther, *Köln, 31. Mai 1942*, 85.
88. LSA (Luftschutzabschnitt) III, Besprechung vom 4. 7. 1942, HStAD, BR 1131/56; see in detail Rüther, 'Reaktionen und Folgen', 66–71.
89. *Meldungen aus dem Reich*, vol. xiii, 24 May 1943, 5277.
90. Pöhlmann, 'Von Versailles nach Armageddon', esp. 366–72.
91. On this compare Pogt, *Vor fünfzig Jahren*.
92. SD-Abschnitt Linz, 23 June 1943, IfZ-Archiv, MA 667.
93. *Meldungen aus dem Reich*, 1 July 1943; see also Dröge, *Widerstand*, 132.
94. This was the view not only of Goebbels and the SD but also of the OLG presidents; see OLG-Präsident Darmstadt to the RJM, 1 December 1944, IfZ-Archiv, MA 430/2; OLG-Präsident Naumburg (Saale) to the RJM, 30 June 1943, IfZ-Archiv, MA 430/1.
95. See Steinert, *Hitlers Krieg*, 32; and Wirl, *Meinung*, 52–4.
96. '*Wollt Ihr den totalen Krieg?*', entry for 10 March 1943, 452; and for the follow-ing see also Boberach, 'Auswirkungen', 265–79.
97. See also Mackay, *Half the Battle*, 144ff.
98. Bristol: reaction to raids (April 1941), Mass-Observation File Report Series, 626; Liverpool: effect of raids (May 1941), Mass-Observation File Report Series, 706.
99. Lysaght, *Brendan Bracken*, 191–218.
100. Memorandum to the War Cabinet, 24 April 1942, PRO, INF 1/679.
101. Quoted in McLaine, *Ministry of Morale*, 128f.
102. Preparation of Air Raid Commentaries, 31 March 1941, PRO, INF 1/174A; for the following see Preparation of Air Raid Commentaries, 31 March 1941, PRO, INF 1/174A.
103. Harrisson, *Living*, 289 and 300f.
104. For an overview see Kushner, *Persistence of Prejudice*.
105. Sixth Weekly Report for Home Intelligence (November 1940), Mass-Observation File Report Series, 486; Air raid casualty news (12 July 1940), Mass-Observation File Report Series, 266.
106. *Liverpool Daily Echo*, 2 October 1940: 'New Homes for Raid Victims'; *Liverpool Express*, 26 September 1940: 'Caring for Homeless'.
107. *Liverpool Daily Echo*, 24 October 1940: 'Communal Feeding'.
108. *Liverpool Post*, 1 November 1940: 'Merseyside Civil Defence'.
109. *Manchester Guardian*, 27 December 1940: 'A Manchester Survey after the Attack'.
110. The Assessment of Air-Raid Morale from the local press. Home Intelligence Report, Social Survey and Damage Reports in Britain (1943), PRO, HO 199/456.

111. *Manchester Guardian*, 30 December 1940:'Air-Raid Damage in Manchester'.
112. *Southern Daily Echo*, 27 November 1940: 'Towns Nazis tried to destroy still live'.
113. *Southern Daily Echo*, 6 December 1940:'King Inspires People of Southampton'.
114. Southampton: effects of recent raids (December 1940), Mass-Observation File Report Series, 516; Southampton: report on raids (December 1940), Mass-Observation File Report Series, 517.
115. Calder, *Myth*, 250; Ward, *Britishness*, 27f.
116. *Liverpool Express*, 7 November 1940:'King and Queen talk to Bomb Victims'.
117. The same is true of Southampton; see, for example, *Southern Daily*, 6 December 1940: 'King Inspires People of Southampton'; *Manchester Guardian*, 16 January 1941:'The Duke talking to Manchester People'.
118. *The Times*, 1 September 1939: 'Evacuation—Today'; Kressel, *Evakuierungen*, 69–88.
119. *The Times*, 1 September 1939:'Keep Calm'.
120. *The Times*, 2 September 1939:'Children Move on'.
121. Westall, *Children of the Blitz*, 48.
122. Compare Ward, *Britishness*, 55–66.
123. Rose, *War*, 207ff.
124. British Movietone News, 14 September 1939.
125. *The Spectator*, 8 September 1939; see also Lowe, *Education and the Second World War*, 5ff.
126. *Glasgow Herald*, 14 September 1939.
127. Liverpool Council of Social Service, Wartime Bulletin of Information, No. 60, 6 April 1942, Liverpool Record Archive.
128. Rose, *War*, 58ff.
129. Calder, *Myth*, 62f.
130. See among others Kressel, *Evakuierungen*, 182–9.
131. National Emergency Bulletin, No. 48, Liverpool Council of Social Service, 27 December 1940, Liverpool Record Archive.
132. *Glasgow Herald*, 14 September 1939, 5.
133. Compare Klee, *'Luftschutzkeller'*, 124f.
134. Merkblatt an alle Gastgeber der Umquartierten aus den Luftkriegsgebieten (n.d., c. summer 1943), IfZ-Archiv, MA 667.
135. See also Klee, *'Luftschutzkeller'*, 117ff.
136. OLG-Präsident Düsseldorf to the RJM, 30 July 1944, IfZ-Archiv, MA 430/2; OLG-Präsident Linz/Donau to the RJM, 5 April 1944, IfZ-Archiv, MA 430/1.
137. Reports from the west of the Reich by contrast contained in some cases strong criticism of the lack of solidarity being shown by the reception Gaus and, contrary to the official propaganda line, made no bones about the conflicts of interest that existed; see Goebbels, *Tagebücher*, part II, vol. ix, 3 July 1943, 36.
138. Notiz für Pg. Wächter, 16 June 1943, IfZ-Archiv, MA 667.

139. Reichspropagandaleitung, Chef des Propagandastabes, to the Reichspropagandaleiter 16 June 1943, IfZ-Archiv, MA 667.
140. See in detail Fetcher, *Joseph Goebbels*.
141. Teleprinter message from the Party Chancellery office in Berlin to Bormann,
22 June 1943, IfZ-Archiv, MA 667.
142. Goebbels, *Tagebücher*, part II, vol. viii, 19 June 1943, 495.
143. Goebbels, *Tagebücher*, part II, vol. viii, 26 May 1943, 367.
144. OLG-Präsident Frankfurt am Main to the RJM, 27 July 1943, IfZ-Archiv, MA
430/1.
145. Meldungen aus dem SD-Abschnittsbereich, 6 August 1943, BA Berlin, NS
6/411.
146. *Meldungen aus dem Reich*, 2 August 1943, vol. xiv, 5562.
147. See Dröge, *Widerstand*, 130; there are similar assessments in the OLG reports,
for example OLG-Munich report to the RJM, 3 August 1943, IfZArchiv, MA
430/1.
148. Goebbels, *Tagebücher*, part II, vol. ix, 4 September 1943, 421.
149. OLG-Präsident Munich to the RJM, 3 August 1943, IfZ-Archiv, MA 430/1.
150. Meldungen aus dem SD-Abschnittsbereich, 6 August 1943, BA Berlin, NS
6/411.
151. OLG-President Hamburg to the RJM, 3 December 1942, IfZ-Archiv, MA
430/1.
152. Notiz für Pg. Tiessler vom 4. Mai 1943, BA Berlin, NS 13/27: article on
'rumours' for the 'relevant authority'.
153. Propagandaparole 14 (n.d. *c.* 1943), BA Berlin, NS 18/80.
154. Reichspropagandaleitung, 18 November 1943, Führungshinweis No. 7, Akten
der Partei-Kanzlei, part II, 56817.
155. See Kirchner, *Psychologische Kriegsführung*, 16.
156. LK-Mitteilung, 14 July 1944: Anlegung eines Luftkriegs-Archivs, BA Berlin,
R 55/447.
157. See Hopf, *Lübeck*.
158. Düwel and Gütschow, *Fortgewischt*, 104ff.
159. On the relevant literature see above all Rolf Sachsse, *Fotografie*; Sachsse, *Erziehung zum Wegsehen*; Deres, Rüther, and Sachsse, *Fotografieren verboten!*; Schlosser,
Fotografie.
160. Verfügung der Kölner Oberstaatsanwaltschaft im Prozess gegen Herrn S. vom
26. 6. 1942, quoted in Deres, Rüther, and Sachsse, *Fotografieren verboten!*, 75 and
80; see in detail, *Fotografie*, 78–84.
161. See Schlosser, *Fotografie*, 96ff.; for the following see Schlosser, *Fotografie*, 96ff.
162. Minutes of 10 September 1940, quoted in Willi A. Boelcke, *Kriegspropaganda*,
498; see also the minutes of 14 May 1940, Boelcke, *Kriegspropaganda*, 349f.
163. Schlosser, *Fotografie*, 100.
164. Minutes of the ministerial conference of 10 June 1940, in *'Wollt Ihr den totalen
Krieg?'*, 81.

165. Quoted in Schlosser, *Fotografie*, 128f.
166. See among others Lowry, *Pathos und Politik*, 116–32.
167. See Chiari, Rogg, and Schmidt (eds), *Krieg und Militär*; see in particular Rogg, 'Luftwaffe'.
168. For the following see Rother, 'Stukas'.
169. Kindler, '"Wo wir sind, da ist immer oben"', 401.
170. NL Beltzig, IFZ-Archiv, ED 323/1.
171. See, for example, *Liverpool Echo*, 6 December 1941: 'Clearance Work in Central Liverpool following Various Air Raids'.
172. *Manchester Guardian*, 20 December 1941: 'A Year Ago in Manchester'.
173. Underdown, *Bristol under Blitz*.
174. Underdown, *Bristol under Blitz*, 12.
175. de Gaulle, *War Memoirs*, 104.
176. Quoted in Cull, *Selling War*, 101.
177. Cull, *Selling War*, 105.
178. Cull, *Selling War*, 103.
179. Cull, *Selling War*, 109.
180. Cull, *Selling War*, 134f.; 'The Blitz on the Provinces'.
181. *Life Magazine*, 23 September 1940 (title picture).
182. See Connelly, *We Can Take it*, 132–5.
183. See Chapman, *British at War*, 98ff.
184. Calder, *Blitz*, 232f.
185. Battle of Britain: criticism of film (November 1940), Mass-Observation, File Report Series, 491.
186. Preliminary Report on Opinion about Ministry of Information Films (24 July 1941), Mass-Observation, File Report Series, 799; MoI shorts: study of MoI and GPO films, Mass-Observation, File Report Series, 458.
187. Chapman, *British at War*, 100f.; for the following see Chapman, *British at War*, 100f.
188. Aldgate and Richards, *England, their England*, 241.
189. *Daily Telegraph*, 24 March 1943.
190. Richards and Sheridan (eds), *Mass Observation at the Movies*, 225, 249.
191. *The Times*, 26 August 1940; see in detail Flemming, 'Haltung', 52ff.
192. *Daily Mirror*, 12 September 1940: 'Bombs on Berlin'.
193. Webster and Frankland, *Strategic Air Offensive*, i. 178ff.
194. On this see in particular McLaine, *Ministry*, 161ff.
195. *Daily Express*, 1 June 1942: 'The VENGEANCE BEGINS! The ruins of Cologne are hidden under a pall of smoke rising 15,000 feet after the first thousand-bomber raid in history'; see also Connelly, 'Öffentlichkeit', 83; Flemming, 'Haltung', 126ff.
196. Quoted in Flemming, 'Haltung', 129–31.
197. *The Times*, 28 July 1942: 'Hamburg in Flames'; *The Times*, 23 December 1942: 'Big Fires in Munich'.
198. *Manchester Guardian*, 31 July 1943: 'The Battering of Hamburg'.

199. *Daily Express*, 28 August 1943: '77 Tons dropped every minute. Berlin is being Hamburged'; *Daily Mirror*, 25 November 1943: 'Berlin burns'.

200. *Daily Express*, 23 May 1944: 'Berlin, Dead City of Troglodytes'.

201. See Connelly, 'Öffentlichkeit', 84ff.

202. *The Times*, 16 February 1945: '14,000 Tons on Germany'.

203. See among others Goebbels, *Tagebücher*, part II, vol. x, 30 November 1943, 386; *Tagebücher*, part II, vol. xi, 25 January 1944, 166.

204. OLG President Braunschweig to the RJM, 30 November 1943, IfZ-Archiv, MA 430/2; see also Longerich, *'Davon haben wir nichts gewusst!'*, 304–11.

205. Quoted in Bajohr, 'Deportation der Juden', 39f.

206. Quoted in Longerich, *'Davon haben wir nichts gewusst'*, 305.

207. Longerich, *'Davon haben wir nichts gewusst'*, 307f.

208. Goebbels, *Das eherne Herz*, 350.

209. Hölsken, *V-Waffen*, 91–3; Boog, 'Strategischer Luftkrieg', 383f.

210. *Hitlers Lagebesprechungen*, 294–7, Mittagslage, 25 July 1943.

211. See Boog, 'Strategischer Luftkrieg', 340f.

212. *Westfälischer Beobachter/Gladbecker Zeitung*, 29 June 1943: 'Gefallen an der Front der Heimat'; quoted in Blank, 'Kriegsalltag', 435.

213. OLG Bamberg report to the RJM, 2. August 1943, IfZ-Archiv, MA 430/1; OLG President Munich to the RJM, 3 August 1943, IfZ-Archiv, MA 430/1.

214. See IfZ-Archiv, MA 430/1.

215. Goebbels, *Tagebücher*, part II, vol. x, 11 December 1943, 457.

216. Goebbels, *Tagebücher*, part II, vol. x, 11 December 1943, 457.

217. Landgerichtsrat Wachinger to the Amtsgerichtsdirektor in Landshut, 7 August 1943, IfZArchiv, MA 430/1.

218. See, for example, *Völkischer Beobachter* (Munich edition), 30 May 1943: 'Das Schuldkonto der Mordbrenner'; *Völkischer Beobachter*, 27 June 1943: 'Britischer Kindermord in Bochum'; *Völkischer Beobachter*, 11 March 1943: 'Das Schuldkonto der britischen Barbaren schwillt an'; *Völkischer Beobachter*, 2/3 July 1944: 'Die Rache der Geschichtslosen'; *National-Zeitung*, 20 April 1944: 'Die Fehlrechnung des Bombenterrors'.

219. See, for example, *National-Zeitung*, 4 August 1944: 'Die Schadensaufstellung'; *Völkischer Beobachter* (Munich edition), 31 October 1943: 'Wohnungshilfswerk für Fliegergeschädigte'.

220. *Völkischer Beobachter* (Munich edition), 8 April 1943: 'Schadensnachweis bei Bombenschäden'.

221. *Völkischer Beobachter* (Munich edition), 1 August 1943: 'Die Selbsthilfe im Bombenkrieg'; for the following see *Völkischer Beobachter* (Munich edition), 1 August 1943.

222. *Völkischer Beobachter* (Munich edition), 14 December 1943: 'Erfahrungen aus Großangriffsnächten'.

223. Mundpropaganda-Richtlinien des Leiters des Reichspropagandaamts Wien, Parteigenosse Frauenfeld, 13 June 1944, in Wette et al., *Das letzte halbe Jahr*, 161, Doc. 7.

224. Hitler, *Hitlers politisches Testament*, 51.
225. OLG President Nuremberg to the RJM, 3 April 1944, IfZ-Archiv, MA 430/1.
226. Bericht des Wehrmacht-Propaganda-Offiziers des Wehrkreiskommandos II vom 30. 11. 1944, in Wette et al., *Das letzte halbe Jahr*, 85, Doc. 25.
227. Zwischenbericht des Wehrmacht-Propaganda-Offiziers des Wehrkreiskommandos XVII, Wien, 21 July 1944, in Wette et al., *Das letzte halbe Jahr*, 64f., Doc. 8.
228. See also Dröge, *Widerstand*, 213.
229. Vortragsnotiz vom Gruppenleiter der Gruppe A im Oberkommando der Wehrmacht, 3 April 1945, in Wette et al., *Das letzte halbe Jahr*, 124f., Doc. 57.
230. 16. Bericht des Wehrmacht-Propaganda-Offizier des Wehrkreiskommandos UU, 1 February 1945, in Wette et al., *Das letzte halbe Jahr*, 228, Doc. 75.
231. See in detail Neutzner, 'Vom Alltäglichen zum Exemplarischen', 112ff.; Bergander, *Dresden im Luftkrieg*; Bergander, 'Gerücht', 605ff.; Taylor, *Tuesday 13 February 1945*, 360–72.
232. Deutsches Nachrichtenbüro DNB-Dienst, 16 February 1945, Bl. 17, IfZ-Archiv, Z 2044.
233. On Dresden see in detail Bergander, *Dresden*; Bergander, 'Kalkül und Routine'.
234. *Svenska Dagbladet*, 25 February 1945: 'Fast 200,000 Opfer der Angriffe auf Dresden', quoted in *Dokumente deutscher Kriegsschäden*, 2nd supplementary number, 469.
235. Quoted from Taylor, *Dresden*, 360.
236. *Der Angriff*, 3 March 1945: 'Ohne Gepäck'; similarly *Der Angriff*, 18 February: 'Bestien'.
237. Goebbels, *Tagebücher*, part II, vol. vii, 9 March 1943, 505.
238. *Das Reich*, 4 March 1945: 'Der Tod von Dresden'; for the following see *Das Reich*, 4 March 1945.
239. See Neutzner, 'Vom Alltäglichen zum Exemplarischen', 126f.
240. See in detail Chapters 9 and 10.

CHAPTER 3

1. O'Brien, *Civil Defence*, 300–3.
2. For an overview see Johnson, *Defence by Committee*.
3. Civil Defence Regional Organization, 12 April 1940, PRO, HO 199/15.
4. Civil Defence Executive Sub-Committee, 8 November 1940, PRO, CAB 73/3.
5. Civil Defence Executive Sub-Committee, 21 September 1940, PRO, CAB 73/3.
6. Civil Defence Executive Sub-Committee, 23 December 1940, PRO, CAB 73/3; For the following see Civil Defence Executive Sub-Committee, 23 December 1940, PRO, CAB 73/3.
7. Civil Defence Executive Sub-Committee, 19 November 1940, PRO, CAB 73/3.

8. Civil Defence Executive Sub-Committee, 2 December 1940, PRO, CAB 73/3.
9. Civil Defence Executive Sub-Committee, Memorandum by the Minister of Home Security, 20 December 1940, PRO, CAB 73/3; For the following see Civil Defence Executive Sub-Committee, Memorandum by the Minister of Home Security, 20 December 1940, PRO, CAB 73/3.
10. Civil Defence Executive Sub-Committee, 16 December 1940, PRO, CAB 73/3.
11. *Hansard, HoC, Debates*, 9 October 1940, vol. 365, 401–9.
12. Evacuation: Memorandum, February 1939, PRO, HLG 7/62; for the following see PRO, HLG 7/62.
13. *The Times*, 1 September 1939: 'Evacuation to-day'.
14. Evacuation: Memorandum, February 1939, Points for Speech at Parents' Meeting, PRO, HLG 7/62; see also among others Brown, *A Child's War*; Parsons, *Evacuation*; Downs, 'A Very British Revolution?'; Welshman, 'Evacuation of Children'.
15. PRO, CAB 73/3.
16. Welshman, 'Evacuation', 35.
17. Welshman, 'Evacuation', 37.
18. Ministry of Health, Circular 1907, 7 November 1939, PRO, MH 101/15; Titmuss, *Social Policy*, 120.
19. On this see in detail Titmuss, *Social Policy*; Harris, 'War'.
20. Welshman, 'Evacuation', 43; For the following see Welshman, 'Evacuation', 43.
21. For Britain see in detail Lemke, *Luftschutz*, 239–680; for the Nazi regime see Süss, 'Steuerung'; Brinkhus, *Luftschutz und Versorgungspolitik*.
22. On the RLM see in detail Lemke, *Luftschutz*, 240–51.
23. On this see Klee, *'Luftschutzkeller'*, 40–70; Krause, *Flucht*.
24. Draft for Milch's presentation to Hitler, Vermerk, 28 January 1942, BA-MA, RL 4/341.
25. For detail on this see Brinkhus, 'Luftschutz'.
26. Blank, 'Kriegsalltag', 399ff.
27. Telex from the RLM and OBdL, 10 January 1944 to the Reich Defence Commissioners in Blank, 'Kriegsalltag', 401.
28. Goebbels, *Tagebücher*, part II, vol. iii, 30 March 1942, 583.
29. Klee, *'Luftschutzkeller'*, 44–70; Kock, *Führer*.
30. Goebbels, *Tagebücher*, part II, vol. ii, 9 December 1941, 458; vol. iii, 2 January 1942, 40; see also Klee, *'Luftschutzkeller'*, 64ff.
31. Goebbels, *Tagebücher*, part II, vol. iii, 17 January 1942, 127.
32. Reichsminister für Volksaufklärung und Propaganda, 28 April 1942 an die Gauleiter, Reichsstatthalter und Reichsverteidigungskommissare, BA Berlin, R2/30.315.
33. Compare Brinkhus, 'Hitler'.
34. Goebbels, *Tagebücher*, part II, vol. v, 8 August 1942, 275–8; vol. v, 9 August 1942, 282–4.

35. On the importance of local government during the war see Brinkhus, 'Auftragsverwaltung der Gemeinden'.

36. Carl Overhues to the Partei-Kanzlei, 8 October 1942, Akten der Partei-Kanzlei, part II, 11363–6; For the following see Akten der Partei-Kanzlei, part II, 11363–6; on this see also Klee, 'Luftschutzkeller', 96–102.

37. Excerpt from a message from Gauleiter Florian to the Partei-Kanzlei, 21 October 1942, Akten der Partei-Kanzlei, part II, 11357–60.

38. On Ley's role see also the note of 21 November 1942 concerning a conversation between DAF chief of staff, Simon, and Reich Housing Commissioner, Wagner, Akten der Partei-Kanzlei, part I, 16336.

39. On this see among others Boog, 'Luftkrieg über Europa'.

40. Lammers to Frick, 31 December 1942, BA Berlin, R 1501/922; on the Reich Chancellery's position see also Lammers to Bormann, 11 December 1942, Akten der Partei-Kanzlei, part II, 10108600–03.

41. See Süss, 'Aufstieg des Karl Brandt'.

42. Lammers to Goebbels, 31 December 1942, BA Berlin, R 1501/922.

43. See also Nicolson, Diaries and Letters, entry of 6 February 1941, 200.

44. On this see Ewen, 'Preparing the British Fire Service'.

45. Ewen, 'Preparing the British Fire Service', 221ff.

46. See, for example, The Times, 19 April 1941: 'Civil Defence'; The Times, 28 April 1941: 'Fire Fighting'.

47. On this see in detail O'Brien, Civil Defence, 445–503.

48. Conversation with the Secretary of the National Council of Social Service on 6 June 1941, PRO, Premier 4/40/14.

49. National Council of Social Service: Welfare Work in Bombed Areas, Notes for Voluntary Social Organisations, 14 May 1941, PRO, Premier 4/40/14.

50. The Case for a Minister of Civil Defence, 30 May 1941, PRO, Premier 4/31/1.

51. Memorandum for the Prime Minister, 4 June 1941, PRO, Premier 4/34/1.

52. Hansard, HoC, Debates, vol. 372, Civil Defence, 11 June 1941, 200–90, above all 215–22.

53. Departmental Reports on Preparations for Heavy Air Attacks next Winter, Memorandum by the Ministry of Home Security, 18 July 1941, PRO, HO 186/927, 4–14; for the following see PRO, HO 186/927, 4–14.

54. O'Brien, Civil Defence, 534.

55. On this see in detail Balfour, Propaganda, 152–6.

56. Departmental Reports on Preparations for Heavy Air Attacks next Winter, Memorandum by the Ministry of Home Security, 18 July 1941, PRO, HO 186/927; For the following see PRO, HO 186/927.

57. O'Brien, Civil Defence, 540f.

58. Civil Defence Executive Sub-Committee, Review of Civil Defence arrangements in the light of the possibilities of future raiding, 18 November 1942, PRO, CAB 73/6.

59. See in detail Boog, 'Luftkrieg über Europa', 506–25.

60. Hölsken, *V-Waffen*, 169ff.

61. The Threat of the Long Range Rockets, Memorandum, 5 July 1943, PRO, HO 186/2973.

62. For the following see O'Brien, *Civil Defence*, 646–50.

63. Civil Defence Committee Meeting, 18 January 1944, PRO, CAB 73/8; Civil Defence Committee Meeting, 2 March 1944, PRO, CAB 73/8; for the following see PRO, CAB 73/8.

64. O'Brien, *Civil Defence*, 663ff.

65. Home Security, 15 September 1944, PRO, HO 101/44 (p). *The Times*, 21 September 1944: 'Services to be Reduced'.

66. Woolven, 'Defence', 256; *The Times*, 23 October 1944: 'Reduction in Civil Defence'.

67. *The Times*, 7 September 1944: 'Black-out to be Eased'.

68. Goebbels, *Tagebücher*, part II, vol. vii, 8 January 1943, 70.

69. List of the members of the Inter-ministerial Air War Damage Committee dated January 1943, BA Berlin, R 2/30316.

70. See also Santana, 'Ein Radikaler'.

71. On Theodor Ellgering see the information in his personal file in Stadtarchiv Duisburg 26/798.

72. Rundschreiben des Reichsministers für Volksaufklärung und Propaganda Joseph Goebbels 14. 6. 1943 an die Gauleiter und Mitglieder des Luftkriegsschädenausschusses, BA Berlin, R 2/24925.

73. Copy of a telex from Reichsleiter Bormann to Goebbels, 18 June 1943, IfZ-Archiv, MA 667, in which Bormann complains about interpretations of the 'Führer's will' by Goebbels and Berndt.

74. Schnellbrief des Reichsministers für Volksaufklärung und Propaganda, Luftkriegsschädenausschuss an die Mitglieder des Luftkriegsschädenausschusses und Gauleiter vom 19. 6. 1943, BA Berlin, R2/24925.

75. Reichsminister für Volksaufklärung und Propaganda an die Mitglieder des Interministeriellen Luftkriegsschädenausschusses und die Gauleiter, LK-Mitteilung No. 6, 10 July 1943, BA Berlin, R 2/24925.

76. See, for example, Niederschrift über die Besprechung der Sofortmaßnahmen nach Fliegerangriffen, 2 March 1943, in Duisburg, BA Berlin, R 36/2697.

77. Erlaß des Führers über die Errichtung einer Reichsinspektion der zivilen Luftkriegsmaßnahmen, 21 December 1943, IfZ-Archiv, MA 470; also published in Moll, 'Führer-Erlasse', 380f.

78. Goebbels, *Tagebücher*, part II, vol. x, 26 November 1943, 362.

79. On Hoffmann see Blank, 'Albert Hoffmann'.

80. Goebbels, *Tagebücher*, part II, vol. x, 19 December 1943, 505; Goebbels, *Tagebücher*, part II, vol. x, 20 December 1943, 511.

81. See Vermerk der Reichskanzlei, 16 December 1943, Akten der Partei-Kanzlei, part II, 10111324–40.

82. Goebbels, *Tagebücher*, part II, vol. 10, 25 November 1943, 354.

83. Reichsministerium für Volksaufklärung und Propaganda, LK-Mitteilung, 10 November 1943, BA Berlin, R 55/447, Bl. 121.
84. Goebbels, Tagebücher, part II, vol. xi, 4 March 1944, 394f.; part II, vol. xi, 29 March 1944, 576.
85. Reichsminister für Volksaufklärung und Propaganda an die Gauleiter, 28 January 1944, BA Berlin, R 2/24925.
86. Goebbels, *Tagebücher*, part II, vol. xi, 20 January 1944, 127.
87. Goebbels, *Tagebücher*, part II, vol. xi, 12 January 1944, 77.
88. Reichsminister für Volksaufklärung und Propaganda, 31 March 1944, LK-Mitteilung No. 112, an die Gauleiter, die geschäftsführenden Behörden der Reichsverteidigungs-kommissare, die Mitglieder des Interministeriellen Luftkriegsschädenausschusses sowie an die Reichspropagandaämter und die M-Beauftragten der Gauleitungen, BA Berlin, R2/24925; for the following see BA Berlin, R2/24925; see also Klee, *'Luftschutzkeller'*, 140ff.
89. Vermerk, 21 January 1944, Reichsinspektion der zivilen Luftkriegsmaßnahmen, BA Berlin, R 1501/619.
90. Bericht über die Inspektion im Reichsgau Wartheland am 22. und 23. 3. 1944, BA Berlin, R 3101/10094.
91. Reichsminister für Volksaufklärung und Propaganda, LK-Mitteilung, 23 December 1943, BA Berlin, R2/24925.
92. See Goebbels, *Tagebücher*, part II, vol. x, 21 October 1943, 142.
93. Reichsminister für Volksaufklärung und Propaganda, 31 March 1944, LK-Mitteilung No. 112, an die Gauleiter, die geschäftsführenden Behörden der Reichsverteidigungskommissare, die Mitglieder des Interministeriellen Luftkriegsschädenausschusses sowie die Reichspropagandaämter und die M-Beauftragten der Gauleitungen, BA Berlin, R 2/24925.
94. Reichsminister für Volksaufklärung und Propaganda, LK-Mitteilung vom 23. 12. 1943, BA Berlin, R 2/24925; Mitteilung des Luftkriegsschädenausschusses, 26 August 1943, BA Berlin, R 2/24925.
95. That was true, for example, in the case of very practical suggestions such as the removal of cellar windows, which the Reich Inspectorate had made during a visitation to Gau Baden-Alsace at the beginning of March 1944; see Reichsminister für Volksaufklärung und Propaganda, Führerinformation 27 März 1944 über die Reichsinspektion zur Durchführung ziviler Luftkriegs-maßnahmen im Gau Baden-Elsass vom 4. bis 6. März 1944, BA Berlin, R 3101/10094.
96. Brinkhus ('Hitler') was the first person to reach this conclusion.
97. Reichsminister für Volksaufklärung und Propaganda, Schnellbrief vom 31. 3. 1944 an die Gauleiter, Reichsverteidigungskommissare und Mitglieder des Interministeriellen Luftkriegsschädenausschusses, BA Berlin, R 2/24925; Goebbels, *Tagebücher*, part II, vol. xiii, 29 March 1944, 576; vol. xiv, 2 November 1944, 138f.
98. Berndt to Himmler, 11 July 1944, IfZ-Archiv, MA 290.

99. Goebbels, *Tagebücher*, part II, vol. xiii, 2 August 1944, 198.
100. Longerich, 'Joseph Goebbels und der Totale Krieg'.
101. Longerich, 'Joseph Goebbels und der Totale Krieg', 310.
102. *RGBl.* 1939, part I, 1679.
103. Freisler, 'Gedanken zur Verordnung gegen Volksschädlinge', *Deutsches Recht* (1939), 1450–2.
104. Weckbecher, *Freispruch und Todesstrafe*, 251.
105. Freisler, 'Rechtsfrage des Kriegsstrafrechts'.
106. Anschütz, *Arbeit der Sondergerichte*, 18.
107. Schwarz, *Strafgesetzbuch*, 1038.
108. Schwarz, *Strafgesetzbuch*, 1038, Ministerialdirigent Dr. Schäfer zum § 4 der Volksschädlingsverordnung, 28ff.
109. Freisler, Grau, Krug, and Rietsch (eds), *Deutsches Strafrecht*, i. 1.
110. On the background to this, by no means uncontroversial, decree see above all Hensle, *Rundfunkverbrechen*, 26–37.
111. Hensle, *Rundfunkverbrechen*, 120–7.
112. *RGBl.* 1939, part I, 1683.
113. On this see Mechler, *Kriegsalltag*, 158f.
114. Compare Schmidt, *Todesstrafe*, 136f.; for the following see Schmidt, *Todesstrafe*, 136f.
115. See Angermund, *Richterschaft*, 248ff.; see also Oehler, *Rechtsprechung*, 107ff.; on the background see Gruchmann, 'Generalangriff auf die Justiz?'
116. *Richterbriefe*, Mitteilung des Reichsministers der Justiz, No. 1, 1 October 1942, 9.
117. Mitteilung des Reichsministers der Justiz, No. 1, 1 October 1942, 10; for the following see Mitteilung des Reichsministers der Justiz, No. 1, 1 October 1942, 10.
118. *Richterbriefe*, No. 7, 1 April 1943: Volksschädlinge bei feindlichen Luftangriffen, 102f.
119. Volksschädlinge bei feindlichen Luftangriffen, 103.
120. OLG President Cologne to RJM, 27 November 1942, IfZ-Archiv, MA 430/1.
121. Reichsminister der Justiz, Führerinformation No. 74, 14 July 1942; see also Bajohr, *Parvenüs und Profiteure*, 166–71.
122. *Richterbriefe*, No. 17, 1 April 1944: Plünderer und Volksschädlinge nach Luftrangriffen, 293ff.; For the following see *Richterbriefe*, No. 17, 1 April 1944: Plünderer und Volksschädlinge nach Luftrangriffen, 293ff.
123. *Richterbriefe*, No. 17, 1 April 1944: Plünderer und Volksschädlinge nach Luftangriffen, 295.
124. See Roeser, *Sondergericht*, 123.
125. OLG President Kiel to RJM, 4 August 1944, IfZ-Archiv, MA 430/1.
126. OLG President Hamburg to RJM, 12 April 1944, IfZ-Archiv, MA 430/1.
127. See Oehler, *Rechtsprechung*, 226.
128. Generalstaatsanwalt bei dem Oberlandesgericht München an den Oberstaatsanwalt München I, 25 January 1945, NARA II, T-178, Roll 9.
129. On this see, for example, Seeger, 'Schwerstverbrecher', 173.

130. Mechler, *Kriegsalltag*, 161; for Essen see Roeser, *Sondergericht*, 121.

131. *Richterbriefe*, No. 17, 1 April 1944, 301.

132. Roeser, *Sondergericht*, 121.

133. Schwarz, *Strafgesetzbuch*, 535.

134. *Richterbriefe*, No. 11, 1 August 1943, 164ff.

135. Reichsminister der Justiz, Führerinformation No. 117, 3 September 1942.

136. Reichsminister der Justiz, Führerinformation No. 117, 3 September 1942, 161f.

137. Luftschutzgesetz vom 26. 6. 1935, *RGBl.* 1935, part I, 827.

138. Runderlass des Reichsführers und Chefs der Polizei, 14 April 1944, Stadtarchiv Düsseldorf, IV/1001.

139. Polizeipräsident München, 11 November 1941, Maßnahmen gegen Zuwiderhandlungen gegen Verdunkelungsvorschriften, Stadtarchiv Munich, Branddirektion 74/3, 11.

140. Letter from the RML, 14 November, Akten der Partei-Kanzlei, Part I, 26872, 10310090.

141. Letter from the deputy Gauleiter of the Gau Munich-Upper Bavaria, 20 August 1940, Staatsarchiv Munich, NSDAP 1547.

142. Reibel, *Fundament*, 372.

143. See also Stammers, *Civil Liberties*, 12–31.

144. Ministry of Home Security: War-Time Lighting Restrictions, 1939, PRO, MEPO 2/7307.

145. Mass-Observation Archive, File Reports, 15A (December 1939).

146. On this see in detail Gardiner, *Wartime*, 53–75.

147. Report of the Committee on Blackout Restrictions in Industrial Establishments, 11 August 1943, War Cabinet, PRO, CAB 21/2049; Committee on Blackout Restriction of 14 February 1944, PRO, MEPO 2/7307. Detailed reports on the effects of the existing blackout regulations in PRO, MEPO 2/7307.

148. Gardiner, *Wartime*, 56.

149. Information in Gardiner, *Wartime*, 57.

150. Metropolitan Police, New Scotland Yard, 5 October 1939: Public Morale, PRO, MEPO 2/7307.

151. Memorandum of 5 October 1939: Private Secretary to the Commissioner, PRO, MEPO 2/27307.

152. See among others *Daily Despatch*, 29 February 1940: 'Two Years for Attacking Women in Black-out'; *Newcastle Journal*, 6 February 1940: 'Women Stabbed in Black-out'.

153. *The Times*, 7 February 1940: 'More Juvenile Crime'.

154. *The Times*, 12 January 1940: 'Increase in Crime At Railway Stations'.

155. *The Times*, 28 September 1940: 'Burglary during the Black-out'.

156. See among others *The Scotsman*, 17 February 1940: 'Prison for Bag-Snatcher'.

157. *The Times*, 28 August 1940: 'Alleged Looting after Raid'.

158. Gardiner, *Wartime*, 597.

159. On this see among other things the debate about juvenile 'delinquency' in Manchester: Ministry of Information, Manchester Information Committee: Conference on Juvenile Delinquency, 15 November 1944, Summary of Proceedings, Manchester Local Record Archive, M 77/1–6.

160. Ziegler, *London*, 148.

161. Gardiner, *Wartime*, 597.

162. Commissioner for Police, Philip Game, New Scotland Yard, 17 July 1944, War Cabinet, Civil Defence Committee, PRO, CAB 73/9.

163. PRO, CAB 73/9.

164. War Cabinet, Civil Defence Committee, Minutes of a Meeting, 3 August 1944, PRO, CAB 73/9; for the following see PRO, CAB 73/9.

165. War Cabinet, Civil Defence Committee, Compensation for Losses by Looting, Memorandum by the Parliamentary Secretary Board of Trade, 9 August 1944, PRO, CAB 73/9.

166. War Damage Commission, *Short History*, 1ff.; for what follows see War Damage Commission, *Short History*, 1ff.

167. *The Times*, 18 October 1939: 'War Damage to Property'; *The Times*, 23 June 1939: 'Compensation for War Damage to Property'; *The Times*, 22 April 1939: 'Compensation for War Damage'; *The Times*, 16 May 1939: 'War Damage to Property'.

168. *The Times*, 12 December 1940: 'Insurance against War Damage'.

169. War Damage Commission, *Short History*, 20.

170. Hansard, HoC, Debates, 13 August 1940, cc 617–18W, vol. 364, Sir K. Wood; *The Times*, 19 November 1940: 'War Damage and Injury'.

171. *The Times*, 29 May 1941: 'Insurance against War Damage'.

172. Developments in German Civil Defence during 1943, 28 February 1944, Note by the Chairman, Ministry of Home Security, PRO, CAB 73/8.

173. *The Times*, 20 August 1941: 'Repair of War Damage'.

174. Hansard, HoC, Debates, vol. 373, 22 June 1941, 823–6.

175. Hansard, HoC, Debates, vol. 120, 11 November 1941, 431–4.

176. Hansard, HoC, Debates, vol. 118, 13 March 1941, 709–84.

177. Hansard, HoC, Debates, vol. 373, 22 July 1941, 823–6, Mr Pethick-Lawrence.

178. War Damage Commission, *Short History*, 21.

179. For appeals against the decisions of the War Damage Commission see the files on individual cases: Appeals against decisions by the War Damage Commission, PRO, IR 34/450–3.

180. *The Times*, 23 August 1943: 'War Damage Clarification'.

181. Hansard, HoC, Debates, vol. 391, 5 August 1943, 2554–77, Mr Assheton.

182. On this see *Das Reich*, 1 August 1943: 'Das Recht der Geschädigten'.

183. *RGBl.* 1940, part I, 1547; on this as one of the first to deal with it see Noakes, *Nazism*, iv: *The German Home Front in World War II*, 562ff.

184. *RGBl.* 1939, part I, 1754.

185. Dr Stuckart, 'Probleme der Kriegsschäden', *Deutsche Verwaltung*, 18 (1941), 6–11, here 10.
186. Regierungsrat Franz Büchner, 'Der Sachschaden im Kriegsschädenrecht', *Deutsche Verwaltung*, 17 (1940), 312–17, here 317.
187. Oberregierungsgerichtsrat Dr Danckelmann, 'Vermögensschäden im Kriegsschädenrecht', *Deutsche Verwaltung*, 17 (1940), 385–90, here 385.
188. On the concept see Martin Weise, 'Das neue Kriegssachschädenrecht', *Deutsche Verwaltung*, 18 (1941), 25–31, 26.
189. Dritte Anordnung über die Entschädigung von Nutzungsschäden vom 23. 4. 1941, MBliV, 778.
190. See Weise, 'Kriegssachschädenrecht', 29.
191. *RGBl.* 1941, part I, 437f.: Verordnung über die Behandlung der Kriegsschäden von Juden.
192. *RGBl.* 1941, part I, 201.
193. Oberregierungsrat Hans Vollprecht, 'Das Reichsverwaltungsgericht (Reichskriegsschädenamt) und die Aufsichtsführung in Kriegsschädensachen', *Deutsche Verwaltung*, 19 (1942), 426–8, here 426.
194. On this see also Reichsrichter Rempel, 'Vertretungsbefugnis in Entschädigungsverfahren', *Deutsche Verwaltung*, 20 (1943), 130.
195. Reichsrichter Rempel to the Reich Minister of the Interior, 27 January 1944, BA Berlin, R 1501/923; For the following see BA Berlin, R 1501/923.
196. On the question of the compensation of war widows see in detail Kramer, *Volksgenossinnen*, 242–69.
197. See Rüther, *Köln, 31. Mai 1942*, 91.
198. Aufzeichnung über die Ausführungen des Herrn Reichsministers der Finanzen in der Besprechung mit Vertretern des Reichsinteresses der Hauptschadensgebiete am 2. 11. 1943, in *Dokumente deutscher Kriegsschäden*, ii/1. 555f.; for the following see BA Berlin, R 1501/923.
199. On local government practice see Chapter 4.
200. Stuckart to the Reichsführer SS, 19 February 1944, BA Berlin, R 1501/923; for what follows see BA Berlin, R 1501/923.
201. Rundschreiben des RMI vom 30. 8. 1943 an die Höheren Verwaltungsbehörden, in *Dokumente deutscher Kriegsschäden*, ii/1. 576f.
202. Stadtarchiv Rostock, 'NSDAP im Luftkrieg. Aufgaben für den Gau Mecklenburg, 1944'.
203. *Völkischer Beobachter* (Munich edition), 16 November 1943: 'Eine Briefmarkensammlung geht verloren'.
204. RMI an die höheren Verwaltungsbehörden vom 30. 9. 1943, in *Dokumente deutscher Kriegsschäden*, ii/1. 577f.
205. Runderlass des RMI, 18 July 1944, *MBliV*, 708.
206. Runderlass des RMI, 4. 8. 1944 an die Höheren Verwaltungsbehörden, in *Dokumente deutscher Kriegsschäden*, ii/2. 580f.

207. Reichsrichter Danckelmann to Oberverwaltungsgerichtsrat Boyens, 13 August 1944, BA Berlin, R 1501/3572.
208. *Richterbriefe*, No. 7, 1 April 1943: 'Volksschädlinge bei feindlichen Luftangriffen', 107ff.
209. *Richterbriefe*, No. 7, 1 April 1943, 100.

CHAPTER 4

  1. Report on the War-work done by Local Government Authorities, 30 May 1940, Mass-Observation File Report Series, 152.
  2. Note of a Conference of Chief Constables held at the Home Office, 18 October 1938, PRO, HO 45/18124; see detail on this in Lemke, *Luftschutz*, 387; for the following see Lemke, *Luftschutz*, 387.
  3. Air Raid Precaution Department, Heads of Divisions Council, 2 December 1938, PRO, HO 45/18198.
  4. Report on the War-work done by Local Government Authorities, 30 May 1940, Mass-Observation File Report Series, 152.
  5. On this see among others Krause, *Flucht*, 81−3; for Nuremberg see Schramm, *Luftschutz in Nürnberg*.
  6. For the case of Munich see detail in Klee, *'Luftschutzkeller'*, 39−44.
  7. For an overview see Gotto, 'Kommunale Krisenbewältigung', 44f.; see also Brinkhus, 'Auftragsverwaltung der Gemeinden', 218.
  8. Bericht über die Tätigkeit des Sozialamtes für Fliegergeschädigte im Kriegsjahr 1942, Hauptstaatsarchiv Düsseldorf, RW 50−53/3344.
  9. Einsatz der NSV-Küchen, 18 July 1942, Stadtarchiv Stuttgart, Luftschutz, 221, Wohlfahrtsamt Stuttgart über die Betreuung der Fliegergeschädigten in Köln vom 23. 6. 1942, Historisches Archiv der Stadt Köln, 659/15.
 10. Merkblatt für Fliegergeschädigte, 1 March 1941, Stadtarchiv Nürnberg, C 52/I, 4.
 11. Hess, 'Leipzig', 218.
 12. Compare Gotto, *Kommunalpolitik*, 361−71.
 13. For Hagen see Blank, *Hagen*, 59ff.
 14. On the history of local government in Britain see among others Dittmar, *Kommunalverwaltung in England*.
 15. On this see in detail Gotto, *Kommunalpolitik*, 80f.
 16. Broszat, *Staat Hitlers*, 426.
 17. See above all Gruner, 'NS-Judenverfolgung'.
 18. For other equally important areas of urban local government activity see Gotto, *Kommunalpolitik*, 318−43.
 19. Bericht über einen Besuch zu Zwecken des Erfahrungsaustausches bei den Feststellungsbehörden in Düsseldorf, Hamburg und Hannover vom 1. bis 7. 3. 1942, 1, Stadtarchiv Nürnberg, C 52/I, 4.
 20. Stadtarchiv Nürnberg, C 52/I, 4.
 21. Stadtarchiv Nürnberg, C 52/I, 12.

22. Vorläufige Richtlinien für die Sachbearbeitung [of the city of Hanover] vom 25. 11. 1941, Stadtarchiv Nürnberg, C 52/I, 42.
23. Niederschrift über die Bezirksstellenbesprechung vom 30. 5. 1944, Stadtarchiv Düsseldorf, IV/3516.
24. AnweisungV 17 vom 15. 2. 1943,Anlage 7, Stadtarchiv Nürnberg, C 52/9;Amt für Kriegsschäden, Dienstblatt Part IVI, Hilfs- und Fürsorgemaßnahmen, 21 May 1943, 1, Landesarchiv Berlin 005–07/519.
25. Vorläufige Richtlinien für die Sachbearbeitung [der Stadt Hannover] vom 25. 11. 1941, 2, Stadtarchiv Nürnberg, C 52/I, 42.
26. Stadtarchiv Nürnberg, C 52/I, 9.
27. Stadtarchiv Nürnberg, C 52/I, 13.
28. Organisation eines Kriegsschädenamtes (n.d., around 1942), Bl. 2, Stadtarchiv Rostock, 1.1.3.30, 520. Compare, for example, the report of the head of the Augsburg city legal office, Seufert: Bezirksbesprechung der Feststellungsbehörden in München am 16. 4. 1943, 15, Stadtarchiv Nürnberg, C 52/I, 62.
29. Excerpt from the Nazi Party district leader and Oberbürgermeister of Ludwigshafen about his experiences during the air raids from 1 August to 15 January 1944, Stadtarchiv Stuttgart, Luftschutz, 222.
30. Bezirksbesprechung der Feststellungsbehörden in München am 16. 4. 1943, Stadtarchiv Nürnberg, C 52/I, 62.
31. Besprechung mit dem Gauleiter am 18. 12. 1943, Kriegsschädenamt, Stadtarchiv Nürnberg, C 52/I, 19.
32. Das Kriegsschädenamt Kiel, 6 (n.d., mid-1942), Stadtarchiv Kiel, 41611.
33. Rundverfügung vom 18. 3. 1944, Stadtarchiv Düsseldorf, IV/3516; Kriegsschädenamt Zentrale an Hauptamt v. 23. 5. 1944, Das Kriegsschädenamt Kiel, 6 (n.d., mid-1942), Stadtarchiv Kiel, 41611 IV/482.
34. Protokoll der Bezirksstellenbesprechung vom 27. Juli 1944, Stadtarchiv Düsseldorf, IV/3516.
35. Amt für Kriegsschäden, Dienstblatt Part IVI, Hilfs- und Fürsorgemaßnahmen, 25 April 1944, 25, Landesarchiv Berlin 005–07/519.
36. Amt für Kriegsschäden,Vermerk über die Besprechung am 19. 11. 1943 beim Hauptamt für Kriegssachschäden, Landesarchiv Berlin,A Rep. 005–007/438.
37. Niederschrift über die Bezirksstellenbesprechung vom 30. 5. 1944, Stadtarchiv Düsseldorf, IV/3516;Vertreter des Reichsinteresses beim Finanzamt Schöneberg, Beschwerdeführung in der Kriegsschädensache Wilhelm Klotz, vom 30. 3. 1944, Landesarchiv Berlin, Pr. Br. Rep. 57 Stadtpräsident Reichshauptstadt Berlin, Bd. 126/b., 480.
38. Letter from the Kriegsschädenamt Nürnberg, 7 March 1943, Stadtarchiv Nürnberg, C 52/I, 22.
39. Rundverfügung des Kriegsschädenamtes No. 81 vom 25. März 1944, Stadtarchiv Düsseldorf, IV/3516.
40. On this see also Blank, *Kriegsalltag*, 425–9.
41. Longerich, *Politik der Vernichtung*, 432f.

42. Express letter from the Reich Finance Minister, 4 November 1941, in Rummel and Rath, *'Reich'*, Doc. 1, 311f.
43. Director Buchholz to the OFP Düsseldorf, 1 November 1943, Stadtarchiv Düsseldorf, IV/474.
44. Quoted in Kuller, 'Erster Grundsatz: Horten für die Reichsfinanzverwaltung', 171.
45. Betreff: Sicherstellung jüdischer Einrichtungsgegenstände für Fliegergeschädigte, vom 26. 11. 1941, Stadtarchiv Nürnberg, C 52/I, 60.
46. *RGBl.* 1941, part I, 722–4.
47. Betreff: Lagerhaltung von Judenmöbeln vom 17. 10. 1941, Stadtarchiv Nürnberg, C 52/60.
48. Niederschrift über eine Besprechung über die Verwertung von Altmöbeln vom 20. 2. 1942, Stadtarchiv Nürnberg, C 52/I, 60.
49. Kuller, 'Erster Grundsatz: Horten für die Reichsfinanzverwaltung', 173.
50. Aly, *Volksstaat*, 150.
51. Unlike in other cities in the Reich, the Gestapo played a much greater role in the process of 'Aryanization'. On this see in detail Kuller, 'Erster Grundsatz: Horten für die Reichsfinanzverwaltung', 174; and Kuller and Drecoll, 'Inszenierter Volkszorn'.
52. Data on the use of Jewish apartments, 3 September 1942, Stadtarchiv Nürnberg, C 52/I, 9; Niederschrift über die Besprechung am 3. 9. 1942 über die Verwaltung von Judenwohnungen und Judenmöbeln, Stadtarchiv Nürnberg, C 52/I, 9.
53. Anweisung V 4 vom 21. 9. 1942, Stadtarchiv Nürnberg, C 52/I, 9.
54. Data in Kuller, 'Erster Grundsatz: Horten für die Reichsfinanzverwaltung', 178.
55. Rummel and Rath, *'Reich'*, 189.
56. For Hamburg see above all Bajohr, *Arisierung*, 331–8.
57. OFP Köln 26. 3. 1942 an die Vorsteher der Finanzämter Bitburg, Saarburg, Prüm: Abschiebung der Juden, in Rummel and Rath, *'Reich'*, Doc. 33, 368f.
58. Rummel and Rath, *'Reich'*, 192.
59. OFP Westfalen, 8 December 1941, in Dressen, *'Aktion 3'*, 78–82, here 80.
60. Vorstand des Finanzamtes Trier an den OFP Köln 24. 8. 1942, in Rummel and Rath, *'Reich'*, Doc. 86, 425ff.
61. Reichsminister der Finanzen 14. 8. 1942: Verwertung des beweglichen Vermögens aus eingezogenem und verfallenem Vermögen, in Rummel and Rath, *'Reich'*, Doc. 84, 423f.
62. Note for the Münster city building officer, Dr Poelzig, on the provision of victims of bomb damage with furniture previously owned by Jews: see Betrifft: Versorgung Bombengeschädigter mit Möbeln und Hausrat, vom 16. 10. 1942, Stadtarchiv Münster, Stadtregistratur, Fach 36, 18d <http://www.westfaelische-geschichte.de/que1242>, most recent use: 24 August 2009.
63. On this see among others Becker, *Gewalt und Gedächtnis*, 77–140; for a Rhenish community see the documents in Dressen, *'Aktion 3'*, 178–84.

64. *Hamburger Fremdenblatt*, 29 March 1941: 'Jüdisches Umzugsgut unter dem Hammer'.
65. On the announcements of the Cologne finance office see Rüther, *im Zweiten Weltkrieg*, 94 and 99.
66. Rummel and Rath, *'Reich'*, 188.
67. See also Aly, *Volksstaat*, 149.
68. A detailed list of the number of railway wagons going to the various Gaus shows that the majority of the possessions of Jews who had been deported ended up in the Rhineland and Westphalia as well as in Hamburg.; see Dressen, *'Aktion 3'*, 51ff.
69. Bajohr, *Arisierung*, 334.
70. Quoted in Bajohr, *Arisierung*, 335.
71. Bajohr, *Arisierung*, 332.
72. See the concluding report on the major raid on Cologne of 30/1 May 1942, in Rüther, *Köln im Zweiten Weltkrieg*, 198–214.
73. On the concept see Gotto, *Kommunalpolitik*.
74. For the following see Woolven, 'Defence', 197.
75. *The Times*, 7 October 1940: 'Civil Defence Powers in Stepney'.
76. Woolven, 'Defence', 203.
77. Woolven, 'Defence', 204.
78. *Daily Herald*, 4 March 1941.
79. Woolven, 'Defence', 206.
80. Titmuss, *Social Policy*, 252ff.
81. Liverpool City Defence, Emergency Committee, Minute Book No. 6, 2 July 1940, Liverpool Record Archive, 352 MIN/DEF.
82. Charlton, Garrat, and Fletcher, *The Air Defence of Britain*, 141.
83. Woolven, 'Defence', 211; for the following see Woolven, 'Defence', 211.
84. Titmuss, *Social Policy*, 15f.; for the following see Titmuss, *Social Policy*, 15f.
85. Titmuss, *Social Policy*, 15f., 282.
86. On this, from the standpoint of the officials involved, see War Damage Commission, *Short History*; Tiratsoo, 'Reconstruction of Blitzed British Cities'.
87. Titmuss, *Social Policy*, 273.
88. Plymouth Council of Social Service, 30 May 1941, Plymouth Record Archive, Lord Mayor Files, 1495/62.
89. Titmuss, *Social Policy*, 282f.
90. Underdown, *Bristol under Blitz*, 38.
91. Liverpool City Defence, Emergency Committee, Minute Book No. 6 (20 May–1 November 1940), 25 September 1940, Liverpool Record Archive, 352 MIN/DEF.
92. An excerpt from the letter is in Liverpool City Defence, Emergency Committee, Minute Book No. 6 (20 May–1 November 1940), 3 October 1940, Liverpool Record Archive, 352 MIN/DEF.
93. Liverpool City Defence, Emergency Committee, Minute Book No. 6, 3 October 1940, Liverpool Record Archive, 352 MIN/DEF.

94. Liverpool City Defence, Emergency Committee, Minute Book No. 7, 2 December 1940, Liverpool Record Archive, 352 MIN/DEF.

95. Liverpool City Defence, Emergency Committee, Minute Book No. 7, 23 December 1940, Liverpool Record Archive, 352 MIN/DEF.

96. Report on Liverpool and Manchester (6 January 1941), Mass-Observation, File Report Series, 516.

97. Report on Liverpool and Manchester (6 January 1941), Mass-Observation, File Report Series, 516.

98. Liverpool City Defence, Emergency Committee, Minute Book No. 10, 24 August 1942, Liverpool Record Archive, 352 MIN/DEF; for the following see Liverpool City Defence, Emergency Committee, Minute Book No. 10, 24 August 1942, Liverpool Record Archive, 352 MIN/DEF.

99. Eastern Civil Defence Region Office of the Regional Commissioner, 10 June 1942, PRO, HO 199/98.

100. Memorandum to the Regions Commissioner in Connection with the Recent Air Raids, 3 June 1942, PRO, HO 199/98.

101. Civil Defence Office for the Regional Commissioner, South West Regional Office Bristol, 17 December 1940, PRO, HO 199/36.

102. Kurki, *Operation Moonlight Sonata*; Longmate, *Air Raid*.

103. Longmate, *Air Raid*, 188ff.

104. Longmate, *Air Raid*, 192.

105. Quoted in Longmate, *Air Raid*, 195.

106. Harrisson, *Living*, 155ff.; Titmuss, *Social Policy*, 317.

107. Lessons of Intensive Air Attacks. Coordination of Action (January 1941), 2–3, PRO, HO 199/394A; for the following see PRO, HO 199/394A.

108. Lessons based on Recent London Raids, Inspector's General Department (n.d. [1941]), PRO, HO 199/394A.

109. Salvage Memorandum No. 1, 26 May 1941, Devon Record Archive, Town Clerk, Group P, Air Raid Precaution, Box 22.

110. Ministry of Information, Plymouth, Emergency Arrangements, Devon Record Archive, Town Clerk Papers, Group P, Air Raid Precaution, Box 22; Ministry of Health to Mr Newman, 10 April 1941, Devon Record Archive, Town Clerk Papers, Group P, Air Raid Precaution, Box 22; Arrangements of Feeding and Accommodation of Civil Defence Reinforcement at Reinforcement Depots, Office of the Regional Commissioner, 16 April 1941, Devon Record Archive, Town Clerk Papers, Group P, Air Raid Precaution, Box 21.

111. Meeting at the Museum & Art Gallery Plymouth, 23 July 1942, Mutual Aid Scheme, Devon Record Archive, Town Clerk Papers, Group O, Air Raid Precaution, Box 21.

112. Mutual Aid Scheme, Devon Record Archive, Town Clerk Papers, Group O, Air Raid Precaution, Box 21; Titmuss, *Social Policy*, 317f.

113. On this see Schönpflug and Aust (eds), *Gegner*.

114. Mass Raids. An appreciation of Civil Defence under altered conditions of enemy action, 9 October 1942, UEA, SZ, OEMU 58/3/3/29; for the following see UEA, SZ, OEMU 58/3/3/29d.
115. On this see above all Blank, *Kriegsalltag*, 394–402.
116. Stand des Führerprogramms vom 9. 12. 1942 Bl. 113, BA-MA, RL 4/341.
117. See, for example, Gotto, *Kommunalpolitik*, 345ff.
118. Niederschrift über die Besprechung der leitenden Baubeamten der rheinischen Stadtkreise am 9. 8. 1941 in Köln, BA Berlin, R 36/2697.
119. For an introduction on this see Argyris and Schön, *Organisation*.
120. Niederschrift über die Besprechung der leitenden Baubeamten der rheinischen Stadtkreise am 9. 8. 1941 in Köln, BA Berlin, R 36/2697.
121. See Brinkhus, 'Auftragsverwaltung', 232–41.
122. Note for the trip to Bremen, 14 January 1941, Stadtarchiv Stuttgart, Luftschutz, 218. On this see in detail Müller, *Stuttgart*.
123. Oberbürgermeister Strölin, Maßnahmen für durch Luftangriffe obdachlos gewordene Volksgenossen, 14 March 1941, Stadtarchiv Stuttgart, Luftschutz, 838.
124. See Beer, *Kriegsalltag*, 151–61, especially 159f.
125. Niederschrift über den vom Deutschen Gemeindetag veranstalteten Erfahrungsaustausch der Luftschutzsachbearbeiter im Nordwesten und Norden des Reiches am 2. 5. 1942 in Hannover, Hauptstaatsarchiv Düsseldorf, RW 53/701.
126. Erfahrungsbericht über den Luftangriff auf Köln vom 30./31. 5. 1942, Stadtarchiv Stuttgart, Luftschutz, 221.
127. Hauptamt für Kommunalpolitik, Niederschrift über die Dienstbesprechung des Hauptamtes für Kommunalpolitik am 10/11 September 1943 in Leipzig, NARA II, RG 242, T 580, Roll 894.
128. On Rostock see among others the report by Gauleiter Hildebrandt on the lessons learnt from combating the major raid on Rostock (end of May/beginning of June 1942), in *Mecklenburg im Zweiten Weltkrieg*, 468–74; on the severe overtaxing of the authorities see *Mecklenburg im Zweiten Weltkrieg*, 468–74. Besprechung des Sonderstabes Gaueinsatzstab) vom 28. 4. 1942, 313–20; Besprechung des Sonderstabes (Gaueinsatzstab) vom 28. 4. 1942, 1. 5. 1942, 379–87; Besprechung des Sonderstabes (Gaueinsatzstab) vom 28. 4. 1942, 1. 5. 1942, 282–5.
129. Compare Rüther, *Köln im Zweiten Weltkrieg*, 76–82.
130. Circular No. 25 from Sonderstab des stellv. Gauleiters bei der Einsatz-Befehlsstelle Köln, 6 1942, Hauptstaatsarchiv Düsseldorf, RW 23/122.
131. Erfahrungsbericht über den Luftangriff auf Köln vom 30./31. 5. 1942, Stadtarchiv Stuttgart, Luftschutz, 221.
132. Hauptamt für Kommunalpolitik, Niederschrift über die Dienstbesprechung des Hauptamtes für Kommunalpolitik am 10/11 September 1943 in Leipzig, 3, NARA II, RG 242, T 580, Roll 894.
133. Niederschrift über den Erfahrungsaustausch von 14 Städten im Süden und Südwesten des Reiches am 13. 8. 1942 in Stuttgart, Stadtarchiv München,

Bayerischer Gemeindetag, 189. For the following see Niederschrift über den Erfahrungsaustausch von 14 Städten im Süden und Südwesten des Reiches am 13. 8. 1942 in Stuttgart, Stadtarchiv München, Bayerischer Gemeindetag, 189.

134. Sondermitteilung Nr. 1 des Deutschen Gemeindetages vom 24. Oktober 1942; Stadtarchiv München, Bayerischer Gemeindetag, 189; also in BA Berlin, R 36/2736.

135. Sondermitteilung Nr. 4 des Deutschen Gemeindetages vom 28. 12. 1942, 1f., Stadtarchiv München, Bayerischer Gemeindetag, 189.

136. Sondermitteilung Nr. 4 des Deutschen Gemeindetages vom 28. 12. 1942, 1f., Stadtarchiv München, Bayerischer Gemeindetag, 189.

137. Hauptamt für Kommunalpolitik, Niederschrift über die Dienstbesprechung des Hauptamtes für Kommunalpolitik am 10/11 September 1943 in Leipzig, 59, NARA II, RG 242, T 580, Roll 894; on this see in detail Brinkhus, 'Auftragsverwaltung der Gemeinden'.

138. Niederschrift über die Sitzung des Oberbürgermeistergremiums bei und nach Fliegerangriffen vom 4. 10. 1941, BA Berlin, NS 25/50.

139. Niederschrift über den Erfahrungsaustausch für besonders luftbedrohte Städte vom 29. 7. 1943, Hauptstaatsarchiv Düsseldorf, RW 50–53/3340. For the following see Niederschrift über den Erfahrungsaustausch für besonders luftbedrohte Städte vom 29. 7. 1943, Hauptstaatsarchiv Düsseldorf, RW 50–53/3340.

140. Gotto, *Kommunalpolitik*, 356ff.

141. For Augsburg see Gotto, *Kommunalpolitik*, 350–8.

142. Kurt Mack to Peter Walter, 14 July 1943, Stadtarchiv Stuttgart, Luftschutz, 218.

143. Closed meeting of the council, 3 February 1944: Luftkriegserfahrungen aus anderen Städten, Stadtarchiv Stuttgart, Luftschutz, 222.

144. Excerpt concerning the discussion of the Oberbürgermeister with councillors on 7 October 1943, Stadtarchiv Stuttgart, Luftschutz, 222.

145. Strölin came to this conclusion after visiting Mannheim: see closed discussion of the Oberbürgermeister with councillors on 7 October 1943, Stadtarchiv Stuttgart, Luftschutz, 221; a similiar assessment was also made of Frankfurt: Luftkriegsschäden in Frankfurt vom 30. 3. 1944, Stadtarchiv Stuttgart, Luftschutz, 222.

146. Closed meeting of the council, 3 February 1944: Luftkriegserfahrungen aus anderen Städten, Stadtarchiv Stuttgart, Luftschutz, 222.

147. Letter from Deutscher Gemeindetag to the Reich Gau, state and provincial agencies, 4 November 1943, BA Berlin R 36/2696.

148. Compare Thorpe, *Parties*, 280ff.

149. Luftwaffen-Dienstvorschrift 751/1, Grundsätze für die Führung des Luftschutzes, December 1942, Beiheft 1, 18.

150. Compare Noack and Weißbecker, 'Partei als Rückgrat'.

151. StdF, Abteilung M: 'Anweisungen und Richtlinien für den Einsatz der NSV. im Kriege' (n.d.: c.6/1939), BA Berlin, NS 6/146, Bl. 23–4.

152. For detail on this see Nolzen, 'Sozialismus der Tat'.

153. *RGBl.* 1940, part I, 45f.; see also Beer, *Kriegsalltag*, 47ff.

154. Sonder-Einsatz der NSDAP vom 5. 4. 1940, Hauptstaatsarchiv Düsseldorf, RW 23/25; on this see also Rüther, *Köln im Zweiten Weltkrieg*, 66ff.

155. See also Blank, *Hagen*, 175–8.

156. On Münster see, for example, Beer, *Kriegsalltag*, 151f.

157. Fürsorge für Fliegergeschädigte. Nach den Unterlagen beim Deutschen Gemeindetag. Stand vom 24. 7. 1942, BA Berlin, R 36/2697. Wohlfahrtsamt Stuttgart vom 23. 6. 1942: Die Betreuung der Fliegergeschädigten in Köln, Stadtarchiv Stuttgart, Luftschutz, 221; Zusammenarbeit zwischen Partei und Gemeinde bei der Bekämpfung von Luftkriegsfolgen (n.d. [autumn 1943]), Stadtarchiv Düsseldorf, IV/478.

158. Sondermitteilung Nr. 5 vom 16. 3. 1943 des Deutschen Gemeindetages, Stadtarchiv München, Bayerischer Gemeindetag, 189.

159. On this see in detail Brinkhus, 'Auftragsverwaltung der Gemeinden', 223–32.

160. NSV-Einsatz in den Hamburger Großkatastrophentagen (n.d.), BA Berlin, NS 26/260.

161. NSDAP Hauptamt für Volkswohlfahrt Kreis Gross-Frankfurt to the Ortsgruppenamtsleiter der NSV, 17 November 1943, NARA II, RG 243, Box 575, 64 b-p (3). Gotto, *Kommunalpolitik*, 364.

162. Carl Vincent Krogmann: 'Die Aufgaben des Oberbürgermeisters nach einem Großangriff', 7, BA Berlin, R 1501/1523; see also Gotto, *Kommunalpolitik*, 364.

163. NSV-Verpflegungsstelle Stuttgart vom 22. 10. 1944, Stadtarchiv Stuttgart, Sozialamt, 840.

164. Klee, 'Nationalsozialistische Wohlfahrtspolitik', 612–20.

165. Zusammenarbeit zwischen Partei und Gemeinde bei der Bekämpfung von Luftkriegsfolgen (n.d. [autumn 1943]), Stadtarchiv Düsseldorf, IV/478.

166. Beer, *Kriegsalltag*, 163–71; Brinkhus, 'Auftragsverwaltung der Gemeinden', 237ff.

167. Tätigkeit der Baueinsatzleiter der Hansestadt Köln (n.d.), Historisches Archiv der Stadt Köln, 517/22. Zusammenarbeit zwischen Partei und Gemeinde bei der Bekämpfung von Luftkriegsfolgen (n.d. [autumn 1943]), B 7, Stadtarchiv Düsseldorf, IV/478.

168. For an overview see also Noakes, 'Selbstverwaltung'.

169. Bajohr, 'Gauleiter in Hamburg'.

170. For an introduction see Mecking and Wirsching, *Stadtverwaltung als Systemstabilisierung?*, 7f.

171. On this see the study by Reibel, *Fundament*, 366; For the following see Reibel, *Fundament*, 366.

172. Einsatzplan der Partei für die Bekämpfung schwerer Notstände bei Fliegerangriffen im Gau München-Oberbayern vom 7 September 1942, BA Berlin, NS 1/275.

173. Oberbefehlshaber der Luftwaffe vom 17. Dezember 1942: Abgrenzung der Befehlsbefugnisse, Akten der Parteikanzlei, 047284–047287. On this see Beer, *Kriegsalltag*, 137–63, here 138f.

174. On this see Nolzen, 'Die NSDAP, der Krieg und die deutsche Gesellschaft'; Ruppert and Riechert, *Herrschaft und Akzeptanz*, 208–21.

175. Kreisleiter der NSDAP Groß-Frankfurt vom 9. 9. 1943: Einsatz der Partei im Luftschutz, IfZ-Archiv, MA 136/2.

176. Referat des Ausbildungsleiters der Ortsgruppe auf der Tagung vom 13. 10. 1944 zum Thema: Die Ausbildung im Luftschutz, Staatsarchiv München, NSDAP 498, I.

177. Dienstanweisung für den Reichsluftschutzbund, Staatsarchiv München, NSDAP 498.

178. Die Führung einer Reviergruppe. Vortrag von HLF. Lange bei einer Tagung der Reviergruppenführer und Reviergruppen-Frauensachbearbeiterinnen des Notbereichs I München-Nord vom 13. 10. 1944, Staatsarchiv München, NSDAP 498.

179. Kreis-Einsatzleiter to the Bereichseinsatzleiter und Einsatzleiter der Ortsgruppen des Notbereichs München I: Luftkriegseinsatz der Partei IV/44 vom 13. 12. 1944, Staatsarchiv München, NSDAP 499.

180. On this see above all Kramer, *Volksgenossinnen*.

181. Gauleitung München-Oberbayern der NSDAP vom 27. 10. 1943 über die Aktivierung der Partei, Staatsarchiv München, NSDAP 52.

182. Letter from the deputy Gauleiter of Gau Munich-Upper Bavaria, 20 August 1940, Staatsarchiv München, NSDAP 1547.

183. Wiggam, 'Blackout', 43–58.

184. *Hamburger Anzeiger*, 25 March 1943: 'Gespräch mit Generalmajor der Polizei v. Heimburg'.

185. *Harburger Anzeiger und Nachrichten*, 18 August 1941: 'Einsatzbereite "Luftschutzgemeinschaft"'; *Hamburger Tagblatt*, 2 July 1943: 'Luftschutzbereitschaft. Mängel müssen abgestellt werden'; Der Polizeipräsident von Hamburg an die Bezirksgruppe des Reichsluftschutzbundes der Hansastadt, 16 January 1943, NARA II, RG 243, Box 579, 64 b-p (3).

186. See Reibel, *Fundament*, 373.

187. Munich police chief, 11 November 1941, Stadtarchiv München, Branddirektion 73/4, 11; Runderlass an alle Polizeibehörden vom 14. 4. 1944, Stadtarchiv Düsseldorf, IV/1001.

188. See the documentation of the events in Stadtarchiv Rostock, Brandschutz, 1.1.8–710.

189. Richtlinien für die Verdunkelungskontrolle (n.d.), Staatsarchiv München, NSDAP 498.

190. Leiter des erweiterten Selbstschutzes an alle Mieter im Haus vom 17. 10. 1944, Stadtarchiv Düsseldorf, IV/1001.

584 NOTES TO PP. 216–222

191. Kreisgruppenführer an den Sonderbeauftragten des Gauleiters und Reichsverteidigungskommissars für den Notbereich München I vom 1. 12. 1944, Staatsarchiv München, NSDAP 498.

192. Ortsgruppe München-Freimann an den Sonderbeauftragten im Notbereich I vom 10. 10. 1944, Staatsarchiv München, NSDAP 498; NSDAP-Ortsgruppe Alte Heide an den Sonderbeauftragten des Gauleiters und Reichsverteidigungskommissars im Notbereich München I vom 12. 10. 1944, NSDAP 498.

193. NSDAP-Ortsgruppe München-Freimann an den Sonderbeauftragten des Gauleiters im Notbereich I vom 10. 10. 1944, Staatsarchiv München, NSDAP 498.

194. See Ruppert and Riechert, *Herrschaft*, 208–21.

195. On this see also Erker, 'Stadt', 457f.

196. On this see also Richtlinien für den Luftkriegseinsatz der Partei (n.d., *c.*1944), Stadtarchiv Rostock, 1.1.3.30.

197. OB Fiehler to Heinrich Himmler, 1 February 1944, Stadtarchiv München, Stadtverteidigung, 512/I; see also Erker, 'Stadt', 457f.

198. See also in particular Beer, *Kriegsalltag*, 137–61.

199. Fings, *Krieg*.

200. Niederschrift über die Dienstbesprechung des Hauptamtes für Kommunalpolitik am 10/11 September 1943 in Leipzig, OB Haidn, 49ff., NARA II, Rg. 243, T 580, Roll 834.

201. Himmler to Kurt Daluege, 9 September 1942, Bl. 114–120, BA Berlin, NS 19/14.

202. Bl. 119, BA Berlin, NS 19/14.

203. On this see in detail Fings, *Krieg*, 34–54.

204. Darstellung der Arbeitskräfte für Sofortmaßnahmen und Luftschutzbauten, Stadtarchiv Duisburg, 600/794, Anweisung vom 28. 7. 1942, Stadtarchiv Düsseldorf, IV/877.

205. Fings, *Krieg*, 58, 60, 64.

206. Fings, *Krieg*, 119–26.

207. Fings, *Krieg*, 90f.

208. RMdL and ObdL on 4 September 1940, Bl. 6385, IfZ-Archiv, MA 414.

209. Fings, *Krieg*, 96.

210. On this compare also Schäfer, 'Rolle der Kommunen'.

211. Goebbels, *Tagebücher*, part II, vol. xi, 13 March 1944, 463f.

212. Fings, *Krieg*, 135.

213. On this see in detail Blank, 'Kriegsendphase'.

214. Quoted in Blank, 'Albert Hoffmann', 193.

215. OB Düsseldorf to the Regierungspräsidenten, 5 August 1942, Stadtarchiv Düsseldorf, Abt. XXIII/552; on this see also Brinkhus, 'Auftragsverwaltung', 228ff.

216. For an overview see Malpass, 'Wartime Planning'.

217. See Royal Commission on the Distribution of the Industrial Population, Report (Chairman, A. Montague-Barlow), Cmd. 6153, 1940.
218. City Treasurer to Town Clerk, 6 April 1946, Plymouth Record Archive, 1673/27/CC/0; Rateable value of shopping centre, Borough Treasurer, 17 April 1946, Southampton City Record Archive, SC/T9/100; see also Hasegawa, 'Rise and Fall', 140.
219. *Picture Post*, 4 January 1941: 'A Plan for Britain'.
220. Lindner and Böckler (eds), *Die Stadt*, 14.
221. See in detail Leendertz, *Ordnung schaffen*.
222. Düwel and Gutschow, *Fortgewischt*, 111.
223. See Düwel and Gutschow, *Fortgewischt*, 40.
224. Düwel and Gutschow, *Fortgewischt*, 40.
225. Quoted in Düwel and Gutschow, *Fortgewischt*, 44.
226. On this see also for the war period Haerendel, *Kommunale Wohnungspolitik*, 407–24.
227. Düwel and Gutschow, *Fortgewischt*, 104.
228. Goebbels, *Tagebücher*, part II, vol. v, 20 August 1942, 358.
229. Albert Speer to the Gauleiters in December 1943, in Durth and Gutschow, *Träume*, i. 51ff.; for the following see Durth and Gutschow, *Träume*, i. 51ff.
230. On this see also Durth, 'Architektur und Stadtplanung', 168f.
231. See in detail Gutschow and Durth, *Träume*, 71–9.
232. Gutschow and Durth, *Träume*, 603–30; for the following see Gutschow and Durth, *Träume*, 603–30.
233. Düwel and Gutschow, *Fortgewischt*, 238f.
234. Konstanty Gutschow, 27 March 1944: 'Das neue Hamburg', published in Durth and Gutschow, *Träume*, 674; quotes in Durth and Gutschow, *Träume*.
235. Gerhard Graubner, 'Der Wehrgedanke als Grundlage der Stadtgestaltung und Stadtplanung', published in Durth and Gutschow, *Träume*, 771–6; for discussion of the concept see Durth and Gutschow, *Träume*, 719–21.
236. *Völkischer Beobachter*, 7 January 1944: 'Bombenterror wirtschaftspolitisch gesehen'; *Meldungen aus dem Reich*, vol. xvi, 13 January 1944, 6242; on this see also Blank, *Kriegsalltag*, 431.
237. Lowe, 'Second World War'.
238. Memorandum submitted on behalf of the Multiple Shops Federation (June 1941), PRO, HLG 71/761.
239. Essex and Brayshaw, 'Town'.
240. Hasegawa, 'Rise and Fall', 145.
241. Essex and Brayshaw, 'Town', 244.
242. *A Plan for Plymouth*, 11.
243. On this see Essex and Brayshaw, 'Town', 248.
244. Meeting of the representatives of local authorities and planning committees to consider the setting up of a Joint Executive Committee, 26 October 1943, Plymouth Record Archive, Lord Mayor Files, 1658/6.

245. Hasegawa, 'Rise and Fall', 159.
246. For criticism of the compensation law see Hasegawa, 'Rise and Fall', 147.
247. PRO, CAB 125/375.
248. Hasegawa, 'Rise and Fall', 160.
249. Tiratsoo, *Reconstruction*, 128ff.
250. Quoted in Tiratsoo, *Reconstruction*, 128ff.
251. Hasegawa, 'Rise and Fall', 146.
252. Tiratsoo, *Reconstruction*, 131.
253. See on this among others D. E. Gibson, Report to Housing Committee of the City of Coventry, 22 March 1943, PRO, HLG 71/914; on this see also Tiratsoo, *Reconstruction*, 6–18.
254. Hasegawa, *Replanning the Blitzed City Centre*, 30–46.
255. For example, a young unnamed academic commented along these lines with reference to the planning euphoria of the war years: 'In fact, if we win the war we shall lose every stronghold of the Home Front'; Mass Observation, *The Journey Home* (London, 1944), 21.
256. *Picture Post*, 7 October 1944: 'London's Bombed Homes: A Defeat on the Home Front'.
257. For the following see Bullock, 'Housing'.
258. On this see Forshaw and Abercrombie, *County of London Plan*.
259. Durth and Gutschow, *Träume*, 305.
260. Meeting of the Metropolitan Boroughs Standing Joint Committee, 28 June 1944, London Metropolitan Archive, CL/HSG/1/15.
261. Woolven, 'Defence', 257; Bullock, 'Housing', 266ff.
262. On the disputes about housing construction see also Malpass, 'Wartime Planning'.
263. Bullock, 'Housing', 281.

CHAPTER 5

1. On this see in detail Marrin, *Last Crusade*; Wilkinson, *The Church of England*.
2. See Wilkinson, *Dissent*, 87.
3. See also Overy, *Morbid Age*, 244–55.
4. Temple, *Thought in War Time*, 53–5.
5. Temple, *Justification of War*.
6. Temple, *Christian Order*, 8f.
7. Alan Don to Bentley, 31 May 1939, Lambeth Palace Library, Lang Papers, 57.
8. Wilkinson, *Dissent*, 266.
9. Kingsley Wood to Archbishop Lang, 12 June 1939, Lambeth Palace Library, Lang Papers, 80.
10. A Report on the Deputation of Pacifist Clergy to the Archbishop of Canterbury and the Archbishop of York, 11 June 1940, Lambeth Palace Library, Lang Papers, 80.
11. See Raven, *War and the Christian*, 138.

12. Bell, 'Function of the Church' (published for the first time in the *Fortnightly Review*, 146 (1939)), 638–43; on Bell and various aspects of his political and theological activities see the special issue of *Kirchliche Zeitgeschichte*, 21 (2008), 'George K. A. Bell (1883–1958)—Bridgebuilding in Desperate Times'.

13. George Bell, Chichester Diocesan Leaflet October 1939, Lambeth Palace Library, Bell Papers, 72.

14. See Chandler, 'Church', 925.

15. Barry, *Mervyn Haigh*, 135–8.

16. See the *Church Times*, 20 December 1940: 'The Bishop of Coventry and Reprisals'.

17. *Church Times*, 20 December 1941: 'Summary'; on the dispute see above all Chandler, 'Church', 927.

18. In fact around 800 people had been killed in Rotterdam. On the city's wartime history see Strupp, 'Stadt'.

19. *Gloucester Diocesan Magazine*, 'Bishop's Letter', January 1941.

20. Parker, *Faith*, 92.

21. *Chronicle of Convocation*, 27 May 1941, London, 1941, 1f.

22. George Bell to Liddell Hart, 31 October 1940, Lambeth Palace Library, Bell Papers, 38, part I.

23. *The Times*, 17 April 1941: 'The Pope's Appeal'.

24. George Bell, 'Night Bombing: The Bishop of Chichester replies to his critics' (n.d. *c.* 14 June 1941), Lambeth Palace Library, Bell Papers, 70.

25. Bell to Temple, 6 May 1942, Lambeth Palace Library, Temple Papers, 57.

26. Sinclair to Temple, 17 July 1943, Lambeth Palace Library, Temple Papers, 57.

27. Temple to Sinclair, 9 July 1943, Lambeth Palace Library, Temple Papers, 57.

28. Sampson to Temple, 5 December 1942, Lambeth Palace Library, Temple Papers, 57.

29. Sampson to Temple, 10 December 1942, Lambeth Palace Library, Temple Papers, 57.

30. Willem A. Visser't Hooft to William Temple, 15 December 1943, in Archiv des Ökumenischen Rats der Kirchen, Genf, Box 301.010; also published in Visser't Hooft, *Welt*, 221.

31. Visser't Hooft, *Welt*, 222.

32. Temple to Sherwood, 1 December 1943, Lambeth Palace Library, Temple Papers, 57.

33. Chandler, 'Church', 937.

34. *Gloucester Diocesan Magazine*, Bishop Headlam, December 1943, Lambeth Palace Library, Temple Papers, 57.

35. *Hansard, House of Lords*, vol. 130, 9 February 1944, 736ff.; for the following see *Hansard, House of Lords*, vol. 130, 9 February 1944; on this see also Jasper, *Bell*, 276–8.

36. On these events see also Carli, 'Illusion'; on the controversy concerning the bombing of Rome see also Archbishop Godfrey to Mr Eden, 24 June 1943,

PRO, FO 371/37253; further references to the diplomatic conflicts arising from a potential bombing of Rome in PRO, FO 371/3725, and PRO, FO 371/46879.

37. *Hansard, House of Lords*, vol. 130, 9 February 1944, 750–5.

38. *Hansard, House of Lords*, vol. 130, 9 February 1944, 747–50.

39. *Völkischer Beobachter*, 12 February 1944: 'Die Schlacht um Berlin'; *Völkischer Beobachter*, 24 January 1944: 'England möchte seine schwere Terrorschuld leugnen.'

40. Goebbels, *Tagebücher*, part II, vol. xi, 10 February 1944, 274.

41. Visser't Hooft to George Bell, 29 February 1944, in Visser't Hooft, *Welt*, 221; on the relationship between Visser't Hooft and George Bell see Besier, 'Intimately Associated', 256.

42. *Daily Mail*, 11 February 1944.

43. *The Times*, 10 February 1944: 'The Bombing of Germany'.

44. *Oxford Diocesan Magazine*, 'Bishop's Letter', March 1944, 20–2.

45. Temple to Bell, 26 February 1944, Lambeth Palace Library, Temple Papers, 57; see also the further correspondence between Temple and Bell in Temple Papers.

46. Hart to Bell, 12 February 1944, Lambeth Palace Library, Bell Papers, 38, part I.

47. The responses are contained in Lambeth Palace Library, Bell Papers, 70; on this see also Chandler, 'Church', 940ff.; Wilkinson, *Dissent*, 269ff.

48. *Catholic Herald*, 18 February 1944.

49. Brittain, *Seed of Chaos*.

50. Brittain and Sayre, *Massacre by Bombing*.

51. *The Tablet, Weekly Newspaper of the Diocese of Brooklyn*, 3 June 1944.

52. Ford, 'Morality of Obliteration Bombing'.

53. Quoted in Ford, 'Morality of Obliteration Bombing', 308.

54. Garett, *Ethics and Airpower*, 115–20.

55. Jasper, *Bell*, 284; Chandler, 'Church', 945f.

56. 'Zur Lage der Kirche' (weekly letter of 31 May 1939), 1154f.

57. All quotes in epd-medien, No. 48, 24 June 2002.

58. On this see Damberg, 'Kriegserfahrung', 324f.; see also Hürten, *Deutsche Katholiken*; Missalla, *Volk und Vaterland*, 37–54; Repgen, 'Bischöfe'.

59. Hürten, *Deutsche Katholiken*, 488f.; see also Uertz, *Gottesrecht*.

60. Kardinal Faulhaber's sermon on All Souls' Day 2 November 1941, AEM, NL Faulhaber, 4222.

61. Kardinal Faulhaber's sermon on the occasion of the reopening of the cathedral 15 August 1943: 'Wiederaufbauen—ein Gebot der Stunde', AEM, NL Faulhaber, 4224.

62. Sermon of the Bishop of Münster on the occasion of the pilgrimage to Telgte on 4 July 1943, AEK, CR II 25. 18, 1; for the following see Sermon of the Bishop of Münster.

63. On this see Leitner, *Gott im Krieg*, 432–4.

64. Theophil Wurm to the Stuttgart pastor on the reading out of his address in the church service of 9 August 1943, in Schäfer (ed.), *Landesbischof*, 458.

65. Theophil Wurm to the pastors of his diocese, 1 August 1944, in *Landesbischof*, 461–4, here 462f.
66. Quoted in Gerlach, *Zeugen*, 350.
67. See among others *Zur Lage der Kirche*, 3 (weekly letter on Luther's birthday 1943), 1663.
68. Kardinal Faulhaber's sermon on the victims of the air war on 3 July 1944, AEM, NL Faulhaber, 4225.
69. Address by the Archbishop of Cologne on 27 September 1944 in Neuss at a church service for the victims of the air raid, AEK, CR II 25.18g, 1.
70. Frings to Pius XII, last Sunday in the church's year 1944, AEK, CR II 2.18d, 1; see also Trippen, *Josef Kardinal Frings*, v. 118f.
71. Theophil Wurm to the parishes in the Rhineland suffering badly from air raids, 20 June 1943, in *Landesbischof*, 453–6, here 454f.
72. Schöffel sermon in St Michael's Church, 25 December 1943, in KKR Alt-HH, NL Boltenstern, 3; I would like to thank Malte Thiessen warmly for this reference; on this see in detail Thiessen, *Gedächtnis*, 79.
73. On this sermon see Thiessen, *Gedächtnis*, 81.
74. Address by the cardinal after the pontifical requiem mass for victims of the air raid on 25 April 1944, given on 19 May 1944, AEM, NL Faulhaber, 4225; for the following see AEM, NL Faulhaber, 4225.
75. The Bishop of Limburg on a visit to Frankfurt after an air raid on 8 October 1943, read out to his parishes on 10 October 1943 in church services held in Greater Frankfurt, AEK, CR II 25.18,1.
76. Letter from Faulhaber to the diocesan clergy, 25 April 1944, AEM, NL Faulhaber, 5912.
77. Frings to Pius XII, last Sunday in the church's year 1944, AEK, CR II 2.18d, 1.
78. Bishop Theophil Wurm to the pastors of his diocese, 1 August 1944, in *Landesbischof*, 461–4, here 463.
79. Wurm to Strölin, 5 August 1943, LKA Stuttgart, D 1, vol. 109.
80. Sermon by the Bishop of Münster on the occasion of the pilgrimage to Telgte on 4 July 1943, AEK, CR II 25.18, 1.
81. On this see also Evangelischer Bund (ed.), *Zerstörte Kirchen—Lebende Gemeinde*.
82. Evangelischer Bund (ed.), *Zerstörte Kirchen—Lebende Gemeinde*, 18.
83. Evangelischer Bund (ed.), *Zerstörte Kirchen—Lebende Gemeinde*, 28.
84. Hanover's Protestant bishop, Marahrens, described his experience of bombing in similar terms; on the church's situation see *Wochenbriefe*, iii, Wochenbrief vom 27. 11. 1943, 1665f.
85. On the Evangelische Bund (Protestant League) and its attitude towards the war see above all Fleischmann-Bisten, *Der Evangelische Bund*, 344ff.
86. Pastoral letter for Sexagesima Sunday: 'Der Krieg ist ein Geheimnis der göttlichen Weltregierung', 20 January 1940, AEM, NL Faulhaber, 4172.

87. Kardinal Adolf Bertram: Pastoral Request to Care for Homeless Families, 1 August 1943, AEK, CR I 25.20b,1.

88. Faulhaber's sermon on the occasion of the reopening of the cathedral on 15 August 1943: 'Wiederaufbauen—ein Gebot der Stunde', AEM, NL Faulhaber, 4224.

89. Sermon by the Bishop of Münster on the occasion of the pilgrimage to Telgte on 4 July 1943, AEK, CR II 25.18, 1.

90. Archbishop of Freiburg, 30 November 1944, AEK, CR II 25.18, 2.

91. On this see Hürten, *Deutsche Katholiken*, 460–78.

92. Pastoral address by Cardinal Faulhaber, 31 December 1944, AEM, NL Faulhaber, 4172.

93. Sermon by the Bishop of Münster on the occasion of the pilgrimage to Telgte on 4 July 1943, AEK, CR II 25.18, 1.

94. Faulhaber to the diocesan clergy, 25 April 1944, AEM, NL Faulhaber, 5912.

95. Kardinal Faulhaber, 28 September 1942: 'Religiöses Verhalten bei Fliegerangriffen', AEM, NL Faulhaber, 5931.

96. Archiepiscopal secretariat to the Apostolic Administrator in Innsbruck, 8 June 1943, AEM, NL Faulhaber, 5931.

97. Cardinal Faulhaber, Absolutio generalis for air raids 30 December 1942, AEM, NL Faulhaber, 5931.

98. Faulhaber to the Rottenburg Episcopal Ordinariate, 9 March 1943, AEM, NL Faulhaber, 5931.

99. Cardinal Faulhaber to the Freiburg Ordinariate, 20 October 1943, AEM, NL Faulhaber, 5931.

100. H. Wagner, Pastoral Office of the Archbishopric of Munich, 7 January 1943, AEM, NL Faulhaber, 5931.

101. Faulhaber to Frings, 9 December 1942, AEM, NL Faulhaber, 5931.

102. P. Albert Schmitt, 6 June 1943, AEM, NL Faulhaber, 5931.

103. Faulhaber to Frings, 9 December 1942, AEM, NL Faulhaber, 5931.

104. Kardinal Faulhaber, Absolutio generalis for air raids, 30 December 1942, AEM, NL Faulhaber, 5931.

105. Cardinal Theodor Innitzer, Pastoral Instruction in the Event of an Air Raid, 29 August 1943, AEM, NL Faulhaber, 5931.

106. Reich Minister for Ecclesiastical Affairs, 29 October 1940, AEM, NL Faulhaber, 3407.

107. Copy of the express letter from the Reich Minister for Ecclesiastical Affairs dated 28 December 1940, Akten der Partei-Kanzlei, part II, 72817.

108. Schulte to Wienken, 31 October 1940, in Akten deutscher Bischöfe V, Doc. 601, 234f.; see also EAF, B 2–35, No. 122; Schulte died on 10 March 1941; his successor was Josef Frings from Neuss.

109. Bertram to Hitler, 1 November 1940, in Akten deutscher Bischöfe V, Doc. 603, 237ff.

110. Minutes of the Conference of the West German Bishops on 6 and 7 November 1940 in Kevelaer, in Akten deutscher Bischöfe V, Doc. 606, 246.
111. Bertram to Kerrl, 21 November 1940, in Akten deutsche Bischöfe V, Doc. 613, 265.
112. Announcement by Cardinal Faulhaber, 25 October 1940, AEM, NL Faulhaber, 5912.
113. Archbishop of Bamberg to Reich Minister for Ecclesiastical Affairs, Kerrl, 17 January 1941, in Akten deutscher Bischöfe V, Doc. 631, 312ff.
114. Göbel to Kerrl 11 December 1940, in Akten deutscher Bischöfe V, Doc. 622, 287–91, here 291.
115. Cardinal Konrad Groeber to Reich Minister Lammers, 9 December 1940, EAF, B2-35, No. 122.
116. The vicar of Waldkirch i. Br. to the Archiepiscopal Ordinariate, EAF, B2-35, No. 122; for the following see EAF, B2-35, No. 122.
117. Ordinariate to the pastoral offices 15 January 1943, AEM, NL Faulhaber, 5912.
118. St Ludwig, pastoral report for 1943 dated 8 February 1944, AEM, Seelsorgsberichte, Dekanat München-Nord, 18; Archiepiscopal Vicar's Office Steffeld to the Archiepiscopal Ordinariate Freiburg, 23 February 1942, EAF, B2-35, No. 122.
119. Frings and Jaeger to Hitler, 1 June 1943, AEK, CR II 25.16, 1; for the following see AEK, CR II 25.16, 1d.
120. Archbishop of Cologne on the last Sunday of the church's year 1944 to the Holy Father AEK, CR II 1.14, 1.
121. See Holzapfel, '"Unter deinen Schutz und Schirm fliegen wir..."'.
122. See Diemer, 'Münchner Mariensäule', 457.
123. Handwritten prayer note of Cardinal Faulhaber's (n.d.), AEM, NL Faulhaber.
124. 'Bei Luftangriffen Gebete zur Erweckung der vollkommenen Reue' (n.d.), AEM, NL Faulhaber; the published version of these prayers was approved on 17 February 1944.
125. To the dispersed members of the Reformed Protestant [Calvinist] parish of Barmen-Gemarke, September 1943, EKiR, 7 NL 120/104.
126. Johannes Mehrhoff, sermon: 'Ich werde bleiben im Haus des Herrn immerdar', Ps. 23: 6b, EKiR Düsseldorf, 7 NL 120/104, for the following see EKiR Düsseldorf, 7 NL 120/104; on this see also the references in Flesch, 'Quellen', 266.
127. From the funeral service on Sunday 20 June 1943, in the Immanuelskirche, Pastor M. Mehrhoff, EKiR, 7 NL 120/104.
128. Johannes Mehrhoff to the members of the parish of Barmen-Gemarke, September 1943, EKiR, 7 NL 120/104.
129. For an example see Lotte Zöller to Johannes Mehrhoff, 21 July 1943; see also the letter from Fr. M. Hesselnberg to Johannes Mehrhoff, 2 October 1943; EKiR, 7 NL 120/106.

130. See Kramer, *Volksgenossinnen*, 358.

131. Johannes Mehrhoff, Reisen zu den Evakuierten in Thüringen. Bericht über meinen Dienst an den Evakuierten in Thüringen (1944), EKiR, 7 NL 120/127.

132. Note of 3 September 1943, AEK, CR II 25.18, 1.

133. For such experiences see Holzapfel, 'Alltagsreligiosität', 68ff.

134. Report by August Lehrmann on the raid on Freiburg on 27 November 1944 (n.d, probably composed around 30 September 1945), AEM, NL Faulhaber, 3014.

135. Pastoral Report 1944, Dekanat München-Nordost, 19 January 1945, AEM, Seelsorgsberichte, 37.

136. Ottendichl, Pastoral Report for 1944/5, AEM, Seelsorgsberichte, 45.

137. Quoted in Thiessen, *Gedächtnis*, 85; for the following see Thiessen, *Gedächtnis*, 85.

138. St Ludwig, Pastoral Report for the Year 1943, 8 February 1944, AEM, Dekanat-München Nord, 18, Seelsorgsberichte; for the following see AEM, Dekanat-München Nord, 18, Seelsorgsberichte.

139. St Sylvester, Pastoral Report for the year 1943, 14 November 1944, AEM, Seelsorgsbericht, Dekanat München-Nord, 23.

140. Terror raid on Augsburg, Church councillor Heinrich Schmid, 'Die Augsburger Schreckensnacht vom 25./26. 2. 1944', Landeskirchliches Archiv Nürnberg, Bayerisches Dekanat Augsburg, 285; I am very grateful to Martina Steber for this reference.

141. St Ludwig, Pastoral Report for the year 1943, 8 February 1944, AEM, Seelsorgsbericht, Dekanat München-Nord, 18; for the following see AEM, Seelsorgsbericht, Dekanat München-Nord, 1.

142. St Ludwig, Pastoral Report for the year 1944, AEM, Seelsorgsbericht, Dekanat-München Nord, 18.

143. *Zur Lage der Kirche*, 3, weekly letter, 27 November 1943, 666.

144. Hering, 'Kirchliches Leben', 78f.

145. Hering, 'Kirchliches Leben', 79f.

146. Overlack, *Aufbruch*, 370ff.

147. See also Kösters, 'Kirche und Glaube', 370.

148. Vicar Riekes, Bochum, October 1943: 'Zur Seelsorge in den bombengeschädigten Städten', AEK, CR II 25.18, 1; for the following see AEK, CR II 25.18, 1.

149. For pastoral care in wartime see also among others Mitzscherlich, *Diktatur und Diaspora*, 358–67; Seidel, *Diktaturen*, 50–9; Kösters, *Katholische Verbände*, 552–72; Blessing, 'Deutschland in Not', 46–60.

150. Bericht über die Reise von Pfarrer Metzger und Dechant Brokam aus Essen-Borbeck zum Schwabenland (n.d. July 1943), AEK, CR II 25.20a, 5; for detail on this see Klee, *'Luftschutzkeller'*; Albert Hassler, Bericht über die Evakuiertenseelsorge im Dekanat Buchen vom 18. Juni 1945, EAF, B 2/32–5.

151. Bericht von nach Mitteldeutschland evakuierten Saarländern (n.d.), Archiv der Armen Schulschwestern in München, Drittes Reich, No. 27. I am very grateful to Nicole Kramer for this reference.
152. Ernst Meininghaus, Essen, 3 December 1943, AEK, CR II 25.20a, 5.
153. 'Zur Sorge der Evakuierten' (n.d. *c.*1943), AEK, CR II 25.20b, 1.
154. Note of the meeting on 28 July 1943 in Frankfurt, AEK, CR II 25.20b, 1.
155. Archbishop of Cologne to the archdiocese concerning the Feast of Christ's Transfiguration 6 August 1944, AEK, CR II 25.20b, 2.
156. Archbishop of Cologne: 'Religiöse Betreuung der aus den Städten Abgewanderten, wichtig aber für alle Pfarrer des Erzbistums', 9 August 1943, AEK, CR II 25.20b, 1.
157. Vicar Riekes, Bochum, October 1943: 'Zur Seelsorge in den bombengeschädigten Städten', AEK, C II 25.18, 1; for the following see AEK, C II 25.18, 1.
158. Faulhaber to the priests from the diocese at the front, 15 November 1944, AEM, NL Faulhaber, 5375.
159. Archbishop of Cologne to the priests of the archdiocese of Cologne caring for the evacuated Rhenish Catholics, AEK, CR II 25.20b, 2.
160. Chambers, '"Defend us from All Perils and Dangers of this Night"', 154–67.
161. Rhodes (ed.), *W. S. Churchill*, vi. 6238.
162. Priestley, *People*, 109.
163. For an overview see Field, 'People'.
164. Tom Harrisson, 'Religious Attitudes in a London Borough', Mass Observation, File Report Series, 2274; see also Calder, *People's War*, 478f.
165. 'Church Services, Spiritual Report' (20 August 1940), Mass Observation, File Report Series, 362.
166. See also Field, 'People', 474f.
167. See also Longmate, *How We Lived*, 386.
168. Parker, *Faith*, 83ff.
169. Wilkinson, *Dissent*, 278.
170. Diarist DR 5420 vom 21. 3. 1941, Special Collection, Mass Observation Archive.
171. Longmate, *How We Lived*, 393.
172. See Parker, *Faith*, 144.
173. Parker, *Faith*, 138.
174. Quoted in Parker, *Faith*.
175. Parker, *Faith*, 142.
176. Central Council for Church Care, 25 September 1939, Lambeth Palace Library, Temple Papers, 86.
177. Carpenter, *Archbishop Fisher*, 91.
178. Longmate, *How We Lived*, 390.
179. St Michael's Parish Magazine, May 1940, Plymouth and West Devon Record Office, 2715/24.
180. Matthews, *Saint Paul's Cathedral*, 55ff.

181. Compare Carpenter, *Exeter Cathedral*, Exeter University Library, Edmund Collection.
182. *Parish Magazine. St Simon*, 'The Vicar's Letter', 23 May 1943, Plymouth and West Devon Record Office, 2711/97 (including an excerpt from the Chief Constable's letter).
183. Harrisson, *Living*, 310.
184. *Hampshire Adviser*, 30 November 1940: 'Service in Bombed Church'.
185. *St Michael's Church, Stoke, Parish Magazine*, December 1940, Plymouth and West Devon Record Office, 2715/24.
186. *St Michael's Church, Stoke, Parish Magazine*, January 1941, Plymouth and West Devon Record Office, 2715/24.
187. *Liverpool Daily Post*, 4 November 1939: 'Religious Problems of Evacuees'.
188. Methodist Church, 18 June 1943, Plymouth and West Devon Record Archive, 1929/47, St Augustine.
189. Hastings, *Christianity*, 392.
190. Letter to *The Times*, 21 December 1940: 'Foundations of Peace'.
191. Hastings, *Christianity*, 392f.
192. Hastings, *Christianity*, 395.
193. *Birmingham Gazette*, 16 November 1937: 'Our Guernica'.
194. *The Times*, 28 April 1937: 'The Tragedy of Guernica'; see also Rankin, *Telegram from Guernica*; Schüler-Springorum, 'Mythos Guernica'.
195. *New York Times*, 16 November 1940: 'Revenge by Nazis'; 17 November 1940: 'King George Visits Coventry'.
196. Goebel, 'Coventry nach der "Coventrierung"', 4.
197. Campbell, *Coventry Cathedral*, 12f.
198. *War Pictures by British Artists*.
199. *War Pictures by British Artists*, 7.
200. Calder, *Myth*, 250.
201. *Daily Mail*, 31 December 1940: 'War's Greatest Picture: St Paul's Stands Unharmed in the Midst of the Burning City'.
202. *Bristol's Bombed Churches*, 3.
203. *Bristol's Bombed Churches*, Foreword, Harry W. Blackburne.
204. *Bristol's Bombed Churches*, 20.
205. AT, Esra 6: 7.
206. *Bristol's Bombed Churches*, 39.
207. *Bristol's Bombed Churches*, 9.
208. Howard, *Ruined and Rebuilt*, 22.
209. On this see Campbell, *Coventry Cathedral*, 22ff.
210. The New Coventry Cathedral Plan.
211. See Campbell, *Coventry Cathedral*, 29.
212. On this see also Trippen, *Josef Kardinal Frings*, i. 98–105.
213. See the report on a Una-Sancta conference held 27–9 April 1943 in Tübingen, in Schäfer (ed.), *Landeskirche*, 1349–51.

214. Mehl and Thierfelder, *Ökumene im Krieg*.

215. Joseph Plettenberg: Verhandlungen mit dem Präsidenten der Thüringischen evangelischen Kirche zu Eisenach, 27 July 1944, AEK, CR II 25.20b, 2. For the following see AEK, CR II 25.20b, 2.

216. On further developments see Notiz über die Abhaltung von Gottesdiensten katholischer Evakuierter in evangelischen Kirchen und kirchlichen Räumen, 27 December 1944, AEK, CR II 25.18, 1.

217. Seidel, *Übergang der Diktaturen*, 50–6.

218. On the internal church instructions and legal regulations see Notiz: Ist es zulässig, in der Diaspora für Evakuierte öffentlichen Gottesdienst (kirchliche religiöse Unterweisung) in nicht der kath. Kirche eigenen Räumen, insbesondere in gemieteten Privatunterkünften, zu veranstalten (n.d. *c.*1944), see AEK, CR II 25.20b, 2.

219. Catholic priests' office in Elrich to the archiepiscopal Generalvikariat in Fulda, 28 August 1943, AEK, CR II 25.20b, 1.

220. Bishop Wurm to the Generalvikar of the Rottenburg diocese, 11 January 1944, in Schäfer (ed.), *Landeskirche*, 1353.

221. 'Terrorangriff auf Augsburg, Evangelisch-Lutherisches Pfarramt St Jakob': on the history of Augsburg's horrific night of 25/6 February 1944, LAELKB, Bayerisches Dekanat Augsburg, 285.

222. See Greschat, 'Stimmen zum Kriegsalltag', 100.

223. 'Terrorangriff auf Augsburg, Gemeinde zu den Barfüßern und der Terrorangriff auf Augsburg vom 25./26. 2. 1944', LAELKB, Bayerisches Dekanat Augsburg, 285.

224. See the interviews in NARA II, RG 243, 64 b-n, Box 571 (4).

225. Superintendent des Kirchenkreises Köln, July 1945: Fragebogen Religion und Kirche, NARA II, RG 243, 64 b-n, Box 571 (4) 7.

226. Generalvikar des Erzbistums Köln, Emmerich David, am 9. Juli, Fragebogen: Religion und Kirche, NARA II, RG 243, 64 b-n, Box 571 (4) 7; for the following see NARA II, RG 243, 64 b-n, Box 571 (4) 7; also published in Akten deutscher Bischöfe V, Doc. 1001, 571–3.

227. Interview with Pfarrer Holstein from the Kreuzkirche in Münster, 17 June 1945, NARA II, RG 243, 64, b-n (4) 6, Box 571.

228. Superintendent des Kirchenkreises Köln, 7 July 1945: Fragebogen Religion und Kirche, NARA II, RG 243, 64 b-n, (4) 7, Box 571.

229. Fisher to Lord Bishop of Winchester, 1 August 1941, Lambeth Palace Library, Fisher Papers, 6.

230. Carpenter, *Exeter Cathedral*, X.

231. Bishop of Winchester to Fisher, 5 August 1941, Lambeth Palace Library, Fisher Papers, 6.

232. See Carpenter, *Archbishop Fisher*, 69–77.

233. Fisher to William (Provost of Coventry), 6 October 1943, Lambeth Palace Library, Fisher Papers, 6.

234. War Damage Act, 1941. Memorandum for the use of Diocesan and Parochial Authorities of the Church of England (n.d. [1941]), Record Archive Southampton, PR 23-8 –29.

235. Wilkinson, *Dissent*, 275.

236. *Church Times*, 12 June 1942: 'Paying the Price'.

237. *Church Times*, 13 February 1942: 'The Church Assembly'.

238. The Methodist Church: Re-Planning. Information for Area Committees, May 1942, Plymouth Record Archive, Plymouth Council Committee Minutes, 586/6/31.

239. Carpenter, *Exeter Cathedral*, X.

240. Abercrombie and Watson, *Plymouth*.

241. Letter to *The Times*, 15 August 1944: 'Ruined City Churches'.

242. Casson, 'Ruins for Remembrance'.

243. Letter to *The Times*, 15 August 1944: 'Ruined City Churches'.

CHAPTER 6

1. See in detail Lemke, *Luftschutz*.

2. Air Raid Shelters. Report of the Lord Privy Seal's Conference, April 1939, House of Commons, Parliamentary Papers, Cmd. 6006.

3. For the following see Blank, 'Kriegsalltag', 403–5.

4. References in Marszolek and Buggeln, *Bunker*, 10f.

5. Hans Hammann, 'Der LS-Bunker in der Städte-Planung des Siedlungsverbandes Ruhrkohlenbezirk', *Baulicher Luftschutz*, 2/4 (1942), 77–81, 77f.

6. Blank, 'Kriegsalltag', 406f.; for the following see Blank, 'Kriegsalltag', 406f.

7. See among others Gerhard Graubner (December 1943), 'Der Wehrgedanke als Grundlage der Stadtgestaltung und Stadtplanung', in Durth and Gutschow, *Träume*, ii. 770–6; 719–29 (December 1943).

8. See in detail Foedrowitz, *Bunkerwelten*, 9–24.

9. Gregg, *Shelter*, 14.

10. Gregg, *Shelter*, 22ff.

11. Newsinger, '"My Country"'.

12. Calder, *Carry on London*, 36–9.

13. See Nash, *Empire*.

14. Calder, *Lessons of London*.

15. Calder, *Carry on London*, 38f.

16. *Daily Worker*, 7 September 1940: 'Sunshine About Raids is Moonshine'; *Daily Worker*, 10 September 1940.

17. Meeting of the Metropolitan Police and Ministry of Health, 6 September 1940, PRO, MH 79/499.

18. RLM/Oberbefehlshaber der Luftwaffe/Inspektion des Luftschutzes, 31 May 1941: 'Bombensichere Luftschutzbauten (Luftschutzbunker) für die Bevölkerung', Akten der Partei-Kanzlei, 10302796–10302800; these regulations were sent to all the

responsible local government offices; see, for example, Stadtarchiv München, Branddirektion 74/3, 6–7.

19. See Knoch, 'Transitstationen der Gewalt'.

20. On the Nazi Party's claims to exercise authority in the air-raid shelters see among others 'Rede des Gauleiters und Reichsstatthalters [Hildebrandt] vor dem Schweriner Amtsträgerkorps des Reichsluftschutzbundes vom 16. 6. 1943', in *Mecklenburg im Zweiten Weltkrieg*, 815–21.

21. Vorläufige Dienstanweisung für die Bunkerverwalter vom 17. 2. 1943, Stadtarchiv Stuttgart, Luftschutz, 94.

22. Quoted in La Speranza, 'Bevölkerung', 105.

23. Foedrowitz, *Bunkerwelten*, 117.

24. Bekanntmachung des Polizeipräsidenten und Luftschutzleiters in Essen betrf. den Einsatz von Männern im Luftschutz und deren Aufenthalt in öffentlichen Luftschutzräumen, 1 June 1944, Stadtarchiv Essen, Rep. 102 XIV/22.

25. Bohl, Keipke, and Schröder (eds), *Bomben*, 162–7.

26. Foedrowitz, *Bunkerwelten*, 118.

27. Erlass des Reichsministers der Luftfahrt, Inspektion des zivilen Luftschutzes, vom 7. 10. 1940: Benutzung der LS-Räume durch Juden, quoted in Pätzold, *Verfolgung, Vertreibung, Vernichtung*, 270.

28. Quoted in Selig and Seligmann, *Schicksal*, 63.

29. Klemperer, *Tagebücher 1945*, entry for 20 January 1945, Sonnabendvormittag, 14f.

30. Entry for 25 August 1944, notes made by the Belgian priest Alphonse Come, in Stadt Essen (ed.), *Stadtarchiv-Materialien*, Quelle 31, 83.

31. On Nuremberg during the last phase of the war see, for example, 1. Bericht des Wehrmacht-Propaganda-Offiziers im Wehrkreiskommando XIII, Nürnberg, Major Müller, für die zweite Hälfte Februar 1945, in Wette et al., *Das letzte halbe Jahr*, Doc. 84, 365f.

32. Entry for 29 November 1944, notes made by the Belgian priest Alphonse Come, in Stadt Essen (ed.), *Stadtarchiv-Materialien*, Quelle 31, 85.

33. Foedrowitz, *Bunkerwelten*, 12f.

34. RML vom 13. 8. 1943: Luftschutz für Ausländer, in Stadtarchiv Düsseldorf, IV/1001.

35. Foedrowitz, *Bunkerwelten*, 121.

36. Use of Underground Railway Stations as Air Raid Shelters: Protective Measures and Control, 1941–1943, PRO, MEPO 2/6354.

37. Harrisson, *Living*, 119.

38. Mass Observation, *The Tube Dwellers*, 102ff.

39. Sheltering in Middlesborough (September 1940), Mass Observation, File Report Series, 407; Report from Mass Observation on Human Adjustments in Air Raids (18 September 1940), Mass Observation, File Report Series, 408.

40. Use of Underground Railway Stations as Air Raid Shelters, Protective Measures and Control, 1941–1943, PRO, MEPO 2/6354.

41. Gregg, *Shelter*, 52.
42. Greswick Atkinson, Air Raid Precaution. Hints for Housewives (1941), Plymouth and West Devon Record Office, 1561-1-CD-SE-1-2.
43. Public Shelter Rules (Plymouth), 20 March 1941, Plymouth and West Devon Record Office, 1561-1-CD-SE-1-2.
44. City of Plymouth, Public Shelter Rules, August 1941, City Archive Plymouth, 1561-1-CDSE-1-2.
45. Meeting of the Air Raid Precaution Committee (Shelter Management), 20 November 1940, Bristol Record Archive, Air Raid Precaution Committee Minute Book 1939–1942, M-B-CC-ARP-2.
46. Meeting of the Air Raid Precaution Sub-Committee, 6 April 1943, Bristol Record Archive, Air Raid Precaution Minute Book 1942–1945, M-B-CC-ARP-5.
47. Report on Interview with Head Shelter Wardens of Lewisham Borough, October 1941, UEA, SZ, OEMU, 56/3/9.
48. Use of Underground Railway Stations as Air Raid Shelters: Protective Measures and Control, 1941–1943, PRO, MEPO 2/6354.
49. Minutes of the Air Raid Precaution Committee, Air Raid Shelter Sub-Committee (19 November 1940), Bristol Record Archive, Air Raid Precaution Minute Book 1939–1942, M-B-CC-ARP-3; Colin Campbell, Town Clerk, Public Shelter Rules (October 1941), Plymouth and West Devon Record Office, 1561-1-CD-SE-1-2.
50. Harrisson, *Living*, 120.
51. *The Swiss Cottager*, Bulletin No. 4, November 1940, 1.
52. Home Intelligence Report 4–11 December 1940, PRO, INF 1/292.
53. Quoted in Field, 'Underground', 19.
54. Mass-Observation Archive, A TC 23/5/E, Special Collection.
55. For the following see Mass-Observation Archive, A TC 23/5/E, Special Collection; see also Gregg, *Shelter*, 53.
56. *The Swiss Cottager*, Bulletin No. 4, November 1940, 1.
57. On this see in detail Kushner, *Persistence*, 53; for the following see Kushner, *Persistence*, 53.
58. Kushner, *Persistence*, 190–202.
59. *The Times*, 27 September 1940: 'News from the Depths'.
60. Kushner, *Persistence*, 197.
61. On the concept see Geyer, *Verkehrte Welt*.
62. *Tube Dwellers* by Mass-Observation, April 1943, Mass Observation Archive, 1948.
63. Note for Meeting of Coordination Committee (24 October 1941), PRO, HO 207/442.
64. Meeting New Shelter Committee with the Minister of Home Security, 2 June 1943, PRO, HO 200/6.
65. Similar reservations had been expressed before: New Shelter Sub-Committee Secretary Report January 1943, PRO, HO 200/5.

66. Ministry of Home Security, Report on an Inquiry into the Accident at Bethnal Green Tube Station Shelter, 3 March 1944, in House of Commons Parliamentary Papers, January 1945, Cmd. 6583.

67. See also Bourke, *Fear*, 236ff.

68. House of Commons, Offical Report, 16 March 1943, Parliamentary Debates, Vol. 387, Column 1062.

69. Bourke, *Fear*, 234.

70. Special Meeting of the General Emergency Committee, 4 March 1943; note of Meeting at Bethnal Green Town Hall, 4 March 1943, PRO, HO 207/1020.

71. Letter to the Ministry of Home Security, signed 'Bethnal Green' (n.d. [March 1943]), PRO, HO 205/236.

72. Ministry of Home Security, Report on an Inquiry into the Accident at Bethnal Green Tube Station Shelter, 3 March 1944, in House of Commons Parliamentary Papers, January 1945, Cmd. 6583, 12.

73. The letters are in PRO, HO 205/236.

74. Agreement for Use of Tubes with the LPTB (London Passenger Transport Board), 1941–1943, PRO, HO 200/3.

75. Woolven, 'Defence', 256.

76. Gregg, *Shelter*, 83.

77. See among others Regional Commissioner to Town Clerk, Exeter, 21 July 1944, Devon Record Archive, Town Clerk Papers, Group O, Air Raid Precaution, Box 49.

78. Occupation of the Tube Shelters, September 1940–June 1945, PRO, HO 207/226.

79. *Essener National-Zeitung*, 10 October 1944: 'Nochmals: Disziplin vor den Bunkern!'

80. Der Polizeipräsident von Stuttgart als örtlicher Luftschutzleiter: Vorläufige LS-Bunker-Ordnung (Mai 1944), Stadtarchiv Stuttgart, Luftschutz, 94; for the following see Stadtarchiv Stuttgart, Luftschutz, 94.

81. Anlage zur Luftschutz-Planbesprechung, Polizeipräsident München vom 15. 1. 1944: Merkblatt für Großbrände, in Stadtarchiv München, Branddirektion, 74/3, 40.

82. Der Polizeipräsident als örtlicher Luftschutzleiter: LS-Pionierstellen vom 4. Mai 1944, Stadtarchiv Stuttgart, Luftschutz, 94.

83. Arnold and Janick, *Sirenen*, 66. The photo shows an advertisement pillar in the Gendarmenmarkt in Berlin in 1943; for the 'Ostmark' see, for example, Beer and Karner, *Krieg aus der Luft*, 119.

84. On the work of the air-raid wardens see Kramer, *Volksgenossinnen*, 186ff.

85. *Hamburger Zeitung*, 3 August 1943, quoted in Thiessen, '"Heimstätte"', 46.

86. *Hamburger Zeitung*, 26 July 1943, quoted in Thiessen, '"Heimstätte"', 46.

87. Quoted in Thiessen, '"Heimstätte"', 46.

88. Arnold and Janick, *Sirenen*, 67.

89. See in detail Kramer, *Volksgenossinnen*, 143–211.

90. *Die Sirene* 1944, No. 7: 'Wir tragen den Luftschutz ins Haus'.

91. See also Kramer, "'Kämpfende Mütter'".
92. See in detail, Kramer, *Volksgenossinnen*, 401ff.
93. *Die Sirene*, 1943, No. 17: 'Kameradschaft von Stadt zu Stadt'.
94. *Die Sirene*, 1944, No. 11: 'Tust Du das auch bei Fliegeralarm?'.
95. *Die Sirene*, 1943, No. 17: 'Bitte etwas mehr Sorgsamkeit'.
96. *Die Sirene*, 1943, No. 21: 'Unsere Ursel'.
97. See among others Albrich and Gisinger, *Tirol und Vorarlberg*, 220, 223.
98. Schmal et al., *Bunker*, 112ff.
99. Schmal et al., *Bunker*, 113.
100. See the photographs in Purpus, Sellen, and Buchen, *Bunker*, 28, ill. 23 and ill. 24.
101. Goebbels, *Tagebücher*, part II, vol. xi, 3 January 1944, 42.
102. *Meldungen aus dem Reich*, SD Report 10 February 1944, 6318.
103. Stargardt, *Opfer der Bomben*, also takes this line; on the debate see also the MA thesis by Barbara Grimm on the murder of Allied pilots: Grimm, 'Lynchmorde'.
104. See among others 13. Bericht des Wehrmacht-Propaganda-Offiziers des Wehrkreiskommandos III, Berlin, Oberstleutnant Wasserfall, über den 'Sondereinsatz Berlin' für die Zeit 1. 1.–7. 1. 1945, in Wette et al., *Das letzte halbe Jahr*, Doc. 71, 203.
105. Purpus, Sellen, and Buchen, *Bunker*, 30f., ill. 27–31.
106. Quoted in *Berichte aus der Abwurfzone*, 177f.
107. Arnold and Janick, *Sirenen*, 82.
108. 21. Bericht des Wehrmacht-Propaganda-Offiziers des Wehrkreiskommandos III, Berlin, Oberstleutnant Wasserfall, über den 'Sondereinsatz Berlin' für die Zeit 28. 2.–6. 3. 1945, in Wette et al., *Das letzte halbe Jahr*, Doc. 80, 299.
109. Discussion of 16 July 1943: Bunker und Stollen, Stadtarchiv Oberhausen, Bestand Tiefbauamt, 47.
110. Paul Sauer, Ratsherr der Stadt Stuttgart, 6 October 1943, to OB Strölin, in Stadtarchiv Stuttgart, Luftschutz, 195.
111. Purpus, Sellen, and Buchen, *Bunker*, 32.
112. Panse, *Angst*, 53
113. Irmgard W., 26 March 1945 (Bremen), in Echternkamp, *Kriegsschauplatz*, Doc. 84, 192; Panse, *Angst*, 58.
114. Letter from Carola Reissner, 15 June 1944, in *Essen im Luftkrieg*, Quelle 27, 79.
115. 13. Bericht des Wehrmacht-Propaganda-Offiziers des Wehrkreiskommandos III, Berlin, Oberstleutnant Wasserfall, über den 'Sondereinsatz Berlin' für die Zeit 1. 1.–7. 1. 1945, in Wette et al., *Das letzte halbe Jahr*, Doc. 71, 204.
116. 21. Bericht des Wehrmacht-Propaganda-Offiziers des Wehrkreiskommandos III, Berlin, Oberstleutnant Wasserfall, über den 'Sondereinsatz Berlin' für die Zeit 28. 2.–6. 3. 1945, in Wette et al., *Das letzte halbe Jahr*, Doc. 80, 299.
117. Quoted in Albrich and Gisinger, *Tirol und Vorarlberg*, 219.
118. Städtisches Hochbauamt Stuttgart, 17 July 1943: Erfahrungsbericht über die Luftangriffe auf Köln vom Juni und Juli 1943, in Stadtarchiv Stuttgart, Luftschutz, 221.

119. Stadt Stuttgart vom 13. 11. 1944: Bericht über das Ergebnis der Nachprüfung von Luftschutzbunkern Stadtarchiv Stuttgart, Luftschutz, 837.
120. *Neue Volksblätter*, 1 March 1945: 'Rücksichtsvoller sein; zit. nach Foedrowitz, Bunkerwelten', 126; see also 24. Bericht des Wehrmacht-Propaganda-Offiziers des Wehrkreiskommandos III, Berlin, Oberstleutnant Wasserfall, über den Sondereinsatz Berlin für die Zeit 3.–29. 3. 1945, in Wette et al., *Das letzte halbe Jahr*, Doc. 81, 318.
121. OLG Düsseldorf to the RJM, 29 November 1944, Berichte der OLG-Präsidenten 1940–1945, If Z-Archiv, MA 430/1.
122. OLG-Präsident Cologne to RJM, 30 November 1943, Berichte der OLG-Präsidenten 1940–1945, If Z-Archiv, MA 430/1.
123. 24. Bericht des Wehrmacht-Propaganda-Offiziers des Wehrkreiskommandos III, Berlin, Oberstleutnant Wasserfall, über den 'Sondereinsatz Berlin' für die Zeit 23. 3.–29. 3. 1945, in Wette et al., *Das letzte halbe Jahr*, Doc. 81, 326.
124. 21. Bericht des Wehrmacht-Propaganda-Offiziers des Wehrkreiskommandos III, Berlin, Oberstleutnant Wasserfall, über den 'Sondereinsatz Berlin' für die Zeit 28. 2.–6. 3. 1945, in Wette et al., *Das letzte halbe Jahr*, Doc. 80, 299.
125. Für ein Beispiel aus Berlin-Karlshorst vgl. 8. Bericht des Wehrmacht-Propaganda-Offiziers des III, Berlin, Oberstleutnant Wasserfall, über den 'Sondereinsatz Berlin' für die Zeit 27. 11–3. 12. 1944 in Wette et al., *Das letzte halbe Jahr*, Doc. 66, 168.
126. Von Kardorff, *Berliner Aufzeichnungen*, entry for 25 January 1944; for the following see Von Kardorff, *Berliner Aufzeichnungen*.
127. Diary entry Rita H., born 1922, quoted in Blank, *Kriegsalltag*, 411; Bronnen, *Geschichte vom Überleben*, 183f.
128. 13. Bericht des Wehrmacht-Propaganda-Offiziers des Wehrkreiskommandos III, Berlin, Oberstleutnant Wasserfall, über den 'Sondereinsatz Berlin' für die Zeit 1. 1.–7. 1. 1945, in Wette et al., *Das letzte halbe Jahr*, Doc. 71, 204.
129. See Süss, 'Dann ist keiner von uns seines Lebens mehr sicher'.
130. *Meldungen aus dem Reich*, SD report, 4 October 1943, 5834.
131. 24. Bericht des Wehrmacht-Propaganda-Offiziers des Wehrkreiskommandos III, Berlin, Oberstleutnant Wasserfall, über den 'Sondereinsatz Berlin' für die Zeit vom 23.–29. 3. 1945, in Wette et al., *Das letzte halbe Jahr*, Doc. 81, 320; 25. Bericht des Wehrmacht-Propaganda-Offiziers des Wehrkreiskommandos III, Berlin, Oberstleutnant Wasserfall, über den 'Sondereinsatz Berlin' für die Zeit 30. 3.–7. 4. 1945, in Wette et al., *Das letzte halbe Jahr*, Doc. 83, 343.
132. On Darmstadt see Schmidt, *Brandnacht*.
133. The accounts in *Überlebensberichte* are particularly gripping. However, these reports were prepared as a contribution to a Nazi cultural politics of memory and are, therefore, themselves part of a specific interpretation of suffering.
134. Panse, *Angst*, 73.
135. Panse, *Angst*, 88f.

136. Panse, *Angst*, 59.
137. *Überlebensberichte*, No. 25.4. Polizei-Revier, 45.
138. Panse, *Angst*, 30f.
139. See among others *Überlebensberichte*, No. 22, Hartwigstraße, 42.
140. Panse, *Angst*, 52f.
141. Calder, *Myth*, 143.
142. Similar things could also be seen in the photos that were published in newspaper articles dealing with life in air-raid shelters. See, for example the *Southern Daily Echo*, 22 January 1941: 'Party Time in Soton Shelter'.
143. *Picture Post*, 3 October 1940: 'Deep Shelters'.
144. See Hardy, *My Life*.
145. See *Picture Post*, 26 October 1940: 'Shelter Life'. The reporters were attempting to create a typology of patterns of behaviour in air-raid shelters and photographed what they considered typical reactions.
146. See also the pictorial narrative narrative in *Ourselves in Wartime*, 71.
147. See *Picture Post*, 12 October 1940: 'Bombed-out'.
148. Priestley, *English Journey*.
149. See Warburton, *Bill Brandt*.
150. See in detail Lewis, 'Shelter Drawings'; Andrews, *London's War*; Zentrum für Kunstausstellungen der DDR: Neue Berliner Galerie (ed.), *Henry Moore*.
151. Andrews, *London's War*, 43ff.
152. Cull, *Selling War*.
153. Quoted in Lewis, 'Shelter Drawings', 120.
154. Keith Vaughan, 'War Artists and the War', in *The Penguin New Writing*, January–March 1943, 112ff.
155. Memorandum on attitude to shelters, 1 November 1941, UEA, Zuckerman Papers, SZ, OPMU/56/3/6.
156. Shelter Warden's Organisation, Visit to Portway Tunnel, 3 September 1942, City Archive Plymouth, 1561-1-CD-SE-1-2.
157. Survey of Shelters in Bermondsey, Lewisham and Southwark, Report on individual Shelter (n.d. [October 1941]), UEA, SZ, OEMU 56/3/18.
158. Dr P. E. Vernon, Head of the Department of Psychology, University of Glasgow: The Conduct of Civil Population in Air-Raids, 30 July 1940, in Mass Observation Archive, University of Sussex Library, Topic Collection, Air Raid, TC 23, Box 6, 6 H.
159. Vernon, 'Psychological Effects of Air Raids', 457–76.
160. Vernon, 'Psychological Effects of Air Raids', 474.
161. Vernon, 'Psychological Effects of Air Raids', 475.
162. Quoted in Shephard, *War of Nerves*, 178.
163. Lewis, 'Incidence of Neurosis in England under War Conditions', 175–83, 179; see also Lewis, Report into the Incidence of Neurosis (n.d. [1942]), PRO, FD 1/6580.

164. *The Lancet*, 23 November 1940: 'Shelter Hygiene', 671. House of Commons Parliamentary Papers, Recommendations of Lord Horder's Committee regarding conditions in air-raid shelters with special reference to health, November 1940, Ministry of Health, Ministry of Home Security.

165. War Cabinet, Home Policy Committee: Additional Powers for Dealing with Infections and Verminous Persons and Children in Shelters and with the Evacuation of Children suffering in Body and Mind, 16 December 1940, PRO, MH 79/499.

166. Living Conditions in the Tube Shelters, 1940–1941, PRO, HO 207/363.

167. *The Lancet*, 14 March 1942: 'Air-Raid Shelters: Natural and Acquired', 329.

168. Use of Underground Railway Shelters: Protective Measures and Control, 1941–1943, in PRO, MEPO 2/6354.

169. Vermin at Tube Station Shelters, 1940–1945, PRO, MH 76/546.

170. 'Health Education in Shelters', *British Medical Journal*, 20 September 1941, 411.

171. On health conditions during the war see above all W. Süss, *'Volkskörper'*.

172. Report of the head of the LS-Sanitätsdienst in Hamm of 21 January 1945 to the Chamber of Doctors of Westphalia South and the Unna Health Office, quoted in Blank, *Kriegsalltag*, 411.

173. A considerably less dramatic assessment for Berlin in the 20. Bericht des Wehrmacht-Propaganda-Offiziers des Wehrkreiskommandos III, Berlin, Oberstleutnant Wasserfall, über den 'Sondereinsatz Berlin' for the period 2–27 February 1945, in Wette et al., *Das letzte halbe Jahr*, Doc. 79, 284; for the consequences for health policy of air raids see in detail Süss, *Volkskörper*, 269–91.

174. 1. Bericht des Wehrmacht-Propaganda-Offiziers im Wehrkreiskommando XIII, Nürnberg, Major Müller, for the second half of February 1945, in Wette et al., *Das letzte halbe Jahr*, Doc. 84, 365.

175. See among others Dr Schröder, Leitender Stadtmedizinaldirektor Berlin: 'Tuberkulosebekämpfung und Luftkrieg', *Der Öffentliche Gesundheitsdienst*, 10 (1944), Nos. 5/6, March 1944, 58–60; see also a set of instructions for those suffering from tuberculosis in *Der Öffentliche Gesundheitsdienst*, 10 (1944), Nos. 5/6, March 1944, 61.

176. See in detail Berger, *Psychiater des deutschen Heeres*, 99–177; Riedesser and Verderber, *Maschinengewehre*.

177. Prof. Voss, 'Beobachtungen aus einer nervenärztlichen Ambulanz im luftbedrohten Gebiet', *Münchner Medizinische Wochenschrift*, 90 (1943), No. 10, 5 March 1943, 185f.; for the following see *Münchner Medizinische Wochenschrift*, 90 (1943), No. 10, 5 March 1943, 185f.

178. Feudell, 'Reaktionen'.

179. For the post-war discussion see Panse, *Angst*.

180. *Münchner Medizinische Wochenschrift*, 88 (1941), No. 46, 14 November 1941, 1245.

CHAPTER 7

1. Lewis, 'Incidence of Neurosis in England under War Conditions', 175–83.
2. 'Disturbances in the mental stability of the worker population remaining in Hull due to the air raids of 1941', Russell Fraser to S. Zuckerman, 1 March 1943 (revised draft), UEA, SZ, OEMU 57/4/5.
3. '1941 in Hull: effects on air raid, Table I, Incidents of Neurosis observed in various groups', UEA, SZ, OEMU 4/57/5.
4. '1941 in Hull: Effects on Air Raid. Conclusions', UEA, SZ, OEMU 4/57/5.
5. 'Group I, Male Workers, Case 1; 1941 in Hull: Effects on Air Raid. Conclusions', UEA, SZ, OEMU 4/57/5.
6. 'Group I, Male Workers, Case 6; 1941 in Hull: Effects on Air Raid. Conclusions', UEA, SZ, OEMU 4/57/5.
7. 'Group I, Male Workers, Case 9; 1941 in Hull: Effects on Air Raid. Conclusions', UEA, SZ, OEMU 4/57/5.
8. 'Group II, Case 16; Mrs. S.; 1941 in Hull: Effects on Air Raid. Conclusions', UEA, SZ, OEMU 4/57/5.
9. 'Group II, Case 22, Mrs. S.; 1941 in Hull: Effects on Air Raid. Conclusions', UEA, SZ, OEMU 4/57/5.
10. 'Group II, Case 12, Mrs. M.; 1941 in Hull: Effects on Air Raid. Conclusions', UEA, SZ, OEMU 4/57/5.
11. Boberach, 'Auswirkungen', 267ff.
12. Pressekonferenz, 10 March 1943, in Boelcke, *Krieg*, 452.
13. See, with a large number of examples, *Berichte aus der Abwurfzone*, 11–30.
14. Report of the Italian Consul General in Cologne, July 1943, Serie Affari Politici, Germania 1931–1945, b. 75, fasc. 3, Archivio Storico del Ministero degli Affari Esteri, Rome (ASMAE). I am grateful to Patrick Bernhard for this reference.
15. Franz-Rudolf von Weiss, entry for 5 June 1942, in Schmitz (ed.), *Humanität und Diplomatie*, 177.
16. Franz-Rudolf von Weiss, entry for 1 May 1944, in Schmitz (ed.), *Humanität und Diplomatie*, 219.
17. Franz-Rudolf von Weiss, entry for 1 May 1944, in Schmitz (ed.), *Humanität und Diplomatie*, 219.
18. Goebbels, *Tagebücher*, part II, vol. xi, 25 January 1944, 166.
19. 'Committee of Historians: Germany's War Potential: An Appraisal, December 1943'; revised version of 18 January 1944, box 164, Map Room Files, FDR Library; quoted in Gentile, *Strategic Bombing*, 21–32; for the following see Gentile, *Strategic Bombing*, 21–32.
20. Most important was the book by the Swedish journalist Arvid Freborg of the *Svenska Dagbladet* translated into English as *Behind the Steel Wall* (London, 1944), in which he reported in detail on the effects of the air raids and on the 'morale' of the population in the air-raid shelters.

21. Quoted in Gentile, *Strategic Bombing*, 29; for the following see Gentile, *Strategic Bombing*, 29.

22. For a contemporary view see Nonne, 'Therapeutische Erfahrungen', 112; see among others Lerner, 'Psychiatry and Casualties of War'; Eckart, 'Aesculap in the Trenches'.

23. Feudell, 'Reaktionen'.

24. For the history of Leipzig during the air war and population developments during the war see Horn, *Leipzig im Bombenhagel*, 190–204.

25. Feudell, 'Reaktionen', 27.

26. Feudell, 'Reaktionen', 4.

27. Feudell, 'Reaktionen', 28.

28. Feudell, 'Reaktionen', 34.

29. Feudell, 'Reaktionen', 34.

30. Feudell, 'Reaktionen', 24.

31. Feudell, 'Reaktionen', 26.

32. Feudell, 'Reaktionen', 34.

33. Fuchs, *Störungen*.

34. Fuchs, *Störungen*, 8.

35. Fuchs, *Störungen*, 16.

36. See Arnold, *The Allied Air War*, 49.

37. I have intentionally used only those documents that were already produced during the war. Contemporary witness accounts produced after 1945 have, to a very large extent, been excluded. On their value as sources and testimony see in detail Thiessen, 'Feuersturm'.

38. Popitz, *Phänomene der Macht*, 44.

39. Franz-Rudolf von Weiss, entry for 11 June 1942, in *Humanität und Diplomatie*, 17.

40. Weiss, entry for 27 February 1943, in *Humanität und Diplomatie*, 388.

41. Weiss, entry for 6 October 1942, in *Humanität und Diplomatie*, 343.

42. Weiss, entry for 23 April 1944, in *Humanität und Diplomatie*, 505.

43. See Rüther, *Köln im Zweiten Weltkrieg*, 565ff.

44. Letter of 19 June 1940, in Rüther, *Köln im Zweiten Weltkrieg*, 571.

45. Letter of 30 November 1940, in Rüther, *Köln im Zweiten Weltkrieg*, 575.

46. Letter at Easter 1942, Anna–Rudolf, in Rüther, *Köln im Zweiten Weltkrieg*, 578.

47. Letter of 31 May 1942, Rudolf–Norway, in Rüther, *Köln im Zweiten Weltkrieg*, 580.

48. For one example among many see the correspondence between Rosalie Schüttler and Theo Hoffmann, in Rüther, *Köln im Zweiten Weltkrieg*, 763–804, esp. 800f.

49. Rosalie Schüttler to Theo Hoffmann, 31 May 1943, in Rüther, *Köln im Zweiten Weltkrieg*, 777.

50. Letter of 31 May 1942, Anna–Köln, in Rüther, *Köln im Zweiten Weltkrieg*, 581.

51. Letter of 4 June 1942, Anna–Rudolf, in Rüther, *Köln im Zweiten Weltkrieg*, 581.

52. Letter of 4 February 1943, Anna–Rudolf, in Rüther, *Köln im Zweiten Weltkrieg*, 583.

53. Letter of 11 July 1943, Anna–Rudolf, in Rüther, *Köln im Zweiten Weltkrieg*, 586.

54. Letter of 8 December 1943, Anna–Rudolf, in Rüther, *Köln im Zweiten Weltkrieg*, 587.

55. Margaret Werner on 14 September 1944, published in Schmidt (ed.), *Brandnacht*, 105f.

56. Letter from Carola K. to Georg K., 11 March 1945, in Echternkamp, *Kriegsschauplatz*, Doc. 42, 154f.

57. Letter from Carola Reissner, 15 June 1944, in *Essen im Luftkrieg*, Quelle 27, 79.

58. Harrisson, *Living*, 77f.

59. Harrisson, *Living*, 76.

60. Harrisson, *Living*, 76.

61. Harrisson, *Living*, 271.

62. Weekly Report by Home Intelligence, 30 September–9 October 1940, PRO, INF 1/292.

63. PRO, INF 1/292.

64. Calder, *War*, 216.

65. *Nella Last's War*, entry for 8 May 1941, 147.

66. Calder, *War*, 216.

67. Quoted in Boberach, 'Auswirkungen', 265.

68. Harrisson, *Living*, 87.

69. Harrisson, *Living*, 91.

70. *Nella Last's War*, entry for 5 May 1941, 141.

71. Longman, *How We Lived*, 353ff.

72. See in detail Summerfield, 'Women Workers'.

73. Weekly Report by Home Intelligence, 7–14 October 1940, PRO, INF 1/292.

74. Jones, 'Civilian', 80f.; for the following see Jones, 'Civilian', 80f.

75. Jones, 'Civilian', 67ff.

76. The Effects of Bombing (9 September 1941), Mass Observation File Report, 844.

77. Report on Portsmouth and Plymouth (29 January 1941), Mass Observation File Report, 559.

78. Second Report on Portsmouth (15 March 1941), Mass Observation File Report, 606.

79. Mass Astrology: public beliefs in the supernatural (July 1941), Mass Observation File Report, 769.

80. Tom Harrisson, 'Civilians in Air Raids', in *Picture Post*, 1 August 1940; 'Civilians in Air Raids' (August 1940), Mass-Observation File Report, 313.

81. *Nella Last's War*, 81.

82. Quoted in Jones, 'Civilian', 146.

83. Weekly Report by Home Intelligence, 18–25 November 1940, PRO, INF 1/292.

84. Weekly Report by Home Intelligence, 24 December 1940–1 January 1941, PRO, INF 1/292.

85. See among others Fraser, Leslie, and Phelps, *Psychiatric Effects*.

86. *Daily Herald*, 13 September 1940: 'Londoners Hear the Music of Guns and Rejoice'.

87. John L. Sweetland, *Growing Up in Wartime London, 1939–1945*, quoted in Rose, *War*, 157.

88. Weekly Report (6 December 1940), Mass Observation File Report, 521.

89. Millgate (ed.), *Mr Brown's War*, entry for 3 November 1940, 72f.

90. *Mr Brown's War*, entry for 21 December 1940, 80f.

91. *Mr Brown's War*, entry for 8 April 1941, 97.

92. Wybrow, *Britain Speaks out*, 16.

93. Quoted in Gardiner, *Wartime*, 640.

94. Weekly Report by Home Intelligence, 11–18 August 1944, PRO, INF 1/292.

95. 'Reactions to V2-bombs', 22 February 1945, Mass-Observation Archive, University of Sussex Library, Topic Collection, Air Raids, TC 23, Box 12, G.

96. 'Pilotless Planes: A Study of the Reaction of Londoners from Information gathered during the period from 16th June 1944 to July 1944', Mass-Observation File Report, 2121.

97. Quoted in Ziegler, *London*, 292.

98. A Report on South East London, M O (February 1945), Mass Observation File Report, 2207.

99. Gardiner, *Wartime*, 648.

100. Reactions to V2-bombs, 20 February 1945, Mass Observation Archive, University of Sussex Library, Topic Collection, Air Raids, TC 23, Box 12, G.

101. Weekly Report by Home Intelligence, 27 June–4 July 1944, PRO, INF 1/292.

102. Weekly Report by Home Intelligence, 29 August–5 September 1944, PRO, INF 1/292.

103. Weekly Report by Home Intelligence, 14–21 November 1944, PRO, INF 1/292.

104. Ziegler, *London*, 294.

105. Cited after Ziegler, *London*, 299.

106. Bolle, 'Ich weiß, dieser Brief wird dich nicht erreichen', Berlin, 2006, letter of 18 January 1944, 227; also reports from the dropping zone, 22.

107. Gustav Schmidt, letter of 1 August 1943, in *Hamburger Katastrophe*, 70f.

108. Quoted in Thiessen, *Gedächtnis*, 36.

109. Thiessen, *Gedächtnis*, 36.

110. Ruth Nöthe, letter of November 1944, in Schmidt, *Brandnacht*, 110.

111. Hermann Holthausen to Hans Meyer, 29 July 1943, in *Hamburger Katastrophe*, 126.

112. Letter from Anni L. to Otto L., 28 February 1944 (in private ownership).

113. Margaret Werner in October 1944, in Schmidt, *Brandnacht*, 106f.

114. Anni L. to Otto L., 28 February 1944 (letter in private posession).

115. Protokoll No. 13: Bildhauer Heinz Wiegel, in *Überlebensberichte*, 31f.; Protokoll No. 71: Frau Christine Wachsmuth, in *Überlebensberichte*, 100.

116. Rosalie Schüttler to Theo Hoffmann, 2 August 1943, in *Köln im Zweiten Weltkrieg*, 779.

117. Friedrich Ruppel, 5 October 1943, in *Hamburger Katastrophe*, 237f.; for the following see *Hamburger Katastrophe*, 237f.

118. Geni S. to Otto S., 28 February 1944 (letter in private possession).

119. Meine liebe E., September 1944, in Schmidt, *Brandnacht*, 108f.

120. Thiessen, *Gedächtnis*, 58.

121. See *Überlebensberichte*, 5ff.

122. Protokoll No. 73: Fensterputzer Otto Pfromm, geboren am 3. 11. 1879, and die Tochter, Frau Katharina Sch., geboren Pfromm, geboren am 19. 2. 1907, in *Überlebensberichte*, 101ff.

123. Protokoll No. 63: Wachtmeister Ludwig B., in *Überlebensberichte*, 88f.

124. Georg Ahrens, 19 August 1943, in *Hamburger Katastrophe*, 225f.

125. Protokoll No. 11: Revieroberwachtmeister Franz Aschemann, recorded on 2 March 1944, in *Überlebensberichte*, 29f.

126. Niederschrift über die Besprechung beim Luftgaukommando VII am 19. 8. 1943 in München, Stadtarchiv Freiburg, C 4/X I/31-8. The minutes were also sent to the Freiburg city councillors among others; for the following see Stadtarchiv Freiburg, C 4/X I/31-8.

127. United States Strategic Bombing Survey, 12f.

128. For the work of the welfare workers see Kramer, *Volksgenossinnen*, 303–15.

129. Fr. Zierach, official in the Hanover department for compensation for personal damage, interview of 13 July 1945, NARA II, RG 243, 64 b-n, Box 571.

130. For the internal debates about the concept of 'morale' see among others Ralph K. White to Gordon Allpor, 7 December 1945, NARA II, RG 243, Entry 6, Box 563.

131. Interview with a Freiburg furniture manufacturer, 25 June 1945, NARA II, RG 243, 64 b-n, Box 571. For Nuremberg see Gregor, 'A Schicksalsgemeinschaft?', 1069.

132. Report of the Ford-Werke Aktiengesellschaft, Köln-Niehl, 19 July 1945, NARA II, RG 243, 64 b-n, Box 571.

133. See in detail Tooze, *Ökonomie der Zerstörung*, 744–50.

134. Quoted in Werner, *'Bleib übrig'*, 266.

135. See Werner, *'Bleib übrig'*, 261.

136. Correspondence and papers concerning school essays 1942–3, UEA, SZ, OEMU 56/8.

137. Barbara Kendall, My Recollection of the Air Raid, 13 February 1942, UEA, SZ, OEMU 56/11.

138. Joan Ray, My Recollection of the Air Raid, 13 February 1942, UEA, SZ, OEMU, 56/11.

139. Lillian Hilton, My Recollection of the Air Raid (Chapman Street Girls' School, Hull), UEA, SZ, OEMU 56/11.

140. Pete Bell, My Recollection of the Air Raid (Constable Street Boys' School, Hull), UEA, SZ, OEMU 56/12.

141. Pauline Day, My Recollection of the Air Raid (Chapman Street Girls' School Hull), UEA, SZ, OEMU 56/12.

142. Gardiner, *Wartime*, 114.

143. Children in Air Raids, 1940, Mass-Observation Archive, University of Sussex Library, Topic Collection, Living through the Blitz, Box 230.

144. Burlingham and Freud, *Young Children in Wartime*, X.

145. Compare Rüther, *Köln im Zweiten Weltkrieg*, 651f.

146. Gertrud L., born 1928, in Rüther, *Köln im Zweiten Weltkrieg*, 652f.; for the following see Rüther, *Köln im Zweiten Weltkrieg*, 652f.

147. Quoted in Stargardt, *Maikäfer*, 283f.; for the following see Stargardt, *Maikäfer*, 283f.

148. Quoted in Stargardt, *Maikäfer*, 275ff.

149. Agnes H., born 1929, in Rüther, *Köln im Zweiten Weltkrieg*, 657f.

150. Hilde K., born 1926, in Rüther, *Köln im Zweiten Weltkrieg*, 659f.

151. Agnes H., born 1929, in Rüther, *Köln im Zweiten Weltkrieg*, 657f.

152. The situation was no different in Frankfurt or Hanover; Effects of Bombing on Morale of Youth and Education. A Topical Report by Otto Springer, Morale Division USSBS, 20 August 1945, 30, NARA II, RG 243, 64 b-q, Box 580.

153. Psychologischer Fragebogen, School, Bremen, 7 July 1945, NARA II, RG 243, 64 b-n, Box 571.

154. Untersuchungen über die Wirkungen der Bombenangriffe auf das Schulleben und die Schulkinder (n.d. unsigned, 13 July 1945), NARA II, RG 243, 64 b-n, Box 571; for the following see NARA II, RG 243, 64 b-n, Box 571.

155. W. Blanke, 9 July 1945, Zu den Fragen über die Auswirkung der Luftangriffe auf die Schuljugend Pychologischer Fragebogen, School, Bremen, 7 July 1945, NARA II, RG 243, 64 b-n, Box 571.

156. By comparison with other factors, for example, forms of compulsory discipline, the increasing importance of outside school activities, the influence of ideology on school lessons, the direct impact of the air raids generally had a less significant impact on the 'morale' of young people. More important were generally the indirect effects of such factors as the consequences of evacuation for the political 'mood' in the Reich. Effects of Bombing on Morale of Youth and Education. A Topical Report by Otto Springer, Morale Division USSBS, 20 August 1945, 60ff., NARA II, RG 243, 64 b-o, Box 580.

157. Fr. Buengener, head of elementary school 36, Hanover: Untersuchungen über die Wirkungen der Bombenangriffe auf das Schulleben und die Schulkinder, 2 July 1945, NARA II, RG 243, 64 b-n, Box 571.

158. Effects of Bombing on Morale of Youth and Education. A Topical Report by Otto Springer, Morale Division USSBS, 20 August 1945, 33, NARA, RG 243, 64 b-q, Box 580.

159. Interview 345, 16 July 1945 (Bonn), Erziehung und Jugend, NARA II, RG 243, 64 b-n, Box 571.
160. W. Blanke, 9 July 1945, responding to questions about the effects of air raids on schoolchildren, Psychological Questionnaire, School, Bremen, 7 July 1945, NARA II, RG 243, 64 b-n, Box 571.
161. Fr. Kaufmann, health worker, report on the questionnaire on the effects of air raids on the provision of welfare, 7 July 1945, NARA II, RG 243, 64 b-n, Box 571.

CHAPTER 8

1. Rugg, 'Civilian Deaths', 156.
2. Burial of war victims. Conference at the Ministry of Health, 24 January 1939, PRO, HO 186/1225; Ministry of Health, Civilian Death due to War Operations, Circular 1779, 28 February 1939, CHC, CD/1/78.
3. Burial Accommodation in London Region, 1 December 1939, PRO, HO 186/376.
4. City of Exeter: Public Health Department, 10 July 1939: Memorandum: Civilian Deaths due to War Operations, Circular 1779, Devon Record Archive, Town Clerk Papers, Group O, Box 17/187.
5. Mortuary accommodation for war dead, 13 July 1939, CHC, CD/1/4/National Emergency Committee.
6. City of Westminster, Civilian Deaths due to War Operations, 26 June 1939, PRO, HO 2311.
7. 'Civilian death through war operations. Arrangements for disposal of bodies', *Municipal Review*, May 1939, 165.
8. Rugg, 'Civilian Deaths', 160; Cremation Society to the Town Clerk of Coventry 26 September 1939, CHC, 3/1/10138/1/3.
9. National Emergency Committee, National Association of Cemetery and Crematorium Superintendents, Report of Executive Committee on the Southern Branch, 22 March 1939, CHC, CD/1/4.
10. See Strange, *Death*, 148–54; for an overview see Cannadine, 'War and Death'.
11. Wilson and Levy, *Burial Reform*, 63f.
12. On Dresden see, for example, Matthias Neutzner, Die Bergung, Registratur und Bestattung der Dresdner Luftkriegstoten. Bericht zum 1. Teilprojekt 'Statistisch-geographische Analyse' der Historikerkommission zu den Luftangriffen auf Dresden zwischen dem 13. und 15. Februar, 24: <http://www.dresden.de/media/pdf/stadtarchiv/Historikerkommission/_Dresden1945_Bericht_TP1_V1_0.pdf.>.
13. Polizeipräsident München, 5 January 1940, Stadtarchiv München, Bestattungsamt, 292.
14. Ministry of Health, Deaths due to War Operations, 1 November 1942, CHC, CD/1/78.

15. Town Clerk to Coventry and Warwickshire Hospital, 21 October 1940, CHC, CD/1/78.
16. National Emergency Committee, General Superintendent Coventry to J. Owen, 7 December 1940, CHC, CD/1/4; Emergency Mortuary for Coventry, 23 December 1940, CHC, 3/1/10138/1/2.
17. Barton, *Blitz*, 150.
18. Longmate, *Air Raid*, 223.
19. *Belfast News Letter* of 23 April 1941: '500 Dead in Belfast'. Barton, *Blitz*, 146ff.
20. Barton, *Blitz*, 148.
21. National Emergency Committee, General Superintendent Coventry to H. W. Welsh, 12 December 1940, CHC, CD/1/4.
22. Compare Strange, *Death*, 164.
23. National Emergency Committee, General Superintendent Coventry to P. W. H. Conn, 26 December 1940, CHC, CD/1/4.
24. National Emergency Committee, Ministry of Health, Circular 2165, Death due to War Operations, 18 October 1940, CHC, CD/1/4.
25. Ministry of Health to Town Councils, 31 January 1941, Bristol Record Office, 3377-II.
26. Town Clerk to Ministry of Health, Funeral Grants to Civilians as a result of War Operations, 10 January 1941, Bristol Record Office, 3377-II.
27. National Emergency Committee, General Superintendent to H. W. Welsh, Hampstead Cemetery, London, 12 December 1940, CHC, CD/1/4.
28. War Cabinet, Home Policy Committee, 18 July 1940, PRO, HO 186/304.
29. Conference and Demonstration on Emergency Arrangements, Plymouth, 10 December 1942, Devon Record Archive, Town Clerk Papers, Group O, Box 17/187.
30. Casualty Survey: Notes on Some Aspects of Casualty Services Mortuaries, 10 December 1943, UEA, SZ, OEMU 42/58/3/1/27.
31. For the treatment of Jewish cemeteries see Wirsching, 'Jüdische Friedhöfe'.
32. OB Stuttgart to Oberbaurat Scheuerle, 9 August 1939, Stadtarchiv Stuttgart, Luftschutz, 281.
33. Compare Black, 'Reburying and Rebuilding', 70.
34. Deutscher Gemeindetag to the Oberbürgermeister of Kiel, Stadtarchiv Kiel, 35200 (the survey covered the major north-west German cities that up till then had been most badly affected, but was later extended to the south-west German cities, including Munich and Stuttgart).
35. Stadt Kiel to the Deutsche Gemeindetag, 15 May 1941, Stadtarchiv Kiel, 35200.
36. Overview: Wer lässt die Beerdigungen ausführen? (n.d., around May/June 1941), Stadtarchiv Kiel, 35200, Bl. 59.
37. Dienststelle für Familienunterhalt, 29 November 1941, Stadtarchiv Kiel, 35200.
38. Letter to the Deutsche Gemeindetag, 24 July 1941, Stadtarchiv Stuttgart, Luftschutz, 281; Amt für Kriegsschäden, Dienstblatt Teil IVI, Hilfs- und Fürsorgemaßnahmen, 31 January 1944, 5, Landesarchiv Berlin 005-07/519.

39. Beratung mit den Beiräten für Luftschutzfragen, 7 October 1941, Stadtarchiv Stuttgart, Luftschutz, 281.

40. Kreisvertrauensmann, Gruppe Bestattungswesen, to the Stadtverwaltung Duisburg 13 July 1942, Stadtarchiv Duisburg, Friedhofsamt, 607/164.

41. Amtsvorstand Friedhofsamt 13 July 1943, Stadtarchiv Duisburg, Friedhofsamt, 607/164.

42. Städtisches Friedhofsamt Stuttgart, 31 October 1941, Stadtarchiv Stuttgart, Luftschutz, 281; OB Stuttgart, 19 April 1942, Stadtarchiv Stuttgart, Luftschutz, 281.

43. Amt für Kriegsschäden, Dienstblatt Teil IVI, Hilfs- und Fürsorgemaßnahmen, 6 April 1944, 7, Landesarchiv Berlin 005-07/519.

44. Städtisches Bestattungsamt München an den Oberbürgermeister der Stadt Duisburg, 8 July 1943, Stadtarchiv Duisburg, Friedhofsamt, 607/164.

45. An den Herrn Oberbürgermeister der Hauptstadt der Bewegung, Bergung und Bestattung von Luftkriegsopfern, 28 July 1943, Stadtarchiv Duisburg, Friedhofsamt, 607/164.

46. For Berlin see Amt für Kriegsschäden, Dienstblatt Teil IVI, Hilfs- und Fürsorgemaßnahmen, 18 April 1944, S. 9, Landesarchiv Berlin 005-07/519.

47. Erfahrungen im Bestattungswesen anlässlich des Katastrophenfalles 12 June 1943, Stadtarchiv Düsseldorf, IV, 477.

48. Luftkriegsmitteilungen des Interministeriellen Luftkriegsschäden-Ausschusses, LKMitteilung No. 72, 18 December 1943, betr. Leichenbergung, BA Berlin, R 55/447; see also Arnold, 'Krieg', 138.

49. Einsatz der Kriminalpolizei: Staatliche Kriminalpolizei, Kriminalpolizeileitstelle Hamburg to the Reichssicherheitshauptamt, Amt V, 23 September 1943, StA Hamburg, 131-1/1529.

50. Oberbürgermeister von Essen to the Stadtverwaltung Düsseldorf, 1 July 1944, Stadtarchiv Düsseldorf, IV, 478.

51. Correspondence of the liaison officer between the Party Chancellery and the Reich propaganda headquarters, Tiessler, with both agencies concerning a ban on references to the Iron Cross in death notices for victims of air raids. Notiz für PG Wächter: Verwendung des Eisernen Kreuzes bei Todesanzeigen für Opfer in der Zivilbevölkerung vom 15. 7. 1942, Akten der Partei-Kanzlei, 42389, 071699.

52. Mitteilung der Reichspressestelle der NSDAP No. 54/43, BA Berlin, NS 18, 1063; on this see also Kramer, 'Kämpfende Mütter', 96.

53. Reichspropagandaamt Weser-Ems to RMVP, 23 February 1942, BA Berlin, NS 18, 1063.

54. Friedrich, *Brand*, 434.

55. On Kassel see Arnold, *The Allied Air War*, 42–4.

56. Direktion des städtischen Bestattungsamtes. 10 October 1942, Stadtarchiv München, Bestattungsamt, 378.

57. Direktion des städtischen Bestattungsamtes München, 25 July 1944: Leichenbehandlung, Stadtarchiv München, Bestattungsamt, 392; Bestattung der Gefallenen,

Besprechung vom 11. 9. 1944, Stadtarchiv München, Bestattungsamt, 519; also references in Permooser, *Luftkrieg*, 258.

58. On Erfurt see Wolf, *Erfurt im Luftkrieg*, 121.

59. Niederschrift über das Ergebnis der Oberbürgermeistertagung in der Regierung Düsseldorf vom 3. 8. 1943, Stadtarchiv Düsseldorf, IV/481.

60. Reichsführer SS und Reichminister des Inneren an die Befehlshaber der Ordnungspolizei und die höheren Verwaltungsbehörden, 14 June 1944, Stadtarchiv Stuttgart, Luftschutz, 283.

61. Deutscher Gemeindetag, Landesdienststelle Hessen/Hessen-Nassau: Vorsorgemassnahmen der Gemeinden für den Fall von Fliegerangriffen, 3 May 1942, Stadtarchiv München, Bayerischer Gemeindetag, 189.

62. Amt für Kriegsschäden, Dienstblatt Teil IVI, Hilfs- und Fürsorgemaßnahmen, 31 January 1944, 1, Landesarchiv Berlin 005-07/519.

63. Bestattungsamt München, Bergung, Abbeförderung und Bestattung von Gefallenen nach Luftangriffen 21. 8. 1944, gez. Hundsdorfer, Stadtarchiv München, Bestattungsamt, 392.

64. Direktion des städtischen Bestattungsamtes, 10 October 1942, Stadtarchiv München, Bestattungsamt, 378.

65. Polizeipräsident Hamburg, 15 October 1943, Staatsarchiv Hamburg, 331-1/ Polizeibehörde I, 1144; for the following see Fings, *Krieg*, 120–33.

66. BA Berlin, NS 19/3661, Bl. 12.

67. Aktennotiz des Beauftragten des OB München für den Notbereich München I, 9 August 1944, Stadtarchiv München, Bestattungsamt, 292; Mitteilung vom 16. 8. durch die Direktion des städtischen Bestattungsamtes, Stadtarchiv München, Bestattungsamt, 292.

68. Städtisches Friedhofsamt Stuttgart: Erfahrungen aus den Luftangriffen auf Hamburg, 4 September 1943, Stadtarchiv Stuttgart, Luftschutz, 281.

69. Aktenvermerk über die Besprechung am 2. 8. 1943: Leichenbeseitigung und Obdachlosenüberstützung nach Großangriffen, Stadtarchiv Stuttgart, Luftschutz, 281.

70. Erfahrungen aus den Luftangriffen auf Hamburg (n.d., *c.* August/September 1943), Stadtarchiv Stuttgart, Luftschutz, 281.

71. Letter from the city administration concerning war decorations for the retrieval of corpses, 3 August 1943, Stadtarchiv Essen, 102 I/1123a.

72. Stadtverwaltung Essen bzgl. Durchführung der Beerdigung der Fliegeropfer nach dem Angriff am 27. 4. 1944, vom 24. 5. 1944 (Jahresbericht Gartenamt 1944), Stadtarchiv Essen, 102/166.

73. See Gräff, *Tod im Luftangriff*, 193ff.

74. Erfahrungen im Bestattungswesen anlässlich des Katastrophenfalles vom 12. 6. 1943, Stadtarchiv Düsseldorf, IV/477; see also the Stuttgarter OB Strölin: Bericht von Oberbürgermeister Dr Strölin über die Luftangriffe vom 19. und 20. 10. 1944, in Badura, *Stuttgart im Luftkrieg*, 234f.

75. For an overview see Wer lässt die Beerdigungen ausführen? (n.d., *c.* May/June 1941), Stadtarchiv Kiel, 35200, Bl. 56.

76. Katholisches Pfarramt St. Oger to Generalvikar Münster (n.d., probably 1946), Bistumsarchiv Münster, A 101–16; I am grateful to Nicole Kramer for this reference.

77. See also Schlechter-Bonnesen, 'Nach dem Bombenangriff', 257ff.

78. Erfahrungen im Bestattungswesen anlässlich des Katastrophenfalles vom 12. 6. 1943, Stadtarchiv Düsseldorf, IV, 477.

79. Thiessen, Gedächtnis, 68.

80. Bauer, Würzburg, 37; see also Dunkhase, 'Würzburg, 16. März 1945'.

81. For Dresden see for example the exceptionally moving letter from Dora Baumgärtel (Meißen) to her children of 15 February 1945, in Neutzner, Leuchten, 309.

82. See Groh, '"Sehen wir Pforzheim!"', 123.

83. For the following see Arnold, 'Krieg', 135.

84. See also Assmann, '"Die Lebenden und die Toten"', 32f.

85. Quoted in Arnold, 'Krieg', 139.

86. See Klemperer, LTI, 164–8.

87. Schmidt, Brandnacht, letter of Margaret Werner (14 September 1944), 105ff., l.c. 106.

88. Schmidt, Brandnacht (letter of September 1944).

89. Überlebensberichte. No. 3: Frau Maria V, 15ff., l.c., 17.

90. Direktor des städtischen Bestattungsamtes München, 25 July 1944, Betreff: Leichenbehandlung, Stadtarchiv München, Bestattungsamt, 392; for the following see Stadtarchiv München, Bestattungsamt, 392.

91. See also Francis, Flyer, 118–25.

92. Hillary, Last Enemy.

93. See among others Rawlinson, Writing, 44.

94. Hillary, Last Enemy, 174f.

95. On this see in detail Kehrt, Moderne Krieger, esp. 82–106 and 245–82.

96. Koestler, Birth of a Myth.

97. Francis, Flyer, 131–45.

98. Rawlinson, Writing, 47.

99. See also Chapman, British at War, 212ff.

100. Wilkinson, 'Changing Attitudes', 160.

101. Town Clerk Coventry to Town Clerk Oxford, 25 January 1941, CHC, 3/1/10138/1/2; for the following see CHC, 3/1/10138/1/2.

102. Strange, Death, 168.

103. General Superintendent Coventry to Wigan Borough Cemetry, 17 February 1941, CHC, CEM/1/18/2.

104. See also Longmate, Air Raid, 226.

105. National Emergency Committee, replies to attached questionnaire, 7 December 1940, CHC, CD/1/4.

106. Town Clerk Coventry to Town Clerk Blackburn, 26 August 1941, CHC, 3/1/10138/1/1.

107. *Sunday Chronicle*, 5 October 1940: 'The Test'.
108. Regional Officer London, 8 October 1940, PRO, HO 186/376.
109. Parks Superintendent Correspondence, General Superintendent Coventry to Medical Officer of Health, Dr Massey, 7 March 1941, CHC, CEM/1/18/2.
110. General Superintendent P. W. H. Conn to F. Smith Esq, Town Clerk, Funeral Arrangements for Air Raid Victims, 20 May 1941, CHC, 3/1/10138/1/1.
111. Parks Superintendent Correspondence, General Superintendent Coventry to Town Clerk, Coventry, 2 May 1941, CHC, CEM/1/18/2.
112. *Manchester Guardian*, 30 December 1940: 'Raid Victim: Manchester Funeral Services'.
113. Parks Superintendent Correspondence, Town Clerk to General Superintendent, Coventry, 8 May 1941, CHC, CEM/1/18/2.
114. Rugg, 'Civilian Deaths', 164; for the following see Rugg, 'Civilian Deaths', 164.
115. Ministry of Health, Circular 2470, 27 August 1940, Devon Record Archive, Town Clerk Papers, Group O, Box 17/187.
116. Rugg, 'Civilian Deaths', 168.
117. Ministry of Health Circular 2192, 1 November 1940, Devon Record Archive, Town Clerk Papers, Group O, Box 17/187.
118. General Superintendent Coventry to Wigan Borough Cemetery, 17 February 1941, CHC, CEM/1/18/2.
119. Bourke, 'Dismembering the Male', 215.
120. Strange, *Death*, 263–73.
121. Ministry of Health, War Death. Emergency Mortuary and Burial Arrangements, 16 (1942), CHC, 3/1/10138/1/4.
122. *Liverpool Post*, 14 May 1941: 'Our Unknown Warriors'; *Daily Dispatch*, 14 May 1941: 'A City Mourns its Dead'.
123. *Liverpool Post*, 6 December 1940: 'Grave of the Unknown'.
124. Wilkinson, 'Changing Attitudes', 159.
125. Hinsley, *The Bond of Peace*, 104.
126. Walton and Lamb, *Raiders over Sheffield*, 77.
127. Quoted in Rugg, 'Civilian Deaths', 168.
128. *The Times*, 28 January 1943: 'Bombed School Dead Buried'.
129. Memorandum (unsigned), 17 November 1941, PRO, HO 45/21922.
130. On the concept see Goebel, *Great War*, 269.
131. Feierliche Beisetzung der weiteren Opfer des Terror-Angriffs auf München, vom 27. 3. 1944, Stadtarchiv München, Branddirektion, 74/3, 34–5.
132. *Warnemünder Zeitung*, 8 July 1940: 'Ganz Warnemünde nahm teil an der Trauerfeier für die Opfer des britischen Luftüberfalls'; published in Bohl, Keipke, and Schröder, *Bomben*, 17f.
133. *Essener National-Zeitung*, 19 February 1942: 'Auch sie starben für Deutschland'.
134. See, for example the *Essener National-Zeitung*, 18 March 1942: 'Über Gräber zum Sieg. Opfer stärken den Willen zum Sieg—Trauerfeier in Hamburg'.

135. Vermerk vom 5. Juni 1944 der Stadtverwaltung Berlin, Deputation für das Siedlungs- und Wohnungswesen, 31450, Landesarchiv Berlin, A Rep. 009/32350.

136. Speech by the OB Düsseldorf on 27 July 1943 on the occasion of the memorial service for the victims of the air raid of 12 June 1943, Stadtarchiv Düsseldorf, IV/477.

137. *Essener National-Zeitung*, 3 May 1944: 'Gefallen für uns alle!'

138. Arnold, *The Allied Air War*, 74–82.

139. *Hamburger Fremdenblatt*, 9 November 1943: 'Führer-Parole, Kampf bis zum Sieg', quoted in Thiessen, 'Gedächtnis', 61.

140. Thiessen, 'Gedächtnis', 61.

141. *Hamburger Fremdenblatt*, 22 November 1943: 'Doch nun höher die Standarten; zur Zeremonie', see Thiessen, 'Gedächtnis', 63ff.

142. See Bohl, Keipke, and Schröder, *Bomben*, 17.

143. *Niederdeutscher Beobachter*, 1 May 1942: 'Feierliche Totenehrung in der Seestadt Rostock'; Rede des Gauleiters [Hildebrandt] in den Stadthallten Schwerin, 1 May 1942, in *Mecklenburg im Zweiten Weltkrieg*, 388–405.

144. *Hamburger Fremdenblatt*, 22 November 1943: 'Gruß an die Toten. Großkundgebung auf dem Adolf-Hitler-Platz.'

145. *Darmstädter Zeitung*, 23 September 1944: 'Darmstadt nahm Abschied von den Opfern des Terrorangriffs'.

146. On the concept see also Behrenbeck, *Kult*, 507.

147. Protokoll der Beratungen der bayerischen Bischöfe in München vom 10. und 11. 3. 1942, EAM, NL Faulhaber 4070.

148. The reference to the variety of local and confessional conflicts may well be one reason why the Nazi Party and the state authorities in Hamburg managed to assert their authority over memorials with increasing success; Thiessen, 'Gedächtnis', 82.

149. Dezernat 7/R, 10 November 1943, Stadtarchiv München, Bestattungsamt, 292.

150. Franz von Weiss, entry for 14 July 1943, Schmitz (ed.), *Humanität und Diplomatie*, 205.

151. Niederschrift über die Besprechung mit den Vertretern der Bezirksverwaltung über die Einrichtung von Bestattungsämtern von 27. 2. 1945, Magistrat der Stadt Berlin/Hauptplanungsamt, Landesarchiv Berlin, A Rep. 009/28636.

152. Polizeipräsident Darmstadt to the American Military Government, 26 March 1946, quoted in Schmidt, *Bombennacht*, 162f.; 3. Polizeirevier Darmstadt, 24 September 1944: Geborgene Leichen, in Schmidt, *Bombennacht*, 154.

153. On this see the photos by Walter Hahn of 25 February 1945, in Neutzner, *Leuchten*, 234.

154. Bauer, *Würzburg*, 35f.

155. See Maciejewski, '"Trauer ohne Riten"', 250.

156. Bauer, *Würzburg*, 35f.

157. This also applied to the crimes during the last phase of the regime and the murdered concentration camp prisoners and forced workers; on this see among others Strebe, *Celle April, 1945*; Keller, '"Verbrechen"'; Grimm, 'Lynchmorde'.
158. A precise reconstruction using all the available sources in Neutzner, 'Bergung'.
159. Goebbels, *Tagebücher*, part II, vol. xiv, 2 November 1944, 139.
160. See the balanced assessment in Schnatz, 'Zerstörung', 37–41; Schnatz, 'Ermittlung von Todesopfern'.
161. Namentliches Verzeichnis der beim Terrorangriff auf Soest in der Nacht zum 6. 12. 1944 Gefallenen, Stadtarchiv Soest, Bestand D, 1757.
162. Brunswig, *Feuersturm über Hamburg*, 279f.
163. *Köln im Luftkrieg*, 91.
164. Stadt Kiel to Hans Rumpf, 21 January 1953, Bombenopfer der Kieler Bevölkerung während des Krieges 1939–1945, Stadtarchiv Kiel, 35200.
165. Figures according to *Köln im Luftkrieg*, 92.

CHAPTER 9

1. *The Times*, 8 May 1945: 'In the Heart of Captured Cologne'.
2. *The Times*, 1 October 1943: 'After the R.A.F. Raids: Damage in Berlin'; *The Times*, 24 March 1944: 'Great Damage to War Factories'.
3. *The Times*, 15 February 1945: 'Cleve to-day'.
4. *Daily Express*, 9 March 1945: 'Over Rhine in Force'; 'These are the ruins of Cologne'.
5. *Daily Mirror*, 10 March 1945: 'Dead cities of "Happy Valley"'; see Flemming, 'Haltung', 204.
6. Flemming, 'Haltung', 209.
7. *The Times*, 1 May 1945: 'Air Power Road to Victory'.
8. Thus *The Times*, for example, published its last picture of Berlin specifically referring to the air war as early as 13 July 1945 under the heading 'Devastated Berlin'. The photo itself had the caption 'New Views From the Air' and showed the bombed Reichstag and Anhalt railway station rather than residential areas.
9. May 1945: German Atrocities: reaction of Londoners to German atrocities in concentration camps from material collected in direct and indirect interviews, Mass-Observation File Reports, 2248.
10. Flemming uses this concept, borrowed from Noelle-Neumann, in the debate about wartime area bombing. See Flemming, 'Haltung', 27–34.
11. Excerpt from the interrogation of Franz von Papen by Mr Thomas J. Dodd in Nuremberg on 12 October 1945, in Overy, *Verhöre*, Doc. 21, 439.
12. Connelly, *Reaching for the Stars*, 40f.; for his recording of Bomber Command see Connelly and Goebel, 'Erinnerungspolitik', 60–5.

13. For a summary see Alter, *Winston Churchill*, 185–91.

14. Probert, *Harris*, 346ff.

15. *The Times*, 17 May 1945: 'Gallant Spirit of Bomber Command'.

16. For the following see Probert, *Harris*, 347f.

17. Connelly, *Reaching for the Stars*, 142.

18. Probert, *Harris*, 349.

19. Connelly takes a different line in 'Image of RAF Bomber Command', 6–16.

20. On the background and the precursors see, for example, USSBS, Morale Division, German Civil Defence Versus Aerial Attack. Prepared for the Morale Division, January 1945, NARA II, RG 243, entry 36, Box 167, 329; this contains a detailed discussion of models and methods and criteria for the measuring of wartime morale.

21. Penton, *Solly Zuckerman*; Zuckerman, *Apes*.

22. British Bombing Survey Unit, The Strategic Air War against Germany 1939–1945. See also the foreword by Cox, 'An Unwanted Child'.

23. Initial Interrogation of Albert Speer, 15 May 1945, in NARA II, RG 243, entry 32, Box 6, Interrogation Albert Speer, US Strategic Bombing Survey, APO 413.

24. See Speer, *Erinnerungen*, 500f.; Süss, 'Nationalsozialistische Deutungen', 107f.

25. See also Probert, *Harris*, 329.

26. Harris, *Bomber Offensive*, 211.

27. Connelly, 'The British People'.

28. Harris, *Bomber Offensive*.

29. Connelly, *Reaching for the Stars*, 143.

30. Quoted in Probert, *Harris*, 362.

31. *The Times*, 14 March 1949: 'Bomber Command Reunion'.

32. For detail see Zweiniger-Bargielowska, *Austerity in Britain*.

33. Gregory, 'Commemoration', 219.

34. Battle of Britain Day 1946 (Ceremonials), PRO, AIR 2/7002.

35. *The Times*, 27 September 1943: 'Thanksgiving in St. Paul's'.

36. *The Times*, 26 August 1943: 'Battle of Britain Sunday'; *The Times*, 13 December 1943: 'Battle of Britain. Memorial Chapel in the Abbey'.

37. Gregory, 'Commemoration', 220.

38. *The Times*, 11 July 1947: 'Battle of Britain Memorial'.

39. Battle of Britain Memorial. Memorandum of the Secretary of State for Air of 9 September 1960, in PRO, CAB 129/102.

40. Conclusion of a Meeting of the Cabinet, 15 September 1960, PRO, CAB 128/34.

41. Conclusions of a Meeting of the Cabinet, 25 April 1961, PRO, CAB 128/35.

42. Mass-Observation Bulletin PB 6, November 1944, Mass-Observation Archive; see also Hewitt, 'Sceptical Generation?', 81ff.

43. Hewitt, 'Sceptical Generation?', 89.

44. Hewitt, 'Sceptical Generation?', 83f.

45. See among others Blank, 'Die Nacht des 16./17. Mai 1943'.

46. Ramsden, 'Refocusing the People's War'.
47. Ramsden, 'Refocusing the People's War', 51.
48. Ramsden, 'Refocusing the People's War', 55.
49. Webster and Frankland, *Strategic Air Offensive*.
50. Churchill, *Second World War*, vi. 470–1.
51. Reynolds, *Command*, 481.
52. Reynolds, *Command*, 481.
53. Frankland, *History at War*, 113.
54. On the history of its reception see among others Connelly, *Reaching for the Stars*, 148ff.
55. *The Times*, 14 December 1961: 'Area Bombing Not Terror Weapon'.
56. Quoted in Frankland, *History*, 119.
57. *Sunday Telegraph*, 1 October 1961: 'Row breaks over last-war bombing: Sir Arthur Harris's retort to charge of costly failure'; *The Times*, 16 October 1961: 'Harris's statue to get royal unveiling'.
58. On this see in detail Nehring, 'Politics'.
59. This is Connelly's argument in *Reaching for the Stars*, 151.
60. *Der Spiegel*, 25 October 1961: 'Bombenkrieg: Im Namen des Herrn', 74–6.
61. Rumpf, *Bombenkrieg*.
62. Rumpf, *Bombenkrieg*, 21.
63. Dokumente über die Alleinschuld Englands am Bombenkrieg gegen die Zivilbevölkerung. Achtes Weißbuch der Deutschen Regierung, ed. by Auswärtiges Amt (Berlin, 1943).
64. See also Benda-Beckmann, 'Katastrophe', 299f.
65. *Der Spiegel*, 6 December 1950: 'Hammer gegen Reptil', 10.
66. *Dokumente deutscher Kriegsschäden*.
67. See in detail Frei, *Vergangenheitspolitik*.
68. Compare Beer, 'Spannungsfeld'.
69. *Dokumentation deutscher Kriegsschäden*, letter of 25 February 1960, BA Koblenz, B 150/5654: Fiche 5.
70. *Dokumente deutscher Kriegsschäden*, i. 68.
71. *Dokumente deutscher Kriegsschäden*, i. 68.
72. *Dokumente über die Alleinschuld Englands*.
73. See Hampe, *Luftschutz*; Schramm, *Luftschutz*.
74. On the concept see Kühne, 'Viktimisierungsfalle'.
75. See in detail Goltermann, *Gesellschaft der Überlebenden*, 165–341.
76. Quoted in 'Die Unfall-(Kriegs-)Neurose', 132.
77. Stier, *Unfallneurosen*.
78. See in detail Goltermann, 'Leid', 428–33; Goltermann, *Gesellschaft der Überlebenden*, 165–216.
79. Bonhoeffer, 'Vergleichende psychopathologische Erfahrungen', 4.
80. See in detail Rüfner, 'Ausgleich', 693–5.
81. On Panse see in detail Heyll, 'Friedrich Panse'.

82. Forsbach, *Medizinische Fakultät*, 356.
83. Panse, *Angst*, 184.
84. Panse, *Angst*, 168f.
85. Panse, *Angst*, 189.
86. See the decision of 4th Senate of the Federal Social Court of 23 October 1958, published in *Die Neurose*, 13.
87. On the conflicts see Freimüller, *Alexander Mitscherlich*, 177–205.
88. Quoted in Goltermann, *Gesellschaft der Überlebenden*, 260.
89. Freimüller, *Mitscherlich*, 195f.
90. See among others *Psychologische Rundschau*, 3 (1952), 220f.
91. See among others Ritter von Baeyer, '"Neurose"', 672f.
92. See Pross, *Wiedergutmachung*, 157; Goschler, *Schuld und Schulden*.
93. Goltermann, 'Leid', 440–51.
94. Foreword in *Dokumente deutscher Kriegsschäden*, i. IX.
95. For the following see Jones, Palmer, and Wessley, *War Pension*.
96. Jones, Palmer, and Wessley, *War Pension*, 377.
97. Guttmann and Baker, 'Neuroses in Firemen'.
98. Carey-Trefzer, 'The Results of a Clinical Study'.
99. Carey-Trefzer, 'The Results of a Clinical Study', 541.
100. Carey-Trefzer, 'The Results of a Clinical Study', 540.
101. See also Penrose, 'Neurosis'.
102. Shephard, 'Psychology', 516–20; for a contemporary overview see Stengel, 'Grossbritannien'.
103. Shephard, 'Psychology', 522, also containing references to other literature.
104. Kral, 'Psychiatric Observations'.
105. *Die 'Neurose'—Ihre versorgungs- und sozialmedizinische Beurteilung*, 5.
106. *Die 'Neurose'—Ihre versorgungs- und sozialmedizinische Beurteilung*, 10.
107. On this see above all Arnold, *The Allied Air War*, 183–219.
108. Gregor takes this line in *Haunted City*, 1–22.
109. Decision of the City Council, 26 November 1945, quoted in Seiderer, 'Würzburg', 147.
110. Seiderer, 'Würzburg', 147.
111. For this argument in relation to Nuremberg see Gregor, 'Erinnerungen'.
112. Arnold, 'Beyond Usable Pasts'.
113. Quoted in Gregor, 'Erinnerungen', 140.
114. *Die Einkehr*, 2 September 1947: 'Michaelisfest'; for the following see *Die Einkehr*, 2 September 1947.
115. *Weg und Wahrheit*, 12 November 1950: 'Kreuz über unserer Zeit'.
116. *Petrusblatt*, 28 April 1946: 'Opfertod: Bericht aus der Bischöflichen Kanzlei Mainz'; *Glaube und Leben*, 22 February 1948: 'Zerstörtes Kloster der Ewigen Anbetung Mainz'.
117. Arnold, *The Allied Air War*, 110.
118. Trippen, 'Erzbischof Frings', 152.

119. Chandler, *Brethren in Adversity*.

120. Howard, *Ruined and Rebuilt*, 87; Meyer, *Leiden und Hoffen*, 109.

121. See also Hein, *Geoffrey Fisher*, 43 ff.

122. Thiessen, *Gedächtnis*, 131.

123. *The Times*, 3 December 1948: 'Young Soldiers in Germany'.

124. *Glaube und Leben*, 4 July 1948: 'Ein Kirchweihfest des Mainzer Domes'; *Kirchenzeitung für das Erzbistum Köln*, 12 May 1946: 'Neues Leben blüht aus den Ruinen'.

125. Quoted in Trippen, *Josef Kardinal Frings*, i. 219.

126. Trippen, *Josef Kardinal Frings*, i. 215.

127. For one example among many see *Weg und Wahrheit*, 16 December 1951: 'Wiederaufbau der Marienkirche in Frankfurt/Seckenbach'.

128. Aufruf zum Wiederaufbau, 1946, Landeskirchliches Archiv Berlin-Brandenburg, Depositum: St Maien/St Nikolai; 12. Bericht zum Schreiben der Superintendantur vom 10. 6. 1946, 18. 6. 1946, Landeskirchliches Archiv Berlin-Brandenburg, Depositum: St Marien/St Nikolai, Rep. II, 19; see also Stupperich, *Otto Dibelius*, 398–406.

129. Thiessen, *Gedächtnis*, 235.

130. Thiessen, *Gedächtnis*, 237.

131. *Würzburger Katholisches Sonntagsblatt*, 20 July 1952: 'Überwältigender Höhepunkt der Kilianswoche'.

132. *The Times*, 8 March 1949: 'Air Raid Shelter As Church'.

133. Kammann, *Carl Klinkhammer*, 161–73.

134. See in detail Steinbacher, *Wie der Sex nach Deutschland kam*.

135. Klinkhammer, 'Kirche', 76.

136. *Rheinische Post*, 31 October 1949: 'Sprengt die Bunker der Seele'.

CHAPTER 10

1. Compare Thiessen, *Gedächtnis*, 238 ff.

2. Howard, *Ruined and Rebuilt*, 30 f.

3. Howard, *Ruined and Rebuilt*, 88.

4. Rennie, *Festival of Britain*.

5. For the following see Goebel, 'Coventry und Dresden', 113 ff.; see also Campbell, *Coventry Cathedral*.

6. *The Times*, 12 May 1962: 'Coventry Cathedral in Perspective'.

7. Tiratsoo, *Reconstruction*, 77 f.

8. Howard, *Ruined and Rebuilt*, 53.

9. Quoted in Howard, *Ruined and Rebuilt*, 54.

10. Meyer, *Leiden*, 115; Heuss, *Tagebuchbriefe 1955–1963*, 354–7.

11. See Kammerer, *Aktion Sühnezeichen Friedensdienste*, 83 f.; on the difficult start see Staffa, 'Aktion Sühnezeichen', 151 f.

12. Erfahrungsbericht einer Reise nach Coventry, 1955, EZA, Bestand 6, 6881; for the following see EZA, Bestand 6, 6881.

13. *The Times*, 18 January 1960: 'Dr. Dibelius on the Change in German Outlook'.

14. Bill Williamson to Lothar Kreyssig, 18 July 1960, EZA 97/464.

15. *The Times*, 4 April 1961: 'Germans to work on Coventry Ruins'.

16. Deutsche Botschaft London, 6 December 1961, EZA, Bestand 6, 6884.

17. See the correspondence in EZA, Bestand 6, 6882.

18. Gerhard Stratenwerth to Pastor Eberhard Bethge, 14 March 1956, EZA, Bestand 6, 6682.

19. *The Times*, 18 May 1962: 'New Cathedral a Spiritual Dynamo'.

20. *The Times*, 26 May 1962: 'Consecration of Coventry Cathedral'.

21. Irving, *Destruction of Dresden*.

22. In the following editions the casualty figures steadily increased in a highly dubious manner; on this see Evans, *Geschichtsfälscher*, 198–229.

23. *New Statesman*, 3 May 1963: 'War Crime'.

24. Frankland, *History*, 120ff.

25. *Der Spiegel*, 19 June 1963: 'Sodom in Sachsen'.

26. *Die Zeit*, 25 September 1964: 'Als Dresden in Trümmer sank'.

27. See Overy, 'The Post War Debate', see also in detail Goebel, 'Coventry und Dresden'; Widera, 'Erinnerung'.

28. Compare Neutzner, 'Anklagen', 134f.

29. On this see Fache, 'Gegenwartsbewältigungen', 222–4.

30. For the following see Margalit, 'Luftangriff', 194.

31. There is evidence pointing to a similar process in other GDR cities; compare, in particular, Arnold, '"Nagasaki"'.

32. Politische Richtlinien zum 10. Jahrestag des amerikanischen Terrorangriffs auf Dresden, 21 January 1955, quoted from Margalit, 'Luftangriff', 199.

33. Margalit, 'Luftangriff', 198; on the celebrations of 1955 see Neutzner, 'Anklagen', 147f.

34. *The Times*, 14 February 1950: 'Bombing of Dresden as a War Crime'; *The Times*, 14 February 1952: 'A Dresden Anniversary'.

35. Margalit, 'Luftangriff', 200.

36. Copy of a letter from David Irving to Richard Crossman, 10 May 1963, PRO, FO 371/169329 CG1851/4; on the background and correspondence see Thomas, *Communing with the Enemy*, 220f.

37. Thomas, *Communing with the Enemy*, 228f.

38. On the reasons see Thomas, *Communing with the Enemy*, 262f.

39. *The Times*, 3 November 1964: 'Coventry Appeal for Dresden'.

40. *The Times*, 15 March 1965: 'Dresden Bombing Atonement'.

41. Quoted in Thomas, *Communing with the Enemy*, 32.

42. Thomas, *Communing with the Enemy*, 260.

43. Goebel, 'Coventry und Dresden', 117ff.

44. See Giebel, 'Tod und Trauer'; see above all Rosenfeld, *Architektur*, 215–22; for the following see Rosenfeld, *Architektur*, 215–22.

45. The New Testament, Romans 11: 33.
46. Rosenfeld, *Architektur*, 220 takes a different view.
47. See also Arnold, *The Allied Air War*, 220–50.
48. For the following see Rosenfeld, *Architektur*, 216ff.
49. Dr Karl von Brentano-Hommeyer to the Münchner Stadtrat, 29 October 1965, Stadtarchiv München, Kulturamt, 1186.
50. For the following see Rosenfeld, *Architektur*, 357–64.
51. See Ziemann, 'Code of Protest'.
52. Quoted in Rosenfeld, *Architektur*, 362; Behnisch had clearly indicated his opposition to a peace monument at an early stage; see Kulturreferat der Stadt München, 16 July 1970: Notiz für Herrn Oberbürgermeister Vogel.
53. CSU-Stadtratsfraktion München an den Oberbürgermeister der Stadt vom 2. 4. 1976, Stadtarchiv München, Kulturamt, 1187.
54. Quoted in Thiessen, 'Erinnerung', 229f.
55. See Arnold, *The Allied Air War*, 285–305.
56. Brunswig, *Feuersturm über Hamburg*.
57. Dettmar, *Zerstörung Kassels*, 54; see also Arnold, *The Allied Air War*, 302–4.
58. Dettmar, *Zerstörung*, 84.
59. Schramm, *Luftschutz*.
60. Domarus, *Untergang des alten Würzburg*, 108.
61. Blank, 'Zerstört und vergessen?', 169.
62. For an example of such a project see Schwanzar, 'Visualisierung des Bombenkriegs'.
63. Compare Arnold, *The Allied Air War*, 306–8.
64. See Thiessen, *Gedächtnis*, 224f.
65. Thiessen, *Gedächtnis*, 263f.
66. Stadt Kiel (ed.), *Wiederaufbau der Innenstädte*.
67. Freiburg is an example of the professionalization of representation as well as the continuity of patterns of memorialization from destruction to reconstruction. See the exhibition catalogue *Zerstörung und Wiederaufbau*, ed. by Stadt Freiburg.
68. For the prehistory, destruction, and reconstruction of Würzburg see among others Seiderer, 'Würzburg'.
69. Oesl, 're-VISION', 9.
70. Quoted in Thiessen, *Gedächtnis*, 320.
71. On the exhibition see '"Hamburgs Weg in den Feuersturm"', in *Memo. Museum für Hamburgische Geschichte—Illustrierte Zeitgeschichte*, 1 (October 1993) (Begleitheft).
72. Richter, '"Action Gomorrha"', 64; for the following see Thiessen, *Gedächtnis*, 334ff.
73. See among others Grass, *Krebsgang*; Forte, *Der Junge*; Ledig, *Vergeltung*; Naumann, '"Leerstelle Luftkrieg"' provides an overview; for the debate on the air war and relevant literature see Vees-Gulani, *Trauma and Guilt*; Vees-Gulani, 'Phantomschmerzen'; Hage, *Zeugen der Zerstörung*.
74. On this change of tone in dealing with the Nazi past see Frei, *1945 und wir*, 21.

75. See Süss, 'Massaker und Mongolensturm'; Süss, 'Erinnerungen'; Moeller, 'Bombing of Germany'.
76. Quoted in Winter, *Öffentliche Erinnerungen*, 9.
77. *Bild-Zeitung*, 20 February 2007: 'Erster britischer Kriegsforscher gibt zu: Bomben auf deutsche Städte waren ein Kriegsverbrechen!'
78. Grayling, *Dead Cities*; for criticism see Süss, 'Memories of the Air War'.
79. See among others Fritze, *Moral des Bombenterrors*.
80. See Fache, 'Gegenwartsbewältigungen'.
81. Quoted in Fache, 'Gegenwartsbewältigungen', 230f.
82. See Thiessen, *Gedächtnis*, 371–9.
83. *Hamburger Abendblatt*, 4 May 1995: 'Weiße und rote Blumen für die Gefallenen'.
84. Deighton, *Bomber*.
85. Calder, *Battle of Britain*.
86. See among others Bowyer, *Bomber Barons*; Raymond, *Yank in Bomber Command*; Smith, *Halifax Crew*.
87. *Daily Telegraph*, 13 December 1991: 'Bomber statue plea by Mayor of Dresden'.
88. *Der Spiegel*, 30 September 1991: 'Eben die Sieger', 152f.
89. *The Independent*, 3 May 1992: 'A night in hell'; *The Independent*, 13 December 1991: 'Harris Tribute Raises a Royal Dilemma'; *The Independent on Sunday*, 5 January 1992: 'A butcher in bronze or just an old softie?'
90. *The Guardian*, 18 May 1992: 'The Firestorm Rages On'; *The Guardian*, 25 May 1992: 'Church snub cheers Harris protesters'.
91. *The Times*, 26 May 1992: 'This is the real memorial'; *The Times*, 5 October 1991: editorial on proposed statue of Sir Arthur Harris.
92. *Daily Telegraph*, 2 October 1991: editorial on proposed statue of Sir Arthur Harris.
93. Leo McKinstry, 'The Revenger's Tragedy', in *The New Statesman*, 17 December 2009.
94. *The New York Times*, 6 January 1992: 'Honor to RAF Leader Wakes Dresden's Ghost'; *The New York Times*, 1 June 1992: 'Britain Unveils Monument to Bomber Harris'.
95. *Hamburger Abendblatt*, 30 May 1992: 'Ein Denkmal reißt Wunden'.
96. *Daily Express*, 1 June 1992: 'Queen Mum is Booed'; Probert, *Harris*, 416ff.
97. *Daily Telegraph*, 13 May 2010: 'Bomber Command: Veterans Celebrate After Memorial Approval'.
98. See for example *The Guardian*, 12 July 2010: 'We have the Cenotaph'.
99. On the 70th Anniversary see among others *The Guardian*, 7 September 2010: 'The Blitz 70 Years on: Share your Stories'.
100. Calder, *War*; Calder, *Myth*; see also the contributions in Smith (ed.), *War and Social Change*.
101. See Geppert, *Thatchers konservative Revolution*, 95–144.

102. Thatcher, *Downing Street Years*, 155; see in detail Noetzel, 'Political Decadence?'
103. Smith, *Britain and 1940*, 126.
104. See Margaret Thatcher's speech in Cheltenham on 3 July 1982, in Thatcher Archive, CCOPR 486/82 <http://www.margaretthatcher.org/search/displaydocument.asp?docid=104989&doctype=1>.
105. Connelly, *We Can Take it*, 78–84.
106. See in detail Summerfield and Peniston-Bird, *Contesting Home Defence*, 170–204.
107. *Daily Mail*, 1 August 1968.
108. *New Society*, 1 April 1971: 'Looking Back in Nostalgia', 542f.
109. *New Society*, 1 April 1971, 542f.
110. *The Guardian*, 15 August 1970; Connelly, *We Can Take it*, 79f.
111. Noakes, 'Making Histories, Experiencing the Blitz'.
112. See Field, 'Nights', 47ff.

CONCLUSION

1. Compare Rowland Manthorpe, 'Spirit of the Brits', in *The Guardian*, 1 July 2006. Subsequent quotations are taken from this source.

Sources and Bibliography

This study is based on archival research in Germany, Britain, Switzerland, and the USA. At national level I made use of the holdings of the Bundesarchiv (Federal Archive) in Berlin, in particular the documents relating to a number of Reich ministries and a range of Nazi Party organizations involved in coping with the effects of the air war. In Britain I used the National Archive for access to the relevant ministerial files and the papers of the War Cabinet and the Civil Defence Cabinet.

In addition I carried out research in many regional and ecclesiastical archives. Unlike those in German towns and cities, the majority of archives in Britain suffered little war damage and hence are relatively complete. German municipal archives vary greatly in what has survived, and those in Berlin especially, though not only those, are badly affected by war damage.

I was able to conduct detailed research using the files of the War Damage Offices, Cemeteries Offices, and Burial Offices in, among other locations, Rostock, Kiel, Hamburg, Berlin, Düsseldorf, Duisburg, Cologne, Stuttgart, Munich, and Nuremberg. In addition, the United States Strategic Bombing Survey (USSBS) files in the National Archives (Washington) were very important for they contain material relating to contemporary surveys conducted on the effects of the bombing raids. This material was produced by social science experts and comprises standardized interviews and questionnaires, interviews with various experts, and the evaluation of statistical data that formed the basis of the USSBS's report. The interviews date back mainly to the early summer of 1945 and were conducted with various clerics, health and civil defence experts.

The holdings of the Mass-Observation Archive at the University of Sussex, which contains many diaries, notebooks, and contemporary surveys relating to people's experiences of the air war, were also very important.

PRIMARY SOURCES

Archives
Bundesarchiv Berlin, Berlin-Lichterfelde (BA Berlin)
NS 1 Reichsschatzmeister der NSDAP

NS 18 Reichspropagandaleiter der NSDAP
NS 19 Persönlicher Stab Reichsführer-SS
NS 22 Reichsorganisationsleiter der NSDAP
NS 25 NSDAP Hauptamt für Kommunalpolitik
NS 37 Hauptamt für Volkswohlfahrt des NSDAP/NS-Volkswohlfahrt e.V.
NS 51 Kanzlei des Führers der NSDAP (Dienstelle Bouhler)
R 2 Reichsfinanzministerium
R 3 Reichsministerium für Rüstung und Kriegsproduktion
R 36 Deutscher Gemeindetag
R 55 Reichsministerium für Volksaufklärung und Propaganda
R 1501 Reichsministerium des Innern
R 3101 Reichswirtschaftsministerium (Teil 2)

Bundesarchiv Koblenz (BA Koblenz)
B 150 Bundesministerium für Vertriebene, Flüchtlinge und Kriegsgeschädigte

Bundesarchiv-Militärarchiv (BA-MA)
RL 4 Chef des Ausbildungswesens/Chef der Fliegerausbildung mit Luftwaffenin-
spektionen und Waffengeneralen
RL 19 Luftkreis- und Luftgaukommandos, Luftgaustäbe
RL 41 Reichsluftschutzbund

Nordrheinwestfälisches Hauptstaatsarchiv Düsseldorf (HStAD)
BR 1131 Polizeipräsident Köln als örtlicher Luftschutzleiter
RW 23 NSDAP-Gauleitung Düsseldorf
RW 53 Deutscher Gemeindetag, Provinzialstelle Rheinland

Bayerisches Hauptstaatsarchiv München (HStAM)
Reichsstatthalter Epp
Staatskanzlei (StK)
Ministerium des Innern (Minn): Bd.22

Landesarchiv Berlin (LAB)
A Rep. 005 Magistrat der Stadt/Deputation für das Siedlungs- und Wohnungswesen
A Rep. 005–07 Hauptamt für Kriegsschäden

Staatsarchiv Augsburg
NSDAP-Gauleitung Schwaben

Staatsarchiv Hamburg
331–1 Polizeibehörde
325–1 Friedhofsverwaltung

Stadtarchiv Düsseldorf
Bestand IV Stadt Düsseldorf, Allgemeine Verwaltungsakten ab 1933

Stadtarchiv Duisburg
Bestand 607 Grünflächen- und Friedhofsamt
Bestand 600 Amt für Sofortmaßnahmen
Bestand 102 Hauptamt

Stadtarchiv Essen
Grünflächenamt 102/166
Rep. XIV/22

Stadtarchiv Freiburg
C 4/XI/31–8

Stadtarchiv Kiel
Amt für Wirtschaft, Stadt- und Regionalentwicklung
Tiefbauamt
Rechnungsprüfungsamt
Sekretariat des OB
Städtische Polizei
Stadtplanungsamt
32877, 34742, 32875.1, 35193, 35200, 41611, 54405, 38392, 34757, 34390, 33417, 33127

Historisches Archiv der Stadt Köln (HASK)
Bestand 517 Luftschutzpolizei
Bestand 659 Verpflegungsstelle für Fliegergeschädigte
Bestand 690 Amt für Krankenanstalten
Bestand 753 Westfriedhof
ZS Kriegschronik 1939–1944/51

Stadtarchiv München
Bayerischer Städtetag, Teil 1 und 2
Bestattungsamt
Brandbekämpfung
Branddirektion, Abgb. Nr. 74/3
Bürgermeister und Rat der Stadt München
Krankenhaus Schwabing
Kulturamt (post-1945 documents)
Luftschutzakten des Polizeipräsidenten
Stadtverteidigung

Stadtarchiv Nürnberg
Kriegsschädenamt C 52 and C52/I

Stadtarchiv Oberhausen
Tiefbauamt

Stadtarchiv Rostock
1.1.8–710 Brandschutz
1.1.3.30–282 Kriegsschäden

Stadtarchiv Soest
Bestand D Akten der Stadtverwaltung Soest, 1933–1950

Stadtarchiv Stuttgart
Bestand 105 Wohnungs- und Siedlungsamt
Bestand 218 Luftschutz
Bestand 246 Bürgermeisteramt
Bestand 837 Bestand Sozialamt

Institut für Zeitgeschichte München-Berlin (IfZ-Archiv)
D 323 NL Beltzig, ED 323/1
Fa 85 Reichsjustizministerium: Lageberichte der Generalstaatsanwaltschaft
MA 136/1 Gau Hessen-Nassau
MA 136/2 Gauleiter Wagner, Stabsamt
MA 290 Persönlicher Stab Reichsführer-SS, Schriftgutverwaltung
MA 314 Persönlicher Stab Reichsführer-SS, Schriftgutverwaltung
MA 414 KZ Natzweiler
MA 430 Reichsjustizministerium: Berichte des Oberreichsanwalts, OLG-Präsidenten
    und Generalstaatsanwälte, 1940–1945
MA 470 Varia
MA 667 Reichsring für Volksaufklärung und Propaganda, Handakten
MA 1566 United States Strategic Bombing Survey

Archiv der Armen Schulschwestern in München
Bestand Drittes Reich

Archiv der Erzbistümer München und Freising (AEM)
NL Faulhaber
Kriegs- und Einmarschberichte
Seelsorgsberichte

Archiv der Evangelischen Kirche im Rheinland, Düsseldorf (EKiR)
7 NL 120 NL Johannes Mehrhoff

Erzbischöfliches Archiv Freiburg (EAF)
B 2 Generalia Erzbischöfliches Ordinariat Freiburg

Landeskirchliches Archiv Berlin-Brandenburg
Depositum: St. Marien/St. Nikolai, Rep. II, 19

Landesarchiv der Evangelisch-Lutherischen Kirche in Bayern (LAELKB)
Bayerisches Dekanat Augsburg

Landeskirchliches Archiv Stuttgart
D-1 Nachlass Landesbischof Wurm

Evangelisches Zentralarchiv (EZA), Berlin
Bestand 6 Kirchliches Außenamt der EKD

Historisches Archiv des Erzbistums Köln (AEK)
Cabinetts-Registratur CR II
25.20a
25.20a,3
25.20b,1
25.20b,2
25.16,1
25.20a,2
25.18.1
25.18,3
2.18d.1
2.18g.1
1.14,1

Bistumsarchiv Münster
A 101–16

The National Archives of the UK: Public Record Office (PRO)
Records of the Cabinet Office:
    CAB 21 Cabinet Office and predecessors: Registered Files
    CAB 65 War Cabinet Minutes
    CAB 73 War Cabinet Committee in Civil Defence
    CAB 125 War Cabinet and Cabinet: Radio Board and successors: Minutes and Papers
    CAB 128 Cabinet: Minutes (CM and CC Series)
Records of the Prime Minister's Office:
    PREM 3 Prime Minister's Office, Operational Papers
    PREM 4 Prime Minister's Office: confidential correspondence and papers
Home Office:
    HO 45 Home Office papers
Ministry of Health:
    HLG 7 Ministry of Health, Special Wartime Functions
    HLG 71 Ministry of Health, Planning Division
    MH 10 Circulars
    MH 79 Ministry of Health: Confidential Registered Files
    MH 101 Ministry of Health: War Diaries, Second World War
Ministry of Information:
    RG 23 Social Survey Reports and Papers
    INF 1
    INF 2
    INF 3

Ministry of Home Security:
   HO 186 Air Raid Precautions
   HO 199 Intelligence Branch
   HO 202 Home Security War Room Daily Reports
   HO 204 Regional Circulars
   HO 205 Ministry of Home Security: 'O' Division: Correspondence and Papers
   HO 207 Regional Commissionars' Registered Files
   HO 208 Air Raid Precaution and Home Security Files
   IR 34 War Damage Commission: Policy Files
MEPO Records of the Metropolitan Police Office
ADM Records of the Admiralty, Naval Forces, Royal Marines, Coastguard,
   and related bodies
AIR2 Air Ministry and Ministry of Defence: Registered Files
FO 371 Foreign Office: Political Departments: General Correspondence

Coventry History Centre (CHC)
CD/1/78
CD/1/80
CD/1/82/
CD/1/83
CA/CD/1/85
CD/1/86
CD/1/102
CD/1/4
CD/1/29
CEM/1/18/1–3
CEM/1/19/10–13
PA501
PA1945
PA408

Bristol Record Office
Air Raid Precaution Committee Minute Book 1939–1942 (M-B-CC-ARP-2
   und 3)
Air Raid Precaution Committee Minutes, 1942–1943 (M-BCC-ARP-4)
Air Raid Precaution Committee 1943–45 (M-BCC-ARP-5)
M-BBC-DEF-2
Town Mayor
P. Avon/PCC/1/b
P. Avon/PCC/1/c
P./CC/PM1/e–g
P. Hen/PCC/3/1
P. StA/PCC/2
P. StC/PCC/1/b
33779 (14)

33779 (5)
33779 (4)
35210/20–1
33779 (13)
33722/9
40519/1 (b)–n

University of Exeter, Library, Edmund Collection
Devon Record Archive, Exeter
Town Clerk Papers:
  482Add15/PZ22
  2359Dadd12
  4085E/98–9
  2178Add2/PM
  2954Add3/PF18
  1939Z/Z4
  2606&adds/3/21
  3741B/F1495
  5200Cadd6/211/6
  1238A/PX94
  3248A/16/13
  1069/PB33–6
  872addA/PB76
  3741B/F885
  70/12
  2513Z/Z17
  5949/Z Z1
  3279Z/Z1-2
  4403 0/Z1-9
  2518A/PW 5
  1179B/WT 53
  4421A/PZ 2
  3248A16/7

Liverpool Record Office
296 ALL/5/2 General correspondence
296 CEN/5 Papers relating to the war damage claim
385 OVE/5/7 Correspondence concerning war damage
720/KIR/170 War damage: correspondence and papers
720/KIR/171 War Damage
M 285: PRE/1/3 Minutes of War Damage Committee
352/BUI/7 Air Raid Precaution reports: 1939–1941
352 MIN/DEF Civil Defence Emergency Committee 1939–1947
M610 MED/2/3/8 War Emergency Committee

352/MD39 City of Liverpool Deaths due to War Operations Register
Council Minute Books
Health Committee

Manchester City Archive
M 77 minutes, correspondence, Manchester Information Committee,
    Public Opinion reports, Newspaper Cuttings: Manchester Blitz

Plymouth and West Devon Record Office
1522 Plymouth Air Raid Precaution
1561 Plymouth Civil Defence Records
1555 Plymouth Blitz
1583 Plymouth Civil Defence
1645 Plymouth City Treasurer
1714 Plymouth, Second World War, Air-raid Casualties
G169 Plymouth Blitz Correspondence
Plymouth Council Committee Minutes
Lord Mayor Files:
    2715/24
    673/27/CC/0
    1658/6

Southampton Archive Office
Town Clerk File
Town Clerk's Miscellaneous boxes
Box 27/8
D/Z/173/4
D/Z 205/2/9
D/Z 291/1
D/Z 551
D/Z 893/1
D/Z 955
D/Z 1058
D/Z/
D/Mat 9/7
D/NC folder 10, 30, 31
SC/BA 1/1
SC/BA 1/2
SC BA 1/48-49
SC/BA/Acc 4109, Box 1–2, 10–12
SC/BA/ARP, Box 12/8/1–4
SC/CD/1
SC/CD 5/1
SC/CD 5/4
SC/EN 2/1–3

SC/EN 4/25/7
SC/H 1/60–6

University of East Anglia Library (UEA)
Solly Zuckerman Archive, World War II Papers (SZ)

Lambeth Palace Library
Bell Papers
Fisher Papers
Lang Papers
Temple Papers

Mass Observation Archive, University of Sussex Library, Brighton
Topic Collection
File Reports 1937–72

Ökumenischer Rat der Kirchen, Genf
Box 301.010 The world council of churches: In process of formation

Archivio Storico del Ministero degli Affari Esteri, Rom (ASMAE)
Serie Affari Politici, Germania 1931–1945, b. 75, fasc. 3.

National Archives and Records Administration, College Park, Maryland (NARA II)
RG 242 National Archives Collection of Foreign Records Seized
RG 243 Records of the United States Strategic Bombing Survey (USSBS)

PRINTED PRIMARY SOURCES

Auswärtiges Amt (ed.), *Dokumente zur Alleinschuld Englands am Bombenkrieg gegen die Zivilbevölkerung. Achtes Weißbuch der Deutschen Regierung* (Berlin, 1943).
Boberach, Heinz (ed.), *Dokumente zur Beeinflussung der deutschen Rechtsprechung 1942–1944* (Boppard am Rhein, 1975).
Boberach, Heinz (ed.), *Meldungen aus dem Reich. Die geheimen Lageberichte des Sicherheitsdienstes der SS 1938–1945*, vols 1–17 (Herrsching, 1984).
Boelcke, Willi A. (ed.), *Kriegspropaganda 1939–1941. Geheime Ministerkonferenzen im Reichspropagandaministerium* (Stuttgart, 1966).
Boelcke, Willi A. (ed.), *'Wollt Ihr den totalen Krieg?' Die geheimen Goebbels-Konferenzen 1939–1943* (Stuttgart, 1967).
Bolle, Miriam, *'Ich weiß, dieser Brief wird Dich nicht erreichen'. Tagebucheinträge aus Amsterdam, Westerbork und Bergen-Belsen* (Berlin, 2006).
Calder, Angus, and Sheridan, Dorothy (eds), *Speak for Yourself: A Mass-Observation Anthology, 1937–49* (London, 1984).
Die Hamburger Katastrophe vom Sommer 1943 in Augenzeugenberichten, ed. Renate Hauschild-Thiessen (Hamburg, 1993).
Die Wehrmachtberichte 1939–1945, Unveränderter photomechanischer Nachdruck (Munich, 1985).

Dokumente deutscher Kriegsschäden. Evakuierte, Kriegssachgeschädigte, Währungsgeschädigte. Die geschichtliche und rechtliche Entwicklung, 5 vols, ed. Bundesminister für Vertriebene, Flüchtlinge und Kriegssachgeschädigte (Bonn, 1958ff.).

Domarus, Max (ed.), *Hitler. Reden und Proklamationen. 1932–1945. Kommentiert von einem Zeitgenossen,* 2 vols (Wiesbaden, 1973).

Evangelischer Bund (ed.), *Zerstörte Kirchen—Lebende Gemeinde. Tatsachen und Zeugnisse zum Luftkrieg* (Berlin, 1944).

Felder, Jakob H., *Durchwachte Nächte. Tagebücher 1939–1944,* ed. Gerhard Felder (Frankfurt am Main, 1994).

Freborg, Arvid, *Behind the Steel Wall* (London, 1944).

Fröhlich, Elke (ed.), *Die Tagebücher von Joseph Goebbels,* part I: *Aufzeichnungen 1923–1941,* part II: *Diktate 1941–1945* (Munich, 1993–2006).

5 Jahre Reichsluftschutzbund. Herausgegeben vom Präsidium des Reichsluftschutzbundes (Berlin, 1938).

Goebbels, Joseph, *Das eherne Herz. Reden und Aufsätze aus den Jahren 1941/42* (Munich, 1943).

Goebbels, Joseph, *Der steile Aufstieg* (Munich, 1944).

Hage, Volker (ed.), *Hamburg 1943. Literarische Zeugnisse zum Bombenkrieg* (Frankfurt am Main, 2003).

Hampe, Erich, *Der zivile Luftschutz im Zweiten Weltkrieg. Dokumentation und Erfahrungsberichte über Aufbau und Einsatz* (Frankfurt am Main, 1963).

Heiber, Helmut, and Longerich, Peter (eds), *Akten der Partei-Kanzlei der NSDAP. Rekonstruktion eines verlorengegangenen Bestandes,* Mircofiche-Edition (Munich, 1983–92).

Heuss, Theodor, *Tagebuchbriefe 1955–1963. Eine Auswahl aus Briefen an Toni Stolper,* ed. Eberhard Pikart (Tübingen, 1970).

Hitlers Lagebesprechungen: die Protokollfragmente seiner militärischen Konferenzen, 1942–1945, ed. Helmut Heiber (Stuttgart, 1962).

Hitlers politisches Testament. Die Bormann-Diktate vom Februar und April 1945 (Hamburg, 1981).

House of Commons Debates, 5th series [Hansard].

Irving, David, *Und Deutschlands Städte starben nicht. Ein Dokumentarbericht* (Zurich, 1963).

Kardorff, Ursula von, *Berliner Aufzeichnungen 1942–1945. Unter Verwendung der Original-Tagebücher,* new edition and commentary by Peter Hartl (Munich, 1992).

Kirchner, Klaus (ed.), *Flugblattpropaganda im 2. Weltkrieg,* vols i–xv (Erlangen, 1974–96).

Klaube, Frank-Roland (ed.), *Überlebensberichte. Der 22. Oktober 1943 in Protokollen der Vermisstensuchstelle des Oberbürgermeisters der Stadt Kassel* (Marburg, 1994).

Klemperer, Victor, *Ich will Zeugnis ablegen bis zum letzten. Tagebücher 1933–1945* (Berlin, 1998).

Klemperer, Victor, *LTI. Notizbuch eines Philologen* (Stuttgart, 2007).

Knipfer, Kurt, and Hampe, Erich (eds), *Der zivile Luftschutz. Ein Sammelwerk über alle Fragen des Luftschutzes* (Berlin, 1937).

Köhn, Gerhard (ed.), *Bomben auf Soest. Tagebücher, Berichte, Dokumente und Fotos zur Erinnerung an die Bombardierungen und das Kriegsende vor 50 Jahren* (Soest, 1994).

Köln im Luftkrieg. Statistische Mitteilungen der Stadt Köln, ed. Statistisches Amt der Stadt Köln (Cologne, 1954).

Last, Nella, *Nella Last's War: The Second World War Diaries of 'Housewife, 49'*, ed. Richard Broad and Suzie Fleming (London, 2006).

Lewis, Aubrey, 'Incidence of Neurosis in England under War Conditions', *The Lancet*, 2 (1942), 175–83.

Lubrich, Oliver (ed.), *Berichte aus der Abwurfzone. Ausländer erleben den Bombenkrieg in Deutschland 1939 bis 1945* (Berlin, 2007).

Mass-Observation, *The Tube Dwellers: The Saturday Book 3* (London, 1943).

Mecklenburg im Zweiten Weltkrieg. Die Tagungen des Gauleiters Friedrich Hildebrandt mit den NS-Führungsgremien des Gaues Mecklenburg 1939–1945. Eine Edition der Sitzungsprotokolle, with an introduction and commentary by Michael Buddrus and with the assistance of Sigrid Fritzlar and Karsten Schröder (Bremen, 2009).

Michelberger, Hans, *Berichte aus der Justiz des Dritten Reiches: Die Lageberichte der Oberlandesgerichtspräsidenten von 1940–1945 unter vergleichender Heranziehung der Lageberichte der Generalstaatsanwälte* (Pfaffenweiler, 1989).

Millgate, Helen D. (ed.), *Mr Brown's War: A Diary of the Second World War* (Stroud, 1998).

Moll, Martin (ed.), *'Führer-Erlasse' 1939–1945. Edition sämtlicher überlieferter, nicht im Reichsgesetzblatt abgedruckter, von Hitler während des Zweiten Weltkrieges schriftlich erteilter Direktiven aus den Bereichen Staat, Partei, Wirtschaft, Besatzungspolitik und Militärverwaltung* (Stuttgart, 1997).

Nicolson, Harold, *Diaries and Letters 1930–1964*, ed. Stanley Olson (London, 1980).

Noakes, Jeremy, and Pridham, Geoffrey (eds), *Nazism 1919–1945: A Documentary Reader*, 4 vols (Exeter, 1983–98).

Nossack, Hans Erich, *Die Tagebücher 1943–1977* (Frankfurt am Main, 1997).

Pätzold, Kurt, *Verfolgung, Vertreibung, Vernichtung. Dokumente des faschistischen Antisemitismus 1933–1942* (Frankfurt am Main, 1984).

Pfister, Peter (ed.), *Das Ende des Zweiten Weltkrieges im Erzbistum München und Freising*, part I and part II (Regensburg, 2005).

Regierungspräsident Arnsberg (ed.), *Luftschutztagesmeldungen 1943 bis 1945* (Arnsberg, 1986).

Rhodes, James Robert (ed.), *W. S. Churchill, Complete Speeches, 1897–1963* (New York, 1974).

Richterbriefe. Dokumente zur Beeinflussung der deutschen Rechtsprechung 1942–1944, ed. Heinz Boberach (Cologne, 1975).

Rüther, Martin (ed.), *Köln, 31. Mai 1942: Der 1000-Bomber-Angriff*, ed. NS-Dokumentationszentrum der Stadt Köln together with the Verein EL-DE-Haus (Cologne, 1992).

Rüther, Martin, *Köln im Zweiten Weltkrieg. Alltag und Erfahrungen zwischen 1939 und 1945. Darstellungen, Bilder, Quellen* (Cologne, 2005).

Schmidt, Klaus (ed.), *Die Brandnacht. Dokumente von der Zerstörung Darmstadts am 11. September 1944* (Darmstadt, 1964).
Schmitz, Markus (ed.), *Humanität und Diplomatie. Die Schweiz in Köln 1940–1949* (Münster, 2001).
Schwarz, Otto, *Strafgesetzbuch. Nebengesetze, Verordnungen und Kriegsstrafrecht* (Munich/Berlin, 1942).
Sollbach, Gerhard E. (ed.), *Aus schwerer Zeit. Das Tagebuch des Hagener Bürgers Bernhard Petersen 1943–1949* (Hagen, 1986).
Sozialdemokratische Partei Deutschlands (ed.), *Deutschland-Berichte der Sozialdemokratischen Partei Deutschlands (Sopade) 1934–1945*, 7 vols (Salzhausen, 1980).
Stasiewski, Bernhard, and Volk, Ludwig (eds), *Akten deutscher Bischöfe über die Lage der Kirche 1933–1945*, 6 vols (Mainz, 1968–85).
Überlebensberichte. Der 22. Oktober in Protokollen der Vermißtensuchstelle des Oberbürgermeisters der Stadt Kassel, ed. Magistrat der Stadt Kassel (Kassel, 1993).
The United States Strategic Bombing Survey: A Collection of the 31 Most Important Reports Printed in 10 Volumes (New York/London, 1976).
Vogt, Helmut, *Bonn im Bombenkrieg. Zeitgenössische Aufzeichnungen und Erinnerungsberichte von Augenzeugen* (Bonn, 1989).
Völker, Karl Heinz, *Dokumente und Dokumentarphotos zur Geschichte der deutschen Luftwaffe. Aus den Geheimakten des Reichswehrministeriums 1919–1933 und des Reichsluftfahrministeriums 1933–1939* (Stuttgart, 1968).
Wette, Wolfram, Bremer, Ricarda, and Vogel, Detlef (eds), *Das letzte halbe Jahr. Stimmungsberichte der Wehrmachtspropaganda 1944–1945* (Essen, 2001).
Zur Lage der Kirche. Die Wochenbriefe von Landesbischof D. August Marahrens, 1934–1947, 3 vols, ed. Thomas Jan Kück (Göttingen, 2009).

Newspapers and Journals
American Journal of Psychiatry
Belfast News Letter
Birmingham Gazette
British Journal of Psychiatry
British Medical Journal
British Movietone News
Catholic Herald
Church Times
Daily Dispatch
Daily Express
Daily Herald
Daily Mail
Daily Mirror
Daily Telegraph
Daily Worker
Darmstädter Zeitung
Das Reich

Der Angriff
Der Nervenarzt
Der Öffentliche Gesundheitsdienst
Der Spiegel
Deutsche Allgemeine Zeitung
Deutsches Nachrichten Büro
Deutsche Verwaltung
Die Sirene
Die Zeit
Einkehr
epd-medien
Farmers Weekly
Glasgow Herald
Glaube und Leben
Gloucester Diocesan Magazine
Hamburger Abendblatt
Hamburger Anzeiger
Hamburger Fremdenblatt
Hampshire Adviser
Horizon
Journal of Abnormal and Social Psychology
Journal of Mental Science
Kirchenzeitung für das Erzbistum Köln
Life Magazine
Liverpool Daily Post
Liverpool Echo
Liverpool Express
Luftschutz und Schule
Manchester Guardian
Münchner Medizinische Wochenschrift
Municipal Review National Zeitung (Essen)
Newcastle Journal
New Society
New Statesman
New York Times
Niederdeutscher Beobachter
Oxford Diocesan Magazine
Parish Magazine S. Simon (Plymouth)
Petrusblatt
Picture Post
Rheinische Post
St. Michael's Church, Stoke, Parish Magazine (Plymouth)
Southern Daily Echo
Süddeutsche Zeitung

Sunday Chronicle
Sunday Telegraph
Svenska Dagblatt
Swiss Cottager
The Independent
The Lancet
The Scotsman
The Spectator
The Tablet
The Times
Völkischer Beobachter (Münchner Ausgabe)
Völkischer Beobachter (Norddeutsche Ausgabe)
Warnemünder Zeitung
Weg und Wahrheit
Westfälischer Beobachter / Gladbecker Anzeiger
Würzburger Katholisches Sonntagsblatt

Secondary Literature

Abercrombie, Patrick, and Watson, Peter, *A Plan for Plymouth: The Report Prepared for the City Council* (Plymouth, 1943).

Addison, Paul, *The Road to 1945: British Politics and the Second World War* (London, 1975).

Addison, Paul, *Churchill on the Home Front, 1900–1955* (London, 1993).

Addison, Paul, 'Churchill and the Price of Victory: 1939–1945', in Tiratsoo (ed.), *From Blitz to Blair*, 53–76.

Addison, Paul, 'National Identity and the Battle of Britain', in Korte and Schneider (eds), *War and the Cultural Construction of Identities*, 225–40.

Addison, Paul, and Calder, Angus (eds), *Time to Kill: The Soldier's Experience of War in the West, 1939–1945* (London, 1997).

Addison, Paul, and Crang, Jeremy A. (eds), *The Burning Blue: A New History of the Battle of Britain* (London, 2000).

Addison, Paul, and Crang, Jeremy A. (eds), *Firestorm: The Bombing of Dresden 1945* (London, 2006).

Aden, Menno, *Hildesheim lebt. Zerstörung und Wiederaufbau. Eine Chronik* (Hildesheim, 1994).

Aders, Gebhard, 'Der Luftangriff auf Bonn am 18. Oktober 1944. Der Versuch einer Rekonstruktion nach englischen Quellen', in Vogt (ed.), *Bonn im Bombenkrieg*, 50–72.

Albrich, Thomas, and Gisinger, Arno, *Tirol und Vorarlberg 1943–1945* (Innsbruck, 1992).

Alderman, Geoffrey, *London Jewry and London Politics, 1889–1986* (London, 1989).

Aldgate, Anthony, and Richards, Jeffrey, *Britain Can Take It: The British Cinema in the Second World War* (Edinburgh, 2007).

Aldgate, Anthony, and Richards, Jeffrey, 'England, their England: Fires Were Started', in Aldgate and Richards, *Britain Can Take It*, 218–45.

Alexander, Axel, *Die Schlacht über Berlin* (Berlin, 1933).

Alter, Peter, *Winston Churchill (1874–1965). Leben und Überleben* (Stuttgart, 2006).

Alte Synagoge Essen (ed.), *Essen unter Bomben. Märztage 1943* (Essen, 1984).

Aly, Götz, *Hitlers Volksstaat. Raub, Rassenkrieg und nationaler Sozialismus* (Frankfurt am Main, 2005).

Aly, Götz (ed.), *Volkes Stimme. Skepsis und Führervertrauen im Nationalsozialismus* (Frankfurt am Main, 2006).

Aly, Götz, 'Historische Demoskopie', in Aly, *Stimme*, 9–21.

Andrews, Julian, *London's War: The Shelter Drawings of Henry Moore* (London, 2002).

Angerer, Henning, *Flakbunker. Betonierte Geschichte* (Hamburg, 2000).

Angermund, Ralph, *Deutsche Richterschaft 1919–1945. Krisenerfahrung, Illusion, politische Rechtsprechung* (Frankfurt am Main, 1990).

Anschütz, Gerhard, *Die Arbeit der Sondergerichte in der Kriegszeit. Abgekürzter Bericht über die Tagung der Sondergerichtsvorsitzenden und Sachbearbeiter für Sondergerichtsstrafsachen bei den Generalstaatsanwälten im Reichsjustizministerium am 24. Oktober 1939* (Berlin, 1939).

Argyris, Chris, and Schön, Donald A., *Die lernende Organisation* (Stuttgart, 2002).

Arnhold, Hermann (ed.), *1945—Im Blick der Fotografie. Kriegsende und Neuanfang* (Münster, 2005).

Arnold, Dietmar, and Janick, Reiner, *Sirenen und gepackte Koffer: Bunkeralltag in Berlin* (Berlin, 2003).

Arnold, Jörg, *The Allied Air War and Urban Memory: The Legacy of Strategic Bombing in Germany* (Cambridge, 2011).

Arnold, Jörg, '"Krieg kann nur der Wahnsinn der Menschheit sein!" Zur Deutungsgeschichte des Luftangriffs vom 22. Oktober 1943 in Kassel', in Süss (ed.), *Deutschland*, 135–49.

Arnold, Jörg, 'Beyond Usable Pasts: Rethinking the Memorialisation of the Strategic Air War in Germany, 1945 to 1965', in Niven and Paver (eds), *Memorialisation*, 26–36.

Arnold, Jörg, '"Nagasaki" in der DDR. Magdeburg und das Gedenken an den 16. Januar 1945', in Arnold, Süss, and Thiessen (eds), *Luftkrieg*, 239–55.

Arnold, Jörg, 'Bombenkrieg und Kriegsmoral. Die Auswirkungen der alliierten Luftoffensive auf die Stimmung und Haltung der deutschen Zivilbevölkerung im Spiegel vertraulicher Berichte und privater Aufzeichnungen' (Heidelberg, 2001) (Magisterarbeit).

Arnold, Jörg, Süss, Dietmar, and Thiessen, Malte (eds), *Luftkrieg, Erinnerungen in Deutschland und Europa* (Göttingen, 2009).

Assmann, Jan, 'Die Lebenden und die Toten', in Assmann, Maciejewski, and Michaels (eds), *Der Abschied von den Toten. Trauerrituale im Kulturvergleich* (Göttingen, 2005), 16–36.

Baeyer, Walter Ritter von, 'Neurose, Psychotherapie und Gesetzgebung', in Frankl, Freiherr von Gebsattel, and Schulz, *Handbuch der Neurosenlehre und Psychotherapie*, 627–90.

Bajohr, Frank, 'Gauleiter in Hamburg. Zur Person und Tätigkeit Karl Kaufmanns', *VfZ* 43 (1995), 267–95.

Bajohr, Frank, 'Hamburgs "Führer": Zur Person und Tätigkeit des Hamburger NSDAP Gauleiters Karl Kaufmann (1900–1969)', in Bajohr and Szodrzynski (eds), *Hamburg in der NS-Zeit* (Hamburg, 1995), 59–91.

Bajohr, Frank, *'Arisierung' in Hamburg. Die Verdrängung der jüdischen Unternehmer 1933–1945* (Hamburg, 1997).

Bajohr, Frank, 'Hamburg—Der Zerfall einer "Volksgemeinschaft"', in Herbert and Schildt (ed.), *Kriegsende*, 318–36.

Bajohr, Frank, *Parvenüs und Profiteure. Korruption in der NS-Zeit* (Frankfurt am Main, 2001).

Bajohr, Frank, 'Die Deportation der Juden: Initiativen und Reaktionen aus Hamburg', in Beate Meyer (ed.), *Die Verfolgung und Ermordung der Hamburger Juden 1933–1945* (Göttingen, 2006), 33–41.

Balfour, Michael, *Propaganda in War 1939–1945: Organisations, Policies and Publics in Britain and Germany* (London, 1979).

Banny, Leopold, *'Dröhnender Himmel—brennendes Land'. Der Einsatz der Luftwaffenhelfer in Österreich 1943–1945* (Vienna, 1988).

Bardua, Heinz, *Stuttgart im Luftkrieg 1939–1945: Mit Dokumentaranhang* (Stuttgart, 1985).

Barry, Frank R., *Mervyn Haigh* (London, 1964).

Barton, Brian, *The Blitz: Belfast in the War Years* (Belfast, 1989).

Bauer, Fritz, *Würzburg im Feuerofen. Tagebuchaufzeichnungen und Erinnerungen an die Zerstörung Würzburgs* (Würzburg, 1985).

Bauer, Richard, *Fliegeralarm. Luftangriffe auf München 1940–1945* (Munich, 1987).

Baumann, Timo, 'Die Entgrenzung taktischer Szenarien. Der Krieg der Zukunft in britischen Militärzeitschriften', in Förster (ed.), *Totaler Krieg*, 179–266.

Baumann, Timo, and Segesser, Daniel, 'Shadows of Total War in French and British Military Journals', in Chickering and Förster (eds), *Shadows*, 197–222.

Baumeister, Werner, *Castrop-Rauxel im Zweiten Weltkrieg 1939–1945* (Castrop-Rauxel, 1988).

Beardmore, George, *Civilians at War: Journals 1938–1946* (Oxford, 1986).

Beaumont, Roger, 'The Bomber Offensive as a Second Front', *Journal of Contemporary History*, 22 (1987), 3–19.

Beaven, Brad, and Griffiths, John, 'The Blitz, Civilian Morale and the City: Mass Observation and Working-Class Culture in Britain, 1940–1941', *Urban History*, 26 (1996), 71–88.

Beaven, Brad, and Griffiths, John, *Mass-Observation and Civilian Morale: Working-Class Communities during the Blitz* (Brighton, 1998).

Beck, Earl R., *Under the Bombs: The German Home Front 1942–1945* (Lexington, Mass., 1986).

Becker, Franziska, *Gewalt und Gedächtnis. Erinnerungen und die nationalsozialistische Verfolgung einer jüdischen Landgemeinde* (Göttingen, 1994).

Becker, Jochen, and Zabel, Hermann (eds), *Hagen unterm Hakenkreuz* (Hagen, 1995).

Beer, Mathias, 'Im Spannungsfeld von Politik und Zeitgeschichte. Das Großforsch- ungsprojekt Dokumentation der Vertreibung der Deutschen aus Ost- Mitteleuropa', *VfZ* 46 (1998), 345–89.

Beer, Siegfried, and Karner, Stefan, *Der Krieg aus der Luft: Kärnten und Steiermark 1941–1945* (Graz, 1992).

Beer, Wilfried, *Kriegsalltag an der Heimatfront. Alliierter Luftkrieg und deutsche Gegen- maßnahmen zur Abwehr und Schadensbegrenzung, dargestellt für den Raum Münster* (Bremen, 1990).

Beevor, Anthony, *Berlin 1945. Das Ende* (Munich, 2002).

Behrenbeck, Sabine, *Der Kult um die toten Helden. Nationalsozialistische Mythen, Riten und Symbole 1923 bis 1945* (Vierow bei Greifswald, 1996).

Behrends, Jan C., 'Soll und Haben. Freundschaftsdiskurs und Vertrauensressourcen in der staatssozialistischen Diktatur', in Frevert (ed.), *Vertrauen*, 338–66.

Bell, George, 'The Function of the Church in Wartime', in Bell, *The Church and Humanity*, 22–31.

Bell, George K. A., *The Church and Humanity, 1939–1946* (London, 1946).

Bell, Helen Amy (ed.), *London was Ours: Diaries and Memoirs of the London Blitz* (London/New York, 2008).

Benda-Beckmann, Bas van, 'De "imperialistische Luftkrieg" en de Koude Oorlog. DDR-historici over de Geallieerde bombardementen op Duitse steden', in Patrick Dassen, Ton Nijhuis, and Krijn Thijs (eds), *Duitsers als slachtoffers. Het einde van een taboe?* (Amsterdam, 2007), 389–430.

Benda-Beckmann, Bas van, 'Eine deutsch–deutsche Katastrophe? Deutungsmuster des Bombenkriegs in der ost- und westdeutschen Geschichtswissenschaft', in Arnold, Süss, and Thiessen (eds), *Luftkrieg*, 297–311.

Bergander, Götz, *Kalkül und Routine. Dresdens Rolle in der britisch-amerikanischen Luftkriegsplanung* (Dresden, 1995).

Bergander, Götz, *Dresden im Luftkrieg* (Würzburg, 1998) [1st edition 1977].

Bergander, Götz, 'Vom Gerücht zur Legende. Der Luftkrieg über Deutschland im Spiegel von Tatsachen, erlebter Geschichte, Erinnerung, Erinnerungsverzerrung', in Thomas Stamm-Kuhlmann, Jürgen Elvert, Birgit Aschmann, and Jens Hohensee (eds), *Geschichtsbilder. Festschrift für Michael Salewski zum 65. Geburtstag* (Stuttgart, 2003), 591–616.

Berger, Georg, *Die beratenden Psychiater des deutschen Heeres 1939 bis 1945* (Frankfurt am Main, 1998).

Berridge, Virginia, *Health and Society in Britain since 1939* (Cambridge, 1999).

Besier, Gerhard, '"Intimately Associated for Many Years": George Bell's and Willem A. Visser't Hooft's Common Life-Work in the Service of the Church Universal', *Kirchliche Zeitgeschichte*, 21 (2008), 246–76.

Bessel, Richard, *Nazism at War* (New York, 2004).

Bessel, Richard, and Schumann, Dirk (eds), *Life after Death: Approaches to a Cultural and Social History of Europe During the 1940s and 1950s* (Cambridge, 2003).

Bessel, Richard, and Schumann, Dirk, 'Introduction: Violence, Normality, and the Construction of Postwar Europe', in Bessel and Schumann (eds), *Life after Death*, 1–13.

Bethge, Eberhard, and Jasper, Ronald (eds), *An der Schwelle zum gespaltenen Europa* (Stuttgart/Berlin, 1974).

Beveridge, Lord William, *Power and Influence: An Autobiography* (London, 1953).

Bevin, Ernst, *The Job to Be Done* (London, 1942).

Bialer, Urs, *The Shadow of the Bomber: The Fear of Air Attack and British Politics 1932–1939* (London, 1980).

Biddle, Tami Davis, 'Wartime Reactions', in Addison and Crang (eds), *Firestorm*, 96–122.

Biddle, Tami Davis, *Rhetoric and Reality in Air Warfare: The Evolution of British and American Ideas about Strategic Bombing: 1914–1945* (Princeton, 2002).

Black, Monica A., 'Reburying and Rebuilding: Reflecting on Proper Burial in Berlin after "Zero Null"', in Confino, Betts, and Schumann (eds), *Mass Death*, 69–90.

Blank, Ralf, 'Ersatzbeschaffung durch "Beutemachen". Die "M-Aktionen"—ein Beispiel nationalsozialistischer Ausplünderungspolitik', in Alfons Kenkmann and Bernd-A. Rusinek (eds), *Verfolgung und Verwaltung. Die wirtschaftliche Ausplünderung der Juden und die westfälischen Finanzbehörden* (Münster, 1999), 87–101.

Blank, Ralf, 'Albert Hoffmann als Reichsverteidigungskommissar im Gau Westfalen-Süd 1943–1945', *Beiträge zur Geschichte des Nationalsozialismus*, 17 (2001), 189–210.

Blank, Ralf, 'Die Kriegsendphase an Rhein und Ruhr 1944/45', in Bernd-A. Rusinek (ed.), *Kriegsende 1945. Verbrechen, Katastrophen, Befreiungen in nationaler und internationaler Perspektive* (Göttingen, 2004), 88–124.

Blank, Ralf, 'Kriegsalltag und Luftkrieg an der "Heimatfront"', in Echternkamp (ed.), *Das Deutsche Reich*, 357–461.

Blank, Ralf, 'Albert Hoffmann. Gauleiter und Reichsverteidigungskommissar in Westfalen-Süd 1943–1945', *Westfälische Lebensbilder*, 17 (Münster, 2005), 255–90.

Blank, Ralf, 'Kriegsendphase und "Heimatfront" in Westfalen', *Westfälische Forschungen*, 55 (2005), 361–421.

Blank, Ralf, *Hagen im Zweiten Weltkrieg. Bombenkrieg, Rüstung und Kriegsalltag in einer westfälischen Großstadt 1939–1945* (Essen, 2008).

Blank, Ralf, 'Die Nacht des 16./17. Mai 1943—"Operation Züchtigung": Die Zerstörung der Möhnetalsperre', Münster, 2006, in Internet Portal Westfälische Geschichte <http://www.westfaelische-geschichte.de/web493>, 22 July 2009.

Blank, Ralf, 'Zerstört und vergessen? Hagen, das Ruhrgebiet und das Gedächtnis des Krieges', in Arnold, Süss, and Thiessen (eds), *Luftkrieg*, 162–82.

Bläsi, Hubert, and Schrenk, Christhard, *Heilbronn 1944/45—Leben und Sterben einer Stadt* (Heilbronn, 1995).

Blessing, Werner K., '"Deutschland in Not, wir glauben...". Kirche und Kirchenvolk in einer katholischen Region 1933–1949', in Martin Broszat, Klaus-Dietmar Henke, and Hans Woller (eds), *Von Stalingrad zur Währungsreform. Zur Sozialgeschichte des Umbruchs* (Munich, 1988), 3–111.

Boberach, Heinz, 'Die Auswirkungen des alliierten Luftkrieges auf die Bevölkerung im Spiegel der SD-Berichte', in Müller and Dilks (eds), *Großbritannien*, 229–41.

Bohl, Hans-Werner, Keipke, Bodo, and Schröder, Karsten (eds), *Bomben auf Rostock. Krieg und Kriegsende in Berichten, Dokumenten, Erinnerungen und Fotos 1940–1945* (Rostock, 1995).

Bonhoeffer, Karl, 'Vergleichende psychopathologische Erfahrungen aus den beiden Weltkriegen', *Der Nervenarzt*, 18 (1947), 1–4.

Boog, Horst, *Die deutsche Luftwaffenführung 1935–1945. Führungsprobleme, Spitzengliederung, Generalstabsausbildung* (Stuttgart, 1982).

Boog, Horst, 'Luftwaffe und unterschiedsloser Bombenkrieg bis 1942', in Wolfgang Michalka (ed.), *Der Zweite Weltkrieg. Analysen, Grundzüge, Forschungsbilanz* (Munich, 1989), 523–31.

Boog, Horst, 'Der anglo-amerikanische strategische Luftkrieg über Europa und die deutsche Luftverteidigung', in Horst Boog, Gerhard Krebs, and Detlef Vogel (eds), *Das Deutsche Reich und der Zweite Weltkrieg*, vi: *Der globale Krieg. Die Ausweitung zum Weltkrieg und der Wechsel der Initiative 1941–1943* (Stuttgart, 1990), 429–565.

Boog, Horst (ed.), *The Conduct of the Air War in the Second World War: An International Comparison* (New York/Oxford, 1992).

Boog, Horst, 'The Luftwaffe and Indiscriminate Bombing up to 1942', in Boog (ed.), *The Conduct of the Air War in the Second World War: An International Comparison* (New York, 1992), 374–404.

Boog, Horst, 'Robert Knauss, the German Douhet', in *Actes du colloque international précurseurs et prophètes de l'aviation militaire, organisé par le Service Historique de l'Armée de l'Air à Paris, École nationale supérieure de techniques avancées* (Paris, 1992), 275–91.

Boog, Horst (ed.), *Luftkriegsführung im Zweiten Weltkrieg. Ein internationaler Vergleich* (Herford/Bonn, 1993).

Boog, Horst, 'Das Ende des Bombenkriegs. Ein militärgeschichtlicher Rückblick', *Aus Politik und Zeitgeschichte*, 45/18–19 (1995), 10–21.

Boog, Horst, *Bombenkrieg, Völkerrecht und Menschlichkeit im Luftkrieg*, in Hans Poeppel, Wilhelm K. von Preussen, and Karl-Günther von Hase (eds), *Die Soldaten der Wehrmacht* (Munich, 1998), 256–323.

Boog, Horst, 'Strategischer Luftkrieg in Europa und die Reichsluftverteidigung 1943–1944', in Horst Boog, Gerhard Krebs, and Detlef Vogel (eds), *Das Deutsche Reich und der Zweite Weltkrieg*, vii: *Das Deutsche Reich in der Defensive* (Stuttgart, 2001), 3–415.

Boog, Horst, *Die strategische Bomberoffensive der Alliierten gegen Deutschland und die Reichsluftverteidigung in der Schlussphase des Krieges*, in Müller (ed.), *Das Deutsche Reich*, 777–884.

Borsdorf, Ulrich, and Jamin, Mathilde (eds), *Über Leben im Krieg. Kriegserfahrungen in einer Industrieregion 1939–1945* (Reinbek bei Hamburg, 1989).

Böttger, Peter, *Winston Churchill und die zweite Front 1941–1943. Ein Aspekt der britischen Strategie im Zweiten Weltkrieg* (Frankfurt am Main, 1984).

Bourke, Joanna, *Dismembering the Male: Men's Bodies, Britain and the Great War* (London, 1996).

Bourke, Joanna, *Fear: A Cultural History* (London, 2005).

Bowyer, Chaz, *Bomber Barons* (London, 1983).

Bowyer, Michael J. F., *2 Group RAF: A Complete History 1936–1945* (London, 1974).

Boyle, Andrew, *Poor, Dear Brendan: The Quest for Brendan Bracken* (London, 1974).

Bracher, Karl Dietrich, Funke, Manfred, and Jacobsen, Hans-Adolf (eds), *Deutschland 1933–1945. Neue Studien zur nationalsozialistischen Herrschaft* (Düsseldorf, 1992).

Briggs, Asa, *The History of Broadcasting in the United Kingdom*, iii: *The War of Words* (London, 1970).

Brinkhus, Jörn, *Luftschutz und Versorgungspolitik. Regionen und Gemeinden im NS-Staat, 1942–1944/45* (Bielefeld, 2010).

Brinkhus, Jörn, 'Auftragsverwaltung der Gemeinden im Krieg. Das Beispiel rheinischer und westfälischer Städt', in Mecking and Wirsching (eds), *Stadtverwaltung*, 215–42.

Brinkhus, Jörn, 'Ziviler Luftschutz im "Dritten Reich"—Wandel einer Spitzenorganisation', in Süss (ed.), *Deutschland*, 27–40.

Brinkhus, Jörn, 'Hitler, "Goebbels und die Herausforderung der Bombardierung. Ziviler Luftschutz im 'Dritten Reich' 1940–1944"' (MS 2005).

Bristol's Bombed Churches: A Descriptive and Pictorial Record of their Histories and Destruction, compiled by Revd S. Paul Shipley and Howard Rankin (Bristol, 1945).

British Bombing Serving Unit (ed.), *The Strategic Air War against Germany 1939–1945: Report of the British Bombing Survey Unit* (London, 1998).

Brittain, Vera, *Seed of Chaos: What Mass Bombing Really Means* (London, 1944).

Brittain, Vera, and Sayre, John Nevin, 'Massacre by Bombing: The Facts behind the British–American Attack on Germany', *Fellowship*, 10/3 (1944), 49–64.

Brooke, Stephan, *Labour's War: The Labour Party during the Second World War* (Oxford, 1992).

Broszat, Martin, *Der Staat Hitlers. Grundlegung und Entwicklung seiner inneren Verfassung* (Munich, 1981).

Broszat, Martin, Fröhlich, Elke, and Wiesemann, Flak (eds), *Bayern in der NS-Zeit*, 6 vols (Munich/Vienna, 1977–83).

Brown, Mike, *A Child's War: Britain's Children in the Second World War* (London, 2000).

Brüggemeier, Franz-Josef, *Geschichte Großbritanniens im 20. Jahrhundert* (Munich, 2010).

Brunswig, Hans, *Feuersturm über Hamburg. Die Luftangriffe auf Hamburg im Zweiten Weltkrieg und ihre Folgen* (Stuttgart, 1994) [1st edition 1978].

Büchner, Franz, 'Der Sachschaden im Kriegsschädenrecht', *Deutsche Verwaltung*, 17 (1940), 312–17.

Bullock, Nicholas, 'Re-assessing the Post-war Housing Achievement: The Impact of War Damage Repairs on the New Housing Programme in London', *20th Century British History*, 16 (2005), 256–82.

Burchhardt, Lothar, 'Die Auswirkungen der Kriegswirtschaft auf die deutsche Zivil-bevölkerung im Ersten und Zweiten Weltkrieg', *Militärgeschichtliche Mitteilungen*, 15 (1974), 65–97.

Burgdorff, Stephan, and Habbe, Christian (eds), *Als Feuer vom Himmel fiel. Der Bombenkrieg in Deutschland* (Munich, 2003).

Burlingham, Dorothy, and Freud, Anna, *Young Children in Wartime: A Year's Work in a Residential Nursery* (London, 1942).

Busch, Dieter, *Der Luftkrieg im Raum Mainz während des Zweiten Weltkrieges 1939–1945* (Mainz, 1988).

Büttner, Ursula, 'Hamburg im Luftkrieg: Die politischen und wirtschaftlichen Fol-gen des "Unternehmens Gomorrha"', in Marlene P. Hiller, Eberhard Jäckel, and Jürgen Rohwer (eds), *Städte im Zweiten Weltkrieg. Ein internationaler Vergleich* (Augsburg, 1991), 272–98.

Calder, Angus, *The People's War: Britain 1939–45* (London, 1969).

Calder, Angus, 'Mass-Observation, 1937–1949', in Martin Bulmer (ed.), *Essays on the History of British Sociological Research* (Cambridge, 1984), 121–36.

Calder, Angus, *The Myth of the Blitz* (London, 1991).

Calder, Angus, 'The Battle of Britain in Pilots' Memoirs', in Addison and Crang (eds), *The Burning Blue*, 191–206.

Calder, Richard, *Carry on London* (London, 1941).

Calder, Richard, *The Lessons of London* (London, 1941).

Campbell, Louise, *Coventry Cathedral: Art and Architecture in Post-War Britain* (Oxford, 1996).

Campion, Garry, *The Good Fight: Battle of Britain Propaganda and the Few* (Basing-stoke/New York, 2009).

Cannadine, David, 'War and Death, Grief and Mourning in Modern Britain', in Joachim Whaley (ed.), *Mirrors and Mortality: Studies in the Social History of Death* (London, 1981), 187–242.

Caplan, Jane (ed.), *Nazi Germany: Short Oxford History of Germany* (Oxford, 2008).

Carey-Trefzer, Charlotte J., 'The Results of a Clinical Study of War-Damaged Chil-dren who Attended the Child Guidance Clinic, the Hospital for Sick Children, Great Ormond Street, London', *Journal of Mental Science*, 95 (1949), 535–59.

Carli, Maddalene, 'Die Illusion von der Unsterblichkeit. Roms Gedenken an das Bom-bardement vom 19. Juli 1943', in Arnold, Süss, and Thiessen (eds), *Luftkrieg*, 101–13.

Carpenter, Edward Frederick, *Archbishop Fisher: His Life and Times* (Norwich, 1991).

Carpenter, Spencer Cecil, *Exeter Cathedral* (Exeter, 1943).

Casson, Hugh, 'Ruins for Remembrance', in *Bombed Churches as War Memorials* (Cheam, 1945), 17–19.

Castan, Joachim, *Der Rote Baron. Die ganze Geschichte des Manfred von Richthofen* (Stuttgart, 2007).

Chambers, Vanessa, '"Defend us from All Perils and Dangers of this Night": Coping with Bombing in Britain during the Second World War', in Richard Overy,

Claudia Baldoli, and Andrew Knapp (eds), *Bombing, States and Peoples in Western Europe, 1940–1945* (London, 2011), 154–67.

Chandler, Andrew, 'The Church of England and the Obliteration Bombing of Germany in the Second World War', *English Historical Review*, 108 (1993), 920–46.

Chandler, Andrew, *Brethren in Adversity: Bishop George Bell and the Crisis of German Protestantism 1933–1938* (London, 1998).

Chapman, James, *The British at War: Cinema, State and Propaganda 1939–1945* (London/New York, 1998).

Charlton, Oswald, Garrat, G. T., and Fletcher, R., *The Air Defence of Britain* (London, 1938).

Chiari, Bernhard, Rogg, Matthias, and Schmidt, Wolfgang (eds), *Krieg und Militär im Film des 20. Jahrhunderts* (Munich, 2003).

Chickering, Roger, *Freiburg im Ersten Weltkrieg. Totaler Krieg und städtischer Alltag 1914–1918* (Paderborn, 2009).

Chickering, Roger, and Förster, Stig (eds), *Great War, Total War: Combat and Mobilization on the Western Front, 1914–1918* (Cambridge, 2000).

Chickering, Roger, and Förster, Stig (eds), *The Shadows of Total War: Europe, East Asia, and the United States, 1919–1939* (Cambridge, 2003).

Chickering, Roger, and Förster, Stig, 'Introduction', in Chickering and Förster (eds), *Shadows*, 1–19.

Chisholm, Anne, and Davie, Michael, *Beaverbrook: A Life* (London, 1992).

Churchill, Winston, *Der Zweite Weltkrieg*, vols i–vi (Hamburg, 1949–54).

Clapson, Mark, and Larkham, Peter J., *The Blitz and its Legacy: Wartime Destruction to Post-War Reconstruction* (Birmingham, 2013).

Clarke, Peter, *Hope and Glory: Britain, 1900–1990* (London, 1990).

Cluet, Marc, 'Danger arièn et architecture du IIIe Reich', *Revue historique des armées*, 4 (1980), 147–56.

Connelly, Mark, *Reaching for the Stars: A New History of Bomber Command in World War II* (London/New York, 2001).

Connelly, Mark, 'The British People, the Press, and the Strategic Air Campaign against Germany', *Contemporary British History*, 16 (2002), 39–58.

Connelly, Mark, 'The Image of RAF Bomber Command in British Popular Culture, 1945–2000', *Historische Literatur. Rezensionszeitschrift von H-Soz-u-Kult*, 2 (2004), 6–16.

Connelly, Mark, *We Can Take It! Britain and the Memory of the Second World War* (Harlow, 2004).

Connelly, Mark, 'Die britische Öffentlichkeit, die Presse und der Luftkrieg gegen Deutschland, 1939–1945', in Kettenacker (ed.), *Ein Volk von Opfern?*, 72–92.

Connelly, Mark, and Goebel, Stefan, 'Zwischen Erinnerungspolitik und Erinnerungskonsum. Der Luftkrieg in Großbritannien', in Arnold, Süss, and Thiessen (eds), *Luftkrieg*, 50–65.

Cooper, Alan, *Air Battle of the Ruhr* (Shrewsbury, 1992).

Costello, David R., 'Searchlight Books and the Quest for a "People's War", 1941–1942', *Journal of Contemporary History*, 24 (1989), 257–76.

Cox, Sebastian, 'An Unwanted Child: The Struggle to Establish a British Bombing Survey', in *The Strategic Air War against Germany 1939–1945: Report of the British Bombing Survey Unit*, Studies in Air Power No. 4 (London, 1998), xviii–xxii.

Cox, Sebastian, 'The Dresden Raids: Why and how', in Addison and Crang (eds), *Firestorm*, 18–61.

Crane, Conrad, *Bombs, Cities, and Civilians: American Airpower Strategy in World War II* (Lawrence, Kan., 1993).

Crawford, Keith, 'Constructing National Memory: The 1940/41 Blitz in British History Textbooks', *Internationale Schulbuchforschung*, 23 (2001), 323–38.

Crew, David, 'Auftakt zum Kalten Krieg? Wie sich die DDR an die Bombardierung Dresdens im Februar 1945 erinnerte', in Daniela Münkel and Jutta Schwartzkopf (eds), *Geschichte als Experiment. Studien zu Politik, Kultur und Alltag im 19. und 20. Jahrhundert* (Frankfurt am Main, 2004), 287–95.

Cronin, James E., *The Politics of the Expansion: War, State and Society in Twentieth-Century Britain* (London/New York, 1991).

Crosby, Travis, *The Impact of Civilian Evacuation in the Second World War* (London, 1986).

Crossick, Geoffrey, 'And what should they know about England? Die vergleichende Geschichtsschreibung im heutigen Großbritannien', in Haupt and Kocka (eds), *Geschichte und Vergleich*, 61–75.

Crowell, Samuel, 'Defending against the Allied Bombing Campaign: Air Raid Shelters and Gas Protection in Germany, 1939–1945', *Journal of Historical Review*, 20/4 (2001), 15–41.

Cull, Nicholas John, *Selling War: The British Propaganda Campaign against American 'Neutrality' in World War II* (Oxford, 1996).

Damberg, Wilhelm, *Der Kampf um die Schulen in Westfalen 1933–1945* (Mainz, 1986).

Damberg, Wilhelm, 'Kriegserfahrung und Kriegstheologie', *Theologie Quartalschrift*, 182 (2002), 321–41.

Danchev, Alex, 'Liddell Hart and the Indirect Approach', *Journal of Military History*, 63 (1999), 313–37.

Darracott, Joseph (ed.), *The First World War in Posters* (New York/Dover, 1974).

David, Hein, *Geoffrey Fisher: Archbishop of Canterbury* (Cambridge, 2008).

Davison, Robson S., 'The Belfast Blitz', *Irish Sword*, 16 (1985), 65–83.

Dear, Ian C. B., *The Oxford Companion to the Second World War* (revised edition) (Oxford, 2001).

Deighton, Len, *Bomber* (London, 1970).

Deist, Wilhelm, 'Die Aufrüstung der Wehrmacht', in Wilhelm Deist, Manfred Messerschmidt, Hans-Erich Volkmann, and Wolfram Wette (eds), *Das Deutsche Reich und der Zweite Weltkrieg*, i: *Ursachen und Voraussetzungen der deutschen Kriegspolitik* (Stuttgart, 1979), 371–532.

Demps, Laurenz, 'Die Luftangriffe auf Berlin. Ein dokumentarischer Bericht', *Jahrbuch des Märkischen Museums*, 4 (1978), 27–68.

Deres, Thomas, and Rüther, Martin (eds), *'Fotografieren verboten!' Heimliche Aufnahmen von der Zerstörung Kölns* (Cologne, 1995).

Dettmar, Werner, *Die Zerstörung Kassels im Oktober 1943. Eine Dokumentation* (Fuldabrück, 1983).

Diefenbacher, Michael, and Fischer-Pache, Wiltrud (eds), *Der Luftkrieg gegen Nürnberg. Der Angriff am 2. Januar 1945 und die zerstörte Stadt* (Nuremberg, 2004).

Diemer, Dorothea, 'Die Münchner Mariensäule', in Hubert Glaser (ed.), *Um Glaube und Reich. Kurfürst Maximilian I. Katalog der Ausstellung in der Residenz am 12.6.– 5.10. 1980* (Munich/Zurich, 1980), 457.

Dines, Peter, and Knoch, Peter, 'Deutsche und britische Erfahrungen im Bombenkrieg 1940–1945', in Dieter Brötel and Hans H. Pöschko (eds), *Krisen und Geschichtsbewußtsein. Mentalitätsgeschichtliche und didaktische Beiträge. Peter Knoch zum Gedenken* (Weinheim, 1996), 53–75.

Dittmar, Raoul, *Kommunalverwaltung in England* (Cologne, 2007).

Dlugoborski, Waclaw (ed.), *Zweiter Weltkrieg und sozialer Wandel* (Göttingen, 1981).

Domarus, Max, *Der Untergang des alten Würzburg im Luftkrieg gegen die deutschen Großstädte* (Würzburg, 1978).

Donnelly, Mark, *Britain in the Second World War* (London, 1999).

Dörner, Bernward, *'Heimtücke': Das Gesetz als Waffe. Kontrolle, Abschreckung und Verfolgung in Deutschland 1933–1945* (Paderborn, 1998).

Dörr, Margarete, *'Wer die Zeit nicht miterlebt hat ...' Frauenerfahrungen im Zweiten Weltkrieg und in den Jahren danach, iii: Das Verhältnis zum Nationalsozialismus und zum Krieg* (Frankfurt am Main, 1998).

Douhet, Guilio, *Il domino dell' aria. Probabili aspetti della guerra futura* (Rome, 1921).

Douhet, Guilio, *Luftschlacht* (Berlin, n.d. [1935]).

Downs, Laura Lee, 'A Very British Revolution? L'évacuation des enfants citadins vers les campagnes anglaises 1939–1945', *Vingtième Siècle*, 89 (2006), 47–60.

Dressen, Wolfgang (ed.), *Betrifft: 'Aktion 3'. Deutsche verwerten jüdische Nachbarn. Dokumente zur Arisierung* (Berlin, 1998).

Dröge, Franz, *Der zerredete Widerstand. Zur Soziologie und Publizistik des Gerüchts im 2. Weltkrieg* (Düsseldorf, 1970).

Dunkhase, Heinrich, 'Würzburg, 16. März 1945, 21.25 Uhr–21.42 Uhr. Hintergründe, Verlauf und Folgen des Luftangriffs der No. 5 Bomber Group', *Mainfränkisches Jahrbuch*, 32 (1980), 1–32.

Düringer, Hermann, and Kaiser, Christoph (ed.), *Kirchliches Leben im Zweiten Weltkrieg* (Frankfurt am Main, 2005).

Durth, Werner, *Deutsche Architekten* (Munich, 1992).

Durth, Werner, 'Architektur und Stadtplanung im Dritten Reich', in Michael Prinz and Rainer Zitelmann (eds), *Nationalsozialismus und Modernisierung* (Darmstadt, 1994), 139–71.

Durth, Werner, and Gutschow, Niels, *Träume in Trümmern. Planungen zum Wiederaufbau zerstörter Städte im Westen Deutschlands 1940–1950*, 2 vols (Brunswick/Wiesbaden), 1988.

Düwel, Jörn, and Gutschow, Niels, *Fortgewischt sind alle überflüssigen Zutaten. Hamburg 1943—Zerstörung und Städtebau* (Berlin, 2008).

Ebbinghaus, Angelika, 'Deutschland im Bombenkrieg: Ein missglücktes Buch über ein wichtiges Thema', *Sozial.Geschichte*, 18 (2003), 101–19.

Echternkamp, Jörg (ed.), *Das Deutsche Reich und der Zweite Weltkrieg*, ix/1: *Die deutsche Kriegsgesellschaft 1939 bis 1945. Politisierung, Vernichtung, Überleben* (Munich, 2004).

Echternkamp, Jörg, 'Im Kampf an der inneren und äußeren Front. Grundzüge der deutschen Gesellschaft im Zweiten Weltkrieg', in Jörg Echternkamp (ed.), *Das Deutsche Reich und der Zweite Weltkrieg*, ix/1: *Die deutsche Kriegsgesellschaft 1939 bis 1945. Politisierung, Vernichtung, Überleben* (Munich, 2004), 1–92.

Echternkamp, Jörg, *Kriegsschauplatz Deutschland 1945. Leben in Angst, Hoffnung auf Frieden. Feldpost aus der Heimat und von der Front* (Munich, 2006).

Echternkamp, Jörg, 'Von der Gewalterfahrung zur Kriegserinnerung—über den Bombenkrieg als Thema einer Geschichte der deutschen Kriegsgesellschaft', in Süss (ed.), *Deutschland im Luftkrieg*, 13–26.

Echternkamp, Jörg, and Martens, Stefan (eds), *Der Zweite Weltkrieg in Europa. Erfahrung und Erinnerung* (Paderborn, 2007).

Echternkamp, Jörg, and Martens, Stefan, 'Der Weltkrieg als Wegmarke? Die Bedeutung des Zweiten Weltkrieges für eine europäische Zeitgeschichte', in Echternkamp and Martens (eds), *Der Zweite Weltkrieg in Europa*, 1–33.

Eckardt, Götz (ed.), *Schicksale deutscher Baudenkmale im Zweiten Weltkrieg. Eine Dokumentation der Schäden und Totalverluste auf dem Gebiet der neuen Bundesländer*, 2 vols (Wiesbaden, 2001).

Eckart, Wolfgang U., 'Aesculap in the Trenches: Aspects of German Medicine in the First World War', in Bernd Hüppauf (ed.), *War, Violence and the Modern Condition* (Berlin/New York, 1997), 177–93.

Eichholtz, Dietrich, *Geschichte der deutschen Kriegswirtschaft*, 3 vols (Berlin, 1969, 1984, 1996).

Eley, Geoff, 'Finding the People's War: Film, British Collective Memory, and World War II', *American Historical Review*, 106 (2001), 818–38.

Erdmann, Jens, 'Zur Entwicklung des britischen Kriegsbegriffs. Ein Kommentar zu Lübeck, Rostock und Köln', *Berliner Monatshefte*, 20 (1942), 364–7.

Erker, Paul, 'Die Stadt im Krieg. Zum Verhältnis von Nationalsozialismus und Kommune in der Katastrophe', in Richard Bauer et al. (eds), *München— 'Hauptstadt der Bewegung'. Bayerns Metropole und der Nationalsozialismus* (Munich, 2002), 454–62.

Esposito, Vincent J., and Elting, John R., *A Military History and Atlas of the Napoleonic Wars* (London, 1964).

Essex, Stephen, and Brayshaw, Mark, 'Town versus Country in the 1940s: Planning the Contested Space of a City Region in the Aftermath of the Second Word War', *Town Planning Review*, 76 (2005), 239–64.

Essex, Stephen, and Brayshaw, Mark, 'Vision, Vested Interest and Pragmatism: Who Re-made Britain's Blitzed Cities?', *Planning Perspectives*, 22 (2007), 417–41.

Euler, Helmut, *Als Deutschlands Dämme brachen. Die Wahrheit über die Bombardierung der Möhne-Eder-Sorpe-Staudämme 1943* (Stuttgart, 1979).

Evans, Richard, *Der Geschichtsfälscher. Holocaust und historische Wahrheit im David-Irving-Prozess* (Frankfurt am Main, 2001).

Evans, Richard, *Third Reich at War* (London, 2008).

Ewen, Shane, 'Preparing the British Fire Service for War: Nationalisation, and Evolutionary Reform, 1935–1941', *Contemporary British History*, 20 (2006), 209–31.

Fache, Thomas, 'Gegenwartsbewältigungen. Dresdens Gedenken an die alliierten Luftangriffe vor und nach 1989', in Arnold, Süss, and Thiessen (eds), *Luftkrieg*, 221–38.

Fegan, Thomas, *The 'Baby Killers': German Air Raids on Britain in the First World War* (Barnsley, 2002).

Fetcher, Irving, *Joseph Goebbels im Berliner Sportpalast 1943: 'Wollt ihr den totalen Krieg?'* (Hamburg, 1998).

Feuchter, Georg W., *Geschichte des Luftkrieges. Entwicklung und Zukunft* (Bonn, 1954).

Feudell, Peter, 'Psychische und nervöse Reaktionen der Zivilbevölkerung im Kriege', Leipzig diss. med. 1944.

Field, Clive D., 'Puzzled People Revisited: Religious Believing and Belonging in Wartime Britain, 1939–45', *20th Century British History*, 19 (2008), 446–79.

Field, Geoffrey, 'Nights Underground in Darkest London: The Blitz, 1940–1941', *International Labor and Working-Class History*, 62 (2002), 11–49.

Fielding, Steven, 'The Good War', in Tiratsoo (ed.), *From Blitz to Blair*, 25–52.

Fielding, Steven, Thompson, Peter, and Tiratsoo, Nick, *'England Arise!' The Labour Party and Popular Politics in 1940s Britain* (Manchester, 1995).

Fings, Karola, *Krieg, Gesellschaft und KZ: Himmlers SS-Baubrigaden* (Munich, 2005).

Fitzgibbon, Constantine, *The Blitz* (London, 1957).

Fitzpatrick, Sheila, and Geyer, Michael (eds), *Beyond Totalitarianism: Stalinism and Nazism Compared* (Cambridge, 2009).

Fleischmann-Bisten, Walter, *Der Evangelische Bund in der Weimarer Republik und im sogenannten Dritten Reich* (Frankfurt am Main, 1989).

Flemming, Jana, '"Let 'em have it—right on the chin". Die Haltung der britischen Öffentlichkeit zum RAF-Flächenbombardement 1939–1945', Mainz University diss. 2007.

Flesch, Stefan, 'Quellen zur Kriegszeit in kirchlichen Archiven', in Düringer and Kaiser, *Leben*, 263–75.

Foedrowitz, Michael, *Bunkerwelten. Luftschutzanlagen in Norddeutschland* (Berlin, 1998).

Ford, John C., 'The Morality of Obliteration Bombing', *Theological Studies*, 5 (September 1944), 261–74, 307–9.

Forsbach, Ralf, *Die Medizinische Fakultät der Universität Bonn im 'Dritten Reich'* (Munich, 2006).

Forshaw, J. H., and Abercrombie, Patrick, *County of London Plan* (London, 1943).

Förster, Stig, '"Vom Kriege". Überlegungen zu einer modernen Militärgeschichte', in Thomas Kühne and Benjamin Ziemann (eds), *Was ist Militärgeschichte?* (Paderborn, 2000), 265–81.

Förster, Stig (ed.), *Totaler Krieg. Militärzeitschriften und die internationale Debatte über den Krieg der Zukunft, 1918–1939* (Paderborn, 2002).

Forte, Dieter, *Der Junge mit den blutigen Schuhen* (Frankfurt am Main, 1995).

Fox, Thomas, 'Writing Dresden', in Laurel Cohen-Pfister and Dagmar Wienroeder-Skinner (eds), *Victims and Perpetrators: 1933–1945: (Re)presenting the Past in Post-Unification Culture* (Berlin/New York, 2006), 136–53.

Francis, Martin, *Ideas and Policies under Labour, 1945–51: Building a New Britain* (Manchester, 1997).

Francis, Martin, *The Flyer: British Culture and the Royal Air Force, 1939–1945* (Oxford, 2009).

Frankl, Viktor E., Gebsattel, Victor E., Freiherr von, and Schulz, J. H., *Handbuch der Neurosenlehre und Psychotherapie*, vol. i (Munich/Berlin, 1959).

Frankland, Noble, *History at War: The Campaigns of an Historian* (London, 1998).

Fraser, R., Leslie, M., and Phelps, D., 'Psychiatric Effects of Severe Personal Experiences during Bombing', *Proceedings of the Royal Society of Medicine*, 36 (1942), 119–23.

Frederiksen, Oliver J., *The American Military Occupation of Germany, 1945–1953* (Washington DC, 1953).

Freeman, Roger A., *The Mighty Eighth: A History of the US Eighth Army Air Force* (London, 1986).

Frei, Norbert, 'Der totale Krieg und die Deutschen', in Norbert Frei and Hermann Kling (eds), *Der nationalsozialistische Krieg* (Frankfurt am Main/New York, 1990), 283–301.

Frei, Norbert, *Vergangenheitspolitik. Die Anfänge der Bundesrepublik und die NS-Vergangenheit* (Munich, 1997).

Frei, Norbert, *1945 und wir. Das Dritte Reich im Bewußtsein der Deutschen* (Munich, 2005) (expanded paperback edition Munich, 2009).

Frei, Norbert, 'Volksgemeinschaft. Erfahrungsgeschichte und Lebenswirklichkeit der Hitler-Zeit', in Frei (ed.), *1945 und wir*, 107–28.

Frei, Norbert, '1945 und wir. Die Gegenwart der Vergangenheit', in Frei (ed.), *1945 und wir*, 7–22.

Frei, Norbert (ed.), *Transnationale Vergangenheitspolitik. Der Umgang mit deutschen Kriegsverbrechern in Europa nach dem Zweiten Weltkrieg* (Göttingen, 2006).

Frei, Norbert, *Der Führerstaat. Nationalsozialistische Herrschaft 1933 bis 1945* (Munich, 2007).

Frei, Norbert, Brunner, José, and Goschler, Constantin (eds), *Die Praxis der Wiedergutmachung. Geschichte, Erfahrung und Wirkung in Deutschland und Israel* (Göttingen, 2009).

Freimüller, Tobias, *Alexander Mitscherlich. Gesellschaftsdiagnosen und Psychoanalyse nach Hitler* (Göttingen, 2007).

Freisler, Roland, 'Eine entscheidende Rechtsfrage des Kriegsstrafrecht', *Deutsche Justiz*, 102 (1940), 885.

Freisler, R., Grau, F., Krug, K., and Rietsch, O. (eds), *Deutsches Strafrecht*, i: *Erläuterungen zu den seit dem 1. 9. 1939 ergangenen strafrechtlichen und strafverfahrensrechtlichen Vorschriften* (Berlin, 1941).

Freisler, R., 'Gedanken zur Verordnung gegen Volksschädlinge', *Deutsches Recht* (1939), 1450–2.

Freser, Derek, *The Evolution of the British Welfare State* (London, 1973).

Frevert, Ute, 'Frauen an der "Heimatfront"', in Christoph Klessmann (ed.), *Nicht nur Hitlers Krieg. Der Zweite Weltkrieg und die Deutschen* (Düsseldorf, 1989), 25–51.

Frevert, Ute (ed.), *Vertrauen. Historische Annäherungen* (Göttingen, 2003).

Friedrich, Jörg, *Der Brand. Deutschland im Bombenkrieg 1940–1945* (Berlin/Munich, 2002).

Friedrich, Jörg, *Brandstätten. Der Anblick des Bombenkriegs* (Berlin/Munich, 2003).

Fritze, Lothar, *Die Moral des Bombenterrors. Alliierte Flächenbombardements im Zweiten Weltkrieg* (Munich, 2007).

Fritzsche, Peter, *A Nation of Fliers: German Aviation and the Popular Imagination* (Cambridge/London, 1992).

Fritzsche, Peter, 'Machine Dreams: Air Mindedness and the Reinvention of Germany', *American Historical Review*, 98 (1993), 685–709.

Fritzsche, Peter, *Wie aus Deutschen Nazis wurden* (Zurich/Munich, 1999).

Fritzsche, Peter, *Life and Death in the Third Reich* (Cambridge/London, 2008).

Fuchs, Theo, 'Psychische Störungen nach Bombenangriffen', diss. med. University of Erlangen, 1944.

Fuller, John F. C., *The Second World War 1939–45: A Strategical and Tactical History* (London, 1948).

Futrell, Robert F., *US Army Air Forces Intelligence in the Second World War* (New York/Oxford, 1992).

Galen, Hans (ed.), *Bomben auf Münster. Ausstellung über die Luftangriffe auf Münster im Zweiten Weltkrieg* (Münster, 1983).

Gardiner, Juliet, *Wartime Britain 1939–1945* (London, 2004).

Gardiner, Juliet, 'The Blitz Experience in British Society', in Richard Overy, Claudia Baldoli, and Andrew Knapp (eds), *Bombing, States and Peoples in Western Europe, 1940–1945* (London, 2011).

Garett, Stephan A., *Ethics and Airpower in World War II: The British Bombing of German Cities* (New York, 1993).

Garnett, Ron, *Liverpool in the 1930s and the Blitz* (Preston, 1995).

Gat, Azar, *Fascist and Liberal Vision of War: Fuller, Liddell Hart, Douhet, and other Modernists* (Oxford, 1998).

Gaulle, Charles de, *War Memoirs: The Call to Honour, 1940–1942* (London, 1960).

Geinitz, Christian, 'The First Air War against Non-combatants: Strategic Bombing of German Cities in World War I', in Chickering and Förster (eds), *Great War, Total War*, 2007–26.

Gentile, Gian P., *How Effective is Strategic Bombing? Lessons Learned from World War II to Kosovo* (New York, 2001).

Geppert, Dominik, *Thatchers konservative Revolution. Der Richtungswandel der britischen Tories 1975–1979* (Munich, 2002).

Gerlach, Wolfgang, *Als die Zeugen schwiegen. Bekennende Kirche und die Juden* (Berlin, 1993).

Gestrich, Andreas, 'Jürgen Habermas' Konzept der bürgerlichen Öffentlichkeit: Bedeutung und Kritik aus historischer Perspektive', in Clemens Zimmermann (ed.), *Politischer Journalismus. Öffentlichkeiten und Medien im 19. und 20. Jahrhundert* (Ostfildern, 2006), 25–40.

Geyer, Martin H., *Verkehrte Welt. Revolution, Inflation und Moderne, München 1914– 1924* (Göttingen, 1998).

Geyer, Michael, 'Krieg als Gesellschaftspolitik. Anmerkungen zu neueren Arbeiten über das Dritte Reich im Zweiten Weltkrieg', *AfS* 26 (1986), 557–601.

Geyer, Michael, 'Eine Kriegsgeschichte, die vom Tod spricht', in Thomas Lindenberger and Alf Lüdtke (eds), *Physische Gewalt. Studien zur Geschichte der Neuzeit* (Frankfurt am Main, 1995), 136–61.

Giebel, Anne, 'Tod und Trauer in München 1945–1955', MA diss. Munich, 2006.

Girbig, Werner, *Im Anflug auf die Reichshauptstadt: die Dokumentation der Bombenangriffe auf Berlin* (Stuttgart, 2001).

Gleichmann, Peter, and Kühne, Thomas (eds), *Massenhaftes Töten. Kriege und Genozide im 20. Jahrhundert* (Essen, 2004).

Glienke, Stephan, 'The Allied Air War and German Society', in Richard Overy, Claudia Baldoli, and Andrew Knapp (eds), *Bombing, States and Peoples in Western Europe, 1940–1945* (London, 2011), 171–83.

Gobsch, Hannes, *Wahn-Europa. Eine Vision* (Hamburg/Berlin/Leipzig, 1931).

Goebel, Stefan, *The Great War and Medieval Memory: War, Remembrance and Medievalism in Britain and Germany, 1914–1940* (Cambridge, 2007).

Goebel, Stefan, 'School', in Jay Winter and Jean-Luis Robert (eds), *Capital Cities at War. Paris, London, Berlin, 1914–1919*, ii: *A Cultural History* (New York, 2007), 188–234.

Goebel, Stefan, 'Coventry und Dresden. Transnationale Netzwerke der Erinnerung in den 1950er und 1960er Jahren', in Süss, *Deutschland*, 111–20.

Goebel, Stefan, 'Coventry nach der "Coventrierung". Der Bombenkrieg im europäischen Gedächtnis', in Heinz-Dietrich Löwe (ed.), 'Europäische Stadt— europäische Identität' (MS).

Goltermann, Svenja, 'Psychisches Leid und psychiatrisches Wissen in der Entschädigung', in Frei, Brunner, and Goschler (eds), *Die Praxis der Wiedergutmachung*, 427–51.

Goltermann, Svenja, *Die Gesellschaft der Überlebenden. Deutsche Kriegsheimkehrer und ihre Gewalterfahrungen im Zweiten Weltkrieg* (Munich, 2009).

Golücke, Friedhelm, *Schweinfurt und der strategische Luftkrieg 1943. Der Angriff der US Air Force vom 14. Oktober 1943 gegen die Schweinfurter Kugellagerindustrie* (Paderborn, 1980).

Goschler, Constantin, *Schuld und Schulden. Die Politik der Wiedergutmachung für NS Verfolgte seit 1945* (Göttingen, 2005).

Gotto, Bernhard, *Nationalsozialistische Kommunalpolitik. Administrative Normalität und Systemstabilisierung durch die Augsburger Stadtverwaltung 1933–1945* (Munich, 2006).

Gotto, Bernhard, 'Kommunale Krisenbewältigung', in Süss (ed.), *Deutschland*, 41–56.

Götz, Norbert, *Ungleiche Schwestern. Die Konstruktion von nationalsozialistischer Volksgemeinschaft und schwedischem Volksheim* (Baden-Baden, 2001).

Gräff, Siegfried, *Der Tod im Luftangriff. Ergebnisse pathologisch-anatomischer Untersuchungen* (Hamburg, 1948).

Grass, Günter, *Im Krebsgang* (Göttingen, 2002).

Grayling, Anthony C., *Among the Dead Cities: Was the Allied Bombing of Civilians in WWII a Necessity or a Crime?* (London, 2006).

Greenfield, Kent Roberts, *American Strategy in World War II* (Baltimore, 1970).

Gregg, John R., *The Shelter of the Tubes: Tube Sheltering in Wartime London* (Harrow Weald, 2001).

Gregor, Neil, 'A Schicksalsgemeinschaft? Allied Bombing, Civilian Morale, and Social Dissolution in Nuremberg, 1942–1945', *Historical Journal*, 43 (2000), 1051–70.

Gregor, Neil, '"Is he still alive or long since dead?" Loss, Absence and Remembrance in Nuremberg, 1945–1956', *German History*, 21 (2003), 183–203.

Gregor, Neil, *Haunted City: Nuremberg and the Nazi Past after 1945* (New Haven, 2008).

Gregor, Neil, 'Erinnerungen an die Bombardierung Nürnbergs zwischen Trauer und städtischer Identitätspolitik', in Arnold, Süss, and Thiessen (eds), *Luftkrieg*, 131–45.

Gregory, Adrian, 'The Commemoration of the Battle of Britain', in Addison and Crang (eds), *The Burning Blue*, 217–28.

Greschat, Martin, 'Religiöse und theologische Stimmen zum Kriegsalltag', in Düringer and Kaiser (eds), *Kirchliches Leben im Zweiten Weltkrieg*, 89–107.

Griffiths, Clare V. J., *Labour and the Countryside: The Politics of Rural Britain, 1918–1939* (Oxford, 2007).

Grimm, Barbara, 'Lynchmorde an alliierten Fliegern im Zweiten Weltkrieg', MA diss., LMU 2006.

Grimm, Barbara, 'Lynchmorde an alliierten Fliegern im Zweiten Weltkrieg', in Süss (ed.), *Deutschland*, 71–84.

Groehler, Olaf, *Geschichte des Luftkriegs 1910 bis 1970* (Berlin (Ost), 1975).

Groehler, Olaf, *Bombenkrieg gegen Deutschland* (Berlin, 1990).

Groehler, Olaf, 'Der strategische Luftkrieg und seine Auswirkungen auf die deutsche Zivilbevölkerung', in Boog (ed.), *Luftkriegsführung im Zweiten Weltkrieg*, 329–49.

Groh, Christian, '"Sehen wir Pforzheim!" Der Bombenkrieg als Trauma der Stadtgeschichte', in Bettina Fraisl and Monika Stromberger (eds), *Stadt und Trauma. City and Trauma. Annäherungen—Konzepte—Analysen* (Würzburg, 2004), 123–43.

Gruchmann, Lothar, *Totaler Krieg. Vom Blitzkrieg zur bedingungslosen Kapitulation* (Munich, 1991).

Gruchmann, Lothar, '"Generalangriff auf die Justiz"? Der Reichstagsbeschluss vom 26. April und seine Bedeutung für die Maßregelung der deutschen Richter durch Hitler', *VfZ* 51 (2003), 509–20.

Grundwaldt, Hans-Heinrich, 'Jugendpsyche und Gefahrenmoment', *Luftschutz und Schule*, 1 (June 1936), 219f.

Gruner, Wolf, 'Die NS-Judenverfolgung und die Kommunen. Zur wechselseitigen Dynamisierung von zentraler und lokaler Politik', *VfZ* 48 (2000), 75–126.

Guttmann, E., and Baker, A. A., 'Neuroses in Firemen', *Journal of Mental Science*, 91 (1945), 454–7.

Hachtmann, Rüdiger, and Süss, Winfried (eds), *Hitlers Kommissare. Sondergewalten in der nationalsozialistischen Diktatur* (Göttingen, 2006).

Haerendel, Ulrike, *Kommunale Wohnungspolitik im Dritten Reich. Siedlungsideologie, Kleinhausbau und »Wohnraumarisierung« am Beispiel Münchens* (Munich, 1999).

Hage, Volker, *Zeugen der Zerstörung. Die Literaten und der Luftkrieg* (Frankfurt am Main, 2003).

Hagemann, Karen, and Schüler-Springorum, Stefanie (eds), *Heimat—Front. Militär und Geschlechterverhältnisse im Zeitalter der Weltkriege* (Frankfurt am Main/New York, 2002).

Hahn, Fritz, *Waffen und Geheimwaffen des deutschen Heeres 1933–1945* (Coblenz, 1987).

Haldane, John B. S., *ARP* (London, 1938).

Hampe, Erich (ed.), *Der Zivile Luftschutz im Zweiten Weltkrieg. Dokumentation und Erfahrungsberichte über Aufbau und Einsatz* (Frankfurt am Main, 1963).

Hanke, Marcus, *Luftkrieg und Zivilbevölkerung. Der kriegsvölkerrechtliche Schutz der Zivilbevölkerung gegen Luftbombardements von den Anfängen bis zum Ausbruch des Zweiten Weltkrieges* (Frankfurt am Main, 1991).

Hansen, Randall, *Fire and Fury: The Allied Bombing of Germany, 1942–1945* (New York, 2009).

Hanson, Neil, *The First Blitz: The Secret German Plan to Raze London to the Ground in 1918* (London, 2008).

Hardy, Bert, *My Life* (London, 1985).

Harlander, Tilman, 'Bombardierung und Städtezerstörung. Neuere Literatur', *Die alte Stadt*, 20 (1993), 400–4.

Harris, Arthur T., *Bomber Offensive* (London, 1947).

Harris, José, 'War and Social History: Britain and the Home Front during the Second World War', *Contemporary European History*, 1 (1992), 17–35.

Harris, José, *William Beveridge* (Oxford, 1997).

Harrisson, Tom, *Living through the Blitz* (London, 1976).

Hasegawa, Junichi, *Replanning the Blitzed City Centre: A Comparative Study of Bristol, Coventry and Southampton, 1941–1950* (Milton Keynes, 1992).

Hasegawa, Junichi, 'The Rise and Fall of Radial Reconstruction in 1940s Britain', *20th Century British History*, 10 (1999), 137–61.

Hastings, Adrian, *A History of English Christianity, 1920–1985* (London, 1986).

Hastings, Max, *Bomber Command* (London, 1982).

Haupt, Heinz-Gerhard, and Kocka, Jürgen (eds), *Geschichte und Vergleich. Ansätze und Ergebnisse vergleichender Geschichtsschreibung* (Frankfurt am Main, 1996).

Heeresgeschichtliches Museum Wien (ed.), *Im Keller. Österreich im Zeichen des Luftschutzes* (Vienna, 2007).

Heidekind, Jürgen, '"People's War or Standing Army"? Die Debatte über Militärwesen und Krieg in den Vereinigten Staaten von Amerika im Zeitalter der Französischen Revolution', in Johannes Kunisch, and Herfried Münkler (eds),

Die Wiedergeburt des Krieges aus dem Geist der Revolution. Studien zum bellizistischen Diskurs des ausgehenden 18. und beginnenden 19. Jahrhunderts (Berlin, 1999), 131–52.

Heidenreich, Bernd, and Neitzel, Sönke (eds), *Der Bombenkrieg und seine Opfer* (Wiesbaden, 2004).

Heimann, Judith M., *The Most Offending Soul Alive: Tom Harrisson and his Remarkable Life* (London, 2002).

Hein, David, *Geoffrey Fisher: Archbishop of Canterbury* (Cambridge, 2008).

Helders, Major, *Luftkrieg 1936. Die Zertrümmerung von Paris* (Berlin, 1932).

Hellmold, Wilhelm, *Die V 1. Eine Dokumentation* (Munich/Esslingen, 1988).

Henke, Klaus-Dietmar, *Die amerikanische Besetzung Deutschlands* (Munich, 1995).

Hensbergen, Gijs van, *Guernica. Biografie eines Bildes* (Munich, 2007).

Hensle, Michael P., *Rundfunkverbrechen. Das Hören von »Feindsendern« im National-sozialismus* (Berlin, 2003).

Herbert, Ulrich, *Fremdarbeiter. Politik und Praxis des 'Ausländereinsatzes' in der Kriegs-wirtschaft des Dritten Reiches* (Bonn, 1985).

Herbert, Ulrich (ed.), *Europa und der 'Reichseinsatz'. Ausländische Zivilarbeiter, Kriegs-gefangene und KZ-Häftlinge in Deutschland 1938–1945* (Essen, 1991).

Herbert, Ulrich, and Schildt, Axel (eds), *Kriegsende in Europa. Vom Beginn des deutschen Machtzerfalls bis zur Stabilisierung der Nachkriegsordnung 1944–1948* (Essen, 1998).

Herbst, Ludolf, *Das nationalsozialistische Deutschland 1933–1945. Die Entfesselung der Gewalt: Rassismus und Krieg* (Frankfurt am Main, 1996).

Hering, Rainer, 'Kirchliches Leben im Zweiten Weltkrieg: Das Beispiel Hamburg', in Düringer and Kaiser (eds), *Kirchliches Leben im Zweiten Weltkrieg*, 60–88.

Hess, Ulrich, 'Leipzig—eine Großstadt im Zweiten Weltkrieg', in Marlis Buchholz et al. (eds), *Nationalsozialismus und Region. Festschrift für Herbert Obenaus* (Bielefeld, 1996), 215–26.

Hewitt, Nick, 'A Sceptical Generation? War Memorials and the Collective Memory of the Second World War in Britain, 1945–2000', in Dominik Geppert (ed.), *The Postwar Challenge: Cultural, Social, and Political Change in Western Europe, 1945–1958* (Oxford, 2003), 81–97.

Heyll, Uwe, 'Friedrich Panse und die psychiatrische Erbforschung', in Michael Esch et al. (eds), *Die Medizinische Akademie in Düsseldorf im Nationalsozialismus* (Essen, 1997), 318–40.

Hildebrand, Klaus, *Das Dritte Reich* (Munich, 2003).

Hill, Russell, *Struggle for Germany* (New York, 1947).

Hillary, Richard, *The Last Enemy* (London, 1942).

Hillmann, Jörg, and Zimmermann, John (eds), *Kriegsende 1945 in Deutschland* (Munich, 2002).

Hinchliffe, Peter, *The Other Battle: Luftwaffe Night Aces versus Bomber Command* (Shrewsbury, 1996).

Hinsley, Arthur, *The Bond of Peace* (London, 1941).

Hinton, James, 'Voluntarism and the Welfare/Warfare State: Women's Voluntary Services in the 1940's', *20th Century British History*, 9 (1998), 274–305.

Hinton, James, *Women, Social Leadership, and the Second World War: Continuities of Class* (Oxford, 2002).

Hinton, James, 'The "Class Complex": Mass-Observation and Cultural Distinction in Pre-War Britain', *Past and Present*, 199 (2008), 207–36.

Hippler, Thomas, 'Krieg aus der Luft. Konzeptuelle Vorüberlegungen zur Entstehungsgeschichte des Bombenkrieges', in Wolfgang Hardtwig (ed.), *Ordnungen in der Krise. Zur politischen Kulturgeschichte Deutschlands 1900–1933* (Munich, 2007), 403–22.

Hoffmann-Heyden, Adolf-Eckhard, *Die Funkmeßgeräte der deutschen Flakartillerie 1938–1945* (Dortmund, 1954).

Hohn, Uta, *Die Zerstörung deutscher Städte im Zweiten Weltkrieg. Regionale Unterschiede in der Bilanz des Luftkrieges unter bevölkerungsgeographischem Aspekt* (Dortmund, 1991).

Hohn, Uta, 'Der Einfluß von Luftschutz, Bombenkrieg und Städtezerstörung auf Städtebau und Stadtplanung im "Dritten Reich"', *Die alte Stadt*, 19 (1992), 326–53.

Holman, Bob, *The Evacuation: A Very British Revolution* (Oxford, 1995).

Hölsken, Heinz Dieter, *Die V-Waffen. Entstehung—Propaganda—Kriegseinsatz* (Stuttgart, 1984).

Holzapfel, Christoph, 'Alltagsreligiosität im Krieg: Die Korrespondenz der Familie B. Zwischen Kriegswende und Kriegsende (1943–1946)', in Andreas Holzem and Christoph Holzapfel (eds), *Zwischen Kriegs- und Diktaturerfahrung. Katholizismus und Protestantismus in der Nachkriegszeit* (Stuttgart, 2005), 53–90.

Holzapfel, Christoph, '"Unter deinen Schutz und Schirm fliegen wir . . .". Marienweihen im Zweiten Weltkrieg', in Gottfried Korff (ed.), *Alliierte im Himmel. Populare Religiosität und Kriegserfahrung* (Tübingen, 2006), 127–40.

Hopf, Eduard, *Das zerstörte Lübeck. Sechzig Kreidezeichnungen aus dem Jahre 1942, zusammengestellt und mit einem Text versehen von Günther Grundmann* (Hamburg, 1973).

Horn, Birgit, *Leipzig im Bombenhagel—Angriffsziel 'Haddock': zu den Auswirkungen der alliierten Luftangriffe im Zweiten Weltkrieg auf die Stadt Leipzig* (Leipzig, 1998).

Horne, Alistair, *Macmillan: 1894–1956*, volume i of the Official Biography (London, 1988).

Howard, Anthony, *Crossman: The Pursuit of Power* (London, 1990).

Howard, Richard T., *Ruined and Rebuilt: The Story of Coventry Cathedral 1939–1962* (Letchworth, 1962).

Howkins, Alan, 'A Country at War: Mass-Observation and Rural England, 1939–1945', *Rural History*, 9 (1998), 75–97.

Hubble, Nick, *Mass Observation and Everyday Life: Culture, History, Theory* (London, 2005).

Hürten, Heinz, *Deutsche Katholiken. 1918–1945* (Munich, 1992).

Hyde, Andrew P., *The First Blitz: The German Air Campaign against Britain in the First World War* (Barnsley, 2002).

Irving, David, *The Destruction of Dresden* (London, 1963).

Irving, David, *Der Untergang Dresdens* (Gütersloh, 1964).

Jacobs, William A., 'Strategic Bombing and American National Strategy, 1941–1943', *Military Affairs*, 50 (1986), 133–9.

James, Robert Rhodes (ed.), *W. S. Churchill, Complete Speeches, 1897–1963* (New York, 1974).

Jasper, Ronald Claud Dudley, *George Bell: Bishop of Chichester* (Oxford, 1967).

Jeffery, Tom, *Mass Observation: A Short History* (Birmingham, 1978).

Jefferys, Kevin, 'British Politics and Social Policy during the Second Word War', *Historical Journal*, 30 (1987), 123–44.

Jefferys, Kevin, *The Churchill Coalition and Wartime Politics, 1940–1945* (Manchester, 1991).

Johe, Werner, 'Strategisches Kalkül und Wirklichkeit: Das "Unternehmen Gomorrha"', in Müller and Dilks (eds), *Großbritannien und der deutsche Widerstand*, 217–27.

Johnson, Franklyn Arthur, *Defence by Committee: The British Committee of Imperial Defence, 1885–1959* (London, 1960).

Jones, Edgar, Palmer, Ian, and Wessley, Simon, 'War Pension (1900–1945): Changing Models of Psychological Understanding', *British Journal of Psychiatry*, 180 (2002), 374–9.

Jones, Edgar, and Wessely, Simon, 'The Impact of Total War on the Practice of British Psychiatry', in Chickering and Förster (eds), *Shadows*, 129–48.

Jones, Edgar, et al., 'Civilian Morale During the Second World War: Responses to Air Raids Re-examined', *Social History of Medicine*, 17 (2004), 463–79.

Jones, Helen, *British Civilians in the Front Line: Air Raids, Productivity and Wartime Culture, 1939–45* (Manchester, 2006).

Jones, Neville, *The Origins of Strategic Bombing: A Study of the Development of British Air Strategic Thought and Practice up to 1918* (London, 1973).

Jünger, Ernst (ed.), *Luftfahrt ist not!* (Leipzig, n.d. [1928]).

Kallis, Aristotle A., 'Der Niedergang der Deutungsmacht. Nationalsozialistische Propaganda im Kriegsverlauf', in Echternkamp (ed.), *Das Deutsche Reich und der Zweite Weltkrieg*, ix/1. 203–50.

Kammann, Bruno, *Carl Klinkhammer. Ruhrkaplan, Sanitätssoldat und Bunkerpastor 1903–1997* (Essen, 2001).

Kammerer, Gabrielle, *Aktion Sühnezeichen Friedensdienste. Aber man kann es einfach tun* (Göttingen, 2008).

Kantorowicz, Alfred, *Spanisches Tagebuch* (Hamburg, 1979).

Kehrt, Christian, *Moderne Krieger. Die Technikerfahrung deutscher Luftwaffenpiloten 1910–1945* (Paderborn, 2010).

Keller, Sven, 'Verbrechen in der Endphase des Zweiten Weltkrieges—Überlegungen zu Abgrenzung, Methodik und Quellenkritik', in Cord Arendes, Edgar Wolfrum, and Jörg Zedler (eds), *Terror nach Innen. Verbrechen am Ende des Zweiten Weltkrieges* (Göttingen, 2006), 25–50.

Kennett, Lee, *A History of Strategic Bombing* (New York, 1982).

Kershaw, Ian, *Der Hitler-Mythos. Führerkult und Volksmeinung* (Stuttgart, 1999).

Kershaw, Ian, *Hitler*, 2 vols (Stuttgart, 1998–9).

Kershaw, Ian, *Wendepunkte. Schlüsselentscheidungen im Zweiten Weltkrieg 1940/41* (Munich, 2008).

Kettenacker, Lothar (ed.), *Ein Volk von Opfern? Die neue Debatte um den Bombenkrieg 1940–1945* (Berlin, 2003).

Kettenacker, Lothar, 'Churchills Dilemma', in Kettenacker (ed.), *Ein Volk von Opfern?*, 48–55.

Kienitz, Sabine, 'Die Kastrierten des Krieges. Körperbilder und Männlichkeitskonstruktionen im und nach dem Ersten Weltkrieg', *Zeitschrift für Volkskunde*, 95 (1999), 63–82.

Kienitz, Sabine, 'Beschädigte Helden. Zur Politisierung des kriegsinvaliden Soldatenkörpers in der Weimarer Republik', in Jost Dülffer and Gerd Krumeich (eds), *Der verlorene Frieden. Politik und Kriegskultur nach 1918* (Essen, 2002), 199–214.

Kienitz, Sabine, 'Körper-Beschädigungen. Kriegsinvalidität und Männlichkeitskonstruktionen in der Weimarer Republik', in Hagemann and Schüler-Springorum (eds), *Heimat—Front*, 188–207.

Killingray, David, '"A Swift Agent of Government": Air Power and British Colonial Africa, 1916–1939', *Journal of African History*, 25 (1986), 429–44.

Kimpel, Harald, *Die vertikale Gefahr. Luftkrieg in der Kunst* (Marburg, 1993).

Kindler, Jan, '"Wo wir sind, da ist immer oben". Zur Inszenierung der Luftwaffe im NSKulturfilm', in Bernhard Chiari et al. (eds), *Krieg und Militär im Film des 20. Jahrhunderts* (Munich, 2003), 401–38.

Kirchner, Klaus, *Psychologische Kriegsführung im Zweiten Weltkrieg in Europa* (Munich, 1974).

Kirkham, Pat, and Thoms, David (eds), *War Culture: Social Change and Changing Experience in World War Two Britain* (London, 1995).

Kirwin, Gerald, 'Waiting for Retaliation: A Study in Nazi Propaganda Behaviour and German Civilian Morale', *Journal of Contemporary History*, 16 (1981), 565–83.

Klee, Katja, *Im 'Luftschutzkeller des Reiches'. Evakuierte in Bayern 1939–1953: Politik, soziale Lage, Erfahrungen* (Munich, 1999).

Klee, Katja, 'Nationalsozialistische Wohlfahrtspolitik am Beispiel der NSV in Bayern', in Hermann Josef Rumschöttel and Walter Ziegler (eds), *Staat und Gaue in der NS-Zeit, Bayern 1933–1945* (Munich, 2004), 557–620.

Klinkhammer, Carl, 'Die stabilste Kirche der Welt', in Bürgerverein Heerdt (eds), *Heerdt im Wandel der Zeit II* (Düsseldorf, 1980), 76.

Knoch, Habbo, 'Transitstationen der Gewalt. Bunker und Baracken als Räume absoluter Verfügbarkeit', in Marszolek and Buggeln (eds), *Bunker*, 309–24.

Koch, Horst-Adalbert, *Flak. Die Geschichte der deutschen Flakartillerie und der Einsatz der Luftwaffenhelfer* (Bad Nauheim, 1965).

Kock, Gerhard, *'Der Führer sorgt für unsere Kinder...'. Die Kinderlandverschickung im Zweiten Weltkrieg* (Paderborn, 1997).

Koestler, Arthur, 'The Birth of a Myth: In Memory of Richard Hillary', *Horizon*, 7 (1943), 227–39.

Konvitz, Josef, 'Représentations urbaines et bombardements stratégiques, 1914–1945', *Annales*, 44 (1989), 823–47.

Korte, Barbara, and Ralf Schneider (eds), *War and the Cultural Construction of Identities in Britain* (Amsterdam, 2002).

Kösters, Christoph, *Katholische Verbände und moderne Gesellschaft. Organisationsgeschichte und Vereinskultur im Bistum Münster 1918–1945* (Paderborn, 1995).

Kösters, Christoph, 'Kirche und Glaube an der "Heimatfront". Katholische Lebenswelt und Kriegserfahrungen 1939–1945', in Karl-Joseph Hummel and Christoph Kösters (eds), *Kirchen im Krieg. Europa 1939–1945* (Paderborn, 2007), 363–98.

Kral, V. A., 'Psychiatric Observations under Severe Chronic Stress', *American Journal of Psychiatry*, 108 (1951), 185–92.

Kramer, Nicole, 'Mobilisierung für die "Heimatfront". Frauen im zivilen Luftschutz', in Sybille Steinbacher (ed.), *'Volksgenossinnen'. Frauen in der NS-Volksgemeinschaft* (Göttingen, 2007), 69–92.

Kramer, Nicole, *Volksgenossinnen an der Heimatfront. Mobilisierung, Verhalten, Erinnerung* (Munich, 2011).

Kramer, Nicole, '"Kämpfende Mütter" und "gefallene Heldinnen". Frauen im Luftschutz', in Süss (ed.), *Deutschland*, 85–98.

Krause, Michael, *Flucht vor dem Bombenkrieg: 'Umquartierungen' im Zweiten Weltkrieg und die Wiedereingliederung der Evakuierten in Deutschland 1943–1963* (Düsseldorf, 1997).

Kressel, Carsten, *Evakuierungen und erweiterte Kinderlandverschickung im Vergleich. Das Beispiel der Städte Liverpool und Hamburg* (Frankfurt am Main, 1996).

Kriham, Pat, and Thoms, David (eds), *War Culture: Social Chance and Changing Experience in World War Britain* (London, 1995).

Kroll, Thomas, *Kommunistische Intellektuelle in Westeuropa. Frankreich, Österreich, Italien und Großbritannien im Vergleich (1945–1956)* (Cologne, 2007).

Krüger, Norbert, 'Die Zerstörung Wuppertal-Barmens im 2. Weltkrieg', *Zeitschrift des Bergischen Geschichtsvereins*, 86 (1974), 164–95.

Krüger, Norbert, '"Wenn Sie nicht ins KZ wollen..." Häftlinge in Bombenräumkommandos', *Aus Politik und Zeitgeschichte*, 27/16 (1977), 25–37.

Krüger, Norbert, 'Die Bombenangriffe auf das Ruhrgebiet im Frühjahr 1943', in Borsdorf and Jamin (eds), *Überleben im Krieg*, 88–100.

Krüger, Norbert, 'Die Luftangriffe auf Essen 1940–1945', *Essener Beiträge*, 113 (2001), 159–330.

Kucklick, Christoph, *Der Feuersturm—Bombenkrieg über Deutschland* (Hamburg, 2003).

Kühne, Thomas, 'Die Viktimisierungsfalle. Wehrmachtsverbrechen, Geschichtswissenschaft und symbolische Ordnung des Militärs', in Michael Th. Greven and Oliver von Wrochem (eds), *Der Krieg in der Nachkriegszeit. Der Zweite Weltkrieg in Politik und Gesellschaft der Bundesrepublik* (Opladen, 2000), 183–96.

Kuller, Christiane, '"Erster Grundsatz: Horten für die Reichsfinanzverwaltung": Die Verwertung des Eigentums der deportierten Nürnberger Juden', *Beiträge zur Geschichte des Nationalsozialismus*, 20 (2004), 160–79.

Kuller, Christiane, and Drecoll, Axel, 'Inszenierter Volkszorn, ausgebliebene Empörung und der Sturz Julius Streichers. Reaktionen auf die wirtschaftliche Ausplünderung der deutschen Juden', in Sabrow (ed.), *Skandal und Diktatur*, 77–101.

Kurki, Allan W., *Operation Moonlight Sonata: The German Raid on Coventry* (London, 1995).

Kurowski, Franz, *Der Luftkrieg über Deutschland* (Düsseldorf, 1977).

Kushner, Tony, *The Persistence of Prejudice: Antisemitism in British Society during the Second World War* (Manchester, 1987).

Kushner, Tony, *We Europeans? Mass Observation, Race, and British Identity in Twentieth-Century History* (Aldershot, 2004).

Labour Party (ed.), *A.R.P.: Labour's Policy* (London, 1939).

Lacker, Erich, *Zielort Karlsruhe. Die Luftangriffe im Zweiten Weltkrieg* (Karlsruhe, 1996).

Lambert, Andrew P. N., *The Psychology of Air Power* (London, 1994).

Lancaster, Bill, and Mason, Tony (eds), *Life and Labour in a Twentieth-Century City: The Experience of Coventry* (Coventry, 1986).

La Speranza, 'Marcello,...und für die Bevölkerung wird angeordnet: Luftschutz-maßnahmen in Wien', in Heeresgeschichtliches Museum (ed.), *Im Keller*, 55–146.

Lawlor, Sheila, *Churchill and the Politics of War, 1940–1941* (Cambridge, 1994).

Le Bon, Gustave, *The Psychology of the Great War* (London, 1916).

Ledig, Gert, *Vergeltung* (Frankfurt am Main, 1956) (reissued 1999).

Leendertz, Ariane, *Ordnung schaffen. Deutsche Raumplanung im 20. Jahrhundert* (Göttingen, 2008).

Leers, Johann von, *'Bomben auf Hamburg'. Vision oder Möglichkeit?* (Leipzig, 1932).

Leitner, Wilhelm, *Gott im Krieg. Die Theologie der österreichischen Bischöfe in den Hirtenbriefen zum Ersten Weltkrieg* (Vienna/Cologne/Weimar, 1997).

Lemke, Bernd, *Luftschutz in Großbritannien und Deutschland 1923–1939. Zivile Kriegs-vorbereitungen als Ausdruck der staats- und gesellschaftspolitischen Grundlagen von Demokratie und Diktatur* (Munich, 1999).

Leonhard, Jörn, 'Die Nationalisierung des Krieges und der Bellizismus der Nation: Die Diskussion um Volks- und Nationalkrieg in Deutschland, Großbritannien und den Vereinigten Staaten seit den 1860er Jahren', in Christian Jansen (ed.), *Der Bürger als Soldat. Die Militärisierung europäischer Gesellschaften im langen 19. Jahrhundert: ein internationaler Vergleich* (Essen, 2004), 83–105.

Leonhard, Jörn, *Bellizismus und Nation. Kriegsdeutung und Nationsbestimmung in Europa und den Vereinigten Staaten 1750–1914* (Munich, 2008).

Lerner, Paul, 'Psychiatry and Casualties of War in Germany, 1914–18', *Contemporary History*, 35 (2000), 13–28.

Levine, Alan J., *The Strategic Bombing of Germany 1940–1945* (Westport, Conn./London, 1992).

Levine, Joshua, *Forgotten Voices of the Blitz and the Battle for Britain* (London, 2006).

Levsen, Sonja, *Elite, Männlichkeit und Krieg. Tübinger und Cambridger Studenten, 1900–1929* (Göttingen, 2006).

Lewis, Adrian, 'Henry Moore's "Shelter Drawings"': Memory and Myth', in Kirkham and Thoms (eds), *War Culture*, 113–27.

Lindner, Werner, and Böckler, Erich (eds), *Die Stadt. Ihre Pflege und Gestaltung* (Berlin, 1939).

Lindqvist, Sven, *A History of Bombing* (London, 2001).

Linehan, Thomas, *British Fascism, 1918–1939: Parties, Ideology and Culture* (Manchester/New York, 2000).

Longerich, Peter, 'Joseph Goebbels und der Totale Krieg. Eine unbekannte Denkschrift des Propagandaministers vom 18. Juli 1944', *VfZ* 35 (1987), 289–314.

Longerich, Peter, *Politik der Vernichtung. Eine Gesamtdarstellung der nationalsozialistischen Judenverfolgung* (Munich/Zurich, 1998).

Longerich, Peter, *'Davon haben wir nichts gewusst!' Die Deutschen und die Judenverfolgung* (Munich, 2006).

Longmate, Norman, *Air Raid: The Bombing of Coventry 1940* (London, 1976).

Longmate, Norman, *The Home Front: An Anthology of Personal Experience 1939–1945* (London, 1981).

Longmate, Norman, *How We Lived Then: A History of Everyday Life during the Second World War* (London, 2002).

Lowe, Keith, *Inferno: The Devastation of Hamburg* (London, 2007).

Lowe, Rodney, 'The Second World War, Consensus, and the Foundation of the Welfare State', *20th Century British History*, 1 (1990), 152–82.

Lowe, Roy, *Education and the Second World War: Studies in Schooling and Social Change* (London, 1992).

Lowry, Stephan, *Pathos und Politik. Ideologie in Spielfilmen des Nationalsozialismus* (Tübingen, 1991).

Ludendorff, Erich, *Der Totale Krieg, München 1935* [New edition] (Remscheid, 1988).

Lynch, Cecelia, *Beyond Appeasement: Interpreting Interwar Peace Movements in World Politics* (Ithaca, NY, 1999).

Lysaght, Charles Edward, *Brendan Bracken* (London, 1979).

McDonough, Frank, *Neville Chamberlain: Appeasement and the British Road to War* (London, 1998).

Maciejewski, Franz, 'Trauer ohne Riten—Riten ohne Trauer. Deutsche Volkstrauer nach 1945', in Assmann, Maciejewski, and Michaelis (eds), *Der Abschied von den Toten*, 245–66.

MacIsaac, David, *Strategic Bombing in World War Two: The Story of the Strategic Bombing Survey* (New York, 1976).

Mackay, Robert, *The Test of War: Inside Britain 1939–1945* (London, 1999).

Mackay, Robert, *Half the Battle: Civilian Morale in Britain during the Second World War* (Manchester, 2002).

MacKenzie, S. P., 'War in the Air: Churchill, the Air Ministry and the BBC Response to Victory at Sea', *Contemporary British History*, 20 (2006), 559–74.

McLachlan, Ian, *Night of the Intruders: First-Hand Accounts Chronicling the Slaughter of Homeward Bound USAAF Mission 311* (London, 1994).

McLaine, Ian, *Ministry of Morale: Home Front Morale and the Ministry of Information in World War Two* (London, 1979).

Macnicol, John, 'The Evacuation of Schoolchildren', in Smith (ed.), *War and Social Change*, 3–31.

Maier, Klaus A., 'Totaler Krieg und operativer Luftkrieg', in Maier et al. (eds), *Das Deutsche Reich und der Zweite Weltkrieg*, ii. 43–69.

Maier, Klaus A., 'Die Luftschlacht um England', in Maier et al. (eds), *Das Deutsche Reich und der Zweite Weltkrieg*, ii. 375–408.

Maier, Klaus A., et al. (eds), *Das Deutsche Reich und der Zweite Weltkrieg*, ii: *Die Errichtung der Hegemonie auf dem europäischen Kontinent* (Stuttgart, 1979).

Malpass, Peter, 'Wartime Planning for Post-War Housing in Britain: The Whitehall Debate, 1941–1945', *Town Planning Perspectives*, 18 (2003), 177–96.

Manesse, Eva, *Der Holocaust vor Gericht: Der Prozeß um David Irving* (Berlin, 2000).

Mann, Michael, *Die dunkle Seite der Demokratie. Eine Theorie der ethnischen Säuberung* (Hamburg, 2007).

Margalit, Gilad, 'Der Luftangriff auf Dresden. Seine Bedeutung für die Erinnerungspolitik der DDR und für die Herauskristallisierung einer historischen Kriegserinnerung im Westen', in Susanne Düwell and Mathias Schmidt (eds), *Narrative der Shoah. Repräsentationen der Vergangenheit in Historiographie, Kunst und Politik* (Paderborn, 2002), 189–207.

Margalit, Gilad, 'Dresden and Hamburg', in Helmut Schmitz (ed.), *A Nation of Victims? Representations of German Wartime Suffering from 1945 to the Present* (Amsterdam, 2007), 125–40.

Marrin, Albert, *The Last Crusade: The Church of England in the First World War* (Durham, 1974).

Marszolek, Inge, and Buggeln, Marc (eds), *Bunker. Kriegsort, Zuflucht, Erinnerungsraum* (Frankfurt am Main, 2008).

Marszolek, Inge, and Buggeln, Marc, 'Bunker: Orte, Erinnerungen und Fantasmen', in Marszolek and Buggeln (eds), *Bunker*, 9–26.

Marwick, Arthur, *War and Social Change in the Twentieth Century: A Comparative Study of Britain, France, Germany, Russia and the United States* (London, 1974).

Marx, Erich (ed.), *Bomben auf Salzburg: die 'Gauhauptstadt' im 'Totalen Krieg'* (Salzburg, 1995).

Mason, Tony, 'Looking Back on the Blitz', in Bill Lancaster and Tony Mason (eds), *Life and Labour in a Twentieth Century City: The Experience of Coventry* (Coventry, 1986), 321–41.

Matheson, Neil, 'National Identity and the "Melancholy of Ruin": Cecil Beaton's Photographs of the London Blitz', *Journal of War and Culture Studies*, 1 (2008), 261–74.

Matthews, Walter R., *Saint Paul's Cathedral in Wartime 1939–45* (London, 1946).

Mattioli, Aram, 'Entgrenzte Kriegsgewalt: Der italienische Giftgaseinsatz in Abessinien', *VfZ* 51 (2003), 311–37.

Mattioli, Aram, *Experimentierfeld der Gewalt. Der Abessinienkrieg und seine internationale Bedeutung 1935–1941* (Zurich, 2005).

May, Alex Charles, *Britain and Europe since 1945* (London/New York, 1999).

Mechler, Wolf-Dieter, *Kriegsalltag an der 'Heimatfront'. Das Sondergericht Hannover 1939–1945* (Hanover, 1997).

Mecking, Sabine, and Wirsching, Andreas (eds), *Stadtverwaltung im Nationalsozialismus. Systemstabilisierende Dimension kommunaler Herrschaft* (Paderborn, 2005).

Mecking, Sabine, and Wirsching, Andreas, 'Stadtverwaltung als Systemstabilisierung? Tätigkeitsfelder und Handlungsspielräume kommunaler Herrschaft im Nationalsozialismus', in Mecking and Wirsching (eds), *Stadtverwaltung im Nationalsozialismus*, 1–19.

Mehl, Christoph, and Thierfelder, Jörg, 'Ökumene im Krieg: Evangelisch-katholische Gespräche und innerprotestantische Vergewisserung in der Endphase des "Dritten Reiches"', *Zeitschrift für Kirchengeschichte*, 108 (1997), 342–75.

Meilinger, Phillip S., 'Trenchard and "Morale Bombing": The Evolution of Royal Air Force Doctrine before World War II', *Journal of Military History*, 60 (1996), 243–70.

Meilinger, Phillip S., *Trenchard, Slessor and Royal Air Force Doctrine before World War II*, in Phillip S. Meisinger (ed.), *The Paths of Heaven: The Evolution of Airpower Theory* (Montgomery, Ala., 1997), 41–78.

Meisel, Joseph S., 'Air Raid Shelter Policy and its Critics in Britain before the Second World War', *20th Century British History*, 5 (1994), 300–19.

Mergner, Gottfried, 'Gläubiger Fatalismus. Zur Mentalitätsgeschichte des "totalen Krieges" am Beispiel der Kriegstagebücher meiner Mutter, 1940–1946', in Marcel van der Linden and Gottfried Mergner (eds), *Kriegsbegeisterung und mentale Kriegsvorbereitung. Interdisziplinäre Studien* (Berlin, 1991), 179–94.

Merrilyn, Thomas, *Communing with the Enemy: Covert Operations, Christianity and Cold War Politics in Britain and the GDR* (Oxford/Frankfurt am Main, 2005).

Messenger, Charles, *Bomber Harris and the Strategic Bombing Offensive 1939–1945* (London, 1984).

Metzner, Karl (ed.), *Luftfahrt, Luftschutz und ihre Behandlung im Unterricht* (Leipzig, 1937).

Meyer, Olaf, *Vom Leiden und Hoffen der Städte. Öffentliches Gedenken an die Zerstörungen in Dresden, Coventry, Warschau und St. Petersburg* (Hamburg, 1996).

Middlebrook, Martin, *The Battle of Hamburg: Allied Bomber Forces against a German City in 1943* (London, 1980).

Middlebrook, Martin, *The Berlin Raids: R.A.F. Bomber Command Winter 1943–44* (London, 1988).

Middlebrook, Martin, and Everitt, Chris, *The Bomber Command War Diaries* (Hillingdon, 1985).

Mierzejewski, Alfred C., *Bomben auf die Reichsbahn. Der Zusammenbruch der deutschen Kriegswirtschaft 1944–1945* (Freiburg, 1993).

Miller, Kristine A., *British Literature of the Blitz: Fighting the People's War* (Basingstoke, 2009).

Mira, Emilio, 'Psychiatric Experience in the Spanish War', *British Medical Journal*, 1 (1939), 1161.

Missalla, Heinrich, *Für Volk und Vaterland. Die Kirchliche Kriegshilfe im Zweiten Weltkrieg* (Königstein i.Ts., 1978).

Mitscherlich, Margarete, and Richter, Hans-Eberhard, *Versteckte Vergangenheit. Über den Umgang mit der NS-Zeit in Köln* (Cologne, 1995).

Mitzscherlich, Birgit, *Diktatur und Diaspora. Das Bistum Meißen 1932–1951* (Paderborn, 2005).

Moeller, Robert G., 'The Bombing of Germany, 2005–1940: Back to the Future?', in Tanaka and Young (eds), *Bombing Civilians*, 46–76.

Moessner-Heckner, Ursula, *Pforzheim, Code Yellowfin. Eine Analyse der Luftangriffe 1944–1945* (Sigmaringen, 1991).

Moll, Martin, 'Steuerungsinstrument im "Ämterchaos"? Die Tagungen der Reichs- und Gauleiter der NSDAP', *VfZ* 49 (2001), 215–73.

Moltmann, Günther, 'Goebbels' Rede zum totalen Krieg', *VfZ* 16 (1964), 13–43.

Mommsen, Hans, 'Forschungskontroversen zum Nationalsozialismus', *Aus Politik und Zeitgeschichte*, 57/15 (2007), 14–21.

Mommsen, Hans, 'Amoklauf der "Volksgemeinschaft". Kritische Anmerkungen zu Michael Wildts Grundkurs zur Geschichte des Nationalsozialismus', *Neue Politische Literatur*, 53 (2008), 15–20.

Mommsen, Hans, and Willems, Susanne (eds), *Herrschaftsalltag im Dritten Reich* (Düsseldorf, 1988).

Morgan, Kenneth O., *The People's Peace: British History since 1945* (Oxford, 1999).

Morris, June, 'Morale under Air Attack: Swansea, 1939–1941', *Welsh History Review*, 11 (1982), 358–87.

Mues, Willi, *Der Grosse Kessel. Eine Dokumentation über das Ende des Zweiten Weltkrieges zwischen Lippe und Ruhr/Sieg und Lenne* (Erwitte, 1984).

Müller, Klaus-Jürgen, and Dilks, David N. (eds), *Großbritannien und der deutsche Widerstand 1933–1944* (Paderborn, 1994).

Müller, Rolf-Dieter, 'Die deutschen Gaskriegsvorbereitungen 1919–1945. Mit Giftgas zur Weltmacht?', *Militärgeschichtliche Forschungen*, 1 (1980), 25–54.

Müller, Rolf-Dieter, 'Albert Speer und die Rüstungspolitik im totalen Krieg', in Bernhard Kroener, Rolf-Dieter Müller, and Hans Umbreit (eds), *Das Deutsche Reich und der Zweite Weltkrieg, v/2: Organisation und Mobilisierung des deutschen Machtbereichs* (Stuttgart, 1999), 275–1001.

Müller, Rolf-Dieter, *Der Bombenkrieg 1939–1945*, with the assistance of Florian Huber and Johannes Eglau (Berlin, 2004).

Müller, Rolf-Dieter, 'Bomben und Legenden', in *einestages—Zeitgeschichte auf Spiegel-Online* <http://einestages.spiegel.de/static/topicalbumbackground/302/bomben_und_ legenden.html>, 15 July 2009.

Müller, Rolf-Dieter, Schönherr, Nicole, and Widera, Thomas (eds), *Die Zerstörung Dresdens 13. bis 15. Februar 1945. Gutachten und Ergebnisse der Dresdner Historikerkommission zur Ermittlung der Opferzahlen* (Göttingen, 2010).

Müller, Rolf-Dieter, and Überschär, Gerd R., *Kriegsende 1945. Die Zerstörung des Deutschen Reiches* (Frankfurt am Main, 1994).

Murphy, Robert, *British Cinema in the Second World War* (London, 2000).

Murray, Williamson, 'The Combined Bomber Offensive', *Militärgeschichtliche Mitteilungen*, 51 (1992), 73–94.

Murray, Williamson, *Der Luftkrieg von 1914–1945* (Berlin, 2000).

Mutius, Albert von, 'Kommunalverwaltung und Kommunalpolitik', in Kurt G. A. Jeserich, Hans Pohl, and Georg-Christoph von Unruh (eds), *Deutsche Verwaltungsgeschichte*, iv: *Das Reich als Republik und in der Zeit des Nationalsozialismus* (Stuttgart, 1985), 1055–81.

Nash, Geoffrey, *From Empire to Orient: Travellers to the Middle East* (London, 2005).

Naumann, Klaus, *Der Krieg als Text. Das Jahr 1945 im kulturellen Gedächtnis der Presse* (Hamburg, 1998).

Naumann, Klaus, 'Leerstelle Luftkrieg. Einwurf zu einer verqueren Debatte', *Mittelweg*, 36/2 (1998), 12–15.

Naumann, Klaus, 'Der Bombenkrieg: Deutsche als Opfer ihrer selbst?', in Naumann, *Der Krieg als Text*, 33–71.

Nebelin, Manfred, *Ludendorff. Diktator im Ersten Weltkrieg* (Munich, 2011).

Nehring, Holger, 'Politics, Symbols and the Public Sphere: The Protests against Nuclear Weapons in Britain and West Germany, 1958–1963', *Zeithistorische Forschungen*, 2 (2005), 180–202.

Neillands, Robin, *Der Krieg der Bomber. Arthur Harris und die Bomberoffensive der Alliierten 1939–1945* (Berlin, 2002).

Neitzel, Sönke, *Der Einsatz der deutschen Luftwaffe über dem Atlantik und der Nordsee 1939–1945* (Bonn, 1995).

Neitzel, Sönke, 'Zum strategischen Misserfolg verdammt? Die deutschen Luftstreitkräfte in beiden Weltkriegen', in Bruno Thoss and Hans-Erich Volkmann (eds), *Erster Weltkrieg—Zweiter Weltkrieg. Ein Vergleich* (Paderborn, 2002), 167–92.

Neitzel, Sönke, 'The City under Attack', in Addison and Crang (eds), *Firestorm*, 62–77.

Neitzel, Sönke, 'Eine Standortbestimmung der deutschen Militärgeschichtsschreibung über die Zeitalter der Weltkriege', in Hans-Christof Kraus and Thomas Nicklas (eds), *Geschichte der Politik. Alte und neue Wege*, Historische Zeitschrift 44 (Munich, 2007), 287–308.

Neufeld, Michael J., *Die Rakete und das Reich. Wernher von Braun, Peenemünde und der Beginn des Raketenzeitalters* (Berlin, 1999).

Neufeld, Michael J., and Berenbaum, Michael (eds), *The Bombing of Auschwitz: Should the Allies have Attempted it?* (New York, 2000).

Neumann, Michael, *Royal Air Force gegen Luftwaffe: Die Eskalation zum strategischen Luftkrieg 3. September 1939 bis 12. Mai 1940* (Munich, 2007).

Neumann, Vera, *Nicht der Rede wert. Die Privatisierung der Kriegsfolgen in der frühen Bundesrepublik* (Münster, 1997).

'Die Neurose'. *Ihre Versorgungs- und Sozialmedizinische Beurteilung*, ed. Bundesminister für Arbeit und Sozialordnung (Bonn, 1960).

Neutzner, Matthias, 'Vom Alltäglichen zum Exemplarischen. Dresden als Chiffre für den Luftkrieg der Alliierten', in Neutzner, Reinhard, and Hesse (eds), *Das rote Leuchten*, 110–27.

Neutzner, Matthias, 'Vom Anklagen zum Erinnern. Die Erzählung vom 13. Februar', in Neutzner, Reinhard, and Hesse (eds), *Das rote Leuchten*, 128–63.

Neutzner, Matthias, Reinhard, Oliver, and Hesse, Wolfgang (eds), *Das rote Leuchten. Dresden und der Bombenkrieg* (Dresden, 2005).

The New Coventry Cathedral Plan and Scheme (Coventry, 1944).

Newsinger, John, '"My Country, Right or Left": Patriotism, Socialism and George Orwell, 1939–1941', in Kirkham and Thoms (eds), *War Culture*, 29–37.

Nicholas, Siân, '"Sly Demagogues" and Wartime Radio: J. B. Priestley and the BBC', *20th Century British History*, 6 (1995), 247–66.

Nicholas, Siân, *The Echo of War: Home Front Propaganda and the Wartime BBC 1939–45* (Manchester, 1996).

Niethammer, Lutz (ed.), *'Die Jahre weiß man nicht, wo man die heute hinsetzen soll'. Faschismus-Erfahrungen im Ruhrgebiet* (Berlin/Bonn, 1983).

Niven, Bill (ed.), *Germans as Victims: Remembering the Past in Contemporary Germany* (New York, 2006).

Niven, Bill, 'The GDR and Memory of the Bombing of Dresden', in Niven (ed.), *Germans as Victims*, 109–29.

Niven, Bill, and Paver, Chloe (eds), *Memorialisation in Germany from 1945 to the Present* (Basingstoke, 2010).

Noack, Gerd, and Weißbecker, Manfred, '"Die Partei als Rückgrat der inneren Front". Mobilmachungspläne der NSDAP für den Krieg (1937 bis 1939)', in Dietrich Eichholtz and Kurt Pätzold (eds), *Der Weg in den Krieg. Studien zur Geschichte der Vorkriegsjahre (1935/36 bis 1939)* (Cologne. 1989), 67–90.

Noakes, Jeremy (ed.), *The Civilian in War: The Home Front in Europe, Japan and the USA in World War II* (Exeter, 1992).

Noakes, Jeremy, 'Die kommunale Selbstverwaltung im Dritten Reich', in Adolf Birke and Magnus Brechtken (eds), *Kommunale Selbstverwaltung—Local Self-Government. Geschichte und Gegenwart im deutsch-britischen Vergleich* (Munich, 1996), 65–81.

Noakes, Jeremy, Preface, in Jeremy Noakes and Geoffrey Pridham, *Nazism 1919–1945*, iv: *The German Home Front in World War II: A Documentary Reader* (Exeter, 1998).

Noakes, Jeremy, *Germany*, in Noakes (ed.), *The Civilian in War*, 35–61.

Noakes, Lucy, 'Making Histories: Experiencing the Blitz in London's Museums in the 1990s', in Martin Evans and Ken Lunn (eds), *War and Memory in the Twentieth Century* (Oxford/New York, 1997), 89–104.

Noakes, Lucy, *War and the British: Gender, Memory and National Identity* (London/ New York, 1998).

Noetzel, Thomas, 'Political Decadence? Aspects of Thatcherite Englishness', *Journal for the Study of British Culture*, 1 (1994), 133–48.

Nolzen, Armin, '"Sozialismus der Tat?" Die Nationalsozialistische Volkswohlfahrt (NSV) und der alliierte Luftkrieg gegen das Deutsche Reich', in Süss (ed.), *Deutschland*, 57–69.

Nolzen, Armin, 'Die NSDAP, der Krieg und die deutsche Gesellschaft', in Echternkamp (ed.), *Das Deutsche Reich und der Zweite Weltkrieg*, ix/1. 99–193.

Nolzen, Armin, '"Politische Führung und Betreuung der Bevölkerung". Die NSDAP im Bombenkrieg, 1939–1945', in Lemke (ed.), *Luft- und Zivilschutz*, 89–108.

Nonne, Max, 'Therapeutische Erfahrungen an den Kriegsneurosen in den Jahren 1914 bis 1918', in Karl Bonhoeffer (ed.), *Handbuch der ärztlichen Erfahrungen im Weltkriege 1914/1918*, iv: *Geistes- und Nervenerkrankungen* (Leipzig, 1922), 102–21.

O'Brien, Terrence Henry, *Civil Defence* (London, 1955).

Oehler, Christiane, *Die Rechtsprechung des Sondergerichts Mannheim 1933–1945* (Berlin, 1997).

Oehlrich, Conrad, 'Vom "Police Bombing" zum Luftterror. Die britische Schuld am Bombenkrieg', *Auswärtige Politik*, 10 (1943), 578–86.

Oesl, Bettina, 're-VISION. Zum Konzept der Ausstellung', in Tippe (ed.), *16. März 1945*, 9–13.

Ohliger, Ernst, *Bomben auf Kohlenstadt. Ein Roman, der Wirklichkeit sein könnte* (Berlin, 1935).

Oram, Alison, '"Bombs Don't Discriminate!" Women's Political Activism in the Second World War', in Christine Gledhill and Gillian S. Swanson (eds), *Nationalising Femininity: Culture, Sexuality and British Cinema in the Second World War* (Manchester, 1996), 53–69.

Overlack, Victoria, *Zwischen nationalem Aufbruch und Nischenexistenz. Evangelisches Leben in Hamburg 1933–1945* (Munich, 2007).

Overy, Richard, *The Air War 1939–1945* (London, 1980).

Overy, Richard, *The Battle* (London, 2000).

Overy, Richard, *The Battle of Britain: The Myth and the Reality* (New York, 2001).

Overy, Richard, *Die Wurzeln des Sieges: Warum die Alliierten den Zweiten Weltkrieg gewannen* (Reinbek bei Hamburg, 2002).

Overy, Richard, *Verhöre. Die NS-Elite in den Händen der Alliierten 1945* (Munich/ Berlin, 2002).

Overy, Richard, 'Allied Bombing and the Destruction of German Cities', in Chickering, Förster, and Greiner (eds), *A World at Total War*, 277–95.

Overy, Richard, 'Die alliierte Bombenstrategie als Ausdruck des "totalen Krieges"', in Kettenacker (ed.), *Ein Volk von Opfern?*, 27–47.

Overy, Richard, 'The Post War Debate', in Addison and Crang (eds), *Firestorm*, 123–42.

Overy, Richard, *The Morbid Age: Britain between the Wars* (London, 2009).

Overy, Richard, Baldoli, Claudia, and Knapp, Andrew (eds), *Bombing, States and Peoples in Western Europe, 1940–1945* (London, 2011).

Panayi, Panikos, *Immigration, Ethnicity and Racism in Britain 1815–1945* (London, 1994).

Panse, Friedrich, *Angst und Schreck in klinisch-psychologischer und sozialmedizinischer Sicht. Dargestellt an Hand von Erlebnisberichten aus dem Luftkrieg* (Stuttgart, 1952).

Parker, Stephen G., *Faith on the Home Front: Aspects of Church Life and Popular Religion in Birmingham 1939–1945* (Oxford/New York, 2006).

Parsons, Martin L., *Evacuation: The True Story* (London, 1999).

Parton, Neville, 'The Development of Early RAF Doctrine', *Journal of Military History*, 72 (2008), 1155–78.

Patel, Kiran Klaus, *Soldaten an der Arbeit. Arbeitsdienste in Deutschland und den USA 1933–1945* (Göttingen, 2003).

Patel, Kiran Klaus, '"All of This Helps Us in Planning". Der New Deal und die NS-Sozialpolitik', in Daniel Schönpflug and Martin Aust (eds), *Vom Gegner lernen. Feindschaften und Kulturtransfers im Europa des 19. und 20. Jahrhunderts* (Frankfurt am Main, 2007), 234–52.

Penrose, Lionel S., 'Neurosis in the Women's Service', *Journal of Mental Science*, 95 (1949), 880–96.

Penton, John, *Solly Zuckerman: Scientist out of the Ordinary* (London, 200).

Permooser, Irmtraud, *Der Luftkrieg über München 1942–1945. Bomben auf die Hauptstadt der Bewegung* (Munich, 1996).

Peukert, Detlev, and Reulecke, Jürgen (eds), *Die Reihen fest geschlossen. Beiträge zur Geschichte des Alltags unterm Nationalsozialismus* (Wuppertal, 1981).

Phillips, Alwyn J., *The Valley of the Shadow of Death: An Account of the Royal Air Force Bomber Command Night Bombing and Minelaying Operations Including 'The Battle of the Ruhr'* (Chippenham, 1991).

Piper, Ernst, *Kurze Geschichte des Nationalsozialismus. Von 1919 bis heute* (Hamburg, 2007).

Pogt, Herbert (ed.), *Vor fünfzig Jahren. Bomben auf Wuppertal* (Wuppertal, 1993).

Pöhlmann, Markus, *'Es war gerade, als würde alles bersten…': Die Stadt Augsburg im Bombenkrieg 1939–1945* (Augsburg, 1994).

Pöhlmann, Markus, 'Von Versailles nach Armageddon: Totalisierungserfahrung und Kriegserwartung in deutschen Militärzeitschriften', in Stig Förster (ed.), *Die militärische Debatte über den Krieg der Zukunft 1919–1939* (Paderborn, 2002), 323–91.

Ponting, Clive, *1940: Myth and Reality* (London, 1990).

Popitz, Heinrich, *Phänomene der Macht* (Tübingen, 1992).

Powell, Lewis F., and Putney, Diane T., *ULTRA and the Army Air Forces in World War II* (Washington, 1987).

Price, Alfred, *Blitz on Britain: The Bomber Attacks on the United Kingdom, 1939–1945* (Shepperton, 1977).

Price, Alfred, *Blitz über England* (Stuttgart, 1978).

Priestley, John B., *English Journey* (London, 1934).

Priestley, John B., *Out of the People* (London, 1941).

Primoratz, Igor (ed.), *Terror from the Sky: The Bombing of German Cities in World War II* (New York, 2010).

Probert, Henry, *Bomber Harris. His Life and Times: The Biography of Marshal of the Royal Air Force, Sir Arthur Harris, the Wartime Chief of Bomber Command* (London, 2001).

Probert, Henry, 'Die Auswirkungen des strategischen Luftkrieges auf die deutsche Moral 1940–1945. Britische Erwartungen und deutsche Reaktionen', in Müller and Dilks (eds), *Großbritannien und der deutsche Widerstand*, 197–216.

Pross, Christian, *Wiedergutmachung. Der Kleinkrieg gegen die Opfer* (Frankfurt am Main, 1988).

Purpus, Elke, Sellen, Günther, and Buchen, Helmut, *Bunker in Köln. Versuch einer Sichtbar-Machung* (Essen, 2006).

Ramsden, John, 'Refocusing the People's War: British War Films of the 1950s', *Journal of Contemporary History*, 33 (1998), 35–63.

Rankin, Nicolas, *Telegram from Guernica: The Extraordinary Life of George Steer, War Correspondent* (London, 2003).

Raven, Charles, *War and the Christian* (London, 1938).

Rawlinson, Alfred, *The Defence of London, 1915–1918* (London, 1929).

Rawlinson, Mark, *British Writing of the Second World War* (New York, 2000).

Ray, Jon, *The Night Blitz: 1940–1941* (London, 1996).

Raymond, Robert S., *A Yank in Bomber Command* (Newton Abbot, 1977).

Reemtsma, Jan Philipp, in *Krieg ist ein Gesellschaftszustand. Reden zur Eröffnung der Ausstellung 'Vernichtungskrieg. Verbrechen der Wehrmacht 1941–1944'*, ed. Hamburger Institut für Sozialforschung (Hamburg, 1998), 8–13.

Reibel, Carl-Wilhelm, *Das Fundament der Diktatur: Die NSDAP-Ortsgruppen 1932–1945* (Paderborn, 2002).

Reichardt, Sven, *Faschistische Kampfbünde. Gewalt und Gemeinschaft im italienischen Squadrismus und in der deutschen SA* (Cologne/Weimar/Vienna, 2002).

Rempel, Reichsrichter, 'Vertretungsbefugnis in Entschädigungsverfahren', *Deutsche Verwaltung*, 20 (1943), 130.

Rennie, Paul, *Festival of Britain 1951* (London, 2007).

Repgen, Konrad, 'Die deutschen Bischöfe und der Zweite Weltkrieg', *Historisches Jahrbuch*, 115 (1995), 411–52.

Reuband, Karl-Heinz, 'Das NS-Regime zwischen Akzeptanz und Ablehnung. Eine retrospective Analyse von Bevölkerungseinstellungen im Dritten Reich auf der Basis von Umfragedaten', *Geschichte und Gesellschaft*, 31 (2006), 315–43.

Reynolds, David, *Britannia Overruled: British Policy & World Power in the 20th Century* (London/New York, 1991).

Reynolds, David, *In Command of History: Churchill Fighting and Writing the Second World War* (London, 2005).

Richardi, Hans-Günter, *Bomber über München: Der Luftkrieg von 1939 bis 1945, dargestellt am Beispiel der 'Hauptstadt der Bewegung'* (Munich, 1992).

Richards, Denis, *The Hardest Victory: RAF Bomber Command in the Second World War* (London, 1994).

Richards, Denis, and Saunders, Hillary, *Royal Air Force 1939–1945*, vols. i–iii (London, 1953–5).

Richards, Jeffrey, *Britain Can Take It: The British Cinema in the Second World War* (London, 1986).

Richards, Jeffrey, and Sheridan, Dorothy (eds), *Mass Observation at the Movies* (London, 1987).

Richter, Horst-Eberhard, '"Action Gomorrha". Gedanken zum 50. Jahrestag des großen Bombenangriffs auf Hamburg' (Address in the main Hamburg church of St Peter on 21 June 1993), in Horst-Eberhard Richter (ed.), *Wer nicht leiden will muss hassen. Zur Epidemie der Gewalt* (Hamburg, 1993), 63–72.

Riedesser, Peter, and Verderber, Axel, *'Maschinengewehre hinter der Front'. Zur Geschichte der deutschen Militärpsychiatrie* (Frankfurt am Main, 1996).

Rittersporn, Gábor T., Behrends, Jan C., and Rolf, Malte, 'Öffentlichkeit und öffentliche Räume in Gesellschaften sowjetischen Typs. Ein erster Blick aus komparativer Perspektive' (Introduction), in Gábor T. Rittersporn, Jan C. Behrends, and Malte Rolf (eds), *Sphären von Öffentlichkeit in Gesellschaften sowjetischen Typs. Zwischen partei-staatlicher Selbstinszenierung und kirchlichen Gegenwelten* (Frankfurt am Main, 2003), 7–21.

Rochat, Giorgio, *Die italienischen Militärinternierten im Zweiten Weltkrieg* (Rome, 1987).

Roeser, Frank, *Das Sondergericht Essen 1942–1945* (Baden-Baden, 2000).

Rogg, Matthias, 'Die Luftwaffe im NS-Propagandafilm', in Chiari, Rogg, and Schmidt (eds), *Krieg und Militär*, 343–8.

Rose, Sonya O., *Which People's War? National Identity and Citizenship in Wartime Britain 1939–1945* (New York, 2003).

Rosenfeld, Gavriel D., *Architektur und Gedächtnis. München und Nationalsozialismus. Strategien des Vergessens* (Munich, 2004).

Rosenfeld, Gavriel D., and Jaskot, Paul B. (eds), *Beyond Berlin: Twelve German Cities Confront the Nazi Past* (Ann Arbor, 2008).

Rother, Rainer (ed.), *Die letzten Tage der Menschheit. Bilder des Ersten Weltkrieges. Eine Ausstellung des Deutschen Historischen Museums, Berlin, der Barbican Art Gallery, London, und der Staatlichen Museen zu Berlin—Preußischer Kulturbesitz in Verbindung mit dem Imperial War Museum, London* (Berlin, 1994).

Rother, Rainer, '"Stukas". Zeitnaher Film und Kriegsbedingungen', in Chiari, Rogg, and Schmidt (eds), *Krieg und Militär*, 349–70.

Rothnie, Niall, *The Baedecker Blitz: Hitler's Attack on Britain's Historic Cities* (Shepperton, 1992).

Rüfner, Wolfgang, 'Ausgleich von Kriegs- und Diktaturfolge', in Günther Schulz (ed.), *Geschichte der Sozialpolitik seit 1945*, iii: *Bundesrepublik Deutschland. Bewältigung der Kriegsfolgen, Rückkehr sozialpolitischer Normalität* (Baden-Baden, 2005), 690–757.

Rugg, Julie, 'Managing "Civilian Deaths due to War Operations": Yorkshire Experiences During World War II', *20th Century British History*, 15 (2004), 152–73.

Rummel, Walther, and Rath, Jochen, *'Dem Reich verfallen'—'den Berechtigten zurückzuerstatten'. Enteignung und Rückerstattung jüdischen Vermögens im Gebiet des heutigen Rheinland-Pfalz 1938–1953* (Coblenz, 2001).

Rumpf, Hans, *Der hochrote Hahn* (Darmstadt, 1952).

Rumpf, Hans, *Das war der Bombenkrieg. Deutsche Städte im Feuersturm. Ein Dokumentarbericht* (Oldenburg/Hamburg, 1961).

Ruppert, Andreas, and Riechert, Hans Jörg, *Herrschaft und Akzeptanz. Der Nationalsozialismus in Lippe während der Kriegsjahre. Analyse und Dokumentation* (Opladen, 1998).

Rürup, Reinhard (ed.), *Berlin 1945. Eine Dokumentation* (Berlin, 1995).

Rusinek, Bernd-A., '"Maskenlose Zeit". Der Zerfall der Zivilgesellschaft im Krieg', in Borsdorf and Jamin (eds), *Über Leben im Krieg*, 180–94.

Rusinek, Bernd-A., *Gesellschaft in der Katastrophe. Terror, Illegalität, Widerstand—Köln 1944/45* (Essen, 1989).

Russell, Edmund P. III, 'Speaking of Annihilation: Mobilizing for War against Human and Insect Enemies 1914–1945', *Journal of American History*, 24 (1996), 1505–29.

Rüther, Martin, 'Reaktionen und Folgen', in Rüther, *Köln, 31. Mai 1942*, 77–93.

Rüther, Martin, *Köln im Zweiten Weltkrieg. Alltag und Erfahrung zwischen 1939–1945* (Cologne, 2005).

Rüther, Martin, *Köln, 31. Mai 1942: Der 1000-Bomber-Angriff* (Cologne, 1992).

Sabrow, Martin (ed.), *Skandal und Diktatur. Formen öffentlicher Empörung im NS-Staat und in der DDR* (Göttingen, 2004).

Sabrow, Martin, 'Politischer Skandal und moderne Diktatur', in Sabrow (ed.), *Skandal und Diktatur*, 7–32.

Sachsse, Rolf, *Die Erziehung zum Wegsehen. Fotografie im NS-Staat* (Dresden, 2003).

Sachsse, Rolf, *Fotografie. Vom technischen Bildmittel zur Krise der Repräsentation* (Cologne, 2003).

Saint-Amour, Paul K., 'Air War Prophecy and Interwar Modernism', *Comparative Literature Studies*, 42 (2005), 130–61.

Saldern, Adelheid von (ed.), *Inszenierte Einigkeit. Herrschaftsrepräsentationen in DDR-Städten* (Stuttgart, 2003).

Saldern, Adelheid von, 'Öffentlichkeiten in Diktaturen. Zu den Herrschaftspraktiken im Deutschland des 20. Jahrhunderts', in Günther Heydemann and Heinrich Oberreuter (eds), *Diktaturen in Deutschland—Vergleichsaspekte. Strukturen, Institutionen und Verhaltensweisen* (Bonn, 2003), 442–75.

Sandler, Stanley, *Segregated Skies: All-Black Combat Squadrons of WW II* (Washington, 1992).

Santana, Marcelle, 'Ein Radikaler im Dienst der Partei. Der nationalsozialistische Propagandist Alfred-Ingemar Berndt (1905–1945)', MA dissertation, LMU, Munich, 2007.

Saward, Dudley, *'Bomber' Harris: The Authorised Biography* (London, 1984).

Schäfer, Annette, 'Zur Rolle der Kommunen bei Zwangsarbeitereinsatz im Zweiten Weltkrieg', *Annali*, 28 (2002), 405–33.

Schäfer, Gerhard (ed.), *Landesbischof D. Wurm und der Nationalsozialistische Staat 1940–1945. Eine Dokumentation* (Stuttgart, 1968).

Schäfer, Gerhard, *Die Evangelische Landeskirche in Württemberg und der Nationalsozialismus—eine Dokumentation zum Kirchenkampf*, vols. i–vi (Stuttgart, 1971–86).

Scheil, Stefan, *Churchill, Hitler und der Antisemitismus. Die deutsche Diktatur, ihre politischen Gegner und die europäische Krise der Jahre 1938/39* (Berlin, 2009).

Schildt, Axel, 'Von der Aufklärung zum Fernsehzeitalter. Neue Literatur zu Öffentlichkeit und Medien', *AfS* 40 (2000), 487–509.

Schildt, Axel, Führer, Karl Christian, and Hickethier, Knut, 'Öffentlichkeit—Medien—Geschichte. Konzepte der modernen Öffentlichkeit und Zugänge ihrer Erforschung', *AfS* 41 (2001), 1–38.

Schlechter-Bonnesen, Käthe, 'Nach dem Bombenangriff', in Horst Matzerath (ed.), *'Vergessen kann man die Zeit nicht, das ist nicht möglich . . .'. Kölner erinnern sich an die Jahre 1929–1945* (Cologne, 1985).

Schlemmer, Thomas, and Süss, Dietmar, 'Vittime degli alleati? La memoria della guerra aerea in Germania e in Italia', *Annali dell'Istituto Storico italo-germanico*, 32 (2006), 325–37.

Schlosser, Yvonne, *Fotografie im Bombenkrieg. Zeitzeugenfotografien in Deutschland 1942–1945*, MA dissertation, Augsburg University, 2005.

Schmal, Helga, and Selke, Tobias, *Bunker—Luftschutz und Luftschutzbau in Hamburg* (Hamburg, 2001).

Schmidt, Herbert, *'Beabsichtige ich die Todesstrafe zu beantragen'. Die nationalsozialistische Sondergerichtsbarkeit im Oberlandesbezirk Düsseldorf 1933 bis 1945* (Essen, 1998).

Schmitz, Hubert, *Die Bewirtschaftung der Nahrungsmittel und Verbrauchsgüter 1939–1950. Dargestellt am Beispiel der Stadt Essen* (Essen, 1956).

Schnabel, Ralf, *Die Illusion der Wunderwaffen. Die Rolle der Düsenflugzeuge und Flugabwehrraketen in der Rüstungspolitik des Dritten Reiches* (Munich, 1994).

Schnatz, Helmut, *Der Luftkrieg im Raum Koblenz 1944/45. Eine Darstellung seines Verlaufs, seiner Auswirkungen und Hintergründe* (Boppard, 1981).

Schnatz, Helmut, *Tiefflieger über Dresden? Legenden und Wirklichkeit* (Cologne/Weimar/Vienna, 2000).

Schnatz, Helmut, 'Die Zerstörung der deutschen Städte und die Opfer', in Bernd Heidenreich and Sönke Neitzel (eds), *Der Bombenkrieg und seine Opfer* (Wiesbaden, 2004), 30–48.

Schnatz, Helmut, 'Die vergleichende Ermittlung von Todesopfern der britischen Luftangriffe (allied bombing) auf deutsche Städte', in Müller, Schönherr, and Widera (eds), *Die Zerstörung Dresdens 13. bis 15. Februar 1945*, 101–18.

Schoenbaum, David, *Hitler's Social Revolution* (New York, 1967).

Schönpflug, Daniel, and Aust, Martin (eds), *Vom Gegner lernen. Feindschaften und Kulturtransfers im Europa des 19. und 20. Jahrhunderts* (Frankfurt am Main, 2007).

Schramm, Georg Wolfgang, *Der zivile Luftschutz in Nürnberg*, 2 vols (Nuremberg, 1983).

Schüler-Springorum, Stefanie, 'Mythos Guernica. Projektion, Propaganda, Politik', in Arnold, Süss, and Thiessen, *Luftkrieg*, 84–100.

Schüler-Springorum, Stefanie, *Krieg und Fliegen. Die Legion Condor im Spanischen Bürgerkrieg* (Paderborn, 2010).

Schütz, Erhard, 'Wahn-Europa, Mediale Gas-Luftkriegsszenarien der Zwischenkriegszeit', in Hans Peter Preusser (ed.), *Krieg in den Medien* (Amsterdam, 2005), 127–47.

Schwanzar, Fabian, 'Visualisierung des Bombenkriegs. Anmerkungen zu Fotografien im Stadtmuseum Münster', *Westfälische Forschungen*, 58 (2008), 461–70.

Searle, Alaric, 'Fuller and Liddell Hart: The Continuing Debate', *War in History*, 8/3 (2001), 341–7.

Sebald, Winfried G., *Luftkrieg und Literatur. Mit einem Essay zu Alfred Andersch* (Munich/Vienna, 1999).

Seeger, Andreas, '"Gegen Schwerstverbrecher ist in Kriegzeiten die zugelassene Todesstrafe grundsätzlich die gebotene"', in Robert Bohn and Uwe Danker (eds), *'Standgericht der inneren Front'. Das Sondergericht Altona/Kiel 1932–1945* (Hamburg, 1998), 166–89.

Seib, Philip, *Broadcasts from the Blitz: How Edward R. Murrow Helped Lead America into War* (Washington DC, 2006).

Seidel, Thomas A., *Im Übergang der Diktaturen. Eine Untersuchung zur kirchlichen Neuordnung in Thüringen 1945–1951* (Stuttgart, 2003).

Seiderer, Georg, 'Der Luftkrieg im öffentlichen Gedenken. Wandlungen der Erinnerungskultur in Nürnberg und Würzburg nach 1945', *Jahrbuch für fränkische Landesforschung*, 67 (2007), 333–55.

Seiderer, Georg, 'Würzburg, 16. März 1945. Vom "kollektiven" Trauma zur lokalen Sinnstiftung', in Arnold, Süss, and Thiessen (eds), *Luftkrieg*, 146–61.

Selig, Wolfram, and Seligmann, Richard, *Ein jüdisches Schicksal* (Munich, 1983).

Shephard, Ben, 'Pitiless Psychology: The Role of Prevention in British Military Psychiatry in the Second World War', *History of Psychiatry*, 10 (1999), 491–524.

Shephard, Ben, *A War of Nerves: Soldiers and Psychiatry 1914–1994* (London, 2000).

Sherry, Michael S., *The Rise of American Air Power: The Creation of Armageddon* (New Haven, 1987).

Slack, Kenneth, *George Bell* (London, 1971).

Smith, Adam, 'The British Experience of Bombing', in Peter H. Liddle, Peter Bourne, and Ian R. Whitehead (eds), *The Great World War 1914–1945*, ii: *Who Won? Who Lost?* (London, 2001), 29–40.

Smith, Arthur C., *Halifax Crew: The Story of a Wartime Bomber Crew* (London, 1983).

Smith, Harold L., *War and Social Change: British Society in the Second World War* (Manchester, 1986).

Smith, Harold L., *Britain in the Second World War: A Social History* (Manchester, 1996).

Smith, Malcolm, *British Air Strategy between the Wars* (Oxford, 1984).

Smith, Malcolm, *Britain and 1940: History, Myth and Popular Memory* (London/New York, 2000).

Smith, Malcolm, 'Die Luftbedrohung und die britische Außen- und Innenpolitik. Der Hintergrund der strategischen Luftoffensive', in Boog (ed.), *Luftkriegsführung im Zweiten Weltkrieg*, 701–21.

Sokoloff, Sally, 'The Home Front in the Second World War and Local History', *Local Historian*, 32 (2002), 22–40.

Sollbach, Gerhard E. (ed.), *Dortmund. Bombenkrieg und Nachkriegsalltag 1939–1948* (Hagen, 1996).

Southworth, Herbert, *Guernica! Guernica! A Study of Journalism, Diplomacy, Propaganda and History* (Berkeley, 1977).

Später, Jörg, *Vansittart. Britische Debatten über Deutsche und Nazis 1902–1945* (Göttingen, 2003).

Speer, Albert, *Erinnerungen* (Frankfurt am Main, 1969).

Sperling, Hans, 'Die deutschen Luftkriegsverluste im Zweiten Weltkrieg', in Statistisches Bundesamt, *Wirtschaft und Statistik* (1962), 139–41.

Spetzler, Eberhard, *Luftkrieg und Menschlichkeit. Die völkerrechtliche Stellung der Zivilpersonen im Luftkrieg* (Göttingen, 1956).

Stadt Essen (ed.), *Stadtarchiv-Materialien für den Unterricht*, i: *Essen im Luftkrieg* (Essen, 2000).

Stadt Freiburg (ed.), *Zerstörung und Wiederaufbau. Begleitbuch zur Ausstellung von Stadtarchiv und Augustinermuseum anlässlich des 50. Jahrestages der Zerstörung Freiburgs im Luftkrieg am 27. November 1944* (Freiburg, 1994).

Stadt Hamm (ed.), *Ortstermin Hamm. Zur Justiz im Dritten Reich* (Hamm, 1991).

Stadt Kiel (ed.), *Wiederaufbau der Innenstädte Kiel, Coventry, Lübeck. Chancen und Pläne. Dokumentation zur Ausstellung im Kieler Rathaus vom 16. Januar bis 4. März 1990* (Kiel, 1990).

Stadtmuseum Dresden (ed.), *Verbrannt bis zur Unkenntlichkeit. Die Zerstörung Dresdens 1945* (Dresden, 1994).

Staffa, Christian, 'Die "Aktion Sühnezeichen". Eine protestantische Initiative zu einer besonderen Art der Wiedergutmachung', in Hans Günter Hockerts and Christiane Kuller (eds), *Nach der Verfolgung. Wiedergutmachung nationalsozialistischen Unrechts in Deutschland?* (Munich, 2003), 139–56.

Stammers, Neil, *Civil Liberties in Britain during the Second World War: A Political Study* (London, 1983).

Stanley, Nicholas S., 'The Extra Dimension: A Study and Assessment of the Methods Employed by Mass-Observation in its First Period, 1937–1940', Birmingham Polytechnic CNAA Ph.D. thesis 1981.

Stansky, Peter, 'Henry Moore and the Blitz', in John M. W. Bean (ed.), *The Political Culture of Modern Britain: Studies in Memory of Stephen Koss* (London, 1987), 228–42.

Stansky, Peter, *The First Day of the Blitz: September 7, 1940* (New Haven, 2007).

Stansky, Peter, and Abrahams, William, *London's Burning: Life, Death and Art in the Second World War* (Stanford, Calif., 1994).

Stargardt, Nicholas, 'Opfer der Bomben und der Vergeltung', in Kettenacker (ed.), *Ein Volk von Opfern*, 56–71.

Stargardt, Nicholas, *'Maikäfer flieg'. Hitlers Krieg und die Kinder* (Munich, 2006).

Steel, Nigel, and Hart, Peter, *Tumult in the Clouds: The British Experience of War in the Air* (London, 1997).

Steer, George L., *The Tree of Gernika* (London, 1938).

Steinbacher, Sybille, *Wie der Sex nach Deutschland kam. Der Kampf um Sittlichkeit und Anstand in der frühen Bundesrepublik* (Munich, 2011).

Steinert, Marlis G., *Hitlers Krieg und die Deutschen. Stimmung und Haltung der deutschen Bevölkerung im Zweiten Weltkrieg* (Düsseldorf/Vienna, 1970).

Steinhilber, Wilhelm, *Die schwersten Stunden der Stadt* (Heilbronn, 1988) [New edition].

Stengel, E., 'Grossbritannien. Gegenwärtiger Stand und Entwicklungstendenzen der Neurosenlehre und Psychotherapie', in Frankl, Freiherr von Gebsattel, and Schulz (eds), *Handbuch der Neurosenlehre und Psychotherapie*, i. 105–12.

Stephenson, Jill, 'The Home Front in "Total War": Women in Germany and Britain in the Second World War', in Chickering, Förster, and Greiner (eds), *A World at Total War*, 207–32.

Stephenson, Jill, *Hitler's Home Front: Württemberg under the Nazis* (London, 2006).

Stevenson, J., 'Planer's Moon? The Second World War and the Planning Movement', in Smith (ed.), *War and Social Change*, 58–77.

Stier, Ewald, *Über die sogenannten Unfallneurosen* (Leipzig, 1926).

Stöver, Bernd, *Volksgemeinschaft im Dritten Reich: Die Konsensbereitschaft der Deutschen aus der Sicht sozialistischer Exilberichte* (Düsseldorf, 1993).

Strachan, Hew, 'Total War: The Conduct of War 1939–1945', in Chickering and Förster (eds), *Shadows*, 33–52.

Stradling, Robert, *Your Children Will Be Next: Bombing and Propaganda in the Spanish Civil War* (Cardiff, 2008).

Strange, Julie-Marie, *Death, Grief and Poverty in Britain 1870–1914* (Cambridge, 2005).

The Strategic Air War against Germany 1939–1945: Report of the British Bombing Survey Unit, Studies in Air Power No. 4 (London, 1998).

Strebe, Bernhard, *Celle April 1945 Revisited. Ein amerikanischer Bombenangriff, deutsche Massaker an KZ-Häftlingen und ein britisches Gerichtsverfahren* (Bielefeld, 2008).

Strupp, Christoph, 'Stadt ohne Herz. Rotterdam und die Erinnerung an den deutschen Luftangriff vom 14. Mai 1940', in Arnold, Süss, and Thiessen, *Luftkrieg*, 27–49.

Stuckart, Wilhelm, 'Probleme der Kriegsschäden', *Deutsche Verwaltung*, 18 (1941), 6–11.

Stupperich, Robert, *Otto Dibelius. Ein evangelischer Bischof im Umbruch der Zeiten*. In collaboration with Martin Stupperich (Göttingen, 1989).

Summerfield, Penny, *Women Workers in the Second World War: Production and Patriarchy in Conflict* (London, 1984).

Summerfield, Penny, 'Mass-Observation: Social Research or Social Movement?', *Journal of Contemporary History*, 20 (1985), 439–52.

Summerfield, Penny, *Reconstructing Women's Wartime Lives: Discourse and Subjectivity in Oral Histories of the Second World War* (Manchester, 1998).

Summerfield, Penny, and Peniston-Bird, Corinna, *Contesting Home Defence: Men, Women and the Home Guard in the Second World War* (Manchester, 2007).

Süss, Dietmar, '"Massaker und Mongolensturm". Anmerkungen zu Jörg Friedrichs umstrittenem Buch "Der Brand. Deutschland im Bombenkrieg 1940–1945"', *Historisches Jahrbuch*, 124 (2004), 521–43.

Süss, Dietmar, 'Erinnerungen an den Luftkrieg in Deutschland und Großbritannien', *Aus Politik und Zeitgeschichte*, 55/18–19 (2005), 19–26.

Süss, Dietmar, 'Steuerung durch Information? Joseph Goebbels als "Kommissar der Heimatfront" und Reichsinspekteur für den zivilen Luftschutz', *Beiträge zur Geschichte des Nationalsozialismus*, 22 (2006), 125–45.

Süss, Dietmar, 'Krieg, Nation und "Heimatfront". Großbritannien und der Zweite Weltkrieg', *AfS* 47 (2007), 437–53.

Süss, Dietmar (ed.), *Deutschland im Luftkrieg. Geschichte und Erinnerung* (Munich, 2007).

Süss, Dietmar, '16. März 1945. Die Bombardierung Würzburgs', in Alois Schmid and Katharina Weigand (eds), *Bayern nach Jahr und Tag. Vierundzwanzig Tage aus der bayerischen Geschichte* (Munich, 2007), 385–99.

Süss, Dietmar, 'Memory of the Air War', *Journal of Contemporary History*, 43 (2008), 333–42.

Süss, Dietmar, 'Kannibalen im eigenen Land. Mass-Observation und britische Sozialanthropologie (1890–1945)', *Jahrbuch für Europäische Ethnologie* (2012), 53–72.

Süss, Dietmar, 'Nationalsozialistische Deutungen des Luftkrieges', in Süss (ed.), *Deutschland im Luftkrieg*, 99–110.

Süss, Dietmar, 'Krieg, Kommune, Katastrophe—München 1944', in *Bayerische Landeszentrale für Politische Bildung, Schlüsseljahr 1944* (Munich, 2007), 105–17.

Süss, Dietmar, 'Luftkrieg, Öffentlichkeit und die Konjunkturen der Erinnerung', in Echternkamp and Martens (eds), *Der Zweite Weltkrieg in Europa*, 207–22.

Süss, Dietmar, and Süss, Winfried (eds), *Das 'Dritte Reich'. Eine Einführung* (Munich, 2008).

Süss, Dietmar, and Süss, Winfried, 'Volksgemeinschaft und Vernichtungskrieg. Gesellschaft im NS-Deutschland', in Süss and Süss (eds), *Das 'Dritte Reich'. Eine Einführung*, 79–100.

Süss, Winfried, 'Der beinahe unaufhaltsame Aufstieg des Karl Brandt. Zur Stellung des Reichskommissars für das Sanitäts- und Gesundheitswesen im Machtgefüge der nationalsozialistischen Diktatur', in Wolfgang Woelk and Jörg Vögele (eds), *Gesundheitspolitik in Deutschland von der Weimarer Republik bis in die Frühgeschichte der Bundesrepublik* (Berlin, 2002), 197–223.

Süss, Winfried, *Der 'Volkskörper' im Krieg. Gesundheitspolitik, Gesundheitsverhältnisse und Krankenmord im nationalsozialistischen Deutschland 1939–1945* (Munich, 2003).

Süss, Winfried, '"Dann ist keiner von uns seines Lebens mehr sicher." Bischof von Galen, der katholische Protest gegen die "Euthanasie" und der Stopp der "Aktion T4"', in Sabrow (ed.), *Skandal und Öffentlichkeit*, 102–29.

Sweetman, John, *The Dams Raid—Epic or Myth? Operation Chastise* (London, 1982).

Szarota, Tomasz, 'Die Luftangriffe auf Warschau im Zweiten Weltkrieg', *Acta Poloniae Historica*, 72 (1994), 121–33.

Szodrzyinski, Joachim, 'Das Ende der "Volksgemeinschaft"? Die Hamburger Bevölkerung in der "Trümmergesellschaft" ab 1943', in Bajohr and Szodrzynski (eds), *Hamburg in der NS-Zeit*, 281–305.

Tanaka, Yuki, and Young, Marilyn B. (eds), *Bombing Civilians: A Twentieth-Century History* (New York/London, 2009).

Taylor, Alan J. P., *English History 1914–1945* (Oxford, 1965).

Taylor, Frederick, *Dresden: Tuesday 13 February 1945* (London, 2004).

Taylor, John, '"London's Latest Immortal"—the Statue to Sir Arthur Harris of Bomber Command', *Kritische Berichte*, 20/3 (1992), 96–102.

Taylor, Philip (ed.), *Britain and the Cinema in the Second World War* (Hong Kong, 1988).

Temple, William, *A Conditional Justification of War* (London, 1940).

Temple, William, *Thought in War Time* (London, 1940).

Temple, William, *Towards a Christian Order* (London, 1942).

Terraine, John, 'Theorie und Praxis des Luftkrieges: Die Royal Air Force', in Boog (ed.), *Luftkriegsführung im Zweiten Weltkrieg*, 537–63.

Thatcher, Margaret, *The Downing Street Years* (London, 1995).

Thiessen, Malte, *Eingebrannt ins Gedächtnis. Hamburgs Gedenken an Luftkrieg und Kriegsende 1943 bis 2005* (Munich/Hamburg, 2007).

Thiessen, Malte, 'Gemeinsame Erinnerungen im geteilten Deutschland. Der Luftkrieg im "kommunalen Gedächtnis" der Bundesrepublik und der DDR', *Deutschland Archiv*, 41 (2008), 226–32.

Thiessen, Malte, 'Generation "Feuersturm" oder Generation "Lebensmittelkarte"? Generationen als biografisches Argument und lebensgeschichtliche Erfahrung in Zeitzeugen-Interviews', in Björn Bohnenkamp, Till Manning, and Eva-Maria Silies (eds), *Generation als Erzählung. Neue Perspektiven auf ein kulturelles Deutungsmuster* (Göttingen, 2009), 33–52.

Thiessen, Malte, 'Zeitzeuge und Erinnerungskultur. Zum Verhältnis von privaten und öffentlichen Erzählungen des Luftkriegs', in Lu Seegers and Jürgen Reulecke (eds), *Die 'Generation der Kriegskinder'. Historische Hintergründe und Deutungen* (Giessen, 2009), 157–82.

Thiessen, Malte, 'Gedenken an die "Operation Gomorrha". Hamburgs Erinnerungskultur und städtische Identität', in Süss, *Deutschland*, 121–33.

Thiessen, Malte, 'Von der "Heimstätte" zum Denkmal: Bunker als städtische Erinnerungsorte—das Beispiel Hamburgs', in Marszolek and Buggeln (eds), *Bunker*, 45–60.

Thomas, Merrilny, *Communing with the Enemy: Covert Operations, Christianity and Cold War Politics in Britian and the GDR* (Oxford/Frankfurt am Main, 2005).

Thoms, David, 'The Blitz, Civilian Morale and Regionalism, 1940–1942', in Kirkham and Thoms (eds), *War Culture*, 3–12.

Thorpe, Andrew, 'Britain', in Noakes (ed.), *The Civilian in War*, 14–34.

Thorpe, Andrew, *Parties at War* (Oxford, 2009).

Tippe, Gundolf (ed.), *16. März 1945. re-VISION. Vorgeschichte, Zerstörung, Wiederaufbau. Ausstellungskatalog zum 50. Jahrestag der Zerstörung Würzburgs am 16. März 1945. Rathaus der Stadt Würzburg 15. März bis 5. April* (Würzburg, 1995).

Tiratsoo, Nick, *Reconstruction, Affluence and Labour Politics: Coventry 1945–1960* (London, 1990).

Tiratsoo, Nick (ed.), *From Blitz to Blair: A New History of Britain since 1939* (London, 1997).

Tiratsoo, Nick, 'The Reconstruction of Blitzed British Cities 1945–55: Myths and Reality', *Contemporary British History*, 14 (1999), 27–44.

Titmuss, Richard Morris, *Problems of Social Policy* (London, 1950).

Tooze, Adam, *Ökonomie der Zerstörung. Die Geschichte der Wirtschaft im Nationalsozialismus* (Munich, 2007).

Toppe, Andreas, *Militär und Kriegsvölkerrecht. Rechtsnorm, Fachdiskurs und Kriegspraxis in Deutschland 1899–1940* (Munich, 2008).

Trahan, E. A., *A History of the Second United States Armored Division 1940 to 1946* (Atlanta, 1946).

Trippen, Norbert, 'Erzbischof Frings und der Neubeginn kirchlichen Lebens in Köln 1945', *Jahrbuch des Kölnischen Geschichtsvereins*, 66 (1995), 151–68.

Trippen, Norbert, *Josef Kardinal Frings (1887–1978)*, i: *Sein Wirken für das Erzbistum Köln und für die Kirche in Deutschland* (Paderborn, 2003).

Trotha, Trutz von, 'Zur Soziologie der Gewalt', in Trutz von Trotha (ed.), *Soziologie der Gewalt*. Special issue 37/1997 of the *Kölner Zeitschrift für Soziologie und Sozialpsychologie*, 9–56.

Ueberschär, Gerd R., *Freiburg im Luftkrieg 1939–1945* (Freiburg/Würzburg, 1990).

Uertz, Rudolf, *Vom Gottesrecht zum Menschenrecht. Das katholische Staatsdenken in Deutschland von der Französischen Revolution bis zum II. Vatikanischen Konzil (1789–1965)* (Paderborn, 2005).

Underdown, Alderman Thomas T. H. J., *Bristol under Blitz: The Record of an Ancient City and her People during the Battle of Britain 1940–1941* (Bristol, 1942).

Die Unfall-(Kriegs-)Neurose. Vorträge und Erörterungen gelegentlich eines Lehrganges für Versorgungsärzte im Reichsarbeitsministerium vom 6.–8. März 1929, Arbeit und Gesundheit 13 (Berlin, 1929).

Vees-Gulani, Susanne, *Trauma and Guilt: Literature of Wartime Bombing in Germany* (Berlin/New York, 2003).

Vees-Gulani, Susanne, '"Phantomschmerzen". Durs Grünbeins Porzellan und neue Wege in der Literatur über den Luftkrieg', in Arnold, Süss, and Thiessen (eds), *Luftkrieg*, 277–96.

Vees-Gulani, Susanne, 'The Politics of New Beginnings: Dresden and the Continued Exclusion of the Nazi Past', in Rosenfeld and Jaskot (eds), *Beyond Berlin*, 25–47.

Vernon, E. P., 'Psychological Effects of Air-Raids', *Journal of Abnormal and Social Psychology*, 36 (1941), 457–76.

Visser't Hooft, Willem A., *Die Welt war meine Gemeinde* (Munich, 1972).

Vogel, Detlef, 'Der Kriegsalltag im Spiegel von Feldpostbriefen (1939–1945)', in Wolfram Wette (ed.), *Der Krieg des kleinen Mannes. Eine Militärgeschichte von unten* (Munich, 1995), 199–212.

Vollprecht, Hans, 'Das Reichsverwaltungsgericht (Reichskriegsschädenamt) und die Aufsichtsführung in Kriegsschädensachen', *Deutsche Verwaltung*, 19 (1942), 426–8.

Vorländer, Herwart, *Die NSV. Darstellung und Dokumentation einer nationalsozialistischen Organisation* (Boppard, 1988).

Wagner, Johannes Volker, 'Bomben auf Bochum. Eine deutsche Stadt im Zweiten Weltkrieg', in Johannes Volker Wagner (ed.), *Krieg als Idylle? Nationalsozialistische Propaganda im Film* (Bochum, 1979).

Walton, Mary, and Lamb, Joseph P., *Raiders over Sheffield* (Sheffield, 1944).

Warburton, Nigel, *Bill Brandt: Selected Texts and Photographs* (Oxford, 1993).

Ward, Paul, *Britishness since 1870* (London, 2004).

War Damage Commission (ed.), *A Short History of the War Damage Commission* (n.d. [London, 1962]).

War Pictures by British Artists: Second Series. Air Raids, with an Introduction by Stephen Spender (London, 1943).

Webster, Charles, and Frankland, Noble, *The Strategic Air Offensive against Germany 1939–1945*, vols i–iv (London, 1961).

Weckbecher, Gerhard, *Zwischen Freispruch und Todesstrafe. Die Rechtsprechung der nationalsozialistischen Sondergerichte* (Frankfurt am Main/Bromberg/Baden-Baden, 1998).

Wegmann, Günther, *Das Kriegsende zwischen Ems und Weser 1945* (Osnabrück, 1982).

Weisbrod, Bernd, 'Der Schein der Modernität: Zur Historisierung der "Volksgemeinschaft"', in Karsten Rudolph et al. (eds), *Geschichte als Möglichkeit. Über die Chancen von Demokratie* (Essen, 1995), 224–42.

Weisbrod, Bernd, 'Öffentlichkeit als politischer Prozeß. Dimensionen der politischen Medialisierung in der Geschichte der Bundesrepublik', in Bernd Weisbrod (ed.), *Die Politik der Öffentlichkeit—Die Öffentlichkeit der Politik. Politische Medialisierung in der Geschichte der Bundesrepublik* (Göttingen, 2003), 11–25.

Wells, Herbert George, *War in the Air* (London, 1908).

Welshman, John, 'Evacuation and Social Politics during the Second World War: Myth and Reality', *20th Century British History*, 9 (1998), 28–53.

Welshman, John, 'Evacuation, Hygiene, and Social Policy: The Our Towns Report of 1943', *Historical Journal*, 42 (1999), 781–807.

Welshman, John, 'The Evacuation of Children in Wartime Scotland: Culture, Behaviour and Poverty', *Journal of Scottish Historical Studies*, 26 (2006), 100–20.

Wenk, Silke (ed.), *Erinnerungsorte aus Beton. Bunker in Städten und Landschaften* (Berlin, 2001).

Werner, Wolfgang Franz, *'Bleib übrig!' Deutsche Arbeiter in der nationalsozialistischen Kriegswirtschaft* (Düsseldorf, 1983).

Werner, Wolfgang Franz, 'Belastungen der deutschen Arbeiterschaft in der zweiten Kriegshälfte', in Borsdorf and Jamin (eds), *Über Leben im Krieg*, 33–42.

Westall, Robert (ed.), *Children of the Blitz: Memories of Wartime Childhood* (Oxford, 1989).

Whiting, Charles, *Britain under Fire: The Bombing of Britain's Cities, 1940–1945* (London, 1999).

Widera, Thomas, 'Gefangene Erinnerung. Die politische Instrumentalisierung der Bombardierung Dresdens', in Widera and Fritze (eds), *Alliierter Bombenkrieg*, 109–34.

Widera, Thomas, and Fritze, Lothar (eds), *Alliierter Bombenkrieg. Das Beispiel Dresden* (Göttingen, 2005).

Wiggam, Marc, 'The Blackout and the Idea of Community in Britain and Germany', in Richard Overy, Claudia Baldoli, and Andrew Knapp (eds), *Bombing, States and Peoples in Western Europe, 1940–1945* (London, 2011), 43–58.

Wiggam, Marc, 'The Blackout in Britain and Germany during the Second World War', Ph.D. thesis, University of Exeter, 2011.

Wildt, Michael, *Geschichte des Nationalsozialismus* (Göttingen, 2008).

Wildt, Michael, and Bajohr, Frank (eds), *Volksgemeinschaft. Neue Perspektiven der NS-Gesellschaftsgeschichte* (Frankfurt am Main, 2009).

Wilkinson, Alan, *The Church of England and the First World War* (London, 1978).

Wilkinson, Alan, *Dissent or Conform? War, Peace and the English Churches 1900–45* (London, 1986).

Wilkinson, Alan, 'Changing Attitudes to Death in the Two World Wars', in Peter C. Jupp and Glennys Howarth (eds), *The Changing Face of Death: Historical Accounts of Death and Disposal* (London, 1997), 149–63.

Wilkinson, Bill, 'Exeter's Baedeker Raid', *Army Quarterly and Defence Journal*, 129 (1999), 201–5.

Wilson, Arnold, and Levy, Herman, *Burial Reform and Funeral Costs* (London, 1938).

Winkler, Heinrich August (ed.), *Die große Krise in Amerika. Vergleichende Studien zur politischen Sozialgeschichte 1929–1939* (Göttingen, 1973).

Winkler, Heinrich August, 'Vom Mythos der Volksgemeinschaft', *AfS* 17 (1977), 484–90.

Winter, Martin Clemens, *Öffentliche Erinnerungen an den Luftkrieg in Nordhausen 1945–2005* (Marburg, 2010).

Wirl, Manfred, *Die öffentliche Meinung unter dem NS-Regime. Eine Untersuchung zum sozialpsychologischen Konzept öffentlicher Meinung auf der Grundlage der geheimen Berichte des Sicherheitsdienstes über die Stimmung und Haltung der Bevölkerung im Zweiten Weltkrieg* (Mainz, 1990).

Wirsching, Andreas, *Vom Weltkrieg zum Bürgerkrieg? Politischer Extremismus in Deutschland und Frankreich 1918–1933/39. Berlin und Paris im Vergleich* (Munich, 1999).

Wirsching, Andreas, 'Jüdische Friedhöfe in Deutschland 1933–1957', *VfZ* 50 (2002), 1–40.

Wolf, Helmut, *Erfurt im Luftkrieg 1939–1945* (Jena, 2005).

Wolf, Werner, *Luftangriffe auf die deutsche Industrie 1942–1945* (Munich, 1985).

Woller, Hans, 'Churchill und Mussolini. Offene Konfrontation und geheime Kooperation?', *VfZ* 49 (2001), 563–94.

Woolven, Robin, 'Civil Defence in London 1935–1945: The Formation and Implementation of the Policy for, and the Performance of, the Air Raid Precautions (later Civil Defence) Services in the London Region', London University, Ph.D. thesis, 2002.

Wybrow, Robert, *Britain Speaks out 1935–1987: A Social History as Seen through the Gallup Data* (London, 1989).

Zehender, Bernadette, 'Die Tarnsprache der Wehrmachtsberichte unter Einbeziehung nationalsozialistischer Sprachelemente', in Albrecht Greule and Waltraud Sennebogen (eds), *Tarnung—Leistung—Werbung. Untersuchungen zur Sprache im Nationalsozialismus* (Frankfurt am Main, 2004), 31–87.

Zentrum für Kunstausstellungen der DDR: Neue Berliner Galerie (ed.), *Henry Moore, Shelter and Coal Mining Drawings. Zeichnungen aus den Jahren 1939–1942. Eine Ausstellung aus Großbritannien* (Berlin (East), 1984).

Ziegler, Philip, *London at War 1939–45* (London, 1995).

Ziemann, Benjamin, 'Code of Protest: Images of Peace in the West German Peace Movement, 1945–1990', *Contemporary European History*, 17 (2008), 237–61.

Zimmer, Arthur, *Gas über Österreich* (Vienna, 1943).

Zimmermann, Volker, *In Schutt und Asche. Das Ende des Zweiten Weltkrieges in Düsseldorf* (Düsseldorf, 1995).

Zuckerman, Solly, *From Apes to Warlords* (London, 1978).

Zweiniger-Bargielowska, Ina, *Austerity in Britain: Rationing, Controls and Consumption, 1939–1955* (Oxford, 2000).

Picture Acknowledgements

Index